Norman Rockwell

A SIXTY YEAR RETROSPECTIVE

Saying Grace. *Original oil painting for* Post *cover, November 24, 1951. Collection Mr. and Mrs. Ken Stuart*

Norman Rockwell

A Sixty Year Retrospective

CATALOGUE OF AN EXHIBITION ORGANIZED BY

Bernard Danenberg Galleries, New York

WITH TEXT BY

Thomas S. Buechner

Harry N. Abrams, Inc., Publishers, New York

DISTRIBUTED BY NEW AMERICAN LIBRARY

SCHEDULE OF THE EXHIBITION

FEBRUARY 11–MARCH 5, 1972	The Fort Lauderdale Museum of the Arts Fort Lauderdale, Florida
MARCH 22–MAY 14, 1972	The Brooklyn Museum Brooklyn, New York
MAY 26–JULY 16, 1972	Corcoran Gallery of Art Washington, D. C.
AUGUST 1–AUGUST 27, 1972	Marion Koogler McNay Art Institute San Antonio, Texas
SEPTEMBER 8–NOVEMBER 5, 1972	M. H. De Young Memorial Museum San Francisco, California
NOVEMBER 12–DECEMBER 10, 1972	Oklahoma Art Center Oklahoma City, Oklahoma
DECEMBER 18–JANUARY 21, 1973	Indianapolis Museum of Art Indianapolis, Indiana
JANUARY 28–FEBRUARY 25, 1973	Joslyn Art Museum Omaha, Nebraska
MARCH 8–APRIL 15, 1973	Seattle Art Museum Seattle, Washington

BOOK DESIGN BY NAI Y. CHANG

Standard Book Number: 8109–2049–2
Library of Congress Catalogue Card Number: 70–38513
Text and reproductions of works of art only

HARRY N. ABRAMS, INCORPORATED, NEW YORK
Printed and bound in Japan

P R E F A C E

In 1913, when the great Armory Show introduced modern art to New Yorkers, Norman Rockwell was busy doing one hundred ink drawings for the *Boy Scouts Hike Book*. What part has our most popular artist played in the upheavals which have made us a major power in the art world? Absolutely none. He—and all those other artists with publishers instead of galleries—are the "meanwhile back at the ranch" branch of modern art.

It's time to take another look. In 1968, Bernard Danenberg did an extraordinary thing: he put Norman Rockwell's *Saying Grace* in the window of his gallery on Madison Avenue and hung forty other paintings by Rockwell inside. He had remembered a man whom, as it turns out, nobody wanted to forget; and had remembered him not as an illustrator but as an artist. The exhibition was immensely popular and launched the Rockwell revival—and the Rockwell reappraisal. Subsequently, Harry N. Abrams published the magnificently illustrated *Norman Rockwell: Artist and Illustrator;* Arthur Guptill's 1946 classic, *Norman Rockwell Illustrator* was reissued; the *Saturday Evening Post* came back to life amidst a flurry of Rockwell stories in the national press; and now Mr. Danenberg has organized this exhibition so that we may judge for ourselves. Rockwell in reproduction is not the same as Rockwell in the original. Most people know his work solely through the magazines for which he has done covers, illustrations, and advertisements by the thousands—paper reflections of paintings and drawings nobody ever saw. Now we have the originals before us and can see how they were made, how the artist manipulated brush and pencil, what the colors really are. We can see beyond subject matter to the technique, and, with perception, to the man himself who created these very surfaces. Is he an artist according to your definition?

He is certainly a phenomenon. To be revived at the height of one's fame is a paradox created as much by our times as by his talents. There are different reasons for different people. For example, some of us have grown used to a new and more rudimentary figurative painting, much of it based on the projection of photographs; his use of this technique is so astonishingly good that he must be regarded as a great master in a medium which has only recently become an acceptable tool for the fine artist. But the essential reason for his current popularity probably lies in the area of his own primary interest, which is neither technique nor aesthetics but the subject itself. Generally speaking, we are fascinated by *what* he has painted rather than by *how*. For many he records the time of our pride with such passionate accuracy and gentle humor that we are overwhelmed with the joys of nostalgia. For others, the young in particular, his visual stories are simply wonderfully entertaining and beautifully told. It is youth's fascination with Rockwell that promises a future as popular as his past.

THOMAS S. BUECHNER
December, 1971

CONTENTS

PUBLISHER'S NOTE

In 1943 a fire in Norman Rockwell's studio destroyed many of his original paintings, and over the years many other Rockwell paintings have simply disappeared. In the process of selecting the subjects for the present book it became evident that some of the lost pictures were absolutely essential, in order to have a characteristic variety of the artist's work. We therefore decided to make such reproductions directly from the SATURDAY EVENING POST *covers for which the paintings were originally commissioned (and where they first appeared). It turned out that some of these covers are now extremely rare, and it was largely through Mr. Rockwell's efforts that several of the most important paintings could be illustrated here.*

Norman Rockwell

A SIXTY YEAR RETROSPECTIVE

1910–1929

One of the earliest surviving original paintings by Rockwell. 1912. Whereabouts unknown

In America, Norman Rockwell is the best-known artist who ever lived. His subject is average America. He has painted it with such benevolent affection for so many years that a truly remarkable history of our century has been compiled. Through wars, depression, civil strife, and the exploration of space, Norman Rockwell has drawn subjects from the everyday happenings of which most lives are made. Millions of people have been moved by his picture stories about the awkwardness of youth and the comforts of age, about pride in country, history, and heritage, about reverence, loyalty, and compassion. The virtues that he admires have been very popular, and because he illustrates them using familiar people in familiar settings with wonderful accuracy, he describes the American Dream.

There is an appealing sense of tradition in being a Rockwell watcher, of seeing man land on the moon through the eyes of an artist who recorded Lindbergh's flight across the Atlantic in 1927 and sketched Admiral Dewey's warships steaming into New York harbor in 1899. Another attraction in Rockwell is accuracy. Illustration is a field where a door opening out when it should open in evokes hundreds of letters, and so it is that in this field Rockwell

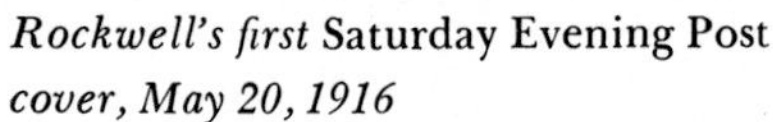
Rockwell's first Saturday Evening Post *cover, May 20, 1916*

Circus Barker. Post *cover, June 3, 1916. Original oil painting, Collection* Saturday Evening Post

has the perfect challenge for his own almost fanatic respect for the visual truth. He is not interested in conveying the idea of a thing, he wants to paint from the thing itself, an actual specific example that he selects with the greatest care.

Here is an account from his autobiography on how to pose a chicken: "You pick up the chicken and rock him back and forth a few times. When you set him down he will stand just as you've placed him for four or five minutes. Of course you have to run behind the easel pretty quickly to do much painting before the chicken moves. But it's better than trying to paint him while he's dashing about the studio. If you want to paint the chicken full face the procedure is even more complicated because the eyes of a chicken are on the sides of his head and when he looks at you he turns his head. I puzzled about that for quite a while. Finally I got a long stick and after I'd set the chicken down and gone behind my easel I'd rap the wall at one side of the chicken and he'd turn his head toward me to look at the wall. It's very strenuous painting a chicken. . . ."

Illustration from Boys' Life, *1915*

Illustration for "The Magic Football" by R. H. Barbour, St. Nicholas, *December, 1914. Collection Norman Rockwell*

Illustration for
"The Magic Football,"
St. Nicholas, *December, 1914.*
Collection Norman Rockwell

Gramercy Park. *1918. Original oil painting. Collection Mr. and Mrs. George J. Arden*

To the Rescue. *1916. Drawing. Collection Patricia and Howard O'Connor*

Party Line. *1918. Original oil painting. Collection Mr. and Mrs. Harold Konner*

The pains Rockwell takes to find the right locations, props, models, and costumes are awe-inspiring: an illustration portraying Martha Washington in a 1939 issue of the *Ladies' Home Journal* was actually painted at Valley Forge; the clothes worn by the models who posed for *Tom Sawyer* and *Huckleberry Finn* were actually purchased off the backs and heads of the citizens of Mark Twain's home town, Hannibal, Missouri; Rockwell's home towns—New Rochelle, New York, Arlington, Vermont, and Stockbridge, Massachusetts—have provided a mob of friends, neighbors, and strangers to back up the professional models so that just the right type can be found for any situation.

The essential factor in understanding why so many people love his work is his own sincerity. Rockwell genuinely likes the people he paints and the people he paints for. When he is amusing them he is

Winter. *Sketch for* St. Nicholas *cover, 1916. Collection* Saturday Evening Post

Saturday Evening Post *cover, January 13, 1917*

amusing himself. Long ago he made the following statement, which was quoted in a 1923 issue of *International Studio*: "People somehow get out of your work just about what you put into it, and if you are interested in the characters that you draw, and understand them and love them, why, the person who sees your picture is bound to feel the same way." An artist's attitude undoubtedly has an impact on his work no matter how professional he is. In Norman Rockwell's case, his sincere interest in his subject causes him to learn a great deal about it, to delve into the characters involved, to explore their actions and reactions in terms of the situation he has conceived. This leads not only to a remarkable degree of definition but also to a

Courting Couple at Midnight. *Original oil painting for* Post *cover, March 28, 1919.*
Collection Harry N. Abrams, Inc., New York

Advertisement for Fisk bicycle tires, 1919

merging of characters and story. Rockwell returns to the same themes again and again, but because the people are different the whole situation is different.

And people, millions of them, enjoy his point of view. It is their point of view, full of things they remember or can imagine or would like to imagine. He does not try to change things; he invites people to chuckle, not to despair; to join the gang of regular fellows, not to stand alone; to reminisce, not to prophesy. He does not mean to confuse or challenge us; he certainly does not want to shock or offend; he rarely even raises a question.

Norman Percevel Rockwell was born on February 3, 1894, in a brownstone on 103rd Street and Amsterdam Avenue in New York City. His father, Jarvis Waring Rockwell, was the manager of the New York office of George Woods, Sons, and Company, a textile firm. According to Rockwell's autobiography, his father's family was "substantial, well to do, character and fortunes founded on three generations of wealth." In addition to reading Dickens aloud after dinner, Waring Rockwell also enjoyed copying illustrations from magazines.

Norman's mother, Nancy Hill Rockwell, was one of twelve children. Her father was an unsuccessful English artist who came to America shortly after the Civil War. "He hoped to open a studio as a portrait and landscape painter . . . instead he became a painter of animals, potboilers and houses. . . . He painted in great detail—every hair on the dog was carefully drawn; the tiny highlights in the pig's eyes—great, watery human eyes—could be clearly seen." Nancy's

Looking Out to Sea. *1919. Original oil painting. Collection Norman Rockwell*

pride centered on her mother's family who traced their English ancestry back to Sir Norman Percevel. Norman, as the first son, received the entire ancestral inheritance—the name (his only brother was named Jarvis). Waring Rockwell was an aloof, gentlemanly father, Nancy a self-indulgent, complaining mother. Norman was never close to either of them. Interestingly, few of his storytelling covers dealt with parental relationships until he himself became a father.

The family was very religious. As a choirboy at St. Luke's and later at the Cathedral of St. John the Divine, Norman sang four services on Sunday after attending four rehearsals during the week. He also marched with a wooden gun in the St. Luke's Battalion. Thin, poorly coordinated, and pigeon-toed, he started wearing corrective shoes when he was ten, eye glasses at twelve. Unable to compete satisfactorily in sports, he used his drawing skill to entertain his contemporaries from an early age. He loved summers in the country and disliked the city, which he found dirty, sordid, and ugly. No theme is more dominant through the first three decades of his work than the idealization of boyhood in the summer in the country. It gradually expands to include adults, and other seasons, but very rarely do city streets appear.

In 1903, the Rockwell family moved to Mamaroneck, and by 1906 Norman had decided what he was going to be: ". . . boys who are athletes are expressing themselves fully. They have an identity, a recognized place among other boys. I didn't have that. All I had was the ability to draw, which as far as I could see didn't count for much. But because it was all I had I began to make it my whole life. I drew all the time. Gradually my narrow shoulders, long neck, and pigeon toes became less important to me. I drew and drew and drew."

By 1908, when he was fourteen, Rockwell commuted to New York on Saturdays and later, with the school principal's permission, on Wednesdays, for his first formal art training—at the Chase School of Fine and Applied Art. He left high school altogether in the middle of his sophomore year and switched to the National Academy School as a full-time student. As might be expected, the curriculum was academic in the grand French tradition. Students began by doing laborious charcoal studies from plaster casts of antique sculptures. When they had learned the fundamentals of proportion, anatomy, and rendering, they graduated to living models—male students in one classroom, female in another. The school was stiff, stilted, and oriented toward winning that classic scholarship, the Prix de Rome.

In 1910, Rockwell left and enrolled at the Art Students League. Founded in 1875, it was the most liberal and exciting art school of its day. Winslow Homer had studied there and so had Charles Dana Gibson, but of the long list of famous alumni none impressed Rock-

Santa. *Original oil painting for* Post *cover, December 4, 1920. Collection Patricia and Howard O'Connor*

Boy and Girl on a Horse. *Original oil painting for* Literary Digest *cover, September 4, 1920. Collection Mrs. Elmer E. Putnam*

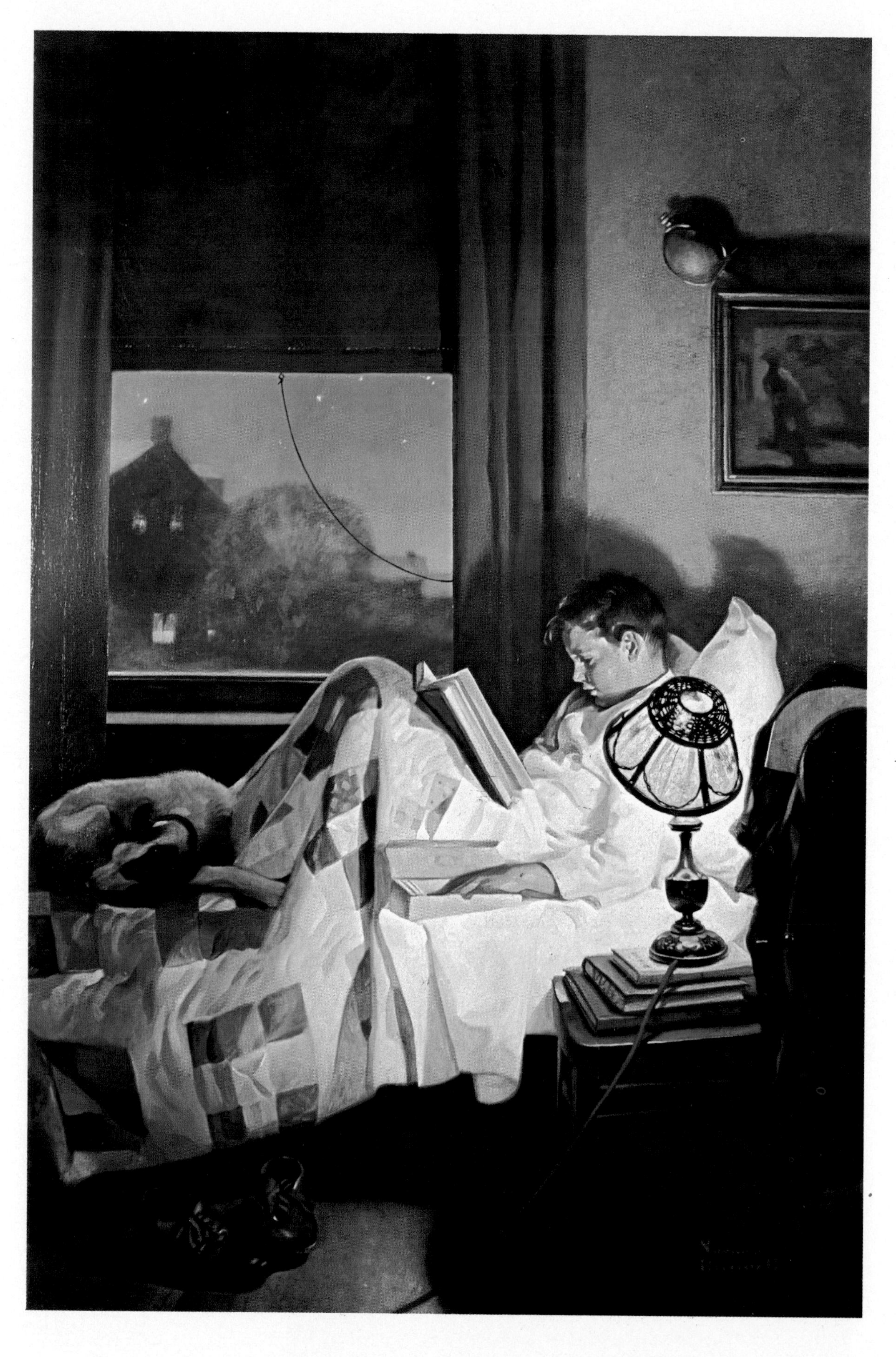

Crackers in Bed. *Original oil painting for advertisement for Edison Mazda Lamp Works, 1921.*
Collection Mr. and Mrs. George J. Arden

Fortune Teller. *Original oil painting for* Post *cover, March 12, 1921.*
Collection Mr. and Mrs. Jerome D. Mack

Christmas: Santa with Elves. *Original oil painting for* Post *cover, December 2, 1922. Collection Jarvis Rockwell*

well more than Howard Pyle, one of the League's founders and the greatest illustrator of his day. Pyle, historian as well as illustrator, gave illustration scholarly status through his historical accuracy, and drama through his portrayal of basic human emotion.

George Bridgman was Rockwell's great teacher. If Pyle's work showed him where he wanted to go, Bridgman gave him the basic equipment for getting there. "You can't paint a house until it's built," he admonished his students. He taught construction: the swivel, hinge, and arch of bone movement, the contraction, rest, and extension of muscles. The body was studied in such detail that once a student knew what any part of the model was doing, he could build that part from the bone up and not have to depend on copying out-

No Swimming. *Original oil painting for* Post *cover, June 4, 1921. Collection Norman Rockwell*

Paying the Bills.
Original oil painting for
Literary Digest *cover, February 26, 1921.*
Collection Mr. and Mrs. Jerome D. Mack

Waking Up Master. *1922. Oil on cardboard. Collection Patricia and Howard O'Connor*

Old Sea Captain. *Original oil painting for* Literary Digest *cover, December 2, 1922. Private collection*

Man Threading a Needle. *Original oil painting for* Post *cover, April 8, 1922. Collection Kayser-Roth Hosiery Company, Inc., New York*

Still Good. *Original oil painting for advertisement for Interwoven socks, 1927. Collection Kayser-Roth Hosiery Company, Inc., New York*

Under the Mistletoe.
1924. Original oil painting.
Collection Patricia and Howard O'Connor

Merry Christmas. *Original oil painting for* Post *cover, December 8, 1928. Collection Mr. and Mrs. Murray L. Pfeffer* ▶

lines. The hands, particularly, in Rockwell's paintings illustrate how much he knows of complex anatomical construction. The fact that he does full-size charcoal drawings before he begins painting shows how seriously he took Bridgman's adage about building before painting. Arthur Burdett Frost, too, had a strong effect; from the very beginning, his careful selection of detail and infusion of quaint humor impressed Rockwell. He worked extraordinarily hard (as he still does) and what he learned he perfected, making each idea his own through the thoroughness of his study and consequent understanding.

Rockwell's other major teacher was Thomas Fogarty, who taught the illustration class. His definition of illustration was simple and straightforward: an author's words in paint. But from this basic approach evolved Rockwell's fascination with authenticity, characterization, supporting detail, and facial expression. In addition to analyzing the work of established illustrators—why they chose par-

Merrie Christmas

Christmas Trio. *Original oil painting for* Post *cover, December 8, 1923. Collection Norman Rockwell*

Saturday Evening Post cover,
December 5, 1925

Saturday Evening Post *cover,*
December 7, 1929

Saturday Evening Post *cover, December 3, 1921*

Farmer and Bird. Post *cover, August 18, 1923. Original oil painting, Collection William W. Waterman*

ticular passages to depict, why a dark instead of a light background, why pen and ink and not oils—Fogarty insisted that his students "live" in their illustrations. They had to know what kinds of people they were painting, why they were behaving as they were, what the weather was like, why they sat in a particular kind of chair—and so on. Obviously, Rockwell accepted Fogarty's lessons as he had Bridgman's, Pyle's, and Frost's.

During this brief period of training, Rockwell had a series of part-time jobs. As monitor the second year in Bridgman's class he had no tuition to pay and, as he continued to live with his parents, his expenses were modest. One summer he earned pocket money by being a paint-box caddy for Ethel Barrymore; during another he bought a mail delivery route in Orienta Point near Mamaroneck. In the winter, while a full-time student at the Art Students League, he worked as a waiter from 8:00 P.M. to midnight at a Child's restaurant then located near the League on Columbus Circle. This uninspiring occupation soon gave way to an exotic one—supernumerary at the Metropolitan Opera (his autobiography contains a delightful account of his relationship with Enrico Caruso) . By 1912, when his family moved back to the city from Mamaroneck, illustrating jobs were coming in fast enough to make other employment unnecessary. At eighteen he was a full-time professional.

Norman Rockwell develops his pictures in a series of separate, self-contained phases: first, a loose sketch of an idea; second, the gathering of models, costumes, background, and props; third, individual drawings of parts or, since about 1937, photographing everything; fourth, a full-scale drawing in great detail; fifth, color sketches; and sixth, putting all the parts together in the final painting. As with most artists, the procedure varies from picture to picture—he may do a whole series of compositional sketches in color or, at

Thanksgiving (The Glutton).
Original oil painting for Life *cover, November 22, 1923.*
Collection Harry N. Abrams, Inc., New York

In Need of Sympathy.
Original oil painting for Post *cover,*
October 2, 1926.
Collection E. A. Elder

Ben Franklin's Sesqui-Centennial.
Original oil painting
for Post *cover, May 29, 1926.*
Collection Mr. and Mrs. Joseph H. Hennage

The Young Artist.
Original oil painting
for Post *cover, June 4, 1927.*
Collection Mr. and Mrs. William M. Young, Jr.

Catching the Big One.
Original oil painting for Post *cover,*
August 3, 1929. Private collection

the other extreme, simply project a photograph onto a white canvas, draw around the image and start painting. The one essential constant in his technique is the rigid separation of drawing and painting. He solves as many problems, makes as many decisions as he can in black-and-white and then takes on the color and textural possibilities of paint as the second phase. Having worked out all the details in black-and-white, he can concentrate fully on color and texture. The tight, frozen aspect of some of Rockwell's work probably comes more from working with photographs and striving for photographic realism than it does from the separation of drawing and painting.

But detailed attention to all parts—with extra attention given to faces—has been a Rockwell hallmark from the very beginning. Capturing just the right expression has long been one of his great if not unique strengths, and he worked hard to get it. In his early work he often overemphasizes what the facial features are doing in an effort to convey the proper emotion—particularly with children.

Norman Rockwell began by being successful. He executed his first commission before he was sixteen (four Christmas cards for Mrs. Arnold Constable), illustrated his first book when he was seventeen (*Tell Me Why Stories*), became art director of *Boys' Life* at nineteen, and reached the pinnacle of his profession by doing a cover for America's most popular magazine, the *Saturday Evening Post*, when he was twenty-two—at which point he married Irene O'Connor.

Illustrations for a book on Samuel de Champlain published in 1912 by the American Book Company were followed by a prodigious effort for Edward Cave, editor of *Boys' Life*: one hundred illustrations for the *Boy Scouts Hike Book* in 1913 and fifty-five more for the *Boys Camp Book* in 1914. In the same years he illustrated at least four novels by Ralph Henry Barbour and, as *Boys' Life* art director, did seventy-eight illustrations for that magazine in 1915 alone. During this period his drawings began to appear regularly in *St. Nicholas*, the *Youth's Companion*, *Everyland*, and the *American Boy*. Rockwell's productivity—enormous from the outset—began in the family apartment in Mamaroneck, but by 1912 he was in his first studio—the attic of a brothel on the Upper West Side. In less than a year he was in his second, near the Brooklyn end of the Brooklyn Bridge. His third studio was beside the boarding house in which his parents lived and the fourth was in New Rochelle, to which they moved in 1915.

The most important single event at this time was the publication of his first *Saturday Evening Post* cover, which appeared in print

Advertisement for Massachusetts Mutual Life Insurance Company

on May 20, 1916. He had done covers of the children's magazines for which he illustrated stories prior to his appearance on the *Post.* Immediately afterward, he began "covering" other national adult publications—many with *Post* rejects. *Collier's, Life* (then a humor magazine), *Leslie's, Judge, Country Gentleman,* the *Literary Digest, People's Popular Monthly, Farm and Fireside* (from Des Moines), and *Popular Science* were among them. He joined the Navy in 1917, and worked for *Afloat and Ashore* two days a week, did portraits of officers, and continued to serve his regular clients. The ever-present signature on covers done between July, 1917, and November, 1918, is sometimes followed by U.S.N.R.F. His first painting for advertisements also appeared during this period.

Certain themes emerge during this first decade that have provided Rockwell with subject matter for more than half a century. They are interesting to follow because his treatment of them changes as he grows older. Other themes are less enduring, and new ones appear all along the way. Situations involving small embarrassments, discomforts, and humiliations have provided humorous covers all the way through. Growing up is another and, closely related, is budding love. Old-fashioned patriotism persists as well as the recording of fads and historical events. Youth contrasted with age is a major

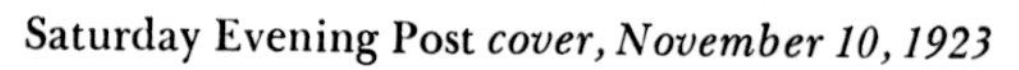
Saturday Evening Post *cover, November 10, 1923*

Saturday Evening Post *cover, April 5, 1924*

category, recurring almost as often as depictions of simple joys for the vicarious delight of the reader. More specific long-term subject matter introduced in this first decade includes, in order of appearance, Santa Claus, Boy Scouts, circus people, dogs, and bandaged big toes. Rockwell's particular ability to combine humor and pathos has not yet appeared as a strong characteristic.

During the twenties, Rockwell became rich and famous. He took up golf and sailing, joined clubs, found his own bootlegger, and spent as much time partying as painting. He toured South America and steamed back and forth across the Atlantic six times. He saw students dueling in Heidelberg, Riffs rebelling in Morocco, and Venezuelans revolting in Caracas. He was accepted by society, pursued by publishers, and divorced by Irene. His work continued to improve.

He became the top cover artist for the *Saturday Evening Post.* His work appeared almost every month, and beginning in 1919 he did a Christmas cover every year without interruption until 1943—but he was tempted by other offers. In 1924, Patterson and McCormick in Chicago founded *Liberty* in competition with the *Post* and *Collier's.* The art director of the new magazine came to New

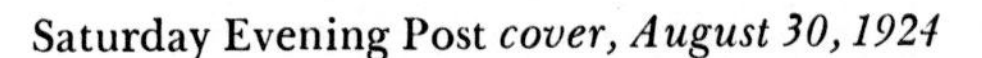

Saturday Evening Post *cover, August 30, 1924*

Saturday Evening Post *cover, April 18, 1925*

Saturday Evening Post *cover,*
August 13, 1927

Rochelle and offered to double whatever the *Post* was paying. Rockwell hesitated, went to Philadelphia, and described the situation to George Horace Lorimer, *Post* editor from 1899 through 1936. Mr. Lorimer's only response was to ask Rockwell what he had decided to do. He decided to stay and Mr. Lorimer decided to double his price. Rockwell's respect for George Horace Lorimer is awesome—no other personality in his autobiography is the subject of such thorough admiration. After this meeting, he illustrated very few covers for other magazines but took on more advertising—at twice his fee for a *Post* cover.

Raleigh Rockwell Travels.
Post *cover, September 28, 1929.*
Original oil painting,
Collection Patricia and
Howard O'Connor

Things were happening fast in the twenties: new clothes, new music, new morals, new art. While in Paris in 1923, Rockwell had enrolled in Colarossi's school. His Bridgman-Pyle approach suddenly seemed hopelessly old-fashioned. He tried to do a "modern" cover emphasizing abstract color. It was rejected by the *Post* and he settled back into what he loves best, telling stories. In a sense, he became two artists and painted in two quite separate styles. One was in the Victorian tradition, sentimental and pretty, full of atmosphere and charm—a direct link with the past and extremely well done. The other style reflected the changes that were taking place:

Illustration for "A Christmas Reunion," Ladies' Home Journal, *December, 1927*

Advertisement for Maxwell House coffee

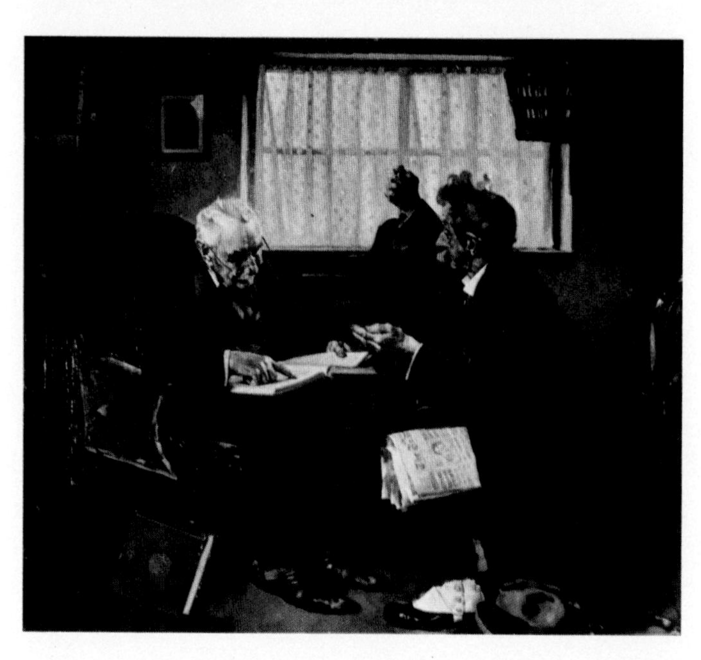

Advertisement for the Encyclopaedia Britannica

Man Painting Flagpole. *Original oil painting for* Post *cover, May 26, 1928. Collection the McCullough Family* ▶

Norman
Rockwell

Saturday Evening Post *cover, July 23, 1927*

Uncle Sam. *Original oil painting for* Post *cover, January 21, 1928. Collection Paul C. Wilmot*

strong silhouettes backed by simple geometric shapes—Art Deco circles and squares, design instead of atmosphere, character instead of idealization, humor instead of sentiment.

Norman Rockwell's subject matter also changes radically during this period. Although children continue to predominate (90 per cent of the *Post* covers illustrated from 1916 to 1919 included children, 50 per cent from 1920 to 1929), the approach changes from that of a boy describing himself to a man looking back on boyhood. More important is the appearance of two new elements in the Rockwell approach. The first is the outside character, who is not one of us and at whom we can laugh; the second is what might be called "pathotic" humor (or humorous pathos). The latter element, pathotic humor, seems almost to have been introduced in order to avoid the danger of derisive laughter. Ridicule is not consistent with Rockwell's personality, and although the characters invite amusement they remain sympathetic, simultaneously funny and sad. Mixing tears and laughter is a delicate job, and the picture that evokes a strong feeling of commiseration can be as successful as the side-splitter. The *Saturday Evening Post* covers painted by Rockwell during the twenties introduced many new subject areas and formats, and several characters that would recur frequently: bums, sheriffs, musicians, and doctors.

THE LAND OF ENCHANTMENT

Original oil painting for Post *illustration, December 22, 1934.*
Collection New Rochelle Public Library, New York

Saturday Evening Post *covers, September 27, 1924—November 21, 1925*

Advertisements for
Massachusetts Mutual Life
Insurance Company

1930 - 1949

Home from Vacation.
Original oil painting
for Post *cover, September 13, 1930.*
Collection Mr. and Mrs. Phil Grace

IN THE THIRTIES, ROCKWELL BEGAN PAINTING FROM PHOTOGRAPHS, returned to illustration, married, and had three sons. From a miserable bachelorhood at the Hotel des Artistes at Sixty-seventh Street and Central Park West following his divorce, he fled to Los Angeles to escape the art editor of *Good Housekeeping* who insisted he illustrate the life of Christ. There he painted Gary Cooper for the May 24, 1930, cover of the *Post* and married Mary Barstow. Back in New Rochelle at 24 Lord Kitchener Road he began to have trouble with his work. Waning self-confidence, indecision, and procrastination reduced both the quality and quantity of his output. He experimented with dynamic symmetry, had another modern art approach rejected, and, in real desperation, left his own charming world for the sordid and ugly: he painted a dead gangster—never published and now lost. In 1932, the Rockwells went to Paris with their newly born first son, Jerry.

Wet Paint. *Original oil painting for* Post *cover, April 12, 1930. Bernard Danenberg Galleries, Inc., New York*

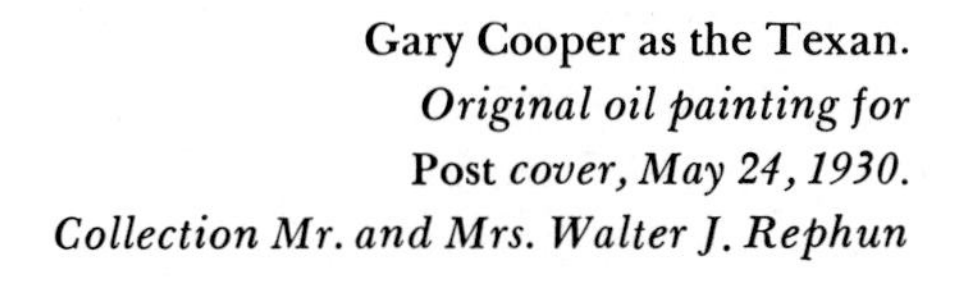

Gary Cooper as the Texan. *Original oil painting for* Post *cover, May 24, 1930. Collection Mr. and Mrs. Walter J. Rephun*

Mother Spanking Her Child.
Original oil painting
for Post *cover, November 25, 1933.*
Collection the McCullough Family

The turning point was 1935. Almost as if he had been saving up for it, Rockwell suddenly began to pour out some of the finest work he has done: illustrations for *Tom Sawyer, Huckleberry Finn,* the life of Louisa May Alcott, the Yankee Doodle mural for the Nassau Tavern in Princeton, and a superb series of magazine illustrations. The *Post* covers done between 1936 and 1939 include some of his very best work.

For purposes of authenticity (if not escape) he traveled whenever possible to the actual site where the story he was to illustrate took place. The whole family traveled to England in 1938, and Rockwell met some of his famous colleagues—Arthur Rackham among them. Twenty-three years earlier, Rockwell had illustrated *The Magic Football* for *St. Nicholas* magazine; Rackham had done the frontispiece for the same issue. During all that period—from *Don*

Charcoal drawing for "Willie Takes a Step" by Don Marquis, American, *January, 1935.*
Collection Mr. and Mrs. Carl Wulff

Final illustration for "Willie Takes a Step" by Don Marquis, American, *January, 1935. Whereabouts unknown*

On Top of the World.
Original oil painting for Ladies' Home Journal, *1933.*
Collection Harry N. Abrams, Inc., New York

Playing Checkers. *1935. Original oil painting.*
Collection Mr. and Mrs. Gustave Seaberg

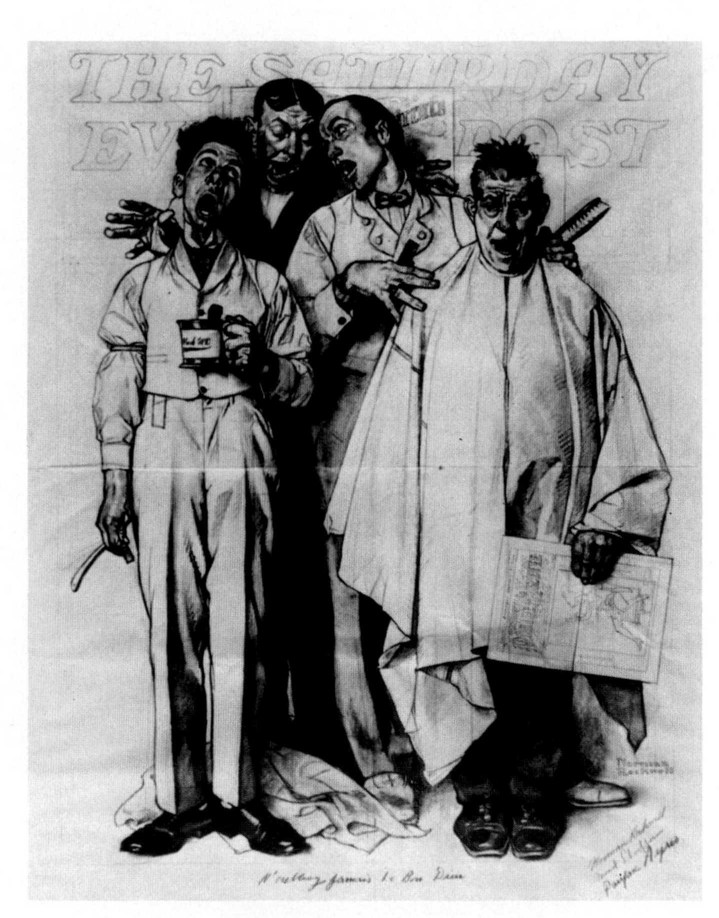

Barbershop Quartet.
Sketch for Post *cover, September 26, 1936.*
Collection Arts International Ltd., Chicago

Boy Flying Kite. *1930s. Drawing.*
Collection Dr. Robert Bakish

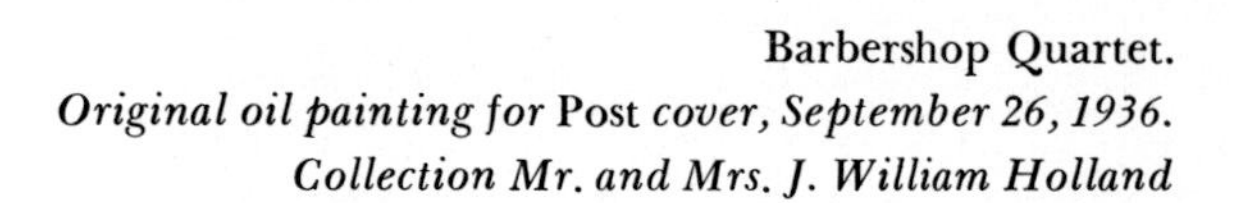

Barbershop Quartet.
Original oil painting for Post *cover, September 26, 1936.*
Collection Mr. and Mrs. J. William Holland

YANKEE DOODLE CAME TO TOWN · RIDING ON A PONY ·

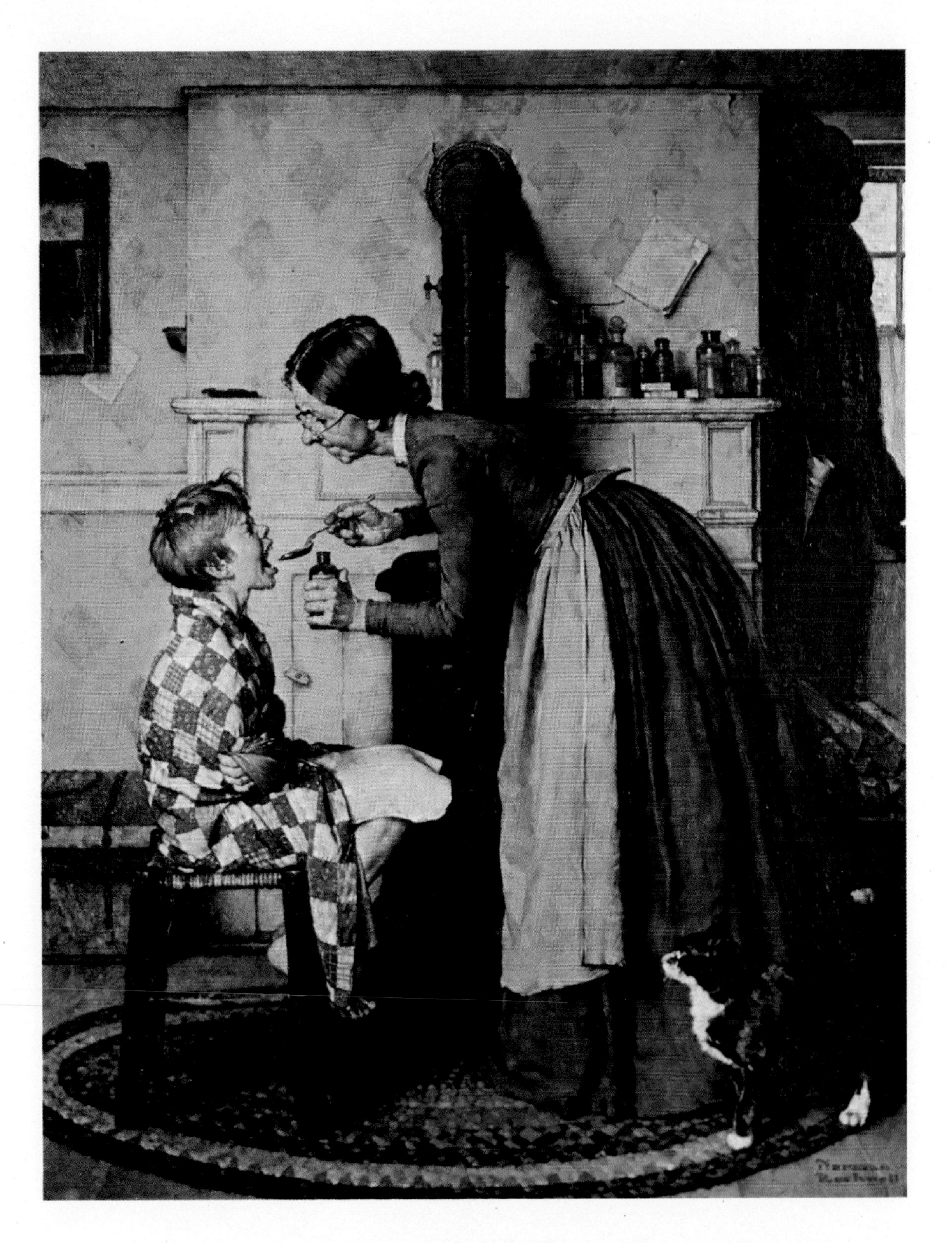

Spring Tonic. *Original oil painting for illustration to* The Adventures of Tom Sawyer, *1936.*
Collection John C. Meeks

◀ YANKEE DOODLE

Mural for the Nassau Tavern, Princeton, New Jersey. 1937

Gaiety Dance Team. *Original oil painting for* Post *cover, June 12, 1937. Collection* Variety, *Inc., New York*

Strong of the Wolf Patrol to the Nassau Tavern mural—Rockwell had lived in New Rochelle. In 1939 the family moved to Arlington, Vermont.

The two major factors affecting Rockwell's work of the thirties are a new interest in illustrating other people's stories and a final surrender to the convenience of the camera. The photographer starts to help about 1937, but illustrations were painted both from living models and from photographs. There is an important but hard-to-define difference. Those painted from photographically supplied information are generally more realistic; forms look flatter, they do not have the same sense of bulk, and, in the beginning at least, the details contribute little to the quality of the design; individual items become less important, and the eye wanders more freely

Harpooner.
1938. Drawing.
Collection Mr. and Mrs. Thomas Rockwell

Harpooner.
1938. Original oil painting.
Collection Pete Martin

Whig and Tory. *1938. Original oil painting. Collection Pete Martin*

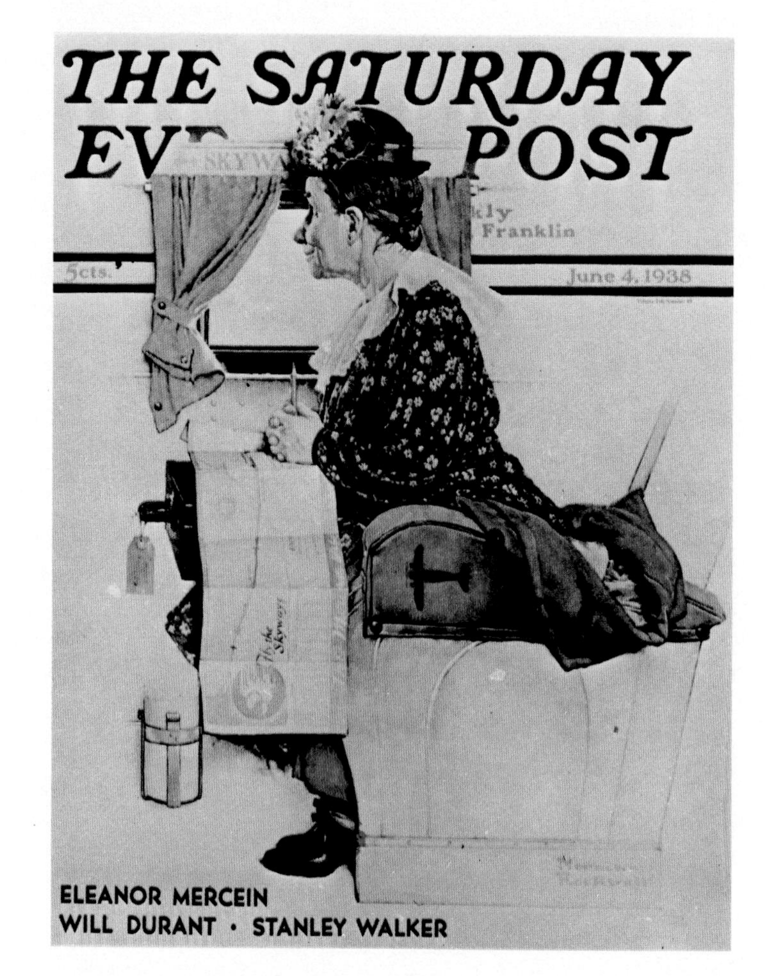

Airplane Trip.
Post *cover, June 4, 1938.*
Original oil painting,
Collection Mr. and Mrs. M. Kunstler

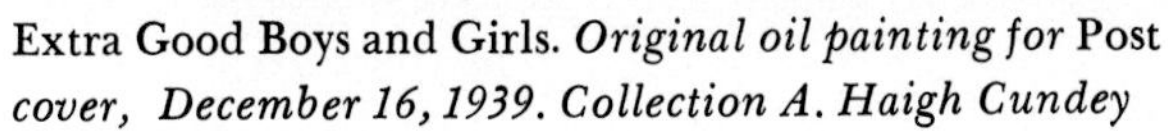
Extra Good Boys and Girls. *Original oil painting for* Post *cover, December 16, 1939. Collection A. Haigh Cundey*

Jester. *Original oil painting for* Post *cover, February 11, 1939. Collection Mrs. G. A. Godwin*

over the surface. If Rockwell found himself too dependent on his photographs at first, he got over it very quickly, and much of this work would be hard to beat for caricature, design, and graphic impact. It is not easy—perhaps it is impossible—to tell the difference between paintings from life and paintings from photographs.

Although he began as an illustrator, assignments for cover designs and commissions for advertisements left little time for less glamorous and less well-paid story illustration. The revival of his interest came in 1935 with the commission to do eight color paintings for a deluxe edition of *Tom Sawyer* and another eight for *Huckleberry Finn,* to be published by Heritage Press. The right job at the right time—twenty years of experience painting barefoot boys, the opportunity to join the grand tradition of illustrating classics, and a welcome change from thinking up his own stories. The results are remarkable. The paintings are free and spontaneous; each has an immediacy about it as if the viewer were there.

Between 1930 and 1939 Rockwell did sixty-seven covers for the *Post*—twenty-two less than he had the previous decade but considerably more than any other artist was doing. Only ten of these covers had children as the main subject. In general terms his approach be-

The Virtuoso. *Original oil painting for* Post *illustration, May 27, 1939.*
Collection Mr. and Mrs. Frank M. Rubinstein

Norman
Rockwell

Homecoming G.I. *Original oil painting for* Post *cover, May 26, 1945*

Santa on Train. *Original oil painting for* Post *cover, December 28, 1940. Collection Mr. and Mrs. Jack D. Emery*

THE HORSESHOE FORGING CONTEST ▶

Original oil painting for illustration to "Blacksmith's Boy—Heel and Toe" by Edward W. O'Brien, Post, *November 2, 1940. Collection Norman Rockwell*

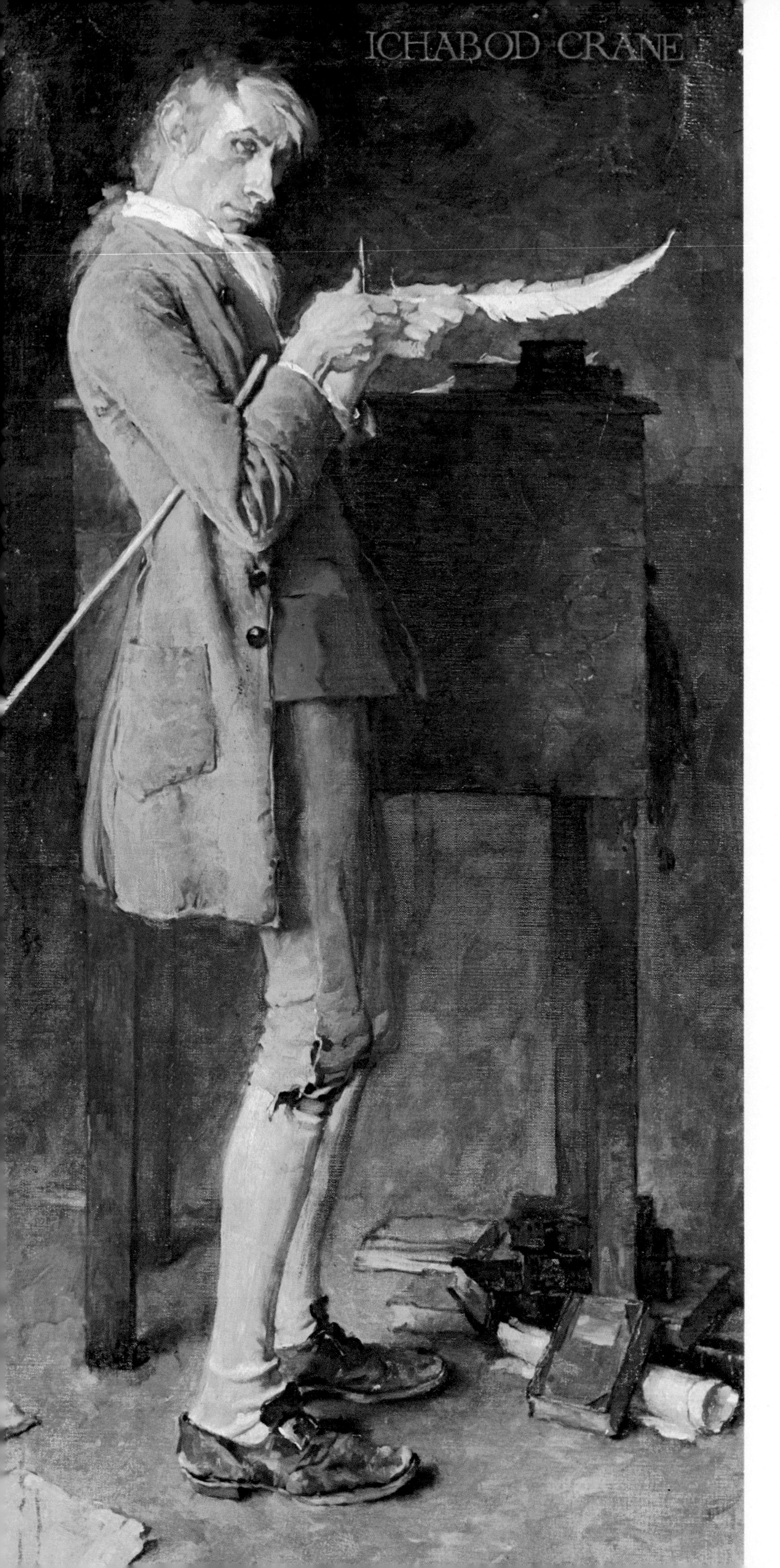

Ichabod Crane. *Late 1930s.*
Original oil painting.
Collection Norman Rockwell

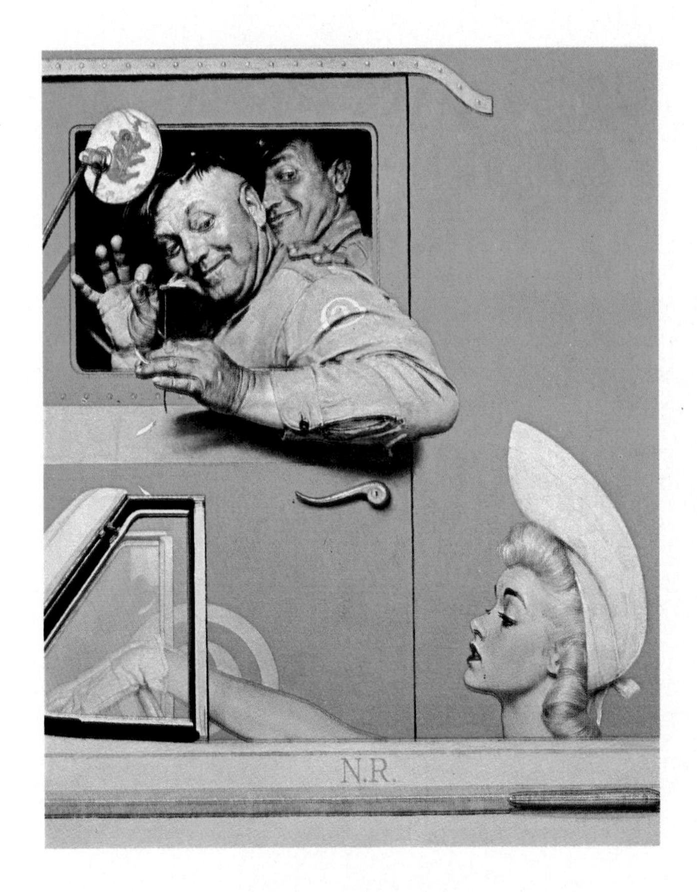

The Flirts. *Original oil painting for* Post *cover, July 26, 1941. Collection Harry N. Abrams, Inc., New York*

April Fools. *Original oil painting for* Post *cover, April 3, 1943. Collection J. and R. S. Schafler*

came less sentimental and the past was treated as decorative rather than nostalgic. More sophisticated subjects were introduced: horseback riding, antiquing, the theater. Sports—football, baseball, hunting, fishing, and croquet—became adult pastimes, and several covers reflect contemporary interest in movie stars, progressive education, rumble seats, and early Americana.

Rockwell took on World War II as if he had discovered it. Twenty-four years earlier he had pictured America's fighting men as Boy Scouts on bivouac—sewing on buttons, thinking of Mom, and singing "Over There." Now he saw soldiers and sailors as civilians in uniform—and the war itself as everybody's fight. He conceived the idea of explaining through pictures what the war was all about. The *Four Freedoms* were the result. Millions of copies were printed and distributed by the government and private agencies all over the world; the Treasury department toured the four originals to sixteen cities where they were seen by 1,222,000 people and used in selling $132,999,537 worth of war bonds. For many Americans World War II made sense because of the goals depicted in the *Four Freedoms.*

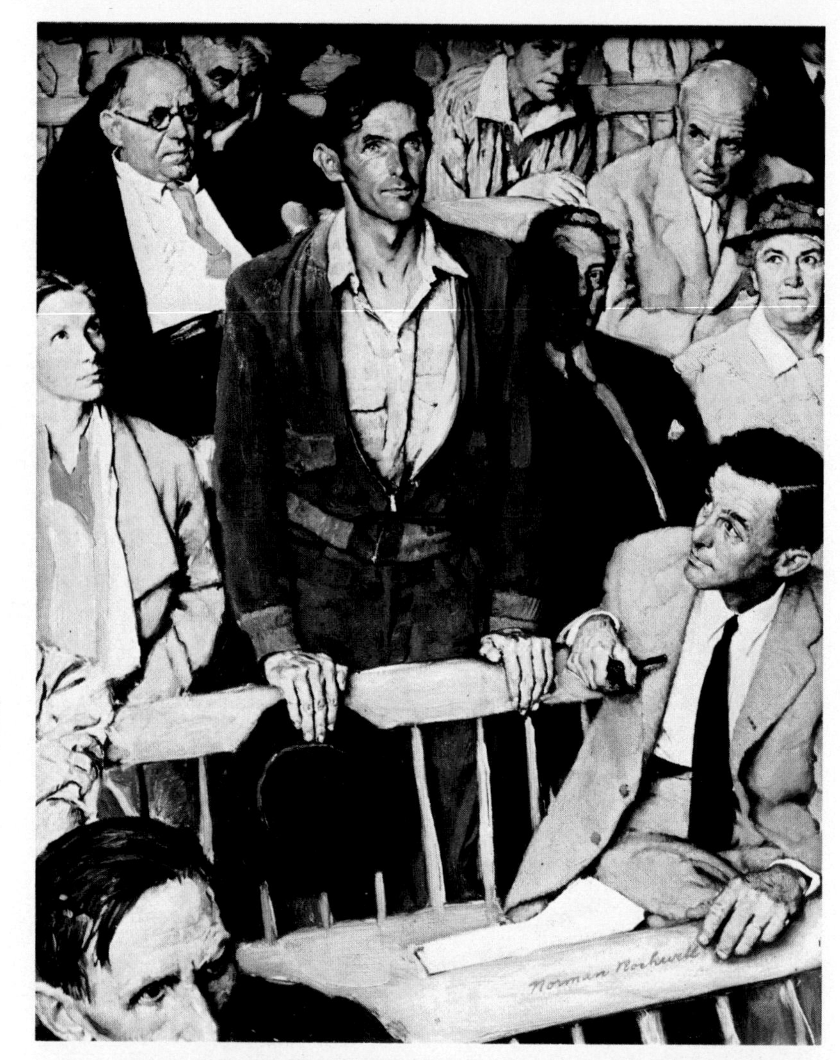

Freedom of Speech.
Original oil painting for poster, 1943.
The Metropolitan Museum of Art, New York.
George A. Hearn Fund, 1952

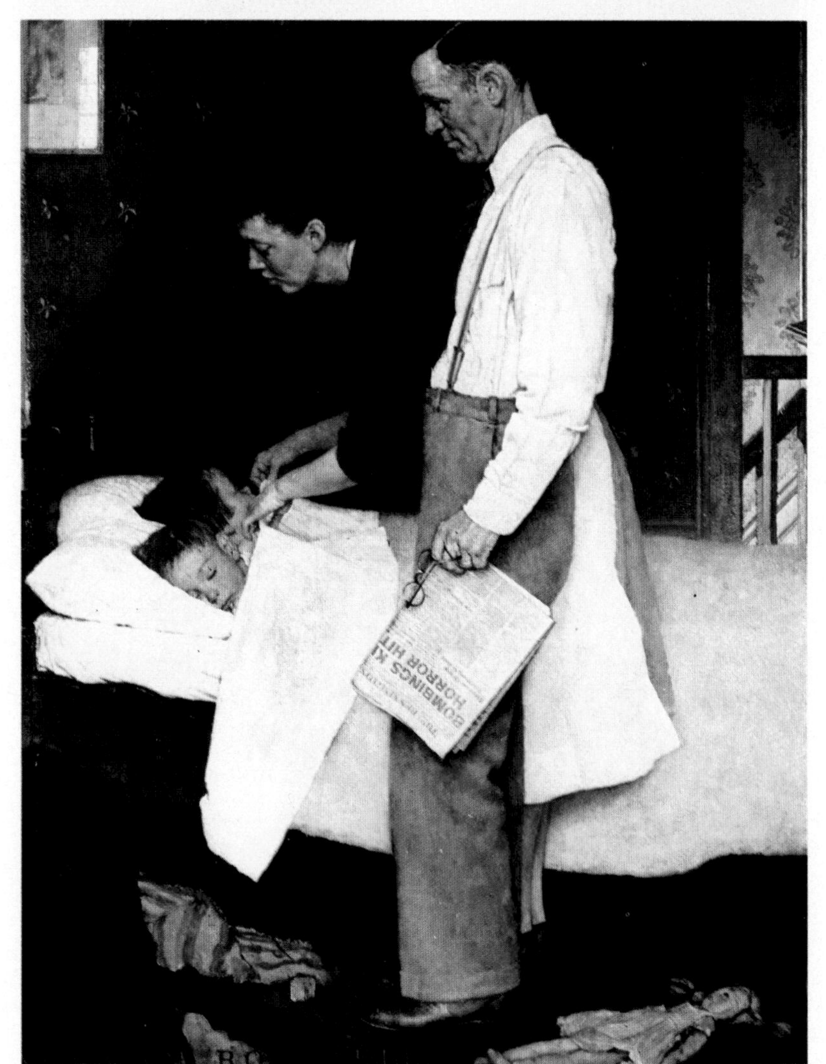

Freedom from Fear.
Original oil painting for poster, 1943.
Collection Norman Rockwell

Freedom of Worship.
Original oil painting
for poster, 1943.
Collection Norman Rockwell

Freedom from Want.
Original oil painting
for poster, 1943.
Collection Norman Rockwell

Fireman. *Original oil painting for* Post *cover, May 27, 1944. Collection Mr. and Mrs. J. Buckhout Johnston*

The Tattoo Artist. *Original oil painting for* Post *cover, March 4, 1944. The Brooklyn Museum* ▶

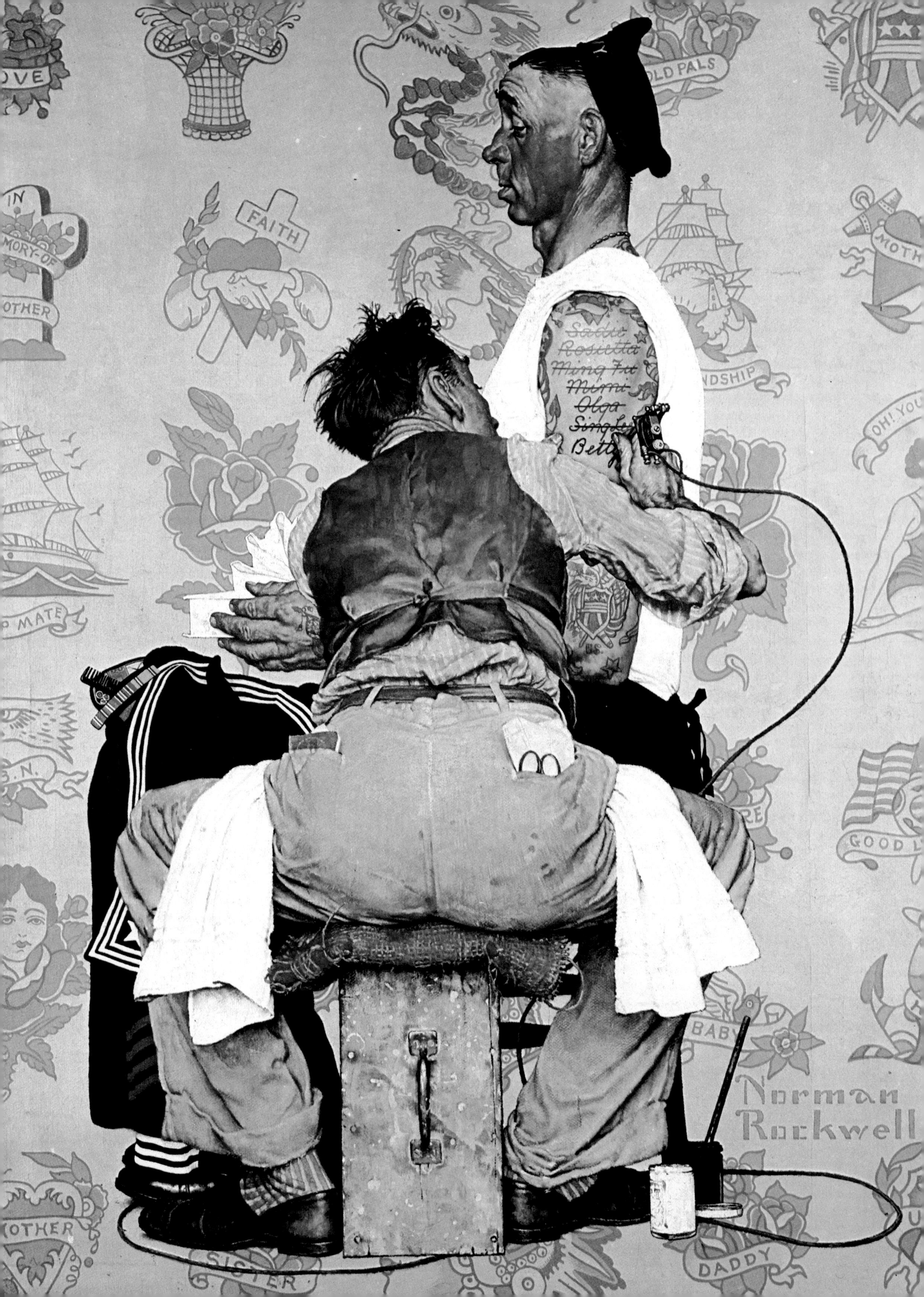

OLD PALS
FAITH
Rosietta
Ming Fu
Mimi
Olga
Betty
BABY
DADDY
SISTER
MOTHER
Norman Rockwell

Willie Gillis. *Original oil painting for* Post *cover, September 16, 1944. Collection Mr. and Mrs. Ken Stuart*

Saturday Evening Post *cover, October 4, 1941*

Norman Rockwell Visits a Country Editor. *Original oil painting for a double-page spread for the* Post, *May 25, 1946. Collection National Press Club, Washington, D.C.*

For Rockwell, departure from reassuring entertainment had been made and was to be made many times thereafter.

Rockwell extended his fight through posters and calendars and ads. Time devoted so successfully to doing illustration in recent years was assigned to pictorial reporting, the nonfiction phase of storytelling. Photographer in tow and sketchbook in hand, Rockwell visited the President, rode a troop train, and stood before his ration board, all of which appeared within the *Saturday Evening Post*. The simplest measure of his involvement is that twenty-five of the thirty-three covers done during this period relate to the war; twenty-four years earlier only four out of eighteen did. G. I. Joe was one of Rockwell's great subjects; on the cover of the *Post* his homecoming was recorded seven times.

For the remainder of the decade, he continued the pictorial documentaries for the *Post*, began a four seasons calendar series for Brown & Bigelow (which still continues), and did his first Christmas cards for Hallmark. Perhaps as a reaction to the war and the realism he brought to it, the work for these new clients is irrepressibly benevolent caricature, still another facet of Rockwell's talent.

Homecoming Marine (The Storyteller). *Original oil painting for* Post cover, *October 13, 1945. Collection Harry Wohl*

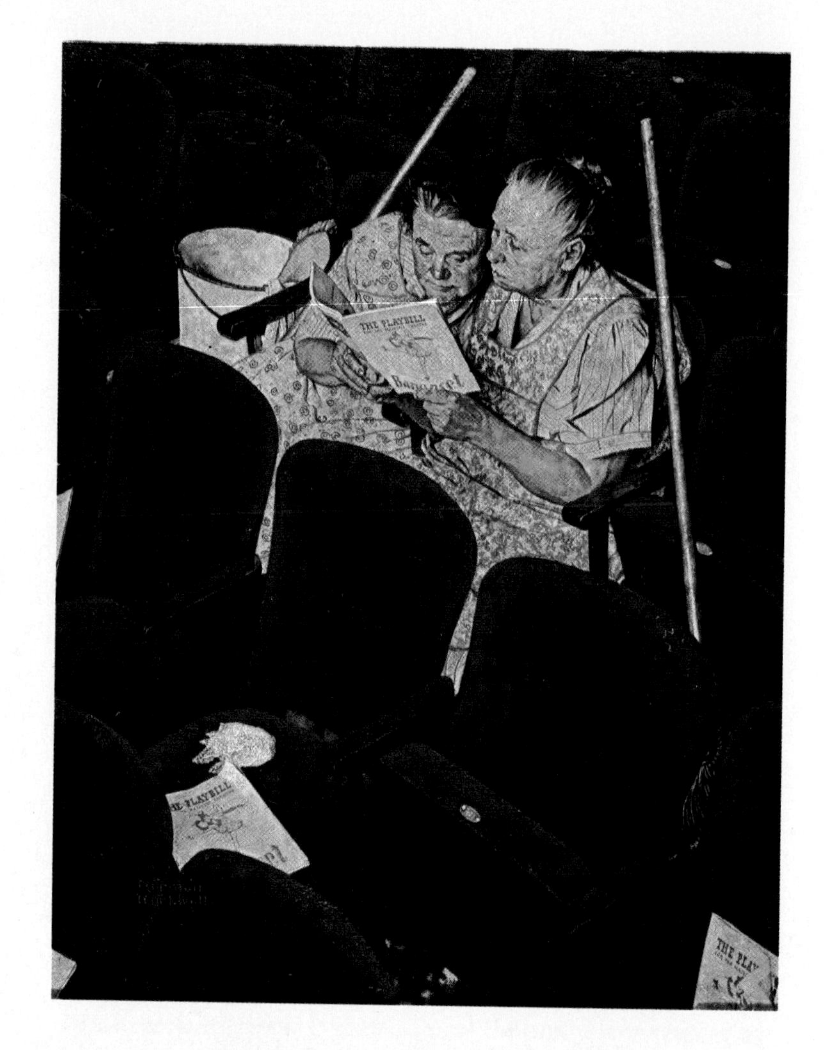

The Chars. *Original oil painting for* Post *cover, April 6, 1946. Collection Newell J. Ward, Jr.*

Red Oaks, Georgia Schoolroom. *Original oil painting for* Post, *November 2, 1946. Private collection*

Little Orphan at the Train. *Late 1930s. Final oil painting for illustration from Rockwell's scrapbooks. Collection Mr. and Mrs. Peter Lind Hayes*

Skater. *1947.*
Original oil painting.
Collection Mr. and Mrs.
Howard Weingrow

Young Boy on High Dive Board.
Original oil painting for Post *cover, August 16, 1947.*
Collection Mr. and Mrs. Robert S. Lubin

Homecoming. *Drawing for* Post *cover, December 25, 1948.*
Bernard Danenberg Galleries, Inc., New York

A personal and professional disaster occurred in 1943 just after the *Four Freedoms* were completed: Rockwell's studio near Arlington burned to the ground. From his point of view it was the loss of twenty-eight years of accumulated props, costumes, materials, and equipment—no more period pieces; from ours it was the loss of an unrecorded number of original paintings and his files of clippings. Today nobody including Rockwell himself has more than a vague idea of the extent of his work. There are no records.

Having "reported" the fire for the *Post* in a sheet of charcoal pencil drawings (July 17, 1943) Rockwell bought a house in the town of Arlington. Two other *Post* cover artists, Mead Schaeffer and John Atherton, lived there and the three became good friends, posing and providing criticism or moral support for each other upon request. Mead Schaeffer posed as the tattooist on the March 4, 1944, cover of the *Post*.

The trade press, beginning with *International Studio* in 1923, has always been interested in Rockwell. *Poster, American Artist, Design,* and *Graphic* have reproduced his work over the years. During the forties, *Arts, Art News,* and *Art Digest* also took notice, usually kindly but rarely enthusiastically. A one-man show at the Milwaukee Art Institute in 1941, a *New Yorker* profile in the March 17

Advertisement for Massachusetts Mutual Life Insurance Company

The Dugout. *Original oil painting for* Post *cover, September 4, 1948. The Brooklyn Museum*

Advertisement for Massachusetts Mutual Life Insurance Company

COUNTY AGRICULTURAL AGENT

Original oil painting for Post, *July 24, 1948. Collection University of Nebraska Art Galleries, Lincoln. Gift of Nathan Gold*

and 24, 1945, issues, and Arthur Guptill's excellent monograph published in 1946 brought him before the most critical of art audiences where he was variously described as a fine artist, a folk artist, and no artist at all.

During this decade, photography seems to continue to present both problems and solutions. With his remarkable abilities in typecasting, arranging, and directing, he reaches new heights in authenticity and realism. His sense of subject often reverts to the *Literary Digest* era of action within a complete setting but with the difference that the setting is now sometimes as important as the actors themselves. In the old days with the model before him hour after hour, the physical relationship between artist and sitter was relatively constant—too far away and he could not see clearly, too close and he could not see the entire subject. Now with the camera recording the scene—totally or in parts—space could be treated in any number of ways, and was. The *Four Freedoms* are a case in point: although obviously intended to be seen together, each puts the viewer, who now stands where Rockwell's photographer stood, in a different relationship with the subject. He is two rows—four or five feet—from the Speaker, inches from the Religious People, at least ten feet from the Fearless Father, and, finally, sits in the midst of Plenty, right on the dining room table. Individually, these vantage points are most successfully used but when the pictures are hung in the same room (as they are in the Old Corner House in Stockbridge) they look as if they had been painted at different settings of a zoom lens.

A second problem inherent in the use of photographs is the artist's dependence on the surface appearance of his subject rather than on its underlying construction. This makes the lines derived from the photographs of great importance because they are the major source of information. Consequently, they cannot be obscured by layers of paint until the artist is absolutely sure of what he is doing. This has two visible effects: first, the painting looks thin and transparent and, second, where the paint is thicker, it piles up in little islands surrounded by valleys where the lines once were or still are. The hampered brushwork that sometimes results is not usually noticeable in reproduction.

On the positive side, this demanding process and the serious subjects to which it was applied produced, in reaction, a delightful freehand style, which may rely on photographs for poses but certainly not for people. Rockwell's natural ability to caricature has been evident on and off from the days when he did illustrations for *Boys' Life*. In some instances, the Nassau Tavern mural and *The Horseshoe Forging Contest*, for example, this ability comes into conflict with his love of authentic reality. The soldiers on the right side of the farmer

Traffic Conditions. *Original oil painting for* Post *cover, July 9, 1949. Collection Mr. and Mrs. Phil Grace*

The New Television Set. *Original oil painting for* Post *cover, November 5, 1949. Los Angeles County Museum of Art. Gift of Mrs. Ned Crowell*

are caricatures compared with the officer on the left; some of the people watching the blacksmiths are exaggerated; others are not. (As an aside on Rockwell's horizontal pictures, they tend to be divisible into two equal halves with composition or action attracting the viewer's attention to the left half.)

Rockwell's treatment of the *Post* cover space from 1940 to 1949 reflected the camera's flexibility and also the new lettering design adopted at the end of June, 1942. Having grown accustomed to going behind or in front of the type that filled the upper fifth of the space, he now appeared under or around it. The name of the magazine had gradually become incidental to the artwork; now it competed for the viewer's attention—and often won. After 1946, lettering describing special features within the magazine was confined within the title panel at the top; no longer does copy cover up parts of the picture.

In addition to the war, the only obviously new subjects were some April Fool covers—fascinating in their juxtaposition of absolute realism and impossible nonsense. The forties treatment of such venerable themes as Santa Claus suggests a certain disillusionment with his own Panglossian vision: The Giver of Good Things slouches in the subway, his beard in his pocket. In using photographs and in accepting the world a little more as it sadly is, Rockwell found and mastered a new subject area: architectural exteriors. The returning soldier's tenement is a good example.

New York Central Diner.
Study for Post *cover, December 7, 1946.*
Collection Richard Rockwell

The Watchmaker.
Original oil painting for advertisement for
The Watchmakers of Switzerland, 1948.
New York and Bienne, Switzerland

Game Called Because of Rain.
Original oil painting for Post *cover, April 23, 1949.*
National Baseball Hall of Fame
and Museum, Cooperstown, New York

Norman
Rockwell

◀ STEAMBOAT RACE

1930s. Original oil painting. Whereabouts unknown

Hallmark Christmas card, 1949

1950–1971

Norman
Rockwell

Homecoming G.I. *Original oil painting for* Post *cover, May 26, 1945. Collection Mr. and Mrs. Ben Hibbs*

Shuffleton's Barber Shop.
Original oil painting for
Post *cover, April 29, 1950.*
Collection Norman Rockwell

IN 1951, ROCKWELL PAINTED THE MOST POPULAR OF ALL HIS *Post* COVERS—the grandmother and grandson saying grace in the railroad station restaurant. In 1952, he painted President Eisenhower, and he has painted every presidential candidate in every election since. But the decade began badly. The discouragement, uncertainty, and dissatisfaction that drove him to Europe in 1932 returned to accompany him through his move in 1953 from Arlington to Stockbridge, Massachusetts; he managed to go on meeting the endless barrage of deadlines with which he has always lived. He also managed to paint two of his best pictures: *Breaking Home Ties,* 1954, and *Marriage License,* 1955. In 1959, his wife Mary died, and he was alone again.

It is impossible to know how, or even if, these troubles affected his work. Changes certainly occurred. The most important one is a turning back to the subject of youth, to the subjects of his youth—boys, dogs, swimming, girls, adolescence, going to church, to the doctor's, to school.

Of the forty-one *Post* covers illustrated during the decade,

Our Heritage. *Original oil painting for Boy Scout calendar, 1950. Collection National Office, Boy Scouts of America, North Brunswick, New Jersey*

A Good Turn All Over the World. *Original oil painting for Boy Scout calendar, 1963. Collection National Office, Boy Scouts of America, North Brunswick, New Jersey*

twenty-two include children—as high a proportion as in the twenties.

These subjects of youth are based on situations typical of his early work but many now appear in new settings with new props—the hypodermic needle instead of the tongue depressor, the veterinarian's office instead of the patent medicine bottle. Although the cards and calendars generally minimize the setting while the *Post* covers emphasize it, a strong tendency, perhaps a compulsion, to caricature unites them stylistically. This can be both an asset and a liability. It can produce charming, lively, properly sentimental calendars—and it can ruin a good picture.

A great many commissions for advertisements were completed during this period. Rockwell did pencil drawings for the Massachusetts Mutual Life Insurance Company for twelve years starting in the early fifties. They describe pleasant, typical moments and milestones in the everyday life of a very Rockwellian family—without a trace of caricature. The same straightforward realism is characteristic of ads for Crest toothpaste, Parker pens, and American Telephone and Telegraph. The creative aspect of all of these illustrations

Scouting is Outing. *Original oil painting for Boy Scout calendar, 1968. Collection National Office, Boy Scouts of America, North Brunswick, New Jersey*

Walking to Church. *Original oil painting for* Post *cover, April 4, 1953. Collection Mr. and Mrs. Ken Stuart*

Lift Up Thine Eyes. *Original oil painting for illustration appearing in* McCall's, *March, 1969. Collection Mr. and Mrs. Phil Grace*

Easter Morning. *Original oil painting for* Post *cover, May 16, 1959. Private collection*

Triple Self-Portrait. *Original oil painting for* Post *cover, February 13, 1960. Collection Norman Rockwell* ▶

Norman
Rockwell

Two Plumbers and a Dog. *Original oil painting for* Post *cover, June 2, 1951. Collection Gordon Andrew*

Breaking Home Ties. *Original oil painting for* Post *cover, September 25, 1954. Collection Don Trachte*

seems to lie more in Rockwell's ability to select, arrange, and direct his subjects than in his abilities as a painter. A series of four cards painted for Hallmark and the sketches done for Pan American World Airways, both in 1957, are exceptions. Although as realistic as everything else, they are painted in a fresh, loose style, quite unlike anything that has come before. Just as Rockwell had blossomed forth with a new approach to illustration after his first session with the doldrums in the late fifties, he came to life again with a new appreciation of the spontaneous.

In knowing only part of his work, it is easy to mistake continuing interest in certain subject themes for a revival of interest. Until everything Rockwell ever did is properly fed into a data bank and a computer is programmed to distinguish all sorts of subtle changes, no one can be sure. Our only certainty is that he always works very

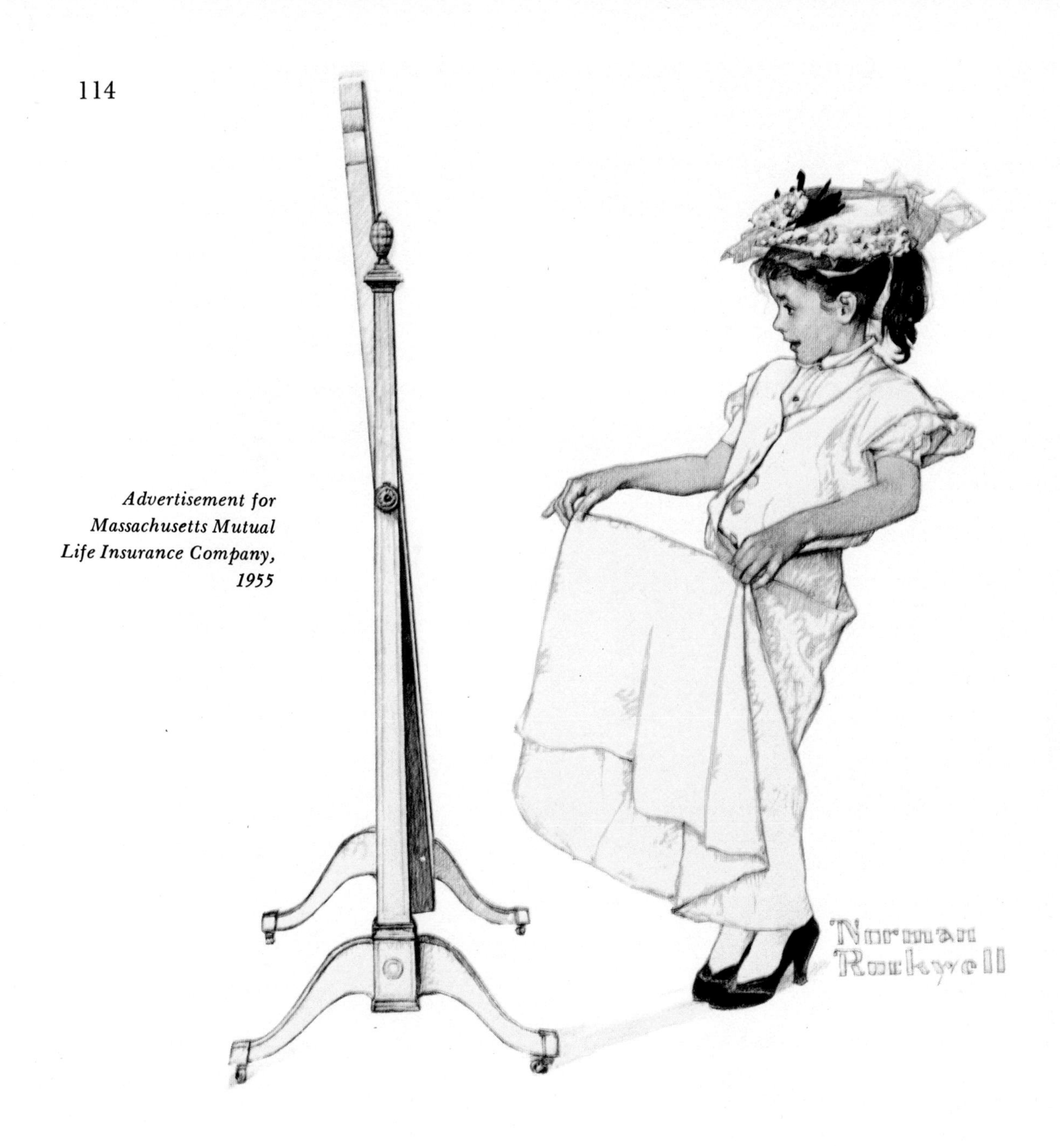

Advertisement for Massachusetts Mutual Life Insurance Company, 1955

hard, produces a prodigious amount, and can keep several approaches to the same subject going simultaneously. His fascination with the dimension of time seems to be one consistent factor. Although he records precise moments, he wants the viewer to know what has just happened or will happen next.

Norman Rockwell's world was changing. The old swimming hole had become polluted, carefree youth came in two colors, and typical, average, ideal Americans were going to fly to the moon. In 1963, he left the *Saturday Evening Post* after an uninterrupted association of forty-seven years and went to work for *Look*. There was a big difference. Instead of painting cheerleaders he painted integration; instead of peace and prosperity, he painted poverty, protest, and the Peace Corps.

Marriage License. *Original oil painting for* Post *cover, June 11, 1955. Collection Norman Rockwell*

Construction Crew.
Original oil painting for
Post *cover, August 21, 1954.*
Collection Saturday Evening Post

Preparing for Winter.
Original oil painting for
Four Seasons calendar, 1960.
Saks Galleries, Denver, Colorado

Checkup. *Original oil painting for* Post *cover, September 7, 1957. Private collection*

Before the Shot. *Original oil painting for* Post *cover, March 15, 1958. Collection Dr. and Mrs. Edward F. Babbott*

What happened? How does a chronicler of nostalgic America turn into a crusader? How can a man spend half a century finding humor and pathos in the daily trivia of American life and suddenly start painting about Russian education, Ethiopian agriculture, and the space program? And how does a man who has prospered by avoiding controversy find himself in Little Rock?

Rockwell is a professional. He accepts assignments, does the work, and gets paid. He and the *Post* worshiped each other; they welcomed his cover ideas almost until the very end—but always subject to editorial approval. The point of view was the magazine's, not

After the Prom. *Original oil painting for* Post *cover, May 27, 1957. Collection Mr. and Mrs. Thomas Rockwell*

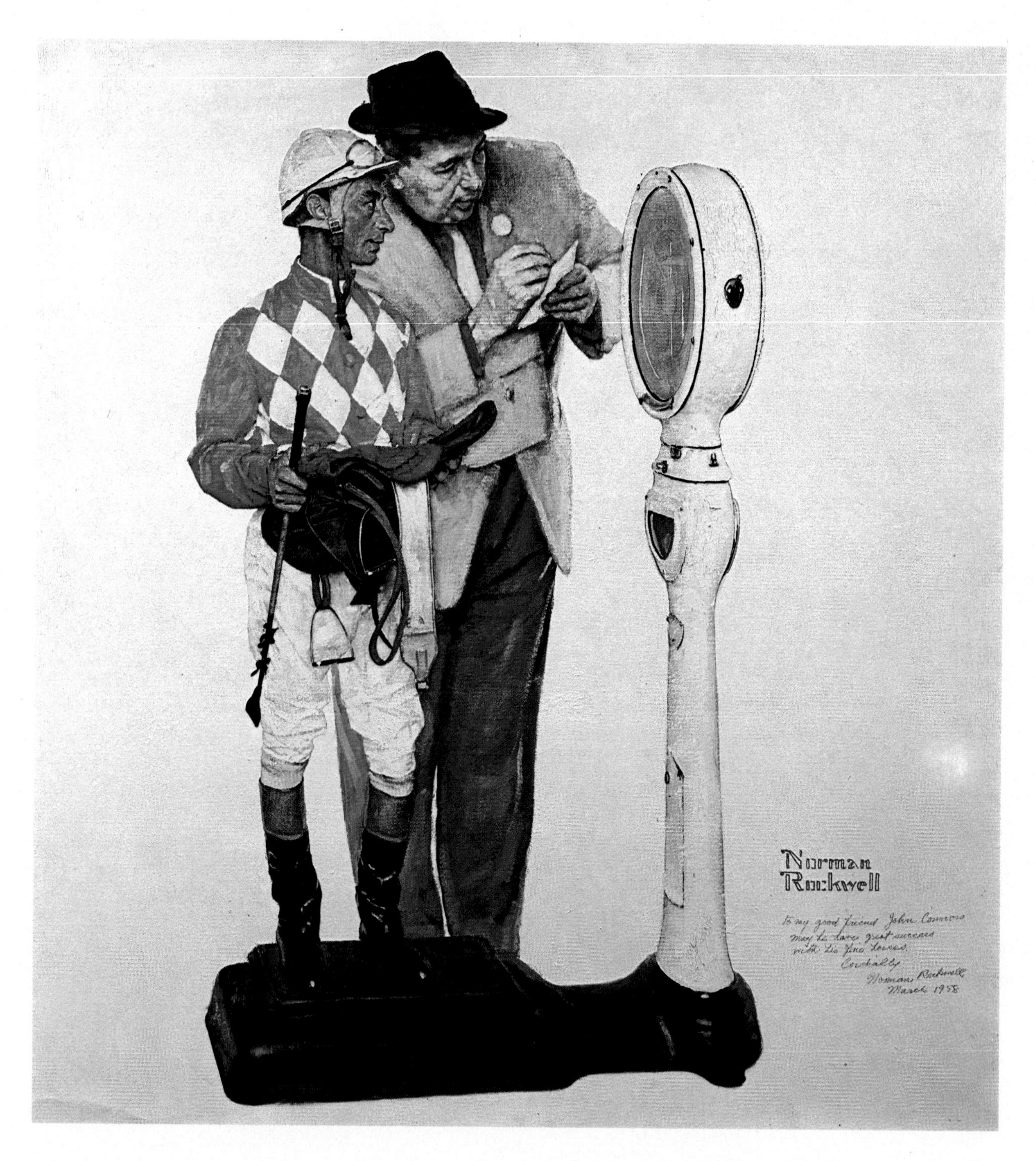

Weighing In. *Original oil painting of first version of* Post *cover, June 28, 1958. Collection Harry N. Abrams, Inc., New York*

Weighing In. *Original oil painting of final version of* Post *cover, June 28, 1958. The New Britain Museum of American Art, Connecticut. Sanford Low Memorial Collection of American Illustration*

Advertisement for Massachusetts Mutual Life Insurance Company, 1959

the artist's. Fortunately, Rockwell shared their point of view most of the time. But no job was done, no painting completed regardless of how strongly he wanted to do it, without their approval, including the *Four Freedoms*.

The *Look* jobs were almost completely special assignments. Rockwell accepted them, did the work, and got paid. The surprising and wonderful elements here are that the jobs were offered and that he did accept them. Imagine approaching the best-known artist in the country, a wealthy, venerable figure sixty-nine years old, and suggesting he change his line! And think of the artist who had just written in his autobiography: "I do ordinary people in everyday situations and that's about all I can do." But even the tenderest moment in the family albums is meager fare compared with a single footprint on the moon. No artist—even Pyle—has had such history to record.

Abstract and Concrete. *Original oil painting for* Post *cover, January 13, 1962. Private collection*

A Family Tree. *Original oil painting for* Post *cover, October 24, 1959. Collection Norman Rockwell*

Rockwell and his wife Molly.
1967. Charcoal sketch.
Collection Norman Rockwell

The decade of the sixties began auspiciously: Rockwell painted *The Golden Rule* in 1960 and married Molly Punderson in 1961. All of the styles and subject themes—even period settings—that developed over the years turn up again: unfinished and partly finished sketches in pencil and paint, silhouetted groups, full interiors, caricatures and portraits, masses of people, exteriors—and, through it all, Boy Scouts. Rockwell's reuse of his own creations occurs surprisingly seldom considering the frequency with which he repeats themes and the length of time he has been working. The fact that he does so at all points up the work involved in creating a single vignette. Once done, it is a tangible property that can save hours of time if applicable to another subject or picture.

The massing of people—usually head-on or in profile—began with the *Freedom of Worship* in 1942, was used in several Boy Scout calendars, and became a major device in the sixties; *The Golden Rule, The Peace Corps in Ethiopia, How Goes the War on Poverty?, The Right to Know,* and *Man's First Step on the Moon* all got this treatment. Based on a studio-arranged composition made from pho-

B. FRANKLIN
PRINTER

Original oil painting for illustration to Poor Richard's Almanacks, *1963. Collection Mrs. Victor H. Neirinckx*

Ben Franklin at a Desk.
Original oil painting for illustration to Poor Richard's Almanacks, *1963.*
Collection Mr. and Mrs. Joseph H. Hennage

Ben Franklin's Belles.
Original oil painting for illustration to Poor Richard's Almanacks, *1963.*
Collection Mr. and Mrs. Joseph H. Hennage

The Tavern.
Original oil painting for illustration to Poor Richard's Almanacks, *1963.*
Collection Mr. and Mrs. Joseph H. Hennage

Almanac Scenes. *Original oil painting for illustration to* Poor Richard's Almanacks, *1963.*
Collection Mr. and Mrs. Joseph H. Hennage

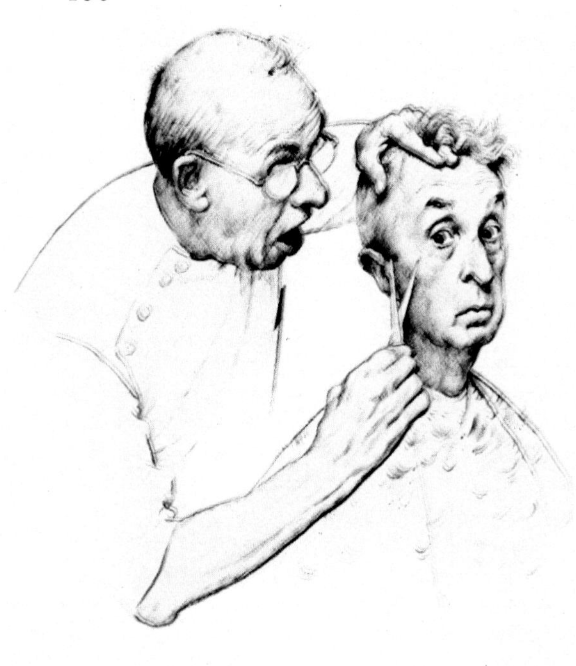

Norman Rockwell at the Barber.
Charcoal drawing for Look, *October 20, 1964.*
Collection Mr. and Mrs. William R. Meyers

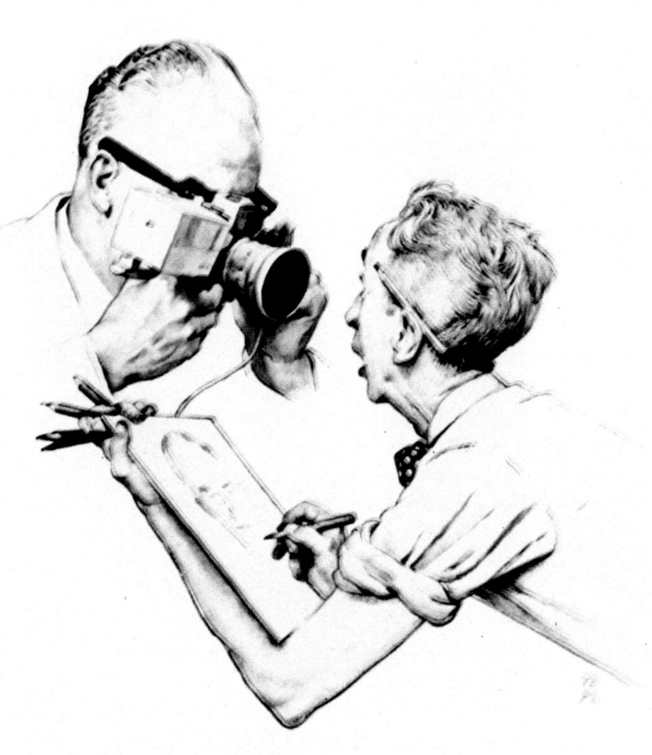

Rockwell and Goldwater.
Charcoal drawing for Look, *October 20, 1964.*
Collection Mr. and Mrs. Irving Lehr

Barry Goldwater.
Sketch for Look, *October 20, 1962.*
Private collection

Elect Casey. *Original oil painting for* Post *cover, November 8, 1958. Collection* Saturday Evening Post

Portrait of Eisenhower.
1952. Original oil painting.
Collection Mr. and Mrs. Ken Stuart

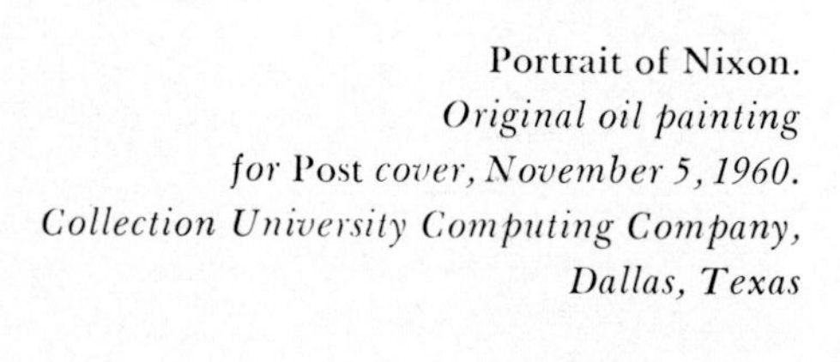

Portrait of Nixon.
Original oil painting
for Post *cover, November 5, 1960.*
Collection University Computing Company,
Dallas, Texas

A Time for Greatness. *Original oil painting for* Look *cover, July 14, 1964. Collection Harry N. Abrams, Inc., New York*

Portrait of Kennedy.
Original oil painting for Post *cover,*
October 29, 1960.
Private collection

JFK's Bold Legacy—Peace Corps.
Oil sketch for Look *cover,*
June 14, 1966.
Collection Mr. and Mrs. Jerome D. Mack

tographs of each individual, the series is characterized by painstaking rendering with emphasis on the unifying effect of common, usually strong, light sources.

In his final year at the *Post,* 1963, all of the covers were portraits. The art editor had approved a group of storytelling ideas, but as the editor did not use them they went with Rockwell when he left.

The assigned subjects Rockwell now accepts are big and important and challenging. Rockwell meets them with enthusiasm and imagination. But he has not changed. He still paints Christmas and funny-sad stories and springtime. He still likes his edges well-defined and, in spite of outer space, he likes his backgrounds close in and parallel to the picture plane. Horizontals and verticals make him

The Peace Corps in Ethiopia. *Original oil painting for* Look *illustration, June 14, 1966. Collection Old Corner House, Stockbridge, Mass.*

THE PROBLEM WE ALL LIVE WITH

Original oil painting for Look, *January 14, 1964. Collection Jack Solomon*

Russian Classroom. *Original oil painting for* Look *illustration, October 3, 1967. Collection Jack Solomon*

Bertrand Russell.
Original oil painting for Ramparts
illustration, May, 1967.
Collection Norman Rockwell

The Golden Rule. *Original oil painting for* Post *cover, April 1, 1961. Collection Norman Rockwell*

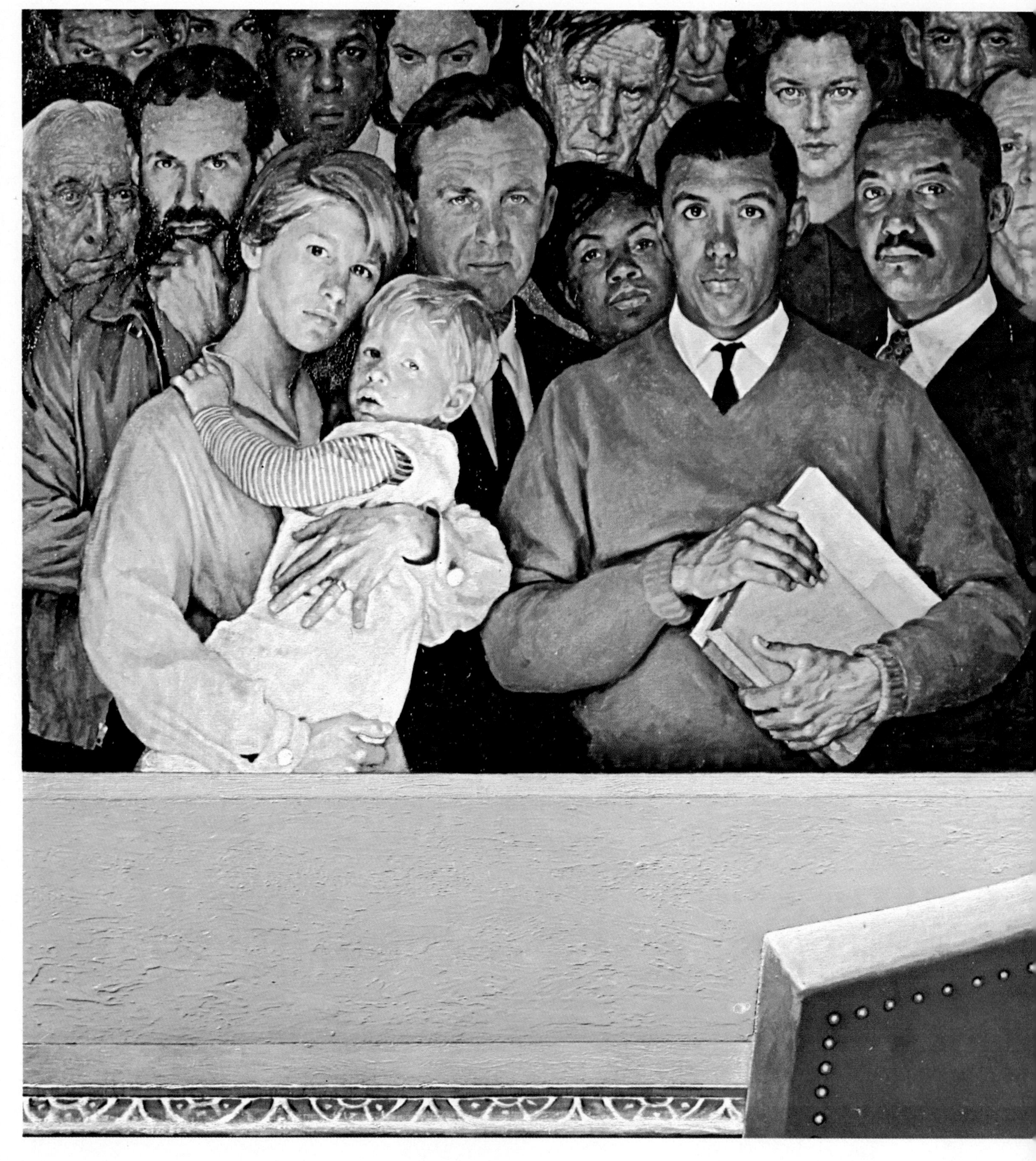

THE RIGHT TO KNOW

Original oil painting for Look *illustration, August 20, 1968. Collection Irving Mitchell Felt*

Portrait of an Astronaut.
Original oil painting for Look,
January 10, 1967.
Collection Aerospace Museum,
Smithsonian Institution,
Washington, D.C.

happier than diagonals, and the object in the foreground still invites us into the picture. Facial expressions are more serious, and the people who wear them are more important, but they still bring things to life as only Rockwell can. He has not abandoned average America, but he has become increasingly specific. His portrait of the nation may be one-sided but it is up-to-date—and, as always, more benevolent than deserved.

Man's First Step on the Moon. *Original oil painting for* Look *illustration, January 10, 1967.* ▶
Collection Aerospace Museum, Smithsonian Institution, Washington, D.C.

UNITED
STATES
norman rockwell

APOLLO 11 SPACE TEAM

LIST OF PLATES

*asterisks * indicate colorplates*

A late Rockwell canvas for the Department of the Interior, Bureau of Reclamation. 1970

Original oil painting for Look *illustration, July 15, 1969. Collection Aerospace Museum, Smithsonian Institution, Washington, D.C.*

Wt 17500
Norman Rockwell

◀ MOVING IN

Original oil painting for Look *illustration, May 16, 1967. Collection Old Corner House, Stockbridge, Mass.*

Detail of
Advertisement for Massachusetts Mutual Life Insurance Company

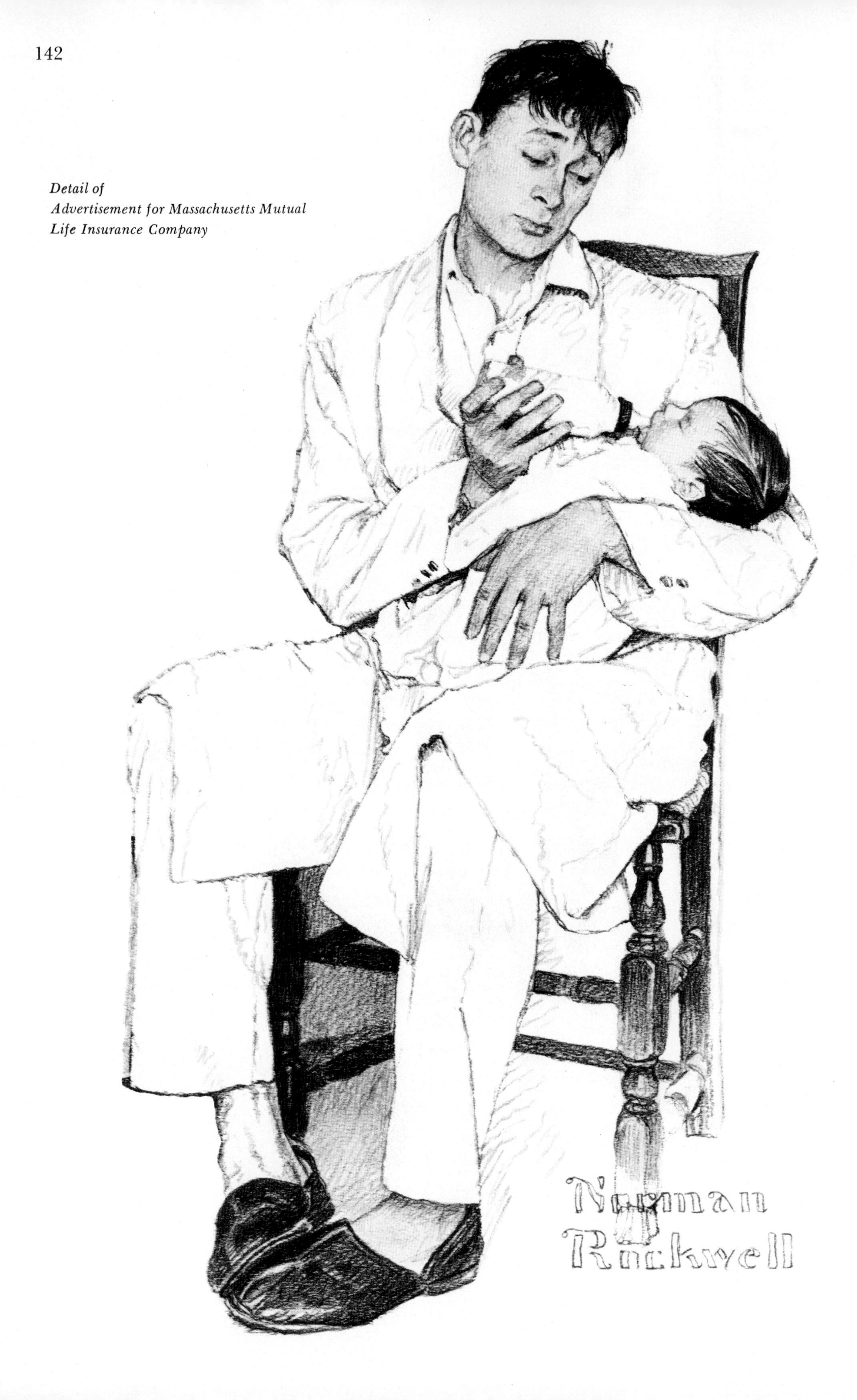

CREDITS

Courtesy Cowles Publications, Inc., LOOK *Magazine, pp. 147, 148–49; Encyclopaedia Britannica, Inc., advertisement, p. 48; Hallmark Cards, Inc., p. 104; George Macy Companies: illustration for The Heritage Press edition of* THE ADVENTURES OF TOM SAWYER, *copyright 1936, 1964 by The George Macy Companies, Inc., p. 65; Massachusetts Mutual Life Insurance Company, pp. 43, 54, 95, 114, 122, 142; Copyright © 1927 Downe Publishing, Inc. Reprinted by special permission of the* LADIES' HOME JOURNAL, *p. 48.*

Microsoft® Excel 2000 Illustrated Complete

Elizabeth Eisner Reding
Tara Lynn O'Keefe

APPROVED COURSEWARE

EXPERT

ONE MAIN STREET, CAMBRIDGE, MA 02142

Australia • Canada • Denmark • Japan • Mexico • New Zealand • Philippines
Puerto Rico • Singapore • South Africa • Spain • United Kingdom • United States

Microsoft Excel 2000—Illustrated Complete is published by Course Technology

Senior Product Manager:	Kathryn Schooling
Product Manager:	Rebecca VanEsselstine
Contributing Author:	Barbara Clemens
Associate Product Manager:	Emily Heberlein
Production Editor:	Jennifer Goguen
Developmental Editors:	Rachel Biheller Bunin, India Koopman
Composition House:	GEX Publishing Services
QA Manuscript Reviewers:	Jeff Schwartz, Alex White, Matt Carroll, John Freitas, Jon Greacan
Text Designer:	Joseph Lee, Joseph Lee Designs
Cover Designer:	Doug Goodman, Doug Goodman Designs

Trademarks

Course Technology and the Open Book logo are registered trademarks of Course Technology.

Illustrated Projects and the Illustrated Series are trademarks of Course Technology.

Some of the product names and company names used in this book have been used for identification purposes only and may be trademarks or registered trademarks of their respective manufacturers and sellers.

For more information contact:

Course Technology
One Main Street
Cambridge, MA 02142

Or find us on the World Wide Web at: www.course.com

Disclaimer

Course Technology reserves the right to revise this publication and make changes from time to time in its content without notice.

ISBN 0-7600-6064-9

Printed in the United States of America

2 3 4 5 6 7 8 9 BM 04 03 02 01 00

The Illustrated Series Offers the Entire Package for your Microsoft Office 2000 Needs

Office 2000 MOUS Certification Coverage

The Illustrated Series offers a growing number of Microsoft-approved titles that cover the objectives required to pass the Office 2000 MOUS exams. After studying with any of the approved Illustrated titles (see list on inside cover), you will have mastered the Core and Expert skills necessary to pass any Office 2000 MOUS exam with flying colors. In addition, **Excel 2000 MOUS Certification Objectives** at the end of the book map to where specific MOUS skills can be found in each lesson and where students can find additional practice.

Helpful New Features

The Illustrated Series responded to Customer Feedback by adding a **Project Files list** at the back of the book for easy reference, Changing the red font in the Steps to green for easier reading, and Adding New Conceptual lessons to units to give students the extra information they need when learning Office 2000.

New Exciting Case and Innovative On-Line Companion

There is an exciting new case study used throughout our textbooks, a fictitious company called MediaLoft, designed to be "real-world" in nature by introducing the kinds of activities that students will encounter when working with Microsoft Office 2000. The **MediaLoft Web site**, available at www.course.com/illustrated/medialoft, is an innovative Student Online Companion which enhances and augments the printed page by bringing students onto the Web for a dynamic and continually updated learning experience. The MediaLoft site mirrors the case study used throughout the book, creating a real-world intranet site for this chain of bookstore cafés. This Companion is used to complete the WebWorks exercise in each unit of this book, and to allow students to become familiar with the business application of an intranet site.

Enhance Any Illustrated Text with these Exciting Products!

Course CBT

Enhance your students' Office 2000 classroom learning experience with self-paced computer-based training on CD-ROM. Course CBT engages students with interactive multimedia and hands-on simulations that reinforce and complement the concepts and skills covered in the textbook. All the content is aligned with the MOUS (Microsoft Office User Specialist) program, making it a great preparation tool for the certification exams. Course CBT also includes extensive pre- and post-assessments that test students' mastery of skills.

SAM 2000

How well do your students *really* know Microsoft Office? SAM 2000 is a performance-based testing program that measures students' proficiency in Microsoft Office 2000. You can use SAM 2000 to place students into or out of courses, monitor their performance throughout a course, and help prepare them for the MOUS certification exams.

Create Your Ideal Course Package with CourseKits™

If one book doesn't offer all the coverage you need, create a course package that does. With Course Technology's CourseKits—our mix-and-match approach to selecting texts—you have the freedom to combine products from more than one series. When you choose any two or more Course Technology products for one course, we'll discount the price and package them together so your students can pick up one convenient bundle at the bookstore.

For more information about any of these offerings or other Course Technology products, contact your sales representative or visit our web site at:

www.course.com

Preface

Welcome to *Microsoft Excel 2000—Illustrated Complete*. This highly visual book offers users a comprehensive hands-on introduction to Microsoft Excel 2000 and also serves as an excellent reference for future use. This book is appropriate for a full semester course, and its modular structure allows for greater flexibility—you can cover the units in any order you choose.

▶ Organization and Coverage

This text contains sixteen units that cover basic to advanced Excel skills. In these units, students learn how to build, edit, and format worksheets and charts, work with formulas and functions, publish workbooks to the Web, automate worksheet tasks, use lists and analyze list data, use PivotTables, exchange data with other programs, and program with Excel.

▶ About this Approach

What makes the Illustrated approach so effective at teaching software skills? It's quite simple. Each skill is presented on two facing pages, with the step-by-step instructions on the left page, and large screen illustrations on the right. Students can focus on a single skill without having to turn the page. This unique design makes information extremely accessible and easy to absorb, and provides a great reference for after the course is over. This hands-on approach also makes it ideal for both self-paced or instructor-led classes.

Each lesson, or "information display," contains the following elements:

Each 2-page spread focuses on a single skill.

Clear step-by-step directions explain how to complete the specific task, with what students are to type in green. When students follow the numbered steps, they quickly learn how each procedure is performed and what the results will be.

Concise text that introduces the basic principles discussed in the lesson. Procedures are easier to learn when concepts fit into a framework.

Excel 2000

Editing a Chart

Once you've created a chart, it's easy to modify it. You can change data values in the worksheet, and the chart will automatically be updated to reflect the new data. You can also easily change chart types using the buttons on the Chart toolbar. Jim looks over his worksheet and realizes he entered the wrong data for the Kansas City store in November and December. After he corrects this data, he wants to see how the same data looks using different chart types.

Steps

Trouble?
If you cannot see the chart and data together on your monitor, click View on the menu bar, click Zoom, then click 75%.

1. If necessary, scroll the worksheet so that you can see both the chart and row 8, containing the Kansas City sales figures, then place your mouse pointer over the data point to display **Series "Kansas City" Point "December" Value "15,500"**
   As you correct the values, the columns for November and December in the chart automatically change.
2. Click cell **F8**, type **18000** to correct the November sales figure, press [→], type **19500** in cell **G8**, then click
   The Kansas City columns for November and December reflect the increased sales figures. See Figure D-9. The totals are also updated in column H and row 10.
3. Select the chart by clicking anywhere within the chart border, then click the **Chart Type list arrow** on the Chart toolbar
   The chart type buttons appear on the Chart Type palette. Table D-3 describes the chart types available.
4. Click the **Bar Chart button** on the palette
   The column chart changes to a bar chart. See Figure D-10. You look at the bar chart, take some notes, and then decide to convert it back to a column chart. You now want to see if the large increase in sales would be better presented with a three-dimensional column chart.
5. Click the **Chart Type list arrow**, then click the **3-D Column Chart button** on the palette
   A three-dimensional column chart appears. You notice that the three-dimensional column format is more crowded than the two-dimensional format but gives you a sense of volume.
6. Click the **Chart Type list arrow**, then click the **Column Chart button** on the palette
7. Save your work

QuickTip
Experiment with different formats for your charts until you get just the right look.

CLUES TO USE

Rotating a chart

In a three-dimensional chart, columns or bars can sometimes be obscured by other data series within the same chart. You can rotate the chart until a better view is obtained. Double-click the chart, click the tip of one of its axes (select the Corners object), then drag the handles until a more pleasing view of the data series appears. See Figure D-8.

FIGURE D-8: 3-D chart rotated with improved view of data series

MediaLoft Sales - Eastern Division

Click to rotate chart

▶ EXCEL D-8 WORKING WITH CHARTS

Hints as well as trouble-shooting advice, right where you need it – next to the step itself.

Clues to Use boxes provide concise information that either expands on one component of the major lesson skill or describes an independent task that is in some way related to the major lesson skill.

Other Features

The two-page lesson format featured in this book provides the new user with a powerful learning experience. Additionally, this book contains the following features:

▶ MOUS Certification Coverage

Each unit opener has a MOUS next to it to indicate where Microsoft Office User Specialist (MOUS) skills are covered. In addition, there is a MOUS appendix which contains a grid that maps to where specific Core and Expert Excel MOUS skills can be found in each lesson and where students can find additional practice. This textbook thoroughly prepares students to learn the skills needed to pass the Excel Core and Expert 2000 exams.

▶ Real-World Case

The case study used throughout the textbook, a fictitious company called MediaLoft, is designed to be "'real-world" in nature and introduces the kinds of activities that students will encounter when working with Microsoft Excel 2000. With a real-world case, the process of solving problems will be more meaningful to students. Students can also enhance their skills by completing the Web Works exercises in each unit by going to the innovative Student Online Companion, available at **www.course.com/illustrated/medialoft**. The MediaLoft site mirrors the case study by acting as the company's intranet site, further allowing students to become familiar with applicable business scenarios.

▶ End of Unit Material

Each unit concludes with a Concepts Review that tests students' understanding of what they learned in the unit. The Concepts Review is followed by a Skills Review, which provides students with additional hands-on practice of the skills. The Skills Review is followed by Independent Challenges, which pose case problems for students to solve. At least one Independent Challenge in each unit asks students to use the World Wide Web to solve the problem as indicated by a Web Work icon. The Visual Workshops that follow the Independent Challenges help students develop critical thinking skills. Students are shown completed Web pages or screens and are asked to recreate them from scratch.

Every lesson features large-size, full-color representations of what the student's screen should look like after completing the numbered steps.

FIGURE D-9: Worksheet with new data entered for Kansas City

MediaLoft Eastern Division Stores

FY 2000 Sales Following Advertising Campaign

	July	August	September	October	November	December	Total
Boston	12,000	12,000	15,500	20,000	21,000	20,500	$103,500
Chicago	14,500	16,000	17,500	18,000	18,500	19,000	$101,000
Kansas City	9,500	10,000	15,000	16,000	18,000	19,500	$103,500
NYC	15,000	13,000	16,500	19,000	20,000	21,000	$ 88,000
Total	$ 51,000	$ 51,000	$ 64,500	$ 73,000	$ 77,500	$ 80,000	$396,000

MediaLoft Sales - Eastern Division

New data

Adjusted data points

Excel 2000

FIGURE D-10: Bar chart

	July	August	September	October	November	December	Total
Boston	12,000	12,000	15,500	20,000	21,000	20,500	$103,500
Chicago	14,500	16,000	17,500	18,000	18,500	19,000	$101,000
Kansas City	9,500	10,000	15,000	16,000	18,000	19,500	$103,500
NYC	15,000	13,000	16,500	19,000	20,000	21,000	$ 88,000
Total	$ 51,000	$ 51,000	$ 64,500	$ 73,000	$ 77,500	$ 80,000	$396,000

MediaLoft Sales - Eastern Division

Row and column data are reversed

TABLE D-3: Commonly used chart type buttons

click	to display a	click	to display a	click	to display a	click	to display a
	area chart		pie chart		3-D area chart		3-D pie chart
	bar chart		(xy) scatter chart		3-D bar chart		3-D surface chart
	column chart		doughnut chart		3-D column chart		3-D cylinder chart
	line chart		radar chart		3-D line chart		3-D cone chart

WORKING WITH CHARTS EXCEL D-9

Quickly accessible summaries of key terms, toolbar buttons, or keyboard alternatives connected with the lesson material. Students can refer easily to this information when working on their own projects at a later time.

The page numbers are designed like a road map. Excel indicates the Excel section, D indicates the fourth unit, and 9 indicates the page within the unit.

Instructor's Resource Kit

The Instructor's Resource Kit is Course Technology's way of putting the resources and information needed to teach and learn effectively into your hands. With an integrated array of teaching and learning tools that offers you and your students a broad range of technology-based instructional options, we believe this kit represents the highest quality and most cutting edge resources available to instructors today. Many of these resources are available at www.course.com. The resources available with this book are:

MediaLoft Web site Available at **www.course.com/illustrated/medialoft**, this innovative Student Online Companion enhances and augments the printed page by bringing students onto the Web for a dynamic and continually updated learning experience. The MediaLoft site mirrors the case study used throughout the book, creating a real-world intranet site for this fictitious company, a national chain of bookstore cafés. This Companion is used to complete the WebWorks exercise in each unit of this book, and to allow students to become familiar with the business application of an intranet site.

Instructor's Manual Available as an electronic file, the Instructor's Manual is quality-assurance tested and includes unit overviews, detailed lecture topics for each unit with teaching tips, an Upgrader's Guide, solutions to all lessons and end-of-unit material, and extra Independent Challenges. The Instructor's Manual is available on the Instructor's Resource Kit CD-ROM, or you can download it from **www.course.com**.

Course Test Manager Designed by Course Technology, this Windows-based testing software helps instructors design, administer, and print tests and pre-tests. A full-featured program, Course Test Manager also has an online testing component that allows students to take tests at the computer and have their exams automatically graded.

Course Faculty Online Companion You can browse this textbook's password-protected site to obtain the Instructor's Manual, Solution Files, Project Files, and any updates to the text. Contact your Customer Service Representative for the site address and password.

Project Files Project Files contain all of the data that students will use to complete the lessons and end-of-unit material. A Readme file includes instructions for using the files. Adopters of this text are granted the right to install the Project Files on any standalone computer or network. The Project Files are available on the Instructor's Resource Kit CD-ROM, the Review Pack, and can also be downloaded from www.course.com.

Solution Files Solution Files contain every file students are asked to create or modify in the lessons and end-of-unit material. A Help file on the Instructor's Resource Kit includes information for using the Solution Files.

Figure Files Figure files contain all the figures from the book in bitmap format. Use the figure files to create transparency masters or in a PowerPoint presentation.

WebCT WebCT is a tool used to create Web-based educational environments and also uses WWW browsers as the interface for the course-building environment. The site is hosted on your school campus, allowing complete control over the information. WebCT has its own internal communication system, offering internal e-mail, a Bulletin Board, and a Chat room.

Course Technology offers pre-existing supplemental information to help in your WebCT class creation, such as a suggested Syllabus, Lecture Notes, Figures in the Book / Course Presenter, Student Downloads, and Test Banks in which you can schedule an exam, create reports, and more.

Brief Contents

Contents

Windows 98

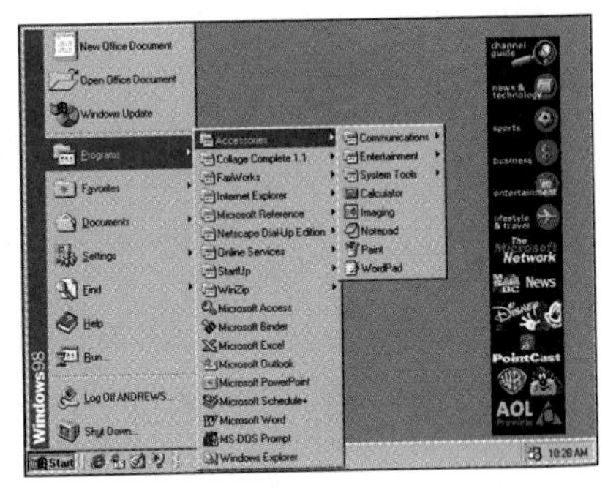

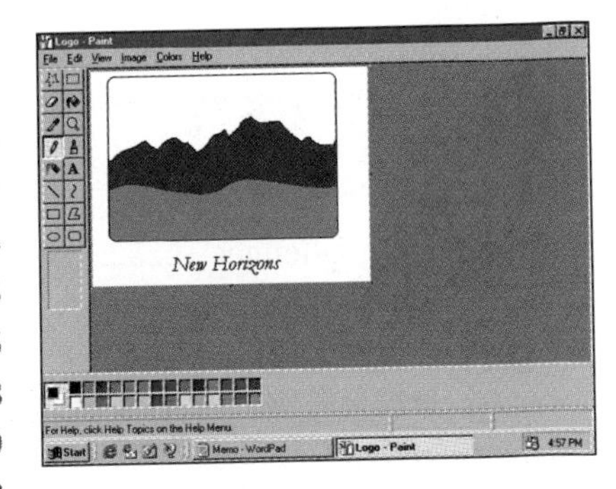

Contents

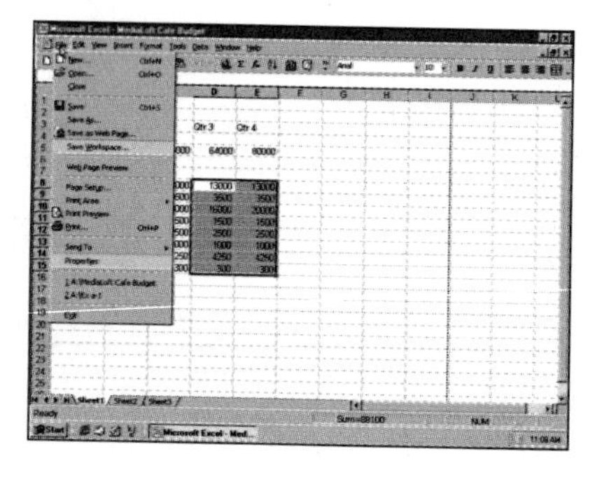

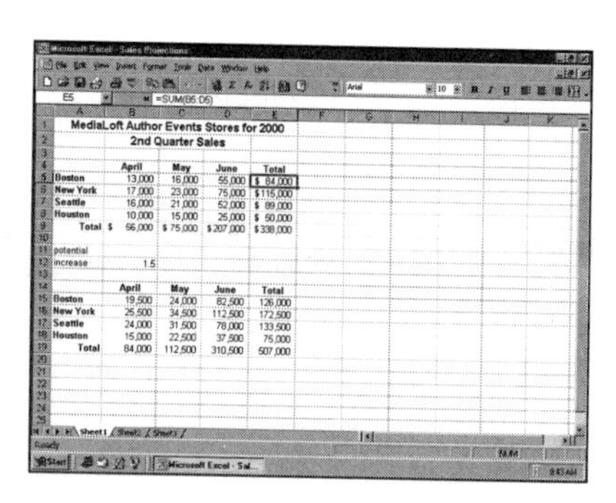

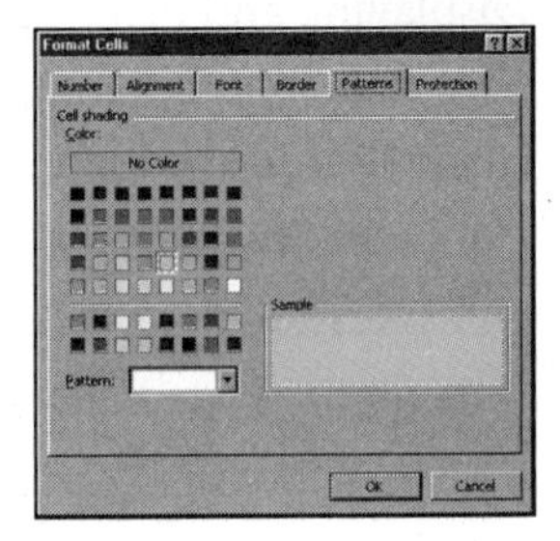

Format Cells
Number
Alignment
Font
Border
Patterns
Protection
Cell shading
Color:
No Color
Sample
Pattern:
OK
Cancel

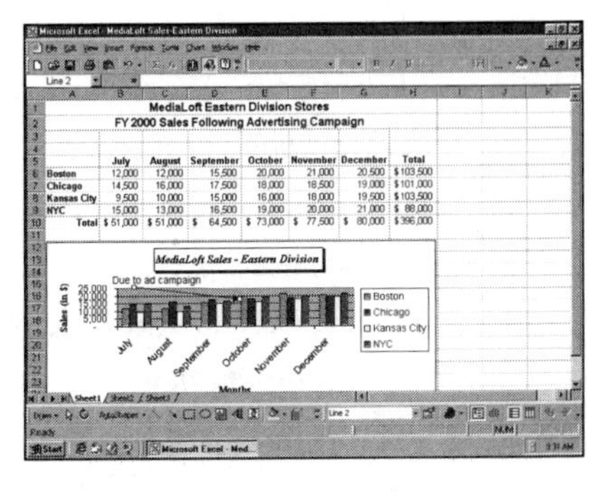

MediaLoft Eastern Division Stores
FY 2000 Sales Following Advertising Campaign
MediaLoft Sales - Eastern Division
Due to ad campaign
Boston
Chicago
Kansas City
NYC

Contents

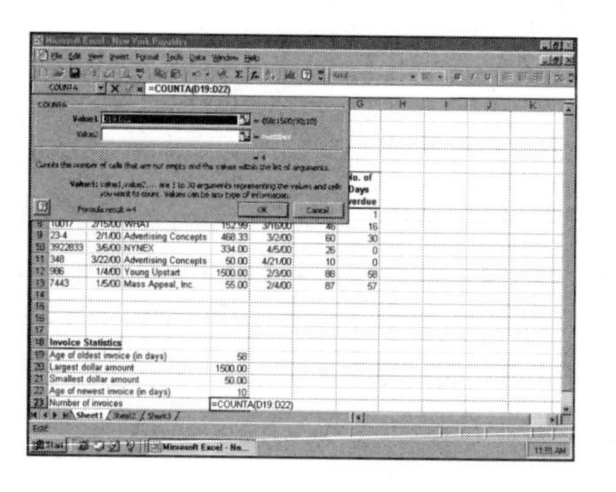

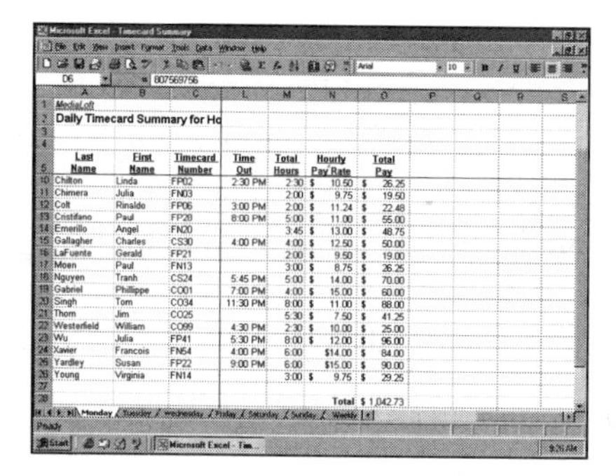

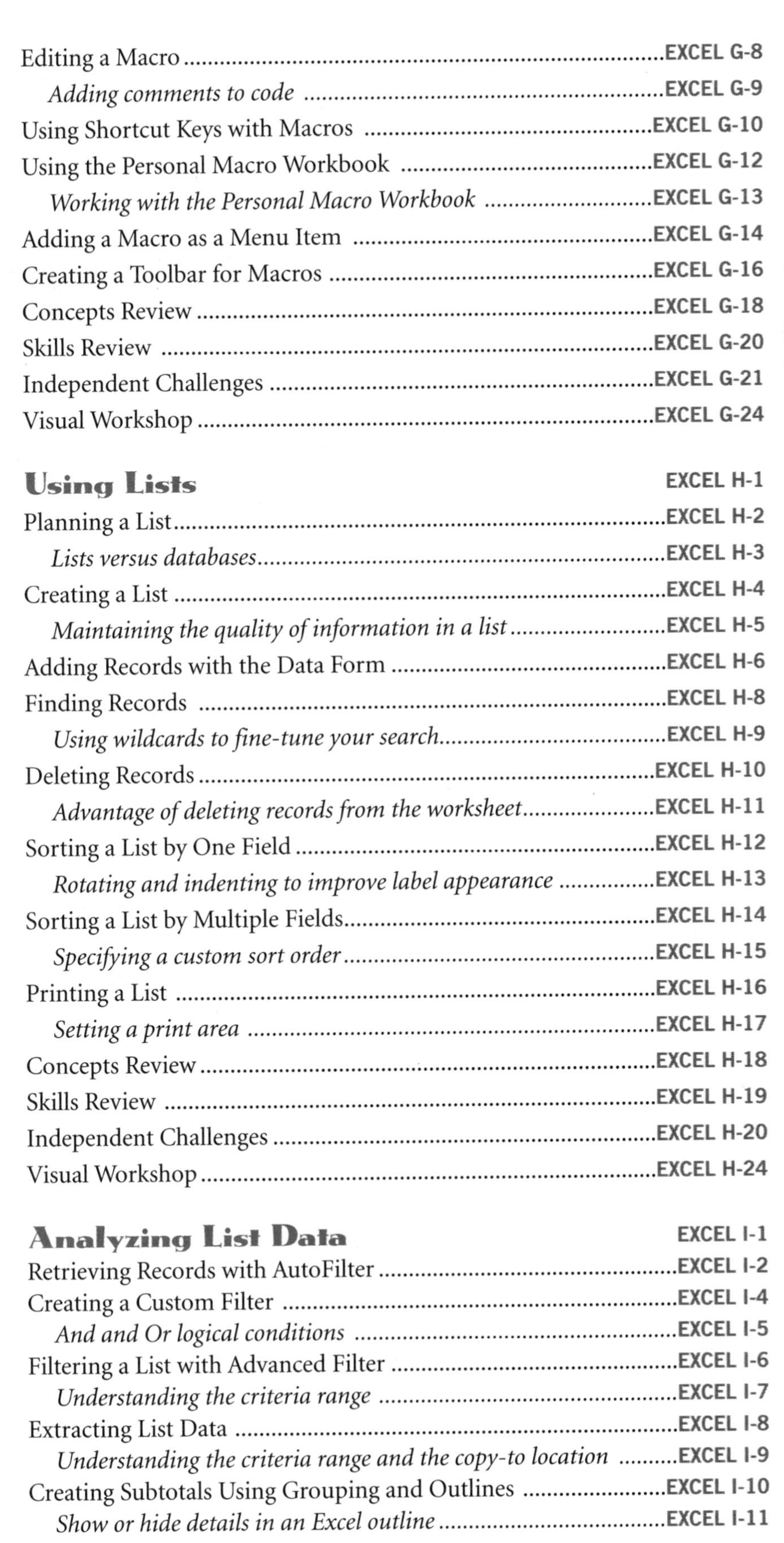

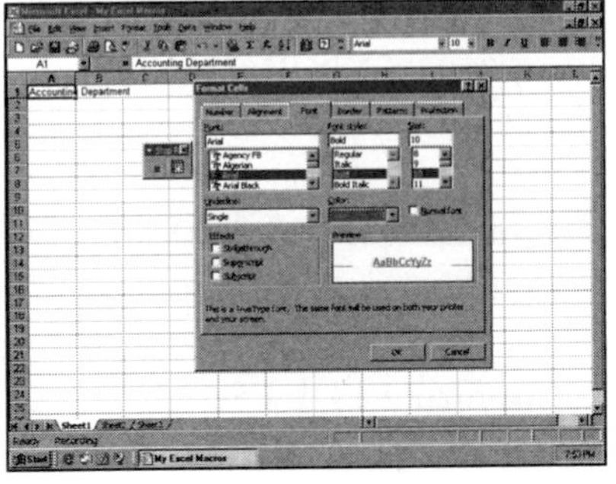

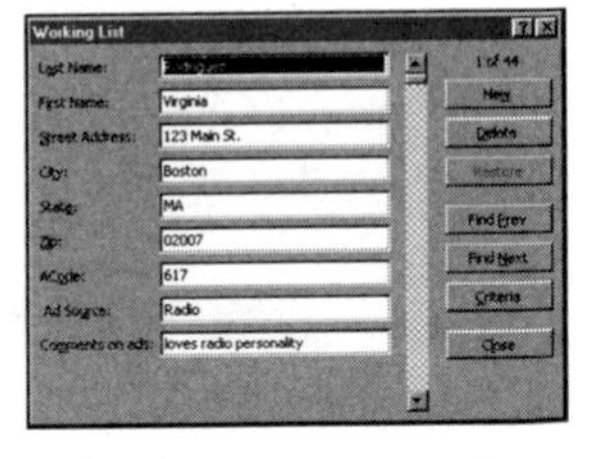

Contents

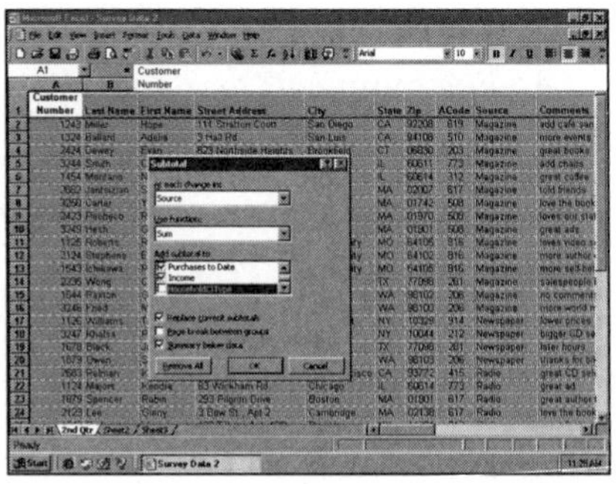

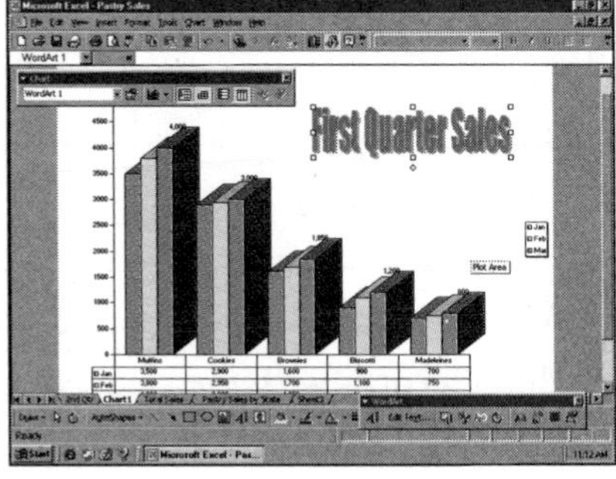

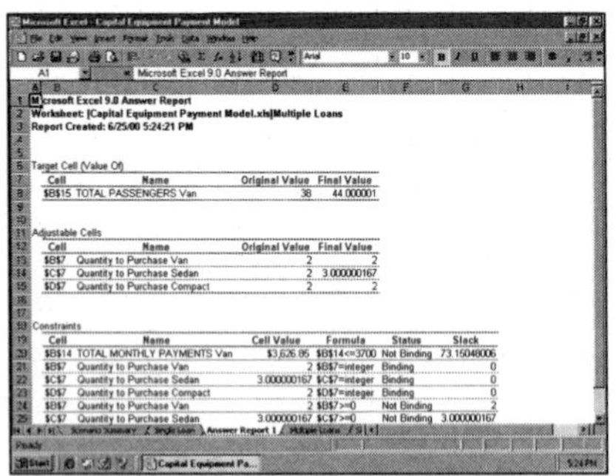

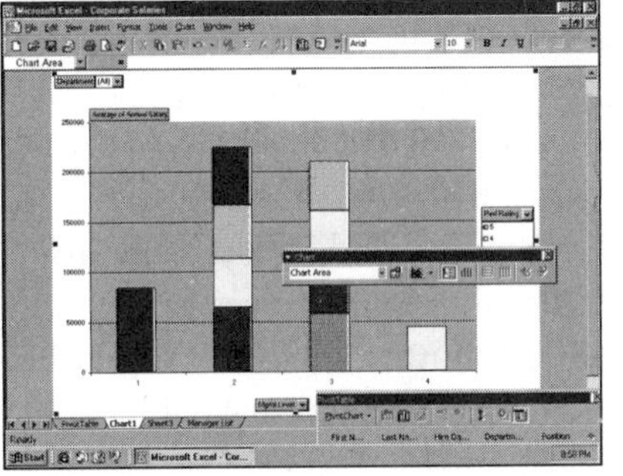

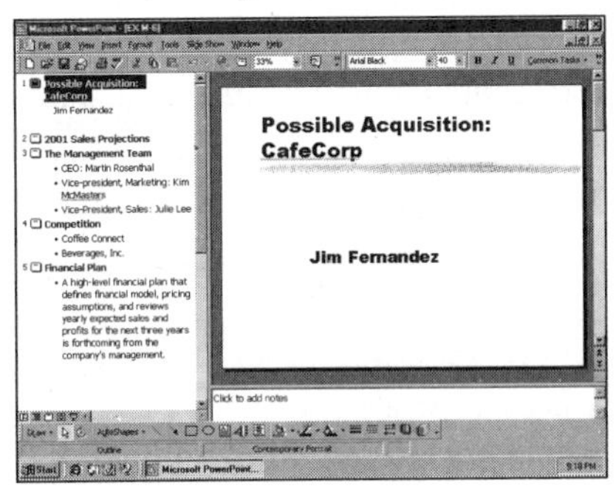

Possible Acquisition:
CafeCorp
Jim Fernandez

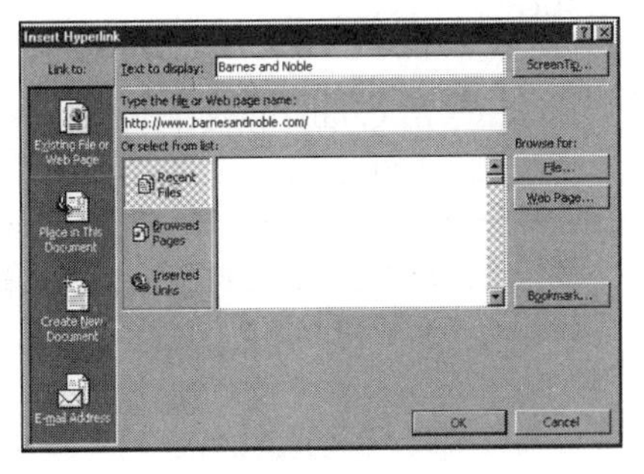

Insert Hyperlink
Text to display:
Barnes and Noble
http://www.barnesandnoble.com/
OK
Cancel

Contents

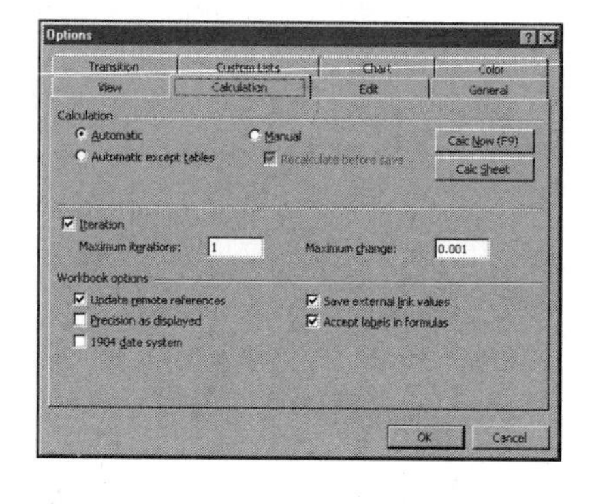

Options
Transition
Custom Lists
Chart
Color
View
Calculation
Edit
General
Calculation
Automatic
Manual
Automatic except tables
Recalculate before save
Calc Now (F9)
Calc Sheet
Iteration
Maximum iterations:
1
Maximum change:
0.001
Workbook options
Update remote references
Save external link values
Precision as displayed
Accept labels in formulas
1904 date system
OK
Cancel

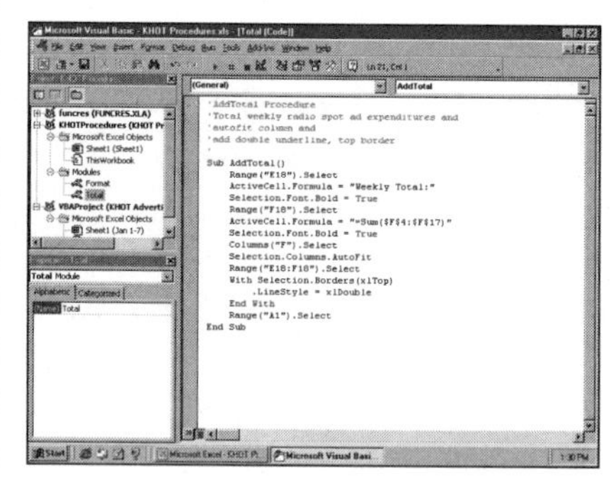

Getting Started with Windows 98

Objectives

- Start Windows and view the Active Desktop
- Use the mouse
- Start a program
- Move and resize windows
- Use menus, keyboard shortcuts, and toolbars
- Use dialog boxes
- Use scroll bars
- Get Help
- Close a program and shut down Windows

Microsoft Windows 98 is an **operating system**, a computer program that controls how the computer carries out basic tasks such as displaying information on your computer screen and running programs. Windows 98 helps you save and organize the results of your work (such as a resume or a list of addresses) as **files**, which are electronic collections of data. Windows 98 also coordinates the flow of information among the programs, printers, storage devices, and other components of your computer system. When you work with Windows 98, you will notice many **icons**, small pictures intended to be meaningful symbols of the items they represent. You will also notice rectangular-shaped work areas known as **windows**, thus the name of the operating system. This use of icons and windows is called a **graphical user interface** (**GUI**, pronounced "gooey"), which means that you interact with the computer through the use of graphics such as windows, icons, and other meaningful words and symbols. This unit introduces you to basic skills that you can use in all Windows programs.

Starting Windows and Viewing the Active Desktop

When you turn on your computer, Windows 98 automatically starts and the Active Desktop appears. The **Active Desktop**, shown in Figure A-1, is where you organize all the information and tools you need to accomplish your computer tasks. From the desktop, you can access, store, share, and explore information seamlessly, whether it resides on your computer, a network, or the Internet. The **Internet** is a worldwide collection of over 40 million computers linked together to share information. The desktop is called "active" because, unlike in other versions of Windows, it allows you to access the Internet. When you start Windows for the first time, the desktop appears with the **default** settings, those preset by the operating system. For example, the default color of the desktop is green. If any of the default settings have been changed on your computer, your desktop will look different than in the figures, but you should be able to locate all the items you need. The bar at the bottom of your screen is called the **taskbar**, which shows what programs are currently running. Use the **Start button** at the left end of the taskbar to start programs, find and open files, access Windows Help and so on. The **Quick Launch toolbar** is next to the Start button; it contains buttons you use to quickly start Internet-related programs and show the desktop when it is not currently displayed. The bar on the right side of your screen is called the **Channel Bar**, which contains buttons you use to access the Internet. Table A-1 identifies the icons and other elements you see on your desktop. If Windows 98 is not currently running, follow the steps below to start it now.

1. **Turn on your computer and monitor**
   Windows automatically starts and the desktop appears, as shown in Figure A-1. If you are working on a network at school or at an office, you might see a password dialog box. If so, continue to Step 2. If not, continue to the next lesson.

2. **Type your password, then press [Enter]**
   Once the password is accepted, the Windows desktop appears on your screen.

Trouble?

If you don't know your password, see your instructor or technical support person.

Accessing the Internet from the Active Desktop

One of the important differences between Windows 98 and previous versions of Windows is that Windows 98 allows you to access the Internet from the desktop using Internet Explorer, a program that is integrated into the Windows 98 operating system. Internet Explorer is an example of a **browser**, a program designed to access the **World Wide Web (WWW, the Web)**. One feature of Internet Explorer is that you can use the Favorites command on the Start menu to access places on the Internet that you visit frequently. Also, you can use the Quick Launch toolbar to launch Internet-related programs and the Channel Bar to view Internet channels, which are like those on television but display Internet content. The integration of a browser into the operating system provides a seamless connection between your desktop and the Internet.

FIGURE A-1: Windows Active Desktop

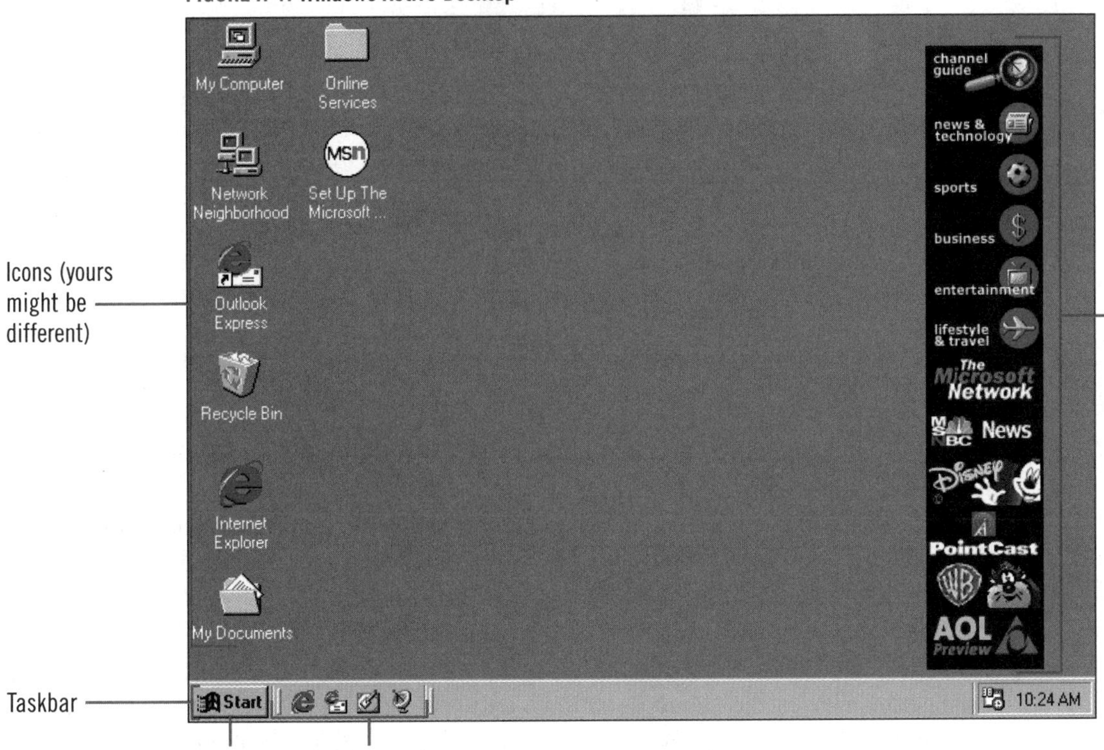

TABLE A-1: Elements of the Windows desktop

desktop element	allows you to
My Computer	Work with different disk drives and printers on your computer
Network Neighborhood	Work with different disk drives and printers on a network
Outlook Express	Start Outlook Express, an electronic mail program
Recycle Bin	Delete and restore files
Internet Explorer	Start Internet Explorer, a program you use to access the Internet
My Documents folder	Store programs, documents, graphics, or other files
Taskbar	Start programs and switch among open programs
Start button	Start programs, open documents, find a file, and more
Channel Bar	Start Internet Explorer and open channels
Quick Launch toolbar	Start Internet Explorer, start Outlook Express, show the desktop, and view channels

Using the Mouse

A **mouse** is a hand-held **input device** that you use to interact with your computer. Input devices come in many shapes and sizes; some, like a mouse, are directly attached to your computer with a cable; others function like a TV remote control and allow you to access your computer without being right next to it. Figure A-2 shows examples of common pointing devices. Because the most common pointing device is a mouse, this book uses that term. If you are using a different pointing device substitute that device whenever you see the term "mouse." When you move the mouse, the **mouse pointer** on the screen moves in the same direction. The **mouse buttons** are used to select icons and commands, which is how you communicate with the computer. Table A-2 shows some common mouse pointer shapes that indicate different activities. Table A-3 lists the five basic mouse actions. Begin by experimenting with the mouse now.

Steps

1. **Locate the mouse pointer on the desktop, then move the mouse across your desk or mousepad**
   Watch how the mouse pointer moves on the desktop in response to your movements. Practice moving the mouse pointer in circles, then back and forth in straight lines.
2. **Position the mouse pointer over the My Computer icon**
   Positioning the mouse pointer over an item is called **pointing**.
3. **With the pointer over the My Computer icon, press and release the left mouse button**
   Pressing and releasing the left mouse button is called **clicking** or single-clicking, to distinguish it from double-clicking, which you'll do in Step 7. When you position the mouse pointer over an icon or any item and click, you select that item. When an item is **selected**, it is **highlighted** (shaded differently than other items), and any action you take will be performed on that item.
4. **With the icon selected, press and hold down the left mouse button, then move the mouse down and to the right and release the mouse button**
   The icon becomes dimmed and moves with the mouse pointer; this is called **dragging**, which you use to move icons and other Windows elements. When you release the mouse button, the icon is moved to a new location.
5. **Position the mouse pointer over the My Computer icon, then press and release the right mouse button**
   Clicking the right mouse button is known as **right-clicking**. Right-clicking an item on the desktop displays a **pop-up menu**, as shown in Figure A-3. This menu lists the commands most commonly used for the item you have clicked. A **command** is a directive that provides access to a program's features.
6. **Click anywhere outside the menu to close the pop-up menu**
7. **Position the mouse pointer over the My Computer icon, then press and release the left mouse button twice quickly**
   Clicking the mouse button twice quickly is known as **double-clicking**, which, in this case, opens the My Computer window. The **My Computer** window contains additional icons that represent the drives and system components that are installed on your computer.
8. **Click the Close button in the upper-right corner of the My Computer window**

Trouble?

If the My Computer window opens, your mouse isn't set with the Windows 98 default mouse settings. See your instructor or technical support person for assistance. This book assumes your computer is set to all Windows 98 default settings

QuickTip

When a step tells you to "click," use the left mouse button. If it says "right-click", use the right mouse button.

TABLE A-2: Common mouse pointer shapes

shape	used to
↖	Select items, choose commands, start programs, and work in programs
I	Position mouse pointer for editing or inserting text; called the insertion point
⌛	Indicate Windows is busy processing a command
↔	Change the size of a window; appears when mouse pointer is on the border of a window
☝	Select and open Web-based data

FIGURE A-2: Common pointing devices

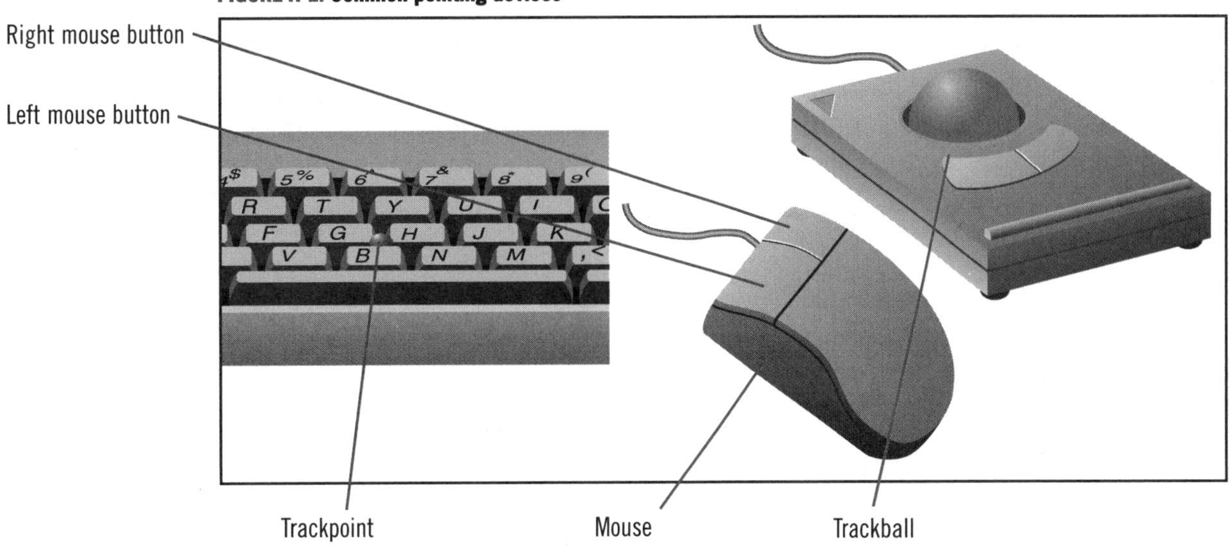

FIGURE A-3: Displaying a pop-up menu

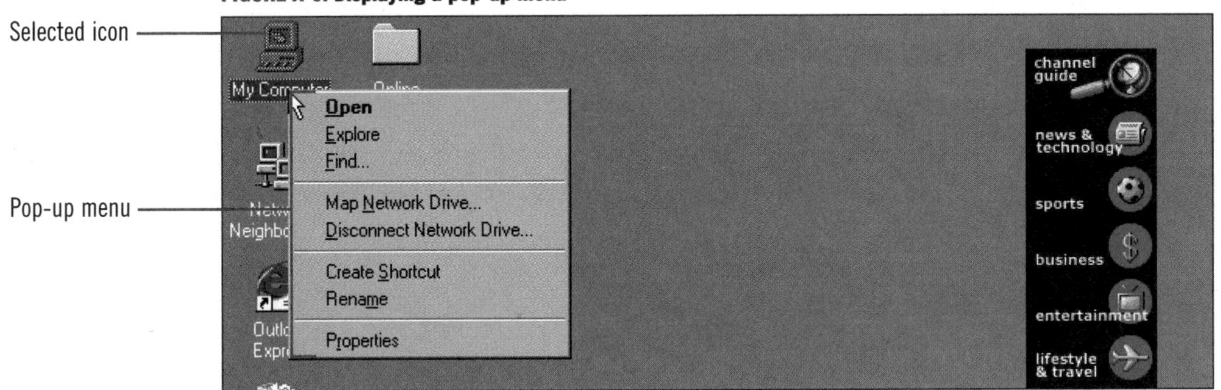

TABLE A-3: Basic mouse techniques

technique	what to do
Pointing	Move the mouse to position the mouse pointer over an item on the desktop
Clicking	Press and release the left mouse button
Double-clicking	Press and release the left mouse button twice quickly
Dragging	Point to an item, press and hold the left mouse button, move the mouse to a new location, then release the mouse button
Right-clicking	Point to an item, then press and release the right mouse button

More about the mouse: Classic style and Internet style

Because Windows 98 integrates the use of the Internet with its other functions, it allows you to choose whether you want to extend the way you click on the Internet to the rest of your computer work. With previous versions of the Windows operating system, and with the default Windows 98 settings, you click an item to select it and double-click an item to open it. When you use the Internet, however, you point to an item to select it and single-click to open it. Therefore, Windows 98 gives you two choices for using the mouse buttons: with the **Classic style**, you double-click to open items, and with the **Internet style** or **Web style**, you single-click to open items. To change from one style to another, click the Start button, point to Settings, click Folder Options, then click the Web style, Classic style, or Custom option.

Windows 98

Starting a Program

To start a program in Windows 98, click the Start button, which lists categories for a variety of tasks described in Table A-4. As you become familiar with Windows, you might want to customize the Start menu to include additional items that you use most often. To start a program from the Start menu, you click the Start menu, point to Programs to open the Programs submenu, then click the program you want to start. Windows 98 comes with several built-in programs, called **accessories**. Although not as feature-rich as many programs sold separately, Windows accessories are useful for completing basic tasks. In this lesson, you start a Windows accessory called **WordPad**, which is a word processing program you can use to create and edit simple documents. Table A-5 describes other popular Windows Accessories.

1. **Click the Start button on the taskbar**
   The Start menu opens.
2. **Point to Programs**
   The Programs submenu opens, listing the programs and categories for programs installed on your computer. WordPad is in the category called Accessories.
3. **Point to Accessories**
   The Accessories menu, shown in Figure A-4, contains several programs to help you complete common tasks. You want to start WordPad, which is probably at the bottom of the list.
4. **Click WordPad**
   WordPad opens and a blank document window opens, as shown in Figure A-5. Note that a **program button** appears on the taskbar, indicating that WordPad is open.

TABLE A-4: Start menu categories

category	description
Windows Update	Connects to a Microsoft Web site and updates your Windows 98 files as necessary
Programs	Opens programs included on the Start menu
Favorites	Connects to favorite Web sites or opens folders and documents that you previously selected
Documents	Opens the most recently opened and saved documents
Settings	Opens tools for selecting settings for your system, including the Control Panel, printers, taskbar and Start menu, folders, icons, and the Active Desktop
Find	Locates programs, files, folders, or computers on your computer network, or finds information and people on the Internet
Help	Provides Windows Help information by topic, alphabetical index, or search criteria
Run	Opens a program or file based on a location and filename that you type or select
Log Off	Allows you to log off the system and log on as a different user
Shut Down	Provides options to shut down the computer, restart the computer in Windows mode, or restart the computer in MS-DOS mode

FIGURE A-4: **Cascading menus**

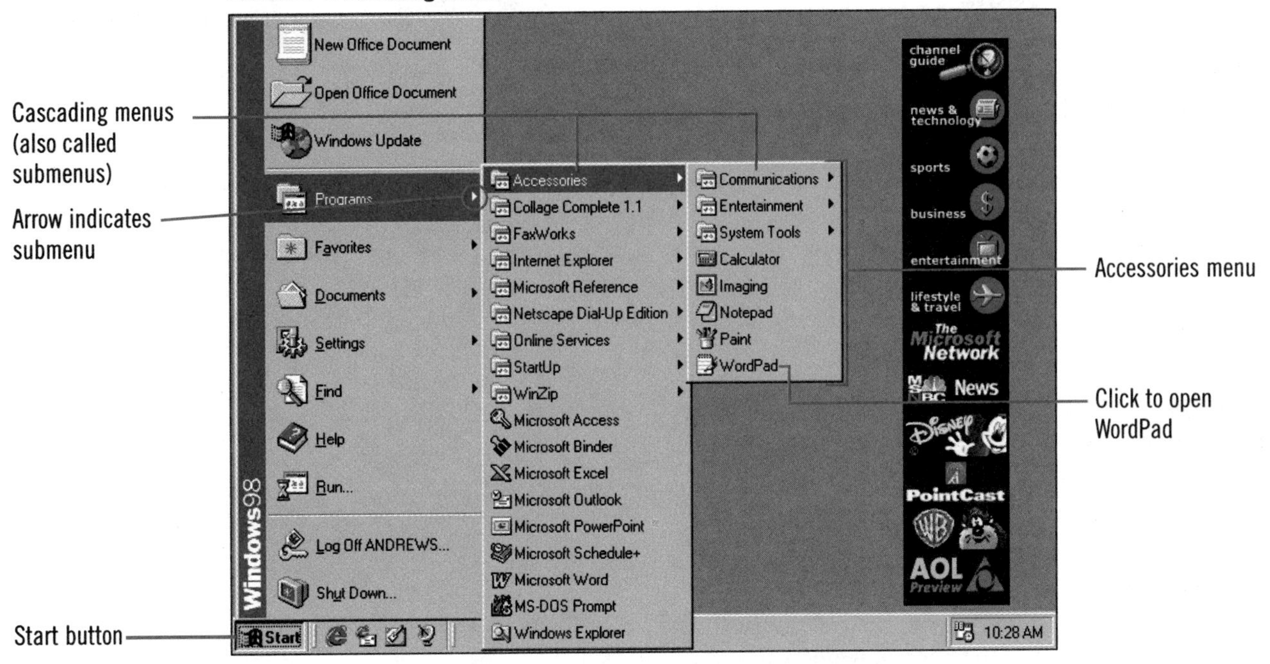

FIGURE A-5: **WordPad window**

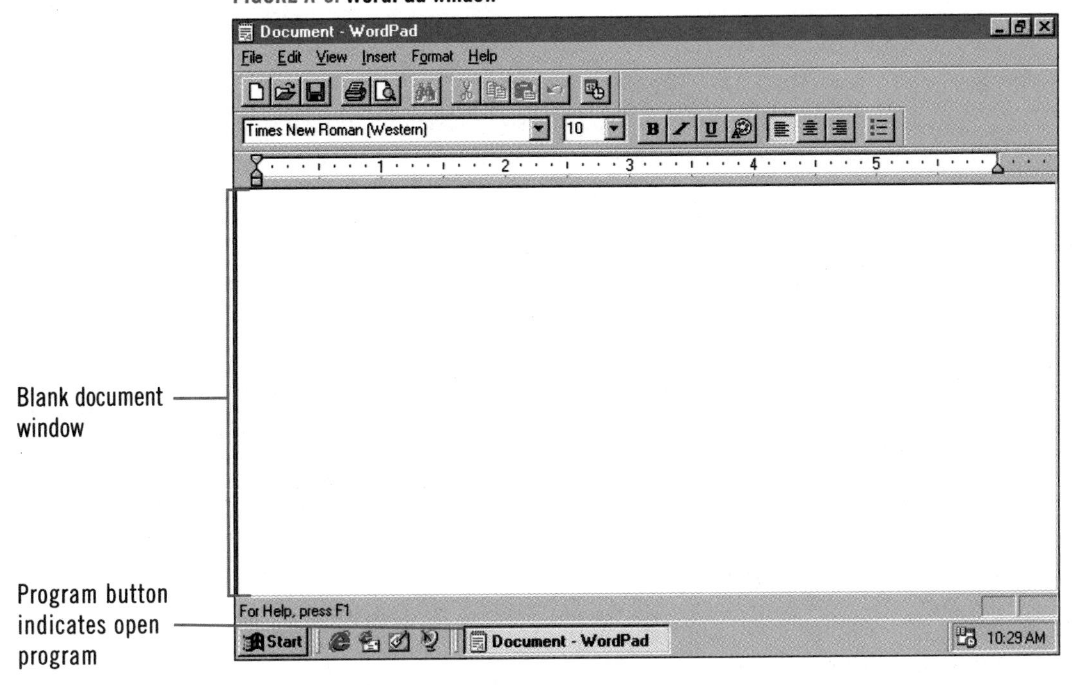

TABLE A-5: **Common Windows Accessories on the Accessories menu**

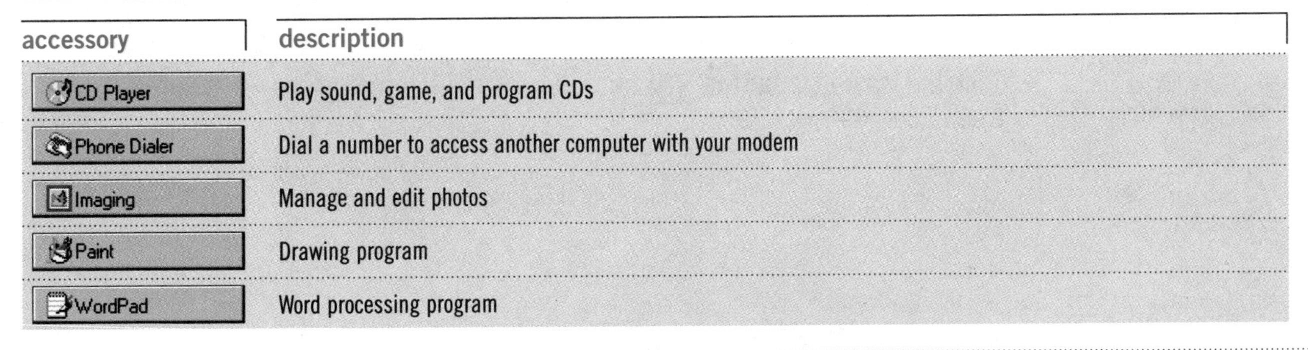

accessory	description
CD Player	Play sound, game, and program CDs
Phone Dialer	Dial a number to access another computer with your modem
Imaging	Manage and edit photos
Paint	Drawing program
WordPad	Word processing program

Windows 98

Moving and Resizing Windows

One of the powerful features of Windows is the ability to open more than one window or program at once. This means, however, that the desktop can get cluttered with the various programs and files you are using. One of the ways to keep your desktop organized is by changing the size of a window or moving it. You can do this using the standard borders and sizing buttons that are part of each window. Practice sizing and moving the WordPad window now.

Steps

1. If the WordPad window does not already fill the screen, click the **Maximize button** in the WordPad window.
   When a window is **maximized**, it takes up the whole screen.
2. Click the **Restore button** in the WordPad window
   To **restore** a window is to return it to its previous size, as shown in Figure A-6. The Restore button only appears when a window is maximized. In addition to minimizing, maximizing, and restoring windows, you can also change the dimensions of any window.
3. Position the pointer on the right edge of the WordPad window until the pointer changes to ↔, then drag the border to the right
   The width of the window increases. You can size the height and width of a window by dragging any of the four sides individually. You can also size the height and width of the window simultaneously by dragging the corner of the window.
4. Position the pointer in the lower-right corner of the WordPad window until the pointer changes to ↘, as shown in Figure A-6, then drag down and to the right
   The height and width of the window increase at the same time. You can also position a restored window wherever you wish on the desktop by dragging its title bar.
5. Click the **title bar** on the WordPad window, as shown in Figure A-6, then drag the window up and to the left
   The window is repositioned on the desktop. The **title bar** is the area along the top of the window that displays the file name and program used to create it. At times, you might wish to close a program window, yet keep the program running and easily accessible. You can accomplish this by minimizing a window.
6. In the WordPad window, click the **Minimize button**
   When you **minimize** a window, it shrinks to a program button on the taskbar, as shown in Figure A-7. WordPad is still running, but it is out of your way.
7. Click the **WordPad program button** on the taskbar to reopen the window
   The WordPad program window reopens.
8. Click the **Maximize button** in the upper-right corner of the WordPad window
   The window fills the screen.

QuickTip

You can resize windows by dragging any corner, not just the lower left. You can also drag any border to make the window taller, shorter, wider, or narrower.

QuickTip

If you have more than one window open and you want to access something on the desktop, you can click the Show Desktop button on the Quick Launch toolbar. All open windows are minimized so the desktop is visible.

FIGURE A-6: Restored WordPad window

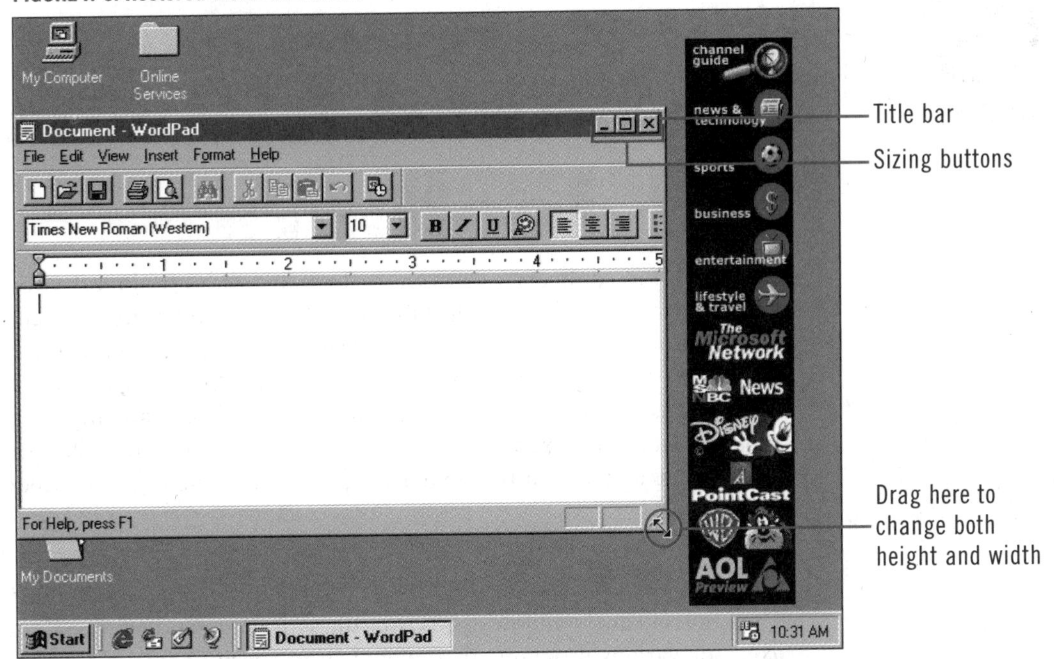

FIGURE A-7: Minimized WordPad window

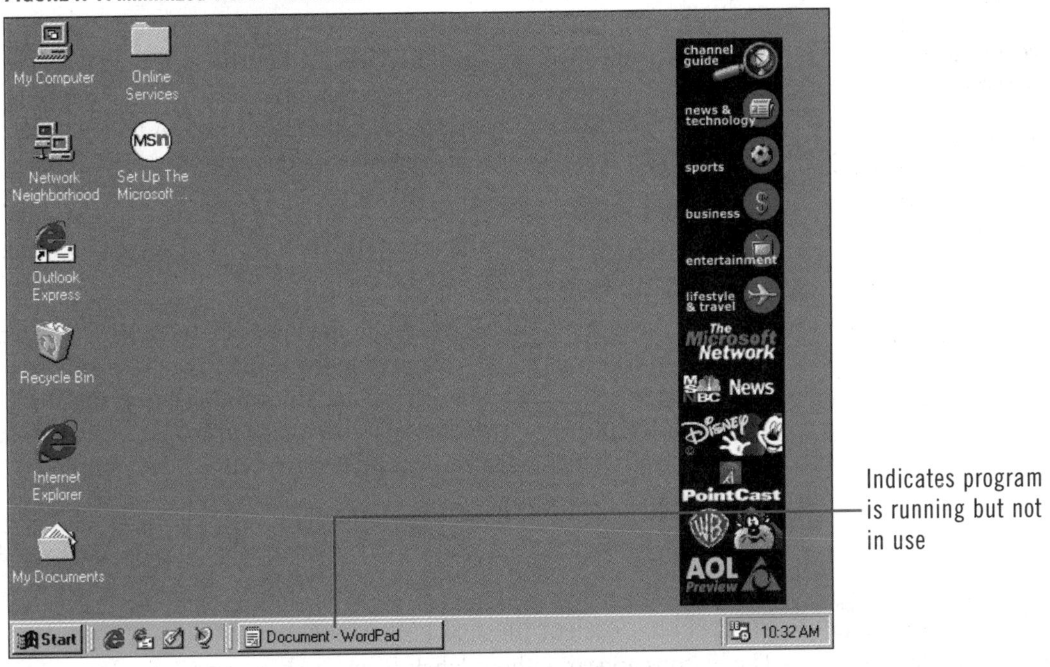

CLUES TO USE

More about sizing windows

Many programs contain two sets of sizing buttons: one that controls the program window itself and another that controls the window for the file with which you are working. The program sizing buttons are located in the title bar and the file sizing buttons are located below them. See Figure A-8. When you minimize a file window within a program, the file window is reduced to an icon in the lower-left corner of the program window, but the size of the program window remains intact.

FIGURE A-8: Program and file sizing buttons

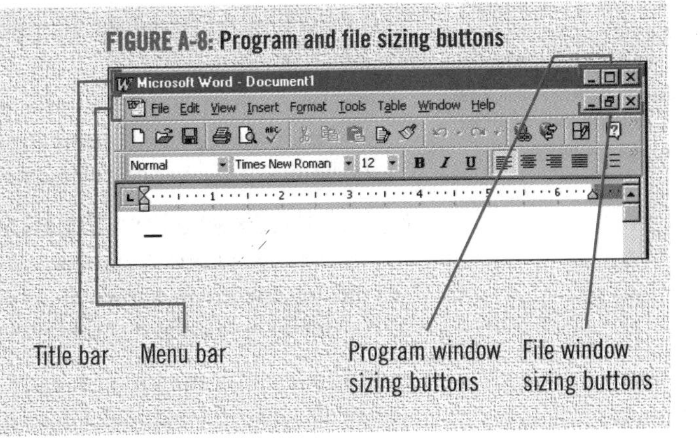

Windows 98

Using Menus, Keyboard Shortcuts, and Toolbars

A **menu** is a list of commands that you use to accomplish certain tasks. You've already used the Start menu to start WordPad. Each Windows program also has its own set of menus, which are located on the **menu bar** under the title bar. The menus organize commands into groups of related operations. See Table A-6 for examples of what you might see on a typical menu. A **toolbar** is a series of buttons, located under the menu bar, that you click to accomplish certain tasks. Buttons are another method for executing menu commands. You will open the Control Panel, then use a menu and toolbar button to change how the contents of the window appear.

QuickTip

You now have two windows open: WordPad and the Control Panel. The Control Panel is the **active window** (or **active program**) because it is the one with which you are currently working. WordPad is **inactive** because it is open but you are not working with it. Working with more than one window at a time is called **multitasking**.

1. Click the **Start button** on the taskbar, point to **Settings**, then click **Control Panel**
   The Control Panel window opens over the WordPad window. The **Control Panel** contains icons for various programs that allow you to specify how your computer looks and performs. You use the Control Panel to practice using menus and toolbars.
2. Click **View** on the menu bar
   The View menu appears, listing the View commands, as shown in Figure A-9. On a menu, a **check mark** identifies a feature that is currently enabled or "on." To disable, or turn "off" the feature, click the command again to remove the check mark. A **bullet mark** can also indicate that an option is enabled. To disable a bulleted option, you must select another option in its place.
3. Click **Small Icons**
   The icons are now smaller than they were before, taking up less room in the window.
4. Press **[Alt][V]** to open the View menu
   The View menu appears again; this time you opened it using the keyboard. Notice that a letter in each command on the View menu is underlined. You can select these commands by pressing the underlined letter. Executing a command using the keyboard is called a **keyboard shortcut**. You might find that you prefer keyboard shortcuts to the mouse if you find it cumbersome to reposition your hands at the keyboard each time you use the mouse.
5. Press **[T]** to select the Toolbars command
   The Toolbars submenu appears with check marks next to the commands that are currently selected.

Trouble?

If the Text Labels command wasn't selected, clicking the command now will select it, and you will see the labels under the buttons. Click View, click Toolbars, then click Text Labels to deselect it.

6. Press **[T]** to deselect the Text Labels command
   The buttons appear without labels below each one; now you can see the entire toolbar.
7. On the Control Panel toolbar, position the pointer over the **Views button** but do not click yet
   When you position the mouse pointer over a button (and other items), a **ScreenTip** appears, showing the name of the item, as shown in Figure A-10. ScreenTips help you learn the names of the various elements in Windows programs.
8. Click the **Views button list arrow**
   Some toolbar buttons have an arrow, which indicates the button contains several choices. Clicking the arrow shows the choices; clicking the button itself automatically selects the command below the one that was previously selected.
9. In the list of View choices, click **Details**
   The Details view includes a description of each program in the Control Panel.

FIGURE A-9: **Opening a menu**

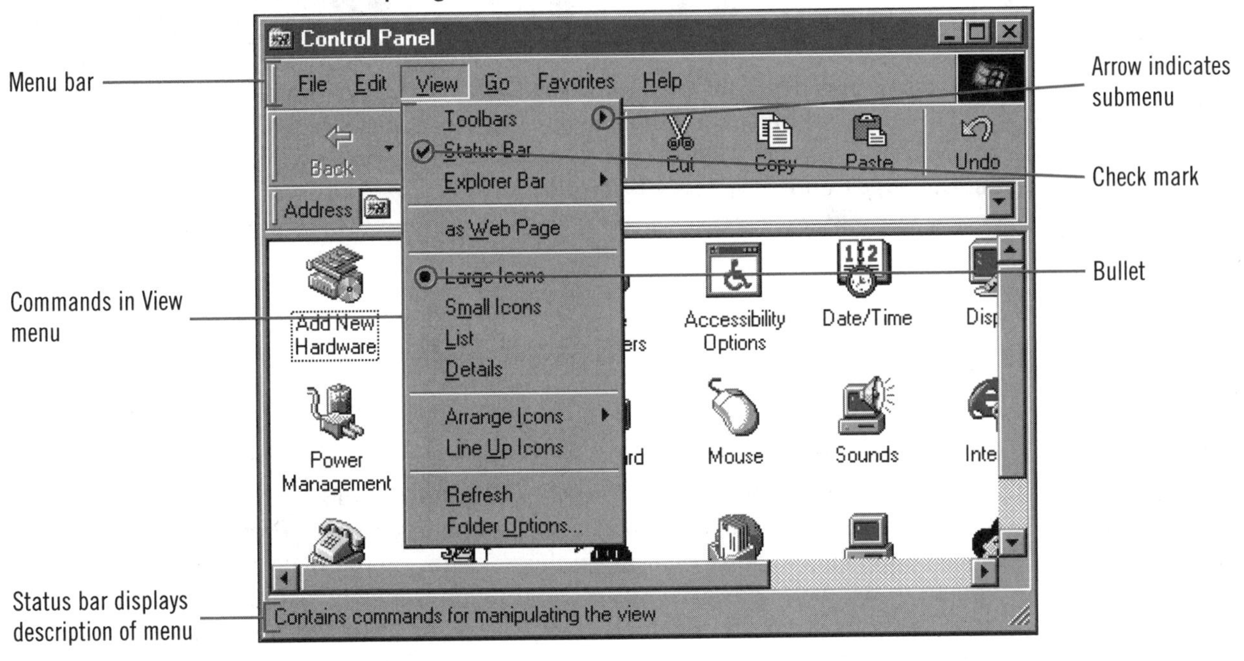

FIGURE A-10: **ScreenTip in Control Panel**

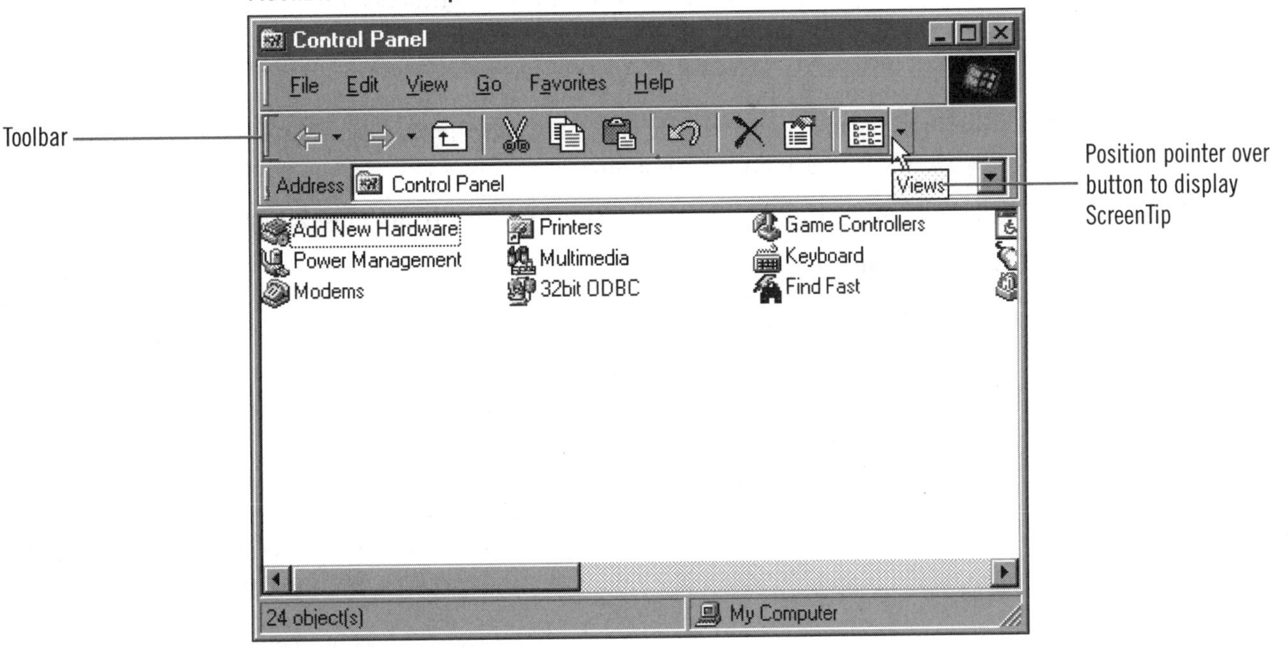

TABLE A-6: **Typical items on a menu**

item	description	example
Dimmed command	A menu command that is not currently available	Undo Ctrl+Z
Ellipsis	Opens a dialog box that allows you to select different or additional options	Save As...
Triangle	Opens a cascading menu containing an additional list of commands	Zoom ▸
Keyboard shortcut	A keyboard alternative to using the mouse for executing a command	Paste Ctrl+V
Underlined letter	Indicates the letter to press for the keyboard shortcut	Print Preview

Windows 98

Using Dialog Boxes

A **dialog box** is a window that opens when you choose a menu command that is followed by an ellipsis (...), or any command that needs more information before the program can carry out the command you selected. Dialog boxes open in other situations as well, such as when you open a program in the Control Panel. See Figure A-11 and Table A-7 for some of the typical elements of a dialog box. Practice using a dialog box to control your mouse settings.

Trouble?

If you can't see the Mouse icon, resize the Control Panel window.

1. **In the Control Panel window, double-click the Mouse icon**
   The Mouse Properties dialog box opens, as shown in Figure A-12. **Properties** are characteristic of a specific computer element (in this case, the mouse) that you can customize. The options in this dialog box allow you to control the way the mouse buttons are configured, select the types of pointers that appear, choose the speed of the mouse movement on the screen, and specify what type of mouse you are using. **Tabs** at the top of the dialog box separate these options into related categories.
2. **Click the Motion tab if it is not already the frontmost tab**
   This tab has two boxes. The first, Pointer speed, has a slider for you to set how fast the pointer moves on the screen in relation to how you move the mouse in your hand. The second, **Pointer trail**, has a check box you can select to add a "trail" or shadow to the pointer on your screen, making it easier to see. The slider in the Pointer trail box lets you determine the degree to which the option is in effect—in this case, the length of the pointer trail.
3. **In the Pointer trail box, click the Show pointer trails check box to select it**
4. **Drag the slider below the check box all the way to the right, then move the mouse pointer across your screen**
   As you move the mouse, notice the pointer trails.
5. **Click the other tabs in the Mouse Properties dialog box and experiment with the options that are available in each category**
   After you select the options you want in a dialog box, you need to select a **command button**, which carries out the options you've selected. The two most common command buttons are OK and Cancel. Clicking OK accepts your changes and closes the dialog box; clicking Cancel leaves the original settings intact and closes the dialog box. The third command button in this dialog box is Apply. Clicking the Apply button accepts the changes you've made and keeps the dialog box open so that you can select additional options. Because you might share this computer with others, it's important to return the dialog box options back to the original settings.
6. **Click Cancel to leave the original settings intact and close the dialog box**

QuickTip

You can also use the keyboard to carry out commands in a dialog box. Pressing [Enter] is the same as clicking OK; pressing [Esc] is the same as clicking Cancel.

FIGURE A-11: Elements of a typical dialog box

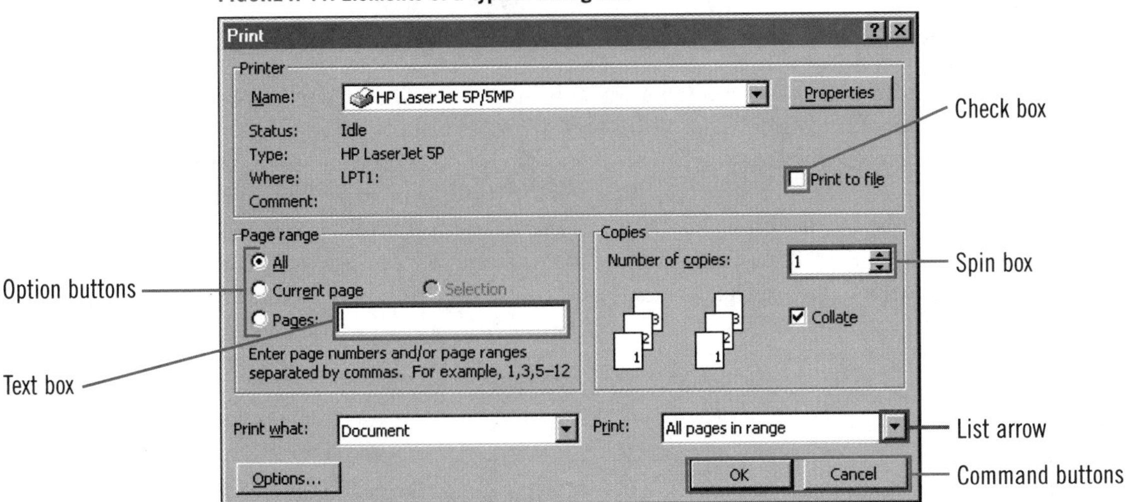

FIGURE A-12: Mouse Properties dialog box

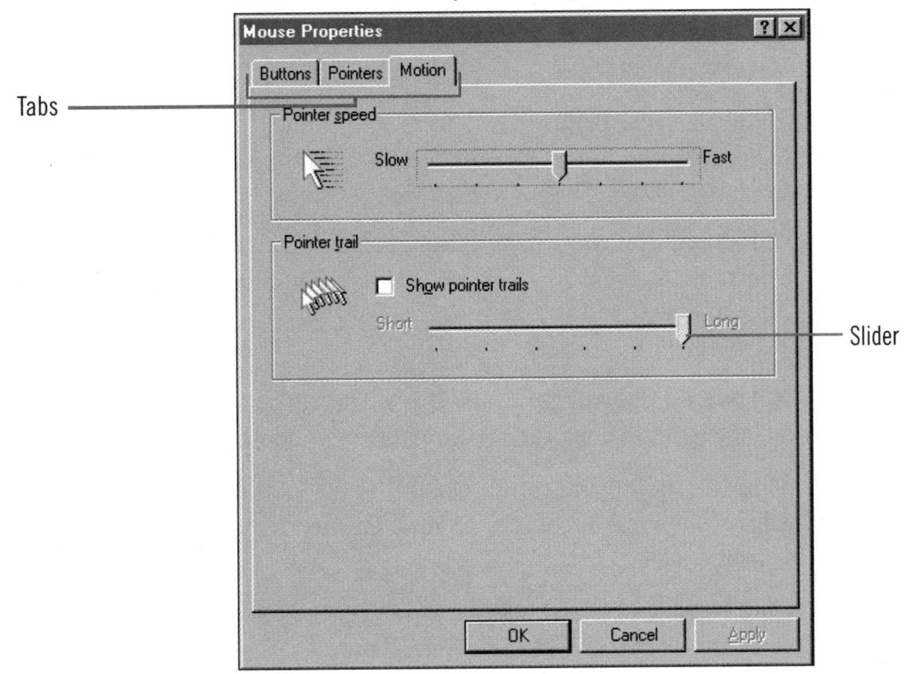

TABLE A-7: Typical items in a dialog box

item	description	item	description
Check box	A box that turns an option on (when the box is checked) and off (when it is blank)	**List box**	A box containing a list of items; to choose an item, click the list arrow, then click the desired item
Text box	A box in which you type text	**Spin box**	A box with two arrows and a text box; allows you to scroll numerical increments or type a number
Option button	A small circle that selects a single dialog box option; you cannot check more than one option button in a list	**Slider**	A shape that you drag to set the degree to which an option is in effect
Command button	A rectangular button in a dialog box with the name of the command on it	**Tab**	A place in a dialog box where related commands and options are organized

Using Scroll Bars

When you cannot see all of the items available in a window, scroll bars appear on the right and/or bottom edges of the window. **Scroll bars** allow you to display the additional contents of the window. There are several ways you can scroll in a window. When you need to scroll only a short distance, you can use the scroll arrows. To scroll the window in larger increments, click in the scroll bar above or below the scroll box. Dragging the scroll box moves you quickly to a new part of the window. See Table A-8 for a summary of the different ways to use scroll bars. With the Control Panel window in Details view, you can use the scroll bars to view all of the items in this window.

Steps

Trouble?

If you can't see the scroll bars, resize the window until both the horizontal and vertical scroll bars appear. Scroll bars don't appear when the window is large enough to include all the information.

QuickTip

The size of the scroll box changes to reflect how many items or the amount of text that does not fit in a window. A larger scroll box indicates that a relatively small amount of the window's contents is not currently visible; you need to scroll only a short distance to see the remaining items. A smaller scroll box indicates that a relatively large amount of information is currently not visible.

1. In the Control Panel window, click the **down scroll arrow**, as shown in Figure A-13
   Clicking this arrow moves the view down one line. Clicking the up arrow moves the view up one line.
2. Click the **up scroll arrow** in the vertical scroll bar
   The screen moves up one line.
3. Click anywhere in the area below the scroll box in the vertical scroll bar
   The view moves down one window's height. Similarly, you can click in the scroll bar above the scroll box to move up one window's height.
4. Drag the **scroll box** all the way down to the bottom of the vertical scrollbar
   The view now includes the items that appear at the very bottom of the window. Similarly, you can drag the scroll box to the top of the scroll bar to view the information that appears at the top of the window.
5. Drag the **scroll box** all the way up to the top of the vertical scroll bar
   This view shows the items that appear at the top of the window.
6. Click the area to the right of the scroll box in the horizontal scroll bar
   The far right edge of the window comes into view. The horizontal scroll bar works the same as the vertical scroll bar.
7. Click the area to the left of the scroll box in the horizontal scroll bar
   You should return the Control Panel to its original settings.
8. On the Control Panel toolbar, click the **Views button list arrow**, click **Large Icons**, then maximize the Control Panel window

FIGURE A-13: Scroll bars in the Control Panel

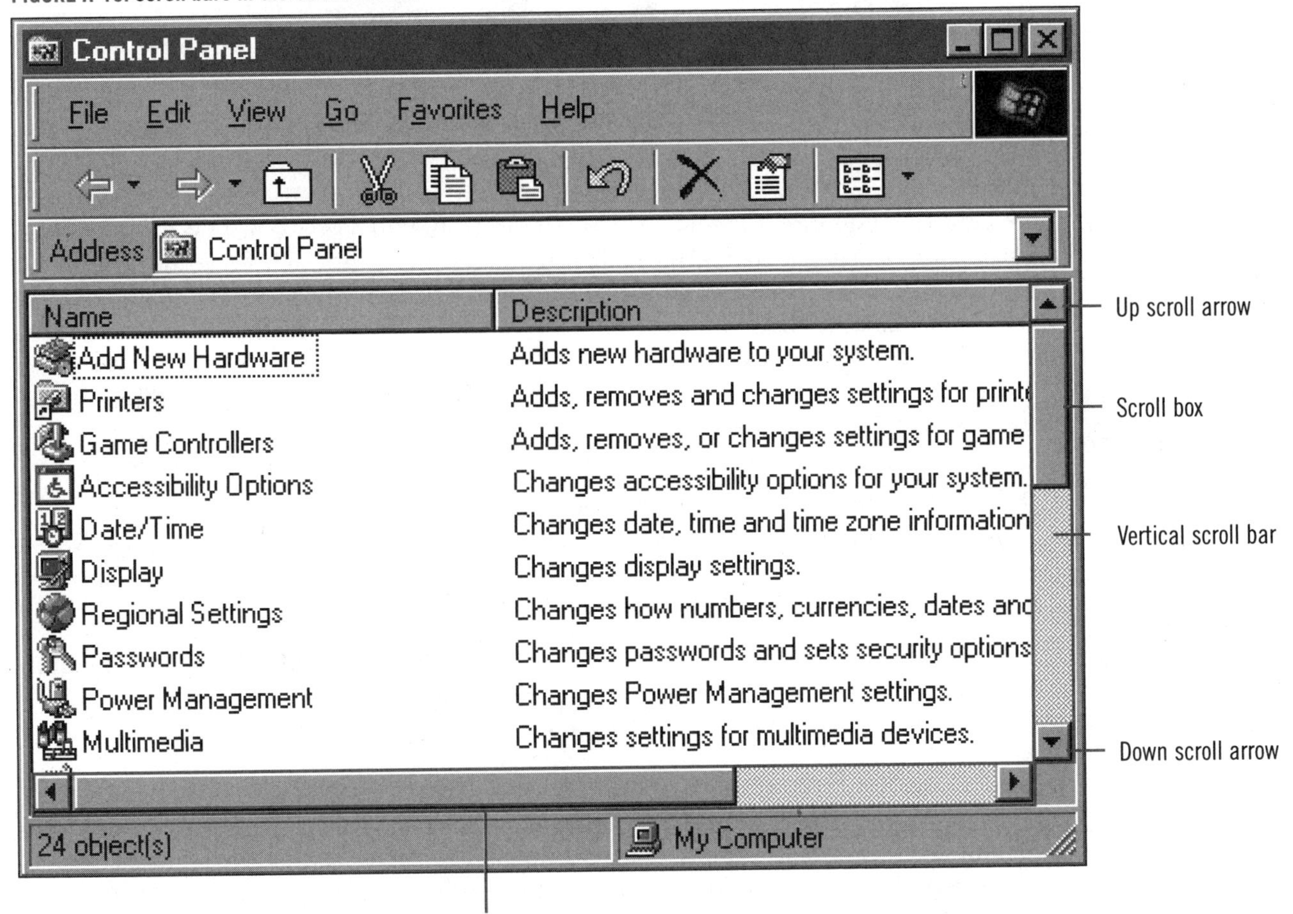

TABLE A-8: Using scroll bars in a window

to	do this
Move down one line	Click the down arrow at the bottom of the vertical scroll bar
Move up one line	Click the up arrow at the top of the vertical scroll bar
Move down one window height	Click in the area below the scroll box in the vertical scroll bar
Move up one window height	Click in the area above the scroll box in the vertical scroll bar
Move up a large distance in the window	Drag the scroll box up in the vertical scroll bar
Move down a large distance in the window	Drag the scroll box down in the vertical scroll bar
Move a short distance side-to-side in a window	Click the left or right arrows in the horizontal scroll bar
Move to the right one window width	Click in the area to the right of the scroll box in the horizontal scroll bar
Move to the left one window width	Click in the area to the left of the scroll box in the horizontal scroll bar
Move left or right a large distance in the window	Drag the scroll box in the horizontal scroll bar

Windows 98

Getting Help

When you have a question about how to do something in Windows 98, you can usually find the answer with a few clicks of your mouse. **Windows Help** works like a book stored on your computer, with a table of contents and an index to make finding information easier. Help provides guidance on many Windows features, including detailed steps for completing a procedure, definitions of terms, lists of related topics, and search capabilities. To open the main Windows 98 Help system, click Help on the Start menu. From here you can browse the Help "book," or you can connect to a Microsoft Web site on the Internet for the latest technical support on Windows 98. To get help on a specific Windows program, click Help on the program's menu bar. You can also access **context-sensitive help**, help specifically related to what you are doing, using a variety of methods such as right-clicking an object or using the question mark button in a dialog box. In this lesson, you get Help on how to start a program. You also get information on the taskbar.

Steps

1. **Click the Start button on the taskbar, then click Help**
   The Windows Help dialog box opens with the Contents tab in front, as shown in Figure A-14. The Contents tab provides you with a list of Help categories. Each "book" has several "chapters" that you can see by clicking the book or the name next to the book.

2. **Click the Contents tab if it isn't the frontmost tab, click Exploring Your Computer, then click Work with Programs to view the Help categories**
   The Help window contains a selection of topics related to running programs.

3. **Click Start a Program**
   The Help window appears in the right pane, as shown in Figure A-15. **Panes** divide a window into two or more sections. At the bottom of the right pane, you can click Related Topics to view a list of topics that may also be of interest. Some Help topics also allow you to view additional information about important words; these words are underlined.

4. **Click the underlined word taskbar**
   A pop-up window appears with a definition of the underlined word.

5. **Read the definition, then press [Enter] or click anywhere outside the pop-up window to close it**

6. **In the left pane, click the Index tab**
   The Index tab provides an alphabetical list of all the available Help topics, like an index at the end of a book. You can enter a topic in the text box at the top of the pane. As you type, the list of topics automatically scrolls to try to match the word or phrase you type. You can also scroll down to the topic. In either case, the topic appears in the right pane, as usual.

7. **In the left pane, click the Search tab**
   You can use the Search tab to locate a Help topic using keywords. You enter a word or phrase in the text box and click List Topics; a list of matching topics appears below the text box. To view a topic, double-click it or select the topic, then click Display.

8. **Click the Web Help button on the toolbar**
   Information on the Web page for Windows 98 Help appears in the right pane (a **Web page** is a document that contains highlighted words, phrases, and graphics that link to other pages on the Internet). You could access this Web page by clicking the "Support Online" underlined text.

9. **In the Windows Help window, click the Close button in the upper-right corner of the window**
   Clicking the Close button closes the active window.

QuickTip

When you point to a Help category, the mouse changes to the hand pointer, the Help category is selected, and the text changes to blue and is underlined. This is similar to selecting items on the Internet.

FIGURE A-14: Windows Help dialog box

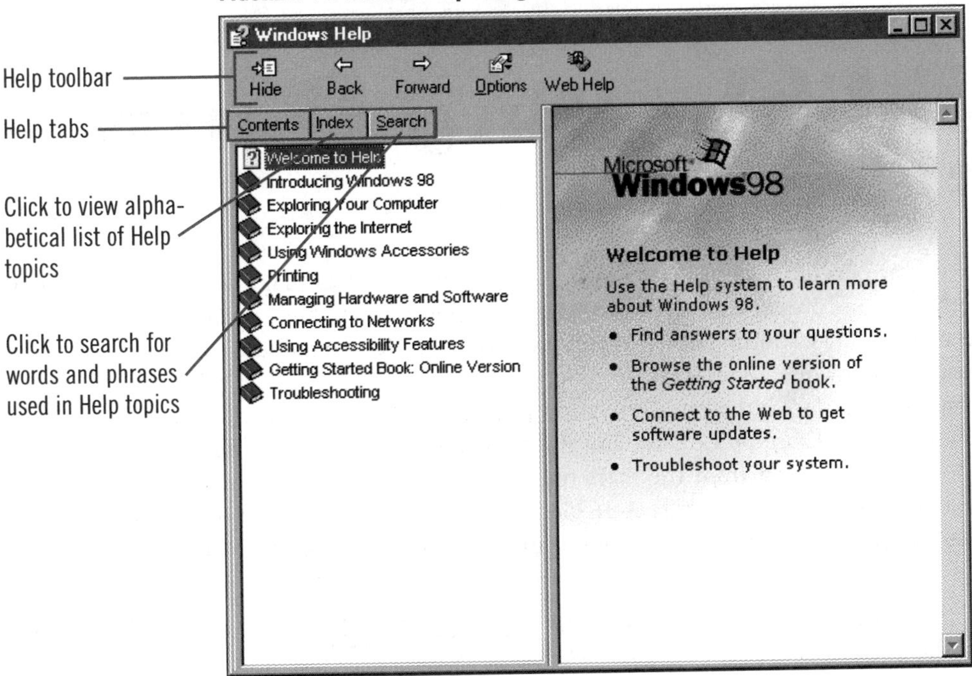

FIGURE A-15: Viewing Help on starting a program

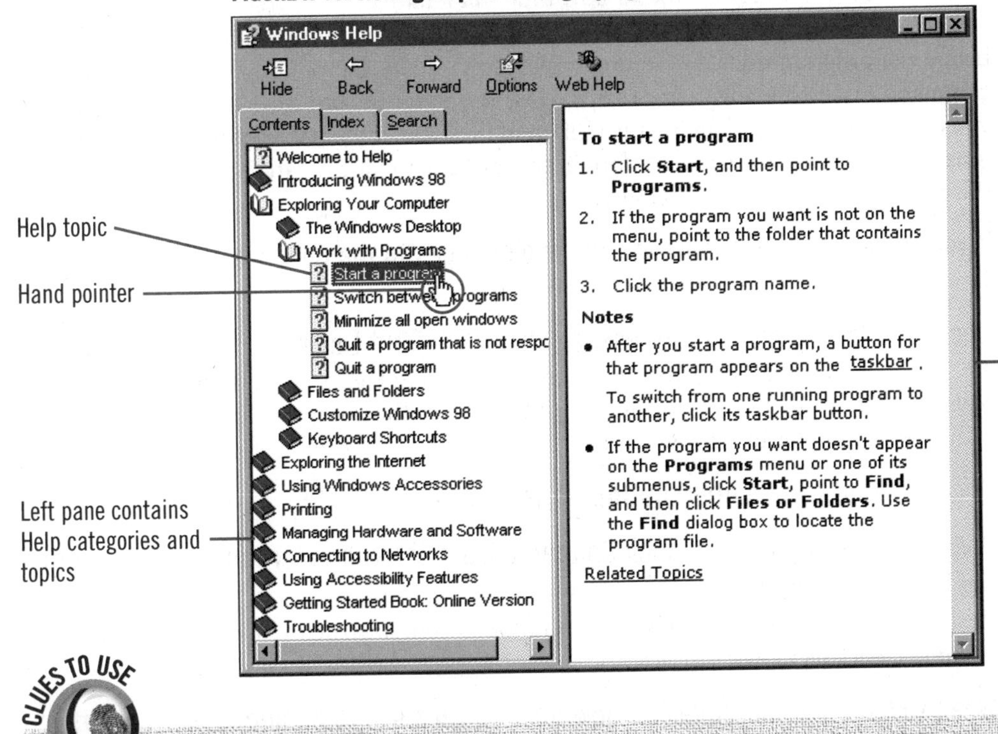

CLUES TO USE

Context-sensitive help

To receive help in a dialog box, click the Help button **?** in the upper-right corner of the dialog box; the mouse pointer changes to ↖?. Click the Help pointer on the item for which you need additional information. A pop-up window provides a brief explanation of the selected feature. You can also click the right mouse button on an item in a dialog box, then click the What's This? button to display the Help explanation. In addition, when you click the right mouse button in a Help topic window, you can choose commands to annotate, copy, and print the contents of the topic window. From the Help pop-up menu, you can also choose to have topic windows always appear on top of the currently active window, so you can see Help topics while you work.

Windows 98

Closing a Program and Shutting Down Windows

When you are finished working on your computer, you need to make sure you shut it down properly. This involves several steps: saving and closing all open files, closing all the open programs and windows, shutting down Windows, and finally, turning off the computer. If you turn off the computer while Windows is running, you could lose important data. To **close** programs, you can click the Close button in the window's upper-right corner or click File on the menu bar and choose either Close or Exit. To shut down Windows after all your files and programs are closed, click Shut Down from the Start menu, then select the desired option from the Shut Down dialog box, shown in Figure A-16. See Table A-9 for a description of shutdown options. Close all your open files, windows, and programs, then exit Windows.

1. In the Control Panel window, click the **Close button** in the upper-right corner of the window
   The Control Panel window closes.
2. Click **File** on the WordPad menu bar, then click **Exit**
   If you have made any changes to the open file, you will be prompted to save your changes before the program quits. Some programs also give you the option of choosing the Close command on the File menu in order to close the active file but leave the program open, so you can continue to work in it with a different file. Also, if there is a second set of sizing buttons in the window, the Close button on the menu bar will close the active file only, leaving the program open for continued use.
3. If you see a message asking you to save changes to the document, click **No**
   WordPad closes and you return to the desktop.
4. Click the **Start button** on the taskbar, then click **Shut Down**
   The Shut Down Windows dialog box opens, as shown in Figure A-16. In this dialog box, you have the option to shut down the computer, restart the computer in Windows mode or restart the computer in MS-DOS mode.
5. Click the **Shut down option button**, if necessary
6. If you are working in a lab, click **Cancel** to leave the computer running and return to the Windows desktop
   If you are working on your own machine or if your instructor told you to shut down Windows, click **OK** to exit Windows.
7. When you see the message **It's now safe to turn off your computer**, turn off your computer and monitor

QuickTip

Complete the remaining steps to shut down Windows and your computer only if you have been told to do so by your instructor or technical support person.

FIGURE A-16: Shut Down Windows dialog box

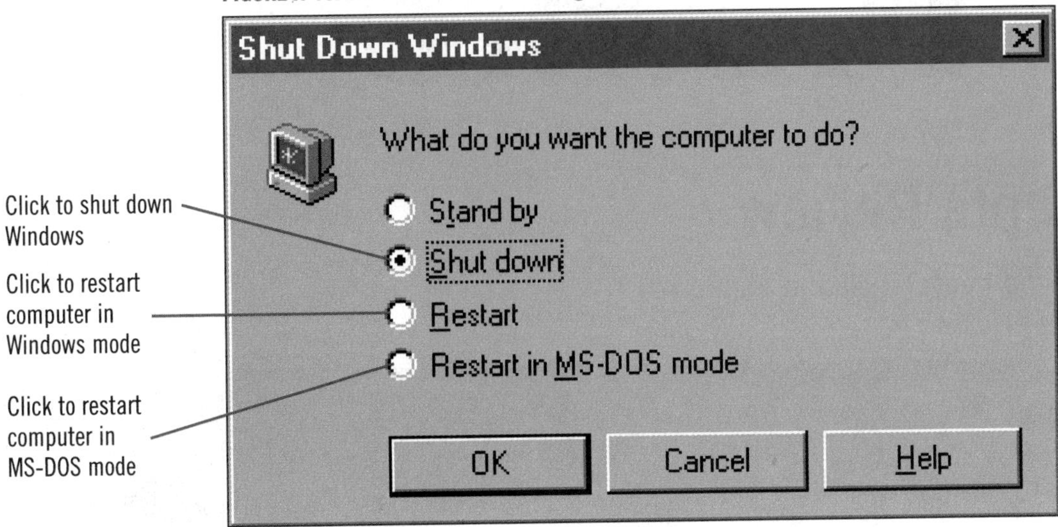

TABLE A-9: Shut down options

shut down option	function	when to use it
Shut down	Prepares the computer to be turned off	When you are finished working with Windows and you want to shut off your computer
Restart	Restarts the computer and reloads Windows	When you want to restart the computer and begin working with Windows again (your programs might have frozen or stopped working).
Restart in MS-DOS mode	Starts the computer in the MS-DOS mode	When you want to run programs under MS-DOS or use DOS commands to work with files

The Log Off command

To change users on the same computer quickly, you can choose the Log Off command from the Start menu. This command identifies the name of the current user. When you choose this command, Windows 98 shuts down and automatically restarts, stopping at the point where you need to enter a password. When the new user enters a user name and password, Windows restarts and the desktop appears as usual.

Practice

► Concepts Review

Identify each of the items labeled in Figure A-17.

FIGURE A-17

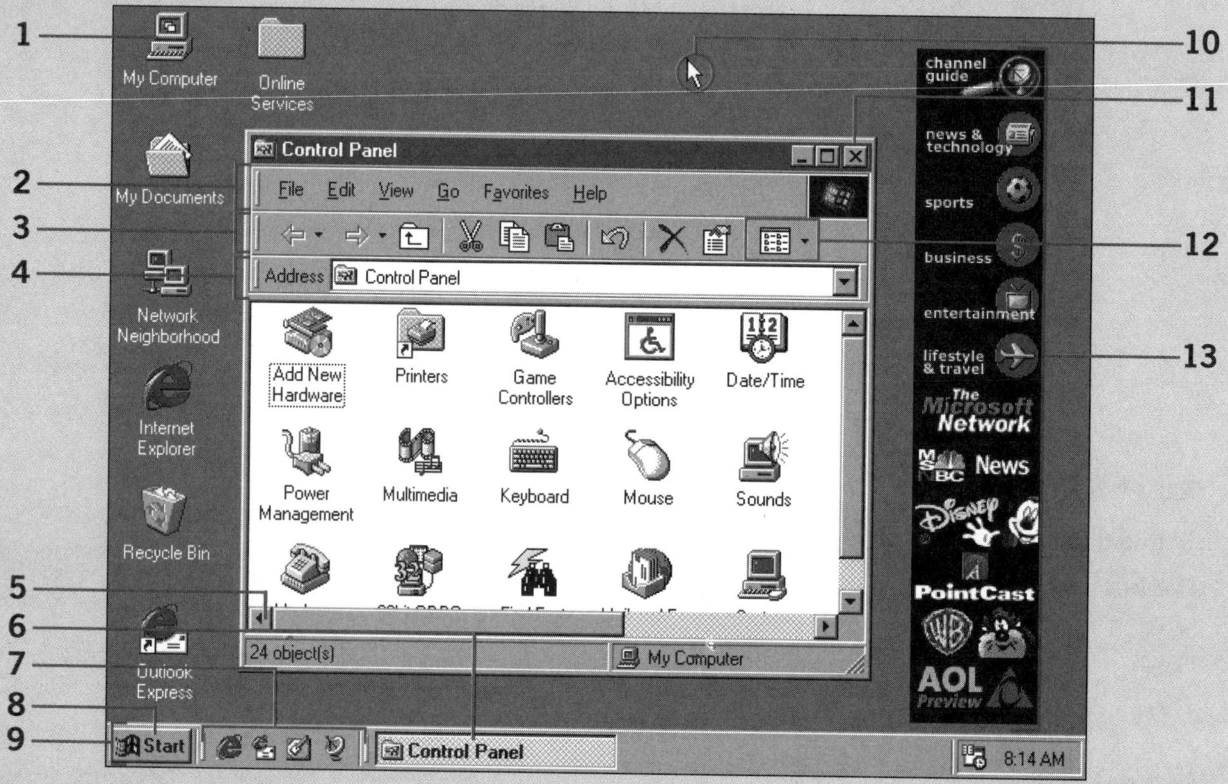

Match each of the statements with the term it describes.

14. Shrinks a window to a button on the taskbar
15. Shows the name of the window or program
16. The item you first click to start a program
17. Requests more information that you supply before carrying out command
18. Shows the Start button, Quick Launch toolbar, and any currently open programs
19. An input device that lets you point to and make selections
20. Graphic representation of program

a. Taskbar
b. Dialog box
c. Start button
d. Mouse
e. Title bar
f. Minimize button
g. Icon

Select the best answer from the list of choices.

21. The acronym GUI means
    a. Grayed user information.
    b. Group user icons.
    c. Graphical user interface.
    d. Group user interconnect.

22. Which of the following is NOT provided by an operating system?
- **a.** Programs for organizing files
- **b.** Instructions to coordinate the flow of information among the programs, files, printers, storage devices, and other components of your computer system
- **c.** Programs that allow you to specify the operation of the mouse
- **d.** Spell checker for your documents

23. All of the following are examples of using a mouse, EXCEPT
- **a.** Clicking the Maximize button.
- **b.** Pressing [Enter].
- **c.** Double-clicking to start a program.
- **d.** Dragging the My Computer icon.

24. The term for moving an item to a new location on the desktop is
- **a.** Pointing.
- **b.** Clicking.
- **c.** Dragging.
- **d.** Restoring.

25. The Maximize button is used to
- **a.** Return a window to its previous size.
- **b.** Expand a window to fill the computer screen.
- **c.** Scroll slowly through a window.
- **d.** Run programs from the Start menu.

26. What appears if a window contains more information than can be displayed in the window?
- **a.** Program icon
- **b.** Cascading menu
- **c.** Scroll bars
- **d.** Check box

27. A window is active when
- **a.** You see its program button on the taskbar.
- **b.** Its title bar is dimmed.
- **c.** It is open and you are currently using it.
- **d.** It is listed in the Programs submenu.

28. You can exit Windows by
- **a.** Double-clicking the Control Panel application.
- **b.** Double-clicking the Program Manager control menu box.
- **c.** Clicking File, then clicking Exit.
- **d.** Selecting the Shut Down command from the Start menu.

Skills Review

1. Start Windows and view the Active Desktop
- **a.** Turn on the computer, if necessary.
- **b.** After Windows starts, identify as many items on the desktop as you can, without referring to the lesson material.
- **c.** Compare your results to Figure A-1.

2. Use the mouse
- **a.** Double-click the Recycle Bin icon.
- **b.** Drag the Recycle Bin window to the upper-right corner of the desktop.
- **c.** Right-click the title bar of the Recycle Bin, then click Close.

3. Start a program.
- **a.** Click the Start button on the taskbar, then point to Programs.
- **b.** Point to Accessories, then click Calculator.
- **c.** Minimize the Calculator window.

4. Practice dragging, maximizing, restoring, sizing, and minimizing windows.
- **a.** Drag the Recycle Bin icon to the bottom of the desktop.
- **b.** Double-click the My Computer icon to open the My Computer window.
- **c.** Maximize the window, if it is not already maximized.
- **d.** Restore the window to its previous size.
- **e.** Resize the window until you see both horizontal and vertical scroll bars.
- **f.** Resize the window until the horizontal scroll bar no longer appears.

g. Click the Minimize button.
h. Drag the Recycle Bin back to the top of the desktop.

5. **Use menus, keyboard shortcuts, and toolbars**
   a. Click the Start button on the taskbar, point to Settings, then click Control Panel.
   b. Click View on the menu bar, point to Toolbars, then click Standard Buttons to hide the toolbar.
   c. Redisplay the toolbar.
   d. Press [Alt][V] to show the View menu, then press [W] to view the Control Panel as a Web page.
   e. Note the change, then use the same keyboard shortcuts to change the view back.
   f. Click the Up One Level button to view My Computer.
   g. Click the Back button to return to the Control Panel.
   h. Double-click the Display icon.
6. **Use dialog boxes.**
   a. Click the Screen Saver tab.
   b. Click the Screen Saver list arrow, select a screen saver, and preview the change but do not click OK.
   c. Click the Effects tab.
   d. In the Visual effects section, click the Use large icons check box to select it, then click Apply.
   e. Note the change in the icons on the desktop and in the Control Panel window.
   f. Click the Use large icons check box to deselect it, Click the Screen Saver tab, return the scrren saver to its original setting, then click Apply.
   g. Click the Close button in the Display Properties dialog box, but leave the Control Panel open.
7. **Use scroll bars**
   a. Click View on the Control Panel toolbar, then click Details.
   b. Resize the Control Panel window, if necessary, so that both scroll bars are visible.
   c. Drag the vertical scroll box down all the way.
   d. Click anywhere in the area above the vertical scroll box.
   e. Click the up scroll arrow until the scroll box is back at the top of the scroll bar.
   f. Drag the horizontal scroll box so you can read the descriptions for the icons.
8. **Get Help**
   a. Click the Start button on the taskbar, then click Help.
   b. Click the Contents tab, then click Introducing Windows 98.
   c. Click Exploring Your Computer, click Customize Windows 98, then click How the Screen Looks.
   d. Click each of the topics and read them in the right pane.
9. **Close a program and shut down Windows.**
   a. Click the Close button to close the Help topic window.
   b. Click File on the menu bar, then click Close to close the Control Panel window.
   c. Click the Calculator program button on the taskbar to restore the window.
   d. Click the Close button in the Calculator window to close the Calculator program.
   e. Click the My Computer program button on the taskbar, then click the Close button to close the window.
   f. If you are instructed to do so, shut down your computer.

Independent Challenges

1. Windows 98 has an extensive help system. In this independent challenge, you will use Help to learn about more Windows 98 features and explore the help that's available on the Internet.

a. Open Windows Help and locate help topics on: adjusting the double-click speed of your mouse; using Print; and, displaying Web content on your desktop.

If you have a printer, print a Help topic for each subject. If you do not have a printer, write a summary of each topic.

b. Follow these steps below to access help on the Internet. If you don't have Internet access, you can't do this step.

- **i.** Click the Web Help button on the toolbar.
- **ii.** Read the introduction, then click the link Support Online. A browser will open and prompt you to connect to the Internet. Once you are connected, a Web site called Support Online will appear.
- **iii.** Click the View Popular Topics link. Write a summary of what you find.
- **iv.** Click the Close button in the title bar of your browser, then disconnect from the Internet and close Windows Help.

2. You may need to change the format of the clock and date on your computer. For example, if you work with international clients it might be easier to show the time in military (24-hour) time and the date with the day before the month. You can also change the actual time and date on your computer, such as when you change time zones.

a. Open the Control Panel window, then double-click the Regional Settings icon.
b. Click the Time tab to change the time to show a 24-hour clock rather than a 12-hour clock.
c. Click the Date tab to change the date to show the day before the month (e.g., 30/3/99).
d. Change the time to one hour later using the Date/Time icon in the Control Panel window.
e. Return the settings to the original time and format and close all open windows.

3. Calculator is a Windows program on the Accessories menu that you can use for calculations you need to perform while using the computer. Follow these guidelines to explore the Calculator and the Help that comes with it:

a. Start the Calculator from the Accessories menu.
b. Click Help on the menu bar, then click Help topics. The Calculator Help window opens, showing several Help topics.
c. View the Help topic on how to perform simple calculations, then print it if you have a printer connected.
d. Open the Tips and Tricks category, then view the Help topic on how to find out what a calculator button does.
e. View the Help topic (under Tips and Tricks) on how to use keyboard equivalents of calculator buttons, then print the topic if you have a printer connected to your computer.
f. Determine how many months you have to work to earn an additional week of vacation if you work for a company that provides one additional day of paid vacation for every 560 hours you work. (*Hint*: First multiply 560 times 5 days, then divide the answer by the number of hours you work in a month.)
g. Close all open windows.

4. You can customize many Windows features to suit your needs and preferences. One way you do this is to change the appearance of the taskbar on the desktop. In this challenge, try the guidelines described to explore the different ways you can customize the appearance of the taskbar.

a. Position the pointer over the top border of the taskbar. When the pointer changes shape, drag up an inch.
b. Resize the taskbar back to its original size.
c. Click the Start button on the taskbar, then point to Settings, and click Taskbar & Start Menu.
d. In the upper-right corner of the Taskbar Properties window, click the Help button, then click each option to view the pop-up window describing the option. You need to click the Help button before clicking each option.
e. Click each option and observe the effect in the preview area. (*Note:* Do not click OK.)
f. Return the options to their original settings or click Cancel.

► Visual Workshop

Use the skills you have learned in this unit to create a desktop that looks like the one in Figure A-18. Make sure you include the following:

- Calculator program minimized
- Scroll bars in Control Panel window
- Details view in Control Panel window
- Rearranged icons on desktop; your icons may be different (*Hint*: If the icons "snap" back to where they were, they are set to be automatically arranged. Right-click a blank area of the desktop, point to Arrange Icons, then click Auto Arrange to deselect it.)
- Channel Bar closed

Use the Print Screen key to make a copy of the screen and then print it from the Paint program (see your instructor or technical support person for assistance.) Be sure to return your settings and desktop back to their original arrangement when you complete this exercise.

FIGURE A-18

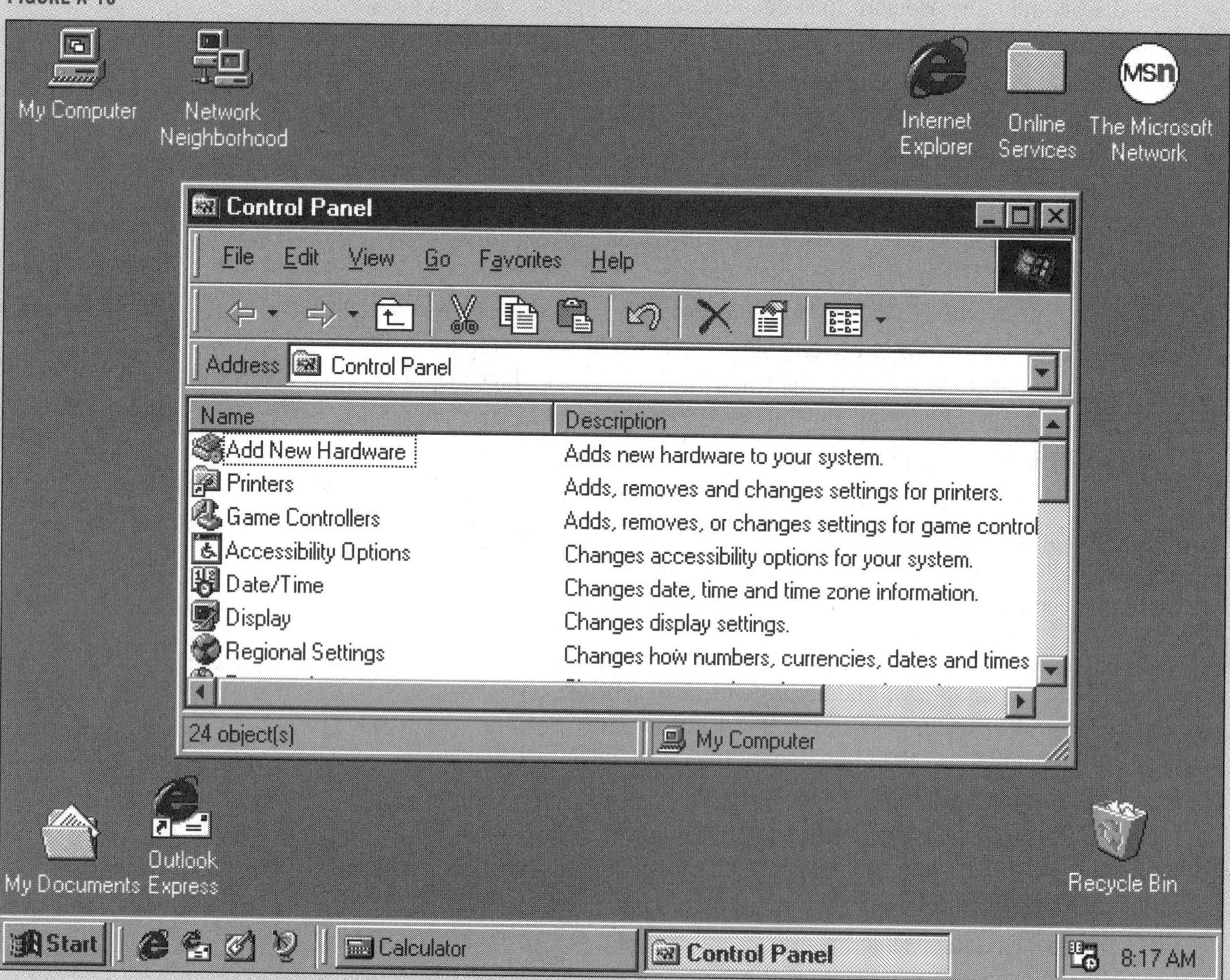

Windows 98

Working

with Programs, Files, and Folders

Objectives

- Create and save a WordPad file
- Open, edit, and save an existing Paint file
- Work with multiple programs
- Understand file management
- View files and create folders with My Computer
- Move and copy files using My Computer
- Manage files with Windows Explorer
- Delete and restore files
- Create a shortcut on the desktop

Most of your work on a computer involves creating files in programs. For example, you might use WordPad to create a resume or Microsoft Excel to create a budget. The resume and the budget are examples of **files**, electronic collections of data that you create and save on a computer. In this unit, you learn how to work with files and the programs you use to create them. You create new files, open and edit an existing file, and use the Clipboard to copy and paste data from one file to another. You also explore the file management features of Windows 98, using My Computer and Windows Explorer. Finally, you learn how to work more efficiently by managing files directly on your desktop.

Windows 98

Creating and Saving a WordPad File

As with most programs, when you start WordPad a new, blank document (or file) opens. To create a new file, such as a memo, you simply begin typing. Your work is automatically stored in your computer's random access memory (RAM) until you turn off your computer, at which point the computer's RAM is erased. To store your work permanently, you must save your work as a file on a disk. You can save files either on an internal hard disk, which is built into your computer, usually drive C, or on a removable 3.5" or 5.25" floppy disk, which you insert into a drive on your computer, usually drive A or B. Before you can save a file on a floppy disk, the disk must be formatted. See the Appendix, "Formatting a Disk," or your instructor or technical support person for more information. When you name a file, you can use up to 255 characters including spaces and punctuation in the File Name box, using either upper or lowercase letters. In this unit, you save your files to your Project Disk. If you do not have a Project Disk, see your instructor or technical support person for assistance. First, you start WordPad and create a file that contains the text shown in Figure B-1. Then you save the file to your Project Disk.

Steps

1. Click the **Start button** on the taskbar, point to **Programs**, point to **Accessories**, click **WordPad**, then click the **Maximize button** if the window does not fill your screen
   The WordPad program window opens with a new, blank document. The blinking insertion point | indicates where the text you type will appear.

Trouble?

If you make a mistake, press [Back Space] to delete the character to the left of the insertion point.

2. Type **Memo**, then press **[Enter]** to move the insertion point to the next line
3. Type the remaining text shown in Figure B-1, pressing **[Enter]** at the end of each line to move to the next line and to insert blank lines
   Now that the text is entered, you can format it. Formatting changes the appearance of text to make it more readable or attractive.

QuickTip

Double-click to select a word or triple-click to select a paragraph.

4. Click in front of the word **Memo**, then drag the mouse to the right to select the word
   The text is now selected and any action you make will be performed on the text.
5. Click the **Center button** on the Formatting toolbar, then click the **Bold button** **B** on the Formatting toolbar
   The text is centered and bold.
6. Click the **Font Size list arrow** 10, then click **16**
   A font is a particular shape and size of type. The text is enlarged to 16 point. One point is 1/72 of an inch in height. Now that your memo is complete, you are ready to save it to your Project Disk.
7. Click **File** on the menu bar, then click **Save As**
   The Save As dialog box opens, as shown in Figure B-2. In this dialog box, you specify where you want your file saved and also give your document a name.

Trouble?

This unit assumes that the drive that contains your Project Disk is drive A. If not, substitute the correct drive any time you are instructed to use the 3½ Floppy (A:) drive. See your instructor or technical support person for assistance.

8. Click the **Save in list arrow**, then click **3½ Floppy (A:)** or whichever drive contains your Project Disk
   The drive containing your Project Disk is now active, meaning that any files currently on the disk are displayed in the list of folders and files and that the file you save now will be saved on the disk in this drive.
9. Double-click the **text** in the File name text box, type **Memo**, then click **Save**
   Your memo is now saved as a WordPad file with the name "Memo" on your Project Disk. Notice that the WordPad title bar contains the name of the file.

FIGURE B-1: Text to enter in WordPad

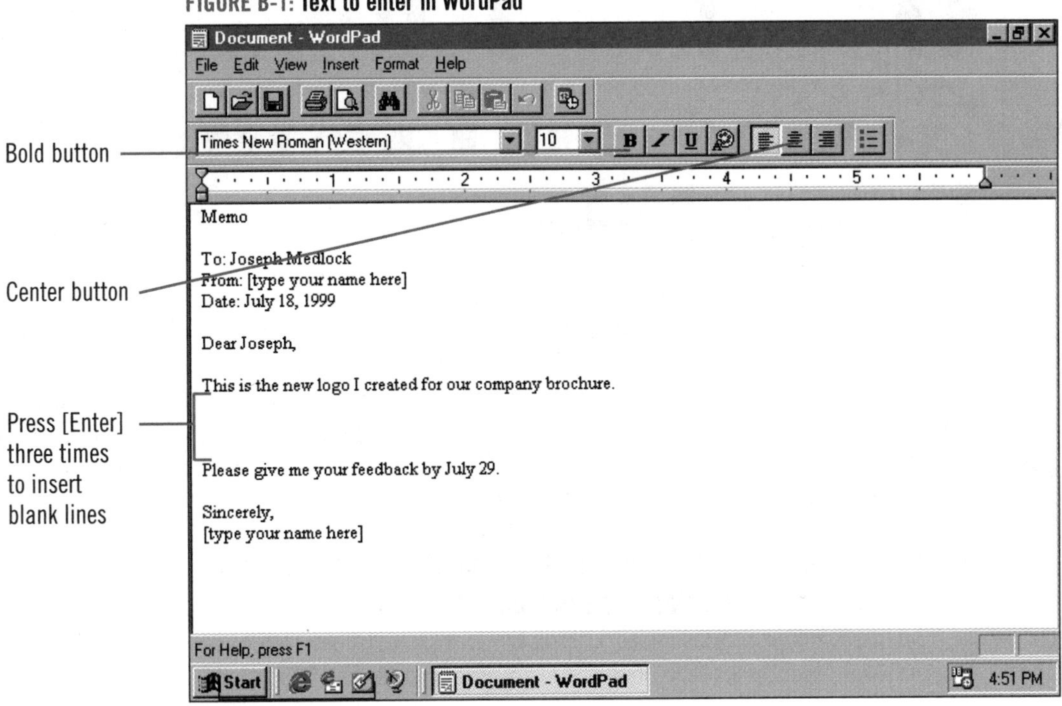

FIGURE B-2: Save As dialog box

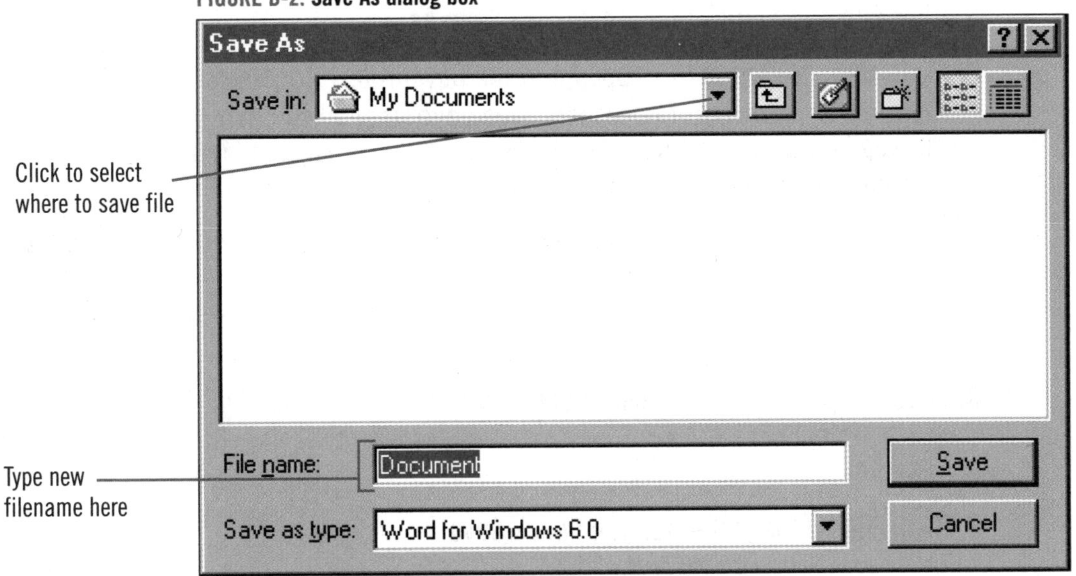

Windows 98

Opening, Editing, and Saving an Existing Paint File

Sometimes you create files from scratch, but often you may want to reopen a file you or someone else has already created. Once you open a file, you can **edit** it, or make changes to it, such as adding or deleting text. After editing a file, you can save it with the same filename, which means that you no longer will have the file in its original form, or you can save it with a different filename, so that the original file remains unchanged. In this lesson, you use **Paint**, a drawing program that comes with Windows 98, to open a file, edit it by changing a color, then save the file with a new filename to leave the original file unchanged.

Steps

1. Click the **Start button** on the taskbar, point to **Programs**, point to **Accessories**, click **Paint**, then click the **Maximize button** if the window doesn't fill the screen
   The Paint program opens with a blank work area. If you wanted to create a file from scratch, you would begin working now.
2. Click **File** on the menu bar, then click **Open**
   The Open dialog box works similarly to the Save As dialog box.
3. Click the **Look in list arrow**, then click **3½ Floppy (A:)**
   The Paint files on your Project Disk are displayed in the Open dialog box, as shown in Figure B-3.
4. Click **Win B-1** in the list of files, then click **Open**
   The Open dialog box closes and the file named Win B-1 opens. Before you make any changes to the file, you decide to save it with a new filename, so that the original file is unchanged.
5. Click **File** on the menu bar, then click **Save As**
6. Make sure **3½ Floppy (A:)** appears in the Save in text box, select the text **Win B-1** in the File name text box if necessary, type **Logo**, then click **Save**
   The Logo file appears in the Paint window, as shown in Figure B-4. Because you saved the file with a new name, you can edit it without changing the original file.
7. Click the **Fill With Color button** in the Toolbox, click the **Blue color box**, which is the fourth from the right in the first row
   Now when you click an area in the image, it will be filled with the color you selected. See Table B-1 for a description of the tools in the Toolbox.
8. Move the pointer into the **white area that represents the sky**, the pointer changes to, then click
   The sky is now blue.
9. Click **File** on the menu bar, then click **Save**
   The change you made is saved.

QuickTip

You can also open a file by double-clicking it in the Open dialog box.

FIGURE B-3: Open dialog box

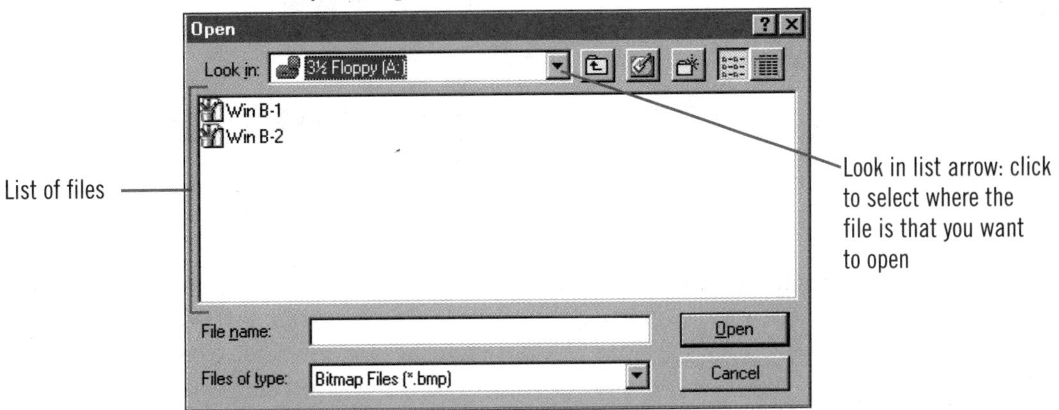

FIGURE B-4: Paint file saved with new filename

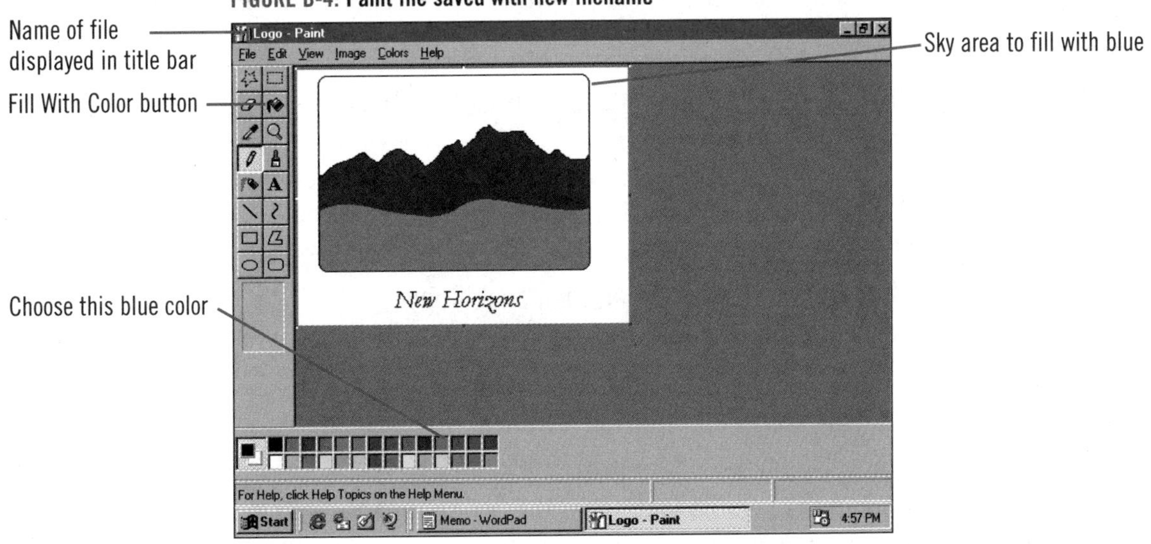

TABLE B-1: Paint Toolbox buttons

tool	description	tool	description
Free-Form Select button	Selects a free-form section of the picture to move, copy, or edit	Airbrush button	Produces a circular spray of dots
Select button	Selects a rectangular section of the picture to move, copy, or edit	Text button	Inserts text into the picture
Eraser button	Erases a portion of the picture using the selected eraser size and foreground color	Line button	Draws a straight line with the selected width and foreground color
Fill With Color button	Fills closed shape or area with the current drawing color	Curve button	Draws a wavy line with the selected width and foreground color
Pick Color button	Picks up a color off the picture to use for drawing	Rectangle button	Draws a rectangle with the selected fill style; also used to draw squares by holding down [Shift] while drawing
Magnifier button	Changes the magnification; lists magnifications under the toolbar	Polygon button	Draws polygons from connected straight-line segments
Pencil button	Draws a free-form line one pixel wide	Ellipse button	Draws an ellipse with the selected fill style; also used to draw circles by holding down [Shift] while drawing
Brush button	Draws using a brush with the selected shape and size	Rounded Rectangle button	Draws rectangles with rounded corners using the selected fill style; also used to draw rounded squares by holding down [Shift] while drawing

Windows 98

Working with Multiple Programs

A powerful feature of Windows is that you can use more than one program at a time. For example, you might be working with a file in WordPad and want to search the Internet to find the answer to a question. You can start your **browser**, a program designed to access information on the Internet, without closing WordPad. When you find the information, you can leave your browser open and switch back to WordPad. Each program that you have open is represented by a program button on the taskbar that you click to switch between programs. You can also copy data from one file to another, whether the files were created with the same program or not, using the **Clipboard**, a temporary area in your computer's memory, and the Cut, Copy, and Paste commands. See Table B-2 for a description of these commands. In this lesson, you copy the logo graphic you worked with in the previous lesson into the memo you created in WordPad.

Steps

Trouble?

If some parts of the image or text are outside the dotted rectangle, click anywhere outside the image, then select the image again, making sure you include everything.

QuickTip

To switch between programs using the keyboard, press and hold down [Alt], press [Tab] until the program you want is selected, then release [Alt].

1. Click the **Select button** on the Toolbox, then drag a rectangle around the entire graphic, including the text
   When you release the mouse button, the dotted rectangle indicates the contents of the selection, as shown in Figure B-5. Make sure the entire image and all the text is inside the rectangle. The next action you take affects the entire selection.
2. Click **Edit** on the menu bar, then click **Copy**
   The logo is copied to the Clipboard. When you **copy** an object onto the Clipboard, the object remains in its original location and is also available to be pasted into another location.
3. Click the **WordPad program button** on the taskbar
   WordPad becomes the active program.
4. Click in the **second line** below the line that ends "for our company brochure."
   The insertion point indicates where the logo will be pasted.
5. Click the **Paste button** on the WordPad toolbar
   The contents of the Clipboard, in this case the logo, are pasted into the WordPad file, as shown in Figure B-6.
6. Click the **Save button** on the toolbar
   The Memo file is saved with the logo inserted.
7. Click the **Close buttons** in both the WordPad and Paint programs to close all open files and exit both programs
   You return to the desktop.

TABLE B-2: Overview of cutting, copying, and pasting

toolbar button	function	keyboard shortcut
Cut	Removes selected information from a file and places it on the Clipboard	[Ctrl][X]
Copy	Places a copy of selected information on the Clipboard, leaving the file intact	[Ctrl][C]
Paste	Inserts whatever is currently on the Clipboard into another location within the same file or in a different file	[Ctrl][V]

FIGURE B-5: Selecting the logo to copy and paste into the Memo file

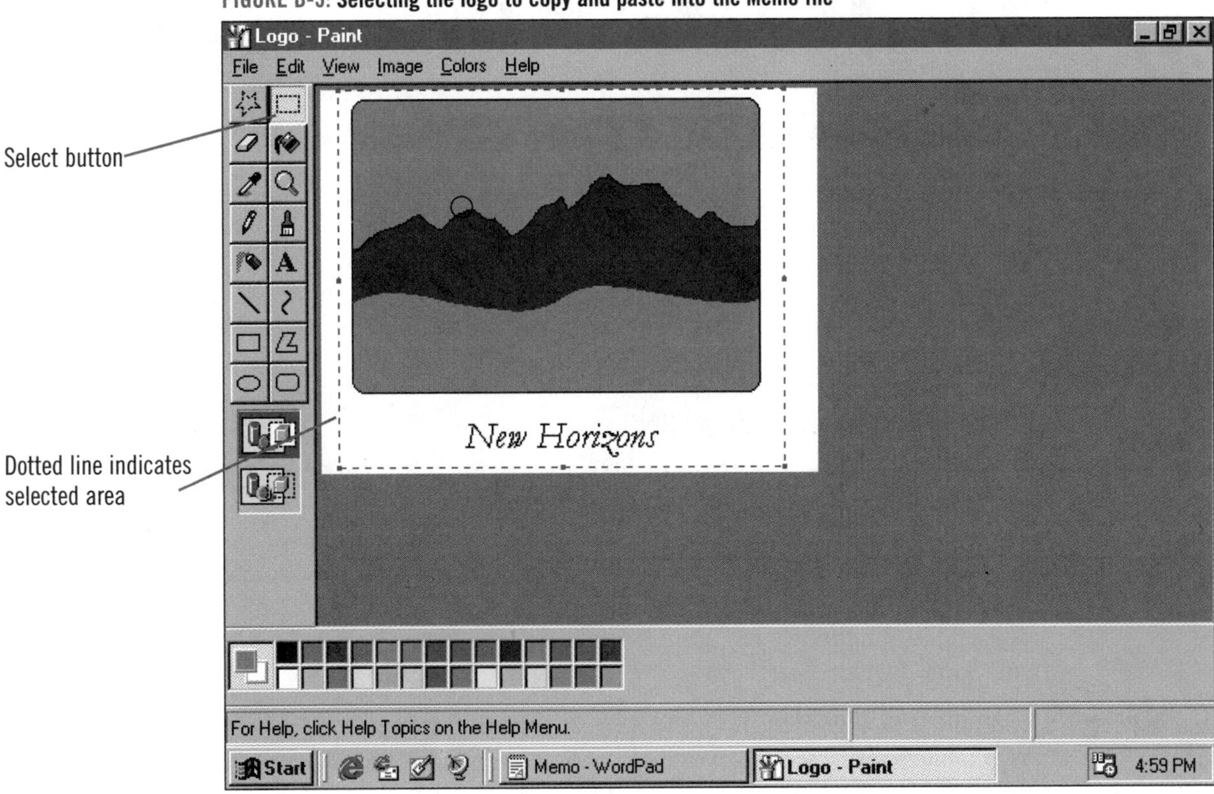

FIGURE B-6: Memo with pasted logo

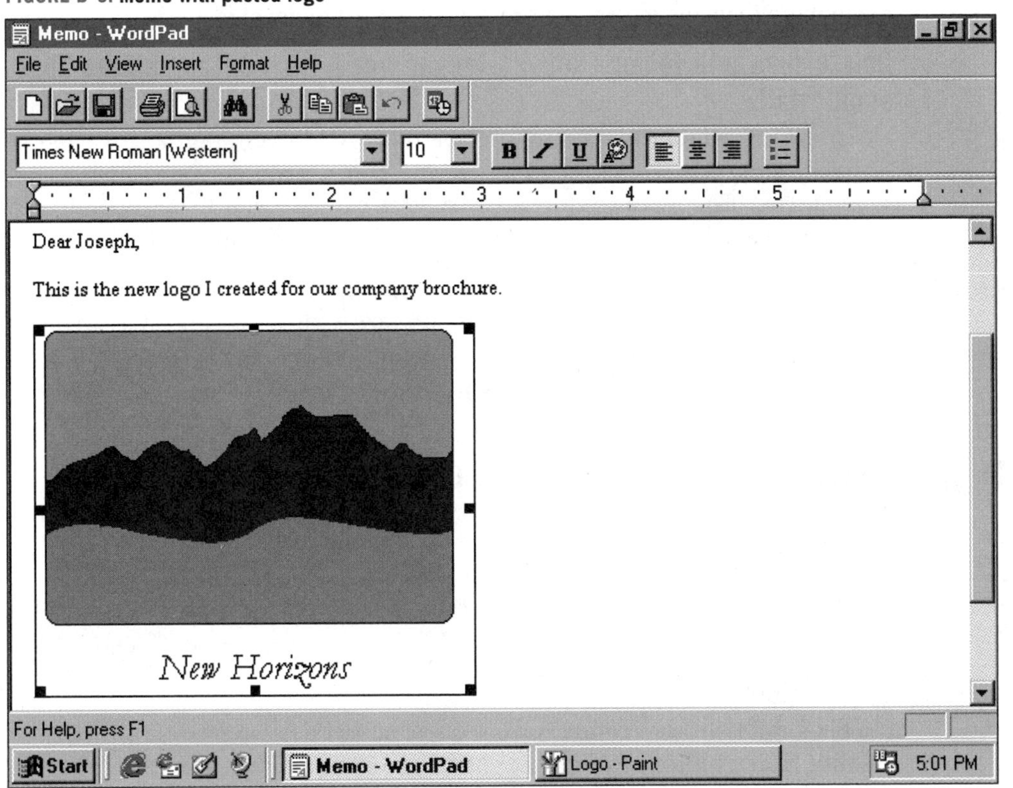

Understanding File Management

After you have created and saved numerous files using various programs, **file management**, the process of organizing and keeping track of all of your files can be a challenge. Fortunately, Windows 98 provides tools to keep everything organized so you can easily locate the files you need. There are two main tools for managing your files: My Computer and Windows Explorer. In this lesson, you preview the ways you can use My Computer and Windows Explorer to manage your files.

Windows 98 gives you the ability to:

Create folders in which you can save your files

Folders are areas on a floppy disk or hard disk in which you can store files. For example, you might create a folder for your documents and another folder for your graphic files. Folders can also contain additional folders, which creates a more complex structure of folders and files, called a **file hierarchy**. See Figure B-7 for an example of how you could organize the files on your Project Disk.

QuickTip

To browse My Computer using multiple windows, click View on the menu bar, then click Folder Options. In the Folder Options dialog box, click the General tab, click Settings, then under Browse folders as follows, click the second option button. Each time you open a new folder, a new window opens, leaving the previous folder's window open so that you can view both at the same time.

Examine and organize the hierarchy of files and folders

When you want to see the overall structure of your files and folders, you can use either My Computer or Windows Explorer. By examining your file hierarchy with these tools, you can better organize the contents of your computer and adjust the hierarchy to meet your needs. Figures B-8 and B-9 illustrate how My Computer and Windows Explorer display folders and files.

Copy, move, and rename files and folders

If you decide that a file belongs in a different folder, you can move it to another folder. You can also rename a file if you decide a new name is more descriptive. If you want to keep a copy of a file in more than one folder, you can copy it to new folders.

Delete files and folders you no longer need, as well as restore files you delete accidentally

Deleting files and folders you are sure you don't need frees up disk space and keeps your file hierarchy more organized. Using the **Recycle Bin**, a space on your computer's hard disk that stores deleted files, you can restore files you deleted by accident. To free up disk space, you should occasionally empty the Recycle Bin by deleting the files permanently from your hard drive.

Locate files quickly with the Windows 98 Find feature

As you create more files and folders, you may forget where you placed a certain file or you may forget what name you used when you saved a file. With Find, you can locate files by providing only partial names or other factors, such as the file type (for example, a WordPad document, a Paint graphic, or a program) or the date the file was created or modified.

Trouble?

If the Quick View command does not appear on the pop-up menu, it means that this feature was not installed on your computer. See your instructor or technical support person for assistance.

Preview the contents of a file without opening the file in its program

After locating a particular file, use Quick View to look at the file to verify that it is the one you want. This saves time because you do not need to open the program to open the file; however, if you decide that you want to edit the file, you can open the program right from Quick View. To preview a file, right-click the selected file in My Computer or Windows Explorer, then click Quick View on the pop-up menu. A preview of the file appears in the Quick View window.

Use shortcuts

If a file or folder you use often is located several levels down in your file hierarchy, in a folder within a folder, within a folder, it might take you several steps to access it. To save time accessing the files and programs you use frequently, you can create shortcuts to them. A **shortcut** is a link that gives you quick access to a particular file, folder, or program.

FIGURE B-7: Example of file hierarchy for Project Disk files

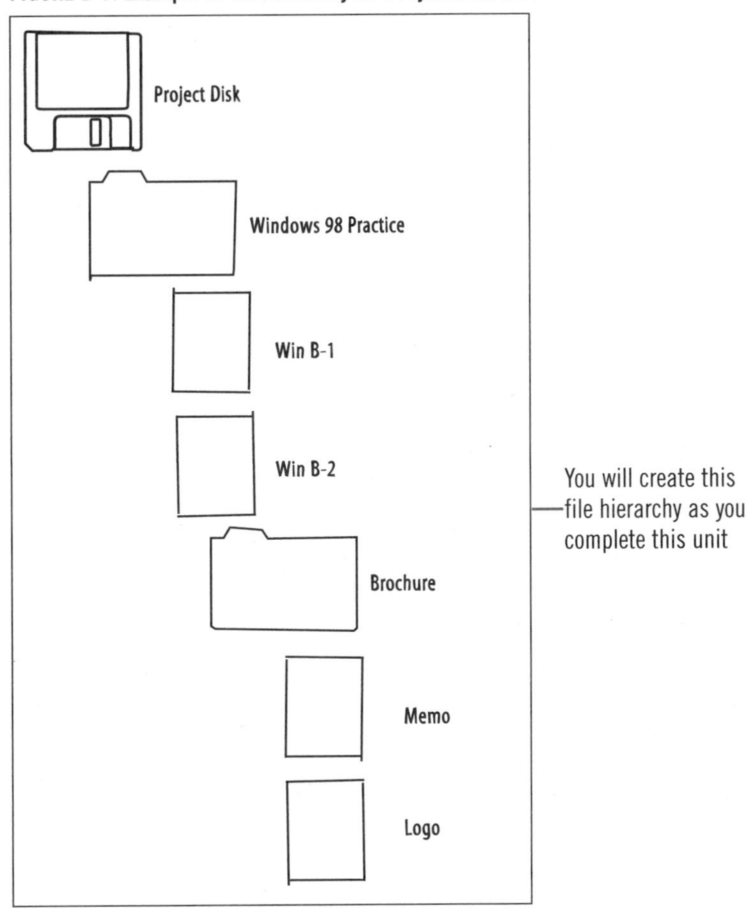

You will create this file hierarchy as you complete this unit

FIGURE B-8: Brochure folder shown in My Computer

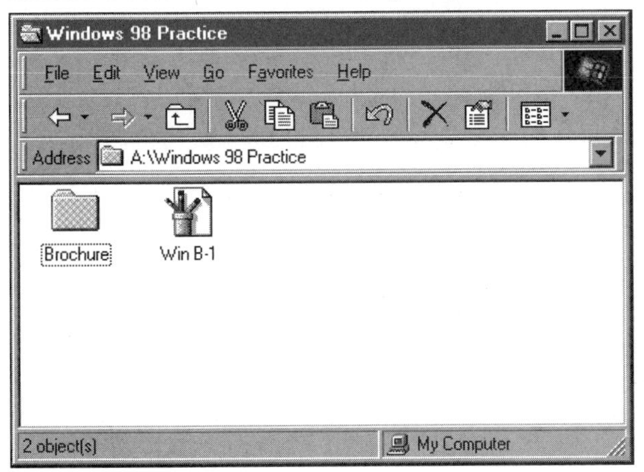

FIGURE B-9: Brochure folder shown in Windows Explorer

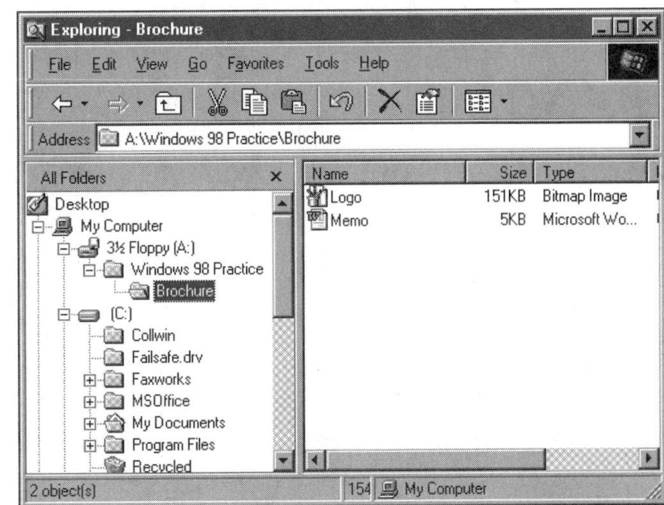

Windows 98

Viewing Files and Creating Folders with My Computer

My Computer shows the contents of your computer, including files, folders, programs, disk drives, and printers. You can click the icons representing these various parts of your computer to view their contents. You can manage your files using the My Computer menu bar and toolbar. See Table B-3 for a description of the toolbar buttons. In this lesson, you begin by using My Computer to move around in your computer's file hierarchy, then you create two new folders on your Project Disk that contain the files you created.

Trouble?

If you do not see the toolbar, click View on the menu bar, point to Toolbars, then click Standard Buttons. If you do not see the Address Bar, click View, point to Toolbar, then click the Address Bar.

Trouble?

This book assumes that your hard drive is drive C. If yours differs, substitute the appropriate drive for drive C wherever it is referenced. See your instructor or technical support person for assistance.

Trouble?

To rename a folder, click the folder to select it, click the folder name so it is surrounded by a rectangle, type the new folder name, then press [Enter].

1. Double-click the **My Computer icon** on your desktop, then click the **Maximize button** if the My Computer window does not fill the screen
   My Computer opens and displays the contents of your computer, as shown in Figure B-10. Your window may contain icons for different folders, drives, printers, and so on.
2. Make sure your Project Disk is in the floppy disk drive, then double-click the **3½ Floppy (A:) icon**
   The contents of your Project Disk are displayed in the window. These are the project files and the files you created using WordPad and Paint. Each file is represented by an icon, which indicates the program that was used to create the file. If Microsoft Word is installed on your computer, the Word icon appears for the WordPad files; if not, the WordPad icon appears.
3. Click the **Address list arrow** on the Address Bar, as shown in Figure B-10, then click **(C:)**, or the letter for the main hard drive on your computer
   The window changes to show the contents of your hard drive. The **Address Bar** allows you to open and display a drive, folder, or even a Web page. You can also type in the Address Bar to go to a different drive, folder, or Web page. For example, typing "C:\" will display drive C; typing "E:\Personal Letters" will display the Personal Letters folder on drive E, and typing "http://www.microsoft.com" opens Microsoft's Web site if your computer is connected to the Internet.
4. Click the **Back button** on the toolbar
   The Back button displays the previous location, in this case, your Project Disk.
5. Click the **Views button list arrow** on the toolbar, then click **Details**
   Details view shows not only the files and folders, but also the size of the file; the type of file, folder, or drive; and the date the file was last modified.
6. Click , then click **Large Icons**
   This view offers less information but provides a large, clear view of the contents of the disk.
7. Click **File** on the menu bar, click **New**, then click **Folder**
   A new folder is created on your Project Disk, as shown in Figure B-11. The folder is called "New Folder" by default. It is selected and ready to be renamed. You can also create a new folder by right-clicking in the blank area of the My Computer window, clicking New, then clicking Folder.
8. Type **Windows 98 Practice**, then press **[Enter]**
   Choosing descriptive names for your folders helps you remember their contents.
9. Double-click the **Windows 98 Practice folder**, repeat Step 7 to create a new folder in the Windows 98 Practice folder, type **Brochure** for the folder name, then press **[Enter]**
10. Click the **Back button** to return to your Project Disk

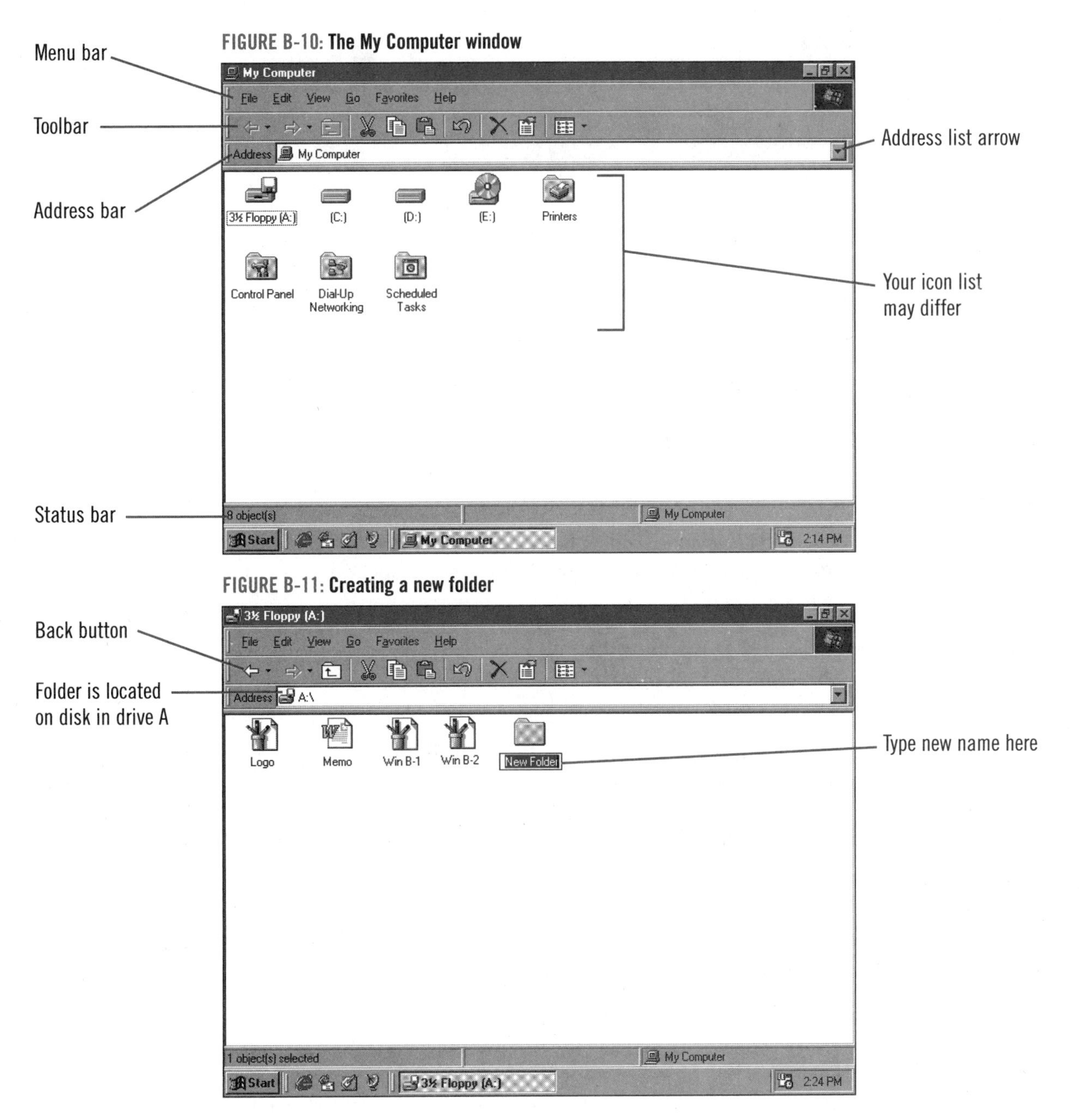

FIGURE B-10: The My Computer window

FIGURE B-11: Creating a new folder

TABLE B-3: Buttons on the My Computer toolbar

button	function
	Moves back to the previous location you have already visited
	Moves forward to the previous location you have already visited
	Moves up one level in the file hierarchy
	Deletes a folder or file and places it on the clipboard
	Copies a folder or file
	Pastes a folder or file
	Undoes the most recent My Computer operation
	Deletes a folder or file permanently
	Shows the properties of a folder or file
	Lists the contents of My Computer using different views

Moving and Copying Files Using My Computer

You can move a file or folder from one location to another using a variety of methods in My Computer or Windows Explorer. If the file or folder and the location to which you want to move it are both visible on the desktop, you can simply drag the item from one location to the other. You can also use the cut, copy and paste commands on the Edit menu or the corresponding buttons on the toolbar. You can also right-click the file or folder and choose the Send to command to "send" it to another location—most often a floppy disk for **backing up** files. Backup copies are made in case you have computer trouble, which may cause you to lose files. In this lesson, you move your files into the folder you created in the last lesson.

Steps

QuickTip

To copy a file so that it appears in two locations, press and hold [Shift] while you drag the file to its new location.

QuickTip

It is easy to confuse the Back button with the Up One Level button. The Back button returns you to the last location you visited, no matter where it is in your folder hierarchy. The Up One Level button displays the next level up in the folder hierarchy, no matter where you last visited.

1. Click **View**, click **Arrange Icons**, then click **By Name**
   In this view, folders are listed first in alphabetical order, followed by files, also in alphabetical order.
2. Click the **Win B-1 file**, hold down the mouse button and drag the file onto the **Windows 98 Practice folder**, as shown in Figure B-12, then release the mouse button
   Win B-1 is moved into the Windows 98 Practice folder.
3. Double-click the **Windows 98 Practice folder** and confirm that it contains the Win B-1 file as well as the Brochure folder
4. Click the **Up button** on the My Computer toolbar, as shown in Figure B–12
   You return to your Project Disk. The Up button displays the next level up in the folder hierarchy.
5. Click the **Logo file**, press and hold **[Shift]**, then click the **Memo file**
   Both files are selected. Table B-4 describes methods for selecting multiple files and folders.
6. Click the **Cut button** on the 3½ Floppy (A:) toolbar
   The icons for the files are gray, as shown in Figure B-13. This indicates that they've been cut and placed on the Clipboard, to be pasted somewhere else. Instead of dragging items to a new location, you can use the Cut, Copy, and Paste toolbar buttons or the cut, copy, and paste commands on the Edit menu.
7. Click the **Back button** to return to the Windows 98 Practice folder, then double-click the **Brochure folder**
   The Brochure folder is currently empty.
8. Click the **Paste button** on the toolbar
   The two files are pasted into the Brochure folder.
9. Click the **Address list arrow**, then click **3½ Floppy (A:)** and confirm that the Memo and Logo files are no longer listed there and that only the Windows 98 Practice folder and the Win B-2 file remain
10. Click the **Close button** in the 3½ Floppy (A:) window

FIGURE B-12: Dragging a file from one folder to another

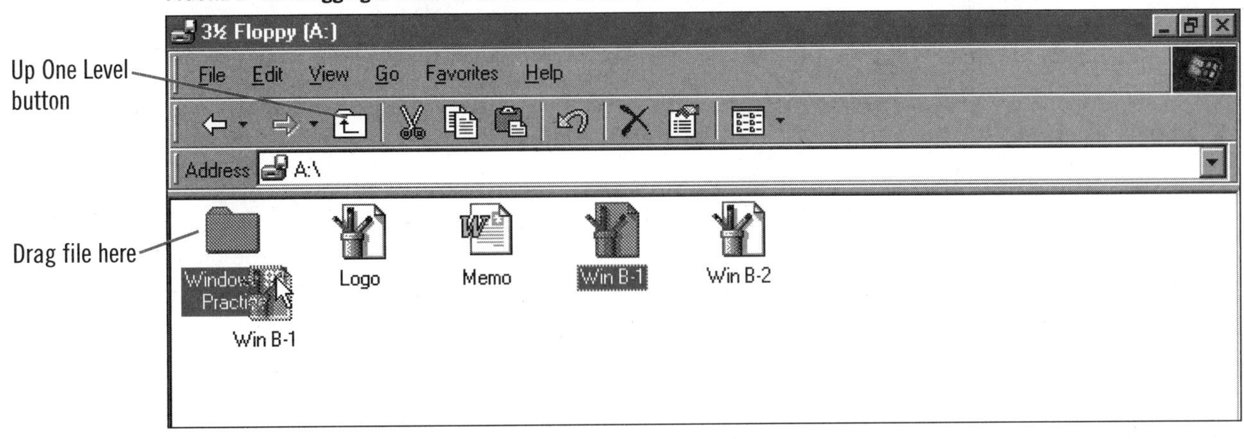

FIGURE B-13: Cutting files to move them

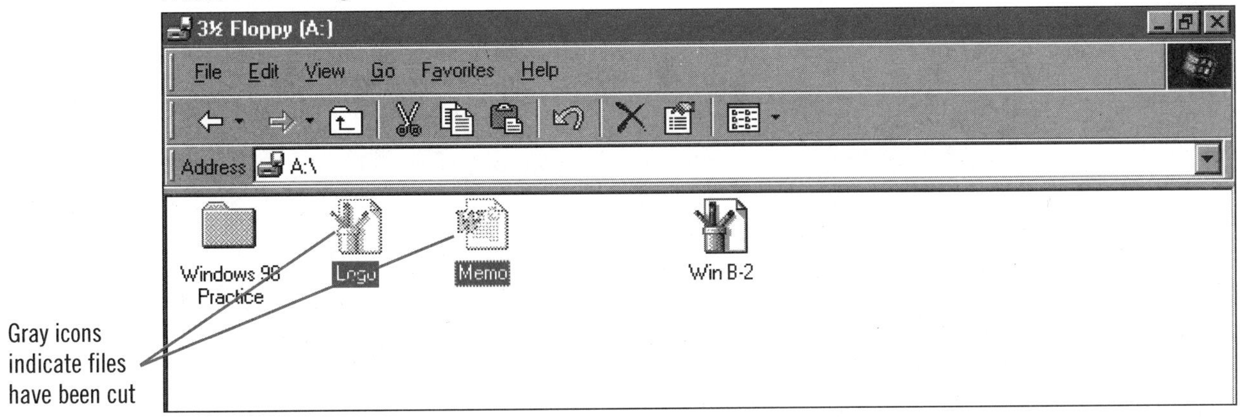

TABLE B-4: Techniques for selecting multiple files and folders

to select	use this technique
Individual objects not grouped together	Click the first object you want to select, then press [Ctrl] as you click each additional object you want to add to the selection
Objects grouped together	Click the first object you want to select, then press [Shift] as you click the last object in the list of objects you want to select; all the objects listed between the first and last objects are selected

Managing Files with Windows Explorer

As with My Computer, you can use Windows Explorer to copy, move, delete, and rename files and folders. However, **Windows Explorer** is more powerful than My Computer: it allows you to see the overall structure of the contents of your computer or network, the file hierarchy, while you work with individual files and folders within that structure. This means you can work with more than one computer, folder, or file at once. In this lesson, you copy a folder from your Project Disk onto the hard drive, then rename the folder.

Steps 1 2 3 4

Trouble?

If you do not see the toolbar, click View on the menu bar, point to Toolbars, then click Standard Buttons. If you do not see the Address Bar, click View, point to Toolbars, then click Address Bar.

1. **Click the Start button, point to Programs, point to Windows Explorer, then click the Maximize button if the Windows Explorer window doesn't already fill the screen**
   Windows Explorer opens, as shown in Figure B-14. The window is divided into two sides called **panes**. The left pane, also known as the **Explorer Bar**, displays the drives and folders on your computer in a hierarchy. The right pane displays the contents of whatever drive or folder is currently selected in the left pane. Each pane has its own set of scroll bars, so that changing what you can see in one pane won't affect what you can see in the other. Like My Computer, Windows Explorer has a menu bar, toolbar, and Address Bar.
2. **Click View on the menu bar, then click Details if it is not already selected**
3. **In the left pane, scroll to and click 3½ Floppy (A:)**
   The contents of your Project Disk are displayed in the right pane.

QuickTip

When neither a + nor a – appears next to an icon, it means that the item does not have any folders in it, although it may have files, which you can display in the right pane by clicking the icon.

4. **In the left pane, click the plus sign (+) next to 3½ Floppy (A:)**
   You can use the plus signs (+) and minus signs (-) next to items in the left pane to show or hide the different levels of the file hierarchy, so that you don't always have to look at the entire structure of your computer or network. A plus sign (+) next to a computer, drive, or folder indicates there are additional folders within that object. A minus sign (-) indicates that all the folders of the next level of hierarchy are shown. Clicking the + displays (or "expands") the next level; clicking the – hides (or "collapses") them.
5. **In the left pane, double-click the Windows 98 Practice folder**
   The contents of the Windows 98 Practice folder appear in the right pane of Windows Explorer, as shown in Figure B-15. Double-clicking an item in the left pane that has a + next to it displays its contents in the right pane and also expands the next level in the hierarchy in the left pane.

Trouble?

If you are working in a lab setting, you may not be able to add items to your hard drive. Skip Steps 6, 7, and 8 if you are unable to complete them.

6. **In the left pane, drag the Windows 98 Practice folder on top of the C: drive icon, then release the mouse button**
   The Windows 98 Practice folder and the files in it are copied to the hard disk.
7. **In the left pane, click the C: drive icon**
   The Windows 98 Practice folder should now appear in the list of folders in the right pane. Now you should rename the folder so you can distinguish the original folder from the copy.

QuickTip

You can also rename a selected file by pressing [F2], or using the Rename command on the File menu.

8. **Right-click the Windows 98 Practice folder in the right pane, click Rename in the pop-up menu, type Practice Copy, then press [Enter]**

FIGURE B-14: The Windows Explorer window

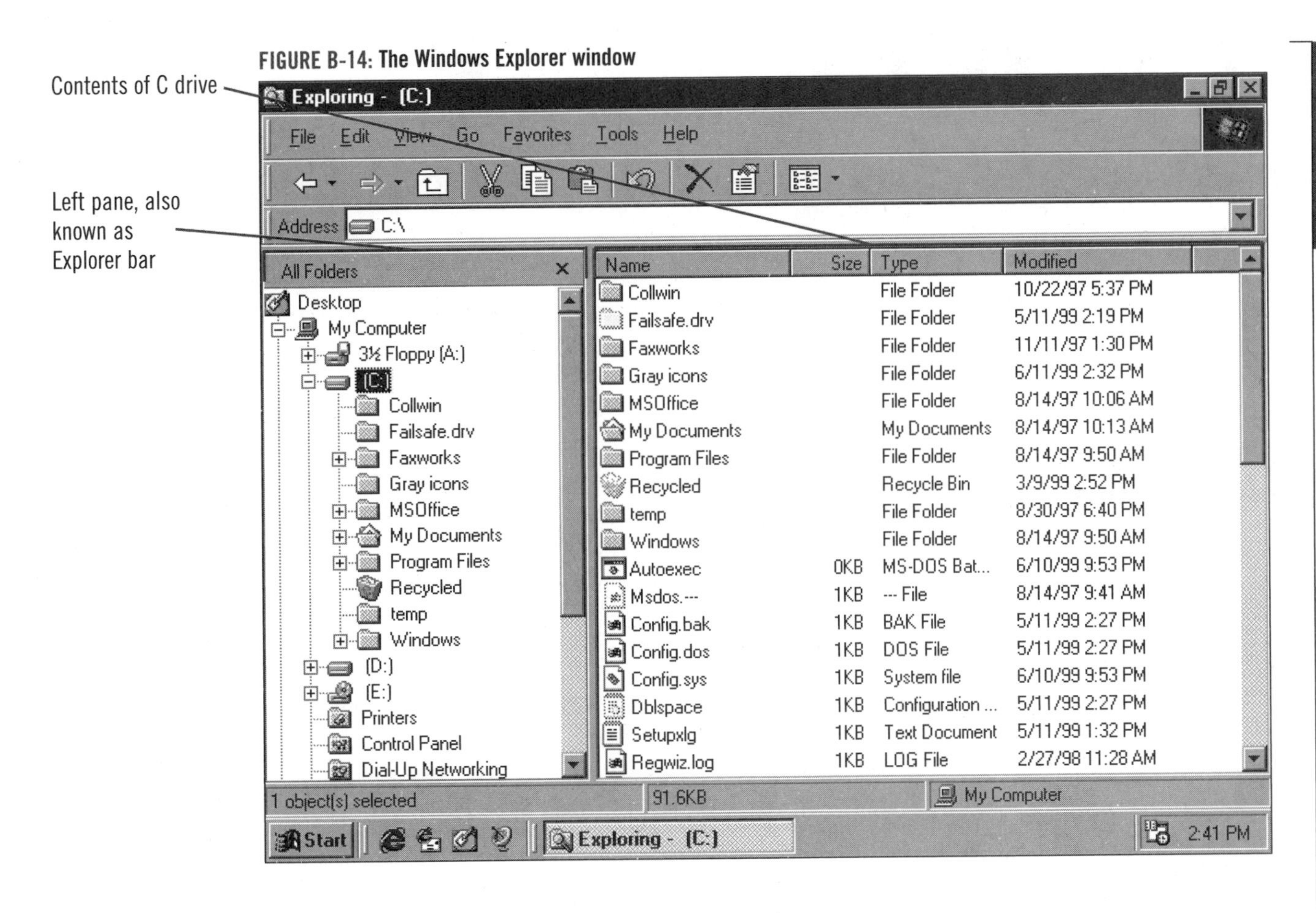

FIGURE B-15: Contents of Windows 98 Practice folder

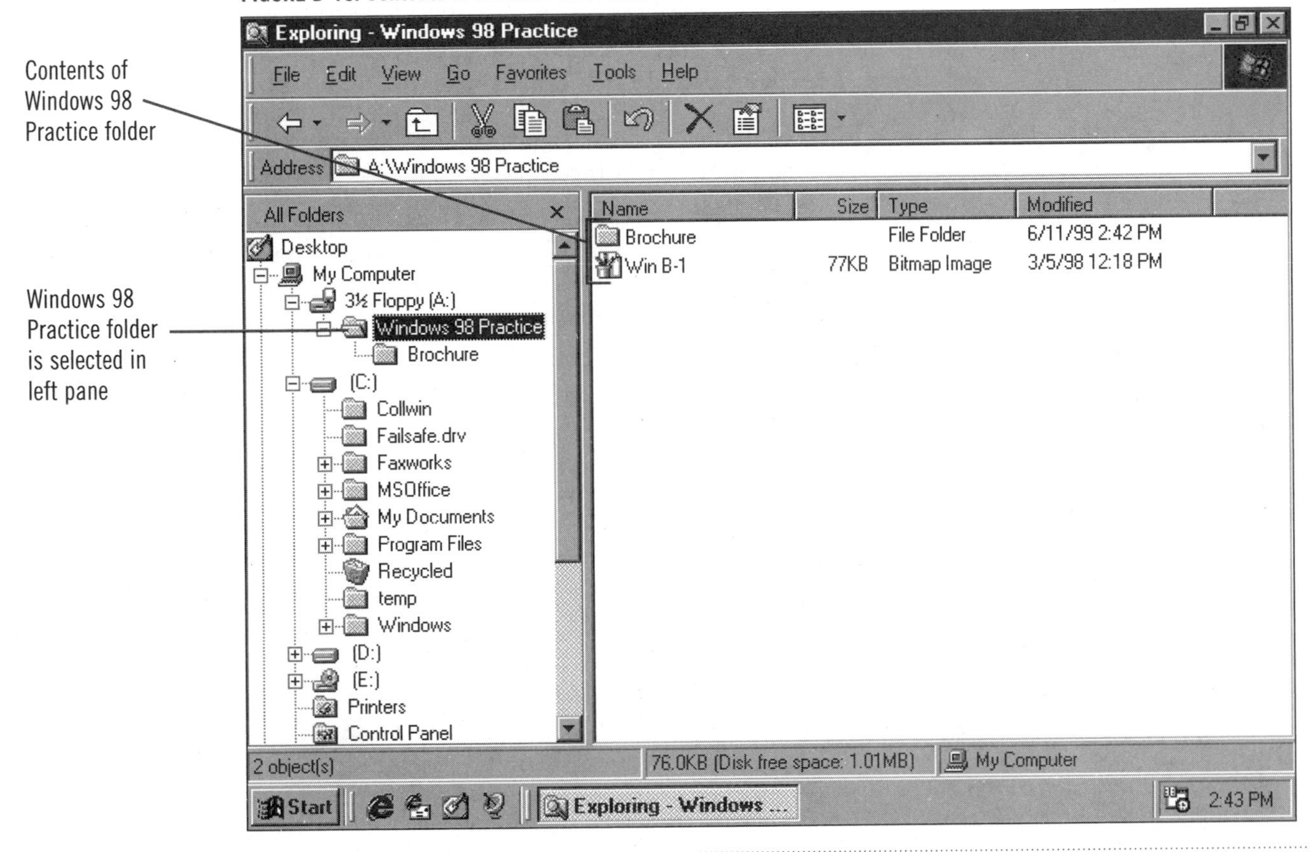

Deleting and Restoring Files

To save disk space and manage your files more effectively, you should **delete** (or remove) files you no longer need. Because files deleted from your hard drive are stored in the Recycle Bin until you remove them permanently by emptying the Recycle Bin, you can restore any files you might have deleted accidentally. However, if you delete a file from your floppy disk it will not be stored in the Recycle Bin—it will be permanently deleted. See Table B-5 for an overview of deleting and restoring files. There are many ways to delete files in Windows 98. In this lesson, you use two different methods for removing files you no longer need. Then, you learn how to restore a deleted file.

1. **Click the Restore button on the Windows Explorer title bar**
   You should be able to see the Recycle Bin icon on your desktop. If you can't see it, resize or move the Windows Explorer window until it is visible. See Figure B-16.

> **QuickTip**
> If you are unable to delete the file, it might be because your Recycle Bin is full, or too small, or the properties have been changed so that files are not stored in the Recycle Bin but are deleted instead. See your instructor or technical support person for assistance.

2. **Drag the Practice Copy folder from the right pane to the Recycle Bin on the desktop, as shown in Figure B-16, then click Yes to confirm the deletion**
   The folder no longer appears in Windows Explorer because you have moved it to the Recycle Bin. Next, you will examine the contents of the Recycle Bin.
3. **Double-click the Recycle Bin icon on the desktop**
   The Recycle Bin window opens, as shown in Figure B-17. Depending on the number of files already deleted on your computer, your window might look different. Use the scroll bar if you can't see the files.
4. **Click Edit on the Recycle Bin menu bar, then click Undo Delete**
   The Practice Copy folder is restored and should now appear in the Windows Explorer window. You might need to minimize your Recycle Bin window if it blocks your view of Windows Explorer, and you might need to scroll the right pane to find the restored folder. Now you should delete the Practice Copy folder from your hard drive.
5. **Click the Practice Copy folder in the right pane, click the Delete button on the Windows Explorer toolbar, resizing the window as necessary to see the button, then click Yes**
   When you are sure you no longer need files you've moved into the Recycle Bin, you can empty the Recycle Bin. You won't do this now, in case you are working on a computer that you share with other people. But, when you're working on your own machine, simply right-click the Recycle Bin icon, then click Empty Recycle Bin in the pop-up menu.

Customizing your Recycle Bin

You can set your Recycle Bin according to how you like to delete and restore files. For example, if you do not want files to go to the Recycle Bin but rather want them to be immediately and permanently deleted, right-click the Recycle Bin, click Properties, then click the Do Not Move Files to the Recycle Bin check box. If you find that the Recycle Bin fills up too fast and you are not ready to delete the files permanently, you can increase the amount of disk space devoted to the Recycle Bin by moving the Maximum Size of Recycle Bin slider to the right. This, of course, reduces the amount of disk space you have available for other things. Also, you can choose not to have the Confirm File Delete dialog box open when you send files to the Recycle Bin. See your instructor or technical support person before changing any of the Recycle Bin settings.

FIGURE B-16: Dragging a folder to delete it

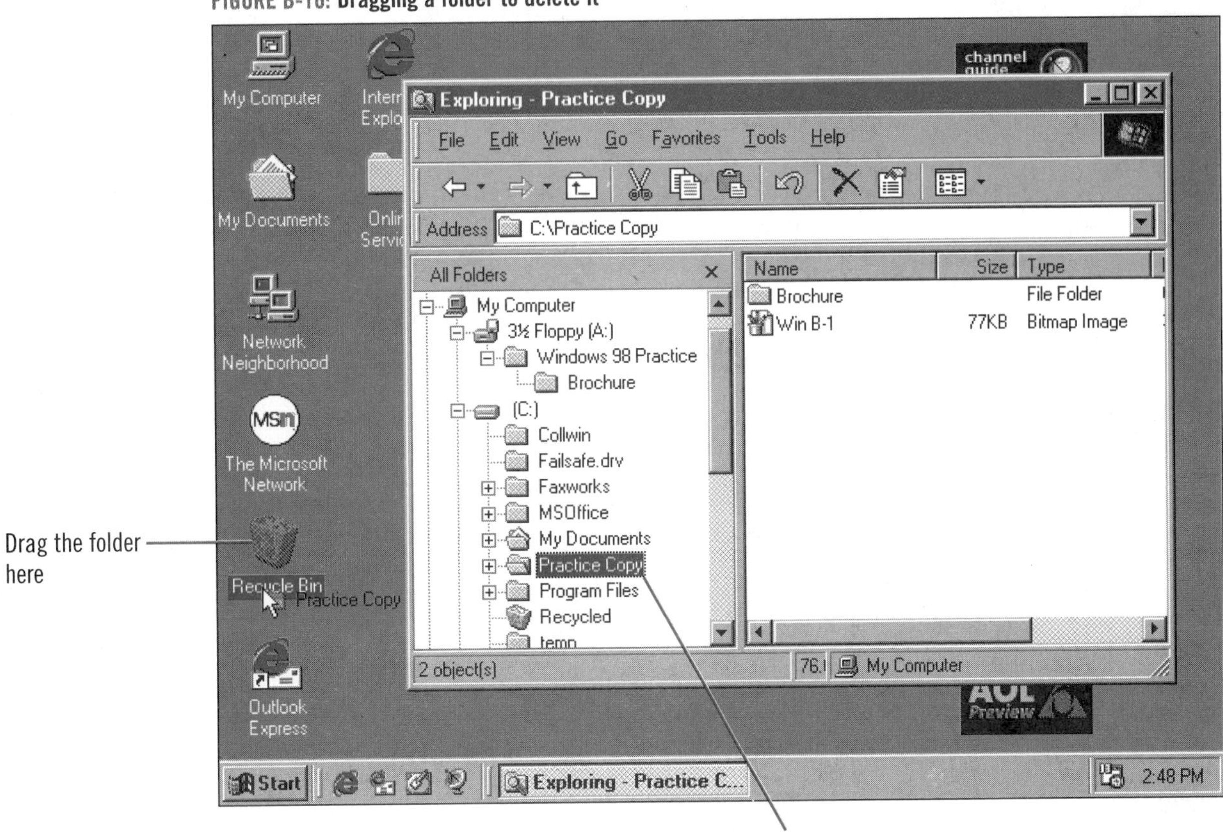

FIGURE B-17: The Recycle Bin window

TABLE B-5: Methods for deleting and restoring files

ways to delete a file	ways to restore a file from the Recycle Bin
Select the file, then click the Delete button on the toolbar	Click the Undo button on the toolbar
Select the file, then press [Delete]	Select the file, click File, then click Restore
Right-click the file, then click Delete on the pop-up menu	Right-click the file, then click Restore
Drag the file to the Recycle Bin	Drag the file from the Recycle Bin to any other location

Creating a Shortcut on the Desktop

When you use a file, folder, or program frequently, it can be cumbersome to open it if it is located several levels down in the file hierarchy. You can create a shortcut to an object and place the icon for the shortcut on the desktop or any other location you find convenient. To open the file, folder, or program using the shortcut, double-click the icon. A **shortcut** is a link between the original file, folder, or program you want to access and the icon you create. In this lesson, you create a shortcut to the Memo file on your desktop.

Steps

1. **In the left pane of the Windows Explorer window, click the Brochure folder**
   The contents of the Brochure folder appear in the right pane.
2. **In the right pane, right-click the Memo file**
   A pop-up menu appears, as shown in Figure B-18.
3. **Click Create Shortcut in the pop-up menu**
   The file named Shortcut to Memo file appears in the right pane. Now you need to move it to the desktop so that it will be accessible whenever you need it.
4. **Click the Shortcut to Memo file with the right-mouse button, then drag the shortcut to an empty area of the desktop**
   Dragging an icon using the left mouse button copies it. Dragging an icon using the right mouse button gives you the option to copy or move it. When you release the mouse button a pop-up menu appears.

   > **QuickTip**
   > Make sure to use the *right* mouse button in Step 4. If you used the left mouse button by accident, right-click the Shortcut to Memo file in the right pane of Windows Explorer, then click Delete.

5. **Click Move Here in the pop-up menu**
   A shortcut to the Memo file now appears on the desktop, as shown in Figure B-19. You might have to move or resize the Windows Explorer window to see it.
6. **Double-click the Shortcut to Memo file icon**
   WordPad starts and the Memo file opens (if you have Microsoft Word installed on your computer, it will start and open the file instead). Using a shortcut eliminates the many steps involved in starting a program and locating and opening a file.
7. **Click the Close button in the WordPad or Word title bar**
   Now you should delete the shortcut icon in case you are working in a lab and share the computer with others. Deleting a shortcut does not delete the original file or folder to which it points.
8. **On the desktop, click the Shortcut to Memo file if necessary, press [Delete], then click Yes to confirm the deletion**
   The shortcut is removed from the desktop and is now in the Recycle Bin.

   > **QuickTip**
   > Deleting a shortcut deletes only the link; it does not delete the original file or folder to which it points.

9. **Close all windows**

FIGURE B-18: Creating a shortcut

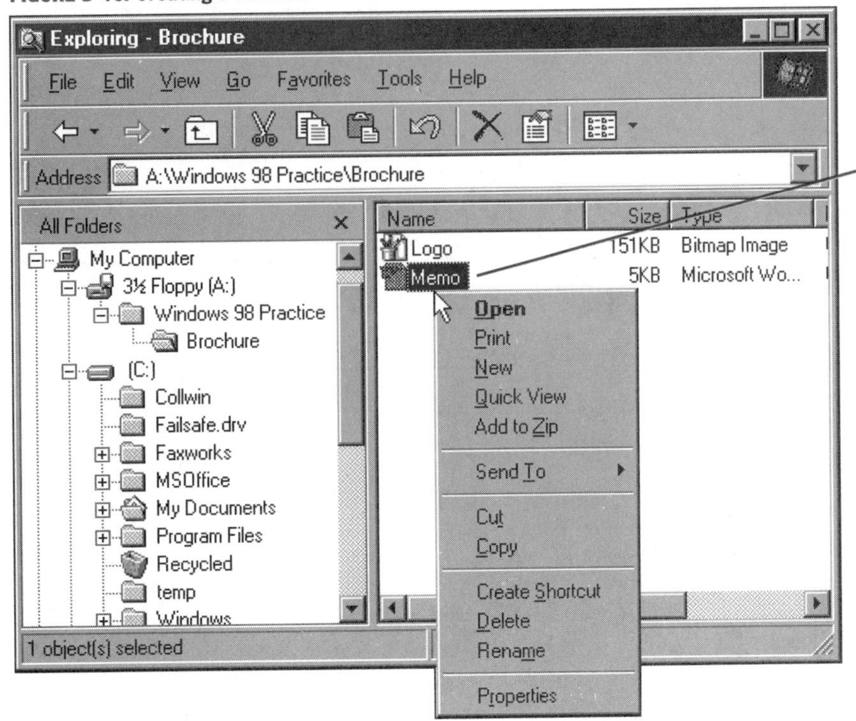

Right-click icon or filename to display pop-up menu. Your menu items may differ.

FIGURE B-19: Shortcut on desktop

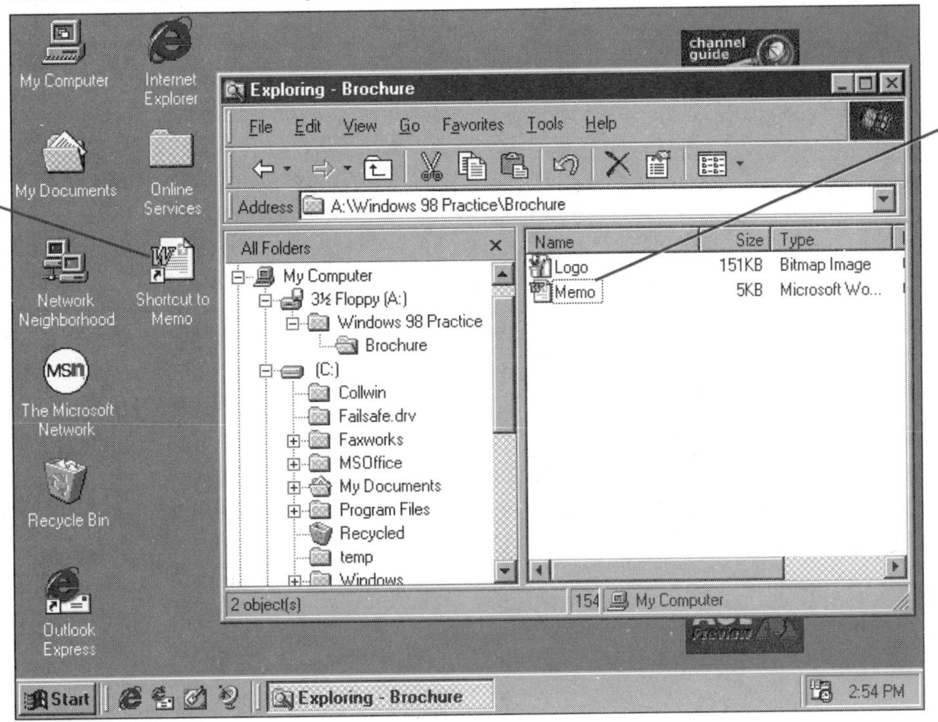

Double-click to open file

Original file located in Brochure folder

CLUES TO USE

Adding shortcuts to the Start menu

If you do not want your desktop to get cluttered with icons but you would still like easy access to certain files, programs, and folders, you can create a shortcut on the Start menu. Drag the file, program, or folder that you want to add to the Start menu from the Windows Explorer window to the Start button. The file, program, or folder will appear on the first level of the Start menu.

Practice

▶ Concepts Review

Label each of the elements of the Windows Explorer window shown in Figure B-20.

FIGURE B-20

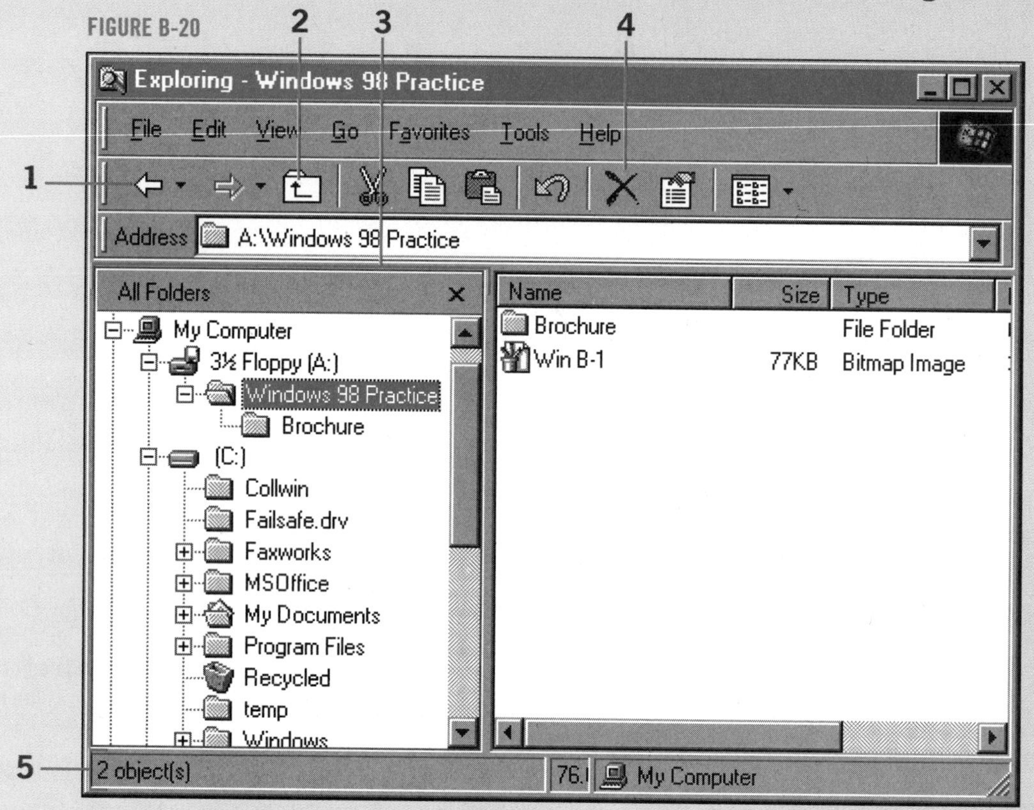

Match each of the statements with the term it describes.

6. **Electronic collections of data**
7. **Your computer's temporary storage area**
8. **Temporary location of information you wish to paste into another program**
9. **Storage areas on your hard drive for files, folders, and programs**
10. **Structure of files and folders**

a. RAM
b. Folders
c. Files
d. File hierarchy
e. Clipboard

Select the best answer from the list of choices.

11. **To prepare a floppy disk to save your files, you must first do which of the following?**
    a. Copy work files to the disk
    b. Format the disk
    c. Erase all the files that might be on the disk
    d. Place the files on the Clipboard
12. **You can use My Computer to**
    a. Create a drawing of your computer.
    b. View the contents of a folder.
    c. Change the appearance of your desktop.
    d. Add text to a WordPad file.
13. **Which of the following best describes WordPad?**
    a. A program for organizing files
    b. A program for performing financial analysis
    c. A program for creating basic text documents
    d. A program for creating graphics

14. Which of the following is NOT a way to move files from one folder to another?
- **a.** Open the file and use the Save As command to save the file in a new location.
- **b.** In My Computer or the Windows Explorer, drag the selected file to the new folder.
- **c.** Use the Cut and Paste commands on the Edit menu while in the My Computer or the Windows Explorer windows.
- **d.** Use the [Ctrl][X] and [Ctrl][V] keyboard shortcuts while in the My Computer or the Windows Explorer windows.

15. In which of the following can you view the hierarchy of drives, folders, and files in a split pane window?
- **a.** Windows Explorer
- **b.** Programs
- **c.** My Computer
- **d.** WordPad

16. To restore files that you have sent to the Recycle Bin:
- **a.** Click File, then click Empty Recycle Bin.
- **b.** Click Edit, then click Undo Delete.
- **c.** Click File, then click Undo.
- **d.** You cannot retrieve files sent to the Recycle Bin.

17. To copy instead of move a file from one folder to another, drag while pressing
- **a.** [Shift].
- **b.** [Alt].
- **c.** [Tab].
- **d.** [Ctrl].

18. To select files that are not grouped together, select the first file, then
- **a.** Press [Shift] while selecting the second file.
- **b.** Press [Alt] while selecting the second file.
- **c.** Press [Ctrl] while selecting the second file.
- **d.** Click on the second file.

19. Pressing [Backspace]
- **a.** Deletes the character to the right of the cursor.
- **b.** Deletes the character to the left of the cursor.
- **c.** Moves the insertion point one character to the right.
- **d.** Moves the insertion point one character to the left.

20. The size of a font is measured in
- **a.** Centimeters.
- **b.** Points.
- **c.** Places.
- **d.** Millimeters.

21. The Back button on the My Computer toolbar:
- **a.** Starts the last program you used.
- **b.** Displays the next level of the file hierarchy.
- **c.** Backs up the currently selected file.
- **d.** Displays the last location you visited.

Skills Review

If you are doing all of the exercises in this unit, you may run out of space on your Project Disk. Use a blank, formatted disk to complete the exercise if this happens.

1. Create and save a WordPad file.
- **a.** Start Windows, then start WordPad.
- **b.** Type a short description of your artistic abilities, pressing [Enter] several times to insert blank lines between the text and the graphic you are about to create.
- **c.** Save the document as "Drawing Ability" to the Windows 98 Practice folder on your Project Disk.

2. Open and save a Paint file.
- **a.** Start Paint and open the file Win B-2 from your Project Disk.
- **b.** Inside the picture frame, create your own unique, colorful design using several colors. Use a variety of tools. For example, create a filled circle and then place a filled square inside the circle.
- **c.** Save the picture as "First Unique Art" to the Windows 98 Practice folder on your Project Disk.

3. Work with multiple programs.
- **a.** Select the entire graphic and copy it to the Clipboard, then switch to WordPad.
- **b.** Place the insertion point in the last blank line, then paste the graphic into your document.
- **c.** Save the changes to your WordPad document using the same filename.
- **d.** Switch to Paint.
- **e.** Using the Fill With Color button, change the color of a filled area of your graphic.

f. Save the revised graphic with the new name, "Second Unique Art," to the Windows 98 Practice folder.
g. Select the entire graphic and copy it to the Clipboard.
h. Switch to WordPad and type "This is another version of my graphic." below the first picture, then press [Enter]. (*Hint*: To move the insertion point to the line below the graphic, click below the graphic, then press [Enter].)
i. Paste the second graphic under the text you just typed.
j. Save the changed WordPad document as "Two Drawing Examples" to the Windows 98 Practice folder.
k. Close Paint and WordPad.

4. View files and create folders with My Computer.
a. Open My Computer, then insert your Project Disk in the appropriate drive if necessary.
b. Double-click the drive that contains your Project Disk.
c. Create a new folder on your Project Disk by clicking File, New, then Folder, and name the new folder "Review."
d. Open the folder to display its contents (it is empty).
e. Use the Address Bar to view your hard drive, usually (C:).
f. Create a folder on the hard drive called "Temporary" then use the Back button to view the Review folder. (*Note:* You may not be able to add items to your hard drive.)
g. Create two new folders in the Review folder. Name one "Documents" and the other "Artwork."
h. Use the Forward button as many times as necessary to view the hard drive.

5. Move and copy files using My Computer.
a. Use the Address Bar to view your Project Disk, then open the Windows 98 Practice folder.
b. Select the two Paint files, then cut and paste them into the Artwork folder.
c. Use the Back button as many times as necessary to view the Windows 98 Practice folder.
d. Select the two WordPad files, then move them into the Documents folder.
e. Close My Computer.

6. View, move and copy files.
a. Open Windows Explorer and display the contents of the Artwork folder in the right pane.
b. Select the two Paint files.
c. Drag the two Paint files from the Artwork folder to the Temporary folder on the hard drive to copy them.
d. Display the contents of the Documents folder in the right pane.
e. Select the two WordPad files.
f. Repeat Step c to copy the files to the Temporary folder on the hard drive.
g. Display the contents of the Temporary folder in the right pane to verify that the four files are there.

7. Delete and restore files and folders.
a. Resize the Windows Explorer window so you can see the Recycle Bin icon on the desktop, then scroll in Windows Explorer so you can see the Temporary folder in the left pane.
b. Delete the Temporary folder from the hard drive by dragging it to the Recycle Bin.
c. Select the Review folder in the left pane, then press [Delete]. Click Yes if necessary to confirm the deletion.
d. Open the Recycle Bin, restore the Review folder and its files to your Project Disk, then close the Recycle Bin. (*Note:* If your Recycle Bin is empty, your computer is set to automatically delete items in the Recycle Bin.)

8. Create a shortcut on the desktop.
a. Use the left pane of Windows Explorer to locate the Windows folder on your hard drive. Select the folder to display its contents in the right pane. (*Note:* If you are in a lab setting, you may not have access to the Windows folder.)
b. In the right pane, scroll through the list of objects until you see a file called Explorer.
c. Drag the Explorer file to the desktop to create a shortcut.
d. Close Windows Explorer.
e. Double-click the new shortcut to make sure it starts Windows Explorer. Then close Windows Explorer again.
f. Delete the shortcut for Windows Explorer and exit Windows.

▶ Independent Challenges

If you are doing all of the Independent Challenges, you will need to use a new floppy disk.

1. You have decided to start a bakery business and you want to use Windows 98 to organize the files for the business.

a. Create two new folders on your Project Disk named "Advertising" and "Customers".
b. Use WordPad to create a form letter inviting new customers to the open house for the new bakery, then save it as "Open House Letter" and place it in the Customers folder.
c. Use WordPad to create a list of five tasks that need to get done before the business opens, then save it as "Business Plan" to your Project Disk, but don't place it in a folder.
d. Use Paint to create a simple logo for the bakery, save it as "Bakery Logo", then place it in the Advertising folder.
e. On a piece of paper, draw out the new organization of all the folders and files on your Project Disk, close all open programs, then exit Windows.

2. On your computer's hard drive, create a folder called "IC3". Follow the guidelines listed here to create the file hierarchy shown in Figure B-21.

a. Start WordPad, create a new file that contains a list. Save the file as "To Do List" to your Project Disk.
b. Start My Computer and copy the Memo file on your Project Disk to the IC3 folder. Rename the file "Article."
c. Copy the Memo file again to the IC3 folder on your hard drive and rename the second copy of the file "Article Two."
d. Use My Computer to copy any Paint file to the IC3 folder and rename the file "Sample Logo."
e. Copy the To Do List from your Project Disk to the IC3 folder and rename the file "Important List."
f. Move the files into the folders shown in Figure B-21.
g. Copy the IC3 folder to your Project Disk. Then delete the IC3 folder on your hard drive. Using the Recycle Bin, restore the file called IC3. To remove all your work on the hard drive, delete this folder again.

FIGURE B-21

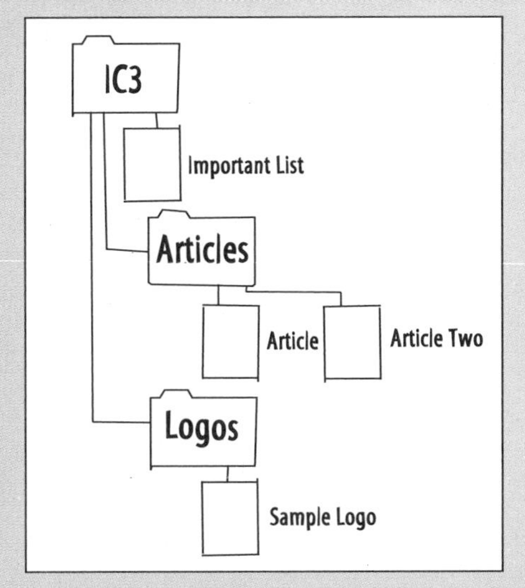

3. With Windows 98, you can access the Web from My Computer and Windows Explorer, allowing you to search for information located not only on your computer or network, but also on any computer connected to the Internet.

a. Start Windows Explorer, then click in the Address Bar so the current location (probably your hard drive) is selected, then type "www.microsoft.com"
b. Connect to the Internet if necessary. The Microsoft Web page displays in the right pane of Windows Explorer.
c. Click in the Address Bar, then type "www.course.com", then wait a moment while the Course Technology Web page opens.
d. Make sure your Project Disk is in the floppy disk drive, then click 3½ Floppy (A:) in the left pane.

e. Click the Back button list arrow, then click Welcome to Microsoft Homepage.
f. Capture a picture of your desktop by using [Print Screen]. Save the file as "Microsoft", then print it. See Independent Challenge 4 for instructions.
g. Click the Close button on the Explorer Bar.
h. Close Windows Explorer and disconnect from the Internet.

4. Create a shortcut to the drive that contains your Project Disk. Then capture a picture of your desktop showing the new shortcut by pressing [Print Screen], located on the upper-right side of your keyboard. The picture is stored temporarily on the Clipboard. Then open the Paint program and paste the contents of the Clipboard into the drawing window. Click No when asked to enlarge the Bitmap. Save the Paint file as Desktop Picture on your Project Disk and print it. Delete the shortcut when you are finished.

▶ Visual Workshop

Recreate the screen shown in Figure B-22, which contains the Brochure window in My Computer, two shortcuts on the desktop, and two files open. Press [Print Screen] to make a copy of the screen, then print it from Paint. See your instructor or technical support person for assistance.

FIGURE B-22

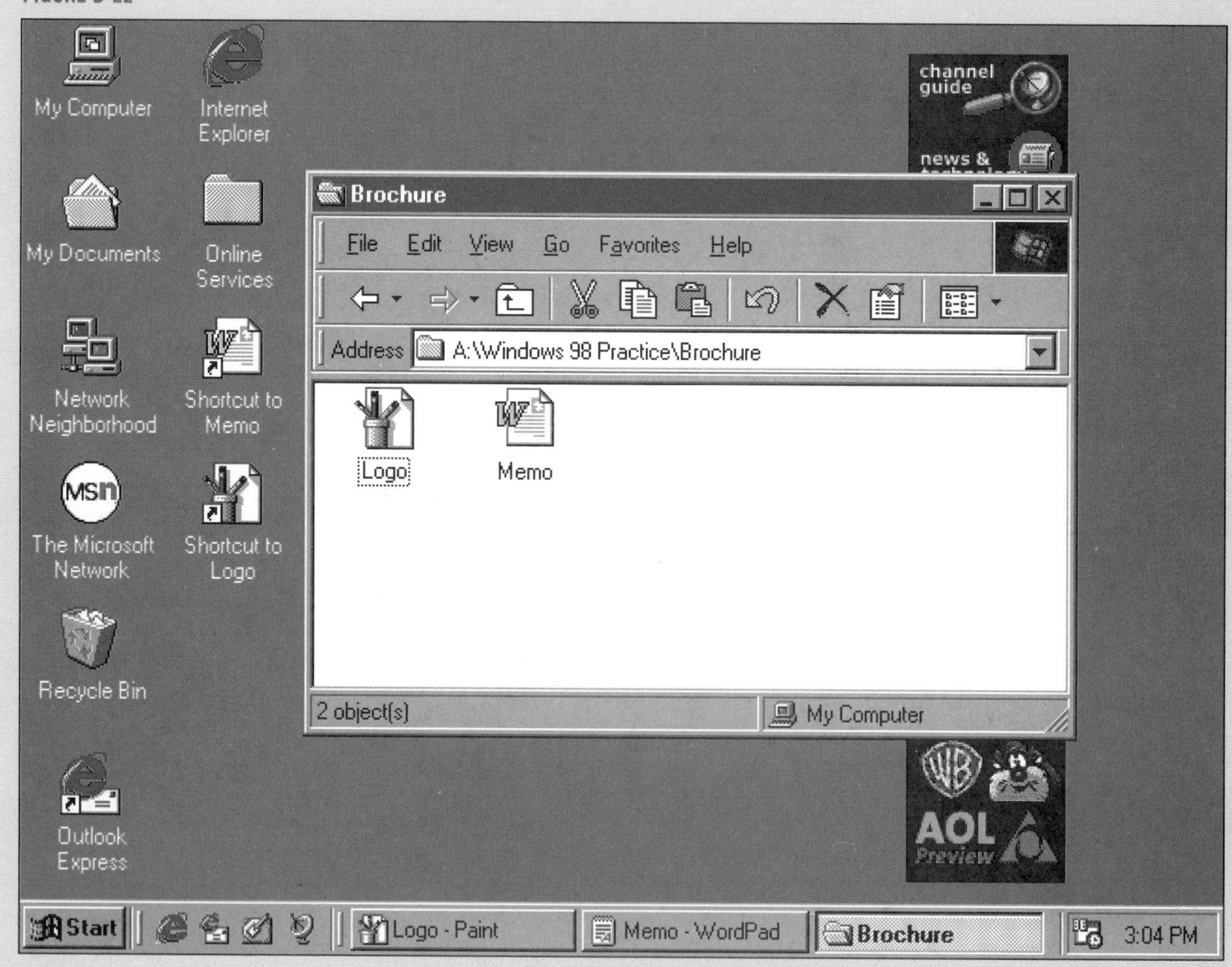

Excel 2000

Getting Started with Excel 2000

Objectives

- Define spreadsheet software
- Start Excel 2000
- View the Excel window
- MOUS Open and save a workbook
- MOUS Enter labels and values
- MOUS Preview and print a worksheet
- MOUS Get Help
- Close a workbook and exit Excel

In this unit, you will learn how to start Microsoft Excel 2000 and use different elements of the Excel window. You will also learn how to open and save existing files, enter data in a worksheet, and use the extensive Help system. Jim Fernandez is the office manager at MediaLoft, a nationwide chain of bookstore cafés selling books, CDs, and videos. MediaLoft cafés also sell coffee and pastries to customers. Jim uses Excel to analyze a worksheet that summarizes budget information for the MediaLoft Café in the New York City store.

Defining Spreadsheet Software

Microsoft Excel is an electronic spreadsheet program that runs on Windows computers. You use an **electronic spreadsheet** to perform numeric calculations rapidly and accurately. See Table A-1 for common ways spreadsheets are used in business. The electronic spreadsheet that you produce when using Excel is also referred to as a **worksheet**. Excel helps Jim produce professional-looking documents that can be updated automatically so they always have accurate information. Figure A-1 shows a budget worksheet that Jim created using pencil and paper, while Figure A-2 shows the same worksheet Jim created using Excel.

Details

The advantages of using Excel include:

Enter data quickly and accurately

With Excel, you can enter information faster and more accurately than when using the pencil-and-paper method. For example, in the MediaLoft NYC Café budget, certain expenses such as rent, cleaning supplies, and products supplied on a yearly plan (coffee, creamers, sweeteners) remain constant for the year. You can copy the expenses that don't change from quarter to quarter, and then use Excel to calculate Total Expenses and Net Income for each quarter by simply supplying the data and formulas.

Recalculate data easily

Fixing typing errors or updating data using Excel is easy, and the results of a changed entry are recalculated automatically. For example, if you receive updated expense figures for Quarter 4, you simply enter the new numbers and Excel recalculates the worksheet.

Perform a what-if analysis

One of the most powerful decision-making features of Excel is the ability to change data and then quickly view the recalculated results. Anytime you use a worksheet to answer the question "what if," you are performing a **what-if analysis.** For instance, if the advertising budget for a quarter is increased to $3,600, you can enter the new figure into the worksheet and immediately see the impact on the overall budget.

Change the appearance of information

Excel provides powerful features for enhancing a spreadsheet so that information is visually appealing and easy to understand. You can use boldface type and shade text headings or numbers to add emphasis to key data in the worksheet.

Create charts

Excel makes it easy to create charts based on information in a worksheet. With Excel, charts are automatically updated as data changes. The worksheet in Figure A-2 includes a pie chart that graphically shows the distribution of the MediaLoft NYC Café's budget expenses for the year 2000.

Share information with other users

Because everyone at MediaLoft is now using Microsoft Office, it's easy to share worksheet data among colleagues. For example, you can complete the MediaLoft budget that your manager started creating in Excel. Simply access the files you need or want to share through the network or from a disk, and then make any changes or additions.

Create new worksheets from existing ones quickly

It's easy to take an existing Excel worksheet and quickly modify it to create a new one. When you are ready to create next year's budget, you can open the file for this year's budget, save it with a new file name, and use the existing data as a starting point.

FIGURE A-1: Traditional paper worksheet

MediaLoft NYC Café Budget

	Qtr1	Qtr 2	Qtr 3	Qtr 4	Total
Net Sales	48,000	76,000	64,000	80,000	268,000
Expenses					
Salary	13,000	13,000	13,000	13,000	52,000
Rent	3,500	3,500	3,500	3,500	14,000
Advertising	3,600	8,000	16,000	20,000	47,600
Cleaners	1,500	1,500	1,500	1,500	6,000
Pastries	2,500	2,500	2,500	2,500	10,000
Milk/Cream	1,000	1,000	1,000	1,000	4,000
Coffee/Tea	4,250	4,250	4,250	4,250	17,000
Sweeteners	300	300	300	300	1,200
Total Expenses	29,650	34,050	42,050	46,050	151,800
Net Income	18,350	41,950	21,950	33,950	116,200

FIGURE A-2: Excel worksheet

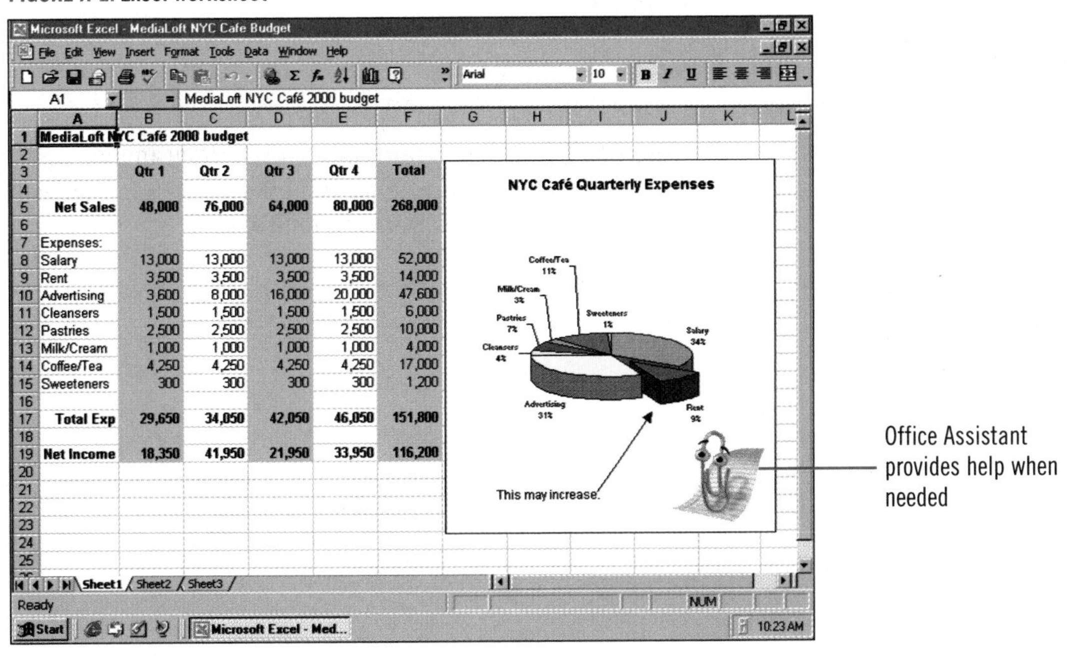

Office Assistant provides help when needed

TABLE A-1: Common business uses for spreadsheets

spreadsheets are used to:	by:
Maintain values	Calculating numbers
Represent values visually	Creating charts based on worksheet figures
Create consecutively numbered pages using multiple workbook sheets	Printing reports containing workbook sheets
Organize data	Sorting data in ascending or descending order
Analyze data	Creating data summaries and short-lists using PivotTables or AutoFilters
Create what-if data scenarios	Using variable values to investigate and sample different outcomes

Starting Excel 2000

To start any Windows program, you use the Start button on the taskbar. A slightly different procedure might be required for computers on a network and those that use Windows-enhancing utilities. If you need assistance, ask your instructor or technical support person. Jim is ready to begin work on the budget for the MediaLoft Café in New York City. He begins by starting Excel.

Steps

1. Point to the **Start button** on the taskbar
   The Start button is on the left side of the taskbar and is used to start programs on your computer.
2. Click
   Microsoft Excel is located in the Programs group, which is at the top of the Start menu, as shown in Figure A-3.
3. Point to **Programs**
   All the programs on your computer, including Microsoft Excel, are listed in this area of the Start menu. See Figure A-4. Your program list might look different depending on the programs installed on your computer.
4. Click the **Microsoft Excel program icon** on the Programs menu
   Excel opens and a blank worksheet appears. In the next lesson, you will familiarize yourself with the elements of the Excel worksheet window.

Trouble?

If you don't see the Microsoft Excel icon, consult your instructor or technical support person.

FIGURE A-3: Start menu

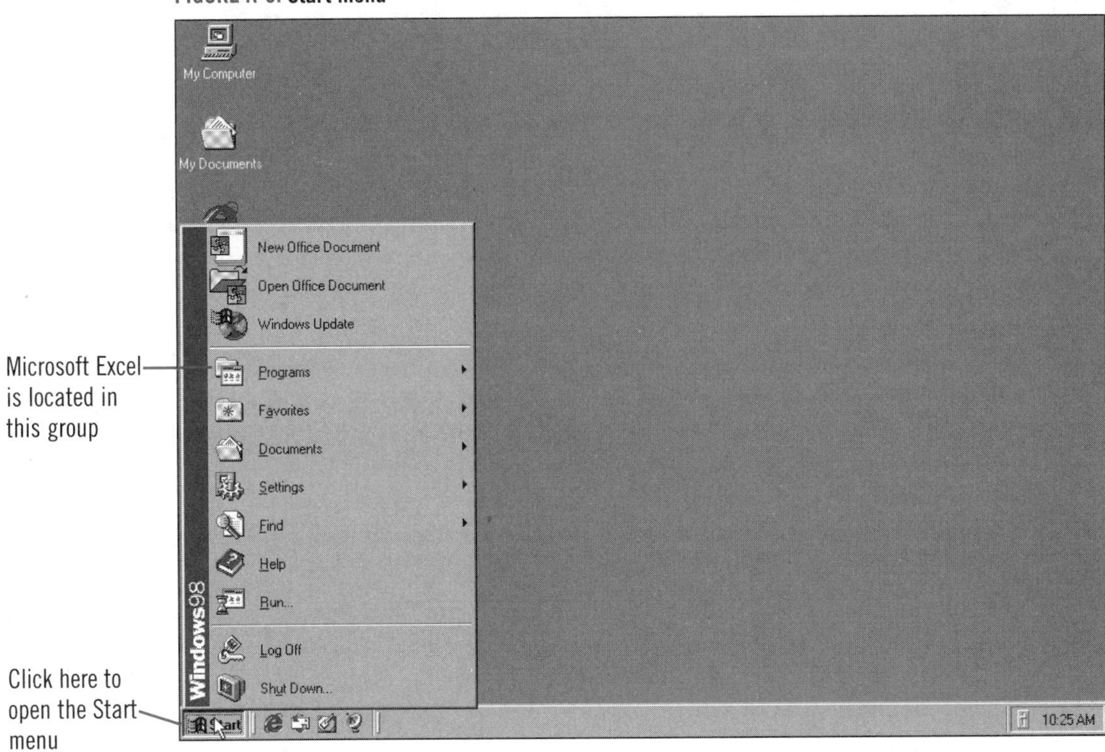

FIGURE A-4: Programs list

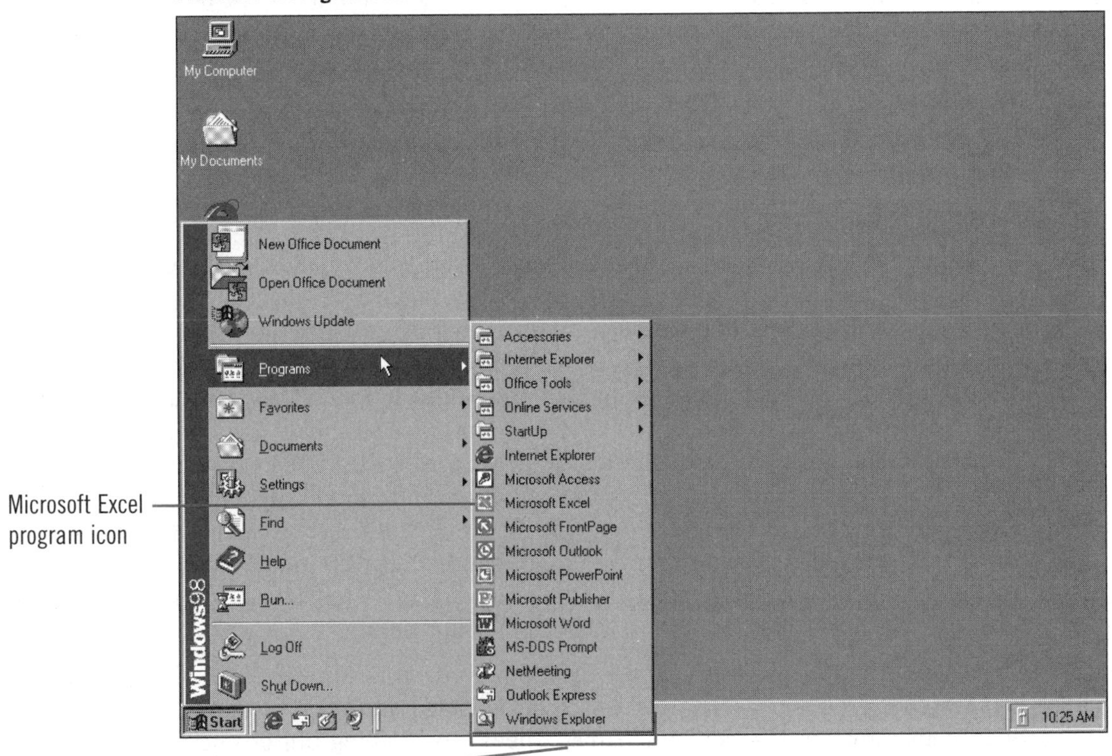

Excel 2000

Viewing the Excel Window

When you start Excel, the **worksheet window** appears on your screen. The worksheet window includes the tools that enable you to create and work with worksheets. Jim needs to familiarize himself with the Excel worksheet window and its elements before he starts working with the budget worksheet. Compare the descriptions below to Figure A-5.

Details

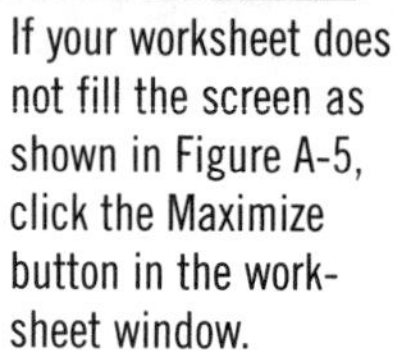

Trouble?

If your worksheet does not fill the screen as shown in Figure A-5, click the Maximize button in the worksheet window.

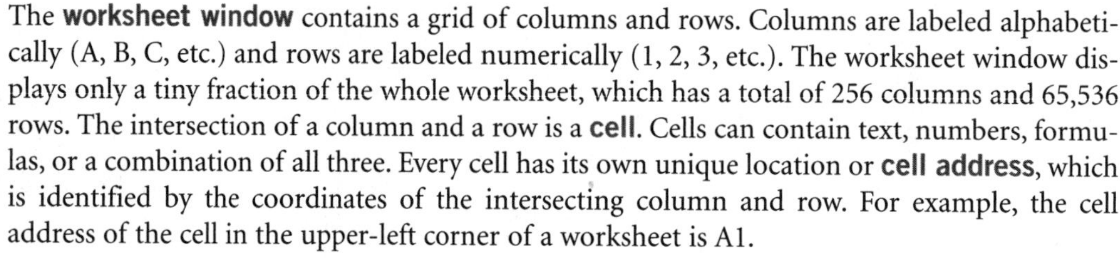

The **worksheet window** contains a grid of columns and rows. Columns are labeled alphabetically (A, B, C, etc.) and rows are labeled numerically (1, 2, 3, etc.). The worksheet window displays only a tiny fraction of the whole worksheet, which has a total of 256 columns and 65,536 rows. The intersection of a column and a row is a **cell**. Cells can contain text, numbers, formulas, or a combination of all three. Every cell has its own unique location or **cell address**, which is identified by the coordinates of the intersecting column and row. For example, the cell address of the cell in the upper-left corner of a worksheet is A1.

The **cell pointer** is a dark rectangle that highlights or outlines the cell you are working in. This cell is called the **active cell**. In Figure A-5, the cell pointer is located at A1, so A1 is the active cell. To activate a different cell, just click any other cell or press the arrow keys on your keyboard to move the cell pointer elsewhere.

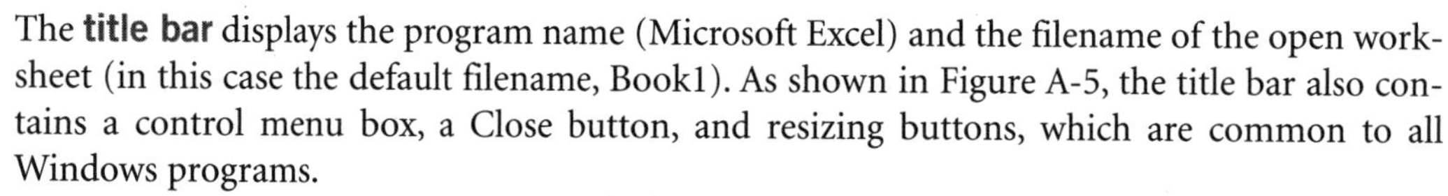

The **title bar** displays the program name (Microsoft Excel) and the filename of the open worksheet (in this case the default filename, Book1). As shown in Figure A-5, the title bar also contains a control menu box, a Close button, and resizing buttons, which are common to all Windows programs.

The **menu bar** contains menus from which you choose Excel commands. As with all Windows programs, you can choose a menu command by clicking it with the mouse or by pressing [Alt] plus the underlined letter in the menu name. When you click a menu, a short list of commonly used commands may appear at first; you can wait or click the double arrows at the bottom of the menu to see expanded menus.

The **name box** displays the active cell address. In Figure A-5, "A1" appears in the name box, indicating that A1 is the active cell.

The **formula bar** allows you to enter or edit data in the worksheet.

The **toolbars** contain buttons for frequently used Excel commands. The **Standard toolbar** is located just below the left edge of the menu bar and contains buttons that effect operations within the worksheet. The **Formatting toolbar**—to the right of the Standard toolbar—contains buttons that change the worksheet's appearance. Each button contains a graphic representation of its function. For instance, the face of the Printing button contains a printer. To choose a button, simply click it with the left mouse button. Not all the buttons on the Standard and Formatting toolbars are visible on the screen. To view other toolbar buttons, click the More Buttons button at the right end of each toolbar to display a list of additional buttons. Throughout the lessons in this book, you will need to remember to click the More Buttons button if a button you are instructed to click is not visible on your screen. When you use a button from the More Buttons list, Excel adds it to your visible toolbar. That's why each user's toolbars look unique. Be sure to read the Clues to Use in this lesson to learn more about working with Excel's toolbars.

Sheet tabs below the worksheet grid let you keep your work in collections called **workbooks.** Each workbook contains three worksheets by default and can contain a maximum of 255 sheets. **Sheet tabs** can be given meaningful names. **Sheet tab scrolling buttons** help you move from one sheet to another.

The **status bar** is located at the bottom of the Excel window. The left side of the status bar provides a brief description of the active command or task in progress. The right side of the status bar shows the status of important keys such as [Caps Lock] and [Num Lock].

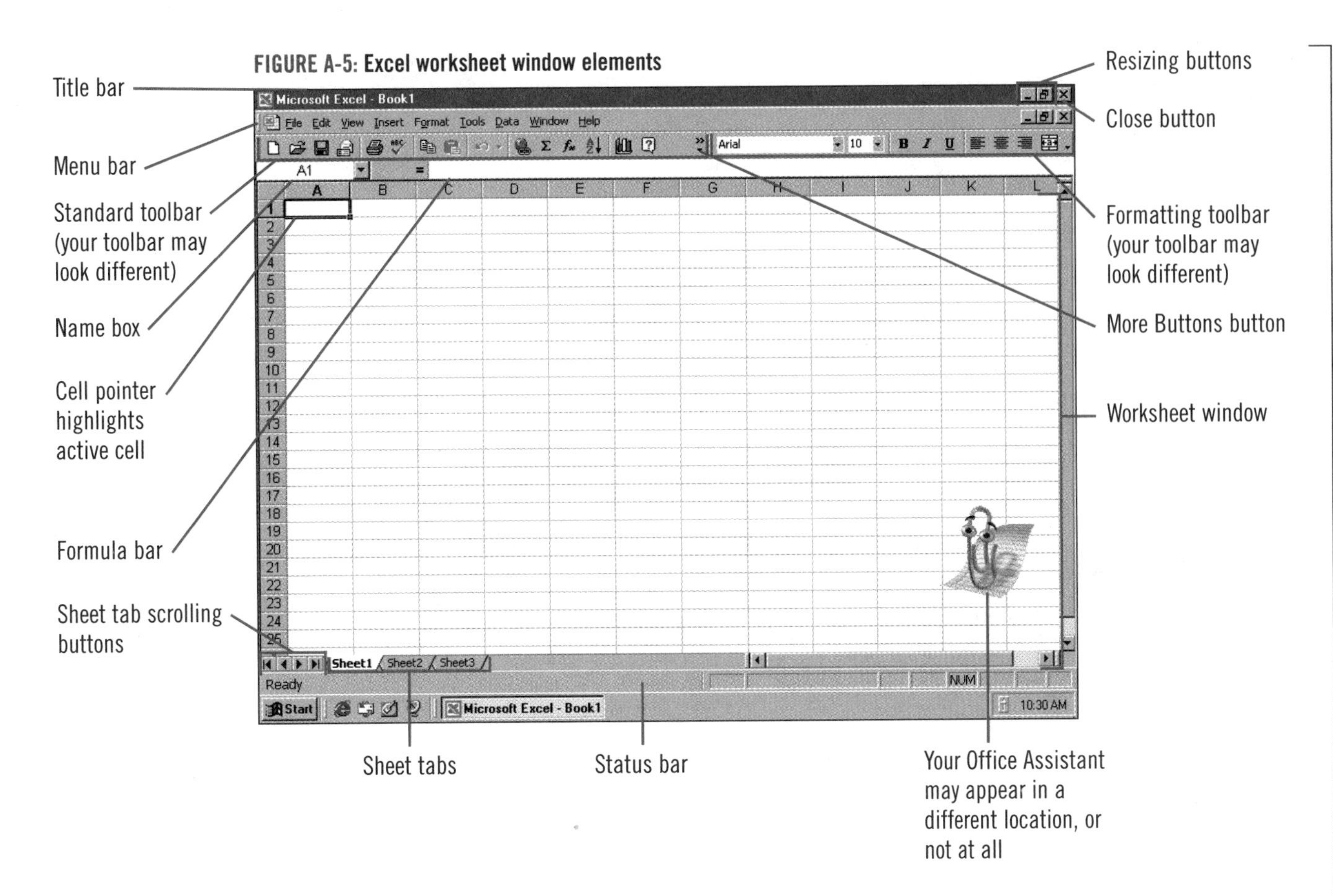

FIGURE A-5: Excel worksheet window elements

Excel 2000

Personalized toolbars and menus in Excel 2000

Excel toolbars and menus modify themselves to your working style. The Standard and Formatting toolbars you see when you first start Excel include the most frequently used buttons. To locate a button not visible on a toolbar, click the **More Buttons button** on that toolbar to see the list of additional toolbar buttons. As you work, Excel promotes the buttons you use to the visible toolbars, and demotes the buttons you don't use to the More Buttons list. Similarly, Excel menus adjust to your work habits, so that the commands you use most often automatically appear on the shortened menus. Click the double arrow at the bottom of a menu to view additional menu commands. You can return toolbars and menus to their default settings by clicking Reset my usage data on the Options tab of the Customize dialog box, as shown in Figure A-6. Resetting your usage data erases changes made automatically to your menus and toolbars. It does not affect the options you customize.

FIGURE A-6: Customize dialog box

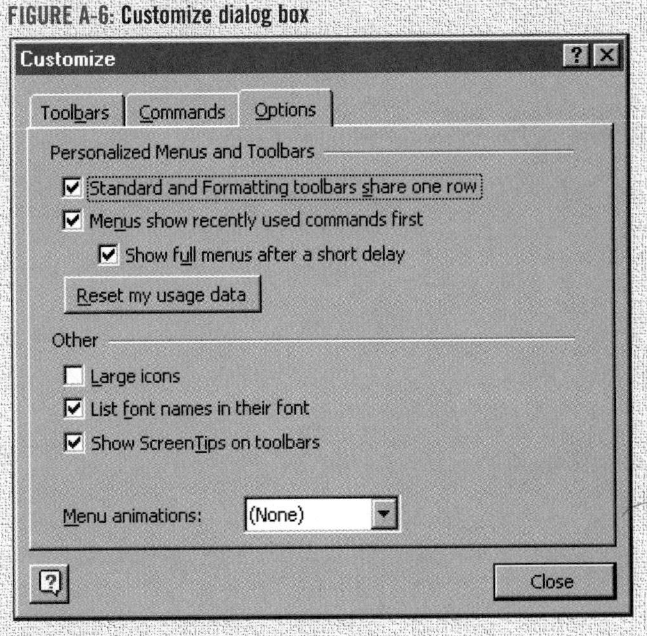

Excel 2000

Opening and Saving a Workbook

Sometimes it's more efficient to create a new worksheet by modifying one that already exists. This saves you from having to retype information that can be reused from previous work. Throughout this book, you will create new worksheets by opening a file from your Project Disk, using the Save As command to create a copy of the file with a new name, and then modifying the new file by following the lesson steps. Use the Save command to store changes made to an existing file. It is a good idea to save your work every 15 minutes or before printing. Saving the files with new names keeps your original Project Disk files intact, in case you have to start the lesson over again or you wish to repeat an exercise. Jim wants to complete the New York City MediaLoft Café budget that a member of the accounting staff has been working on. Jim opens the budget workbook and then uses the Save As command to create a copy with a new name.

Steps 1 2 3 4

1. **Insert your Project Disk in the appropriate disk drive**
2. **Click the Open button on the Standard toolbar**
   The Open dialog box opens. See Figure A-7.
3. **Click the Look in list arrow, then click the drive that contains your Project Disk**
   A list of the files on your Project Disk appears in the Open dialog box.
4. **Click the file EX A-1, then click Open**
   The file EX A-1 opens.
5. **Click File on the menu bar, then click Save As**
   The Save As dialog box opens with the drive containing your Project Disk displayed in the Save in list box. You should save all your files to your Project Disk, unless instructed otherwise.
6. **In the File name text box, select the current file name (if necessary), type MediaLoft Cafe Budget, as shown in Figure A-8, then click Save**
   Both the Save As dialog box and the file EX A-1 close, and a duplicate file named MediaLoft Café Budget opens, as shown in Figure A-9. The Office Assistant may or may not appear on your screen. As you will learn, toolbars and menus change as you work with Excel. It is a good idea to return toolbars and menus to their default settings when you begin these lessons.
7. **Click Tools on the menu bar, click Customize, make sure the Options tab in the Customize dialog box is displayed, click Reset my usage data to restore the default settings, click Yes in the alert box or dialog balloon, then click Close**

QuickTip

You could also double-click the filename in the Open dialog box to open the file.

QuickTip

You can click or use the shortcut key [Ctrl][S] to save a workbook using the same filename.

FIGURE A-7: **Open dialog box**

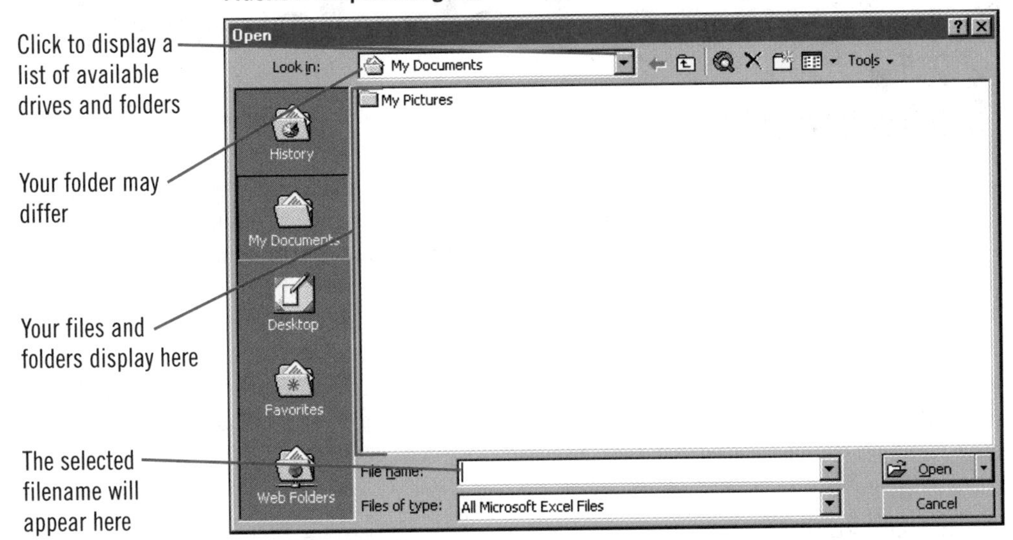

FIGURE A-8: **Save As dialog box**

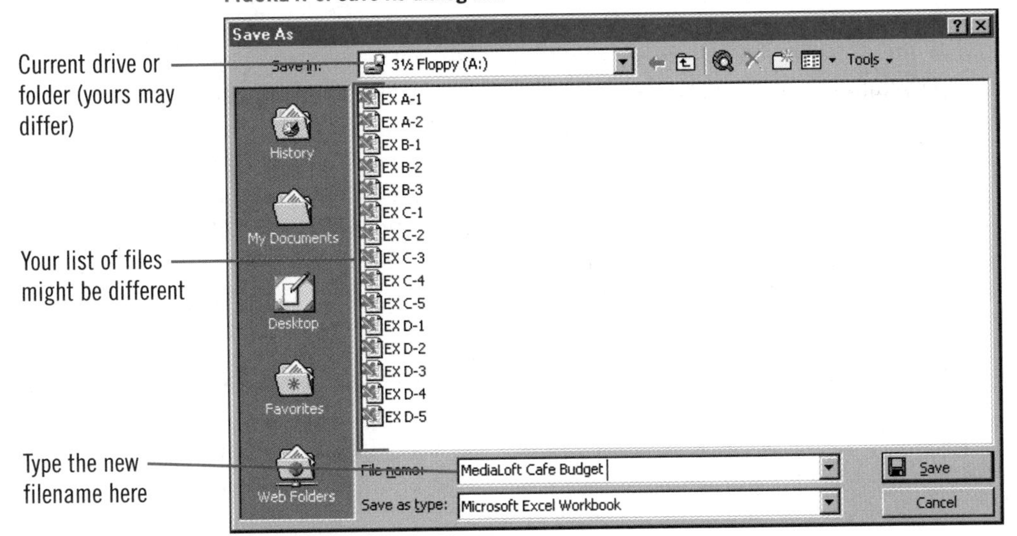

FIGURE A-9: **MediaLoft Cafe Budget workbook**

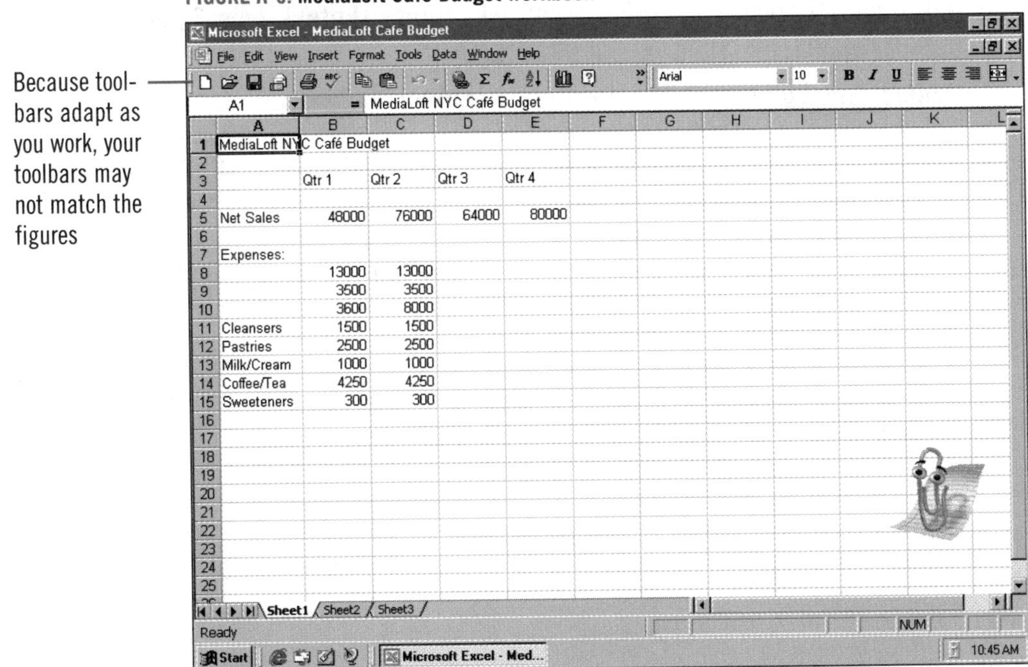

Excel 2000

Excel 2000

Entering Labels and Values

Labels are used to identify the data in the rows and columns of a worksheet. They also make your worksheet more readable and understandable. You should try to enter all labels in your worksheet before entering the data. Labels can contain text and numerical information not used in calculations, such as dates, times, or addresses. Labels are left-aligned by default. **Values**, which include numbers, formulas, and functions, are used in calculations. Excel recognizes an entry as a value when it is a number or begins with special symbols: +, -, =, @, #, or $. All values are right-aligned by default. When a cell contains both text and numbers it is not a valid formula; Excel recognizes the entry as a label. Jim needs to enter labels identifying the rest of the expense categories, and the values for Qtr 3 and Qtr 4 into the MediaLoft Café Budget worksheet.

Steps

1. **Click cell A8 to make it the active cell**
   Notice that the cell address A8 appears in the name box. As you work, the mouse pointer has a variety of appearances, depending on where it is and what Excel is doing. Table A-2 lists and identifies some mouse pointers. The labels in cells A1:A15 identify the expenses.
2. **Type Salary, as shown in Figure A-10, then click the Enter button on the formula bar**
   The label is entered in cell A8 and its contents display in the formula bar. You can also confirm a cell entry by pressing [Enter], pressing [Tab], or by pressing one of the arrow keys on the keyboard. If a label does not fit in a cell, Excel displays the remaining characters in the next cell to the right as long as it is empty. Otherwise, the label is **truncated**, or cut off.
3. **Click cell A9, type Rent, press [Enter] to complete the entry and move the cell pointer to cell A10, type Advertising in cell A10, then press [Enter]**
   The remaining expense values have to be added to the worksheet.
4. **Click cell D8, press and hold the left mouse button, drag the pointer to cell E8 then down to cell E15, then release the mouse button**
   Two or more selected cells is called a **range**. The active cell is still cell D8, the cells in the range are shaded in purple. Since entries often cover multiple columns and rows, selecting a range makes working with data entry easier.
5. **Type 13000, press [Enter], type 3500 in cell D9, press [Enter], type 16000 in cell D10, press [Enter], type 1500 in cell D11, press [Enter], type 2500 in cell D12, press [Enter], type 1000 in cell D13, press [Enter], type 4250 in cell D14, press [Enter], type 300 in cell D15, then press [Enter]**
   All the values in the Qtr 3 column have been added. The cell pointer is now in cell E8.
6. **Using Figure A-11 as a guide, type the remaining values for cells E8 through E15**
   Before confirming a cell entry you can click the Cancel button on the formula bar or press [Esc] to cancel or delete the entry.
7. **Type your name in cell A17, then click the Save button on the Standard toolbar**
   Your name identifies the worksheet as yours when it is printed.

Trouble?

If you notice a mistake in a cell entry after it has been confirmed, double-click the cell, use [Backspace] or [Delete] to make your corrections, then press [Enter]. You can also click Edit on the menu bar, point to Clear, then click Contents to remove a cell's contents.

QuickTip

To enter a number that will not be used as part of a calculation, such as a telephone number, type an apostrophe (') before the number.

TABLE A-2: Commonly used pointers

name	pointer	use to
Normal or Cross	✚	Select a cell or range; indicates Ready mode
I-beam	I	Edit contents of formula bar
Select	↖	Select objects and commands

FIGURE A-7: Open dialog box

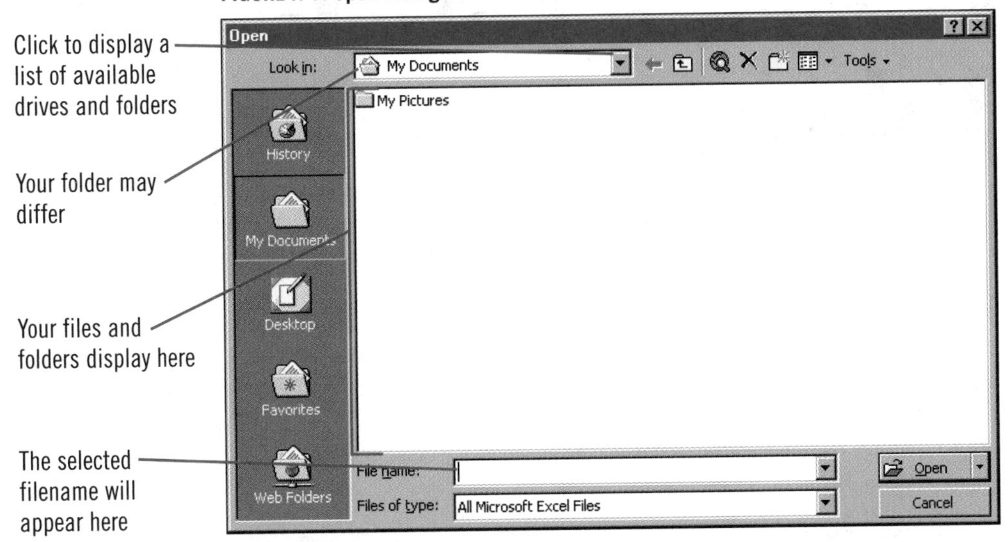

FIGURE A-8: Save As dialog box

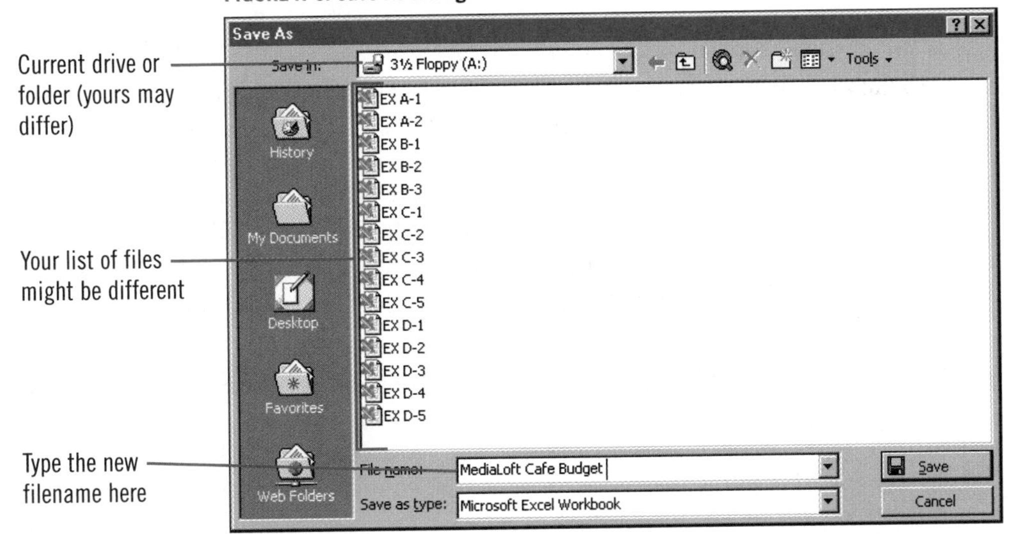

FIGURE A-9: MediaLoft Cafe Budget workbook

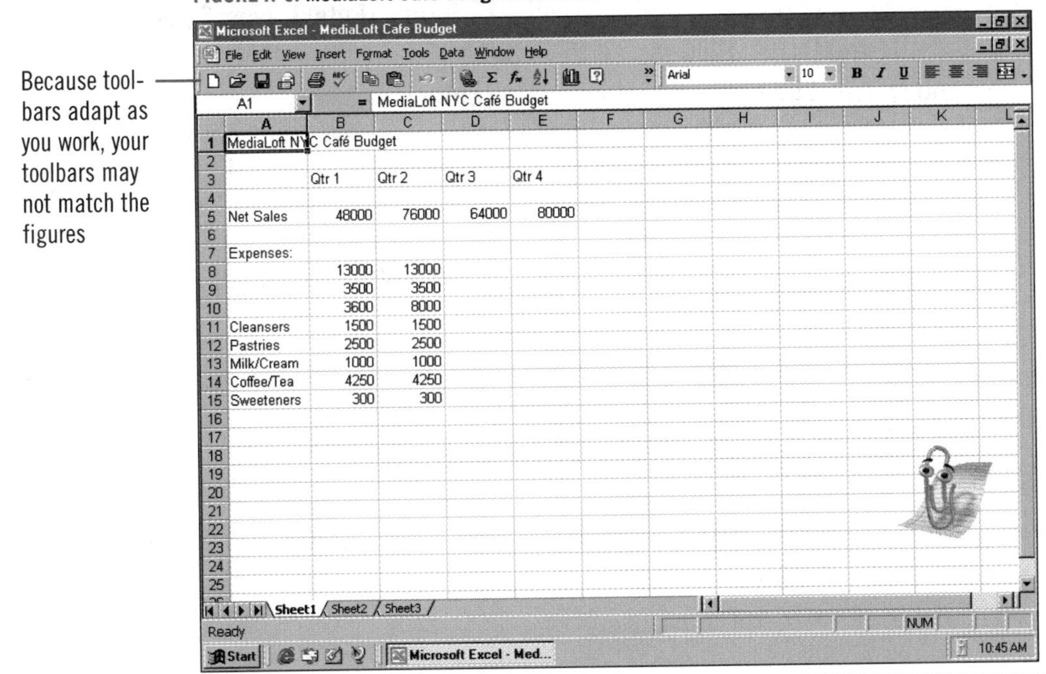

	A	B	C	D	E
1	MediaLoft NYC Café Budget				
2					
3		Qtr 1	Qtr 2	Qtr 3	Qtr 4
4					
5	Net Sales	48000	76000	64000	80000
6					
7	Expenses:				
8		13000	13000		
9		3500	3500		
10		3600	8000		
11	Cleansers	1500	1500		
12	Pastries	2500	2500		
13	Milk/Cream	1000	1000		
14	Coffee/Tea	4250	4250		
15	Sweeteners	300	300		

Excel 2000

Excel 2000

Entering Labels and Values

Labels are used to identify the data in the rows and columns of a worksheet. They also make your worksheet more readable and understandable. You should try to enter all labels in your worksheet before entering the data. Labels can contain text and numerical information not used in calculations, such as dates, times, or addresses. Labels are left-aligned by default. **Values**, which include numbers, formulas, and functions, are used in calculations. Excel recognizes an entry as a value when it is a number or begins with special symbols: +, -, =, @, #, or $. All values are right-aligned by default. When a cell contains both text and numbers it is not a valid formula; Excel recognizes the entry as a label. Jim needs to enter labels identifying the rest of the expense categories, and the values for Qtr 3 and Qtr 4 into the MediaLoft Café Budget worksheet.

Steps

1. **Click cell A8 to make it the active cell**
   Notice that the cell address A8 appears in the name box. As you work, the mouse pointer has a variety of appearances, depending on where it is and what Excel is doing. Table A-2 lists and identifies some mouse pointers. The labels in cells A1:A15 identify the expenses.
2. **Type Salary, as shown in Figure A-10, then click the Enter button on the formula bar**
   The label is entered in cell A8 and its contents display in the formula bar. You can also confirm a cell entry by pressing [Enter], pressing [Tab], or by pressing one of the arrow keys on the keyboard. If a label does not fit in a cell, Excel displays the remaining characters in the next cell to the right as long as it is empty. Otherwise, the label is **truncated**, or cut off.
3. **Click cell A9, type Rent, press [Enter] to complete the entry and move the cell pointer to cell A10, type Advertising in cell A10, then press [Enter]**
   The remaining expense values have to be added to the worksheet.
4. **Click cell D8, press and hold the left mouse button, drag the pointer to cell E8 then down to cell E15, then release the mouse button**
   Two or more selected cells is called a **range**. The active cell is still cell D8, the cells in the range are shaded in purple. Since entries often cover multiple columns and rows, selecting a range makes working with data entry easier.
5. **Type 13000, press [Enter], type 3500 in cell D9, press [Enter], type 16000 in cell D10, press [Enter], type 1500 in cell D11, press [Enter], type 2500 in cell D12, press [Enter], type 1000 in cell D13, press [Enter], type 4250 in cell D14, press [Enter], type 300 in cell D15, then press [Enter]**
   All the values in the Qtr 3 column have been added. The cell pointer is now in cell E8.
6. **Using Figure A-11 as a guide, type the remaining values for cells E8 through E15**
   Before confirming a cell entry you can click the Cancel button on the formula bar or press [Esc] to cancel or delete the entry.
7. **Type your name in cell A17, then click the Save button on the Standard toolbar**
   Your name identifies the worksheet as yours when it is printed.

Trouble?

If you notice a mistake in a cell entry after it has been confirmed, double-click the cell, use [Backspace] or [Delete] to make your corrections, then press [Enter]. You can also click Edit on the menu bar, point to Clear, then click Contents to remove a cell's contents.

QuickTip

To enter a number that will not be used as part of a calculation, such as a telephone number, type an apostrophe (') before the number.

TABLE A-2: Commonly used pointers

name	pointer	use to
Normal or Cross	✚	Select a cell or range; indicates Ready mode
I-beam	I	Edit contents of formula bar
Select	↖	Select objects and commands

FIGURE A-10: Worksheet with initial label entered

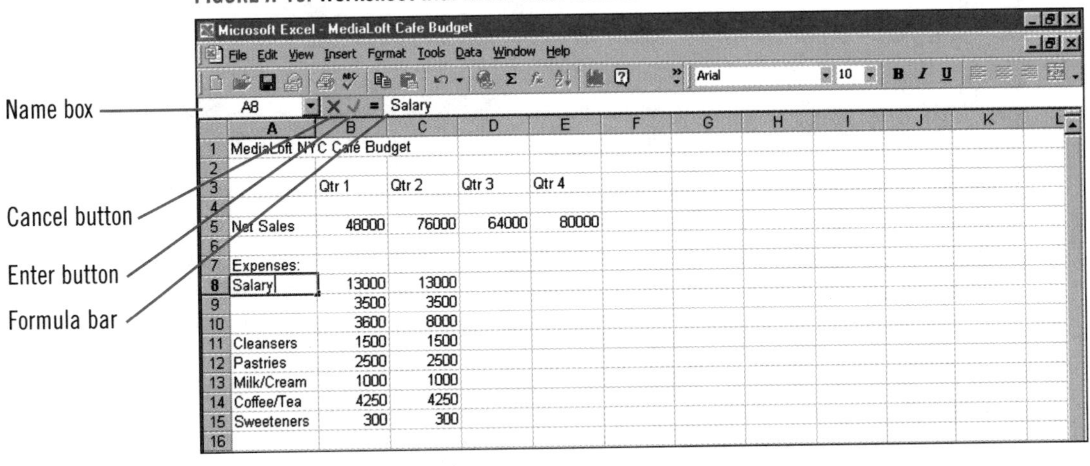

FIGURE A-11: Worksheet with new labels and values

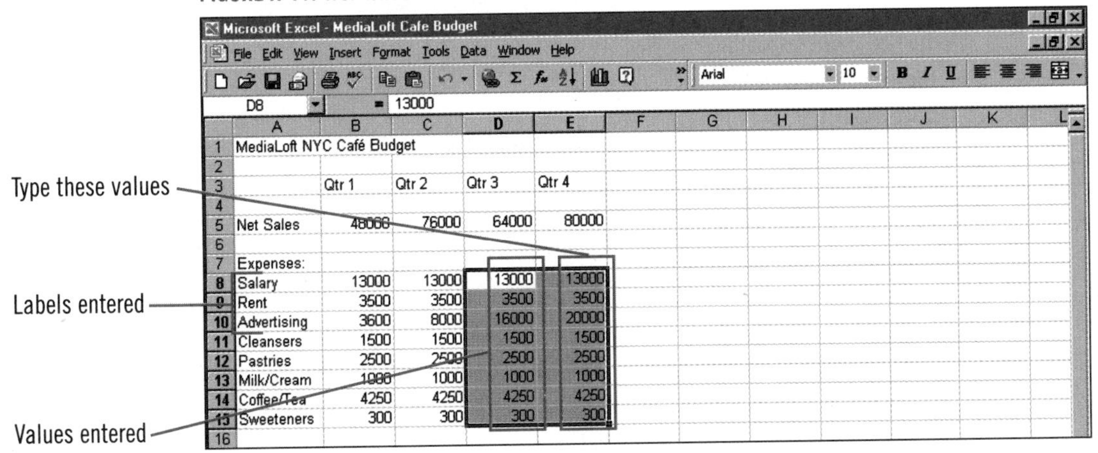

Navigating a worksheet

With over a million cells available to you, it is important to know how to move around, or **navigate**, a worksheet. You can use the arrow keys on the keyboard ([↑], [↓], [←], [→]) to move a cell or two at a time, or [Page Up] or [Page Down] to move a screenful at a time. To move a screen to the left press [Alt] [Page Up]; to move a screen to the right press [Alt] [Page Down]. You can also simply use your mouse pointer to click the desired cell. If the desired cell is not visible in the worksheet window, use the scroll bars or the Go To command to move the location into view. To return to the first active cell in a worksheet, click cell A1, or press [Ctrl][Home].

Excel 2000

Previewing and Printing a Worksheet

When a worksheet is completed, you may want to print it to have a paper copy to reference, file, or give to others. You can also print a worksheet that is not complete to review your work when you are not at a computer. Before you print a worksheet, you should save any changes. That way, if anything happens to the file as it is being sent to the printer, you will have your latest work saved to your disk. Then you should preview it to make sure it will fit on a page the way you want. When you preview a worksheet, you see a copy of the worksheet exactly as it will appear on paper. Table A-3 provides additional printing tips. Jim is finished entering the labels and values into the MediaLoft Café budget. Since he already saved his changes, he previews and prints a copy of the worksheet to review on the way home.

Steps 1 2 3 4

1. **Make sure the printer is on and contains paper**
   If a file is sent to print and the printer is off, an error message appears.

2. **Click the Print Preview button on the Standard toolbar**
   A miniature version of the worksheet appears on the screen, as shown in Figure A-13. If there were more than one page, you could click the Next button or the Previous button to move between pages. You can also enlarge the image by clicking the Zoom button.

3. **Click Print**
   The Print dialog box opens, as shown in Figure A-14. To print, you could also click File on the menu bar, then click Print Preview.

4. **Make sure that the Active Sheet(s) option button is selected and that 1 appears in the Number of copies text box**
   Adjusting the value in the Number of copies text box enables you to print multiple copies. You could also print the selected range, the values you just entered, by clicking the Selection option button.

5. **Click OK**
   The Printing dialog box appears briefly while the file is sent to the printer. Note that the dialog box contains a Cancel button. You can use it to cancel the print job provided you can catch it before the file is sent to the printer.

Trouble?

If the Print Preview button is not visible on your Standard toolbar, click the More Buttons button to view additional toolbar buttons.

CLUES TO USE

Using Zoom in Print Preview

When you are in the Print Preview window, you can enlarge the image by clicking the Zoom button. You can also position the mouse pointer over a specific part of the worksheet page, then click it to view that section of the page. Figure A-12 shows a magnified section of a document. While the image is zoomed in, use the scroll bars to view different sections of the page.

FIGURE A-12: Enlarging the preview using Zoom

MediaLoft NYC Café Budget

	Qtr 1	Qtr 2	Qtr 3	Qtr 4
Net Sales	48000	76000	64000	80000
Expenses:				
Salary	13000	13000	13000	13000
Rent	3500	3500	3500	3500
Advertising	3600	8000	16000	20000
Cleansers	1500	1500	1500	1500
Pastries	2500	2500	2500	2500
Milk/Cream	1000	1000	1000	1000
Coffee/Tea	4250	4250	4250	4250
Sweeteners	300	300	300	300

FIGURE A-13: **Print Preview screen**

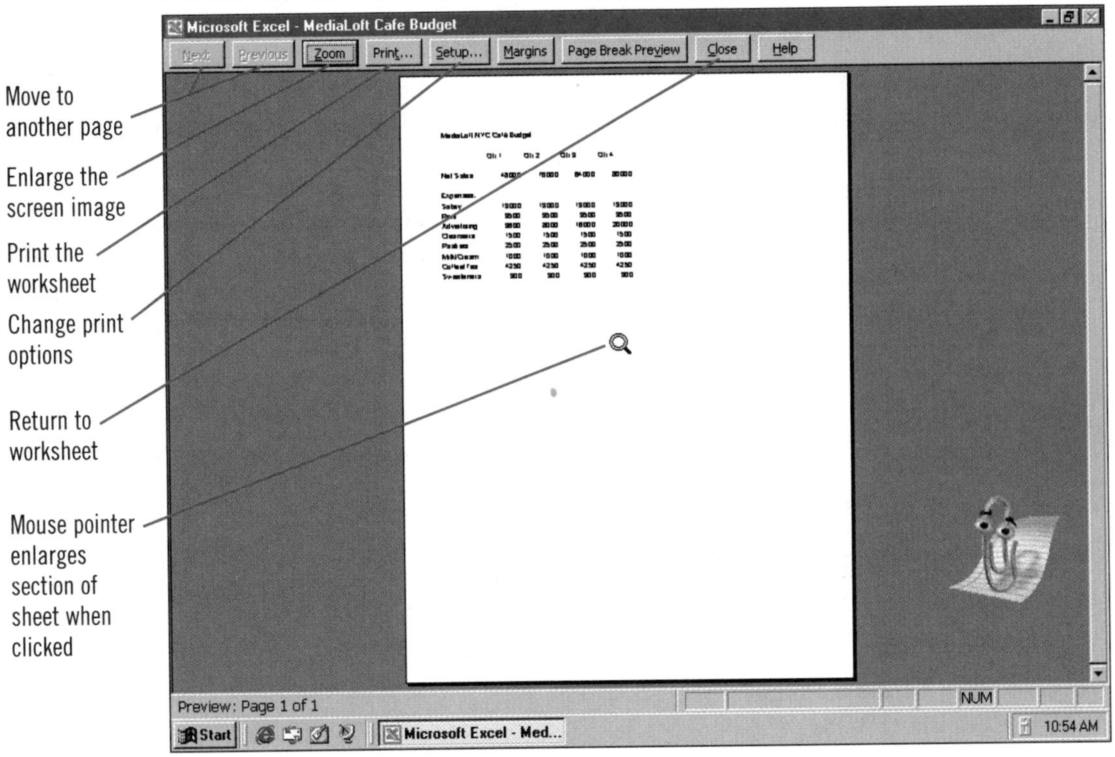

Move to another page

Enlarge the screen image

Print the worksheet

Change print options

Return to worksheet

Mouse pointer enlarges section of sheet when clicked

FIGURE A-14: **Print dialog box**

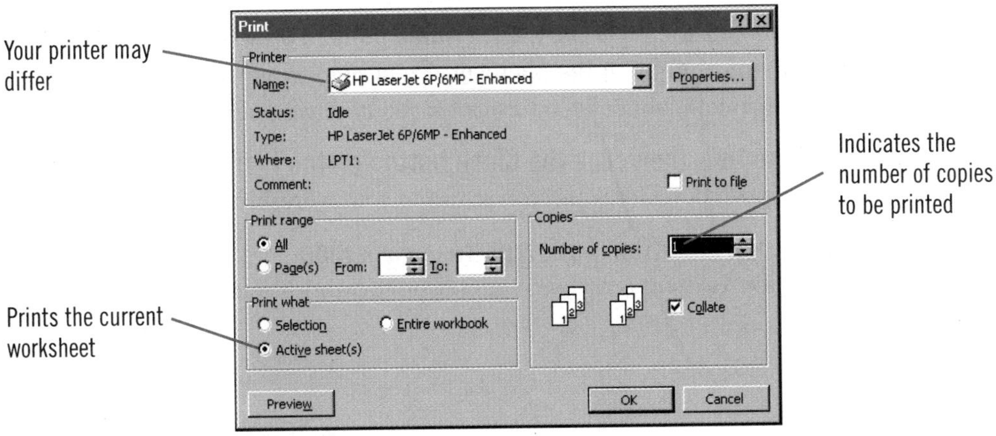

Your printer may differ

Prints the current worksheet

Indicates the number of copies to be printed

TABLE A-3: **Worksheet printing tips**

before you print	recommendation
Save your work	Make sure your work is saved to a disk
Check the printer	Make sure that the printer is turned on and is online, that it has paper, and that there are no error messages or warning signals
Preview the worksheet	Check the formatted image for page breaks, page setup (vertical or horizontal), and overall appearance of the worksheet
Check the printer selection	Use the Printer setup command in the Print dialog box to verify that the correct printer is selected
Check the Print what options	Verify that you are printing either the active sheet, the entire workbook, or just a selected range

Excel 2000

Getting Help

Excel features an extensive **Help system** that gives you immediate access to definitions, explanations, and useful tips. The animated Office Assistant provides help in two ways. You can type a keyword to search on, or access a question and answer format to research your help topic. The Office Assistant provides **ScreenTips** (indicated by a light bulb) on the current action you are performing. You can click the light bulb to access further information in the form of a dialog box that you can resize and refer to as you work. In addition, you can press [F1] at any time to get immediate help. Jim wants to find out more about ranges so he can work more efficiently with them. He knows he can find more information using the animated Office Assistant.

Steps

QuickTip

If it's displayed, you can also click the Office Assistant to access Help.

1. **Click the Microsoft Excel Help button on the Standard toolbar**
   An Office Assistant dialog box opens. You can get information by typing a word to search on in the query box, or by typing a question. If the text within the query box is already selected, any typed text will automatically replace what is highlighted. The Office Assistant provides help based on text typed in the query box.
2. **Type Define a range**
   See Figure A-16.
3. **Click Search**
   The Office Assistant searches for relevant topics from the help files in Excel and then displays the results.

QuickTip

Clicking the Print button in the Microsoft Excel Help window prints the information.

4. **Click See More if necessary, click Name cells in a workbook, then click Name a cell or a range of cells in the Microsoft Excel Help window**
   A Help window containing information about ranges opens. See Figure A-17.
5. **Read the text, then click the Close button on the Help window title bar**
   The Help window closes and you return to your worksheet.
6. **Right-click the Office Assistant, then click Hide**
   The Office Assistant is no longer visible on the worksheet.

Changing the Office Assistant

The default Office Assistant character is Clippit, but there are others from which you can choose. To change the appearance of the Office Assistant, right-click the Office Assistant, then click Choose Assistant. Click the Gallery tab, click the Back and Next buttons until you find an Assistant you want to use, then click OK. (You may need to insert your Microsoft Office 2000 CD to perform this task.) Each Office Assistant makes its own unique sounds and can be animated by right-clicking its window and clicking Animate! Figure A-15 shows the Office Assistant dialog box.

FIGURE A-15: Office Assistant dialog box

FIGURE A-16: Office Assistant

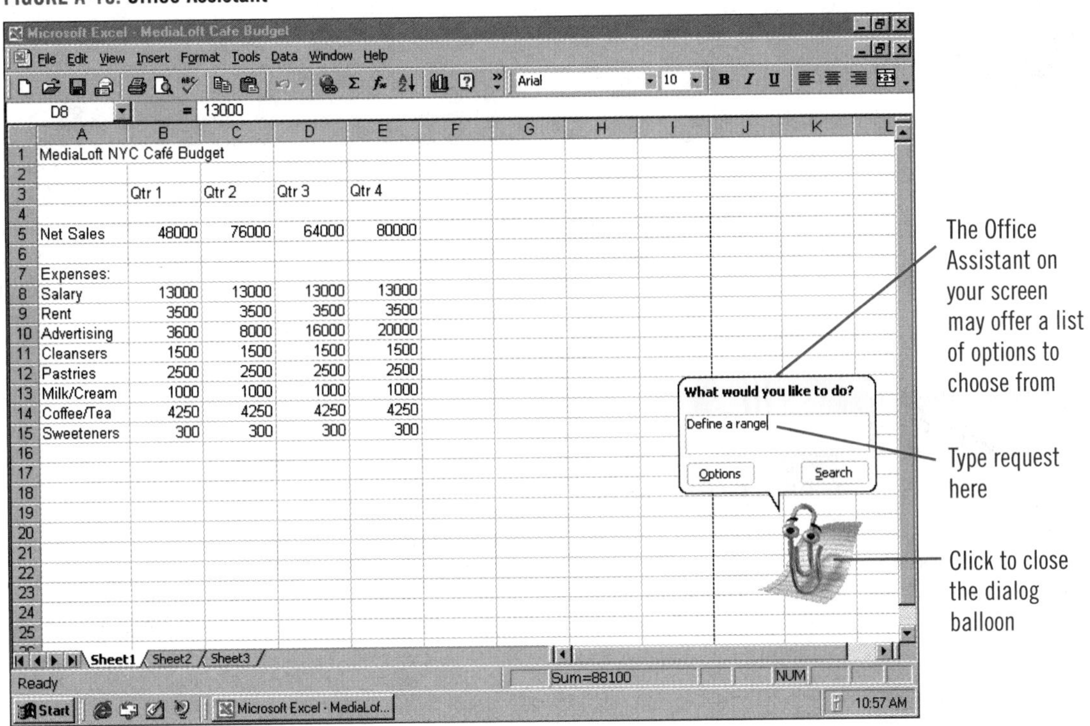

FIGURE A-17: Help window

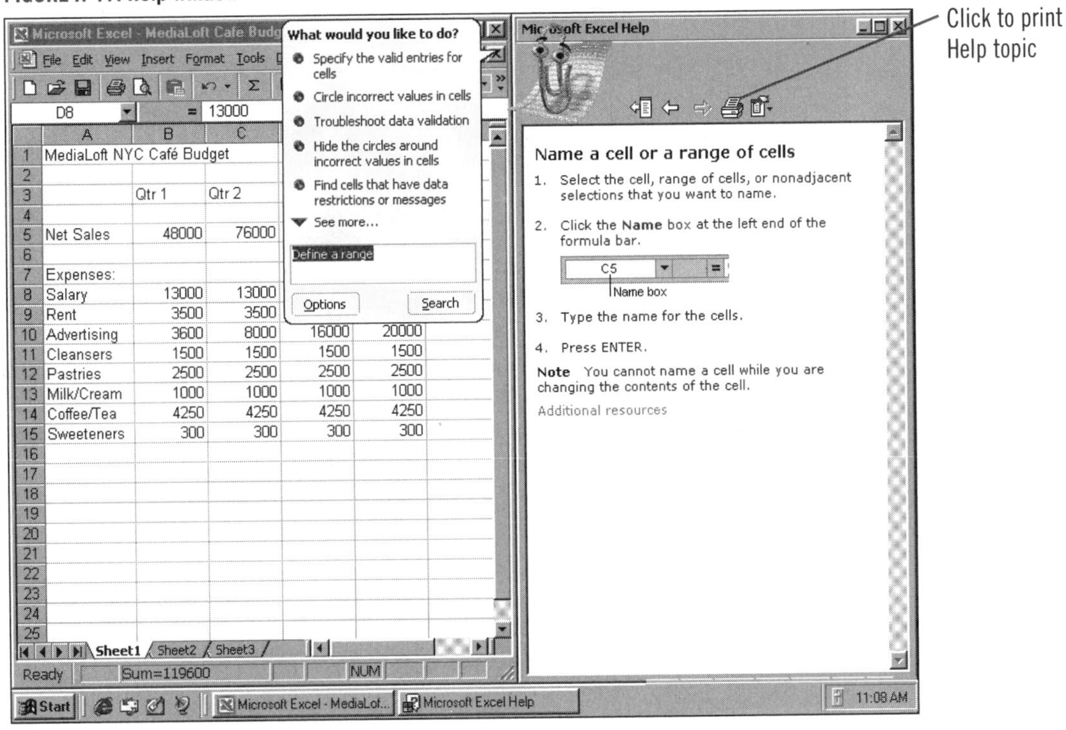

Closing a Workbook and Exiting Excel

When you have finished working you need to save the file and close it. When you have completed all your work in Excel you need to exit the program. You can exit Excel by clicking Exit on the File menu. Since Jim has completed his work on the MediaLoft Café budget, he is finished using Excel for the day. He closes the workbook and then exits Excel.

QuickTip

You could also click the workbook Close button instead of clicking the File menu.

1. Click **File** on the menu bar
   The File menu opens. See Figure A-18.
2. Click **Close**
   Excel closes the workbook and asks if you want to save your changes; if you have made any changes be sure to save them.

Trouble?

To exit Excel and close several files at once, click Exit on the File menu. Excel will prompt you to save changes to each open workbook before exiting.

3. Click **File** on the menu bar, then click **Exit**
   You could also click the program Close button to exit the program. Excel closes and you return to the desktop. Memory is now freed up for other computing tasks.

FIGURE A-18: Closing a workbook using the File menu

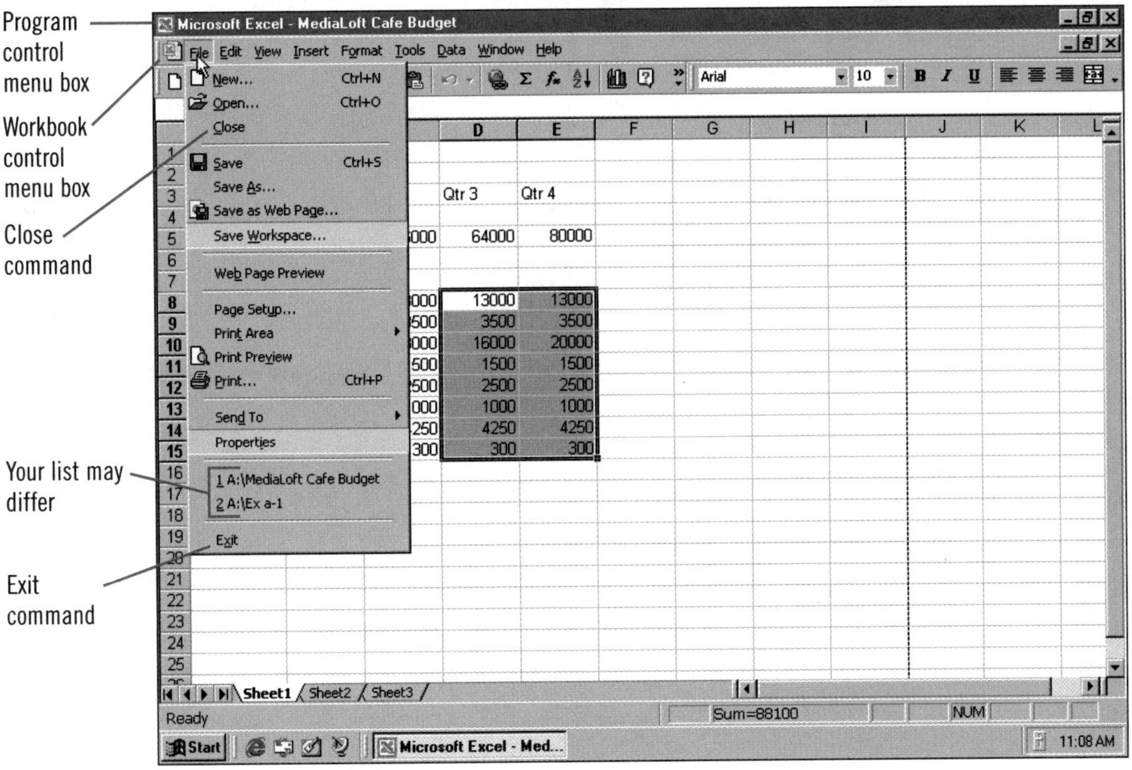

Program control menu box

Workbook control menu box

Close command

Your list may differ

Exit command

Microsoft Excel - MediaLoft Cafe Budget

File Edit View Insert Format Tools Data Window Help

Arial 10

New... Ctrl+N
Open... Ctrl+O
Close
Save Ctrl+S
Save As...
Save as Web Page...
Save Workspace...
Web Page Preview
Page Setup...
Print Area
Print Preview
Print... Ctrl+P
Send To
Properties
1 A:\MediaLoft Cafe Budget
2 A:\Ex a-1
Exit

	D	E	F	G	H	I	J	K	L
3	Qtr 3	Qtr 4							
5	64000	80000							
8	13000	13000							
9	3500	3500							
10	16000	20000							
11	1500	1500							
12	2500	2500							
13	1000	1000							
14	4250	4250							
15	300	300							

Sheet1 / Sheet2 / Sheet3

Ready Sum=88100 NUM

Start Microsoft Excel - Med... 11:08 AM

Excel 2000

Practice

► Concepts Review

Label the elements of the Excel worksheet window shown in Figure A-19.

FIGURE A-19

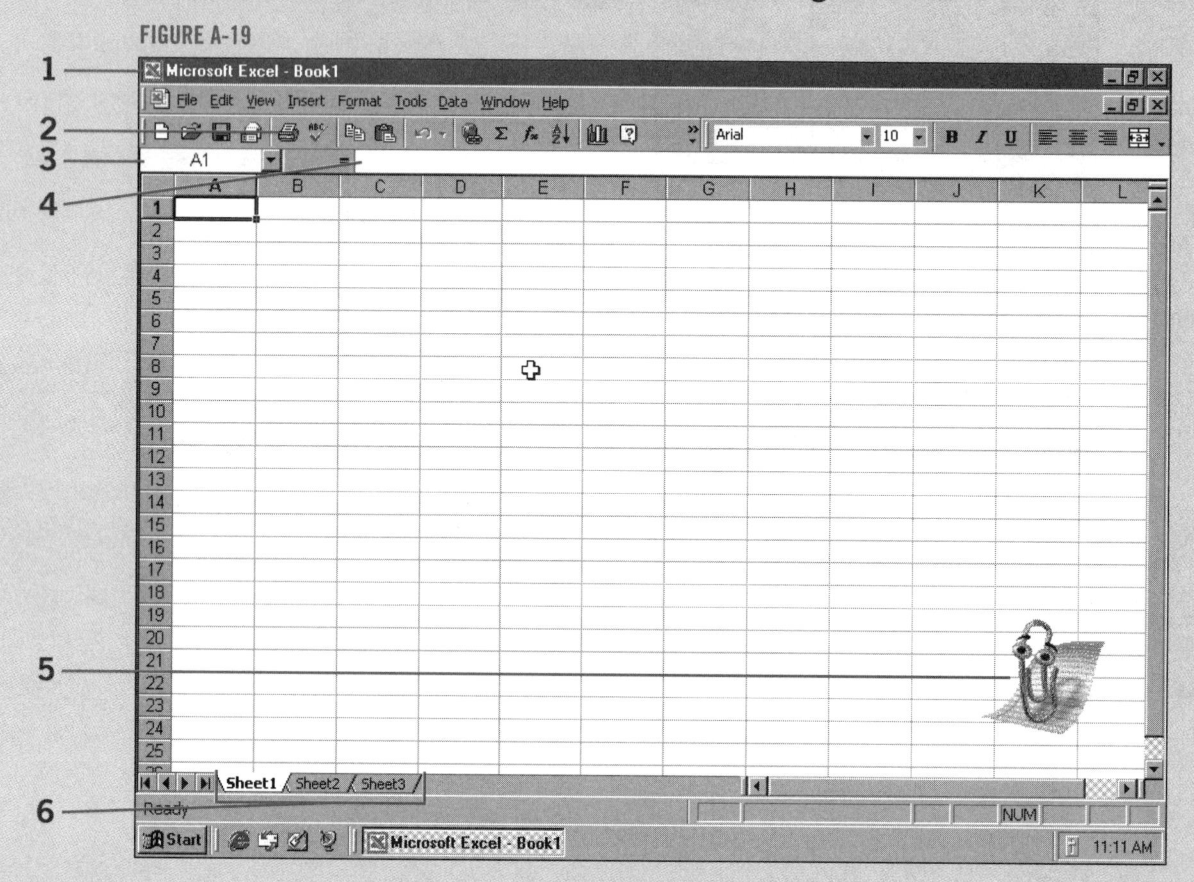

Match each term with the statement that describes it.

7. Cell pointer
8. Button
9. Worksheet window
10. Name box
11. Cell
12. Workbook

a. Area that contains a grid of columns and rows
b. The intersection of a column and row
c. Graphic symbol that depicts a task or function
d. Collection of worksheets
e. Rectangle indicating the active cell
f. Displays the active cell address

Select the best answer from the list of choices.

13. An electronic spreadsheet can perform all of the following tasks, *except*
- **a.** Display information visually.
- **b.** Calculate data accurately.
- **c.** Plan worksheet objectives.
- **d.** Recalculate updated information.

14. Each of the following is true about labels, *except*
- **a.** They are left-aligned by default.
- **b.** They are not used in calculations.
- **c.** They are right-aligned by default.
- **d.** They can include numerical information.

15. Each of the following is true about values, *except*
- **a.** They can include labels.
- **b.** They are right-aligned by default.
- **c.** They are used in calculations.
- **d.** They can include formulas.

16. What symbol is typed before a number to make the number a label?
- **a.** "
- **b.** !
- **c.** '
- **d.** ;

17. You can get Excel Help any of the following ways, *except*
- **a.** Clicking Help on the menu bar.
- **b.** Pressing [F1].
- **c.** Clicking .
- **d.** Minimizing the program window.

18. Each key(s) can be used to confirm cell entries, *except*
- **a.** [Enter].
- **b.** [Tab].
- **c.** [Esc].
- **d.** [Shift][Enter].

19. Which button is used to preview a worksheet?
- **a.** 
- **b.**
- **c.**
- **d.**

20. Which feature is used to enlarge a print preview view?
- **a.** Magnify
- **b.** Enlarge
- **c.** Amplify
- **d.** Zoom

21. Each of the following is true about the Office Assistant, *except*
- **a.** It provides tips based on your work habits.
- **b.** It provides help using a question and answer format.
- **c.** You can change the appearance of the Office Assistant.
- **d.** It can complete certain tasks for you.

Skills Review

1. Start Excel 2000.
- **a.** Point to Programs in the Start menu.
- **b.** Click the Microsoft Excel program icon.

2. View the Excel window.
- **a.** Identify as many elements in the Excel worksheet window as you can without referring to the unit material.

3. Open and save a workbook.
- **a.** Open the workbook EX A-2 from your Project Disk by clicking the Open button.
- **b.** Save the workbook as "Totally Together Fashions" by clicking File on the menu bar, then clicking Save As.

4. Enter labels and values.
- **a.** Enter the labels shown in Figure A-20, the Totally Together Fashions worksheet.
- **b.** Enter values shown in Figure A-20.
- **c.** Type the label "New Data" in cell A2, then clear the cell contents in A2 using the Edit menu.
- **d.** Type your name in cell A10.
- **e.** Save the workbook by clicking the Save button.

FIGURE A-20

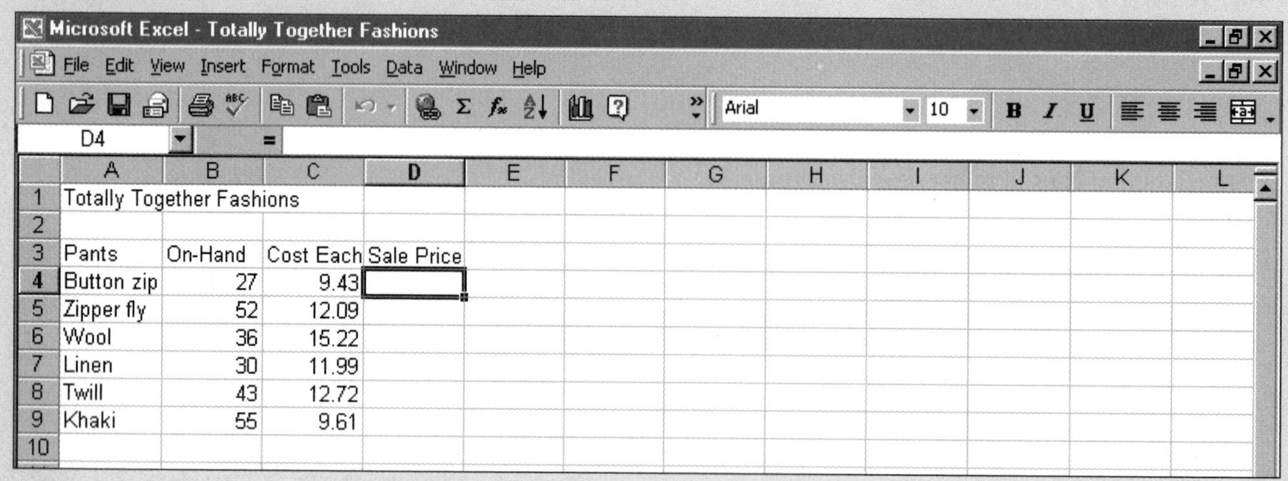

5. Preview and print a worksheet.

a. Click the Print Preview button.
b. Use the Zoom button to see more of your worksheet.
c. Print one copy of the worksheet.

6. Get Help.

a. Click the Office Assistant button if the Assistant is not displayed.
b. Ask the Office Assistant for information about changing the Excel Office Assistant.
c. Print information offered by the Office Assistant using the Print topic command on the Options menu.
d. Close the Help window.

7. Close a workbook and exit Excel.

a. Click File on the menu bar, then click Close.
b. If asked if you want to save the worksheet, click No.
c. If necessary, close any other worksheets you might have opened.
d. Click File on the menu bar, then click Exit.

► Independent Challenges

1. The Excel Help feature provides definitions, explanations, procedures, and other helpful information. It also provides examples and demonstrations to show you how Excel features work. Topics include elements such as the active cell, status bar, buttons, and dialog boxes, as well as detailed information about Excel commands and options.

To complete this independent challenge:

a. Start Excel and open a new workbook.
b. Click the Office Assistant.
c. Type a question that will give you information about opening and saving a workbook. (*Hint*: You may have to ask the Office Assistant more than one question.)
d. Print the information.
e. Return to your workbook when you are finished.
f. Exit Excel.

2. Spreadsheet software has many uses that can affect the way work is done. Some examples of how Excel can be used are discussed in the beginning of this unit. Use your own personal or business experiences to come up with five examples of how Excel could be used in a business setting.

To complete this independent challenge:

a. Start Excel.
b. Open a new workbook.
c. Think of five business tasks that you could complete more efficiently by using an Excel worksheet.
d. Sketch a sample of each worksheet. See Figure A-21, a sample payroll worksheet, as a guide.
e. Open a new workbook and save it as "Sample Payroll" on your Project Disk.
f. Give your worksheet a title in cell A1, type your name in cell B1.
g. Enter the labels shown in Figure A-21.
h. Enter sample data for Hours Worked and Hourly Wage in the worksheet.
i. Save your work, then preview and print the worksheet.
j. Close the worksheet and exit Excel.

FIGURE A-21

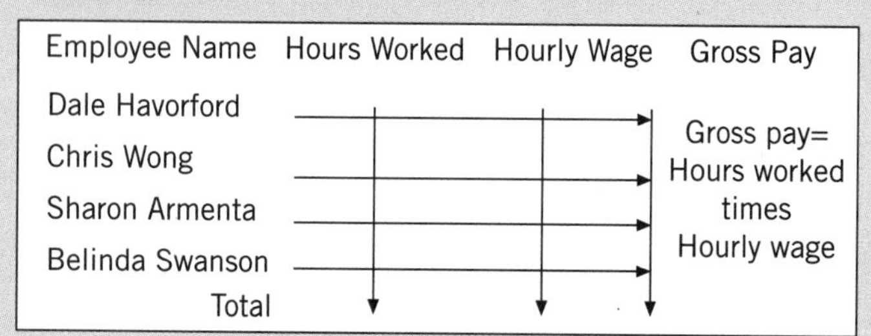

3. You are the office manager for Christine's Car Parts, a small auto parts supplier. Although the company is just three years old, it is expanding rapidly, and you are continually looking for ways to make your job easier. Last year you began using Excel to manage and maintain data on inventory and sales, which has greatly helped you to track information accurately and efficiently. The owner of the company has just approved your request to hire an assistant. This person will need to learn how to use Excel. Create a short training document that your new assistant can use as a reference while becoming familiar with Excel.

To complete this independent challenge:

a. Draw a sketch of the Excel worksheet window and label the key elements, such as toolbars, title bar, formula bar, scroll bars, etc.
b. For each labeled element, write a short description of its use.
c. List three ways to get Help in Excel. (*Hint*: Use the Office Assistant to learn all of the ways to get Help in Excel.)
d. Create a sketch for three of the following spreadsheet uses: accounts payable schedule, accounts receivable, payroll, list of inventory items, employee benefits data, income statement, cash flow report, or balance sheet. (*Hint*: Make up data for these sketches.)
e. Start Excel.
f. Create a new workbook and enter the values and labels for a sample spreadsheet. Make sure you have labels in column A. Enter a title for the worksheet and put your name in cell A1.
g. Select the range which includes the column labels.
h. Use the Print dialog box to print the selected range.
i. Preview the entire worksheet.
j. Save the workbook as "Christine's Car Parts" on your Project Disk, and then exit Excel.

4. To make smart buying decisions, you can use the World Wide Web to gather the most up-to-date information available. MediaLoft employees have access to the Web through the company's intranet. An **intranet** is a group of connected networks owned by a company or organization that is used for internal purposes. Intranets use Internet software to handle the data communications, such as e-mail and Web pages, within an organization. These pages often provide company-wide information. As with all intranets, the MediaLoft intranet limits access to MediaLoft employees.

Imagine that your supervisor at MediaLoft has just given you approval for buying a new computer. Cost is not an issue, and you need to provide a list of hardware and software requirements. You use Excel to create a worksheet using data found on the World Wide Web to support your purchase decision.

To complete this independent challenge:

a. Start Excel, open a new workbook and save it on your Project Disk as "New Computer Data."
b. List the features you want your ideal computer to contain (e.g. CD-ROM drive, etc.).
c. Connect to the Internet, go to the MediaLoft intranet site at http://www.course.com/illustrated/MediaLoft, then click the Research Center link.
d. Use any of the links to computer companies provided at the Research Center to compile your data.
e. Compile data for the components you want. When you find a system that meets your needs, include that in your list. Be sure to identify the system's key features, such as the processor chip, hard drive capacity, RAM, and monitor size. List any extra/upgrade items you want to purchase.
f. When you are finished gathering data, disconnect from the Internet.
g. Make sure all components are listed and totaled. Include any tax and shipping costs the manufacturer charges.
h. Indicate on the worksheet your final purchase decision. Enter your name in one of the cells.
i. Save, preview, and then print your worksheet.
j. Close and exit Excel.

► Visual Workshop

Create a worksheet similar to Figure A-22 using the skills you learned in this unit. Save the workbook as "Carrie's Camera and Darkroom" on your Project Disk. Type your name in cell A11, then preview and print the worksheet.

FIGURE A-22

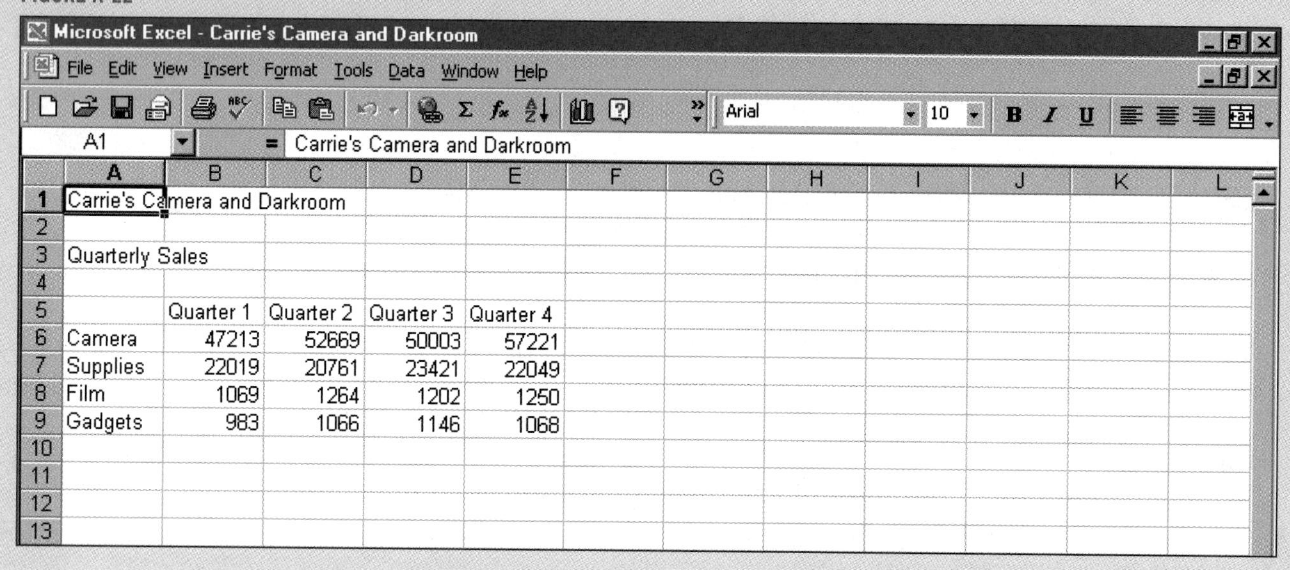

Excel 2000

Unit B

Building and Editing Worksheets

Objectives

- Plan and design a worksheet
- MOUS Edit cell entries and work with ranges
- MOUS Enter formulas
- MOUS Introduce Excel functions
- MOUS Copy and move cell entries
- MOUS Understand relative and absolute cell references
- MOUS Copy formulas with relative cell references
- MOUS Copy formulas with absolute cell references
- MOUS Name and move a sheet

Using your understanding of the basics of Excel, you can now plan and build your own worksheets. When you build a worksheet, you enter text, values, and formulas into worksheet cells. Once you create a worksheet, you can save it in a workbook file and then print it. Jim Fernandez has received a request from the Marketing department for a forecast of this summer's author events and an estimate of the average number of author appearances. Marketing hopes that the number of appearances will increase 20% over last year's figures. Jim needs to create a worksheet that summarizes appearances for last year and forecasts the summer appearances for this year.

Planning and Designing a Worksheet

Before you start entering data into a worksheet, you need to know the purpose and approximate layout of the worksheet. You should also familiarize yourself with the mouse pointers you will encounter; refer to Table B-1. MediaLoft encourages authors to come to stores and sign their books. These author events are great for sales. Jim wants to forecast MediaLoft's 2001 summer author appearances. The goal, already identified by the Marketing department, is to increase the year 2000 signings by 20%. Using the planning guidelines below, work with Jim as he plans this worksheet.

In planning and designing a worksheet it is important to:

Determine the purpose of the worksheet and give it a meaningful title

Jim needs to forecast summer appearances for 2001. Jim titles the worksheet "Summer 2001 MediaLoft Author Events Forecast."

Determine your worksheet's desired results, or "output"

Jim needs to begin scheduling author events and will use these forecasts to determine staffing and budget needs if the number of author events increases by 20%. He also wants to calculate the average number of author events since the Marketing department uses this information for corporate promotions.

Collect all the information, or "input", that will produce the results you want

Jim gathers together the number of author events that occurred at four stores during the 2000 summer season, which runs from June through August.

Determine the calculations, or formulas, necessary to achieve the desired results

First, Jim needs to total the number of events at each of the selected stores during each month of the summer of 2000. Then he needs to add these totals together to determine the grand total of summer appearances. Because he needs to determine the goal for the 2001 season, the 2000 monthly totals and grand total are multiplied by 1.2 to calculate the projected 20% increase for the 2001 summer season. He'll use the Paste Function to select the Average function, which will determine the average number of appearances for the Marketing department.

Sketch on paper how you want the worksheet to look; identify where to place the labels and values

Jim decides to put store locations in rows and the months in columns. He enters the data in his sketch and indicates where the monthly totals and the grand total should go. Below the totals, he writes out the formula for determining a 20% increase in appearances for 2000. He also includes a label for the location of the average number of events calculations. Jim's sketch of his worksheet is shown in Figure B-1.

Create the worksheet

Jim enters the labels first to establish the structure of the worksheet. He then enters the values—the data about the events—into his worksheet. Finally, he enters the formulas necessary to calculate totals, averages, and forecasts. These values and formulas will be used to calculate the necessary output. The worksheet Jim creates is shown in Figure B-2.

FIGURE B-1: Worksheet sketch showing labels, values, and calculations

Summer 2001 MediaLoft Author Events Forecast

	June	July	August	Total	Average
Boston	15	10	23		
New York	14	10	12		
Seattle	12	13	6		
San Diego	10	24	15		
Total	June Total	July Total	August Total	Grand Total	
20% rise	Total X 1.2				

FIGURE B-2: Jim's forecasting worksheet

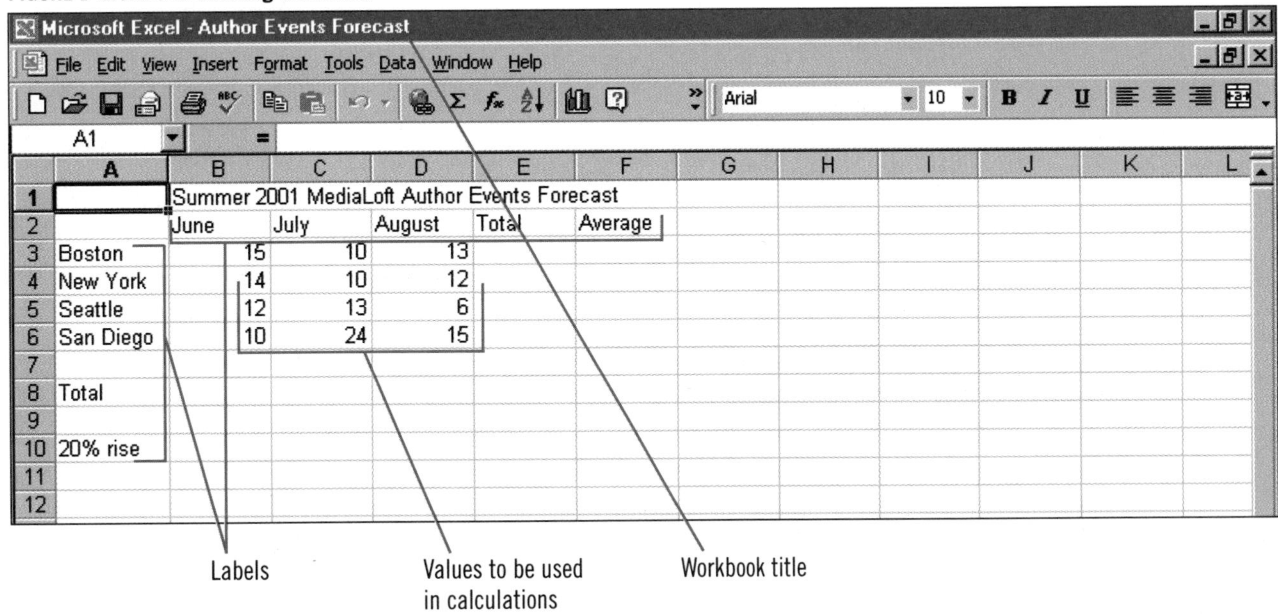

TABLE B-1: Commonly used pointers

name	pointer	use to
Normal		Select a cell or range; indicates Ready mode
Copy		Create a duplicate of the selected cell(s)
Fill handle		Create an alphanumeric series in a range
I-beam		Edit contents of formula bar
Move		Change the location of the selected cell(s)

Editing Cell Entries and Working with Ranges

You can change the contents of any cell at any time. To edit the contents of a cell, you first select the cell you want to edit. Then you have three options: you can click the formula bar, double-click the selected cell, or press [F2]. This puts Excel into Edit mode. To make sure you are in Edit mode, look at the **mode indicator** on the far left side of the status bar. After planning and creating his worksheet, Jim notices that he entered the wrong value for the August Seattle events, and that Houston should be entered instead of San Diego. He fixes the event figures, replaces the San Diego label, and corrects the value for July's Houston events.

Steps

1. Start Excel, click **Tools** on the menu bar, click **Customize**, click the **Options tab** in the Customize dialog box, click **Reset my usage data** to restore the default settings, click **Yes**, then click **Close**
2. Open the workbook **EX B-1** from your Project Disk, then save it as **Author Events Forecast**
3. Click cell **D5**
   This cell contains August Seattle events, which you want to change to reflect the correct numbers for the year 2000.
4. Click to **the right of 6** in the formula bar
   Excel goes into Edit mode, and the mode indicator on the status bar displays "Edit." A blinking vertical line called the **insertion point** appears in the formula bar, and if you move the mouse pointer to the formula bar, the pointer changes to I, which is used for editing. See Figure B-3.
5. Press **[Backspace]**, type **11**, then click the **Enter button** on the formula bar
   The value in cell D5 is changed or edited from 6 to 11. Additional modifications can also be made using the [F2] key.
6. Click cell **A6**, then press **[F2]**
   Excel is in Edit mode again, and the insertion point is in the cell.
7. Press **[Backspace]** nine times, type **Houston**, then press **[Enter]**
   The label changes to Houston. If you make a mistake, you can either click the Cancel button on the formula bar *before* accepting the cell entry, or click the Undo button on the Standard toolbar if you notice the mistake *after* you have accepted the cell entry. The Undo button allows you to reverse up to 16 previous actions, one at a time.
8. Double-click cell **C6**
   Double-clicking a cell also puts Excel into Edit mode with the insertion point in the cell.
9. Press **[Delete]** twice, then type **14**
   The number of book signings for July in Houston has been corrected. See Figure B-4.
10. Click to confirm the entry, then click the **Save button** on the Standard toolbar

QuickTip

The Redo command reverses the action of the Undo command. Click the Redo button on the Standard toolbar if you change your mind after an undo.

FIGURE B-3: **Worksheet in Edit mode**

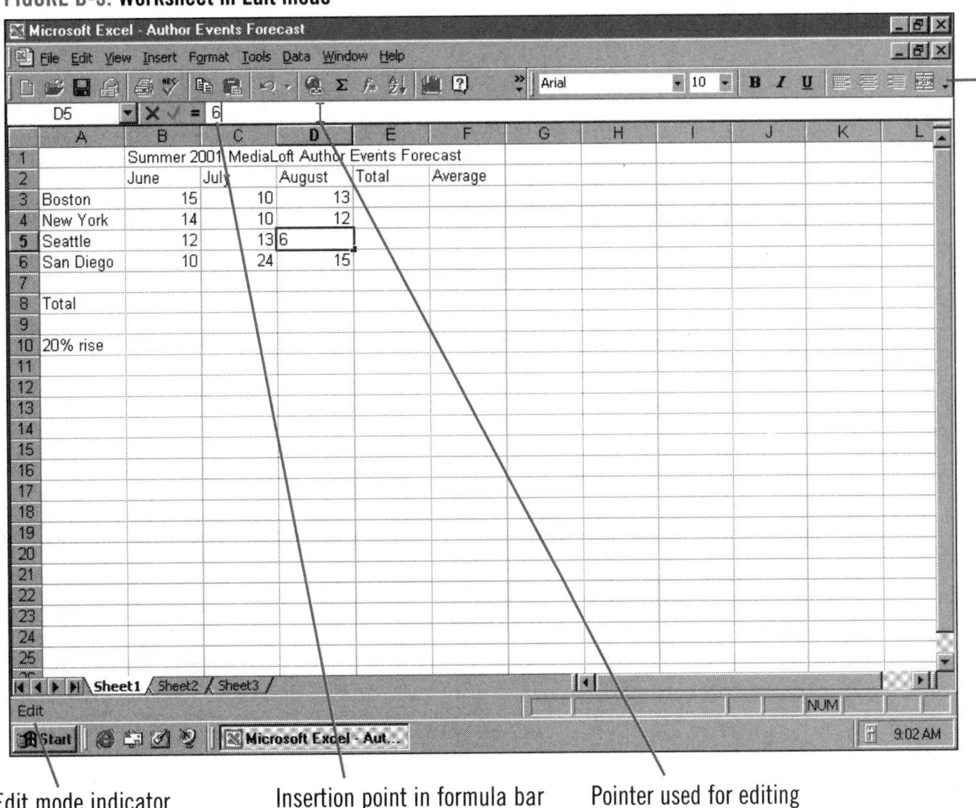

FIGURE B-4: **Edited worksheet**

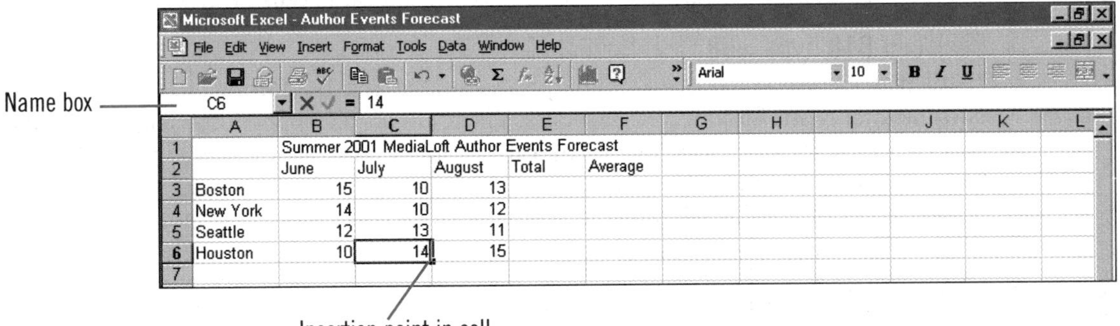

CLUES TO USE

Using range names in a workbook

Any group of cells (two or more) is called a **range**. To select a range, click the first cell and drag to the last cell you want to include in the range. The range address is defined by noting the first and last cells in the range separated by a colon, for example A8:B16. Once you select a range, the easiest way to give it a name is by clicking the name box and typing in a name. Range names—meaningful English names— are usually easier to remember than cell addresses. You can use a range name in a formula (for example, Income-Expenses) or to move around the workbook more quickly. Simply click the name box list arrow, then click the name of the range you want to go to. The cell pointer moves immediately to select that range. To clear the name from a range, click Insert on the menu bar, point to Name, then click Define. Select the range name you want to delete from the Define Name dialog box, click Delete, then click OK.

Excel 2000

Entering Formulas

You use **formulas** to perform numeric calculations such as adding, multiplying, and averaging. Formulas in an Excel worksheet usually start with the formula prefix—the equal sign (=) and contain cell addresses and range names. Arithmetic formulas use one or more **arithmetic operators** to perform calculations; see Table B-2. Using a cell address or range name in a formula is called **cell referencing**. If you change a value in a cell, any formula containing that cell reference will be automatically recalculated using the new value. In formulas using more than one arithmetic operator, Excel uses the order of precedence rules to determine which operation to perform first. Jim needs to total the values for the monthly author events for June, July, and August, and forecast what the 20% increase in appearances will be. He performs these calculations using formulas.

Steps

1. **Click cell B8**
   This is the cell where you want to enter the calculation that totals the June events.
2. **Type = (the equal sign)**
   Placing an equal sign at the beginning of an entry tells Excel that a formula is about to be entered, rather than a label or a value. "Enter" appears on the status bar. The total number of June events is equal to the sum of the values in cells B3, B4, B5, and B6.
3. **Type b3+b4+b5+b6, then click the Enter button on the formula bar**
   Notice that the result of 51 appears in cell B8, and the formula appears in the formula bar. Also, Excel is not case-sensitive: it doesn't matter if you type upper or lower-case characters when you enter cell addresses. See Figure B-5.

Trouble?

If the formula instead of the result appears in the cell after you click , make sure you began the formula with = (the equal sign).

4. **Click cell C8, type =c3+c4+c5+c6, press [Tab]; in cell D8, type =d3+d4+d5+d6, then press [Enter]**
   The total appearances for July, 47, and for August, 51, appear in cells C8 and D8 respectively.
5. **Click cell B10, type =B8*1.2, then click**
   To calculate the 20% increase, you multiply the total by 1.2. The formula in cell B10 multiplies the total events for June, cell B8, by 1.2. The result of 61.2 appears in cell B10 and is the projected value for an increase of 20% over the 51 June events. Now you need to calculate the 20% increase for July and August. You can use the **pointing method**, by which you specify cell references in a formula by selecting the desired cell with your mouse instead of typing its cell reference into the formula. Pointing is a preferred method because it eliminates typing errors.
6. **Click cell C10, type =, then click cell C8**
   When you click cell C8, a moving border surrounds the cell. This **moving border**—as well as the mode indicator—indicates the cell that is copied in this operation. Moving borders can display around a single cell or a range of cells.

QuickTip

Press [Esc] to turn off a moving border.

7. **Type *1.2, then press [Tab]**
   The calculated value 56.4 appears in cell C10.
8. **In cell D10, type =, click cell D8, type *1.2, then click**
   Compare your results with Figure B-6.
9. **Click the Save button on the Standard toolbar**

FIGURE B-5: Worksheet showing formula and result

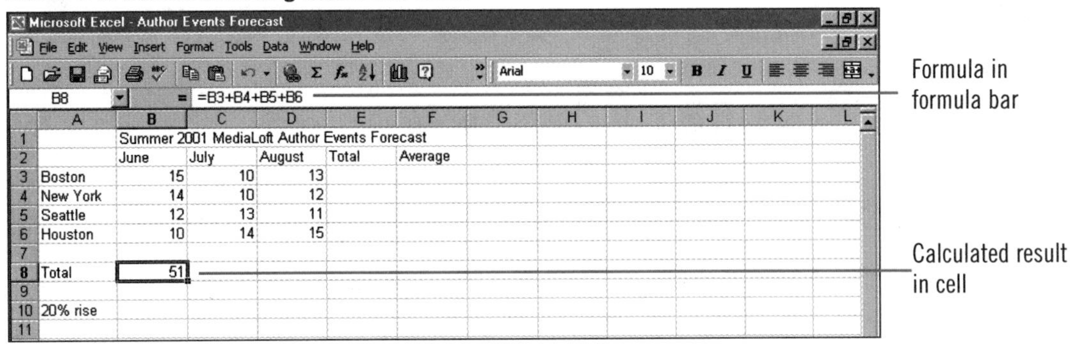

FIGURE B-6: Calculated results for 20% increase

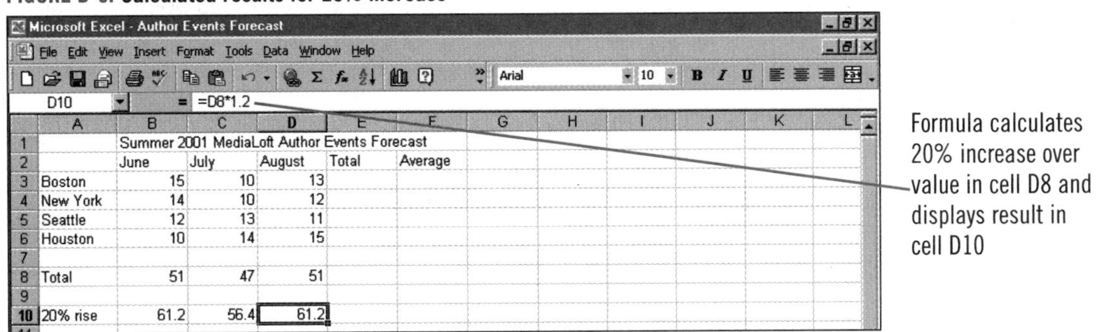

Excel 2000

TABLE B-2: Excel arithmetic operators

operator	purpose	example
+	Addition	=A5+A7
–	Subtraction or negation	=A5-10
*	Multiplication	=A5*A7
/	Division	=A5/A7
%	Percent	=35%
^ (caret)	Exponent	=6^2 (same as 6*6)

Order of precedence in Excel formulas

A formula can include several mathematical operations. When you work with formulas that have more than one operator, the **order of precedence** is very important. If a formula contains two or more operators, such as 4 + .55/4000 * 25, the computer performs the calculations in a particular sequence based on these rules: Operations inside parentheses are calculated before any other operations. Exponents are calculated next, then any multiplication and division—from left to right. Finally, addition and subtraction is calculated from left to right. In the example 4 + .55/4000 * 25, Excel performs the arithmetic operations by first dividing 4000 into .55, then multiplying the result by 25, then adding 4. You can change the order of calculations by using parentheses. For example, in the formula (4+.55)/4000 * 25, Excel would first add 4 and .55, then divide that amount by 4000, then finally multiply by 25.

Excel 2000

Introducing Excel Functions

Functions are predefined worksheet formulas that enable you to do complex calculations easily. Like formulas, functions always begin with the formula prefix = (the equal sign). You can enter functions manually, or you can use the Paste Function to select the function you need from a list. Jim uses the SUM function to calculate the grand totals in his worksheet and the AVERAGE function to calculate the average number of author events per store.

1. **Click cell E3**

   This is the cell where you want to display the total of all author events in Boston for June, July, and August. You use **AutoSum** to create the totals. By default, AutoSum sets up the SUM function to add the values in the cells above the cell pointer. If there are one or fewer values in the cells above the cell pointer, AutoSum adds the values in the cells to the left of the cell pointer—in this case, the values in cells B3, C3, and D3.

2. **Click the AutoSum button on the Standard toolbar, then click the Enter button on the formula bar**

   The formula =SUM(B3:D3) appears in the formula bar. The result, 38, appears in cell E3. The information inside the parentheses is the **argument**, or the information to be used in calculating a result of the function. An argument can be a value, a range of cells, text, or another function.

Trouble?

If you don't see on your toobar, click the More Buttons button on the Standard toolbar.

3. **Click cell E4, click , then click**

   The values for the Boston and New York events are now totaled.

4. **Click cell E5, then click**

   By default, AutoSum sets up a function to add the two values in the cells above the active cell, as you can see by the formula in the formula bar. You can override the current selection by manually selecting the correct range for this argument.

5. **Click cell B5, drag to cell D5 to select the range B5:D5, then click**

   As you drag, the argument in the SUM function changes to reflect the selected range, and a ScreenTip appears telling you the size of the range by row and column.

6. **Click cell E6, type =SUM(, point to cell B6, drag to cell D6, press [Enter], click cell E8, type =SUM(, point to cell B8, drag to cell D8, press [Enter], click cell E10, type =SUM(, point to cell B10, drag to cell D10, then click to confirm the entry**

   See Figure B-7 to verify your results. Now the Paste Function can be used to select the function needed to calculate the average number of author events.

7. **Click cell F3, then click the Paste Function button on the Standard toolbar**

   The Paste Function dialog box opens. See Table B-3 for frequently used functions. The function needed to calculate averages—named AVERAGE—is included in the Most Recently Used function category.

Trouble?

If the Office Assistant opens, click No, don't provide help now.

8. **Click AVERAGE in the Function name list box, click OK, the AVERAGE dialog box opens; type B3:D3 in the Number 1 text box, as shown in Figure B-8, then click OK**

QuickTip

Modify a function's range by clicking the Collapse dialog box button, defining the range with your mouse, then clicking the Expand dialog box button to return to the Paste Function window.

9. **Click cell F4, click , verify that AVERAGE is selected, click OK, type B4:D4, click OK, click cell F5, click , click AVERAGE, click OK, type B5:D5, click OK, click cell F6, click , click AVERAGE, click OK, type B6:D6, then click OK**

   The result in Boston (cell F3) is 12.6667; the result in New York (cell F4) is 12; the result in Seattle (cell F5) is 12; and the result in Houston (cell F6) is 13, giving you the averages for all four stores.

FIGURE B-7: **Worksheet with SUM functions entered**

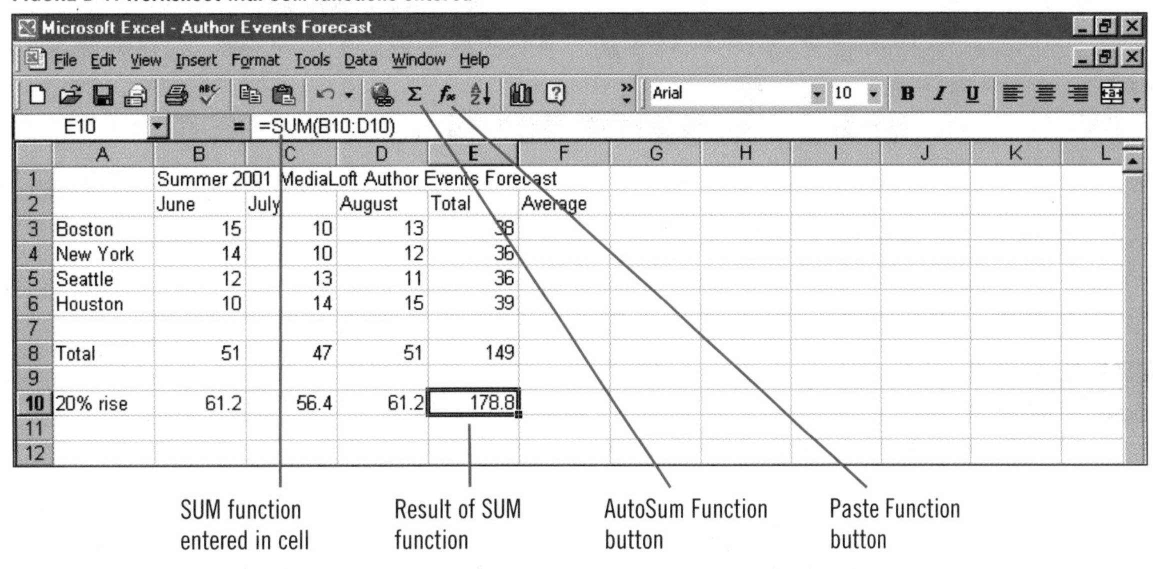

FIGURE B-8: **Using the Paste Function to create a formula**

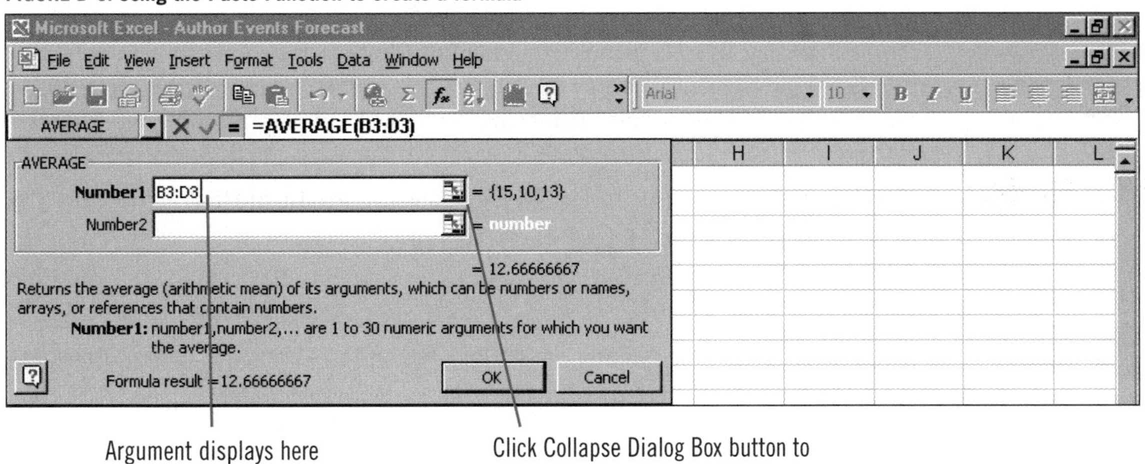

TABLE B-3: **Frequently used functions**

function	description
SUM(*argument*)	Calculates the sum of the arguments
AVERAGE(*argument*)	Calculates the average of the arguments
MAX(*argument*)	Displays the largest value among the arguments
MIN(*argument*)	Displays the smallest value among the arguments
COUNT(*argument*)	Calculates the number of values in the arguments

Using the MIN and MAX functions

Other commonly used functions include MIN and MAX. You use the MIN function to calculate the minimum or smallest value in a selected range; the MAX function calculates the maximum or largest value in a selected range. The MAX function is included in the Most Frequently Used function category in the Paste Function dialog box, while the MIN function can be found in the Statistical category. Like AVERAGE, MIN and MAX are preceded by an equal sign and the argument includes a range.

Excel 2000

Excel 2000

Copying and Moving Cell Entries

Using the Cut, Copy, and Paste buttons or the Excel drag-and-drop feature, you can copy or move information from one cell or range in your worksheet to another. You can also cut, copy, and paste data from one worksheet to another to make corrections, and add information using the Office Clipboard, which can store up to 12 items. Jim needs to include the 2001 forecast for spring and fall author events in his Author Events Forecast workbook. He's already entered the spring report in Sheet2 and will finish entering the labels and data for the fall report. Jim copies information from the spring report to the fall report.

Steps

1. Click **Sheet 2** of the Author Events Forecast workbook
   To work more efficiently, existing labels can be copied from one range to another and from one sheet to another. You see that the store names have to be corrected in cells A6:A7.

2. Click **Sheet 1**, select the range **A5:A6**, then click the **Copy button** on the Standard toolbar
   The selected range (A5:A6) is copied to the **Office Clipboard**, a temporary storage file that holds the selected information you copy or cut. A moving border surrounds the selected range until you press [Esc] or copy additional information to the Clipboard. To copy the most recent item copied to the Clipboard to a new location, you click a new cell and then use the Paste command.

3. Click **Sheet 2**, select the range **A6:A7**, click the **Paste button** on the Standard toolbar, select the range **A4:A9**, then click
   The Clipboard toolbar opens when you copy a selection to the already occupied Clipboard. You can use the Clipboard toolbar to copy, cut, store, and paste up to 12 items.

4. Click cell **A13**, place the pointer on the last on the Clipboard toolbar, the contents of range A4:A9 display in a ScreenTip, click to paste the contents in cell A13, then close the Clipboard toolbar
   The item is copied into the range A13:A18. When pasting an item from the Clipboard into the worksheet, you only need to specify the top left cell of the range where you want the selection to go.The moving border remains active. Now you can use the drag-and-drop technique to copy the Total label, which does not copy the contents to the Clipboard.

5. Click cell **E3**, position the pointer on any edge of the cell until the pointer changes to , then press and hold down **[Ctrl]**
   The pointer changes to the copy pointer . When you copy cells, the original data remains in the original cell. When you move cells, the original data does *not* remain in the original cell.

6. While still pressing **[Ctrl]**, press and hold the **left mouse button**, drag the cell contents to cell **E12**, release the mouse button, then release **[Ctrl]**
   As you drag, an outline of the cell moves with the pointer, as shown in Figure B-9, and a ScreenTip appears tracking the current position of the item as you move it. When you release the mouse button, the Total label appears in cell E12. You now decide to move the worksheet title over to the left. To use drag and drop to move data to a new cell, do not press [Ctrl].

7. Click cell **C1**, position the pointer on the edge of the cell until it changes to , then drag the cell contents to **A1**
   Once the labels are copied, you can easily enter the fall events data into the range B13:D16.

8. Using the information shown in Figure B-10, enter the author events data for the fall into the range B13:D16
   Compare your worksheet to Figure B-10.

QuickTip

The Cut button removes the selected information from the worksheet and places it on the Office Clipboard.

Trouble?

If the Clipboard toolbar does not open, click View on the menu bar, point to toolbars, then click Clipboard.

QuickTip

To use the pop-up menu, right-click, click Copy, click the target cell, right-click, then click Paste to paste the last item copied to the Clipboard.

Trouble?

When you drag and drop into occupied cells, Excel asks if you want to replace the existing cells. Click OK to replace the contents with the cell you are moving.

FIGURE B-9: Using drag and drop to copy information

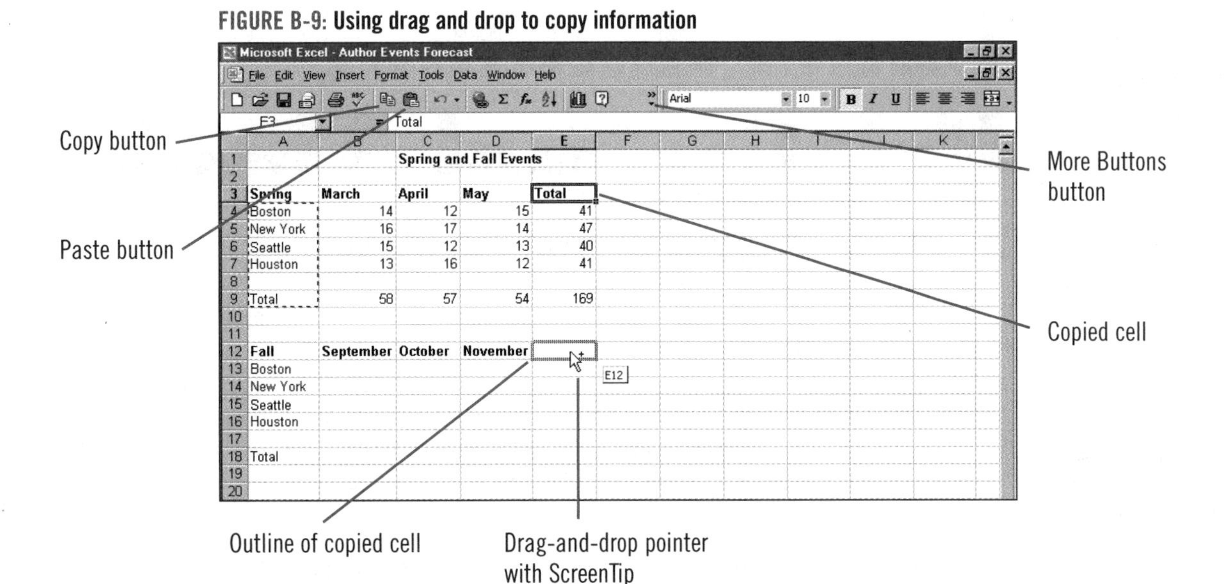

	A	B	C	D	E
1			Spring and Fall Events		
2					
3	Spring	March	April	May	Total
4	Boston	14	12	15	41
5	New York	16	17	14	47
6	Seattle	15	12	13	40
7	Houston	13	16	12	41
8					
9	Total	58	57	54	169
10					
11					
12	Fall	September	October	November	
13	Boston				
14	New York				
15	Seattle				
16	Houston				
17					
18	Total				

FIGURE B-10: Worksheet with Fall author event data entered

12	Fall	September	October	November	Total
13	Boston	16	10	13	
14	New York	12	15	16	
15	Seattle	17	10	18	
16	Houston	14	11	12	
17					
18	Total				

Sheet1 Sheet2 Sheet3 — Ready — Sum=164 — NUM

Sum of selected range displays in status bar

Using the Office Clipboard

The Office Clipboard lets you copy and paste multiple items such as text, images, tables, or Excel ranges within or between the Microsoft Office applications. The Office Clipboard can hold up to 12 items copied or cut from any Office program. The Clipboard toolbar, shown in Figure B-11, displays the items stored on the Office Clipboard. You choose whether to delete the first item from the Clipboard when you copy the thirteenth item. The collected items remain in the Office Clipboard and are available to you until you close all open Office applications.

FIGURE B-11: The Office Clipboard

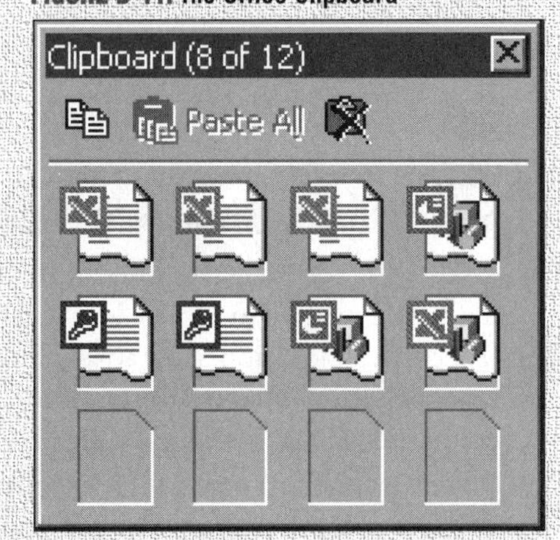

Excel 2000

Understanding Relative and Absolute Cell References

Like a label or value, an existing formula can be copied to a new location. This enables you to work efficiently by copying a working formula to multiple locations. When copied, a cell reference within a formula is automatically copied *relative* to its new location. This is called a **relative reference**. You can, however, choose to copy a cell reference with an absolute reference or a mixed reference. An **absolute reference** always cites a specific cell when the formula is copied. Jim often copies existing worksheet formulas and makes use of many types of cell references.

Use relative references when cell relationships remain unchanged

When Excel copies a formula, all the cell references change to reflect the new location automatically. Each copied formula is identical to the original, except that the column or row is adjusted for its new location. The outlined cells in Figure B-12 contain formulas that contain relative references. For example, the formula in cell E5 is =SUM(B5:D5). When copied to cell E6, the resulting formula is =SUM(B6:D6). The original formula was copied from row 5 to row 6 within the same column, so the cell referenced in the copied formula increased by one row.

Use an absolute cell reference when one relationship changes

In most cases, you will use relative cell references—the default. Sometimes, however, this is not what is needed. In some cases, you'll want to reference a specific cell, even when copying a formula. You create absolute references by placing a $ (dollar sign) before both the column letter and row number for a cell's address using the [F4] function key (on the keyboard). Figure B-13 displays the formulas used in Figure B-11. Notice that each formula in range B15:D18 contains both a relative and absolute reference. By using an absolute reference when referring to cell $B$12 in a formula, Excel keeps that cell reference (representing the potential increase) constant when copying that formula.

Using a mixed reference

When copying formulas, the alternative to changing a cell reference relative to its new location and referring to a specific cell location as an absolute reference, is a mixed reference. A **mixed reference** contains both a relative and absolute reference. When copied, the mixed reference C$14 changes the column relative to its new location but prevents the row from changing. In the mixed reference $C14, the column would not change but the row would be updated relative to its location. Like the absolute reference, a mixed reference can be created using the [F4] function key. With each press of the [F4] key, you cycle through all the possible combinations of relative, absolute, and mixed references ($C$14, C$14, $C14, C14).

FIGURE B-12: Location of relative references

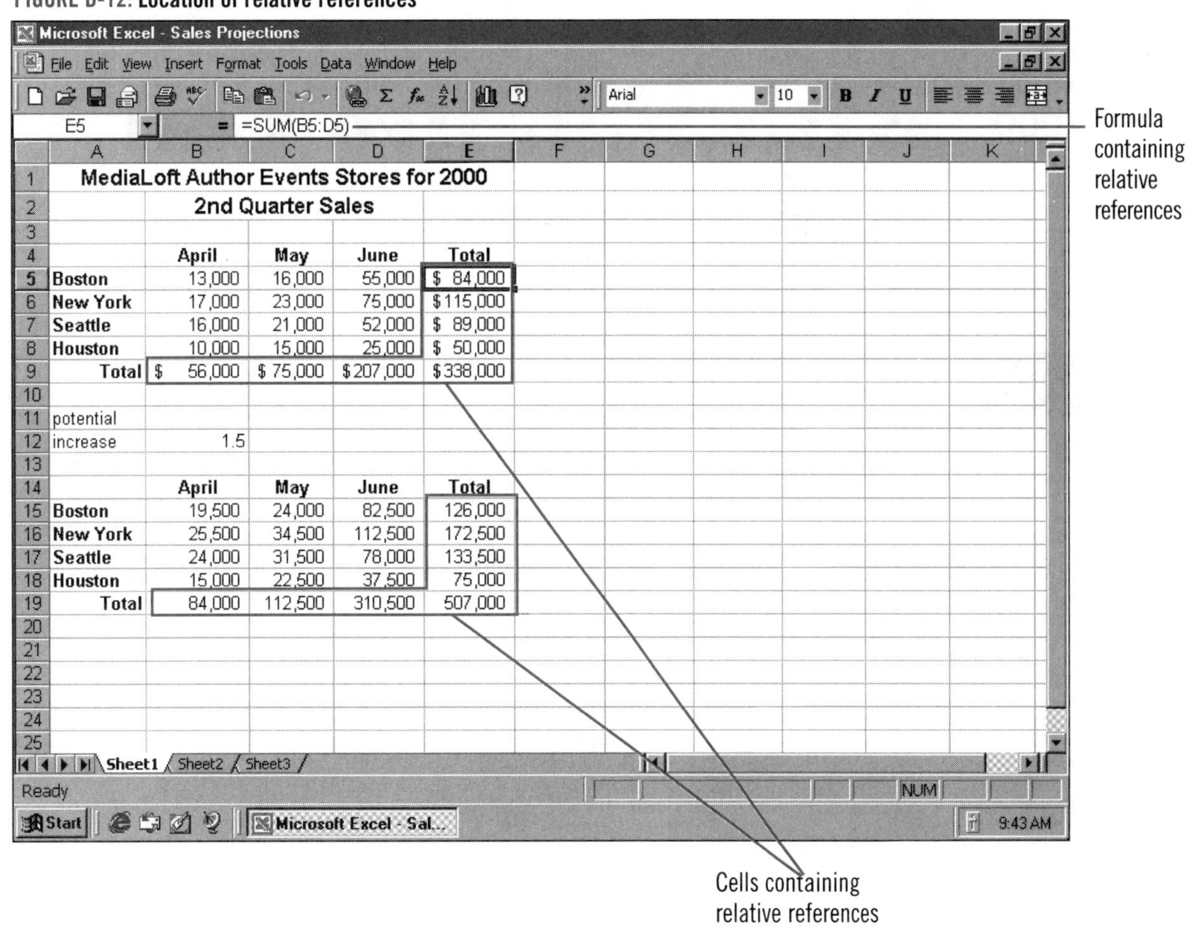

FIGURE B-13: Absolute and relative reference formulas

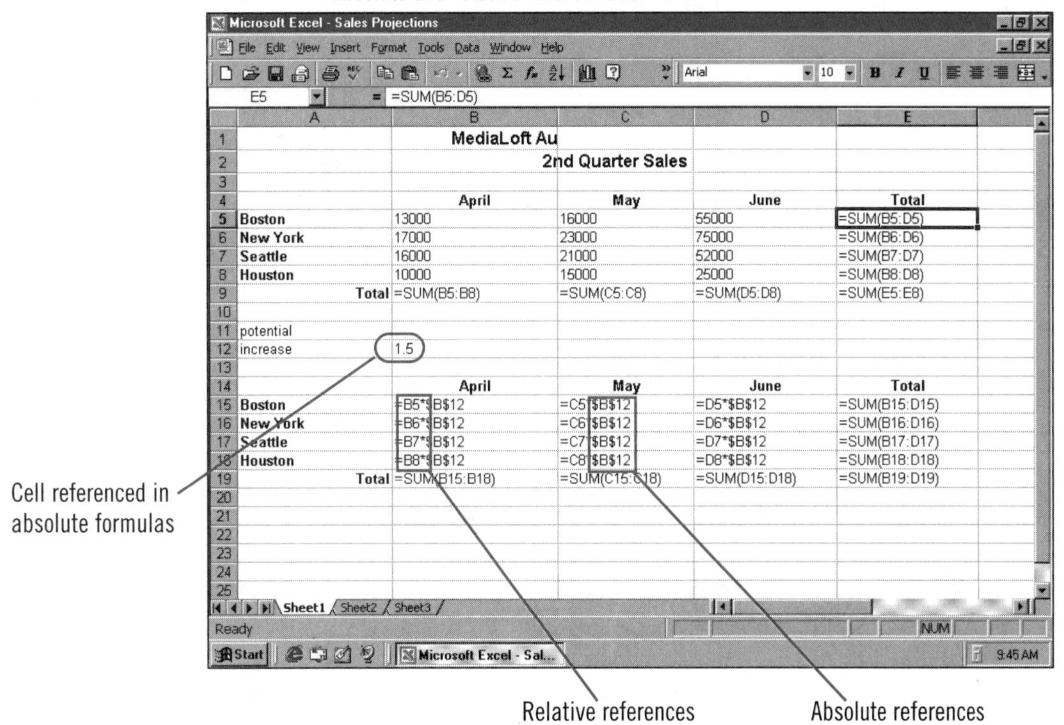

Copying Formulas with Relative Cell References

Copying and moving formulas allows you to reuse formulas you've already created. Copying formulas, rather than retyping them, is faster and helps to prevent typing errors. Jim wants to copy the formulas that total the appearances by region and by month from the spring to the fall. He can use Copy and Paste commands and the Fill Right method to copy this information.

Steps

1. **Click cell E4, then click the Copy button on the Standard toolbar**
   The formula for calculating the total number of spring Boston author events is copied to the Clipboard. Notice that the formula =SUM(B4:D4) displays in the formula bar.

2. **Click cell E13, then click the Paste button on the Standard toolbar**
   The formula from cell E4 is copied into cell E13, where the new result of 39 appears. Notice in the formula bar that the cell references have changed, so that the range B13:D13 appears in the formula. This formula contains **relative cell references** which tell Excel to copy the formula to a new cell, but to substitute new cell references so that the relationship of the cells to the formula in its new location remains unchanged. In this case, Excel adjusted the formula so cells D13, C13, and B13—the three cell references immediately to the left of E13—replaced cells D4, C4, and B4, the three cell references to the left of E4.
   Notice that the bottom right corner of the active cell contains a small square, called the **fill handle**. You can use the fill handle to copy labels, formulas, and values. You use the fill handle to copy the formula in cell E13 to cells E14, E15, and E16.

3. **Position the pointer over the fill handle until it changes to +, press the left mouse button, then drag the fill handle to select the range E13:E16**
   See Figure B-14.

4. **Release the mouse button**
   Once you release the mouse button, the fill handle copies the formula from the active cell (E13) and pastes it into each cell of the selected range. Again, because the formula uses relative cell references, cells E14 through E16 correctly display the totals for the fall author events.

5. **Click cell B9, click Edit on the menu bar, then click Copy**

6. **Click cell B18, click Edit on the menu bar, then click Paste**
   See Figure B-15. The formula for calculating the September events appears in the formula bar. You can use the Fill Right command to copy the formula from cell B18 to cells C18, D18, and E18.

7. **Select the range B18:E18**

8. **Click Edit on the menu bar, point to Fill, then click Right**
   The rest of the totals are filled in correctly. Compare your worksheet to Figure B-16.

9. **Click the Save button on the Standard toolbar**

QuickTip

Click Edit on the menu bar, then click Paste Special to specify components of the copied cell or range prior to pasting. You can selectively copy formulas, values, comments, validation, and formatting attributes, as well as transpose cells or paste the contents as a link.

QuickTip

As you drag the fill handle, the contents of the last filled cell appear in the name box.

Trouble?

If the Clipboard toolbar opens, click the Close button. If the Office Assistant appears, right-click it, then click Hide.

CLUES TO USE

Filling cells with sequential text or values

Often, we fill cells with sequential text: months of the year, days of the week, years, and text plus a number (Quarter 1, Quarter 2, . . .). You can easily fill cells using sequences by dragging the fill handle. As you drag the fill handle, Excel automatically extends the existing sequence. (The contents of the last filled cell appears in the name box.) Use the Fill Series command on the Edit menu to examine all of the available fill series options.

FIGURE B-14: Selected range using the fill handle

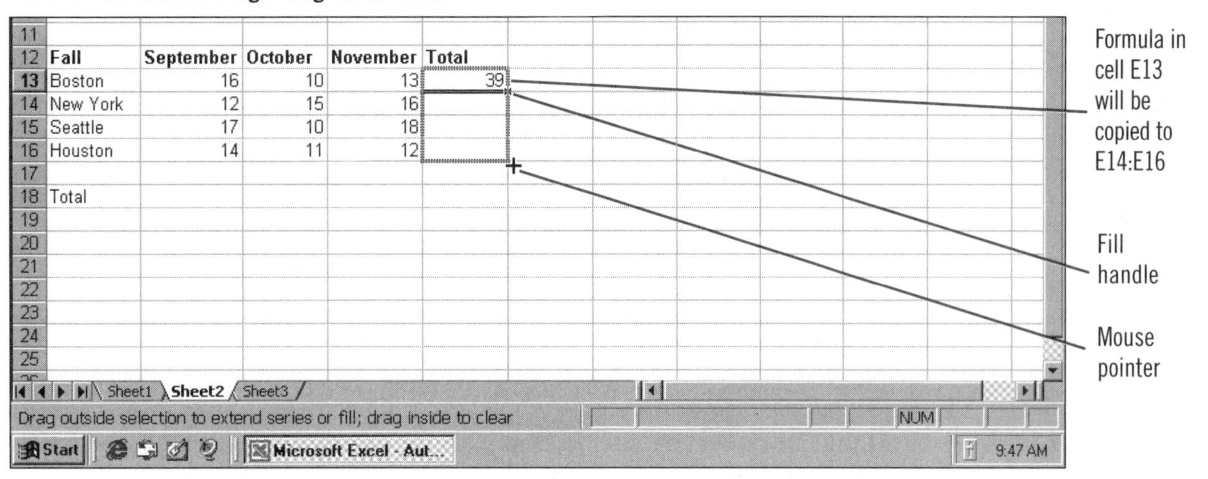

FIGURE B-15: Worksheet with copied formula

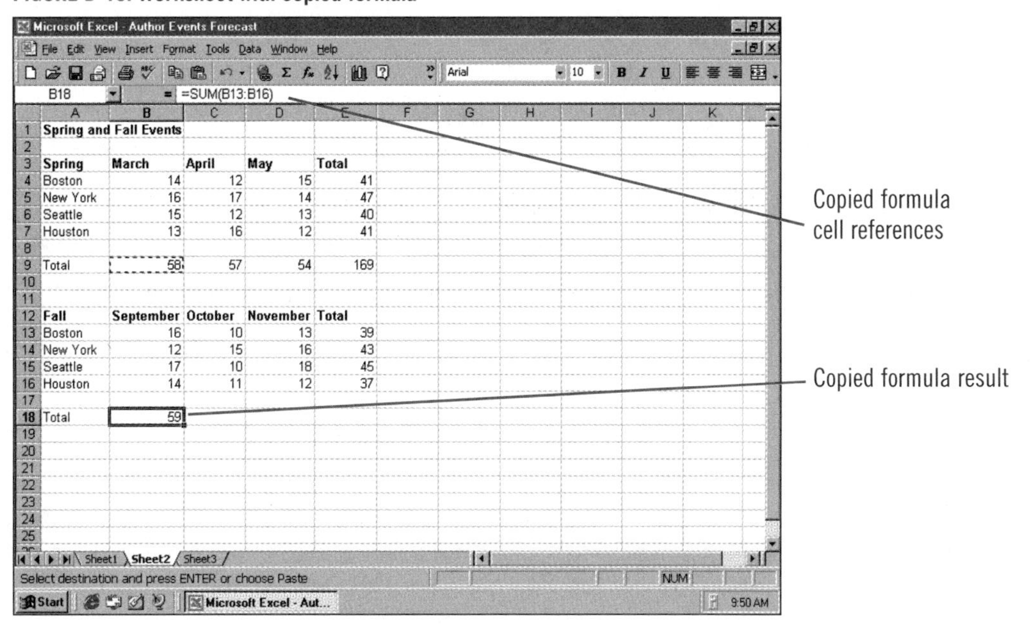

FIGURE B-16: Completed worksheet with all formulas copied

10					
11					
12	**Fall**	**September**	**October**	**November**	**Total**
13	Boston	16	10	13	39
14	New York	12	15	16	43
15	Seattle	17	10	18	45
16	Houston	14	11	12	37
17					
18	Total	59	46	59	164

Sheet1 Sheet2 Sheet3

Ready Sum=328 NUM

Start Microsoft Excel - Aut... 9:49 AM

Excel 2000

Excel 2000

Copying Formulas with Absolute Cell References

When copying formulas, you might want a cell reference to always refer to a particular cell address. In such an instance, you would use an **absolute cell reference.** An absolute cell reference always refers to a specific cell address when the formula is copied. You identify an absolute reference by placing a dollar sign ($) before the row letter and column number of the address (for example $A$1). The staff in the Marketing department hopes the number of author events will increase by 20% over last year's figures. Jim decides to add a column that calculates a possible increase in the number of spring events in 2001. He wants to do a what-if analysis and recalculate the spreadsheet several times, changing the percentage that the number of appearances might increase each time.

1. **Click cell G1, type Change, then press [→]**
   You can store the increase factor that will be used in the what-if analysis in cell H1.
2. **Type 1.1, then press [Enter]**
   The value in cell H1 represents a 10% increase in author events.
3. **Click cell G3, type What if?, then press [Enter]**
   Now you create a formula that references a specific address: cell H1.
4. **In cell G4, type =E4*H1, then click the Enter button on the formula bar**
   The result of 45.1 appears in cell G4. This value represents the total spring events for Boston if there is a 10% increase. To determine the value for the remaining stores, you copy the formula in cell G4 to the range G5:G7.
5. **Drag the fill handle to select the range G4:G7**
   The resulting values in the range G5:G7 are all zeros. When you copy the formula it adjusts so the formula in cell G5 is =E5*H2. Since there is no value in cell H2, the result is 0, an error. You need to use an absolute reference in the formula to keep the formula from adjusting. That way, cell H1 will always be referenced. You can change the relative cell reference to an absolute cell reference using [F4].
6. **Click cell G4, press [F2] to change to Edit mode, then press [F4]**
   When you press [F2], the **range finder** outlines the equation's arguments in blue and green. When you press [F4], dollar signs appear, changing the H1 cell reference to an absolute reference. See Figure B-17.
7. **Click the Enter button on the formula bar**
   The formula correctly contains an absolute cell reference and the value remains unchanged at 45.1. The fill handle can be used to copy the corrected formula in cell G4 to G5:G7.
8. **Drag the fill handle to select the range G4:G7**
   The correct values for a 10% increase display in cells G4:G7. You complete the what-if analysis by changing the value in cell H1 from 1.1 to 1.25 to indicate a 25% increase in events.
9. **Click cell H1, type 1.25, then click**
   The values in the range G4:G7 change to reflect the 25% increase. Compare your worksheet to Figure B-18. Since events only occur in whole numbers, the numbers' appearance can be changed later.

QuickTip

Before you copy or move a formula, check to see if you need to use an absolute cell reference.

FIGURE B-17: Absolute cell reference in cell G4

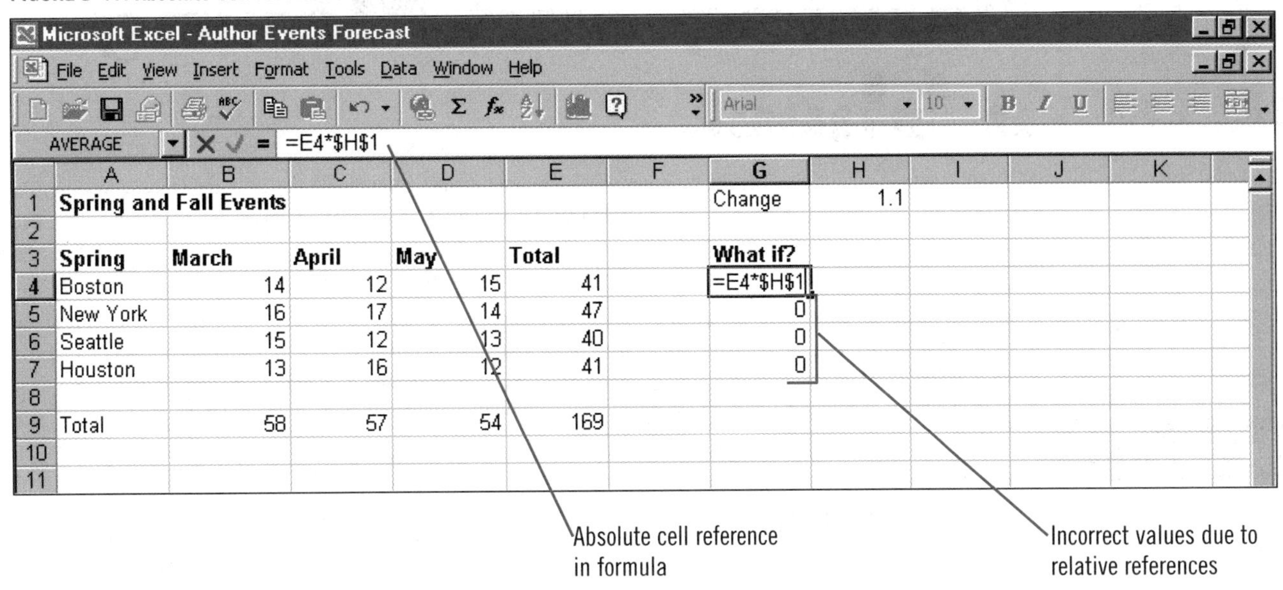

FIGURE B-18: Worksheet with what-if value

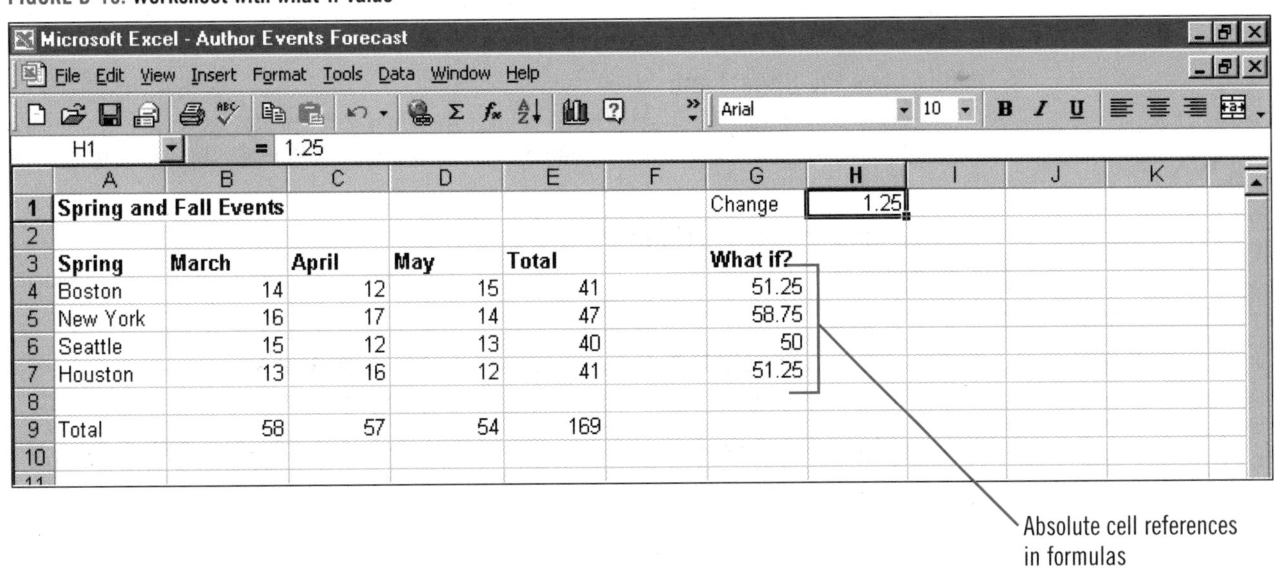

Copying and moving using named ranges

You can give a range of cells an easy-to-remember meaningful name, such as "2001 Sales." If you move the named range, its name moves with it. Like any range, a named range can be referenced absolutely in a formula by using the $ symbol. To copy or move a named range, you can "go to" it quickly by clicking the name box list arrow and selecting its name.

Naming and Moving a Sheet

Each workbook initially contains three worksheets named Sheet1, Sheet2, and Sheet3. When the workbook is opened, the first worksheet is the active sheet. To move from sheet to sheet, click the desired sheet tab located at the bottom of the worksheet window. Sheet tab scrolling buttons, located to the left of the sheet tabs, allow rapid movement among the sheets. To make it easier to identify the sheets in a workbook, you can rename each sheet and then organize them in a logical way. The name appears on the sheet tab. For instance, sheets within a single workbook could be named for individual salespeople to better track performance goals, and the sheets can be moved so they appear in alphabetical order. Jim wants to be able to easily identify the actual author events and the forecast sheets. He decides to name two sheets in his workbook, then changes their order.

Steps

1. Click the **Sheet1 tab**
   Sheet1 becomes active; this is the worksheet that contains the summer information you compiled for the Marketing department. Its tab moves to the front, and the tab for Sheet2 moves to the background.
2. Click the **Sheet2 tab**
   Sheet2, containing the spring and fall data, becomes active. Once you have confirmed which sheet is which, you can rename Sheet1 so it has a name that you can easily remember.
3. Double-click the **Sheet1 tab**
   The Sheet1 text becomes selected with the default sheet name ("Sheet1") selected. You could also click Format in the menu bar, point to Sheet, then click Rename to select the sheet name.
4. Type **Summer**, then press **[Enter]**
   See Figure B-19. The new name automatically replaces the default name in the tab. Worksheet names can have up to 31 characters, including spaces and punctuation.
5. Double-click the **Sheet2 tab**, then rename this sheet **Spring-Fall**
   Jim decides to rearrange the order of the sheets, so that Summer comes after Spring-Fall.
6. Click the **Summer sheet tab**, then drag it to the right of the **Spring-Fall sheet tab**
   As you drag, the pointer changes to the sheet relocation pointer. See Figure B-20. The first sheet in the workbook is now the Spring-Fall sheet. When there are multiple sheets in a workbook, the navigation buttons can be used to scroll through the sheet tabs. Click the leftmost navigation button to display the first sheet tab; click the rightmost navigation button to display the last sheet tab. The left and right buttons move one sheet in their respective directions.
7. Type your name in cell A12, click **File** on the menu bar, click **Print**, click the **Entire workbook option button**, then click the **Preview button**
   The Preview screen opens. Each worksheet is displayed on a separate page. You can preview the workbook sheets by clicking the Next and Previous buttons.
8. Click the **Print button** on the Preview toolbar
9. Save and close the workbook, then exit Excel

QuickTip

To delete a worksheet, select the worksheet you want to delete, click Edit on the menu bar, then click Delete sheet. To insert a worksheet, click Insert on the menu bar, then click Worksheet.

FIGURE B-19: Renamed sheet in workbook

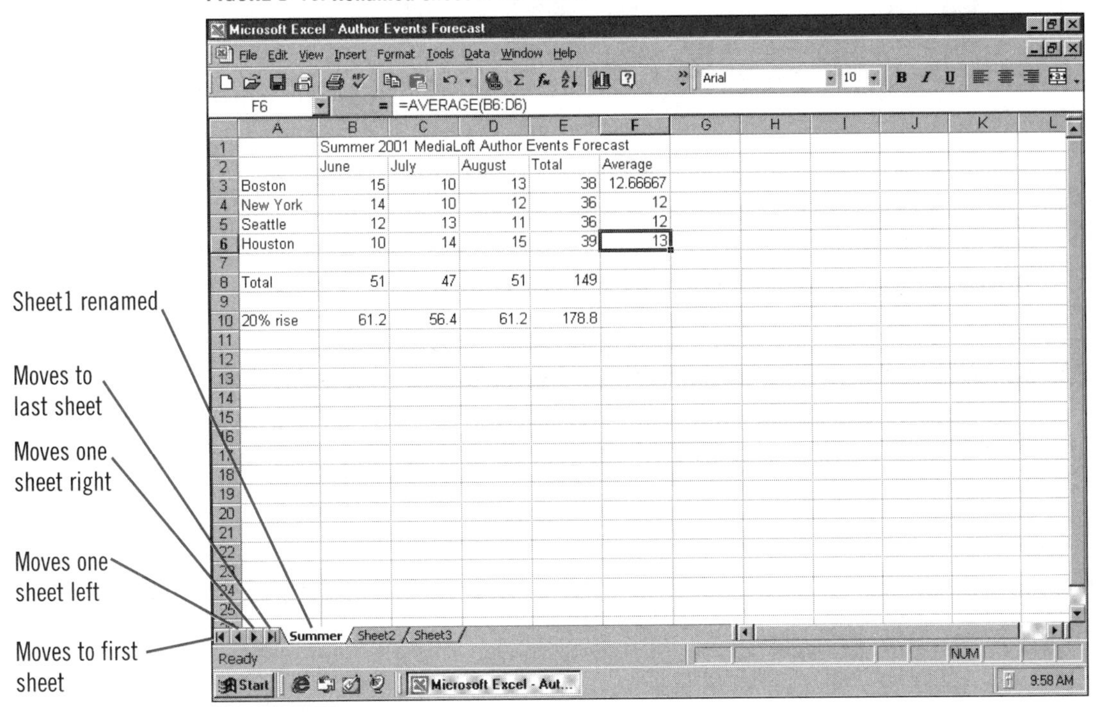

FIGURE B-20: Moving Summer after Spring-Fall sheet

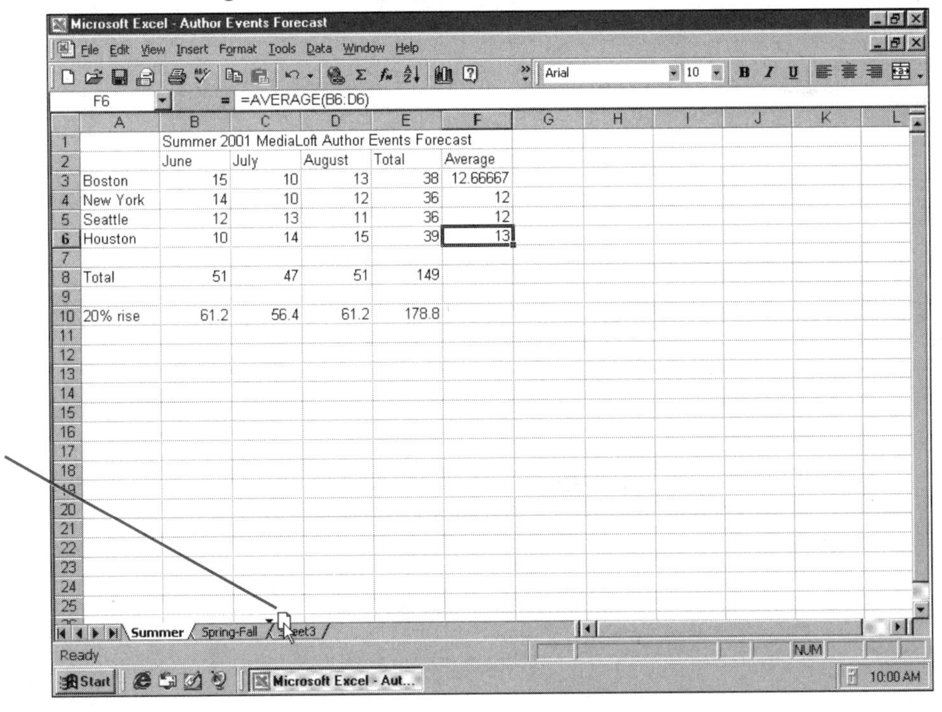

CLUES TO USE

Moving and copying worksheets

There are times when you may want to move or copy sheets. To move sheets within the current workbook, drag the selected sheet tab along the row of sheet tabs to the new location. To copy, simply press CTRL as you drag the sheet tab and release the mouse button before you release CTRL. Although you have to be careful and carefully check the calculations when doing so, moving and copying worksheets to new workbooks is a relatively simple operation. You must have the workbook that you are copying to, as well as the workbook that you are copying from, open. Select the sheet to copy or move, click File on the menu bar, click Edit, then click Move or Copy sheet. Complete the information in the Move or Copy dialog box. Be sure to click the Create a Copy check box if you are copying rather than moving the worksheet.

Practice

► Concepts Review

Label each element of the Excel worksheet window shown in Figure B-20.

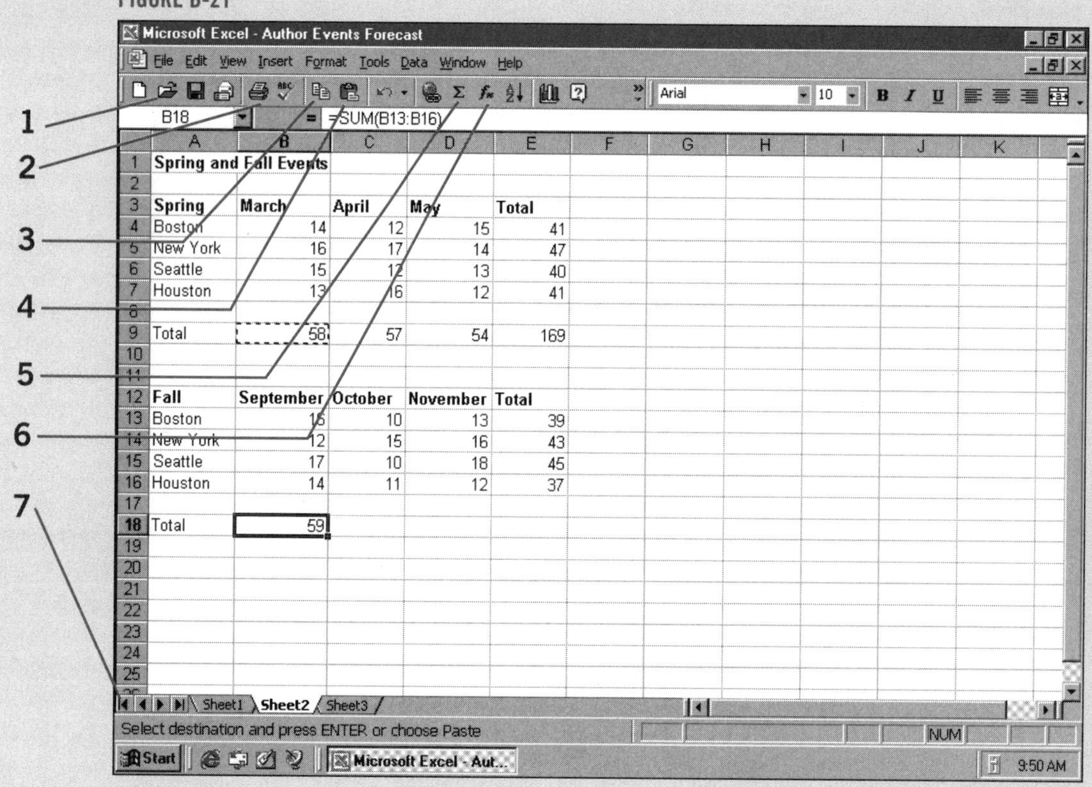

FIGURE B-21

Match the term or button with the statement that describes it.

8. Range
9. Function
10. [paste button]
11. [copy button]
12. Formula

a. A predefined formula that provides a shortcut for commonly used calculations
b. A cell entry that performs a calculation in an Excel worksheet
c. A specified group of cells, which can include the entire worksheet
d. Used to copy cells
e. Used to paste cells

Select the best answer from the list of choices.

13. What type of cell reference changes when it is copied?

a. Absolute
b. Circular
c. Looping
d. Relative

14. What character is used to make a reference absolute?

a. &
b. ^
c. $
d. @

15. Which button is used to enter data in a cell?

a.
b.
c.
d.

Skills Review

1. Edit cell entries and work with ranges.

a. Start Excel, open the workbook EX B-2 from your Project Disk and save it as "Office Furnishings."
b. Change the quantity of Tables to 25.
c. Change the price of each of the Desks to 250.
d. Change the quantity of Easels to 17.
e. Name the range B2:B5 "Quantity" and name the range C2:C5 "Price."
f. Type your name in cell A20, then save and preview the worksheet.

2. Enter formulas.

a. Click cell B6, then enter the formula B2+B3+B4+B5.
b. Save your work, then preview the data in the Office Furnishings worksheet.

3. Introduce Excel functions.

a. Type the label "Min Price" in cell A8.
b. Click cell C8; enter the function MIN(C2:C5).
c. Type the label "Max Price" in cell A9.
d. Create a formula in cell C9 that determines the maximum price.
e. Save your work, then preview the data.

4. Copy and move cell entries.

a. Select the range A1:C6, then copy the range to cell A12.
b. Use drag and drop to copy the range D1:E1 to cell D12.
c. Save your work, then preview the worksheet.

5. Copy formulas with relative cell references.

a. Click cell D2, then create a formula that multiplies B2 and C2.
b. Copy the formula in D2 into cells D3:D5.
c. Copy the formula in D2 into cells D13:D16.
d. Save and preview the worksheet.

6. Copy formulas with absolute cell references.

a. Click cell G2 and type the value 1.375.
b. Click cell E2, then create a formula containing an absolute reference that multiplies D2 and G2.
c. Use the Office Clipboard to copy the formula in E2 into cells E3:E5.
d. Use the Office Clipboard to copy the formula in E2 into cells E13:E16.
e. Change the amount in cell G2 to 2.873.
f. Save the worksheet.

7. Name and move a sheet.

a. Name the Sheet1 tab "Furniture."
b. Move the Furniture sheet so it comes after Sheet3.
c. Name the Sheet2 tab "Supplies."
d. Move the Supplies sheet after the Furniture sheet.
e. Save, preview, print and close the workbook, then exit Excel.

▶ Independent Challenges

1. You are the box-office manager for Brazil Nuts, a popular jazz band. Your responsibilities include tracking seasonal ticket sales for the band's concerts and anticipating ticket sales for the next season. Brazil Nuts sells four types of tickets: reserved seating, general admission, senior citizen tickets, and student tickets.

The 2000–2001 season includes five scheduled concerts: Spring Hop, Summer Blast, Fall Leaves, Winter Snuggle, and Early Thaw. You will plan and build a worksheet that tracks the sales of each of the four ticket types for all five concerts.

To complete this independent challenge:

a. Think about the results you want to see, the information you need to build into these worksheets, and what types of calculations must be performed.
b. Sketch sample worksheets on a piece of paper to indicate how the information should be laid out. What information should go in the columns? In the rows?
c. Start Excel, open a new workbook and save it as "Brazil Nuts" on your Project Disk.
d. Plan and build a worksheet that tracks the sales of each of the four ticket types for all five concerts. Build the worksheets by entering a title, row labels, column headings, and formulas.
e. Enter your own sales data, but assume the following: the Brazil Nuts sold 1000 tickets during the season; reserved seating was the most popular ticket type for all of the shows except for Winter Snuggle; no concert sold more than 20 student tickets.
f. Calculate the total ticket sales for each concert, the total sales for each of the four ticket types, and the total sales for all tickets. Name the worksheet "Sales Data."
g. Copy the Sales Data worksheet and name the copied worksheet "5% Increase." Modify this worksheet in the workbook so that it reflects a 5% increase in sales of all ticket types.
h. Use named ranges to make the worksheet easier to use. (*Hint*: If your columns are too narrow, position the cell pointer in the column you want to widen. To widen the column, click Format on the menu bar, click Column, click Width, choose a new column width, and then click OK.)
i. Type your name in a worksheet cell.
j. Save your work, preview and print the worksheets, then close the workbook and exit Excel.

2. You have been promoted to computer lab manager at Learn-It-All, a local computer training center. It is your responsibility to make sure there are enough computers for students during scheduled classes. Currently, you have five classrooms: four with IBM PCs and one with Macintoshes. Classes are scheduled Monday, Wednesday, and Friday in two-hour increments from 9 a.m. to 5 p.m. (the lab closes at 7 p.m.), and each room can currently accommodate 35 computers.

You plan and build a worksheet that tracks the number of students who can currently use available computers per two-hour class. You create your enrollment data, but assume that current enrollment averages at 80% of each room's daily capacity. Using an additional worksheet, you show the impact of an enrollment increase of 20%.

To complete this independent challenge:

a. Think about how to construct these worksheets to create the desired output.
b. Sketch sample paper worksheets to indicate how the information should be laid out.
c. Start Excel, open a new workbook and save it as "Learn-it-All" on your Project Disk.
d. Build the worksheets by entering a title, row labels, column headings, and formulas. Use named ranges to make the worksheets easier to use, and rename the sheets to identify their contents easily.
e. Use separate sheets for actual enrollment and projected changes.
f. Name each sheet so you know what's on it.
g. Type your name in a worksheet cell.
h. Save your work, preview and print the worksheets, then close the workbook and exit Excel.

3. The Beautiful You Salon is a small but growing beauty salon that has hired you to organize its accounting records using Excel. The store hopes to track its supplies using Excel once its accounting records are under control. Before you were hired, one of the bookkeepers entered expenses in a workbook, but the analysis was never completed.

To complete this independent challenge:

- **a.** Start Excel, open the workbook EX B-3 and save it as "Beautiful You Finances" on your Project Disk. The worksheet includes labels for functions such as the Average, Maximum, and Minimum amounts of each of the expenses in the worksheet.
- **b.** Think about what information would be important for the bookkeeping staff to know.
- **c.** Use the existing worksheet to create a list of the types of functions and formulas you will use, and the cells where they will be located. Indicate where you will have named ranges.
- **d.** Create your sketch using the existing worksheet as a foundation. Your worksheet should use range names in its formulas and functions.
- **e.** Rename Sheet1 "Expenses."
- **f.** Type your name in a worksheet cell.
- **g.** Save your work, then preview and print the worksheet.
- **h.** Close the workbook and exit Excel.

4. MediaLoft offers eligible employees a variety of mutual fund options in their 401(k) plan. These mutual funds are posted on MediaLoft's intranet site. As a newly eligible MediaLoft employee, you need to determine which mutual funds you want to invest in.

To complete this independent challenge:

- **a.** Start Excel, open a new workbook and save it on your Project Disk as "Mutual Fund Data."
- **b.** Connect to the Internet and go to the MediaLoft intranet site at http://www.course.com/illustrated/MediaLoft, click the link for the Human Resources page, then click the Employee Benefits link.
- **c.** Copy the available mutual fund data from the intranet site to Sheet1 of your workbook.
- **d.** Disconnect from the Internet.
- **e.** Name Sheet1 "Current Funds."
- **f.** On Sheet2, assume this year's annual contribution to your mutual funds will be $10,000. Name this sheet "Investment."
- **g.** Choose no more than 4 of the listed mutual funds for your investment, and decide on a percentage for each fund in your contribution.
- **h.** Create formulas that multiply those percentages by the total contribution ($10,000). (*Hint:* Use an absolute reference to determine the dollar amount for each mutual fund.)
- **i.** Assume that MediaLoft will match your contribution at a rate of 50¢ to your $1. Create formulas that determine how much your total annual investment will be, including the MediaLoft matching funds.
- **j.** Type your name in a worksheet cell.
- **k.** Preview, then print the Investment worksheet.
- **l.** Save and print your work.
- **m.** Exit Excel.

Visual Workshop

Create a worksheet similar to Figure B-22 using the skills you learned in this unit. Save the workbook as "Annual Budget" on your Project Disk. Type your name in cell A13, then preview and print the worksheet. (Your toolbars may look different from those shown in the figure.)

FIGURE B-22

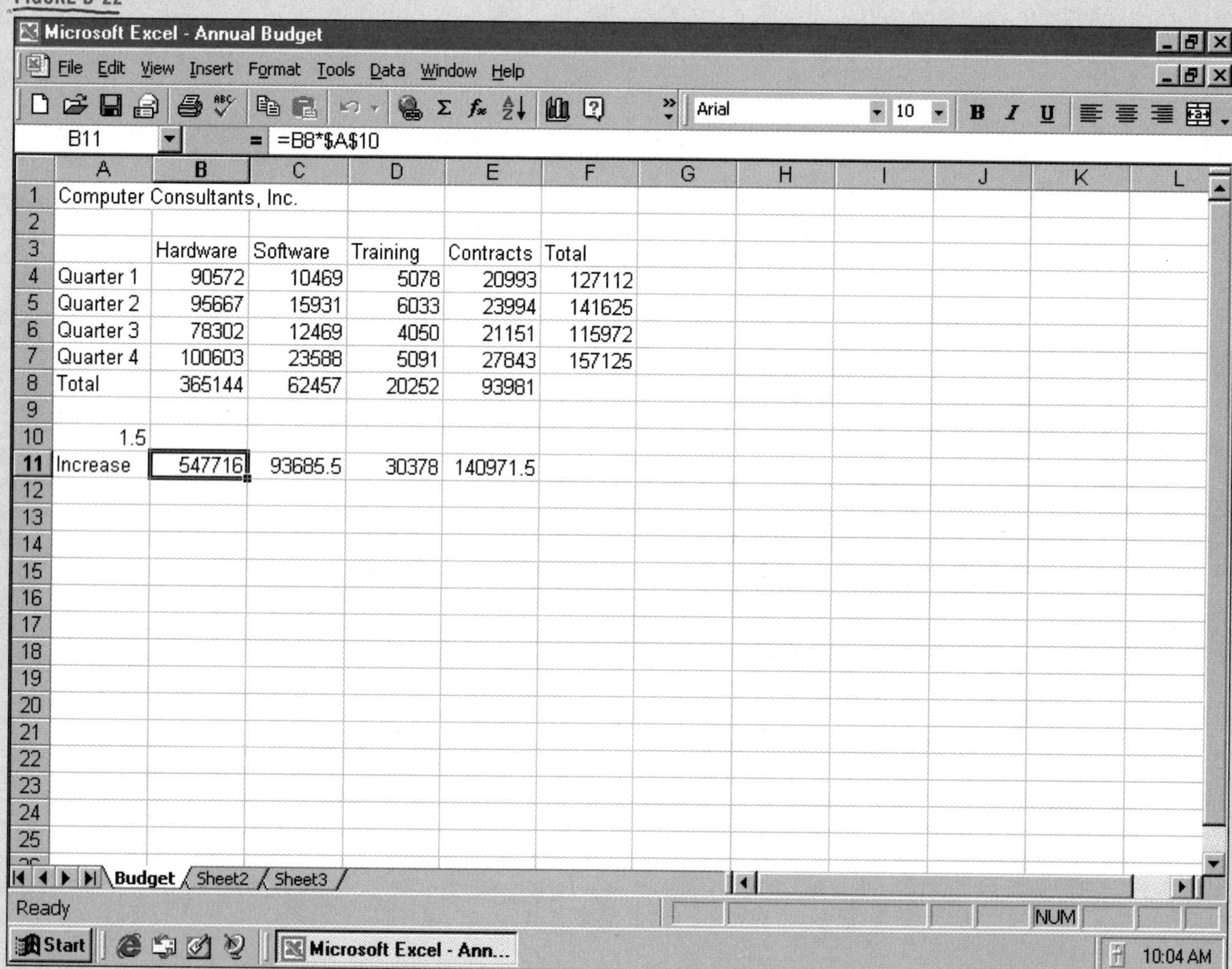

Formatting
a Worksheet

Objectives

- MOUS ▶ Format values
- MOUS ▶ Use fonts and font sizes
- MOUS ▶ Change attributes and alignment of labels
- MOUS ▶ Adjust column widths
- MOUS ▶ Insert and delete rows and columns
- MOUS ▶ Apply colors, patterns, and borders
- MOUS ▶ Use conditional formatting
- MOUS ▶ Check spelling

You use Excel's formatting features for a variety of reasons: to make a worksheet more attractive, to make it easier to read, or to emphasize key data. You do this by using colors and different fonts for the cell contents, adjusting column widths, and inserting and deleting columns and rows. The marketing managers at MediaLoft have asked Jim Fernandez to create a workbook that tracks advertising expenses for all MediaLoft stores. Jim has prepared a worksheet for the New York City store containing this information, which can be adapted later for the other stores. Now he uses formatting techniques to make the worksheet easier to read and to call attention to important data.

Excel 2000

Formatting Values

Formatting determines how labels and values appear in cells; it does not alter the data in any way. To format a cell, first select it, then apply the formatting. Cells and ranges can be formatted before or after data is entered. If you enter a value in a cell and the cell appears to display the data incorrectly, adjust the cell's format to display the value correctly. The Marketing department has requested that Jim begin by tracking the New York City store's advertising expenses. Jim developed a worksheet that tracks advertising invoices. He entered all the information and now wants to format some of the labels and values. Because some of the changes might also affect column widths, Jim makes all his formatting changes before changing the column widths.

Steps

1. Start Excel, click **Tools** on the menu bar, click **Customize**, click the **Options tab** in the Customize dialog box, click **Reset my usage data** to restore the default settings, click **Yes**, then click **Close**
2. Open the worksheet **EX C-1** from your Project Disk, then save it as **Ad Expenses**
   The store advertising worksheet appears in Figure C-1. Numeric data can be displayed in a variety of ways, such as having a leading dollar sign. When formatting, you select the range to be formatted up to the last entry in a column or row by selecting the first cell, pressing and holding [Shift], pressing [End], then pressing [→] for the row, or [↓] for the column.
3. Select the range **E4:E32**, then click the **Currency Style button** on the Formatting toolbar
   Excel adds dollar signs and two decimal places to the Cost ea. column data. Excel automatically resizes the column to display all the information supplied by the new formatting. Another option for formatting dollar values is to apply the comma format, which does not include the $ sign.
4. Select the range **G4:I32**, then click the **Comma Style button** on the Formatting toolbar
   The values in columns G, H, and I display the comma format. You can also format percentages using the Formatting toolbar.
5. Select the range **J4:J32**, click the **Percent Style button** on the Formatting toolbar, then click the **Increase Decimal button** on the Formatting toolbar to show one decimal place
   The % of Total column is now formatted with a percent sign (%) and one decimal place. Dates can be reformatted to display ranges in a variety of ways.
6. Select the range **B4:B31**, click **Format** on the menu bar, then click **Cells**
   The Format Cells dialog box opens with the Number tab in front and the Date format already selected. See Figure C-2. There are many types of date formats from which to choose.
7. Select the (first) format **14-Mar-98** in the Type list box, then click **OK**
   You decide you don't need the year to appear in the Inv Due column.
8. Select the range **C4:C31**, click **Format** on the menu bar, click **Cells**, click **14-Mar** in the Type list box, then click **OK**
   Compare your worksheet to Figure C-3.
9. Save your work

Trouble?

Click the More Buttons button to locate buttons that are not visible on your toolbars.

QuickTip

Select any range by clicking the top left cell, pressing and holding [Shift], then clicking the bottom right cell. [Shift] acts as a "connector" for contiguous cells.

QuickTip

The first DD-MM-YY format displays a single-digit date (such as May 1, 2000) as 1-May-00. The second format would display the same date as 01-May-00.

FIGURE C-1: Advertising expense worksheet

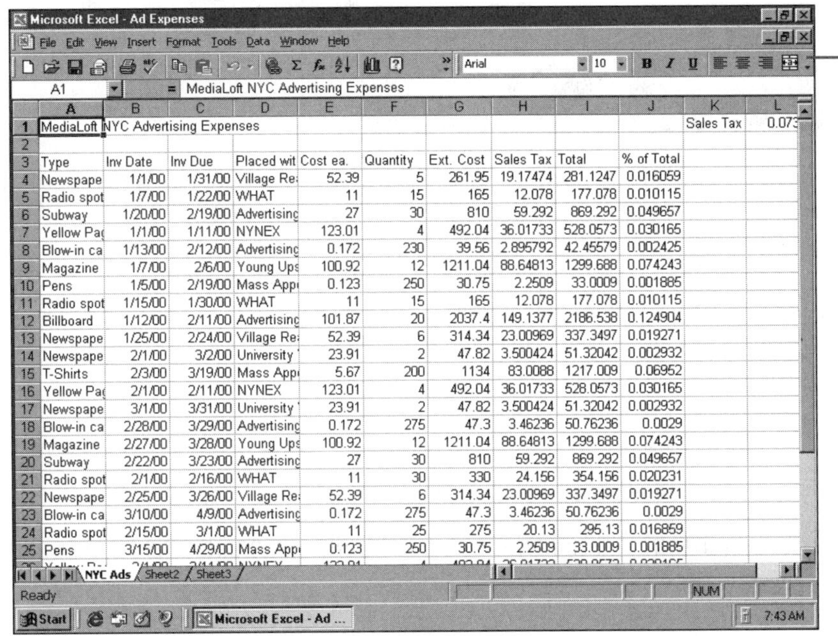

Your toolbars may not match the toolbars in the figures

FIGURE C-2: Format Cells dialog box

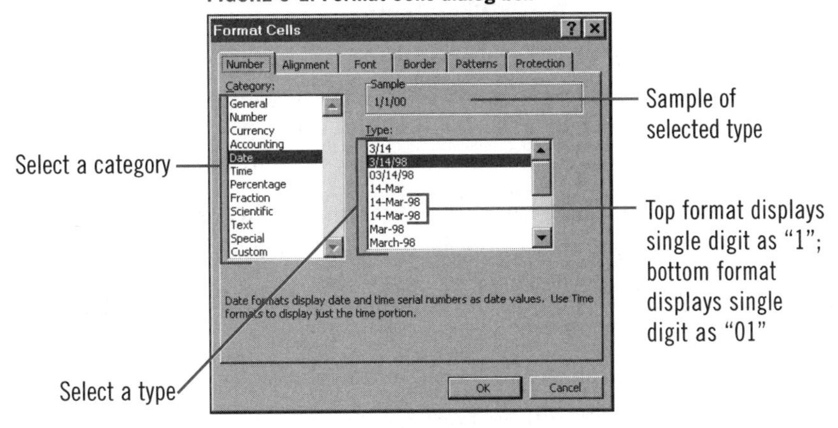

FIGURE C-3: Worksheet with formatted values

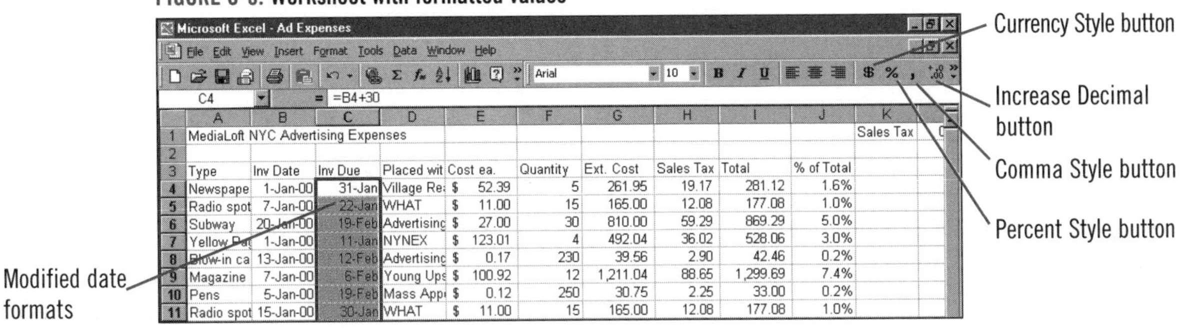

Using the Format Painter

A cell's format can be "painted" into other cells using the Format Painter button on the Standard toolbar. This is similar to using drag and drop to copy information, but instead of copying cell contents, you copy only the cell format. Select the cell containing the desired format, then click . The pointer changes to . Use this pointer to select the cell or range you want to contain the painted format.

Using Fonts and Font Sizes

A **font** is the name given to a collection of characters (letters, numerals, symbols, and punctuation marks) with a specific design. The **font size** is the physical size of the text, measured in units called **points**. The default font in Excel is 10 point Arial. You can change the font, the size, or both of any entry or section in a worksheet by using the Format command on the menu bar or by using the Formatting toolbar. Table C-1 shows several fonts in different sizes. Now that the data is formatted, Jim wants to change the font and size of the labels and the worksheet title so that they are better distinguished from the data.

Steps

QuickTip

You can also open the Format Cells dialog box by right-clicking selected cells, then clicking Format Cells.

1. Press **[Ctrl][Home]** to select cell A1
2. Click **Format** on the menu bar, click **Cells**, then click the **Font tab** in the Format Cells dialog box
   See Figure C-5.
3. Scroll down the **Font list** to see an alphabetical listing of the many fonts available on your computer, click **Times New Roman** in the Font list box, click **24** in the Size list box, then click **OK**
   The title font appears in 24 point Times New Roman, and the Formatting toolbar displays the new font and size information. Column headings can be enlarged to make them stand out. You can also change a font and increase the font size using the Formatting toolbar.
4. Select the range **A3:J3**, then click the **Font list arrow** on the Formatting toolbar
   Notice that the fonts on this font list actually look like the font they represent.
5. Click **Times New Roman** in the Font list, click the **Font Size list arrow,** then click **14** in the Font Size list
   Compare your worksheet to Figure C-6. Notice that some of the column headings are now too wide to display fully in the column. Excel does not automatically adjust column widths to accommodate formatting, you have to adjust column widths manually. You'll learn to do this in a later lesson.
6. Save your work

Using the Formatting toolbar to change fonts and font sizes

The font and font size of the active cell appear on the Formatting toolbar. Click the Font list arrow, as shown in Figure C-4, to see a list of available fonts. Notice that each font name is displayed in the selected font. If you want to change the font, first select the cell, click the Font list arrow, then click the font you want. You can change the size of selected text in the same way, by clicking the Font Size list arrow to display a list of available point sizes.

FIGURE C-4: Available fonts on the Formatting toolbar

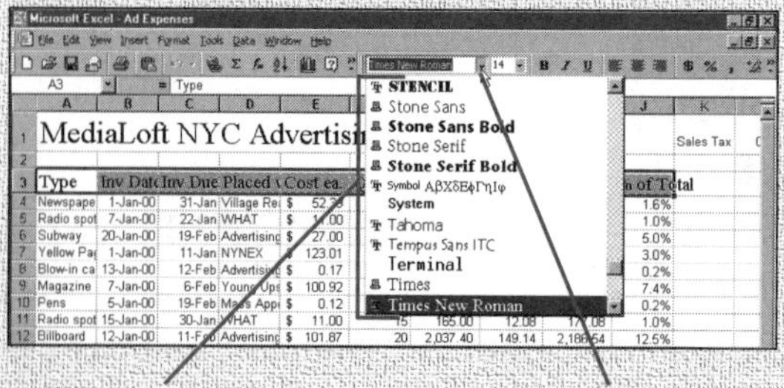

Available fonts installed on your computer (yours may differ)

Font list arrow

FIGURE C-5: Font tab in the Format Cells dialog box

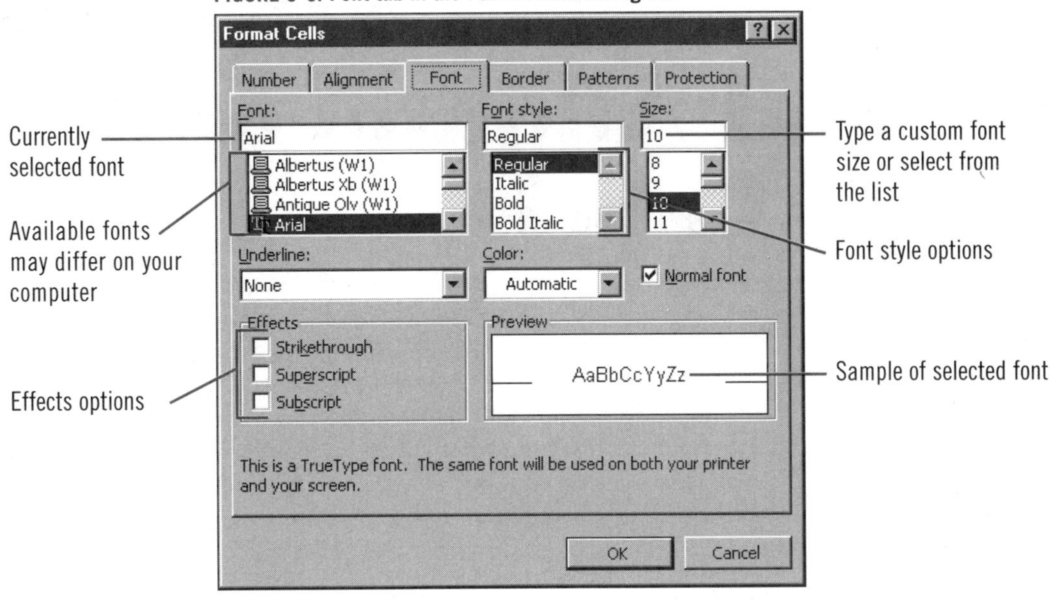

FIGURE C-6: Worksheet with formatted title and labels

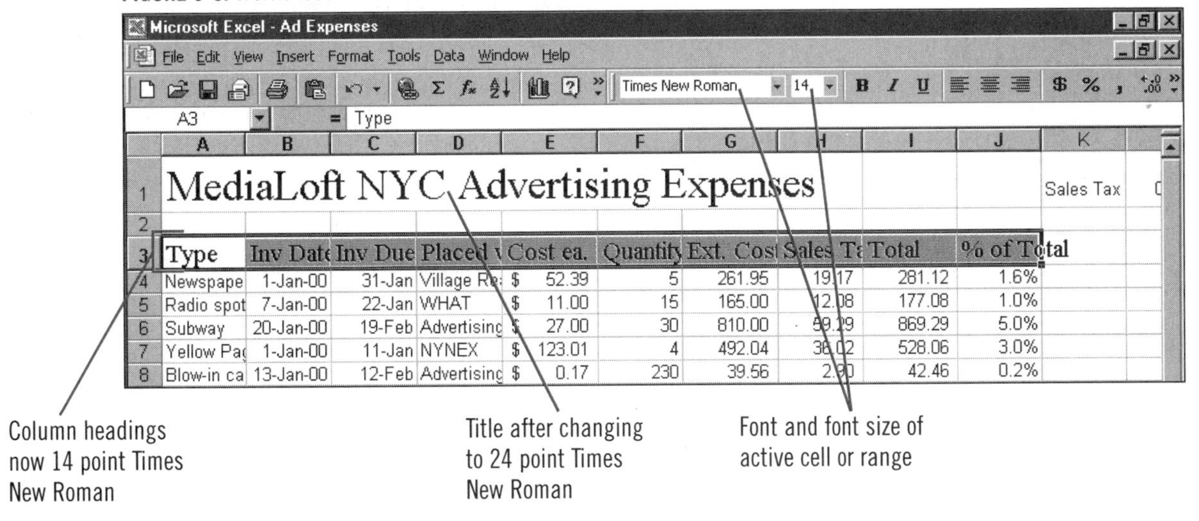

TABLE C-1: Types of fonts

font	12 point	24 point	font	12 point	24 point
Arial	Excel	Excel	Palatino	Excel	Excel
Comic Sans MS	Excel	Excel	Times	Excel	Excel

Changing Attributes and Alignment of Labels

Attributes are styling features such as bold, italics, and underlining that you can apply to affect the way text and numbers look in a worksheet. You can also change the **alignment** of labels and values in cells to be left, right, or center. Attributes and alignment can be applied from the Formatting toolbar, or from the Alignment tab of the Format Cells dialog box. See Table C-2 for a list and description of the available attribute and alignment buttons. Now that he has applied the appropriate fonts and font sizes to his worksheet labels, Jim wants to further enhance the worksheet's appearance by adding bold and underline formatting and centering some of the labels.

Steps

1. Press **[Ctrl][Home]** to move to cell A1, then click the **Bold button** on the Formatting toolbar
   The title Advertising Expenses appears in bold.
2. Select the range **A3:J3**, then click the **Underline button** on the Formatting toolbar
   Excel underlines the text in the column headings in the selected range.
3. Click cell **A3**, click the **Italics button** on the Formatting toolbar, then click
   The word "Type" appears in boldface italic type. Notice that the Bold, Italics, and Underline buttons are indented. You can apply one or more attributes to text simultaneously.
4. Click
   Excel removes italics from cell A3 but the bold and underline formatting attributes remain.
5. Select the range **B3:J3**, then click
   Bold formatting is added to the rest of the labels in the column headings. You want to center the title over the data columns A through J.
6. Select the range **A1:J1**, then click the **Merge and Center button** on the Formatting toolbar
   Merge creates one cell out of the 10 cells across the row, then Center centers the text in that newly created large cell. The title "MediaLoft NYC Advertising Expenses" is centered across ten columns. The alignment within individual cells can be changed using toolbar buttons.
7. Select the range **A3:J3**, then click the **Center button** on the Formatting toolbar
   Compare your screen to Figure C-7. Although they may be difficult to read, notice that all the headings are centered within their cells.
8. Save your work

QuickTip

Overuse of any attribute can be distracting and make a workbook less readable. Be consistent, adding emphasis the same way throughout.

QuickTip

Use formatting shortcuts on any selected range: [Ctrl][B] to bold, [Ctrl][I] to italicize, and [Ctrl][U] to underline.

QuickTip

To clear all formatting, click Edit on the menu bar, point to Clear, then click Formats.

TABLE C-2: Attribute and Alignment buttons on the Formatting toolbar

button	description	button	description
B	Bolds text		Aligns text on the left side of the cell
I	Italicizes text		Centers text horizontally within the cell
U	Underlines text		Aligns text on the right side of the cell
	Adds lines or borders		Centers text across columns, and combines two or more selected adjacent cells into one cell

FIGURE C-7: Worksheet with formatting attributes applied

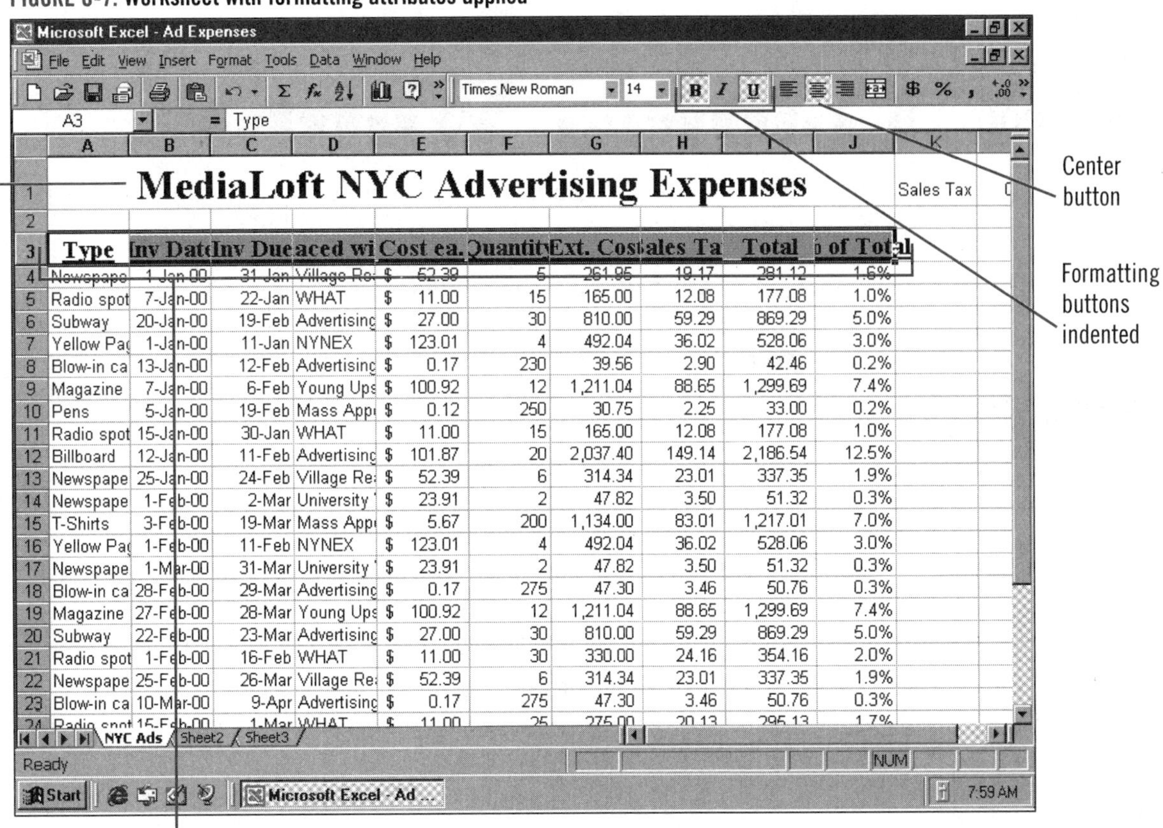

Using AutoFormat

Excel also has 17 predefined worksheet formats to make formatting easier and to give you the option of consistently styling your worksheets. AutoFormats are designed for worksheets with labels in the left column and top rows, and totals in the bottom row or right column. To use AutoFormatting, select the data to be formatted instantly—or place your mouse pointer anywhere within the range to be selected—click Format on the menu bar, click AutoFormat, then select a format from the sample boxes, as shown in Figure C-8.

FIGURE C-8: AutoFormat dialog box

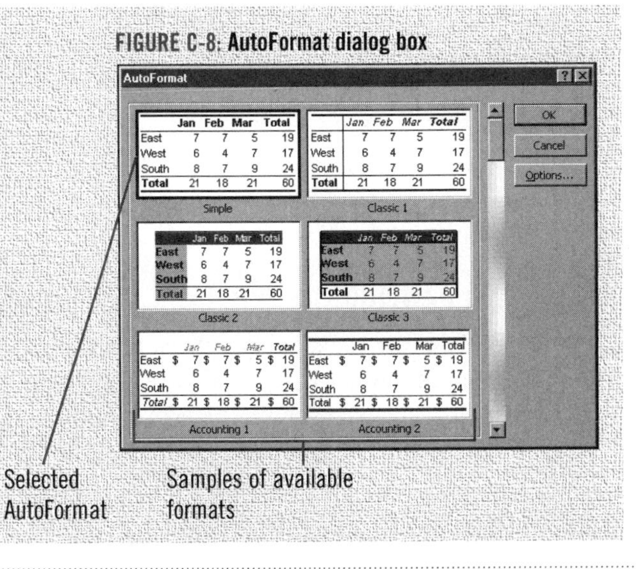

Excel 2000

Adjusting Column Widths

As your worksheet formatting continues, you might need to adjust the width of the columns to make your worksheet more usable. The default column width is 8.43 characters wide, a little less than one inch. With Excel, you can adjust the column width for one or more columns using the mouse or the Column command on the Format menu. Table C-3 describes the commands available on the Format Column menu. You can also adjust the height of rows to accommodate larger font sizes. Jim notices that some of the labels in column A have been truncated and don't fit in the cells. He decides to adjust the widths of the columns so that the labels display fully.

Steps

1. **Position the pointer on the column line between columns A and B selector buttons**
   The pointer changes to ↔, as shown in Figure C-9. You position the pointer on the right edge of the column that you are adjusting. Then you can drag the column edge, resizing it using the mouse.
2. **Click and drag the ↔ pointer to the right until column A is wide enough to accommodate all of the text entries in column A**
   Yellow Pages is the widest entry. The **AutoFit** feature lets you use the mouse to resize a column so it automatically accommodates the widest entry in a cell.
3. **Position the pointer on the column line between columns B and C in the column selector until it changes to ↔, then double-click**
   The width of column B is automatically resized to fit the widest entry, in this case, the column label.
4. **Use AutoFit to resize columns C, D, and J**
   You can also use the Column Width command on the Format menu to adjust several columns to the same width. Columns can be adjusted by selecting any cell in the column.
5. **Select the range F5:I5**
6. **Click Format on the menu bar, point to Column, then click Width**
   The Column Width dialog box appears. Move the dialog box, if necessary, by dragging it by its title bar so you can see the contents of the worksheet. The column width measurement is based on the number of characters in the Normal font (in this case, Arial).
7. **Type 11 in the Column Width text box, then click OK**
   The column widths change to reflect the new settings. See Figure C-10. If "#######" displays after you adjust a column of values, the column is too narrow to display the contents. You need to increase column width until it is wide enough to display the values.
8. **Save your work**

QuickTip

To reset columns to the default width, select the columns, then use the Column Standard Width command on the Format menu. Click OK in the dialog box to accept the default width.

Specifying row height

The Row Height command on the Format menu allows you to customize row height to improve readability. Row height is calculated in points, units of measure also used for fonts—one inch equals 72 points. The row height must exceed the size of the font you are using. Normally, you don't need to adjust row heights manually. If you format something in a row to be a larger point size, Excel will adjust the row to fit the largest point size in the row. You can also adjust row height by placing the ↕ pointer under the row selector button and dragging to the desired height.

FIGURE C-9: Preparing to change the column width

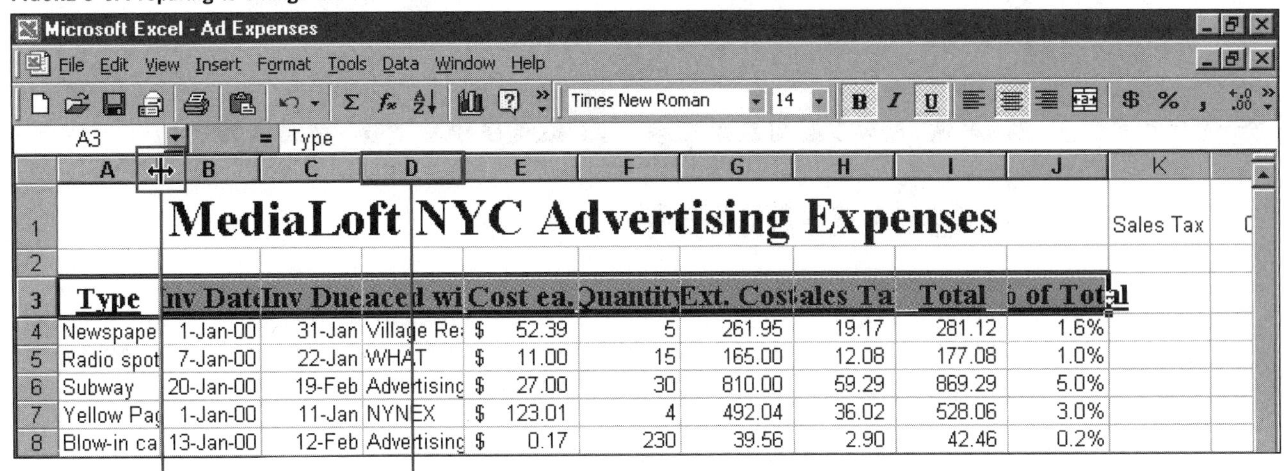

FIGURE C-10: Worksheet with column widths adjusted

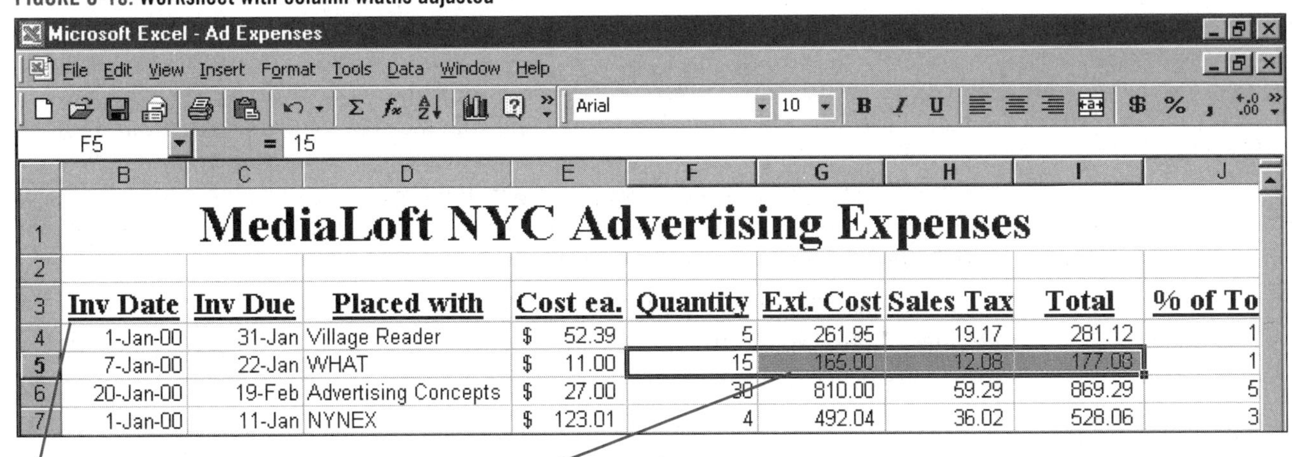

Excel 2000

TABLE C-3: Format Column commands

command	description
Width	Sets the width to a specific number of characters
AutoFit Selection	Fits the widest entry
Hide	Hide(s) column(s)
Unhide	Unhide(s) column(s)
Standard Width	Resets to default widths

Excel 2000

Inserting and Deleting Rows and Columns

As you modify a worksheet, you might find it necessary to insert or delete rows and columns to keep your worksheet current. For example, you might need to insert rows to accommodate new inventory products or remove a column of yearly totals that are no longer current. Jim has already improved the appearance of his worksheet by formatting the labels and values in the worksheet. Now he decides to improve the overall appearance of the worksheet by inserting a row between the last row of data and the totals. Jim has located a row of inaccurate data that should be deleted, as well as a column that is not necessary.

Steps

1. **Right-click cell A32, then click Insert**
   The Insert dialog box opens. See Figure C-11. You can choose to insert a column or a row, or you can shift the data in the cells in the active column right or in the active row down. An additional row between the last row of data and totals will visually separate the totals.

QuickTip

Inserting or deleting rows or columns that are specifically referenced in formulas can cause problems. Be sure to check formulas after inserting or deleting rows or columns.

2. **Click the Entire Row option button, then click OK**
   A blank row is inserted between the totals and the Billboard data for March 2000. Excel inserts rows above the cell pointer and inserts columns to the left of the cell pointer. When you insert a new row, the contents of the worksheet shift down from the newly inserted row. Notice that the formula result in cell E33 has not changed. When you insert a new column, the contents of the worksheet shift to the right from the point of the new column. To insert a single row, you can also click the row selector immediately below where you want the new row, right-click, and then click Insert. To insert multiple rows, select the same number of rows as you want to insert. A row can easily be selected for deletion using its **row selector button**, the gray box containing the row number to the left of the worksheet.
3. **Click the row 27 selector button**
   Hats from Mass Appeal Inc. will no longer be part of the advertising campaign. All of row 27 is selected, as shown in Figure C-12.

QuickTip

Use the Edit menu—or right-click the selected row and click Delete—to remove a selected row. Pressing [Delete] removes the contents of a selected row; the row itself remains.

4. **Click Edit in the menu bar, then click Delete**
   Excel deletes row 27, and all rows below this shift up one row.
5. **Click the column J selector button**
   The percentage information is calculated elsewhere and is no longer needed in this worksheet.
6. **Click Edit in the menu bar, then click Delete**
   Excel deletes column J. The remaining columns to the right shift left one column. You are satisfied with the appearance of the worksheet and decide to save the changes.
7. **Save your work**

FIGURE C-11: Insert dialog box

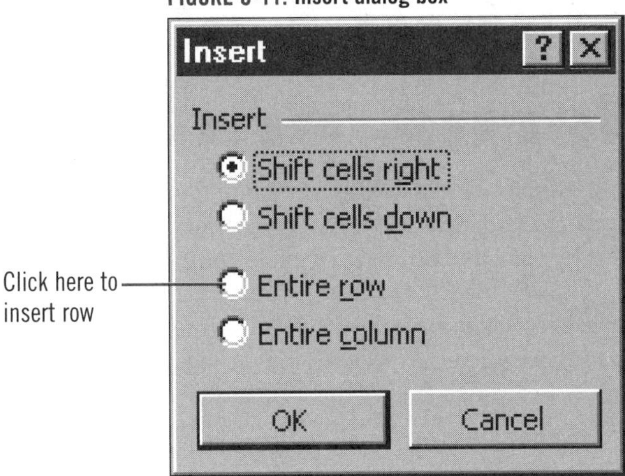

Click here to insert row

FIGURE C-12: Worksheet with row 27 selected

24	Radio spot	15-Feb-00	1-Mar	WHAT	$ 11.00	25	275.00	20.13	295.1
25	Pens	15-Mar-00	29-Apr	Mass Appeal, Inc.	$ 0.12	250	30.75	2.25	33.0
26	Yellow Pages	1-Mar-00	11-Mar	NYNEX	$ 123.01	4	492.04	36.02	528.0
27	Hats	20-Mar-00	4-May	Mass Appeal, Inc.	$ 7.20	250	1,800.00	131.76	1,931.7
28	Subway	20-Mar-00	19-Apr	Advertising Concepts	$ 27.00	30	810.00	59.29	869.2
29	Newspaper	1-Apr-00	1-May	University Voice	$ 23.91	2	47.82	3.50	51.3
30	Subway	10-Apr-00	10-May	Advertising Concepts	$ 27.00	30	810.00	59.29	869.2
31	Billboard	28-Mar-00	27-Apr	Advertising Concepts	$ 101.87	20	2,037.40	149.14	2,186.5
32									
33					$1,169.14	2034	16,311.75	1,194.02	17,505.7

NYC Ads / Sheet2 / Sheet3
Ready Sum=77375.83035 NUM
Start Microsoft Excel - Ad ... 8:04 AM

Row 27 selector button

Inserted row

CLUES TO USE

Using dummy columns and rows

When you add or delete a column or row within a range used in a formula, Excel automatically adjusts the formula to reflect the change. However, when you add a column or row at the end of a range used in a formula, you must modify the formula to reflect the additional column or row. To eliminate having to edit the formula, you can include a dummy column and dummy row which is a blank column or row included at the bottom of—but within—the range you use for that formula, as shown in Figure C-13. Then if you add another column or row to the end of the range, the formula will automatically be modified to include the new data.

FIGURE C-13: Formula with dummy row

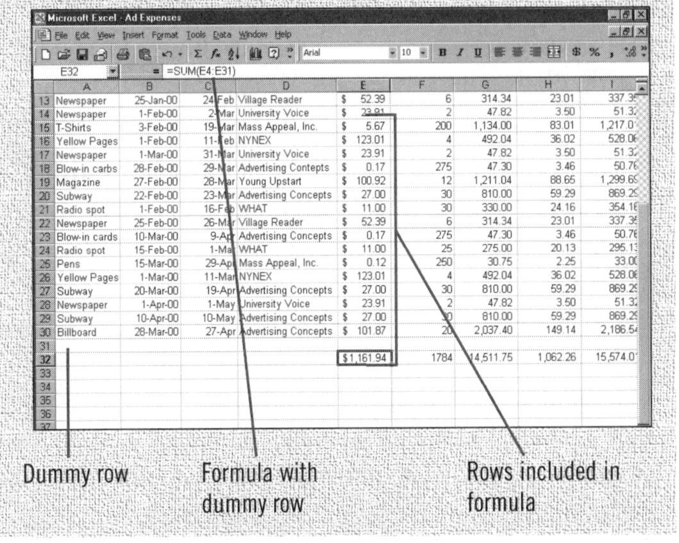

Excel 2000

Applying Colors, Patterns, and Borders

You can use colors, patterns, and borders to enhance the overall appearance of a worksheet and to improve its readability. You can add these enhancements using the Patterns tab in the Format Cells dialog box or by using the Borders and Color buttons on the Formatting toolbar. You can apply color or patterns to the background of a cell or range or to cell contents. And, you can apply borders to all the cells in a worksheet or only to selected cells. See Table C-4 for a list of border buttons and their functions. Jim decides to add a pattern, a border, and color to the title of the worksheet. This will give the worksheet a more professional appearance.

Steps

1. Press **[Ctrl][Home]** to select cell **A1**, then click the **Fill Color list arrow** on the Formatting toolbar
   The color palette appears.
2. Click **Turquoise** (fourth row, fourth color from the right)
   Cell A1 has a turquoise background, as shown in Figure C-14. Notice that Cell A1 spans columns A-I because of the Merge and Center command used for the title.
3. Click **Format** on the menu bar, then click **Cells**
   The Format Cells dialog box opens.
4. Click the **Patterns tab**, as shown in Figure C-15, if it is not already displayed
   When choosing a background pattern, consider that a high contrast between foreground and background increases the readability of the cell contents.
5. Click the **Pattern list arrow**, click the **Thin Diagonal Crosshatch Pattern** (third row, last pattern on the right), then click **OK**
   A border also enhances a cell's appearance. Unlike underlining, which is a text formatting tool, borders extend the width of the cell.
6. Click the **Borders list arrow** on the Formatting toolbar, then click the **Thick Bottom Border** (second row, second border from the left) on the Borders palette
   It can be difficult to view a border while the cell or range formatted with a border is selected.
7. Click cell **A3**
   The border is a nice enhancement. Font color can distinguish labels in a worksheet.
8. Select the range **A3:I3**, click the **Font Color list arrow** on the Formatting toolbar, then click **Blue** (second row from the top, third color from the right) on the palette
   The text changes color, as shown in Figure C-16.
9. Click the **Print Preview button** on the Standard toolbar, preview the first page, click **Next** to preview the second page, click **Close** on the Print Preview toolbar, then save your work

QuickTip

Use color sparingly. Excessive use can divert the reader's attention away from the data in the worksheet.

QuickTip

The default color on the Fill Color and Font Color buttons changes to the last color you selected.

CLUES TO USE

Using color to organize a worksheet

You can use color to give a distinctive look to each part of a worksheet. For example, you might want to apply a light blue to all the rows containing one category of data and a light green to all the rows containing another category of data. Be consistent throughout a group of worksheets, and try to avoid colors that are too bright and distracting.

FIGURE C-14: Background color added to cell

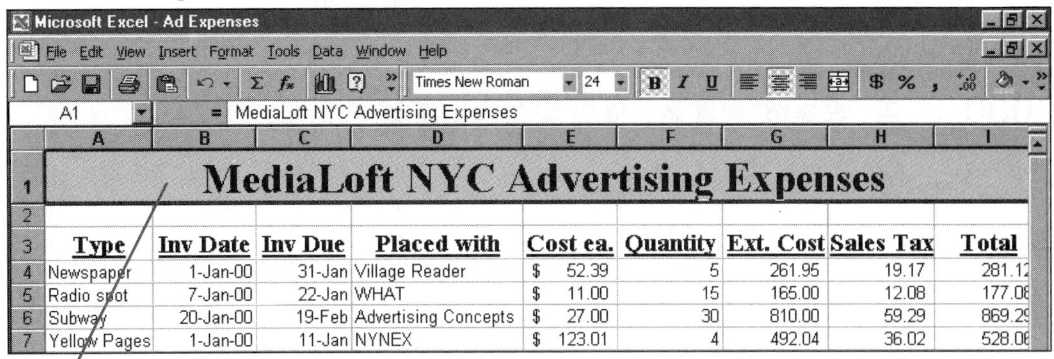

Cell A1 is affected by fill color

FIGURE C-15: Patterns tab in the Format Cells dialog box

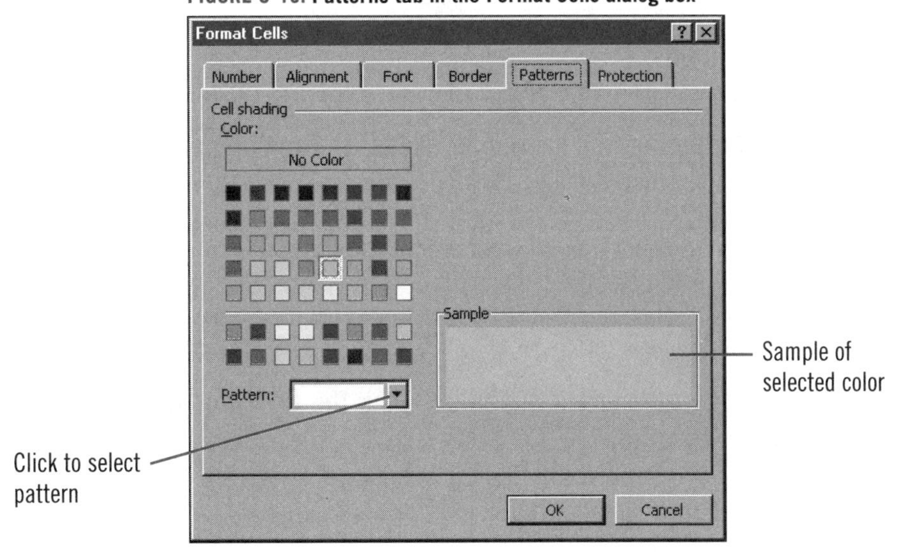

Click to select pattern

Sample of selected color

FIGURE C-16: Worksheet with colors, patterns, and border

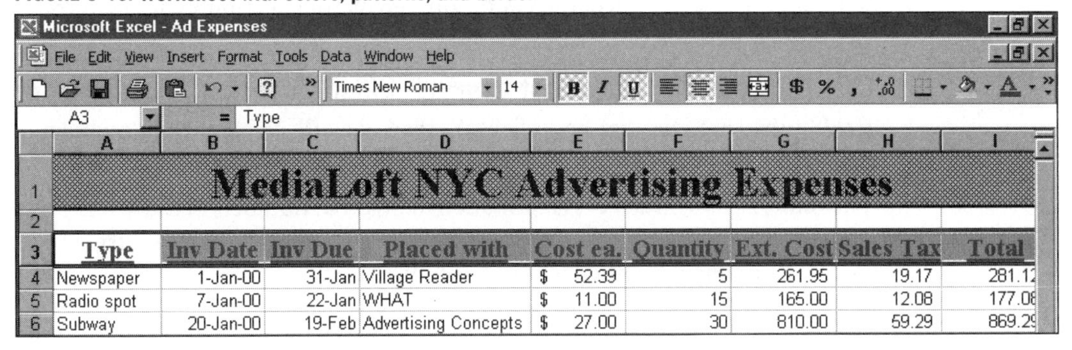

TABLE C-4: Border buttons

button	function	button	function	button	function
	Top Border		Inside Horizontal Border		Thick Bottom Border
	Bottom Border		Inside Vertical Border		Top and Bottom Border
	Left Border		Outside Border		Top and Double Bottom Border
	Right Border		No Border		Top and Thick Bottom Border
	Inside Border		Bottom Double Border		Thick Border

Excel 2000

Using Conditional Formatting

Formatting attributes make worksheets look professional and help distinguish different data. These same attributes can be applied depending on specific outcomes in cells. Automatically applying formatting attributes based on cell values is called **conditional formatting.** If the data meets your criteria, Excel applies the formats you specify. You might, for example, want advertising costs above a certain number to display in red boldface and lower values to display in blue. Jim wants the worksheet to include conditional formatting so that extended advertising costs greater than $175 display in red boldface. He creates the conditional format in the first cell in the extended cost column.

1. Click cell **G4**
   Use the scroll bars if necessary, to make column G visible.
2. Click **Format** on the menu bar, then click **Conditional Formatting**
   The Conditional Formatting dialog box opens, as shown in Figure C-17. Depending on the logical operator you've selected (such as "greater than" or "not equal to"), the Conditional Formatting dialog box displays different input fields. You can define up to three different conditions that let you determine outcome parameters, and then assign formatting attributes to each one. The condition is defined first. The default setting for the first condition is "Cell Value Is" "between."
3. To change the current condition, click the **Operator list arrow**, then click **greater than or equal to**
   The first condition is that the cell value must be greater than or equal to some value. See Table C-5 for a list of options. You can use a constant, formula, cell reference, or date. That value is set in the third box.

Trouble?

If the Office Assistant appears, close it by clicking the No, don't provide help now button.

4. Click the **Value text box**, then type **175**
   Once the value is assigned, the condition's formatting attributes are defined in the Format Cells dialog box.
5. Click **Format**, click the **Color list arrow**, click **Red** (third row, first column on the left), click **Bold** in the Font style list box, click **OK**, then click **OK** to close the Conditional Formatting dialog box
   The value, 261.95, in cell G4 is formatted in bold red numbers because it is greater than 175, meeting the condition to apply the format. The conditional format, like any other formatting, can be copied to other cells in a column.
6. With cell G4 selected, click the **Format Painter button** on the Standard toolbar, then drag the Formatting pointer to select the range **G5:G30**
   Once the formatting is copied, you reposition the cell pointer to review the results.
7. Click cell **G4**
   Compare your results to Figure C-18. All cells with values greater than or equal to 175 in column G are displayed in bold red text.
8. Press **[Ctrl][Home]** to move to cell A1
9. Save your work

FIGURE C-17: Conditional Formatting dialog box

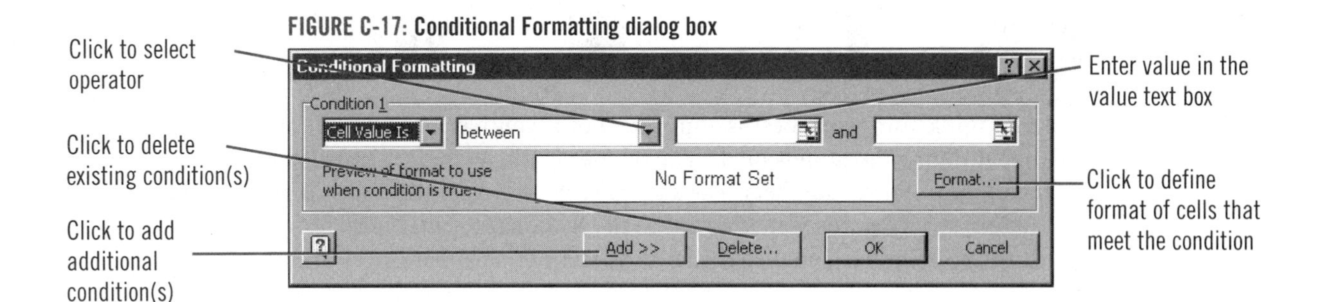

FIGURE C-18: Worksheet with conditional formatting

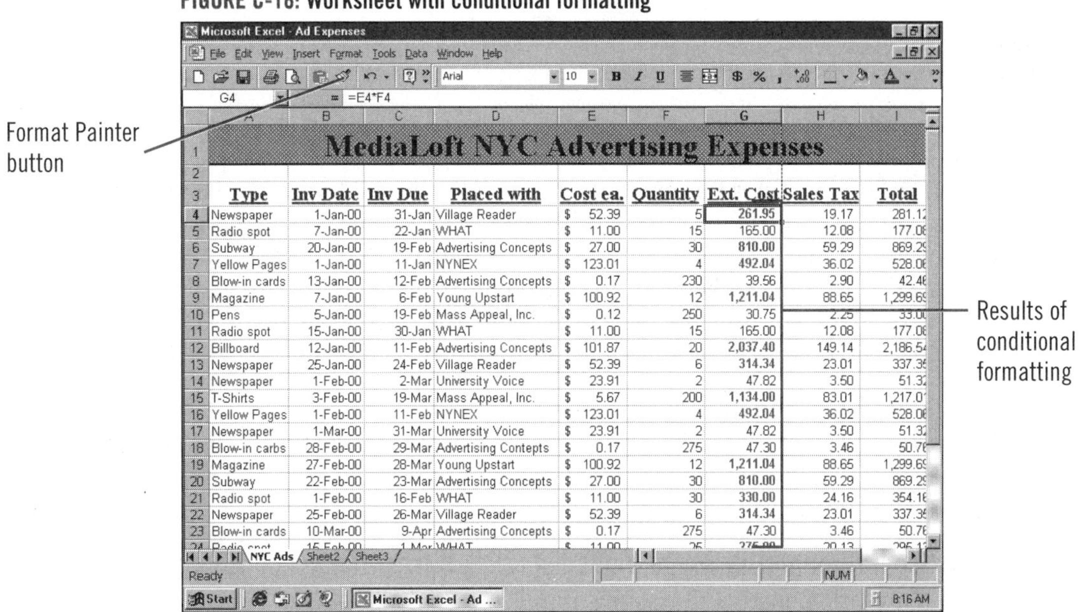

TABLE C-5: Conditional Formatting Options

option	mathematical equivalent	option	mathematical equivalent
Between	X>Y<Z	**Greater than**	Z>Y
Not between	B≯C≮A	**Less than**	Y<Z
Equal to	A=B	**Greater than or equal to**	A>=B
Not equal to	A≠B	**Less than or equal to**	Z<=Y

Deleting conditional formatting

Because it's likely that the conditions you define will change, any of the conditional formats defined can be deleted. Select the cell(s) containing conditional formatting, click Format on the menu bar, click Conditional Formatting, then click the Delete button. The Delete Conditional Format dialog box opens, as shown in Figure C-19. Click the checkboxes for any of the conditions you want to delete, then click OK. The previously assigned formatting is deleted—leaving the cell's contents intact.

FIGURE C-19: Delete Conditional Format dialog box

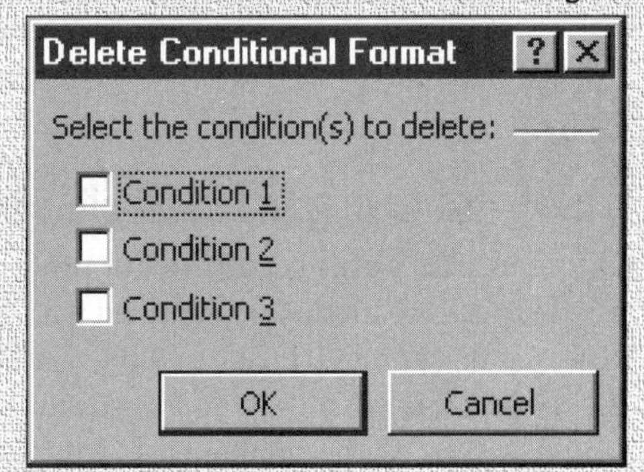

Excel 2000

Excel 2000

Checking Spelling

You may think your worksheet is complete, but if you haven't checked for spelling errors, you risk undermining the professional value of your work. A single misspelled word can cast doubt on the validity of your numbers. The spell checker in Excel is also shared by Word, PowerPoint, and Access, so any words you've added to the dictionary using those programs are available in Excel. Jim has completed the formatting for his worksheet and is ready to check its spelling.

Steps

1. Click the **Spelling button** on the Standard toolbar
   The Spelling dialog box opens, as shown in Figure C-20, with MediaLoft selected as the first misspelled word in the worksheet. The spell checker starts from the active cell and compares words in the worksheet to those in its dictionary. Any word not found in the dictionary causes the spell checker to stop. At that point, you can decide to Ignore, Change, or Add the word to the active dictionary. For any word, (such as MediaLoft or "Inv", the abbreviation of invoice) you have the option to Ignore or Ignore All cases the spell checker cites as incorrect.
2. Click **Ignore All** for MediaLoft
   The spell checker found the word "cards" misspelled and offers "crabs" as one possible alternative. As words are found, you can choose to ignore them, fix the error, or select from a list of alternatives.
3. Scroll through the Suggestions list, click **cards**, then click **Change**
   The word "Concepts" is also misspelled and the spell checker suggests the correct spelling.
4. Click **Change**
   When no more incorrect words are found, Excel displays the message box shown in Figure C-21.
5. Click **OK**
6. Press **[Ctrl][Home]**
7. Type your name in cell A2
8. Save your work, then preview and print the worksheet
9. Click **File** on the menu bar, then click **Exit** to close the workbook and exit Excel

Modifying the spell checker

Each of us uses words specific to our profession or task. Because the dictionary supplied with Microsoft Office cannot possibly include all the words that each of us needs, it is possible to add words to the dictionary shared by all the components in the suite. To customize the Microsoft Office dictionary used by the spell checker, click Add when a word that you know to be correct (but was not in the dictionary) is found. From then on, that word will no longer be considered misspelled by the spell checker.

FIGURE C-20: **Spelling dialog box**

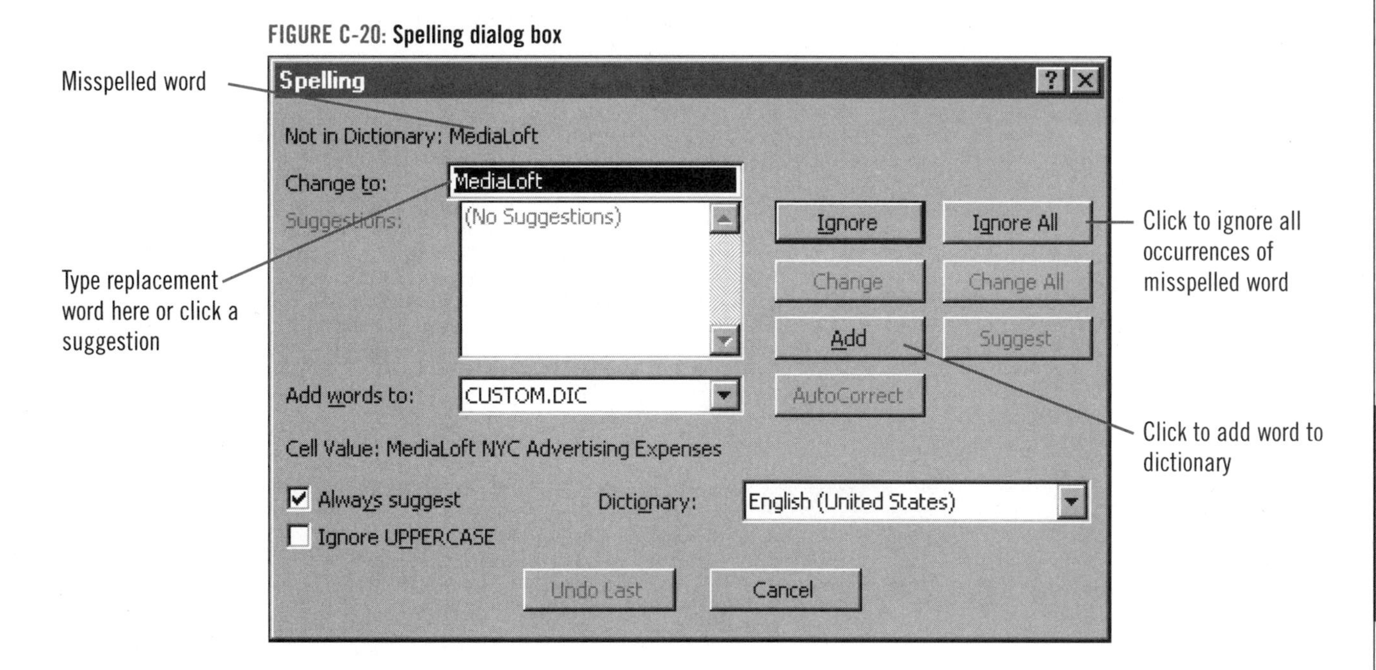

FIGURE C-21: **Spelling completed alert box**

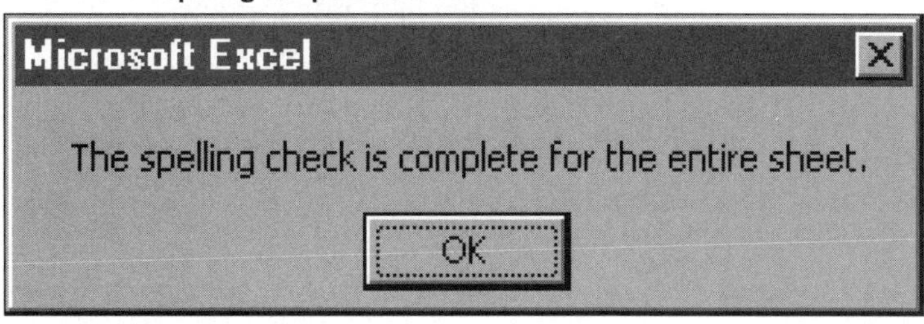

Practice

► Concepts Review

Label each element of the Excel worksheet window shown in Figure C-22.

FIGURE C-22

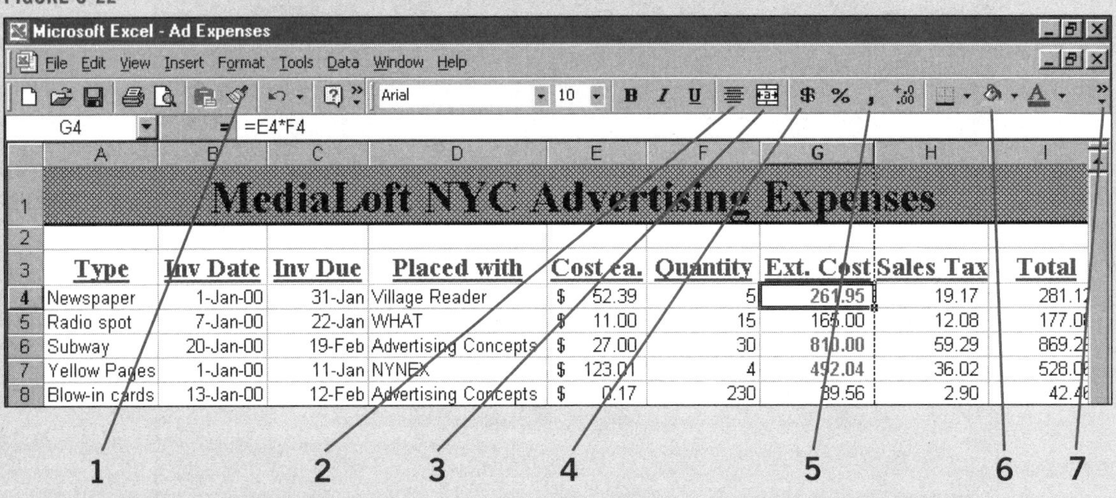

Match command or button with the statement that describes it.

8. **Format Cells**
9. **Edit Delete**
10. **Format Conditional Formatting**
11.
12.
13.

- **a.** Changes appearance of cell depending on result
- **b.** Erases the contents of a cell
- **c.** Checks the spelling in a worksheet
- **d.** Changes the appearance of selected cells
- **e.** Pastes the contents of the Clipboard in the current cell
- **f.** Changes the format to Currency

Select the best answer from the list of choices.

14. Which button increases the number of decimal places in selected cells?

a.
b.
c.
d.

15. Each of the following operators can be used in conditional formatting, *except*

a. Equal to.
b. Greater than.
c. Similar to.
d. Not between.

16. How many conditional formats can be created in any cell?

a. 1
b. 2
c. 3
d. 4

17. Which button center-aligns the contents of a single cell?

a. [button]
c. [button]
b. [button]
d. [button]

18. Which of the following is an example of the comma format?

a. $5,555.55
c. 55.55%
b. 5555.55
d. 5,555.55

Skills Review

1. Format values.

a. Start Excel and open a new workbook.
b. Enter the information from Table C-6 in your worksheet. Begin in cell A1, and do not leave any blank rows or columns.
c. Add the bold attribute to the equipment descriptions, as well as the Description and Totals labels.
d. Add the italics attribute to the Price and Sold labels.
e. Apply the Comma format to the Price and Sold data.
f. Insert formulas in the Totals column (multiply the price by the number sold).
g. Apply the Currency format to the Totals data.
h. Save this workbook as "Sports Equipment" on your Project Disk.

TABLE C-6

Best Sports Supreme, Inc.

Quarterly Sales Sheet

Description	Price	Sold	Totals
Ski boots	250	1104	
Rollerblades	175	1805	
Baseball bats	95	1098	
Footballs	35	1254	

2. Use fonts and font sizes.

a. Select the range of cells containing the column titles.
b. Change the font of the column titles to Times New Roman.
c. Increase the font size of the column titles to 14 point.
d. Resize the columns as necessary.
e. Select the range of values in the Price column.
f. Format the range using the Currency Style button.
g. Resize the columns, if necessary.
h. Save your changes.

3. Change attributes and alignment of labels.

a. Select the worksheet title Best Sports Supreme, Inc., then click the Bold button to apply boldface to the title.
b. Use the Merge and Center button to center the title over columns A through D.
c. Select the label Quarterly Sales Sheet, then click the Underline button to apply underlining to the label.
d. Select the range of cells containing the column titles, then click the Center button to center the column titles.
e. Save your changes, then preview and print the workbook.

4. Adjust column widths.

a. Use the AutoFit feature to resize the Price column.
b. Use the Format menu to resize the Description column to 16 and the Sold column to 9.
c. Save your changes.

5. Insert and delete rows and columns.

a. Insert a new row between rows 4 and 5.

b. Add Best Sports Supreme's newest product—a baseball jersey—in the newly inserted row. Enter "45" for the price and "360" for the number sold.

c. Use the fill handle to copy the formula in cell D4 to cell D5.

d. Add a new column between the Description and Price columns with the title "Location."

e. Delete the "Location" column.

f. Save your changes, then preview the workbook.

6. Apply colors, patterns, and borders.

a. Add a border around the value data.

b. Apply a lime background color to the Description column.

c. Apply a green background to the column labels in cells B3:D3. A3:D3

d. Change the color of the font in the first row of the data to green.

e. Add a pattern fill to the title in Row 1.

f. Type your name in an empty cell, then save your work.

g. Print the worksheet, then close the workbook.

7. Use conditional formatting.

a. Open the file EX C-2 from your Project Disk and save it as "Quarterly Report."

b. Create conditional formatting that changes values to blue if they are greater than 2500, ~~and changes them to green if less than 700~~.

c. Use the Bold button and Center button to format the column headings ~~and row titles~~.

d. Column A should be wide enough to accommodate the contents of cells A3:A9.

e. AutoFit the remaining columns.

f. Use Merge and Center in Row 1 to center the title over columns A:E.

g. Format the title Reading Room, Inc. using 14 point Times New Roman text. Fill the cell with a color and pattern of your choice.

h. Type your name in an empty cell, ~~then apply a green background and make the text color yellow~~.

i. Use the Edit menu to clear the cell formats of the cell with your name, then save your changes.

8. Check spelling.

a. Check the spelling in the worksheet using the spell checker.

b. Correct any spelling errors.

c. Save your changes, then preview and print the workbook.

d. Save, close the workbook, then exit Excel.

► Independent Challenges

1. Now that the Beautiful You Salon's accounting records are on Excel, they would like you to work on the inventory. Although more items will be added later, enough have been entered in a worksheet for you to begin your modifications.
To complete this independent challenge:

a. Start Excel, open the workbook EX C-3 on your Project Disk, and save it as "BY Inventory."
b. Create a formula that calculates the value of the inventory on hand for each item.
c. Use an absolute reference to calculate the sale price of each item.
d. Use enhancements to make the title, column headings, and row headings more attractive.
e. Make sure all columns are wide enough to see the data.
f. Add a row under #2 Curlers for "Nail Files," price paid $0.25, sold individually (each), with 59 on hand.
g. Before printing, preview the file so you know what the worksheet will look like. Adjust any items as needed, check spelling, and print a copy.
h. Use conditional formatting to display which items have 25 or less on hand. Choose colors and formatting.
i. Use cell formatting to add borders around the data in the Item column.
j. Delete the row with #3 Curlers.
k. Type your name in an empty cell, then preview and print the worksheet.
l. Save, close the workbook, then exit Excel.

2. Continuing your efforts with the Community Action Center, you need to examine the membership in comparison to the community more closely. To make the existing data look more professional and easier to read, you've decided to use attributes and your formatting abilities.
To complete this independent challenge:

a. Start Excel, open the workbook EX C-4 on your Project Disk, and save it as "Community Action."
b. Remove any blank columns.
c. Format the Annual Revenue column using the Currency format.
d. Make all columns wide enough to fit their data.
e. Use formatting enhancements, such as fonts, font sizes, and text attributes to make the worksheet more attractive.
f. Center-align the contents of cells containing column labels.
g. Design conditional formatting so that Number of Employee data greater than 50 employees displays in blue.
h. Before printing, preview the file so you know what the worksheet will look like. Adjust any items as needed, check spelling, type your name in an empty cell, save your work, and then print a copy.
i. Close the workbook and exit Excel.

3. Classic Instruments is a Miami-based company that manufactures high-quality pens and markers. As the finance manager, one of your responsibilities is to analyze the monthly reports from your five district sales offices. Your boss, Joanne Bennington, has just asked you to prepare a quarterly sales report for an upcoming meeting. Since several top executives will be attending this meeting, Joanne reminds you that the report must look professional. In particular, she asks you to emphasize the company's surge in profits during the last month and to highlight the fact that the Northeastern district continues to outpace the other districts.

To complete this independent challenge:

a. Plan and build a worksheet that shows the company's sales during the last three months. Make sure you include:

- The number of pens sold (units sold) and the associated revenues (total sales) for each of the five district sales offices. The five Classic Instruments sales districts include: Northeastern, Midwestern, Southeastern, Southern, and Western.
- Calculations that show month-by-month totals and a three-month cumulative total.
- Calculations that show each district's share of sales (percent of units sold).
- Formatting enhancements to emphasize the recent month's sales surge and the Northeastern district's sales leadership.

b. Prepare a worksheet plan that states your goal, lists the worksheet data you'll need, and identifies the formulas for the different calculations.

c. Sketch a sample worksheet on a piece of paper, indicating how the information should be organized and formatted. How will you calculate the totals? What formulas can you copy to save time and keystrokes? Do any of these formulas need to use an absolute reference? How will you show dollar amounts? What information should be shown in bold? Do you need to use more than one font? More than one point size?

d. Start Excel, then build the worksheet with your own sales data. Enter the titles and labels first, then enter the numbers and formulas. Save the workbook as "Classic Instruments" on your Project Disk.

e. Make enhancements to the worksheet. Adjust the column widths as necessary. Change the row height of row 1 to 30 points. Format labels and values, and change attributes and alignment.

f. Add a column that calculates a 15% increase in sales. Use an absolute cell reference in this calculation.

g. Type your name in an empty cell.

h. Before printing, preview the file so you know what the worksheet will look like. Adjust any items as needed, check spelling, and then print a copy.

i. Save your work before closing the file and exiting Excel.

4. As the MediaLoft office manager, you've been asked to assemble data on currently available office suites for use in a business environment. You use the World Wide Web to retrieve information about current software and then post the information on the MediaLoft intranet site. You also create an attractive worksheet for distribution to department managers.
To complete this independent challenge:

a. Start Excel, then open a new workbook and save it as "Software Comparison" on your Project Disk.
b. Connect to the Internet, go to the MediaLoft intranet site at http://www.course.com/illustrated/MediaLoft, then click the link for the Accounting page.
c. Print the Office Suite Analysis, disconnect from the Internet, then enter the data in the Software Comparison workbook.
d. Create a title for the worksheet in cell A1. Use the Merge and Center command to center the title over the worksheet columns.
e. Make sure each column is resized to accommodate its widest contents.
f. Format the labels for each suite manufacturer in bold, 12 point, Times New Roman font.
g. Format the labels for the type of program (for example, spreadsheets) in italics, 12 point, Times New Roman font.
h. Create a background color and a border for the title. Use a pattern to enhance the text.
i. Right-align the label for the suite price.
j. Use conditional formatting so that suites costing more than $375 display in red.
k. Type your name in a visible worksheet cell.
l. Save and print your work, then exit Excel.

Visual Workshop

Create the worksheet shown in Figure C-23, using skills you learned in this unit. Open the file EX C-5 on your Project Disk and save it as "Projected March Advertising Invoices." Create a conditional format in the Cost ea. column so that entries greater than 60 are displayed in red. (*Hint:* The only additional font used in this exercise is Times New Roman. It is 22 points in row 1, and 16 points in row 3.)

FIGURE C-23

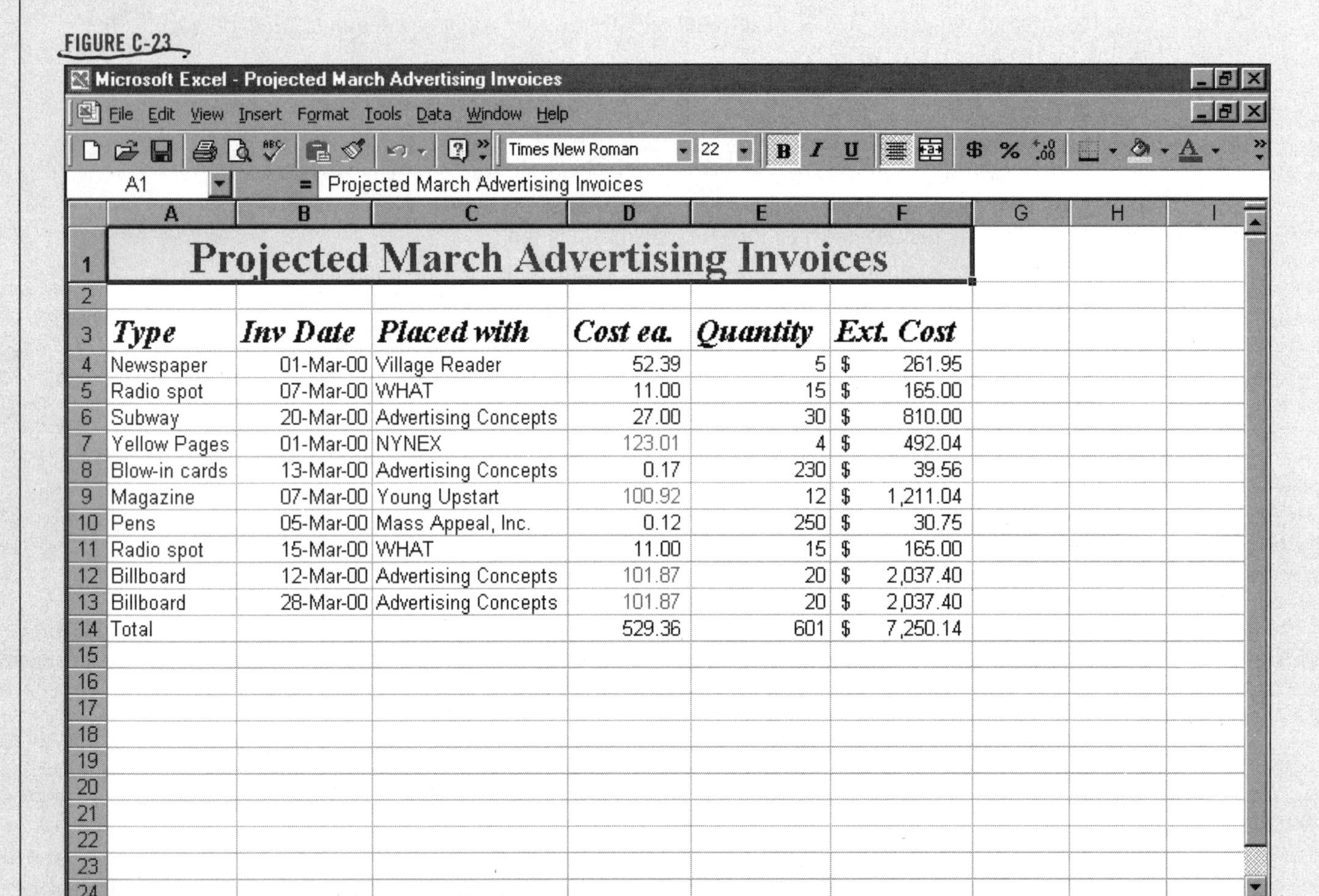

Projected March Advertising Invoices

Type	Inv Date	Placed with	Cost ea.	Quantity	Ext. Cost
Newspaper	01-Mar-00	Village Reader	52.39	5	$ 261.95
Radio spot	07-Mar-00	WHAT	11.00	15	$ 165.00
Subway	20-Mar-00	Advertising Concepts	27.00	30	$ 810.00
Yellow Pages	01-Mar-00	NYNEX	123.01	4	$ 492.04
Blow-in cards	13-Mar-00	Advertising Concepts	0.17	230	$ 39.56
Magazine	07-Mar-00	Young Upstart	100.92	12	$ 1,211.04
Pens	05-Mar-00	Mass Appeal, Inc.	0.12	250	$ 30.75
Radio spot	15-Mar-00	WHAT	11.00	15	$ 165.00
Billboard	12-Mar-00	Advertising Concepts	101.87	20	$ 2,037.40
Billboard	28-Mar-00	Advertising Concepts	101.87	20	$ 2,037.40
Total			529.36	601	$ 7,250.14

Excel 2000

Working with Charts

Objectives

- Plan and design a chart
- MOUS Create a chart
- MOUS Move and resize a chart
- MOUS Edit a chart
- MOUS Format a chart
- MOUS Enhance a chart
- MOUS Annotate and draw on a chart
- MOUS Preview and print a chart

Worksheets provide an effective way to organize information, but they are not always the best format for presenting data to others. Information in a selected range or worksheet can easily be converted to the visual format of a chart. Charts graphically communicate the relationships of data in a worksheet. In this unit, you will learn how to create a chart, how to edit a chart and change the chart type, how to add text annotations and arrows to a chart, and how to preview and print a chart. For the annual meeting Jim Fernandez needs to create a chart showing the six-month sales history at MediaLoft for the stores in the eastern division. He wants to illustrate the trend of growth in this division.

Excel 2000

Planning and Designing a Chart

Before creating a chart, you need to plan the information you want your chart to show and how you want it to look.  In early June, the Marketing department launched a regional advertising campaign for the eastern division. The results of the campaign were increased sales during the fall months. Jim wants his chart for the annual meeting to illustrate the growth trend of sales in MediaLoft's eastern division stores and to highlight this dramatic sales increase.

Jim uses the worksheet shown in Figure D-1 and the following guidelines to plan the chart:

Determine the purpose of the chart, and identify the data relationships you want to communicate visually

You want to create a chart that shows sales throughout MediaLoft's eastern division from July through December. In particular, you want to highlight the increase in sales that occurred as a result of the advertising campaign.

Determine the results you want to see, and decide which chart type is most appropriate to use

Different charts have different strengths and display data in various ways. How you want your data displayed—and how you want that data interpreted—can help you determine the best chart type to use. Table D-1 describes several different types of charts and when each one is best used. Because you want to compare data (sales in multiple locations) over a time period (the months July through December), you decide to use a column chart.

Identify the worksheet data you want the chart to illustrate

You are using data from the worksheet titled "MediaLoft Eastern Division Stores" as shown in Figure D-1. This worksheet contains the sales data for the four stores in the eastern division from July through December.

Sketch the chart, then use your sketch to decide where the chart elements should be placed

You sketch your chart as shown in Figure D-2. You put the months on the horizontal axis (the **x-axis**) and the monthly sales figures on the vertical axis (the **y-axis**). The **tick marks** on the y-axis create a scale of measure for each value. Each value in a cell you select for your chart is a **data point**. In any chart, a **data marker** visually represents each data point, which in this case is a column. A collection of related data points is a **data series**. In this chart, there are four data series (Boston, Chicago, Kansas City, and New York), so you include a **legend** to make it easy to identify them.

FIGURE D-1: Worksheet containing sales data

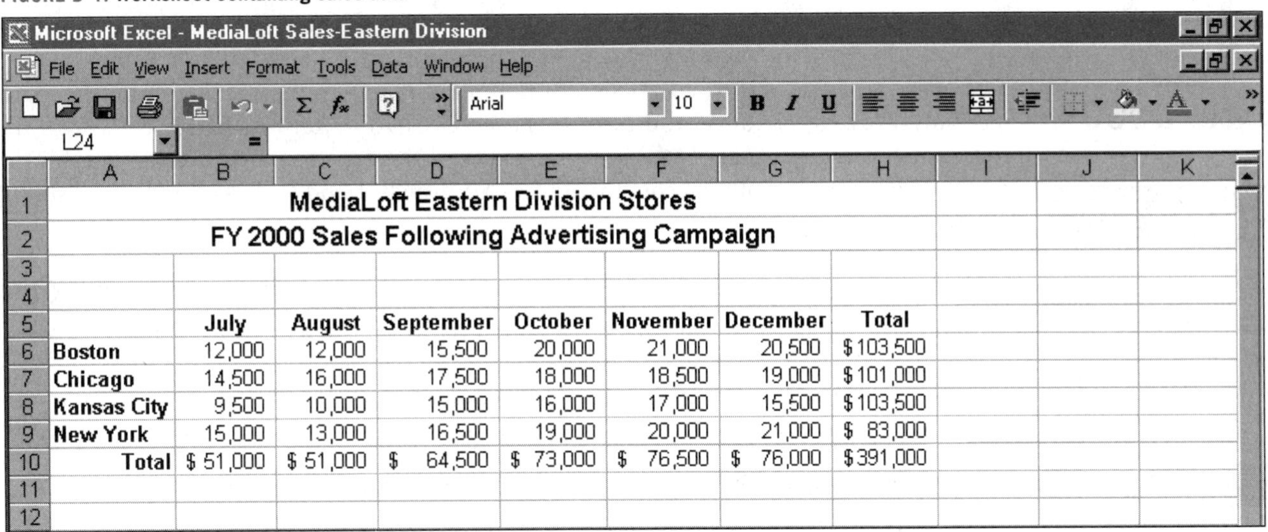

Microsoft Excel - MediaLoft Sales-Eastern Division

MediaLoft Eastern Division Stores

FY 2000 Sales Following Advertising Campaign

	July	August	September	October	November	December	Total
Boston	12,000	12,000	15,500	20,000	21,000	20,500	$103,500
Chicago	14,500	16,000	17,500	18,000	18,500	19,000	$101,000
Kansas City	9,500	10,000	15,000	16,000	17,000	15,500	$103,500
New York	15,000	13,000	16,500	19,000	20,000	21,000	$ 83,000
Total	$ 51,000	$ 51,000	$ 64,500	$ 73,000	$ 76,500	$ 76,000	$391,000

FIGURE D-2: Sketch of the column chart

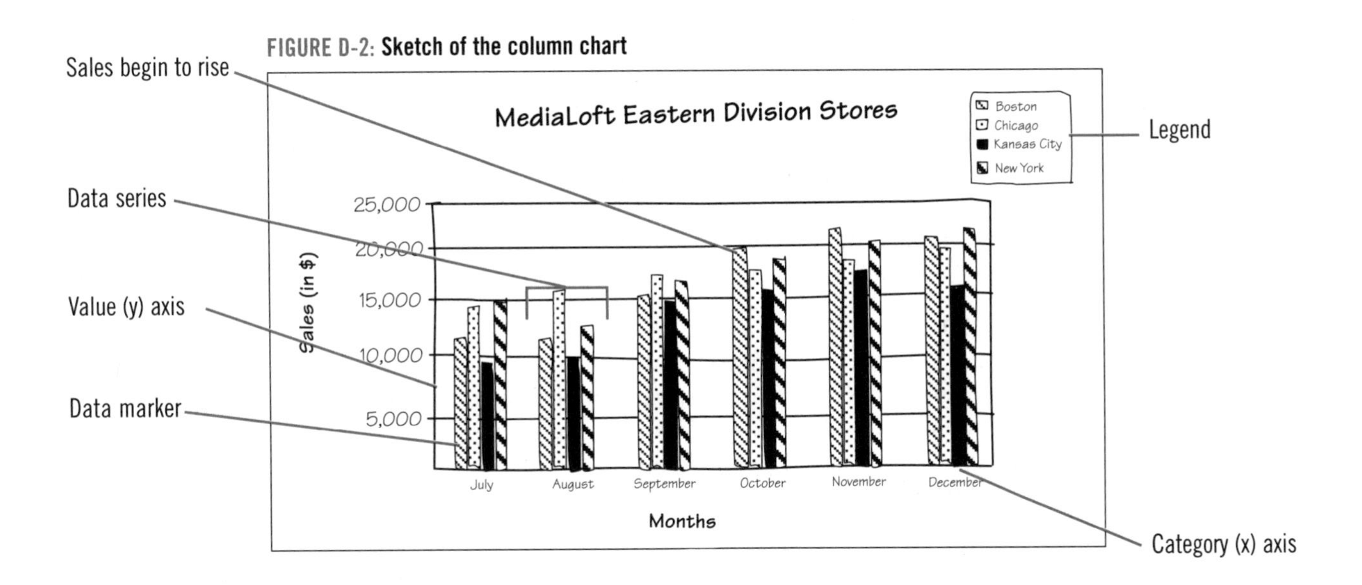

TABLE D-1: Commonly used chart types

type	button	description
Area		Shows how volume changes over time
Bar		Compares distinct objects over time using a horizontal format; sometimes referred to as a horizontal bar chart in other spreadsheet programs
Column		Compares distinct objects over time using a vertical format; the Excel default; sometimes referred to as a bar chart in other spreadsheet programs
Line		Compares trends over even time intervals; similar to an area chart
Pie		Compares sizes of pieces as part of a whole; can have slices pulled away from the pie, or "exploded"
XY (scatter)		Compares trends over uneven time or measurement intervals; used in scientific and engineering disciplines for trend spotting and extrapolation
Combination	none	Combines a column and line chart to compare data requiring different scales of measure

Excel 2000

Creating a Chart

To create a chart in Excel, you first select the range containing the data you want to chart. Once you've selected a range, you can use the Excel Chart Wizard to lead you through the process of creating the chart. Using the worksheet containing the sales data for the eastern division, Jim creates a chart that shows the growth trend that occurred as a result of the advertising campaign.

QuickTip

To reset toolbars, click Tools on the menu bar, click Customize, click Reset my usage data, click Yes, then click Close.

Trouble?

Click the More Buttons button to locate buttons that are not visible on your toolbars.

1. **Start Excel, reset your toolbars to their default settings, open the workbook EX D-1 from your Project Disk, then save it as MediaLoft Sales-Eastern Division**
   You want the chart to include the monthly sales figures for each of the eastern division stores, as well as month and store labels. You don't include the Total columns because the monthly figures make up the totals and these figures would skew the chart.
2. **Select the range A5:G9, then click the Chart Wizard button on the Standard toolbar**
   This range includes the cells that will be charted. The Chart Wizard opens. The Chart Wizard - Step 1 of 4 - Chart Type dialog box lets you choose the type of chart you want to create. See Figure D-3. You can see a preview of the chart by clicking and holding the Press and Hold to View Sample button.
3. **Click Next to accept Column, the default chart type**
   The Chart Wizard - Step 2 of 4 - Chart Source Data dialog box lets you choose the data being charted and whether the series are in rows or columns. You want to chart the effect of sales for each store over the time period. Currently, the rows are accurately selected as the data series, as specified by the Series in option button located under the Data range. Since you selected the data before clicking the Chart Wizard button, Excel converted the range to absolute values and the correct range =Sheet1!$A$5:$G$9 displays in the Data range text box.
4. **Click Next**
   The Chart Wizard - Step 3 of 4 - Chart Options dialog box shows a sample chart using the data you selected. Notice that the store locations (the rows in the selected range) are plotted according to the months (the columns in the selected range), and that the months were added as labels for each data series. Notice also that there is a legend showing each location and its corresponding color on the chart. Here, you can choose to keep the legend, add a chart title, gridlines, data labels, data table, and add axis titles.
5. **Click the Chart title text box, then type MediaLoft Sales - Eastern Division**
   After a moment, the title appears in the Sample Chart box. See Figure D-4.
6. **Click Next**
   In the Chart Wizard - Step 4 of 4 - Chart Location dialog box, you determine the placement of the chart in the workbook. You can display a chart as an object on the current sheet, on any other existing sheet, or on a newly created chart sheet. A **chart sheet** in a workbook contains only a chart that is linked to the worksheet data. Displaying the chart as an object in the sheet containing the data will help Jim emphasize his point at the annual meeting.
7. **Click Finish**
   The column chart appears and the Chart toolbar opens, either docked, as shown in Figure D-5, or floating. Your chart might be in a different location and look slightly different. You will adjust the chart's location and size in the next lesson. The **selection handles**, the small squares at the corners and sides of the chart's border, indicate that the chart is selected. Anytime a chart is selected, as it is now, a blue border surrounds the data range, a green border surrounds the row labels, and a purple border surrounds the column labels. If you want to delete a chart, select it, then press [Delete].
8. **Save your work**

Trouble?

If you are using a small monitor, your chart may appear distorted. If so, you'll need to move it to a blank area of the worksheet and then enlarge it before continuing with the lessons in this unit. See your instructor or technical support person for assistance.

FIGURE D-3: First Chart Wizard dialog box

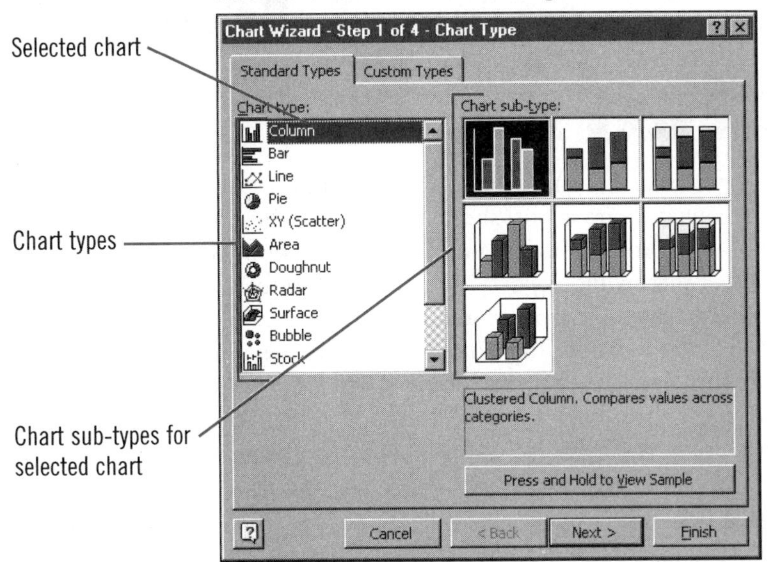

FIGURE D-4: Third Chart Wizard dialog box

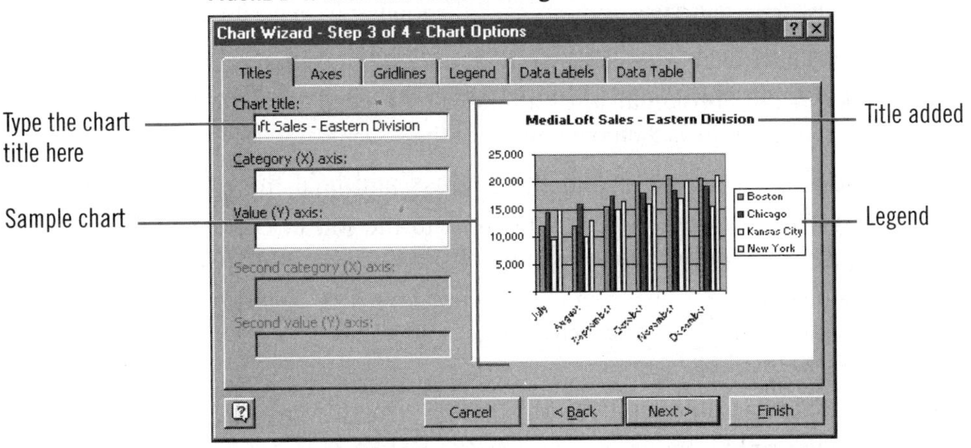

FIGURE D-5: Worksheet with column chart

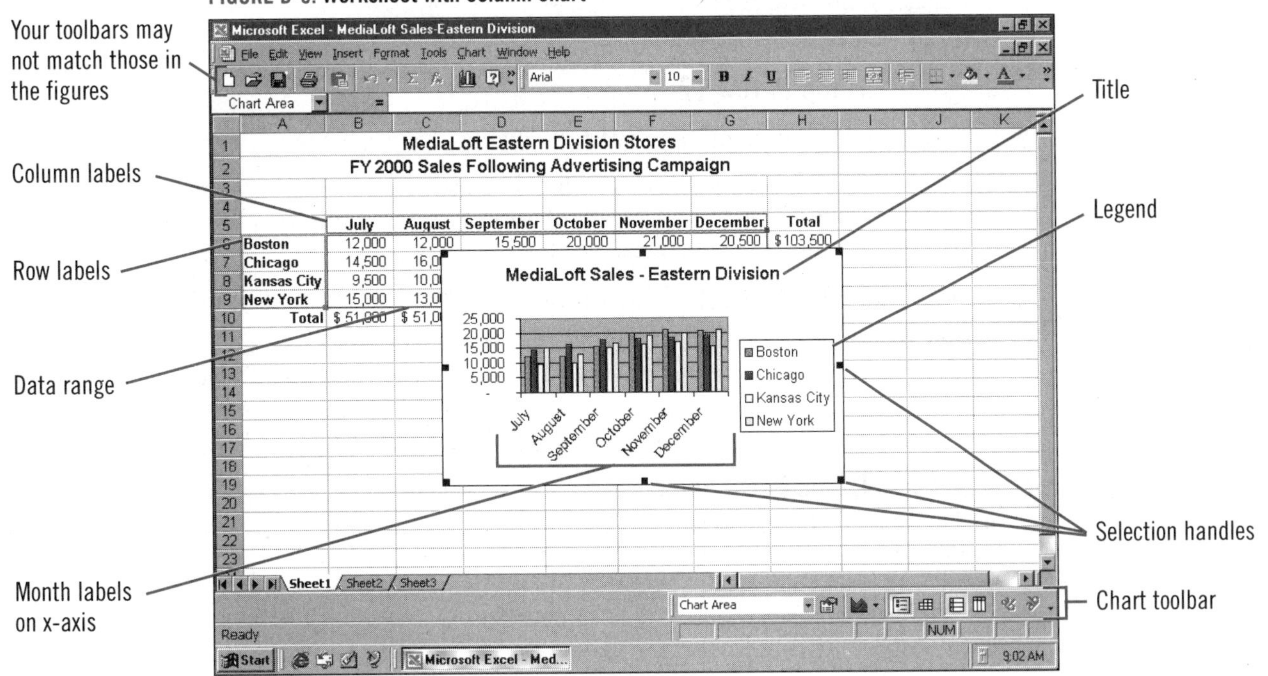

Excel 2000

Moving and Resizing a Chart

Charts are graphics, or drawn **objects**, and are not in a specific cell or range address. You can move a chart anywhere on a worksheet without affecting formulas or data in the worksheet. Resize a chart to improve its appearance by dragging the selection handles. You can even put a chart on another sheet without worrying about cell formulas. Drawn objects such as charts contain other objects that you can move and resize. To move an object, select it, then drag it or cut and copy it to a new location. To resize an object, use the selection handles. When you select a chart object, the name of the selected object appears in the Chart Objects list box on the Chart toolbar, and in the name box. Jim wants to increase the size of the chart and position it below the worksheet data. He also wants to change the position of the legend.

QuickTip

When a chart is selected, the Chart menu appears on the menu bar.

1. **Make sure the chart is still selected, then position the pointer over the chart**
   The pointer shape indicates that you can move the chart or use a selection handle to resize it. For a table of commonly used pointers, refer to Table D-2. On occasion, the Chart toolbar obscures your view. You can dock the toolbar to make it easier to see your work.
2. **If the chart toolbar is floating, click the Chart toolbar's title bar, drag it to the right edge of the status bar until it docks, then release the mouse button**
   The toolbar is docked on the bottom of the screen.
3. **Place the pointer on the chart, press and hold the left mouse button, using ✥ drag the upper left edge of the chart to the top of row 13 and the left edge of the chart to the left border of column A, then release the mouse button**
   A dotted outline of the chart perimeter appears as the chart is being moved. The chart is in the new location. Resizing a chart doesn't affect the data in the chart, only the way the chart looks on the sheet.
4. **Position the pointer on the right-middle selection handle until it changes to ↔, then drag the right edge of the chart to the right edge of column H**
   The chart is widened. See Figure D-6.
5. **Position the pointer over the top middle selection handle until it changes to ↕, then drag it to the top of row 12**
6. **If the labels for the months do not fully display, position the pointer over the bottom middle selection handle until it changes to ↕, then drag down to display the months**
   You can move the legend to improve the chart's appearance. You want to align the top of the legend with the top of the plot area.
7. **Click the legend to select it, then drag the legend using the pointer to the upper-right corner of the chart until it is aligned with the plot area**
   Selection handles appear around the legend when you click it; "Legend" appears in the Chart Objects list box on the Chart toolbar as well as in the name box, and a dotted outline of the legend perimeter appears as you drag. Changing the original Excel data modifies the legend text.
8. **Click cell A9, type NYC, then click ✓**
   See Figure D-7. The legend is repositioned and the legend entry for the New York City store is changed.
9. **Save your work**

FIGURE D-6: Worksheet with resized and repositioned chart

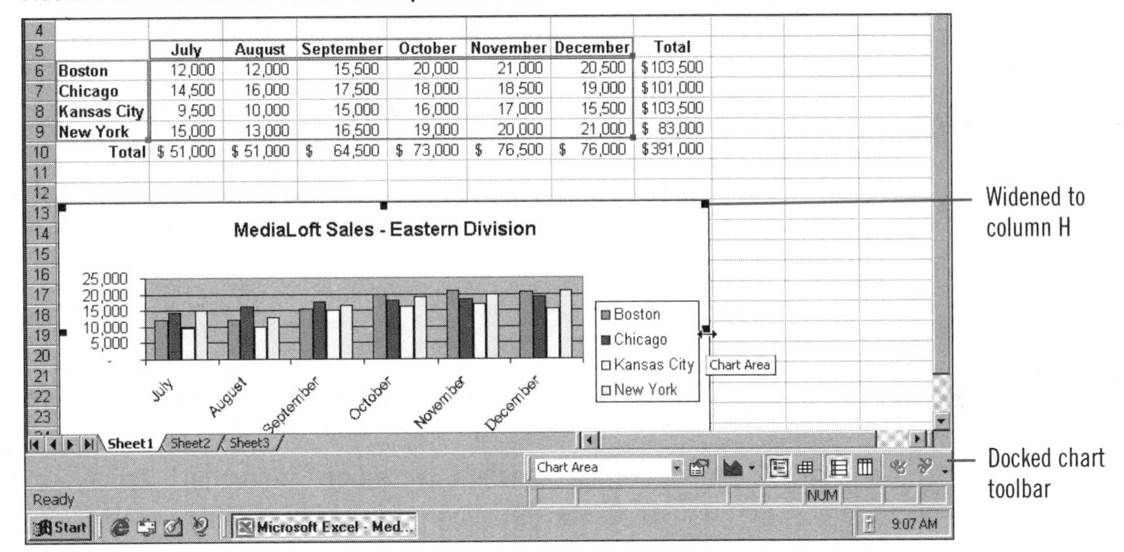

FIGURE D-7: Worksheet with repositioned legend

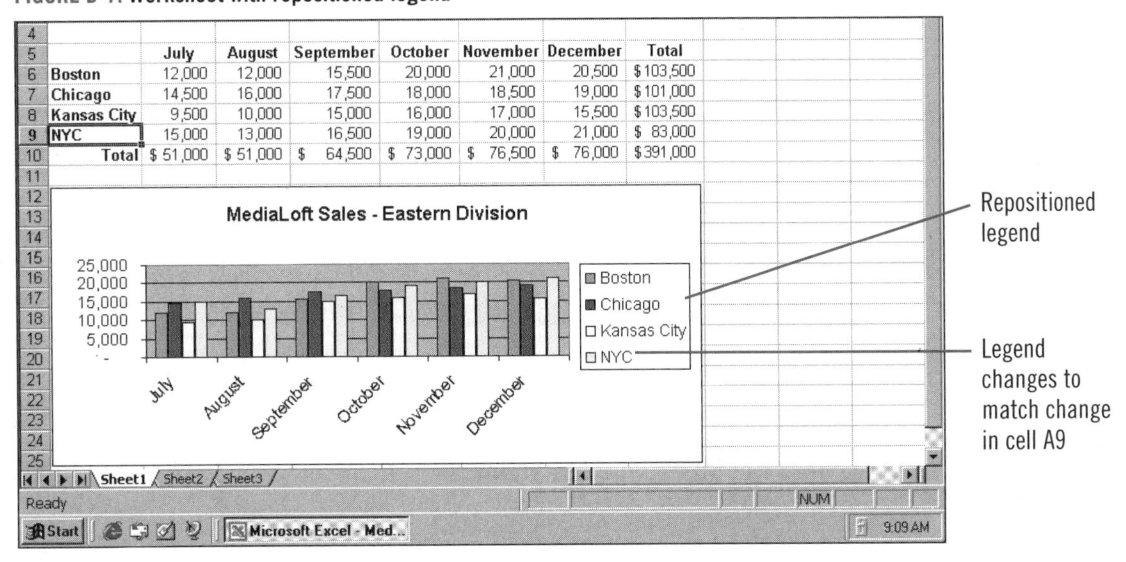

TABLE D-2: Commonly used pointers

name	pointer	use	name	pointer	use
Diagonal resizing	⤢ or ⤡	Change chart shape from corners	**I-beam**	I	Edit chart text
Draw	+	Create shapes	**Move chart**	✥	Change chart location
Horizontal resizing	↔	Change chart shape from left to right	**Vertical resizing**	↕	Changes chart shape from top to bottom

Identifying chart objects

There are many objects within a chart and Excel makes it easy to identify each of them. Placing your mouse pointer over a chart object causes a ScreenTip for that object to appear, whether the chart is selected or not. If a chart—or any object in it—is selected, the ScreenTips still appear. In addition, the name of the selected chart object appears in the name box and the Chart Object list box on the Chart toolbar.

Excel 2000

Excel 2000

Editing a Chart

Once you've created a chart, it's easy to modify it. You can change data values in the worksheet, and the chart will automatically be updated to reflect the new data. You can also easily change chart types using the buttons on the Chart toolbar. Jim looks over his worksheet and realizes he entered the wrong data for the Kansas City store in November and December. After he corrects this data, he wants to see how the same data looks using different chart types.

Trouble?

If you cannot see the chart and data together on your monitor, click View on the menu bar, click Zoom, then click 75%.

1. If necessary, scroll the worksheet so that you can see both the chart and row 8, containing the Kansas City sales figures, then place your mouse pointer over the data point to display **Series "Kansas City" Point "December" Value "15,500"**
   As you correct the values, the columns for November and December in the chart automatically change.
2. Click cell **F8**, type **18000** to correct the November sales figure, press [→], type **19500** in cell **G8**, then click
   The Kansas City columns for November and December reflect the increased sales figures. See Figure D-9. The totals are also updated in column H and row 10.
3. Select the chart by clicking anywhere within the chart border, then click the **Chart Type list arrow** on the Chart toolbar
   The chart type buttons appear on the Chart Type palette. Table D-3 describes the chart types available.
4. Click the **Bar Chart button** on the palette
   The column chart changes to a bar chart. See Figure D-10. You look at the bar chart, take some notes, and then decide to convert it back to a column chart. You now want to see if the large increase in sales would be better presented with a three-dimensional column chart.
5. Click the **Chart Type list arrow**, then click the **3-D Column Chart button** on the palette
   A three-dimensional column chart appears. You notice that the three-dimensional column format is more crowded than the two-dimensional format but gives you a sense of volume.
6. Click the **Chart Type list arrow**, then click the **Column Chart button** on the palette
7. Save your work

QuickTip

Experiment with different formats for your charts until you get just the right look.

CLUES TO USE

Rotating a chart

In a three-dimensional chart, columns or bars can sometimes be obscured by other data series within the same chart. You can rotate the chart until a better view is obtained. Double-click the chart, click the tip of one of its axes (select the Corners object), then drag the handles until a more pleasing view of the data series appears. See Figure D-8.

FIGURE D-8: 3-D chart rotated with improved view of data series

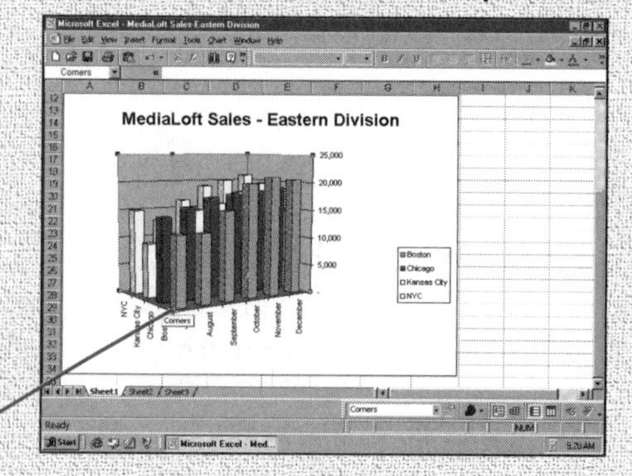

Click to rotate chart

FIGURE D-9: Worksheet with new data entered for Kansas City

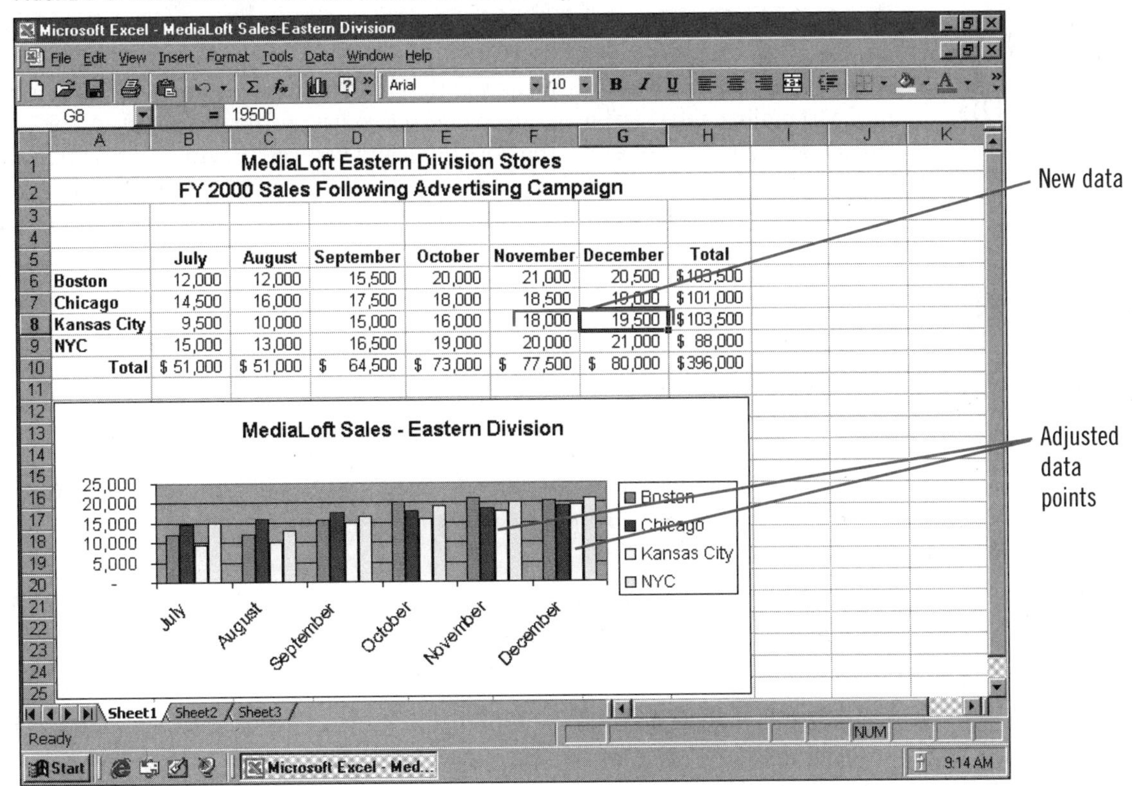

FIGURE D-10: Bar chart

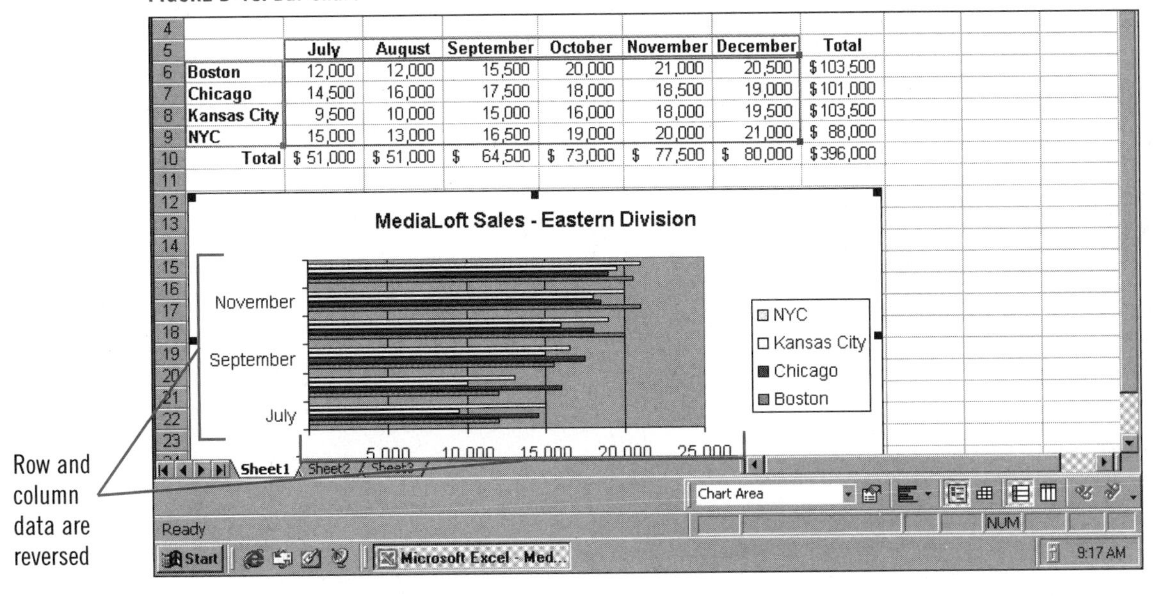

TABLE D-3: Commonly used chart type buttons

click	to display a	click	to display a	click	to display a	click	to display a
	area chart		pie chart		3-D area chart		3-D pie chart
	bar chart		(xy) scatter chart		3-D bar chart		3-D surface chart
	column chart		doughnut chart		3-D column chart		3-D cylinder chart
	line chart		radar chart		3-D line chart		3-D cone chart

Excel 2000

Formatting a Chart

After you've created a chart using the Chart Wizard, you can easily modify its appearance. Use the Chart toolbar and Chart menu to change the colors of data series and add or eliminate a legend and gridlines. **Gridlines** are the horizontal and vertical lines in the chart that enable the eye to follow the value on an axis. The button that selects the chart type changes to the last chart type selected. The corresponding Chart toolbar buttons are listed in Table D-4. Jim wants to make some changes in the appearance of his chart. He wants to see if the chart looks better without gridlines, and he wants to change the color of a data series.

Steps

1. Make sure the chart is still selected
   Horizontal gridlines currently appear in the chart.
2. Click **Chart** on the menu bar, click **Chart Options**, click the **Gridlines tab** in the Chart Options dialog box, then click the **Major Gridlines checkbox** for the Value (Y) axis to remove the check
   The gridlines disappear from the sample chart in the dialog box, as shown in Figure D-11. Even though gridlines extend from the tick marks on an axis across the plot area, they are not always necessary to the chart's readability.
3. Click the **Major Gridlines checkbox** for the Value (Y) axis, then click the **Minor Gridlines checkbox** for the Value (Y) axis
   Both major and minor gridlines appear in the sample.
4. Click the **Minor Gridlines checkbox** for the Value (Y) axis, then click **OK**
   The minor gridlines disappear, leaving only the major gridlines on the Value axis. You can change the color of the columns to better distinguish the data series.
5. With the chart selected, double-click any **light blue column** in the NYC data series
   Handles appear on all the columns in the NYC data series, and the Format Data Series dialog box opens, as shown in Figure D-12.
6. Click the **Patterns tab**, if necessary, click the **fuschia box** (in the fourth row, first on the left), then click **OK**
   All the columns for the series are fuschia, and the legend changes to match the new color. Compare your finished chart to Figure D-13.
7. Save your work

QuickTip

Minor gridlines show the values between the tick marks.

QuickTip

Add values, labels, and percentages to your chart using the Data Labels tab in the Chart Options dialog box.

TABLE D-4: Chart enhancement buttons

button	use
	Displays formatting dialog box for the selected object on the chart
	Selects chart type (chart type on button changes to last chart type selected)
	Adds/Deletes legend
	Creates a data table within the chart
	Charts data by row
	Charts data by column
	Angles selected text downward
	Angles selected text upward

FIGURE D-11: Chart Options dialog box

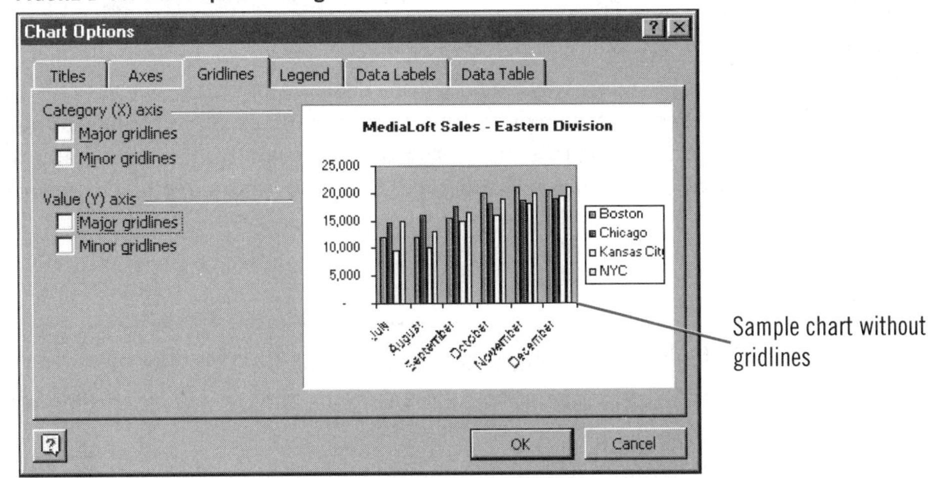

FIGURE D-12: Format Data Series dialog box

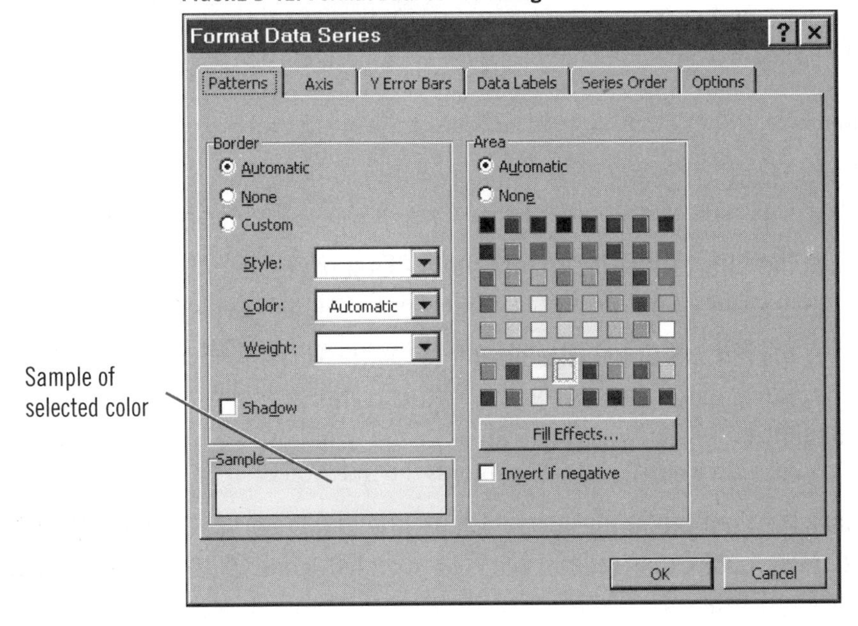

FIGURE D-13: Chart with formatted data series

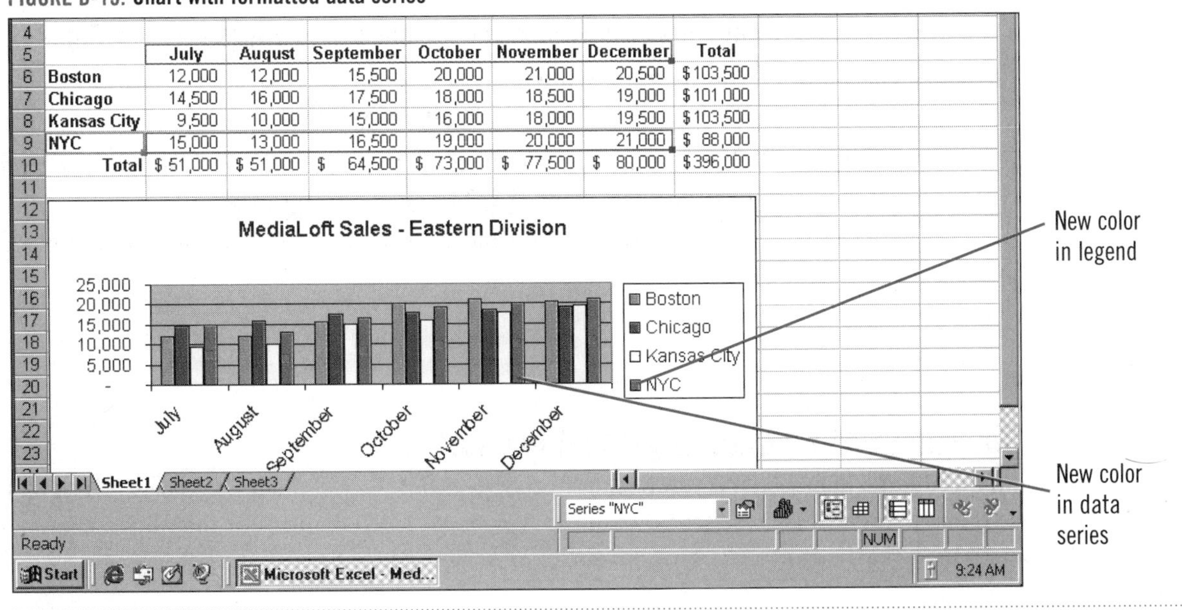

Excel 2000

Enhancing a Chart

There are many ways to enhance a chart to make it easier to read and understand. You can create titles for the x-axis and y-axis, add graphics, or add background color. You can even format the text you use in a chart. Jim wants to improve the appearance of his chart by creating titles for the x-axis and y-axis. He also decides to add a drop shadow to the title.

1. **Make sure the chart is selected, click Chart on the menu bar, click Chart Options, click the Titles tab in the Chart Options dialog box, then type Months in the Category (X) axis text box**
   Descriptive text on the x-axis helps a user understand the chart. The word "Months" appears below the month labels in the sample chart, as shown in Figure D-14.

QuickTip
To edit the text, position the pointer over the selected text box until it changes to I, click, then edit the text.

2. **Click the Value (Y) axis text box, type Sales (in $), then click OK**
   A selected text box containing "Sales (in $)" appears rotated 90 degrees to the left of the y-axis. Once the Chart Options dialog box is closed, you can move the Value or Category axis titles to new positions by clicking on an edge of the object and dragging it.
3. **Press [Esc] to deselect the Value-axis title**
   Next you decide that a border with a drop shadow will enhance the chart title.
4. **Click the chart title MediaLoft Sales – Eastern Division to select it**
   You can create a drop shadow using the Format button on the Chart toolbar.

QuickTip
The Format button opens a dialog box with the appropriate formatting options for the selected chart element. The ScreenTip for the button changes depending on the selected object.

5. **Click the Format Chart Title button on the Chart toolbar to open the Format Chart Title dialog box, make sure the Patterns tab is selected, then click the Shadow checkbox**
   A border with a drop shadow surrounds the title. You can continue to format the title.
6. **Click the Font tab in the Format Chart Title dialog box, click Times New Roman in the Font list, click Bold Italic in the Font style list, click OK, then press [Esc] to deselect the chart title**
   A border with a drop shadow appears around the chart title, and the chart title text is reformatted.
7. **Click the Category Axis Title, click , click the Font tab, select Times New Roman in the Font list, then click OK**
   The Category Axis Title appears in the Times New Roman font.
8. **Click the Value Axis Title, click , click the Font tab, click Times New Roman in the Font list, click OK, then press [Esc] to deselect the title**
   The Value Axis Title appears in the Times New Roman font. Compare your chart to Figure D-15.
9. **Save your work**

Changing text font and alignment in charts

The font and the alignment of axis text can be modified to make it more readable or to better fit within the plot area. With a chart selected, double-click the axis text to be modified. The Format Axis dialog box appears. Click the Font or the Alignment tab, make the desired changes, then click OK.

FIGURE D-14: Sample chart with Category (X) axis text

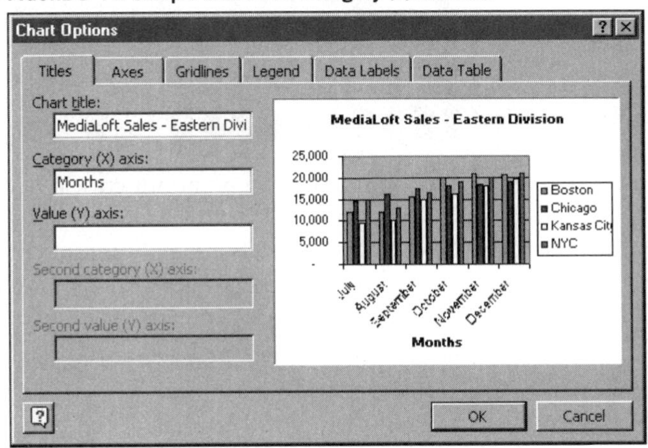

FIGURE D-15: Enhanced chart

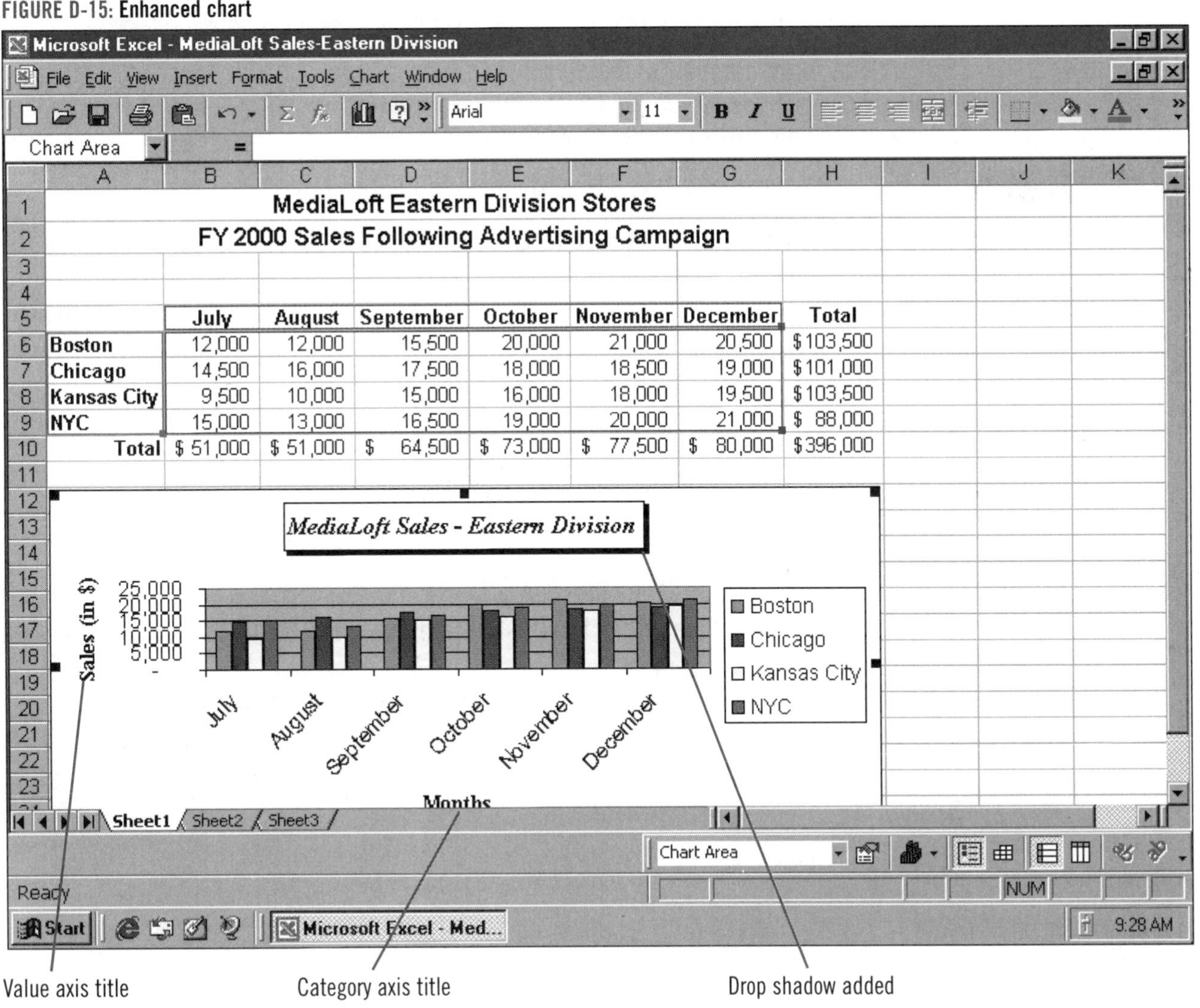

Excel 2000

Annotating and Drawing on a Chart

You can add arrows and text annotations to point out critical information in your charts. Text annotations are labels that you add to a chart to further describe the data in it. You can draw lines and arrows that point to the exact locations you want to emphasize. Jim wants to add a text annotation and an arrow to highlight the October sales increase.

Steps

1. Make sure the chart is selected
   To call attention to the Boston October sales increase, you can draw an arrow that points to the top of the Boston October data series with the annotation, "Due to ad campaign." With the chart selected, simply typing text in the formula bar creates annotation text.
2. Type **Due to ad campaign**, then click the **Enter button**
   As you type, the text appears in the formula bar. After you confirm the entry, the text appears in a selected text box within the chart window.
3. Point to an edge of the text box so the pointer changes to
4. Drag the text box **above the chart**, as shown in Figure D-16, then release the mouse button
   You can add an arrow to point to a specific area or item in a chart using the Drawing toolbar.
5. Click the **Drawing button** on the Standard toolbar
   The Drawing toolbar appears.
6. Click the **Arrow button** on the Drawing toolbar
   The pointer changes to + and the status bar displays "Click and drag to insert an AutoShape." When you draw an arrow, the point farthest from where you start will have the arrowhead.
7. Position + under the '**t**' in the word "to" in the text box, press and hold the **left mouse button**, drag the line to the **Boston column in the October sales series**, then release the mouse button
   An arrowhead appears, pointing to Boston October sales. The arrowhead is a selected object in the chart and can be resized, formatted, or deleted just like any other object. Compare your finished chart to Figure D-17.
8. Click to close the Drawing toolbar
9. Save your work

Trouble?

If the pointer changes to I or ↔, release the mouse button, click outside the text box area to deselect it, then select the text box and repeat Step 3.

QuickTip

You can insert text and an arrow in the data section of a worksheet by clicking the Text Box button on the Drawing toolbar, drawing a text box, typing the text, and then adding the arrow.

FIGURE D-16: Repositioning text annotation

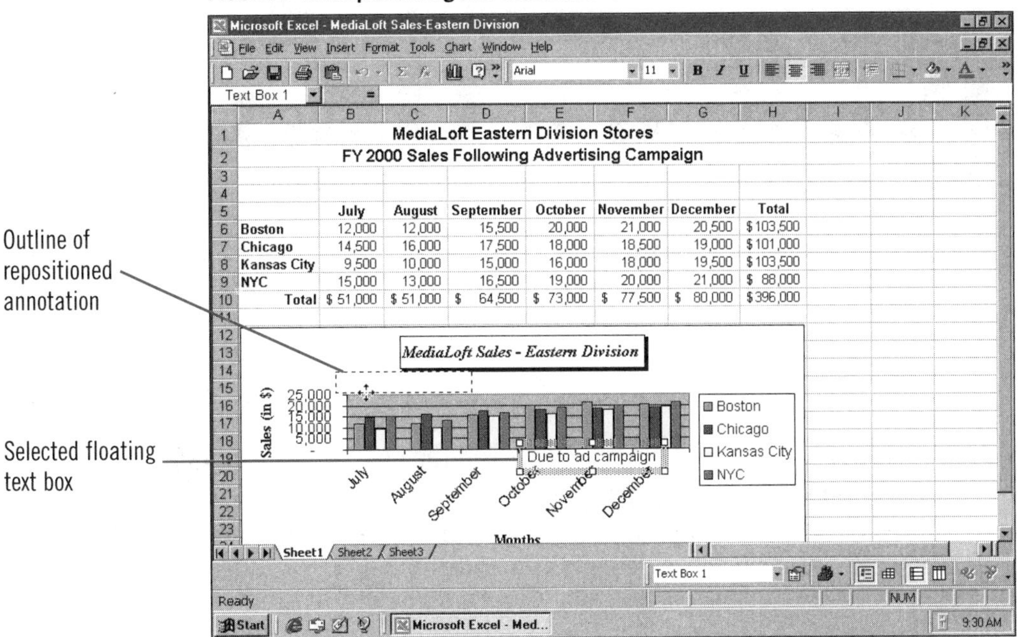

FIGURE D-17: Completed chart with text annotation and arrow

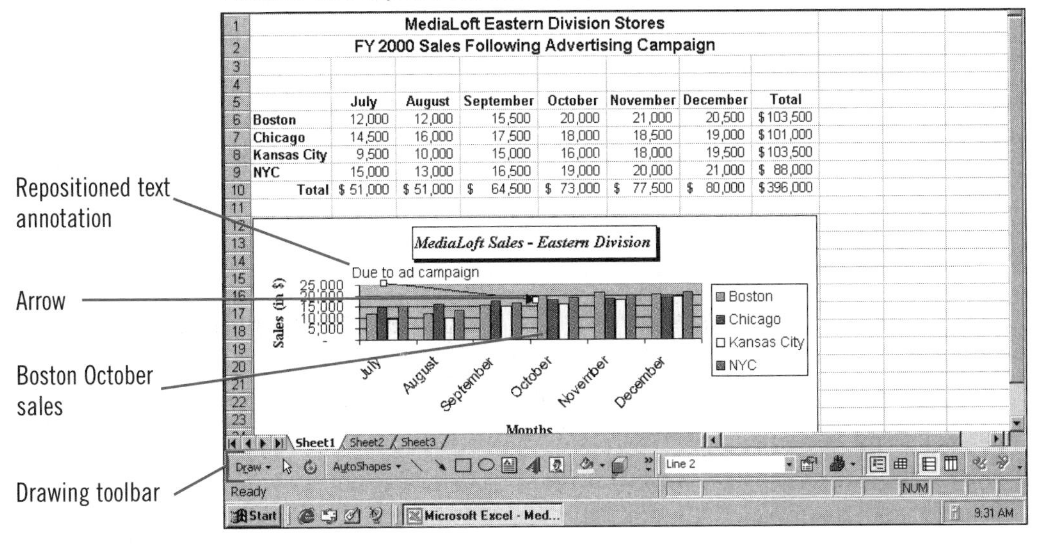

CLUES TO USE

Exploding a pie slice

Just as an arrow can call attention to a data series, you can emphasize a pie slice by exploding it, or pulling it away from, the pie chart. Once the pie chart is selected, click the pie to select it, click the desired slice to select only the slice, then drag the slice away from the pie, as shown in Figure D-18. After you change the chart type, you may need to adjust arrows within the chart.

FIGURE D-18: Exploded pie slice

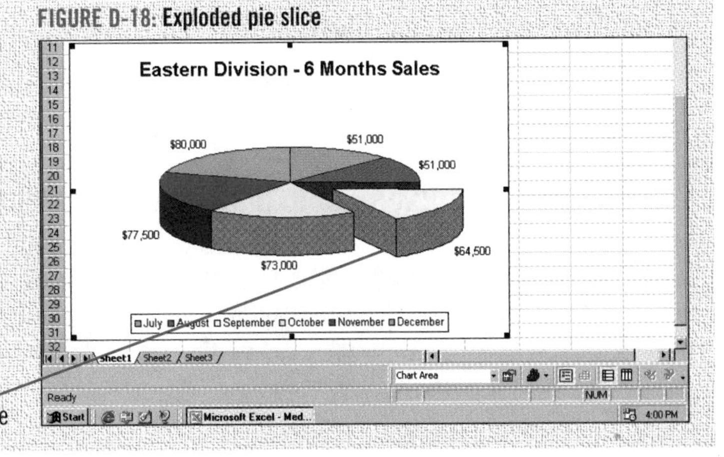

Excel 2000

Previewing and Printing a Chart

After you complete a chart to your satisfaction, you will need to print it. Previewing a chart gives you a chance to see what your chart looks like before you print it. You can print a chart by itself, or as part of the worksheet. Jim wants to print the chart for the annual meeting. He will print the worksheet and the chart together, so that the shareholders can see the actual sales numbers for the eastern division stores.

Steps

1. Press **[Esc]** twice to deselect the arrow and the chart, click cell **A35**, type your name, press **[Enter]**, then press **[Ctrl][Home]**
   If you wanted to print only the chart without the data, you would leave the chart selected. Including your name on a worksheet insures that you'll be able to identify your work when it is printed.
2. Click the **Print Preview button** on the Standard toolbar
   The Print Preview window opens. You decide that the chart and data would make better use of the page if they were printed in **landscape** orientation—that is, with the text running the long way on the page. Altering the page setup changes the orientation of the page.
3. Click **Setup** on the Print Preview toolbar to open the Page Setup dialog box, then click the **Page tab**
4. Click the **Landscape option button** in the Orientation section as shown in Figure D-19, then click **OK**
   Because each page has a left default margin of 0.75", the chart and data will print too far over to the left of the page. You can change this setting using the Margins tab.
5. Click **Setup**, click the **Margins tab**, click the **Center on page Horizontally checkbox**, then click **OK**
   The data and chart are positioned horizontally on the page. See Figure D-20.
6. Click **Print** to display the Print dialog box, then click **OK**
   The data and chart print and you are returned to the worksheet. If you want, you can choose to preview (and print) only the chart.
7. Select the **chart**, then click the **Print Preview button**
   The chart appears in the Print Preview window. If you wanted to, you could print the chart by clicking the Print button on the Print Preview toolbar.
8. Click **Close** on the Print Preview toolbar
9. Save your work, then close the workbook and exit Excel

Trouble?

Click Margins on the Print Preview toolbar to display Margin lines in the Print Preview window.

Using the Page Setup dialog box for a chart

When a chart is selected, a different Page Setup dialog box opens than when neither the chart nor data is selected. The Center on Page options are not always available. To accurately position a chart on the page, you could click the Margins button on the Print Preview toolbar. Margin lines appear on the screen and show you exactly how the margins display on the page. The exact placement appears in the status bar when you press and hold the mouse button on the margin line. You can drag the lines to the exact setting you want.

FIGURE D-19: Page tab of the Page Setup dialog box

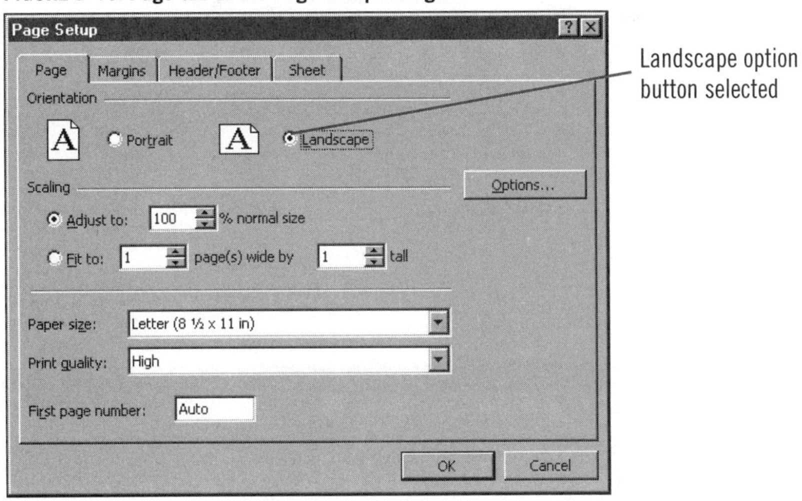

FIGURE D-20: Chart and data ready to print

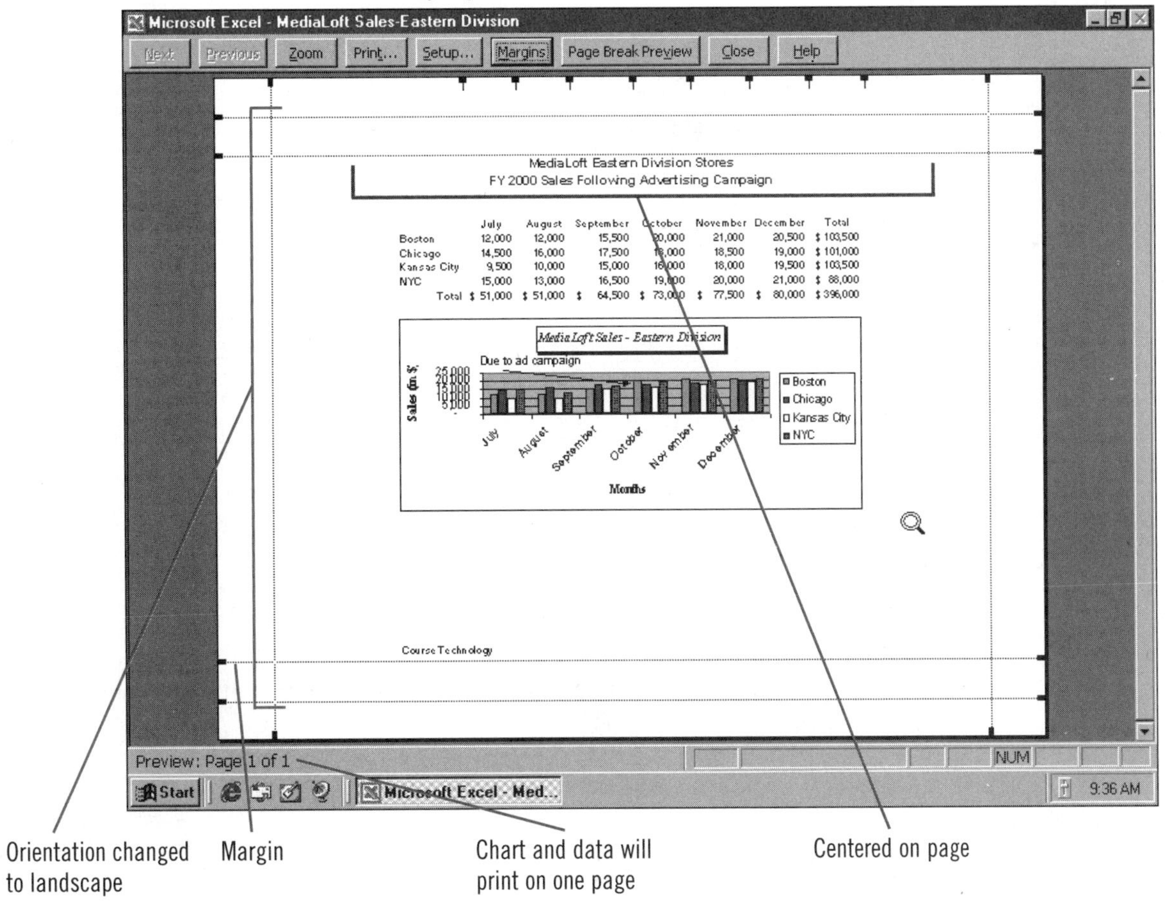

Excel 2000

Practice

► Concepts Review

Label each element of the Excel chart shown in Figure D-21.

FIGURE D-21

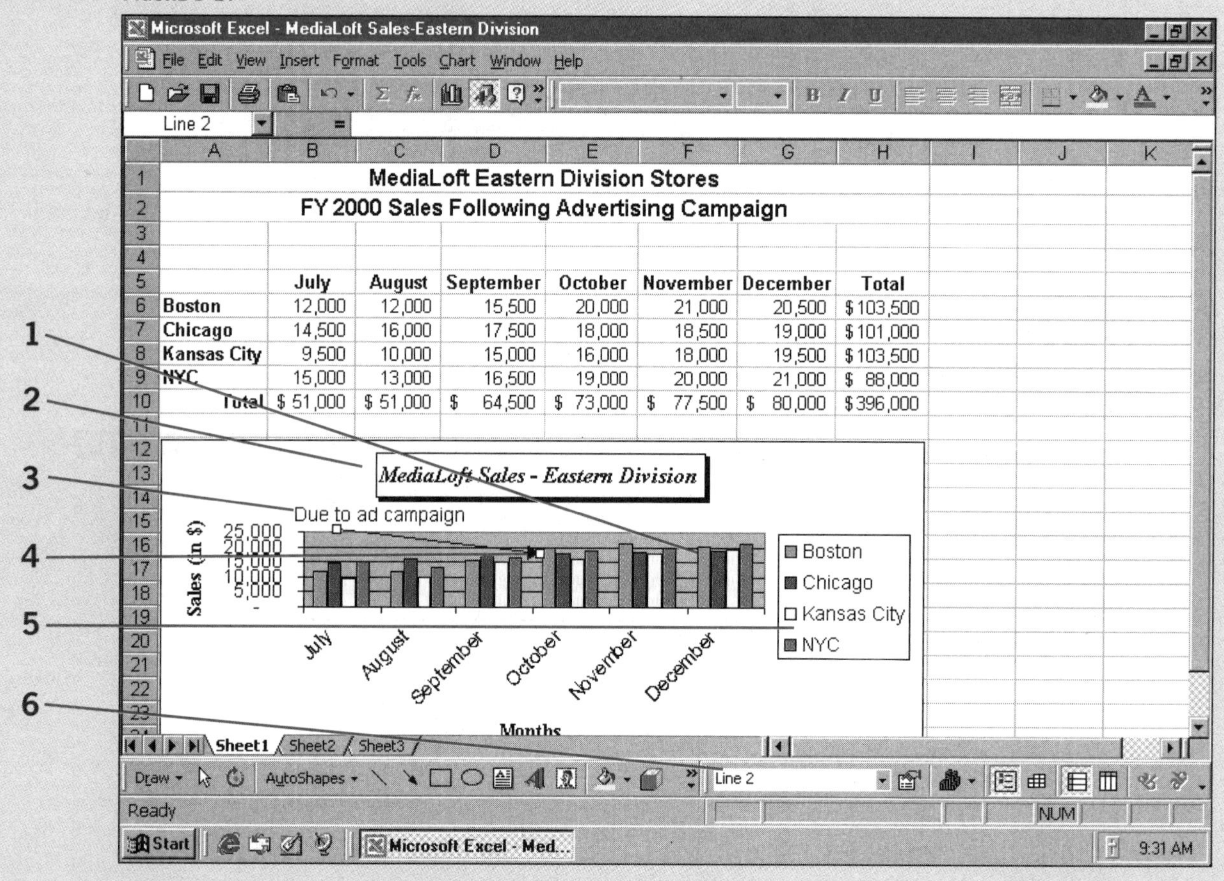

Match each chart type with the statement that describes it.

7. Column	**a.** Shows how volume changes over time
8. Area	**b.** Compares data as parts of a whole
9. Pie	**c.** Displays a column and line chart using different scales of measurement
10. Combination	**d.** Compares trends over even time intervals
11. Line	**e.** Compares data over time—the Excel default

Select the best answer from the list of choices.

12. The object in a chart that identifies patterns used for each data series is a
- **a.** Data point.
- **b.** Plot.
- **c.** Legend.
- **d.** Range.

13. What is the term for a row or column on a chart?
- **a.** Range address
- **b.** Axis title
- **c.** Chart orientation
- **d.** Data series

14. The orientation of a page whose dimensions are 11" by 8½" is
- **a.** Sideways.
- **b.** Longways.
- **c.** Portrait.
- **d.** Landscape.

15. The Value axis is the
- **a.** X-axis.
- **b.** Z-axis.
- **c.** D-axis.
- **d.** Y-axis.

16. The Category axis is the
- **a.** X-axis.
- **b.** Z-axis.
- **c.** D-axis.
- **d.** Y-axis.

17. Which pointer is used to resize a chart object?
- **a.** I
- **b.** ⤢
- **c.** ✥
- **d.** +

Skills Review

1. Create a chart.

a. Start Excel, open a new workbook, then save it as "Software Usage" to your Project Disk.
b. Enter the information from Table D-5 in your worksheet in range A1:F6. Resize columns and rows.
c. Save your work.
d. Select the range you want to chart.
e. Click the Chart Wizard button.
f. Complete the Chart Wizard dialog boxes and build a column chart on the same sheet as the data, having a different color bar for each department. Title the chart "Software Usage by Department."
g. Save your work.

TABLE D-5

	Excel	Word	PowerPoint	Access	Publisher
Accounting	22	15	2	2	1
Marketing	13	35	35	5	32
Engineering	23	5	3	1	0
Personnel	10	25	10	2	25
Production	6	5	22	0	22

2. Move and resize a chart.

a. Make sure the chart is still selected.
b. Move the chart beneath the data.
c. Drag the chart's selection handles so it is as wide as the screen.
d. Move the legend below the charted data. (*Hint:* Change the legend's position using the Legend button on the Chart toolbar.)
e. Save your work.

3. Edit a chart.

a. Change the value in cell B3 to "6." Notice the change in the chart.
b. Select the chart by clicking it.
c. Click the Chart Type list arrow on the Chart toolbar.
d. Click the 3-D Column Chart button.
e. Rotate the chart to move the data.
f. Change the chart back to a column chart.
g. Save your work.

4. Format a chart.

a. Make sure the chart is still selected.
b. Use the Chart Options dialog box to turn off the displayed gridlines.
c. Change the font used in the Category and Value labels to Times New Roman.
d. Turn the major gridlines back on.
e. Change the title's font to Times New Roman.
f. Save your work.

5. Enhance a chart.

- **a.** Make sure the chart is still selected, click Chart on the menu bar, click Chart Options, then click the Titles tab.
- **b.** Click the Category (X) axis text box, then type "Software" in the selected text box below the x-axis.
- **c.** Click the Value (Y) axis text box, type "Users" in the selected text box to the left of the y-axis, then click OK.
- **d.** Change the legend entry for "Production" to "Art."
- **e.** Add a drop shadow to the title.
- **f.** Save your work.

6. Annotate and draw on a chart.

- **a.** Select the chart.
- **b.** Create the text annotation "Need More Users."
- **c.** Drag the text annotation under the title.
- **d.** Click the Arrow button on the Drawing toolbar.
- **e.** Click below the text annotation, drag the arrow so it points to the area containing the Access columns, then release the mouse button.
- **f.** Save your work.

7. Preview and print a chart.

- **a.** Deselect the chart and type your name in cell A30.
- **b.** Preview the chart and data to see how it will look when printed.
- **c.** Change the paper orientation to landscape.
- **d.** Center the data and chart horizontally and vertically on the page.
- **e.** Click Print in the Print Preview window.
- **f.** Select the chart.
- **g.** Preview, then print only the chart.
- **h.** Save your work, close the workbook, then exit Excel.

▶ Independent Challenges

1. You are the operations manager for the Springfield Theater Group. Each year the city of Springfield applies to various state and federal agencies for matching funds. The city's marketing department wants you to create charts for a report that will be used to document the number of productions in previous years. You need to create charts that show the number of previously produced plays.

To complete this independent challenge:

a. Sketch a sample worksheet on a piece of paper describing how you will create the charts. Which type of chart is best suited for the information you need to display? What kind of chart enhancements will be necessary? Will a 3-D effect make your chart easier to understand?
b. Start Excel, open the workbook EX D-2 from your Project Disk, then save it as "Theater Group."
c. Create a column chart for the data.
d. Change at least one of the colors used in a data series.
e. Create at least two additional charts for the same data to show how different chart types display the same data.
f. After creating the charts, make the appropriate enhancements. Include chart titles, legends, and value and category titles.
g. Add data labels.
h. Type your name in a cell in the worksheet.
i. Before printing, preview the file so you know what the charts will look like. Adjust any items as needed.
j. Save your work. Print the worksheet (charts and data).
k. Close the workbook and exit Excel.

2. One of your responsibilities at the Beautiful You Salon is to re-create the company's records using Excel. Another is to convince the current staff that Excel can make daily operations easier and more efficient. You've decided to create charts using the previous year's operating expenses. These charts will be used at the next monthly meeting.

To complete this independent challenge:

a. Decide which data in the worksheet should be charted. Sketch two sample charts. What type of charts are best suited for the information you need to display? What kind of chart enhancements will be necessary?
b. Start Excel, open the workbook EX D-3 from your Project Disk, and save it as "BY Expense Charts."
c. Create a column chart containing the expense data for all four quarters.
d. Using the same data, create two additional charts using different chart types.
e. Add annotated text and arrows (to the initial chart) highlighting any important data or trends that you can see from the charts.
f. In one chart, change the colors of data series, and in another chart, use black-and-white patterns only.
g. Type your name in a cell in the worksheet.
h. Before printing, preview the file so you know what the charts will look like. Adjust any items as needed.
i. Print the charts. Save your work.
j. Close the workbook and exit Excel.

3. The Step Lightly Ad Agency is delighted with the way you've organized their membership roster using Excel. The Board of Directors wants to assess certain advertising expenses and has asked you to prepare charts that can be used in their presentation.

To complete this independent challenge:

a. Start Excel, open the workbook EX D-4 from your Project Disk, and save it as "Step Lightly."
b. Use the raw data for the sample shown in the range A16:B24 to create charts.
c. Decide what types of charts would be best suited for this type of data. Sketch two sample charts. What kind of chart enhancements will be necessary?
d. Create at least three different chart types that show the distribution of advertising expenses.
e. Add annotated text and arrows highlighting important data, such as the largest expense.
f. Change the color of at least one data series.
g. Add Category and Value axis titles; add a chart title. Format the titles with a font of your choice. Place a drop shadow around the chart title.
h. Type your name in a cell in the worksheet.
i. Before printing, preview the file so you know what the charts will look like. Adjust any items as needed. Be sure the chart is placed appropriately on the page.
j. Print the charts, save your work, then close the workbook and exit Excel.

4. During the second quarter of the year, the New York City MediaLoft store decided to analyze sales by type of book for a three-month period. Sales have been steadily increasing and the manager of the store is planning to renovate the space. Depending on which books sell best for the store location, the manager will reallocate the selling floor space accordingly. To be able to present this information to see which types of books are the best sellers, you will chart the analysis to get a graphical representation of the distributions. You decide to create two types of charts for the same data.

To complete this independent challenge:

a. Start Excel, open a new workbook, and save it on your Project Disk as "New York Analysis."
b. Connect to the Internet, go to the MediaLoft intranet site at http://www.course.com/illustrated/MediaLoft, then click the link for the Accounting page.
c. Copy the New York Analysis data into your worksheet.
d. Create a column chart with the data series in rows on the same worksheet as the data. Include a descriptive title and the following text: "Type of Book" in the Category axis, and "Sales" in the Value axis.
e. Place the chart on the same sheet as the data.
f. Move the chart so that it is below the data and the left side of the chart is in column A.
g. Format the legend so that it is placed along the bottom of the chart.
h. Change the color of the Science Fiction data series to fuschia.
i. Remove the gridlines.
j. Using the same data, create a 3-D bar chart (use the Clustered bar with the 3-D visual effect) with the data series in rows on a new sheet.
k. Add appropriate title(s) to the worksheet and axes.
l. Format the Value axis so the numbers display no decimal places, and a 1000 separator (comma).
m. Type your name in a visible cell in the worksheet containing the data.
n. Preview the chart and change margins as needed.
o. Print the worksheet data and column chart, making setup modifications as necessary.
p. Print the 3-D bar chart making any setup modifications as necessary.
q. Save the workbook and exit Excel.

► Visual Workshop

Modify a worksheet using the skills you learned in this unit, using Figure D-22 for reference. Open the file EX D-5 from your Project Disk, and save it as "Quarterly Advertising Budget." Create the chart, then change the data to reflect Figure D-22. Type your name in cell A13, save, preview, and then print your results.

FIGURE D-22

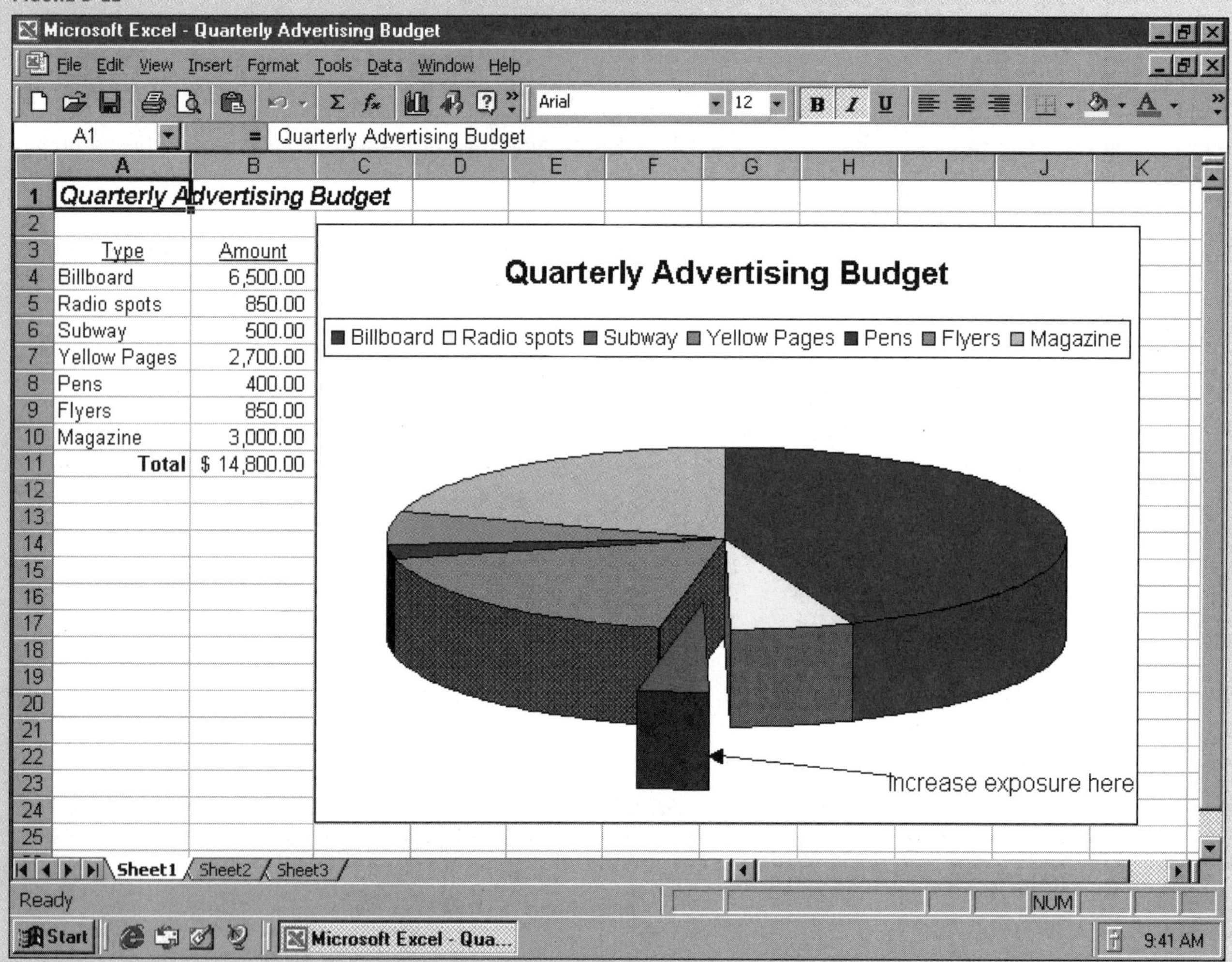

Working with Formulas and Functions

Objectives

- MOUS ► Create a formula with several operators
- MOUS ► Use names in a formula
- MOUS ► Generate multiple totals with AutoSum
- MOUS ► Use dates in calculations
- MOUS ► Build a conditional formula with the IF function
- MOUS ► Use statistical functions
- MOUS ► Calculate payments with the PMT function
- MOUS ► Display and print formula contents

Without formulas, Excel would simply be an electronic grid with text and numbers. Used with formulas, Excel becomes a powerful data analysis software tool. As you learn how to analyze data using different types of formulas, including those that call for functions, you will discover more ways to use Excel. In this unit, you will gain a further understanding of Excel formulas and learn how to build several Excel functions. Top management at MediaLoft has asked Jim Fernandez to analyze various company data. To do this, Jim creates several worksheets that require the use of formulas and functions. Because management is considering raising salaries for store managers, Jim's first task is to create a report that compares the payroll deductions and net pay for store managers before and after a proposed raise.

Creating a Formula with Several Operators

You can create formulas that contain a combination of cell references (for example, Z100 and B2), operators (for example, * [multiplication] and – [subtraction]), and values (for example, 99 or 1.56). You also can create a single formula that performs several calculations. If you enter a formula with more than one operator, Excel performs the calculations in a particular sequence based on algebraic rules called **precedence**; that is, Excel performs the operation(s) within the parentheses first, then performs the other calculations. See Table E-1. Jim has been given the gross pay and payroll deductions for the first payroll period and needs to complete his analysis. He also has preformatted, with the Comma style, any cells that are to contain values. Jim begins by entering a formula for net pay that subtracts the payroll deductions from gross pay.

Steps

QuickTip

To return personalized toolbars and menus to their default state, click Tools on the menu bar, click Customize, click the Options tab in the Customize dialog box, click Reset my usage data to restore the default settings, click Yes, click Close, then close the Drawing toolbar if it is displayed.

Trouble?

If you receive a message box indicating "Parentheses do not match," make sure you have included both a left and a right parenthesis.

1. **Start Excel if necessary, open the workbook titled EX E-1, then save the workbook as Pay Info for Store Mgrs**
   The first part of the net pay formula will go in cell B11.
2. **Click Edit on the menu bar, click Go To, then type B11 in the Reference box and click OK**
   The Go To command is especially useful when you want to select a cell in a large worksheet.
3. **Type =B6-**
   Remember that you can type cell references in either uppercase or lowercase letters. (Excel automatically converts lowercase cell reference letters to uppercase.) If you make a mistake while building a formula, press [Esc] and begin again. You type the equal sign (=) to tell Excel that a formula follows, B6 to reference the cell containing the gross pay, and the minus sign (–) to indicate that the next entry will be subtracted from cell B6.
4. **Type (B7+B8+B9+B10) then click the Enter button on the formula bar**
   The net pay for Payroll Period 1 appears in cell B11, as shown in Figure E-1. (*Note:* Your toolbars may differ from those in the figure.) Because Excel performs the operations within parentheses first, you can control the order of calculations on the worksheet. (In this case, Excel sums the values in cells B7 through B10 first.) After the operations within the parentheses are completed, Excel performs the operations outside the parentheses. (In this case, Excel subtracts the total of range B7:B10 from cell B6.)
5. **Copy the formula in cell B11 into cells C11:F11, then return to cell A1**
   The formula in cell B11 is copied to the range C11:F11 to complete row 11. See Figure E-2.
6. **Save the workbook**
   Jim is pleased with the formulas that calculate net pay totals.

TABLE E-1: Example formulas using parentheses and several operators

formula	order of precedence	calculated result
=36+(1+3)	Add 1 to 3; then add the result to 36	40
=(10–20)/10–5	Subtract 20 from 10; divide that by 10; then subtract 5	–6
=(10*2)*(10+2)	Multiply 10 by 2; add 10 to 2; then multiply the results	240

FIGURE E-1: Worksheet showing formula and result

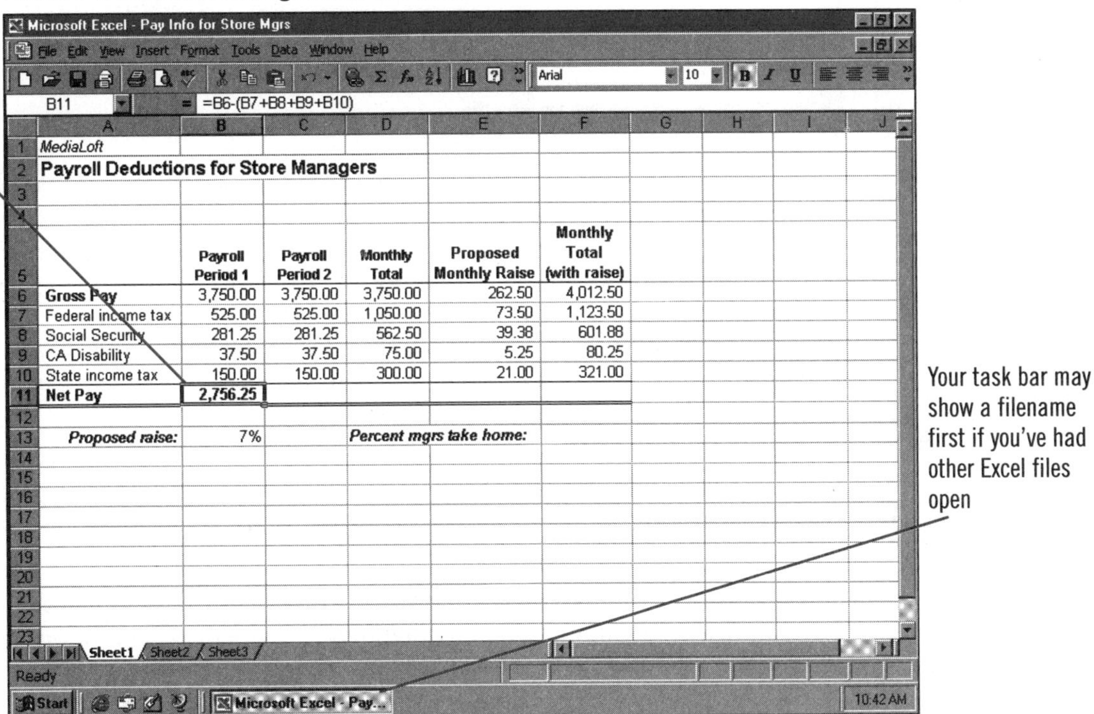

FIGURE E-2: Worksheet with copied formulas

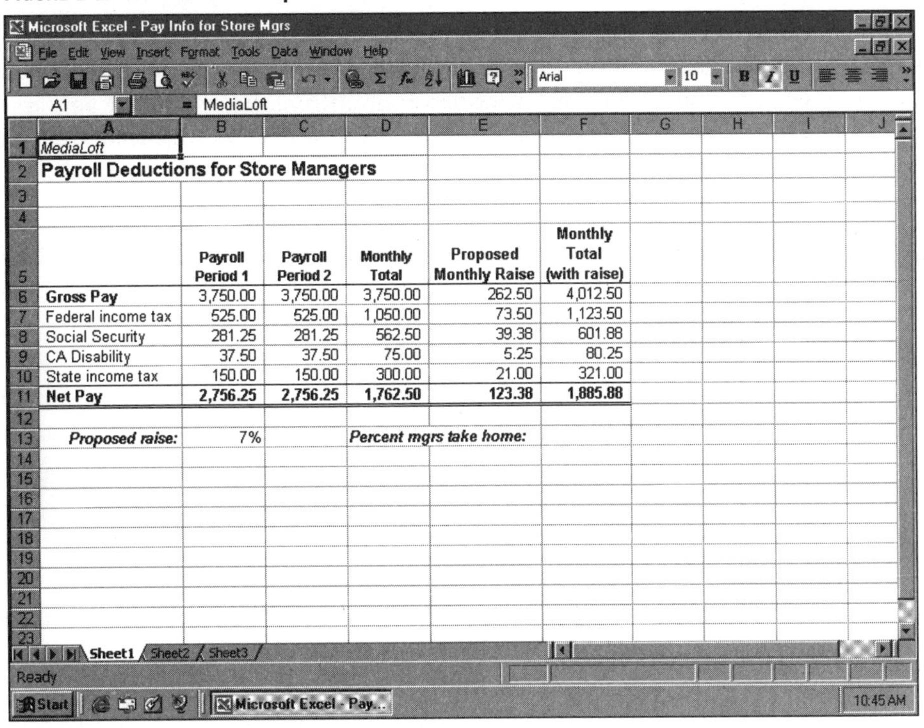

Excel 2000

CLUES TO USE

Using Paste Special to paste formulas and values and to perform calculations

You can use the Paste Special command to quickly enter formulas and values or even to perform quick calculations. Click the cell(s) containing the formula or value you want to copy, click the Copy button on the Standard toolbar, then right-click the cell where you want the result to appear. In the pop-up menu, choose Paste Special, then choose the feature you want to paste and click OK.

Using Names in a Formula

You can assign names to cells and ranges. Doing so reduces errors and makes a worksheet easier to follow. You also can use names in formulas. Using names in formulas facilitates formula building and provides a frame of reference for formula logic—the names make formulas easy to recognize and maintain. The formula Revenue – Cost, for example, is much easier to comprehend than the formula A2 – D3. You can produce a list of workbook names and their references at any time. Jim wants to include a formula that calculates the percentage of monthly gross pay the managers would actually take home (net pay) if a 7% raise is granted. He starts by naming the cells he'll use in the calculation.

Steps

1. **Click cell F6, click the name box on the formula bar to select the active cell reference, type Gross_with_Raise, then press [Enter]**
   The name assigned to cell F6, Gross_with_Raise, appears in the name box. Note that you must type underscores instead of spaces between words. Cell F6 is now named Gross_with_Raise to refer to the monthly gross pay amount that includes the 7% raise. The name box displays as much of the name as fits (Gross_with_...). The net pay cell needs a name.

QuickTip

To delete a name, click Insert on the menu bar, point to Name, then click Define. Select the name, click Delete, then click OK.

2. **Click cell F11, click the name box, type Net_with_Raise, then press [Enter]**
   The new formula will use names instead of cell references.
3. **Click cell F13, type =Net_with_Raise/Gross_with_Raise, then click the Enter button on the formula bar (make sure you begin the formula with an equal sign)**
   The formula bar now shows the new formula, and the result, 0.47, appears in the cell. If you add names to a worksheet after all the formulas have been entered, you must click Insert on the menu bar, point to Name, click Apply, click the name or names, then click OK. Cell F13 needs to be formatted in Percent style.

QuickTip

If you don't see on your toolbar, click the More Buttons button on the Formatting toolbar.

4. **Select cell F13, click Format on the menu bar, click Style, click the Style name list arrow, click Percent, then click OK**
   Notice that the result shown in cell F13, 47%, is rounded to the nearest whole percent as shown in Figure E-3. A **style** is a combination of formatting characteristics, such as bold, italic, and underlined. You can use the Style dialog box instead of the Formatting toolbar to apply styles. You can also use it to remove styles: select the cell that has a style and select Normal in the Style name list. To define your own style, select a cell, format it using the formatting toolbar (such as bold, italic, and 14 point), then open the Style dialog box and type a name for your style. Later, you can apply all those formatting characteristics simply by applying your new style from the dialog box.
5. **Enter your name into cell D1, return to cell A1, then save and print the worksheet**
   You can use the Label Ranges dialog box (Insert menu, Name submenu, Label command) to designate existing column or row headings as labels. Then instead of using cell references for the column or row in formulas, you can use the labels instead. (This feature is turned off by default. To turn it on, go to Tools/Options/Calculation tab/Accept labels in formulas.)
6. **Close the workbook**

FIGURE E-3: **Worksheet formula that includes cell names**

Formula with cell names

Name box

F13 | =Net_with_Raise/Gross_with_Raise

	A	B	C	D	E	F
1	*MediaLoft*					
2	**Payroll Deductions for Store Managers**					
3						
4						
5		**Payroll Period 1**	**Payroll Period 2**	**Monthly Total**	**Proposed Monthly Raise**	**Monthly Total (with raise)**
6	**Gross Pay**	3,750.00	3,750.00	3,750.00	262.50	4,012.50
7	Federal income tax	525.00	525.00	1,050.00	73.50	1,123.50
8	Social Security	281.25	281.25	562.50	39.38	601.88
9	CA Disability	37.50	37.50	75.00	5.25	80.25
10	State income tax	150.00	150.00	300.00	21.00	321.00
11	**Net Pay**	**2,756.25**	**2,756.25**	**1,762.50**	**123.38**	**1,885.88**
12						
13	***Proposed raise:***	7%		***Percent mgrs take home:***		47%

Cell named Gross_with_Raise

Result of calculation

Cell named Net_with_Raise

Producing a list of names

You might want to verify the names you have in a workbook and the cells they reference. To paste a list of names in a workbook, select a blank cell that has several blank cells beside and beneath it. Click Insert on the menu bar, point to Name, then click Paste. In the Paste Name dialog box, click Paste List. Excel produces a list that includes the sheet name and the cell or range the name identifies. See Figure E-4.

FIGURE E-4: **Worksheet with pasted list of names**

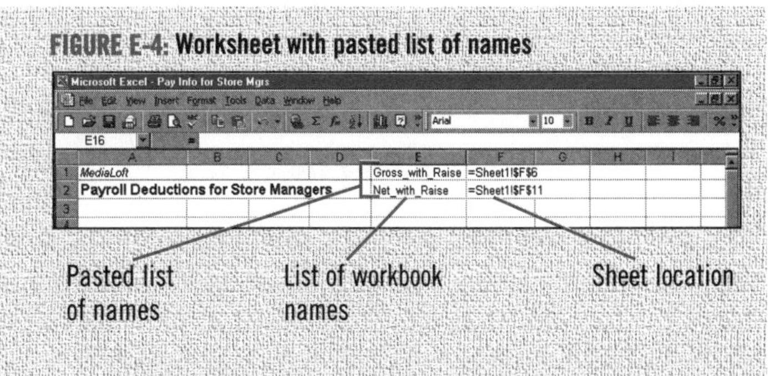

Excel 2000

Excel 2000

Generating Multiple Totals with AutoSum

In most cases, the result of a function is a value derived from a calculation. Functions can also return results such as text, references, or other information about the worksheet. You enter a function, such as AVERAGE, directly into a cell; you can use the Edit Formula button; or you can insert it with the Paste Function. You can use cell references, ranges, names, and formulas as arguments between the parentheses. (Recall that arguments are the information used in calculating the results of a function.) As with other cell entries, you can cut, copy, and paste functions from one area of the worksheet to another and from one workbook to another. The most widely used Excel function, SUM, calculates worksheet totals and can be entered easily using the AutoSum button on the Standard toolbar. Maria Abbot, MediaLoft's general sales manager, has given Jim a worksheet summarizing store sales. He needs to complete the worksheet totals.

1. **Open the workbook titled EX E-2, type your name into cell D1, then save the workbook as MediaLoft Sales**
   You can use AutoSum to generate two sets of totals at the same time.
2. **Select range B5:E9, press and hold [Ctrl], then select range B11:E15**
   To select nonadjacent cells, you must press and hold [Ctrl] while selecting the additional cells. Compare your selections with Figure E-5. The totals will appear in the last line of each selection.
3. **Click the AutoSum button on the Standard toolbar**
   When the selected range you want to sum (B5:E9 and B11:E15, in this example) includes a blank cell with data values above it, AutoSum enters the total in the blank cell.
4. **Select range B5:F17, then click**
   Whenever the selected range you want to sum includes a blank cell in the bottom row or right column, AutoSum enters the total in the blank cell. In this case, Excel ignores the data values and totals only the sums. Although Excel generates totals when you click the AutoSum button, it is a good idea to check the results.
5. **Click cell B17**
   The formula bar reads =SUM(B15,B9). See Figure E-6. When generating grand totals, Excel automatically references the cells containing SUM functions with a comma separator between cell references. Excel uses commas to separate multiple arguments in all functions, not just in SUM.
6. **Print the worksheet, then save and close the workbook**

Trouble?

If you select the wrong combination of cells, simply click on a single cell and begin again.

FIGURE E-5: Selecting nonadjacent ranges using [Ctrl]

	A	B	C	D	E	F
1	*MediaLoft*			Jim Fernandez		
2	**1999 Sales Summary**					
3						
4	***MediaLoft East***	**Qtr 1**	**Qtr 2**	**Qtr 3**	**Qtr 4**	**Total**
5	Boston	$ 147,000	$ 162,000	$ 157,000	$ 174,000	
6	Chicago	175,000	259,000	244,000	257,000	
7	Kansas City	152,000	207,000	215,000	225,000	
8	New York	183,000	230,000	225,000	247,000	
9	**Total**					
10	***MediaLoft West***					
11	Houston	$ 80,000	$ 117,000	$ 148,000	$ 182,000	
12	San Diego	63,000	95,000	152,000	186,000	
13	San Francisco	103,000	145,000	182,000	220,000	
14	Seattle	90,000	132,000	183,000	198,000	
15	**Total**					
16						
17	**Grand Total**					

Sheet1 / Sheet2 / Sheet3

Ready Sum= $ 5,535,000

Start Microsoft Excel - Med... 11:09 AM

FIGURE E-6: Completed worksheet

B17 = =SUM(B15,B9)

Comma used to separate multiple arguments

	A	B	C	D	E	F
1	*MediaLoft*			Jim Fernandez		
2	**1999 Sales Summary**					
3						
4	***MediaLoft East***	**Qtr 1**	**Qtr 2**	**Qtr 3**	**Qtr 4**	**Total**
5	Boston	$ 147,000	$ 162,000	$ 157,000	$ 174,000	$ **640,000**
6	Chicago	175,000	259,000	244,000	257,000	**935,000**
7	Kansas City	152,000	207,000	215,000	225,000	**799,000**
8	New York	183,000	230,000	225,000	247,000	**885,000**
9	**Total**	$ **657,000**	$ **858,000**	$ **841,000**	$ **903,000**	$ **3,259,000**
10	***MediaLoft West***					
11	Houston	$ 80,000	$ 117,000	$ 148,000	$ 182,000	$ **527,000**
12	San Diego	63,000	95,000	152,000	186,000	$ **496,000**
13	San Francisco	103,000	145,000	182,000	220,000	$ **650,000**
14	Seattle	90,000	132,000	183,000	198,000	$ **603,000**
15	**Total**	$ **336,000**	$ **489,000**	$ **665,000**	$ **786,000**	$ **2,276,000**
16						
17	**Grand Total**	$ **993,000**	$ **1,347,000**	$ **1,506,000**	$ **1,689,000**	$ **5,535,000**

Sheet1 / Sheet2 / Sheet3

Ready

Start Microsoft Excel - Med... 11:19 AM

Excel 2000

CLUES TO USE

Quick calculations with AutoCalculate

To check a total quickly without entering a formula, just select the range you want to sum, and the answer appears in the status bar next to SUM=. You also can perform other quick calculations, such as averaging or finding the minimum value in a selection. To do this, right-click the AutoCalculate area in the status bar and select from the list of options. The option you select remains in effect and in the status bar until you make another selection. See Figure E-7.

FIGURE E-7: Using AutoCalculate

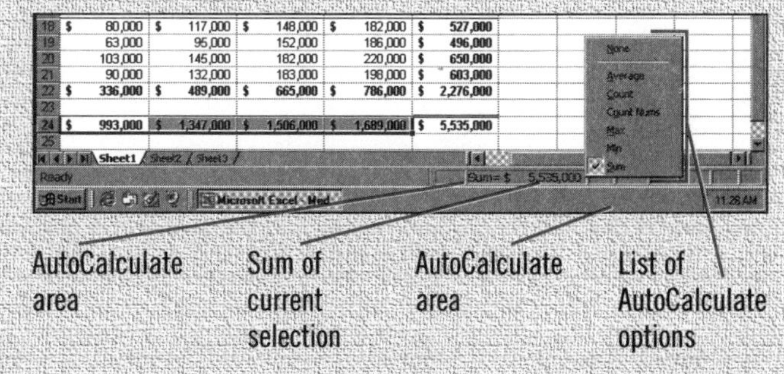

Excel 2000

Using Dates in Calculations

If you enter dates in a worksheet so that Excel recognizes them as dates, you can sort (arrange) the dates and perform date calculations. For example, you can calculate the number of days between your birth date and today, which is the number of days you have been alive. When you enter an Excel date format, Excel considers the entry a date function, converts the date to a serial date number, and stores that number in the cell. A date's converted serial date is the number of days to that date. Excel automatically assigns the serial date of "1" to January 1, 1900 and counts up from there; the serial date of January 1, 2000, for example, is 36,526. Jim's next task is to complete the New York Accounts Payable worksheet. He remembers to enter the worksheet dates in a format that Excel recognizes so that he can use date calculation.

1. Open the workbook titled **EX E-3**, then save the workbook as **New York Payables** to the appropriate folder on your Project Disk
   The calculations will be based on the current date, 4/1/00.
2. Click cell **C4**, type **4/1/00**, then press **[Enter]**
   The date appears in cell C4 just as you typed it. You want to enter a formula that calculates the invoice due date, which is 30 days from the invoice date. The formula adds 30 days to the invoice date.
3. Click cell **E7**, type =, click cell **B7**, type **+30**, then click the **Enter button** on the formula bar
   Excel calculates the result by converting the 3/1/00 invoice date to a serial date number, adding 30 to it, then automatically formatting the result as a date. See Figure E-8. You can use the same formula to calculate the due dates of the other invoices.
4. Drag the fill handle to copy the formula in cell E7 into cells **E8:E13**
   Cell referencing causes the copied formula to contain the appropriate cell references. Now you are ready to enter the formula that calculates the age of each invoice. You do this by subtracting the invoice date from the current date. Because each invoice age formula must refer to the current date, you must make cell C4, the current date cell, an absolute reference in the formula.
5. Click cell **F7**, type =, click cell **C4**, press **[F4]** to add the absolute reference symbols ($), type −, click **B7**, then click
   The formula bar displays the formula $C$4−B7. The numerical result, 31, appears in cell F7 because there are 31 days between 3/1/00 and 4/1/00. You can use the same formula to calculate the age of the remaining invoices.
6. Drag the fill handle to copy the formula in F7 to the range **F8:F13**, then press **[Ctrl][Home]**
   The age of each invoice appears in column F, as shown in Figure E-9.
7. Save the worksheet

QuickTip

You also can perform time calculations in Excel. For example, you can enter an employee's starting time and ending time, then calculate how many hours and minutes he or she worked. You must enter time in a format that Excel recognizes; for example, 1:35 PM (h:mm AM/PM).

QuickTip

If you perform date calculations and the intended numeric result displays as a date, format the cell(s) using a number format.

Using date functions

When you want Excel to perform a calculation using the current date, you can choose date and time options such as NOW, DATE, and TODAY. DATE inserts any date whose month, day, and year you specify as arguments in the formula palette: =DATE(2000,7,6) will produce July 6, 2000, NOW inserts the current date and time, while TODAY inserts today's date only (you don't have to enter arguments for NOW or TODAY).

FIGURE E-8: Worksheet with formula for invoice due date

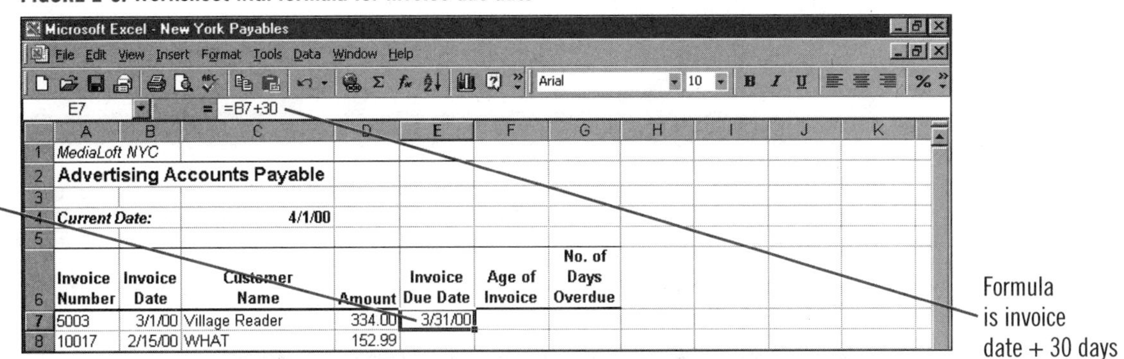

	A	B	C	D	E	F	G
1	MediaLoft NYC						
2	Advertising Accounts Payable						
3							
4	Current Date:		4/1/00				
5							
6	Invoice Number	Invoice Date	Customer Name	Amount	Invoice Due Date	Age of Invoice	No. of Days Overdue
7	5003	3/1/00	Village Reader	334.00	3/31/00		
8	10017	2/15/00	WHAT	152.99			

FIGURE E-9: Worksheet with copied formulas

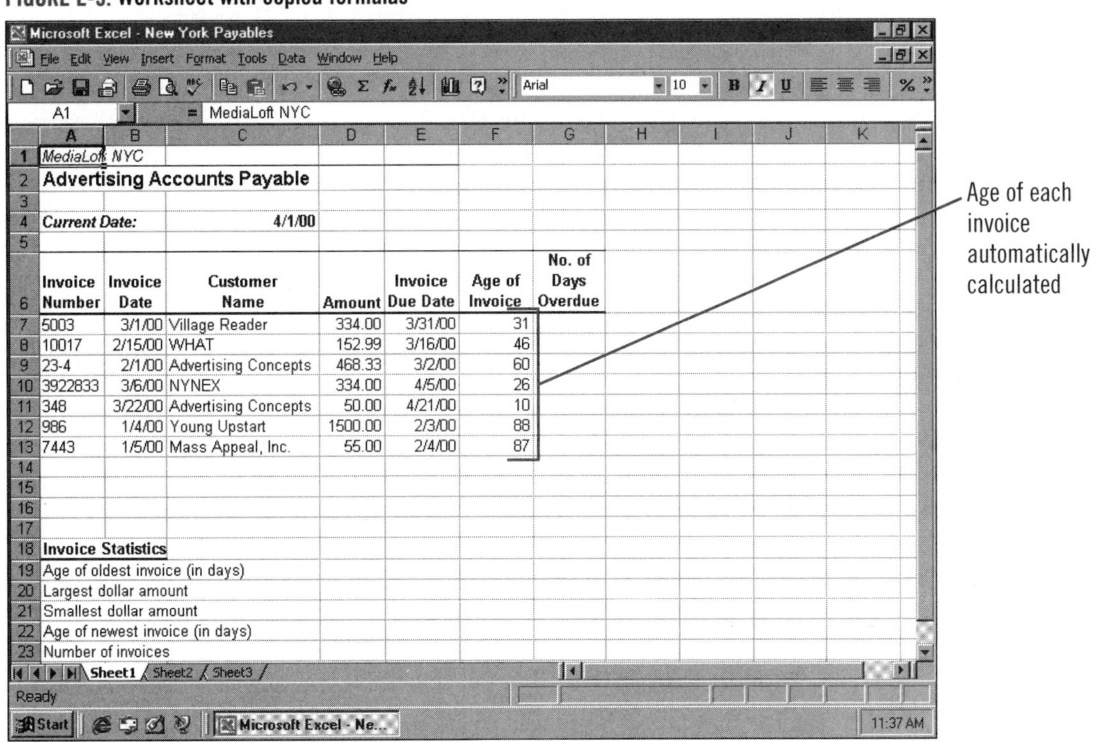

	A	B	C	D	E	F	G
1	MediaLoft NYC						
2	Advertising Accounts Payable						
3							
4	Current Date:		4/1/00				
5							
6	Invoice Number	Invoice Date	Customer Name	Amount	Invoice Due Date	Age of Invoice	No. of Days Overdue
7	5003	3/1/00	Village Reader	334.00	3/31/00	31	
8	10017	2/15/00	WHAT	152.99	3/16/00	46	
9	23-4	2/1/00	Advertising Concepts	468.33	3/2/00	60	
10	3922833	3/6/00	NYNEX	334.00	4/5/00	26	
11	348	3/22/00	Advertising Concepts	50.00	4/21/00	10	
12	986	1/4/00	Young Upstart	1500.00	2/3/00	88	
13	7443	1/5/00	Mass Appeal, Inc.	55.00	2/4/00	87	
14							
15							
16							
17							
18	Invoice Statistics						
19	Age of oldest invoice (in days)						
20	Largest dollar amount						
21	Smallest dollar amount						
22	Age of newest invoice (in days)						
23	Number of invoices						

Custom number and date formats

When you use numbers and dates in worksheets or calculations, you can use built-in Excel formats or create your own. The date you entered, 9/1/00, uses the Excel format m/d/yy. You could change it to the format d-mmm, or 1-Sep. The value $3,789 uses the number format $#,### where # represents positive numbers. To apply number formats, click Format on the menu bar, click Cells, then click the Number tab. In the category list, click a category, then specify the exact format in the list or scroll box to the right. To create a custom format, click Custom in the category list, then click a format that resembles the one you want. In the Type box, edit the symbols until they represent the format you want, then click OK. See Figure E-10.

FIGURE E-10: Custom formats on the Number tab in the Format Cells dialog box

Format Cells
Number | Alignment | Font | Border | Patterns | Protection
Category: General, Number, Currency, Accounting, Date, Time, Percentage, Fraction, Scientific, Text, Special, Custom
Sample: MediaLoft NYC
Type: #,##0
General, 0, 0.00, #,##0, #,##0.00, #,##0_);(#,##0), #,##0_);[Red](#,##0)
Delete
Type the number format code, using one of the existing codes as a starting point.
OK | Cancel

Edit these symbols to customize this format

Custom formats category

Custom formats

Excel 2000

Building a Conditional Formula with the IF Function

You can build a conditional formula using an IF function. A **conditional formula** is one that makes calculations based on stated conditions. For example, you can build a formula to calculate bonuses based on a person's performance rating. If a person is rated a 5 (the stated condition) on a scale of 1 to 5, with 5 being the highest rating, he or she receives 10% of his or her salary as a bonus; otherwise, there is no bonus. When the condition is a question that can be answered with a true or false response, Excel calls this stated condition a **logical test**. The IF function has three parts, separated by commas: a condition or logical test, an action to take if the logical test or condition is true, then an action to take if the logical test or condition is false. Another way of expressing this is: IF(test_cond,do_this,else_this). Translated into an Excel IF function, the formula to calculate bonuses would look something like this: IF(Rating=5,Salary*0.10,0). The translation would be: If the rating equals 5, multiply the salary by 0.10 (the decimal equivalent of 10%), then place the result in the selected cell. If the rating does not equal 5, place a 0 in the cell. When entering the logical test portion of an IF statement, you typically use some combination of the comparison operators listed in Table E-2. Jim is almost finished with the worksheet. To complete it, he needs to use an IF function that calculates the number of days each invoice is overdue.

Steps

1. **Click cell G7**
   The cell pointer is now positioned where the result of the function will appear. You want the formula to calculate the number of days overdue as follows: If the age of the invoice is greater than 30, calculate the days overdue (Age of Invoice − 30), and place the result in cell G7; otherwise, place a 0 (zero) in the cell. The formula will include the IF function and cell references.
2. **Type =IF(F7>30, (be sure to type the comma)**
   You have entered the first part of the function, the logical test. Notice that you used the symbol for greater than (>). So far, the formula reads: If Age of Invoice is greater than 30 (in other words, if the invoice is overdue). The next part of the formula tells Excel the action to take if the invoice is over 30 days old.
3. **Type F7-30, (be sure to type the comma)**
   This part of the formula, between the first and second commas, is what you want Excel to do if the logical test is true (that is, if the age of the invoice is over 30). Continuing the translation of the formula, this part means: Take the Age of Invoice value and subtract 30. The last part of the formula tells Excel the action to take if the logical test is false (that is, if the age of the invoice is 30 days or less).
4. **Type 0, then click the Enter button on the formula bar (you do not have to type the closing parenthesis) to complete the formula**
   The formula is complete, and the result, 1 (the number of days overdue), appears in cell G7. See Figure E-11.
5. **Copy the formula in cell G7 into cells G8:G13 and return to cell A1**
   Compare your results with Figure E-12.
6. **Save the workbook**

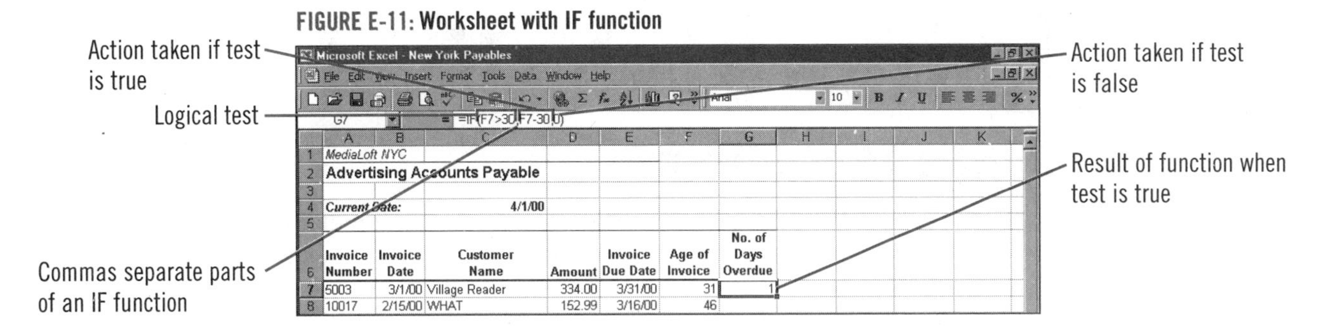

FIGURE E-11: Worksheet with IF function

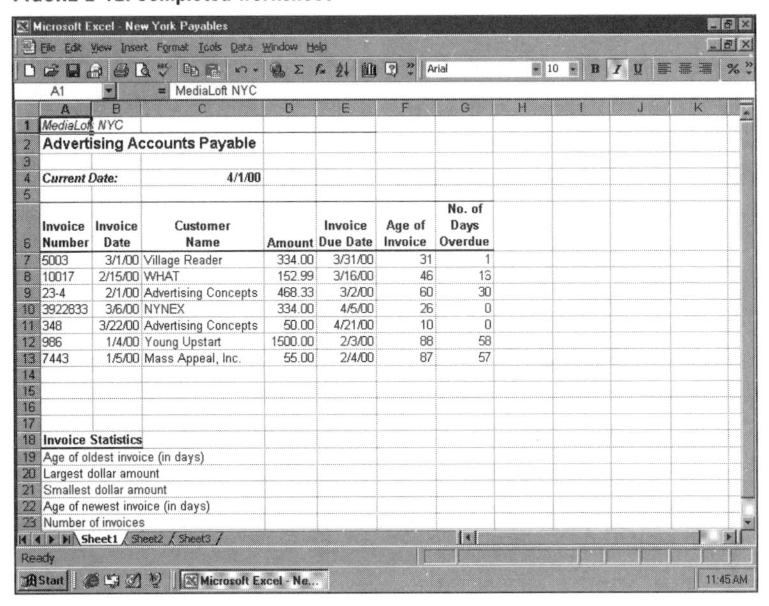

FIGURE E-12: Completed worksheet

TABLE E-2: Comparison operators

operator	function
<	Less than
>	Greater than
=	Equal to
<=	Less than or equal to
>=	Greater than or equal to
<>	Not equal to

Inserting and deleting selected cells

As you add formulas to your workbook, you may need to insert or delete cells, not entire rows or columns. When you do this, Excel automatically adjusts cell references to reflect their new locations. To insert cells, click Insert on the menu bar, then click Cells. The Insert dialog box opens, asking if you want to insert a cell and move the selected cell down or to the right of the new one. To delete one or more selected cells, click Edit on the menu bar, click Delete, and, in the Delete dialog box, indicate which way you want to move the adjacent cells. Be careful when using this option that you do not disturb row or column alignment that may be necessary to make sense of the worksheet.

Using Statistical Functions

Excel offers several hundred worksheet functions. A small group of these functions calculates statistics such as averages, minimum values, and maximum values. See Table E-3 for a brief description of these commonly used functions. Jim wants to present detailed information about open accounts payable. To do this, he adds some statistical functions to the worksheet. He begins by using the MAX function to calculate the maximum value in a range.

Steps

Trouble?

If you have difficulty clicking cells or ranges when you build formulas, try scrolling to reposition the worksheet area until all participating cells are visible.

Trouble?

If your results do not match those shown here, check your formulas and make sure you did not type a comma following each open parentheses. The formula in cell D20, for example, should be =MAX(D7:D13)

QuickTip

If you don't see the desired function in the Function name list, scroll to display more function names.

1. Click cell **D19**, type **=MAX(**, select range **G7:G13**, then press **[Enter]**
   Excel automatically adds the right parenthesis after you press [Enter]. The age of the oldest invoice (or maximum value in range G7:G13) is 58 days, as shown in cell D19. Next, Jim builds a formula to calculate the largest dollar amount among the outstanding invoices.
2. In cell D20, type **=MAX(**, select range **D7:D13**, then press **[Enter]**
   The largest outstanding invoice, for $1500.00, is shown in cell D20. The MIN function finds the smallest dollar amount and the age of the newest invoice.
3. In cell D21, type **=MIN(**, select range **D7:D13**, then press **[Enter]**; in cell D22, type **=MIN(**, select range **F7:F13**, then press **[Enter]**
   The smallest dollar amount owed is $50.00, as shown in cell D21, and the newest invoice is 10 days old. The COUNT function calculates the number of invoices by counting the number of entries in column A.
4. In cell D23, type =, then click the **Paste Function button** on the Standard toolbar to open the Paste Function dialog box
5. Under Function category, click **Statistical**, then under Function name, click **COUNT**
   After selecting the function name, notice that the description of the COUNT function reads, "Counts the number of cells that contain numbers..." Because the invoice numbers are formatted in General rather than in the Number format, they are considered text entries, not numerical entries, so the COUNT function will not work. There is another function, COUNTA, that counts the number of cells that are not empty and therefore can be used to count the number of invoice number entries.
6. Under Function name, click **COUNTA**, then click **OK**
   Excel opens the Formula Palette and automatically references the range that is directly above the active cell as the first argument (in this case, range D19:D22, which is not the range you want to count). See Figure E-13. You need to select the correct range of invoice numbers. Because the desired invoice numbers are not visible, you need to collapse the dialog box so that you can select the correct range.
7. With the Value1 argument selected in the Formula Palette, click the Value1 **Collapse Dialog Box button**, select range **A7:A13** in the worksheet, click the **Redisplay Dialog Box button**, then click **OK**
   Cell D23 confirms that there are seven invoices. Compare your worksheet with Figure E-14.
8. Type your name into cell D1, press **[Ctrl][Home]**, then save, print, and close the workbook

FIGURE E-13: Formula Palette showing COUNTA function

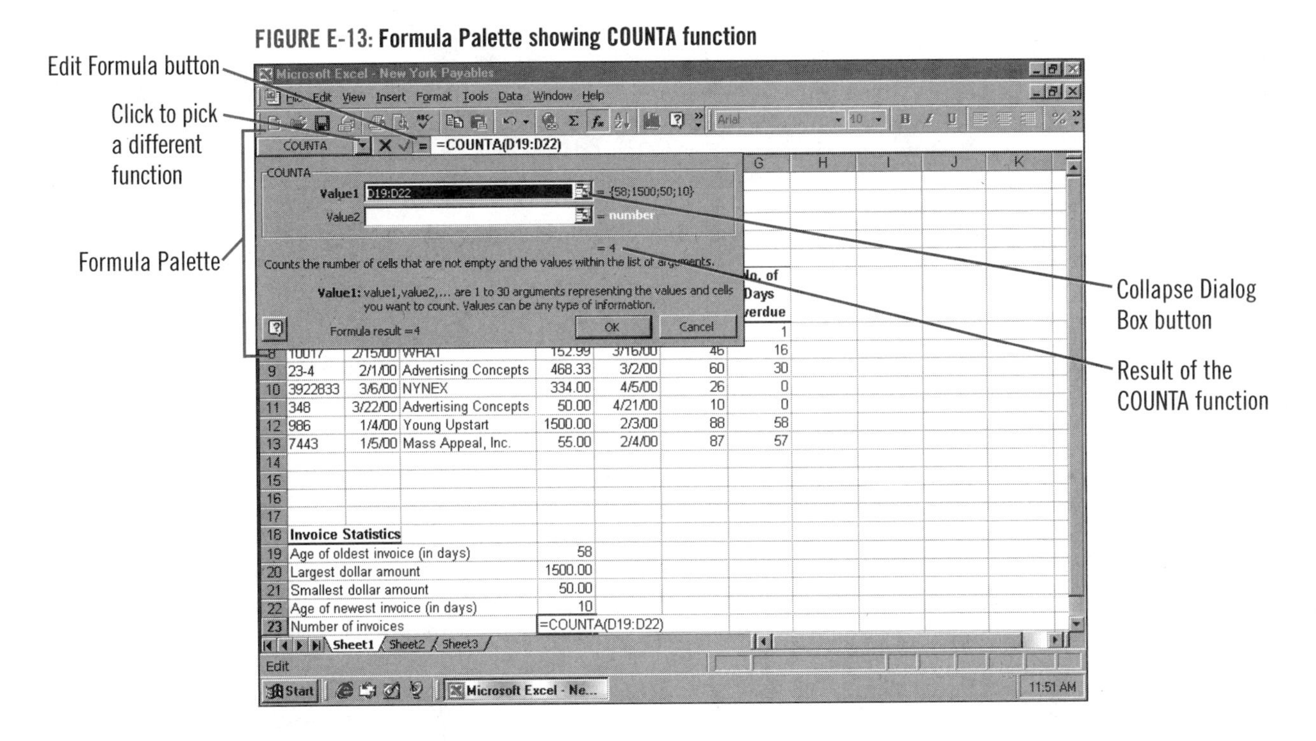

FIGURE E-14: Worksheet with invoice statistics

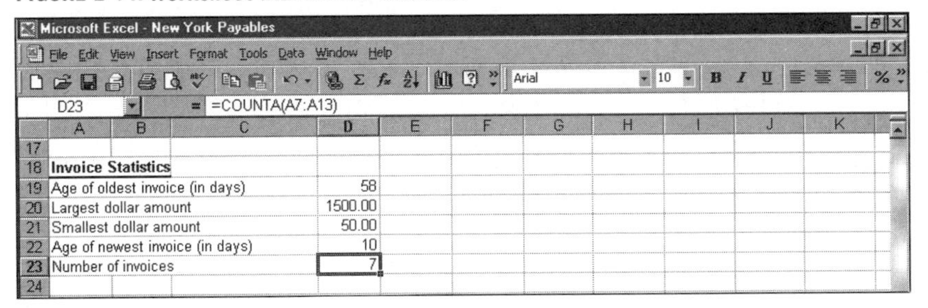

TABLE E-3: Commonly used statistical functions

function	worksheet action
AVERAGE	Calculates an average value
COUNT	Counts the number of values
COUNTA	Counts the number of nonblank entries
MAX	Finds the largest value
MIN	Finds the smallest value
SUM	Calculates a total

Using the Formula Palette to enter and edit formulas

When you use the Paste Function to build a formula, the Formula Palette displays the name and description for the function and each of its arguments, the current result of the function, and the current result of the entire formula. You also can use the Formula Palette to edit functions in formulas. To open the Formula Palette from either a blank cell or one containing a formula, click the Edit Formula button on the formula bar.

Excel 2000

Calculating Payments with the PMT Function

PMT is a financial function that calculates the periodic payment amount for money borrowed. For example, if you want to borrow money to buy a car, the PMT function can calculate your monthly payment on the loan. Let's say you want to borrow $15,000 at 9% interest and pay the loan off in five years. The Excel PMT function can tell you that your monthly payment will be $311.38. The parts of the PMT function are: PMT(rate, nper, pv, fv, type). See Figure E-15 for an illustration of a PMT function that calculates the monthly payment in the car loan example. For several months, MediaLoft management has been discussing the expansion of the San Diego store. Jim has obtained quotes from three different lenders on borrowing $25,000 to begin the expansion. He obtained loan quotes from a commercial bank, a venture capitalist, and an investment banker. Now Jim can summarize the information using the Excel PMT function.

1. Open the workbook titled **EX E-4**, then save the workbook as **San Diego Financing**
   Jim has already entered all the lender data; you are ready to calculate the commercial loan monthly payment in cell E5.
2. Click cell **E5**, type **=PMT(C5/12,D5,B5)** (make sure you type the commas); then click the **Enter button** on the formula bar
   You must divide the annual interest by 12 because you are calculating monthly, not annual, payments. Note that the payment of ($543.56) in cell E5 is a negative amount. (It appears in red on a color monitor.) Excel displays the result of a PMT function as a negative value to reflect the negative cash flow the loan represents to the borrower. Because you want to show the monthly payment value as a positive number, you can convert the loan amount to a positive number by placing a minus sign in front of the cell reference.
3. Edit cell E5 so it reads **=PMT(C5/12,D5,−B5)**, then click
   A positive value of $543.56 now appears in cell E5. See Figure E-16. You can use the same formula to generate the monthly payments for the other loans.
4. With cell **E5** selected, drag the fill handle to select range **E5:E7**
   A monthly payment of $818.47 for the venture capitalist loan appears in cell E6. A monthly payment of $1,176.84 for the investment banker loan appears in cell E7. The loans with shorter terms have much higher payments. You will not know the entire financial picture until you calculate the total payments and total interest for each lender.
5. Click cell **F5**, type **=E5*D5**, then press **[Tab]**; in cell G5, type **=F5−B5**, then click
6. Copy the formulas in cells F5:G5 into the range **FG:G7**, then return to cell A1
   You can experiment with different interest rates, loan amounts, or terms for any one of the lenders; the PMT function generates a new set of values automatically. Compare your results with those in Figure E-17.
7. Enter your name into cell **D1**, save the workbook, then print the worksheet

QuickTip

It is important to be consistent about the units you use for *rate* and *nper.* If, for example, you express *nper* as the number of *monthly* payments, then you must express the interest rate as a *monthly* rate, not an annual rate.

FIGURE E-15: Example of PMT function for car loan

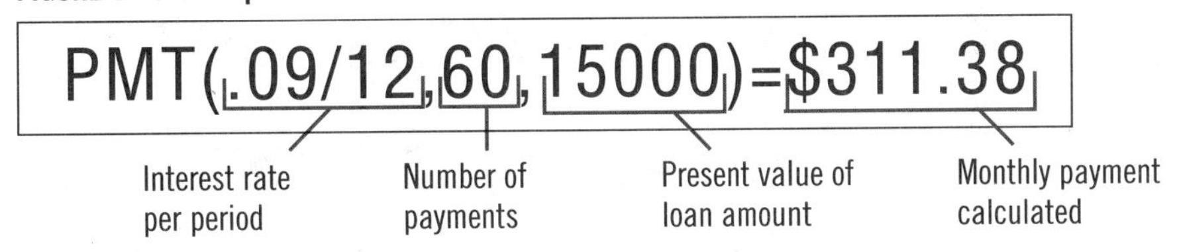

FIGURE E-16: PMT function calculating monthly loan payment

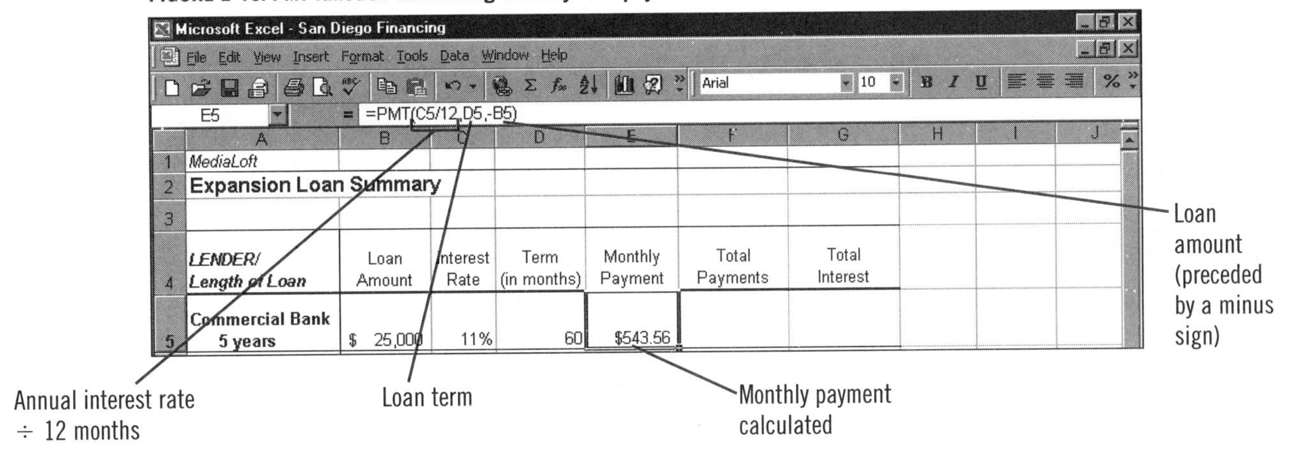

FIGURE E-17: Completed worksheet

Microsoft Excel - San Diego Financing

A1 = MediaLoft

	A	B	C	D	E	F	G
1	*MediaLoft*						
2	Expansion Loan Summary						
3							
4	***LENDER/ Length of Loan***	Loan Amount	Interest Rate	Term (in months)	Monthly Payment	Total Payments	Total Interest
5	**Commercial Bank 5 years**	$ 25,000	11%	60	$543.56	$ 32,613.63	$ 7,613.63
6	**Venture Capitalist 3 years**	$ 25,000	11%	36	$818.47	$ 29,464.85	$ 4,464.85
7	**Investment Banker 2 years**	$ 25,000	12%	24	$1,176.84	$ 28,244.08	$ 3,244.08

CLUES TO USE

Calculating future value with the FV function

You can use the FV (Future Value) function to determine the amount of money a given monthly investment will amount to, at a given interest rate after a given number of payment periods. The syntax is similar to that of the PMT function: FV(rate,nper,pmt,pv,type). For example, suppose you want to invest $1,000 every month for the next 12 months into an account that pays 12% a year, and you want to know how much you will have at the end of 12 months (that is, its future value). You would enter the function FV(.01,12,−1000), and Excel would return the value $12,682.50 as the future value of your investment. As with the PMT function, the units for the rate and nper must be consistent. If you make monthly payments on a three-year loan at 6% annual interest, you would use the rate 6%/12 and 36 periods (12*3). The arguments pv and type are optional; pv is the present value, or the total amount the series of payments is worth now. If you omit it, Excel assumes the pv is 0. The Type argument indicates when the payments are made; 0 is the end of the period and 1 is the beginning of the period.

Excel 2000

Displaying and Printing Formula Contents

Excel usually displays the result of formula calculations in the worksheet area and displays formula contents for the active cell in the formula bar. However, you can instruct Excel to display the formulas directly in the worksheet locations in which they were entered. You can document worksheet formulas by first displaying the formulas, then printing them. These formula printouts are valuable paper-based worksheet documentation. Because formulas are often longer than their corresponding values, landscape orientation is the best choice for printing formulas. Jim is ready to produce a formula printout to submit with the worksheet.

Steps

1. Click **Tools** on the menu bar, click **Options**, then click the **View tab**
   The View tab of the Options dialog box appears, as shown in Figure E-18.
2. Under Window options, click the **Formulas** check box to select it, then click **OK**
   The columns widen and retain their original formats.
3. Scroll horizontally to bring columns E through G into view
   Instead of formula results appearing in the cells, Excel shows the actual formulas. The column widths adjusted automatically to accommodate the formulas.
4. Click the **Print Preview button** on the Standard toolbar
   The status bar reads Preview: Page 1 of 3, indicating that the worksheet will print on three pages. You want to print it on one page and include the row number and column letter headings.
5. Click the **Setup button** in the Print Preview window, then click the **Page tab**
6. Under Orientation, click the **Landscape option button**; then under Scaling, click the **Fit to option button**
   Selecting Landscape instructs Excel to print the worksheet sideways on the page. The Fit to option ensures that the document is printed on a single page.
7. Click the **Sheet tab**, under Print click the **Row and column headings check box** to select it, click **OK**, then position the **Zoom pointer** over **column A** and click
   The worksheet formulas now appear on a single page, in landscape orientation, with row (number) and column (letter) headings. See Figure E-19.
8. Click **Print** in the Print Preview window, then click **OK**
   After you retrieve the printout, you want to return the worksheet to display formula results. You can do this easily by using a key combination.
9. Press **[Ctrl][`]** to redisplay formula results, save and close the workbook, then exit Excel
   [Ctrl][`] (grave accent mark) toggles between displaying formula results and displaying formula contents.

QuickTip

All Page Setup options—such as Landscape orientation, Fit to scaling—apply to the active worksheet and are saved with the workbook.

FIGURE E-18: View tab of the Options dialog box

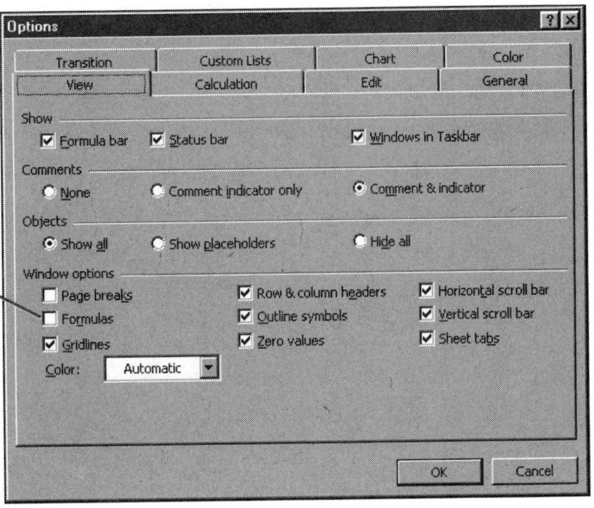

Click here to view formulas

FIGURE E-19: Print Preview window

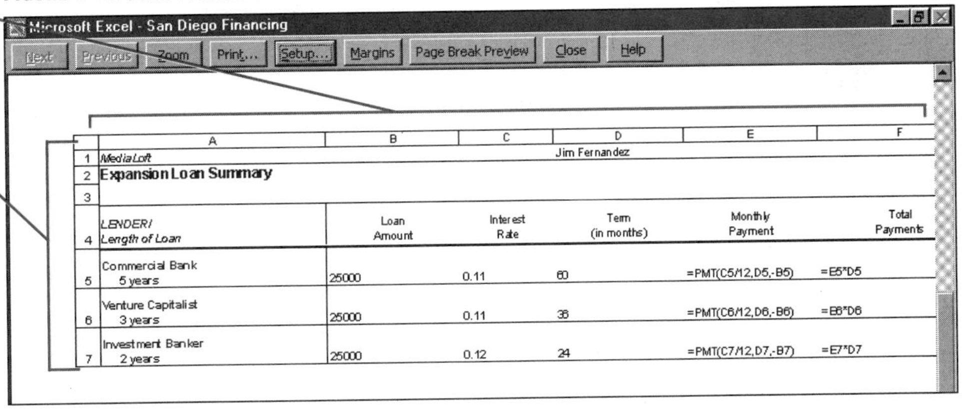

Column headings

Row headings

Excel 2000

Setting margins and alignment when printing part of a worksheet

CLUES TO USE

Sometimes you want to print one part of a worksheet. While you may have set margins for printing the whole worksheet, you can set custom margins to print the smaller section. Select the range you want to print, click File on the menu bar, click Print, under Print what click Selection, then click Preview. In the Print Preview window, click Setup, then click the Margins tab. See Figure E-20. Double-click the margin numbers and type new ones. Use the Center on page check boxes to center the range horizontally or vertically. If you plan to print the range again in the future, save the view after you print: Click View on the menu bar, click Custom Views, click Add, then type a view name and click OK.

FIGURE E-20: Margins tab in the Page Setup dialog box

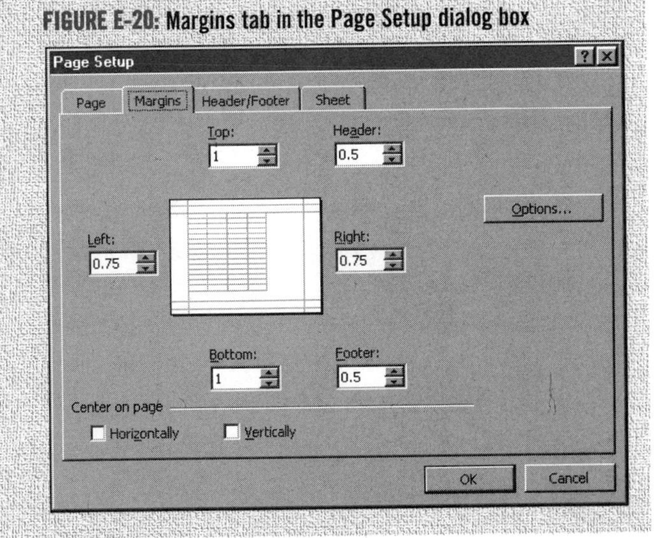

Excel 2000

Practice

► Concepts Review

Label each element of the Excel screen shown in Figure E-21.

FIGURE E-21

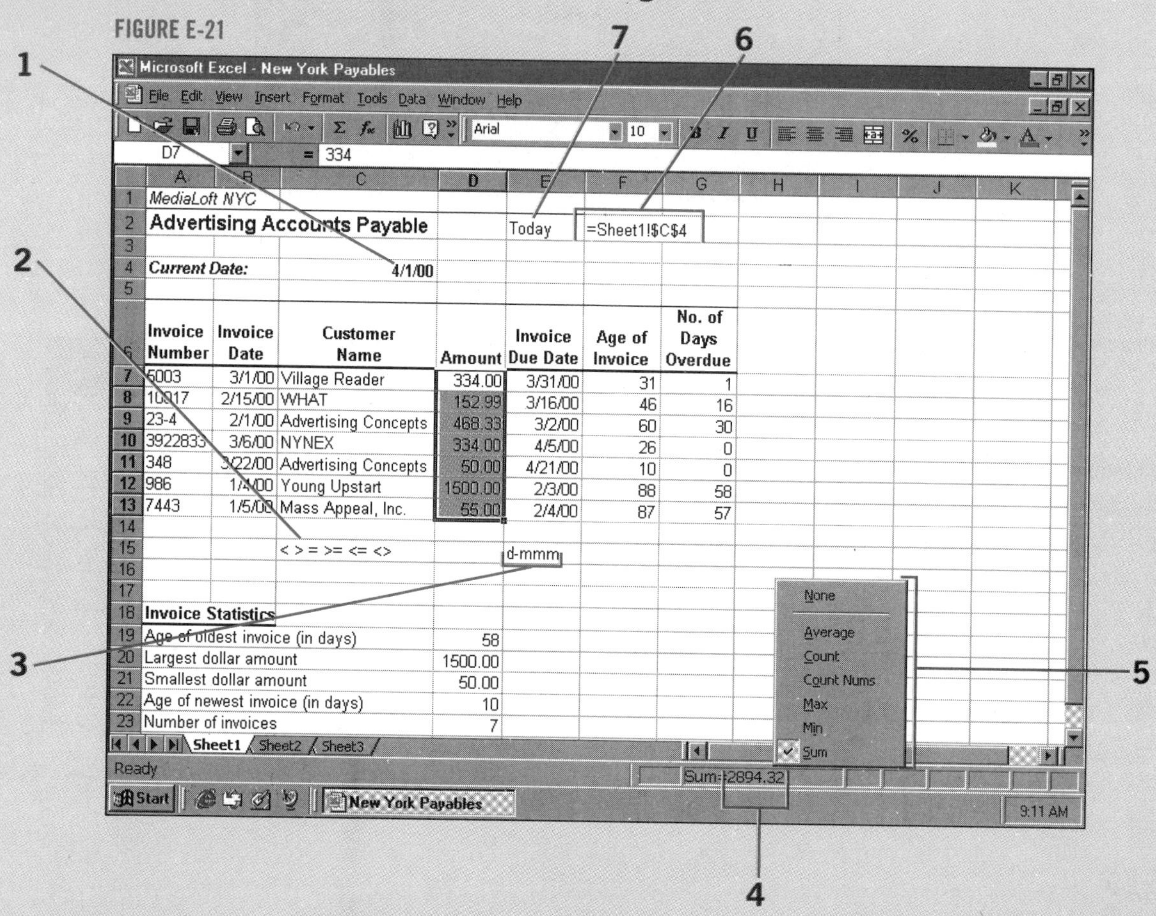

Match each term with the statement that best describes its function.

8. Parentheses
9. COUNTA
10. test_cond
11. COUNT
12. pv

a. Part of the IF function in which the conditions are stated
b. Function used to count the number of numerical entries
c. Part of the PMT function that represents the loan amount
d. Function used to count the number of nonblank entries
e. Symbols used in formulas to control formula calculation order

Select the best answer from the list of choices.

13. To generate a positive payment value when using the PMT function, you must
- **a.** Enter the function arguments as positive values.
- **b.** Enter the function arguments as negative values.
- **c.** Enter the amount being borrowed as a negative value.
- **d.** Enter the interest rate divisor as a negative value.

14. When you enter the rate and nper arguments in a PMT function,
- **a.** Multiply both units by 12.
- **b.** Be consistent in the units used.
- **c.** Divide both values by 12.
- **d.** Use monthly units instead of annual units.

15. To express conditions such as less than or equal to, you can use a(n)
- **a.** IF function.
- **b.** Comparison operator.
- **c.** AutoCalculate formula.
- **d.** PMT function.

16. Which of the following statements is false?
- **a.** $#,### is an Excel number format.
- **b.** You can create custom number and date formats in Excel.
- **c.** You can use only existing number and date formats in Excel.
- **d.** m/d/yy is an Excel date format.

▶ Skills Review

1. Create a formula with several operators.
- **a.** Open workbook EX E-5, enter your name into cell D1, and save the workbook as "Manager Bonuses".
- **b.** Select cell C15 using the Go To command.
- **c.** Enter the formula C13+(C14*7).
- **d.** Use the Paste Special command to paste the values in B4:B10 to G4:G10.

2. Use names in a formula.
- **a.** Name cell C13 "Dept_Bonus".
- **b.** Name cell C14 "Project_Bonus".
- **c.** In cell E4, enter the formula Dept_Bonus*D4+Project_Bonus.
- **d.** Copy the formula in cell E4 into the range E5:E10.
- **e.** Format range E4:E10 with the Comma Style button.
- **f.** In cell F4, enter a formula that sums C4 and E4.
- **g.** Copy the formula in cell F4 into the range F5:F10.
- **h.** Return to cell A1, then save your work.

3. Generate multiple totals with AutoSum.
- **a.** Select range E4:F11.
- **b.** Enter the totals using AutoSum.
- **c.** Format range E11:F11 using the Currency Style button.
- **d.** Return to cell A1, save your work, then preview and print this worksheet.

4. **Use dates in calculations.**
   a. Make the Merit Pay sheet active.
   b. In cell D6, enter the formula B6+183.
   c. Copy the formula in cell D6 into the range D7:D14.
   d. Use the NOW function to insert the date and time in cell A3, widening the column as necessary.
   e. In cell E18, enter the text "Next Pay Date", and, in cell G18, use the Date function to enter the date 10/1/00.
   f. Save your work.
5. **Build a conditional formula with the IF function.**
   a. In cell F6, enter the formula IF(C6=5,E6*0.05,0).
   b. Copy the formula in cell F6 into the range F7:F14.
   c. Apply the comma format with no decimal places to F6:F14.
   d. Select the range A4:G4 and delete the cells using the Delete command on the Edit menu. Shift the remaining cells up.
   e. Repeat the procedure to delete the cells A15:G15.
   f. Use the Cells command on the Insert menu to insert a cell between Department Statistics and Average Salary, moving the remaining cells down.
   g. Check your formulas to make sure the cell references have been updated.
   h. Save your work.
6. **Use statistical functions.**
   a. In cell C18, enter a function to calculate the average salary in the range E5:E13 with no decimal places.
   b. In cell C19, enter a function to calculate the largest bonus in the range F5:F13.
   c. In cell C20, enter a function to calculate the lowest performance rating in the range C5:C13.
   d. In cell C21, enter a function to calculate the number of entries in range A5:A13.
   e. Enter your name in cell F3, then save, preview, and print this worksheet.
7. **Calculate payments with the PMT function.**
   a. Make the Loan sheet active.
   b. In cell B9, enter the formula PMT(B5/12,B6,−B4).
   c. In cell B10, enter the formula B9*B6.
   d. AutoFit column B, if necessary.
   e. In cell B11, enter the formula B10−B4.
   f. Enter your name in cell C1, then save and print the worksheet.
8. **Display and print formula contents.**
   a. Use the View tab in the Options dialog box to turn formulas on.
   b. Adjust the column widths as necessary.
   c. Save, preview, and print this worksheet in landscape orientation with the row and column headings.
   d. Close the workbook.

Independent Challenges

1. As manager of Mike's Ice Cream Parlor, you have been asked to create a worksheet that totals the monthly sales of all store products. Your monthly report should include the following:

- Sales totals for the current month for each product
- Sales totals for the last month for each product
- The percent change in sales from last month to this month

To document the report further, you decide to include a printout of the worksheet formulas.

To complete this independent challenge:

a. Open the workbook titled EX E-6, type your name into cell D1, then save the workbook as "Mike's Sales" to the appropriate folder on your Project Disk.
b. Enter today's date in cell A3. Create and apply a custom format.
c. Complete the headings for weeks 2 through 4. Enter totals for each week and current month totals for each product. Calculate the percent change in sales from last month to this month. (*Hint:* The formula in words would be (Current Month-Last Month)/Last Month.)
d. After you enter the percent change formula for regular ice cream, copy the formula down the column and format the column with the percentage style.
e. Apply a comma format with no decimal places to all numbers and totals.
f. Save, preview, then print the worksheet on a single page. If necessary, print in landscape orientation. If you make any page setup changes, save the worksheet again.
g. Display and print the worksheet formulas, then print the formulas on one page with row and column headings.
h. Close the workbook without saving the changes for displaying formulas.

2. You are an auditor with a certified public accounting firm. Fly Away, a manufacturer of skating products, including roller skates and skateboards, has contacted you to audit its financial records. The managers at Fly Away have asked you to assist them in preparing their year-end sales summary. Specifically, they want to add expenses and show the percent of annual expenses that each expense category represents. They also want to show what percent of annual sales each expense category represents. You should include a formula calculating the difference between sales and expenses and another formula calculating expenses divided by sales. The expense categories and their respective dollar amounts are as follows: Building Lease $45,000; Equipment $203,000; Office $23,000; Salary $345,000; Taxes $302,000. Use these expense amounts to prepare the year-end sales and expenses summary for Fly Away.

To complete this independent challenge:

a. Open the workbook titled EX E-7, type your name into cell D1, then save the workbook as "Fly Away Sales".
b. Name the cell containing the formula for total annual expenses "Annual_Expenses". Use the name Annual_Expenses in the first formula calculating percent of annual expenses. Copy this formula as appropriate and apply the percentage style. Make sure to include a formula that sums all the values for percent of annual expenses, which should equal 1 or 100%.
c. Enter a formula calculating what percent of annual sales each expense category represents. Use the name Annual_Sales in the formula and format it appropriately. Enter formulas calculating annual sales minus annual expenses and expenses divided by sales using only the names Annual_Sales and Annual_Expenses. Add formulas for totals as appropriate.
d. Format the cells using the Currency, Percent, or Comma style. Widen the columns as necessary to display cell contents.
e. Save, preview, then print the worksheet on a single page. If necessary, use landscape orientation. Save any page setup changes you make.
f. Display and print worksheet formulas on a single page with row and column headings.
g. Close the workbook without saving the changes for displaying formulas.

3. As the owner of Custom Fit, a general contracting firm specializing in home-storage projects, you are facing yet another business challenge at your firm. Because jobs are taking longer than expected, you decide to take out a loan to purchase some new power tools. According to your estimates, you need a $5,000 loan to purchase the tools. You check three loan sources: the Small Business Administration (SBA), your local bank, and a consortium of investors. Each source offers you a loan on its own terms. The local bank offers you the loan at 9.5% interest over four years. The SBA will loan you the money at 9% interest, but you have to pay it off in three years. The consortium offers you an 8% loan, but they require you to pay it back in two years. To analyze all three loan options, you decide to build a tool loan summary worksheet. Using the loan terms provided, build a worksheet summarizing your options.

To complete this independent challenge:

a. Open a new workbook, type your name in cell A1, then save it as "Custom Fit Loan Options".
b. Enter today's date in cell A3.
c. Enter labels and worksheet data. You need headings for the loan source, loan amount, interest rate, term or number of payments, monthly payment, total payments, and total interest. Fill in the data provided for the three loan sources.
d. Enter formulas as appropriate: a PMT formula for the monthly payment; a formula calculating the total payments based on the monthly payment and term values; and a formula for total interest based on the total payments and the loan amount.
e. Format the worksheet as desired.
f. Save, preview, then print the worksheet on a single page using landscape orientation. Create a printout of worksheet formulas showing row and column headings. Do not save the worksheet with these settings.

4. The MediaLoft accounting department has asked you to analyze overall MediaLoft CD sales and look at ways to improve them. The figures you will need are on the MediaLoft intranet site. This site gives employees access to companywide information. Accounting is considering taking out a $25,000 loan to buy new CD display cases for some of its stores.

To complete this independent challenge:

a. Start Excel, then open the File EX E-8, save it as CD Analysis on your Project Disk, and make sure the CD Sales tab is active.
b. Connect to the Internet, go to the MediaLoft intranet site at http://www.course.com/Illustrated/MediaLoft. Click the Accounting link, then click the CD Sales Analysis link. Print the CD Sales Analysis, disconnect from the Internet, and then, starting in cell A2, enter this data on the CD Sales sheet in the CD Analysis workbook, except for the Totals row. Enter formulas to calculate the totals in row 11 and label the row. Enter formulas to calculate the category totals in column F and label the column totals.
c. In row 13, enter a label in column A that reads "Goals", and enter the following sales goals for each quarter:

Q1	Q2	Q3	Q4
317,000	327,000	372,000	400,000

d. Enter a formula that totals the goals figures in cell F13.
e. In row 15, enter a label called "Real to Goal", and enter formulas for each loan that calculate the difference between goal and actual sales for each quarter and for the year's total.
f. In row 17, enter another label called "Status". For each quarter, use the IF function that displays the text "Over Goal" if the Real to Goal total is a positive number (in other words, >0). Otherwise, have it print "Under Goal". Format the cells, AutoFit the columns as necessary, and save the worksheet.
g. Go to the CD Loan worksheet and use the PMT function to calculate the monthly payment for each loan, making sure it displays as a positive number.
h. Enter a formula in column F that calculates the total interest for each loan. It should multiply the monthly payment by the term of the loan, and then subtract the original loan amount from the result.

i. For each loan, the respective banks have given MediaLoft a certain number of days to respond, after which their loan offers will no longer be valid. In the Inform by column, enter a formula for each loan that adds the number of days in column G to today's date, displaying the date by which MediaLoft must respond. (*Hint:* Use the TODAY function to enter today's date in the formula.)

j. In cells B8:B10, use Excel functions to enter the shortest term, the lowest rate, and the average interest rate, then display and print the formulas for the CD Loan sheet.

k. Print the CD Sales and CD Loan worksheets, then save and close the workbook.

Visual Workshop

Create the worksheet shown in Figure E-22. (Hint: Enter the items in range C9:C11 as labels by typing an apostrophe before each formula.) Type your name in row 1, and save the workbook as "Car Payment Calculator" to the appropriate folder on your Project Disk. Preview, then print, the worksheet.

FIGURE E-22

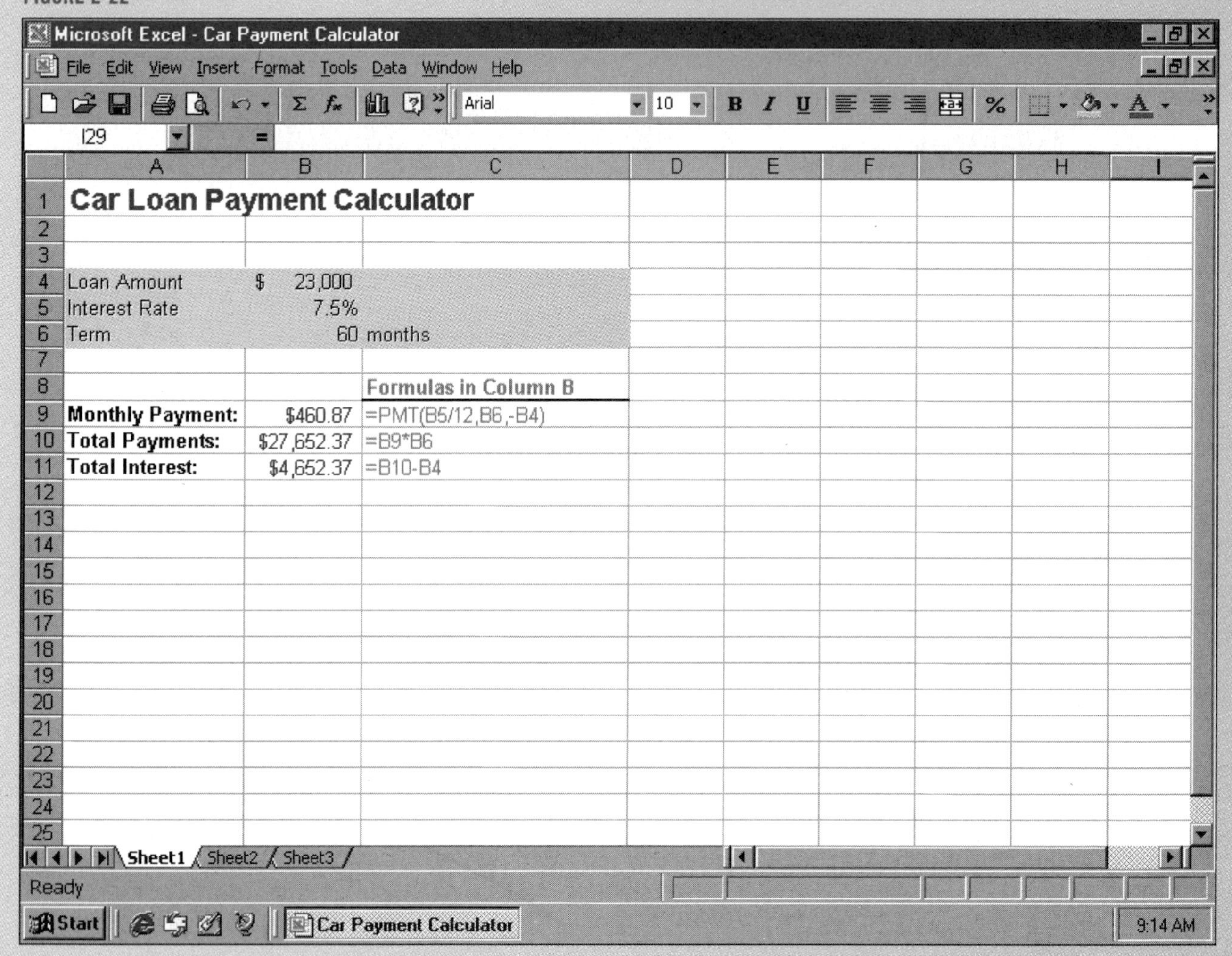

Excel 2000

Managing

Workbooks and Preparing Them for the Web

Objectives

- MOUS ► Freeze columns and rows
- MOUS ► Insert and delete worksheets
- MOUS ► Consolidate data with 3-D references
- MOUS ► Hide and protect worksheet areas
- ► Save custom views of a worksheet
- MOUS ► Control page breaks and page numbering
- MOUS ► Create a hyperlink between Excel files
- MOUS ► Save an Excel file as an HTML document

In this unit you will learn several Excel features to help you manage and print workbook data. You will also learn how to prepare workbooks for publication on the World Wide Web. MediaLoft's accounting department asks Jim Fernandez to design a timecard summary worksheet to track salary costs for hourly workers. He designs a worksheet using some employees from the MediaLoft Houston store. When the worksheet is complete, the accounting department will add the rest of the employees and place it on the MediaLoft intranet site for review by store managers. Jim will save the worksheet in HTML format for viewing on the site.

Freezing Columns and Rows

As rows and columns fill up with data, you might need to scroll through the worksheet to add, delete, modify, and view information. Looking at information without row or column labels can be confusing. In Excel, you can temporarily freeze columns and rows, which enables you to view separate areas of your worksheets at the same time. **Panes** are the columns and rows that **freeze**, or remain in place, while you scroll through your worksheet. The freeze feature is especially useful when you're dealing with large worksheets. Sometimes, though, even freezing is not sufficient. In those cases, you can create as many as four areas, or panes, on the screen at one time and move freely within each of them. Jim needs to verify the total hours worked, hourly pay rate, and total pay for salespeople Paul Cristifano and Virginia Young. Because the worksheet is becoming more difficult to read as its size increases, Jim needs to freeze the column and row labels.

QuickTip

To return personalized toolbars and menus to their default state, click Tools on the menu bar, click Customize, click Reset my usage data on the Options tab, click Yes, then click Close.

1. **Start Excel if necessary, open the workbook titled EX F-1, save it as Timecard Summary, scroll through the Monday worksheet to view the data and click cell D6**
   You move to cell D6 because you want to freeze columns A, B, and C. By doing so, you will be able to see each employee's last name, first name, and timecard number on the screen when you scroll to the right. Because you want to scroll down the worksheet and still be able to read the column headings, you also freeze the labels in rows 1 through 5. Excel freezes the columns to the left and the rows above the cell pointer.

2. **Click Window on the menu bar, then click Freeze Panes**
   A thin line appears along the column border to the left of the active cell, and another line appears along the row above the active cell indicating that columns A through C and rows 1 through 5 are frozen.

QuickTip

To easily change worksheet data without manual scrolling, click Edit on the menu bar, click Replace, then enter text you want to find and text you want to replace it with. Use the Find Next, Replace, and Replace All buttons to find and replace occurrences of the found text with the replacement text.

3. **Scroll to the right until columns A through C and L through O are visible**
   Because columns A, B, and C are frozen, they remain on the screen; columns D through K are temporarily hidden from view. Notice that the information you are looking for in row 13 (last name, total hours, hourly pay rate, and total pay for Paul Cristifano) is readily available. You jot down Paul's data but still need to verify Virginia Young's information.

4. **Scroll down until row 26 is visible**
   Notice that in addition to columns A through C, rows 1 through 5 remain on the screen as well. See Figure F-1. Jim jots down the information for Virginia Young. Even though a pane is frozen, you can click in the frozen area of the worksheet and edit the contents of the cells there, if necessary.

QuickTip

When you open an existing workbook, the cell pointer is in the cell it was in when you last saved the workbook. Press [Ctrl][Home] to return to cell A1 prior to saving and closing a workbook.

5. **Press [Ctrl][Home]**
   Because the panes are frozen, the cell pointer moves to cell D6, not A1.

6. **Click Window on the menu bar, then click Unfreeze Panes**
   The panes are unfrozen.

7. **Return to cell A1, then save the workbook**

FIGURE F-1: Scrolled worksheet with frozen rows and columns

Microsoft Excel - Timecard Summary

D6 = 807569756

	A	B	C	L	M	N	O
1	*MediaLoft*						
2	Daily Timecard Summary for Ho						
3							
4							
5	Last Name	First Name	Timecard Number	Time Out	Total Hours	Hourly Pay Rate	Total Pay
10	Chilton	Linda	FP02	2:30 PM	2:30	$ 10.50	$ 26.25
11	Chimera	Julia	FN03		2:00	$ 9.75	$ 19.50
12	Colt	Rinaldo	FP06	3:00 PM	2:00	$ 11.24	$ 22.48
13	Cristifano	Paul	FP28	8:00 PM	5:00	$ 11.00	$ 55.00
14	Emerillo	Angel	FN20		3:45	$ 13.00	$ 48.75
15	Gallagher	Charles	CS30	4:00 PM	4:00	$ 12.50	$ 50.00
16	LaFuente	Gerald	FP21		2:00	$ 9.50	$ 19.00
17	Moen	Paul	FN13		3:00	$ 8.75	$ 26.25
18	Nguyen	Tranh	CS24	5:45 PM	5:00	$ 14.00	$ 70.00
19	Gabriel	Phillippe	CO01	7:00 PM	4:00	$ 15.00	$ 60.00
20	Singh	Tom	CO34	11:30 PM	8:00	$ 11.00	$ 88.00
21	Thorn	Jim	CO25		5:30	$ 7.50	$ 41.25
22	Westerfield	William	CO99	4:30 PM	2:30	$ 10.00	$ 25.00
23	Wu	Julia	FP41	5:30 PM	8:00	$ 12.00	$ 96.00
24	Xavier	Francois	FN54	4:00 PM	6:00	$14.00	$ 84.00
25	Yardley	Susan	FP22	9:00 PM	6:00	$15.00	$ 90.00
26	Young	Virginia	FN14		3:00	$ 9.75	$ 29.25
27							
28						Total	$ 1,042.73

Monday / Tuesday / Wednesday / Friday / Saturday / Sunday / Weekly

Ready

Start | Microsoft Excel - Tim... | 9:26 AM

Break in row numbers due to frozen rows 1-5

Break in column letters due to frozen columns A-C

Excel 2000

Splitting the worksheet into multiple panes

Excel provides a way to split the worksheet area into vertical and/or horizontal panes, so that you can click inside any one pane and scroll to locate desired information in that pane while the other panes remain in place. See Figure F-2. To split a worksheet area into multiple panes, drag the split box (the small box at the top of the vertical scroll bar or at the right end of the horizontal scroll bar) in the direction you want the split to appear. To remove the split, move the mouse over the split until the pointer changes to a double pointed arrow ÷, then double-click.

FIGURE F-2: Worksheet split into two horizontal panes

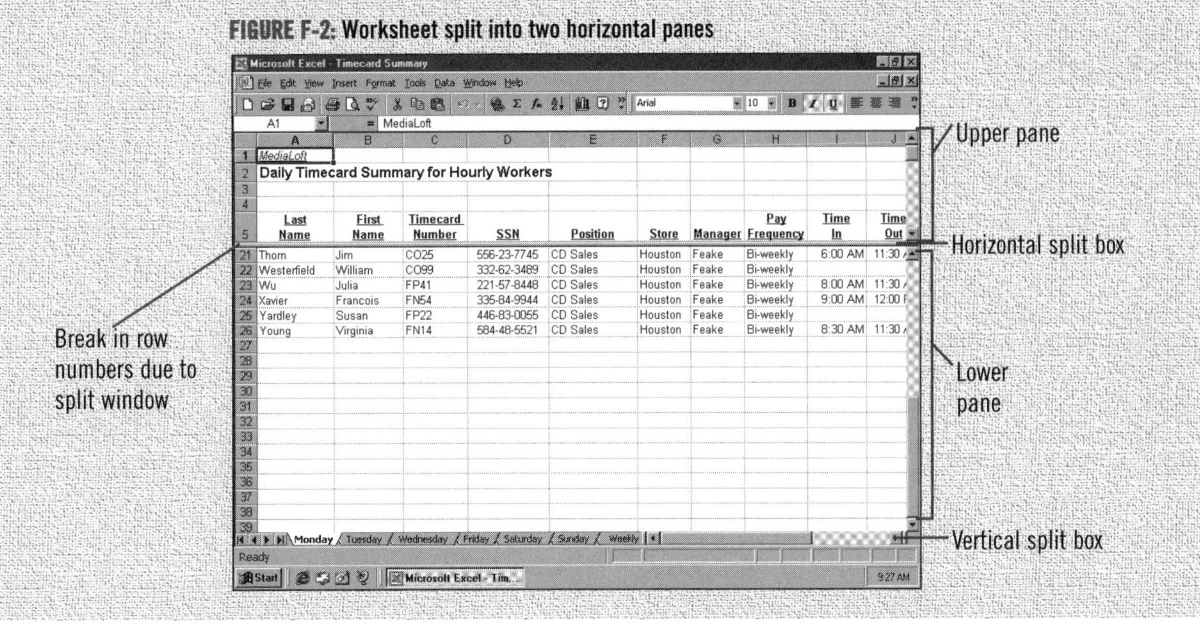

Excel 2000

Inserting and Deleting Worksheets

You can insert and delete worksheets in a workbook as needed. For example, because new workbooks open with only three sheets available (Sheet1, Sheet2, and Sheet3), you need to insert at least one more sheet if you want to have four quarterly worksheets in an annual financial budget workbook. You can do this by using commands on the menu bar or pop-up menu. Jim was in a hurry when he added the sheet tabs to the Timecard Summary workbook. He needs to insert a sheet for Thursday and delete the sheet for Sunday because these Houston workers do not work on Sundays.

QuickTip

You also can copy the active worksheet by clicking Edit on the menu bar, then clicking Move or Copy Sheet. Choose the sheet the copy will precede, then select the Create a copy check box.

1. Click the **Friday sheet tab**, click **Insert** on the menu bar, then click **Worksheet**
   Excel automatically inserts a new sheet tab labeled Sheet1 to the left of the Friday sheet.
2. Rename the Sheet1 tab **Thursday**
   Now the tabs read Monday, Tuesday, Wednesday, Thursday, Friday, and Saturday. The tab for the Weekly Summary is not visible, but you still need to delete the Sunday worksheet.
3. Click the **Sunday sheet tab**, move the pointer over the **Sunday tab**, then click the **right mouse button**
   A pop-up menu appears. See Figure F-3. The pop-up menu allows you to insert, delete, rename, move, or copy sheets, select all the sheets, or view any Visual Basic programming code in a workbook.
4. Click **Delete** on the pop-up menu
   A message box warns that the selected sheet will be deleted permanently. You must acknowledge the message before proceeding.
5. Click **OK**
   The Sunday sheet is deleted. Next, to check your work, you view a menu of worksheets in the workbook.

QuickTip

You can scroll several tabs at once by pressing [Shift] while clicking one of the middle tab scrolling buttons.

6. Move the mouse pointer over any tab scrolling button, then **right-click**
   When you right-click a tab scrolling button, Excel automatically opens a menu of the worksheets in the active workbook. Compare your list with Figure F-4.
7. Click **Monday**, return to cell A1, then save the workbook

FIGURE F-3: Worksheet pop-up menu

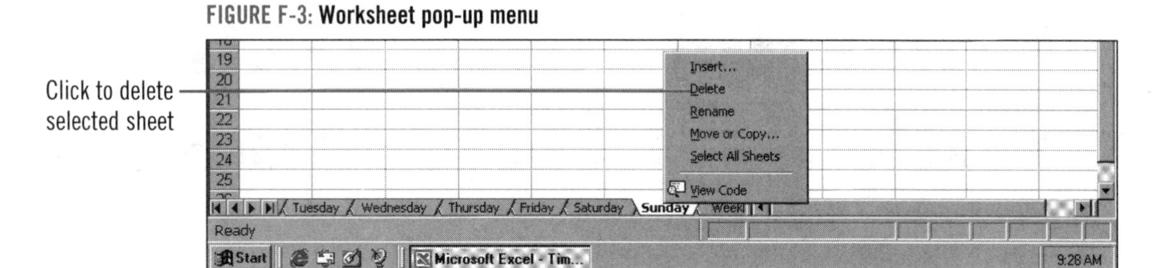

FIGURE F-4: Workbook with menu of worksheets

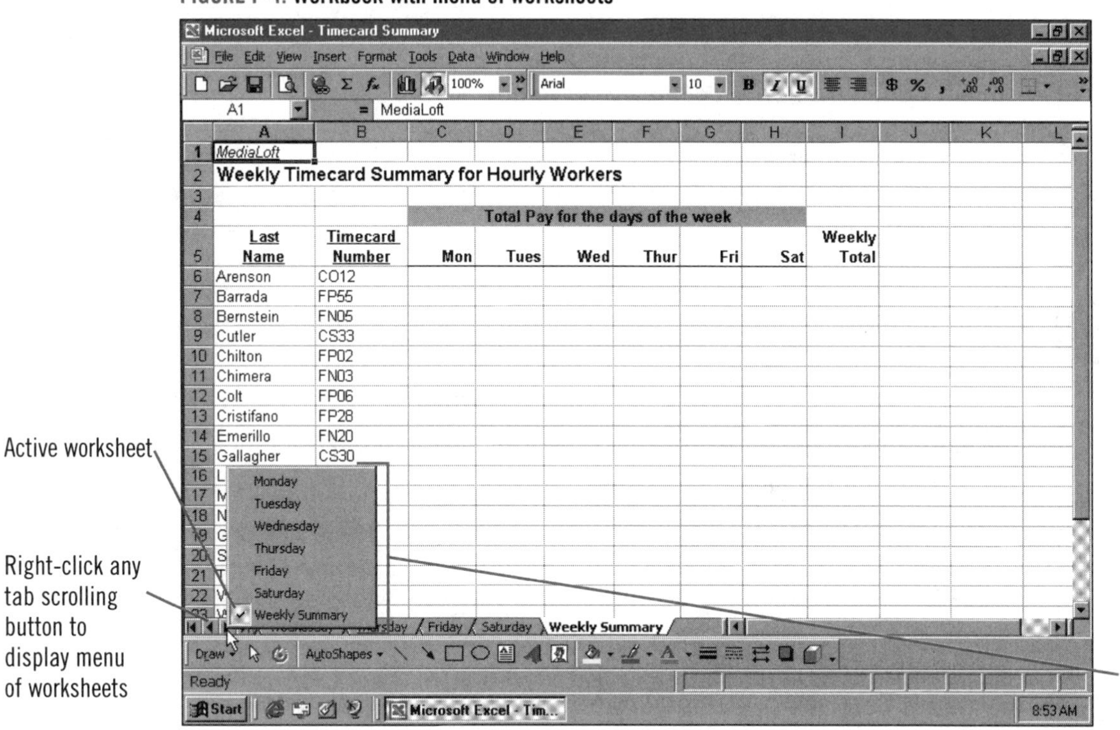

Specifying headers and footers

As you prepare a workbook for others to view, it is helpful to give them as much data as possible about the worksheet—how many pages, who created it on what date, and the like. You can do this easily in a **header** or **footer**, information that prints at the top or bottom of each printed page. Headers and footers are visible on screen only in Print Preview. To add a header, for example, click View on the menu bar, click Header and Footer, click Custom Header, and you see a dialog box similar to that in Figure F-5. Both the header and the footer are divided into three sections, and you can enter information in any or all of them. Type information such as your name and click the icons to enter the page number, total pages, date, time, filename, or sheet name to enter codes that represent these items. Click OK, view the preview on the Header and Footer tab, then click OK again.

FIGURE F-5: Header dialog box

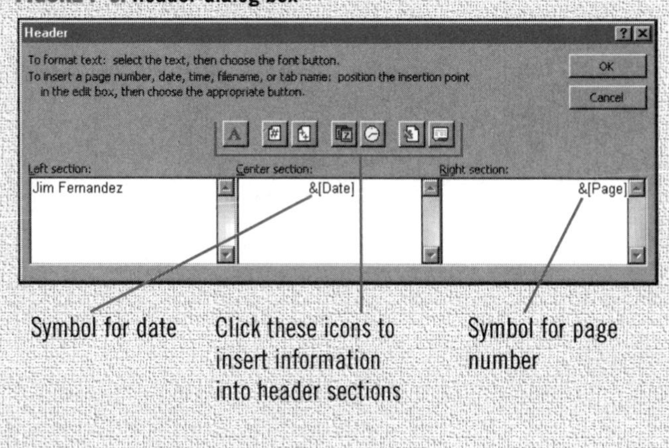

Excel 2000

Consolidating Data with 3-D References

When you want to summarize similar data that exists in different sheets or workbooks, you can combine and display it in one sheet. For example, you might have departmental sales figures on four different store sheets that you want to add together, or **consolidate**, on one summary sheet that shows total departmental sales for all stores. The best way to consolidate data is to use cell references to the various sheets on a consolidation, or summary, sheet. Because they reference other sheets that are usually behind the summary sheet, such references effectively create another dimension in the workbook and are called **3-D references.** You can reference data in other sheets and in other workbooks. Referencing cells is a better method than retyping calculated results because the data values on which calculated totals depend might change. If you reference the values instead, any changes to the original values are automatically reflected in the consolidation sheet. Although Jim does not have timecard data for the remaining days of the week, he wants to test the Weekly Summary sheet that will consolidate the timesheet data. He does this by creating a reference from the total pay data in the Monday sheet to the Weekly Summary sheet. First, he freezes panes to improve the view of the worksheets prior to initiating the reference between them.

1. On the Monday sheet, click cell **D6**, click **Window** on the menu bar, click **Freeze Panes**, then scroll horizontally to bring columns L through O into view
2. Right-click a **tab scrolling button**, then click **Weekly Summary**
   Because the Weekly Summary sheet (which is the consolidation sheet) will contain the reference, the cell pointer must reside there when you initiate the reference. To make a simple **reference** within the same sheet or between sheets, position the cell pointer in the cell to contain the reference, type = (equal sign), position the cell pointer in the cell to be referenced, and then enter the information.
3. While in the Weekly Summary sheet, click cell **C6**, type **=**, activate the Monday sheet, click cell **O6**, then click the **Enter button** on the formula bar
   The formula bar reads =Monday!O6. See Figure F-6. *Monday* references the Monday sheet. The ! (exclamation point) is an **external reference indicator** meaning that the cell referenced is outside the active sheet; O6 is the actual cell reference in the external sheet. The result, $33.00, appears in cell C6 of the Weekly Summary sheet, showing the reference to the value displayed in cell O6 of the Monday sheet.
4. While in the Weekly Summary sheet, copy cell **C6** into cells **C7:C26**
   Excel copies the contents of cell C6 with its relative reference down the column. You can test a reference by changing one cell that it is based on and seeing if the reference changes.
5. Activate the Monday sheet, edit cell L6 to read **6:30 PM**, then activate the Weekly Summary sheet
   Cell C6 now shows $41.25. Changing Beryl Arenson's "time out" from 5:30 to 6:30 increased her pay from $33.00 to $41.25. This makes sense because Beryl's hours went from four to five, and her hourly salary is $8.25. The reference to Monday's total pay was automatically updated in the Weekly Summary sheet. See Figure F-7.
6. Preview, then print the Weekly Summary sheet
   To preview and print an entire workbook, click File on the menu bar, click Print, click to select the Entire Workbook option button, then click Preview. In the Preview window, you can page through the entire workbook. When you click Print, the entire workbook will print.
7. Activate the Monday sheet, then unfreeze the panes
8. Save the workbook

Trouble?

If you have difficulty referencing cells between sheets, press [Esc] and begin again.

FIGURE F-6: Worksheet showing referenced cell

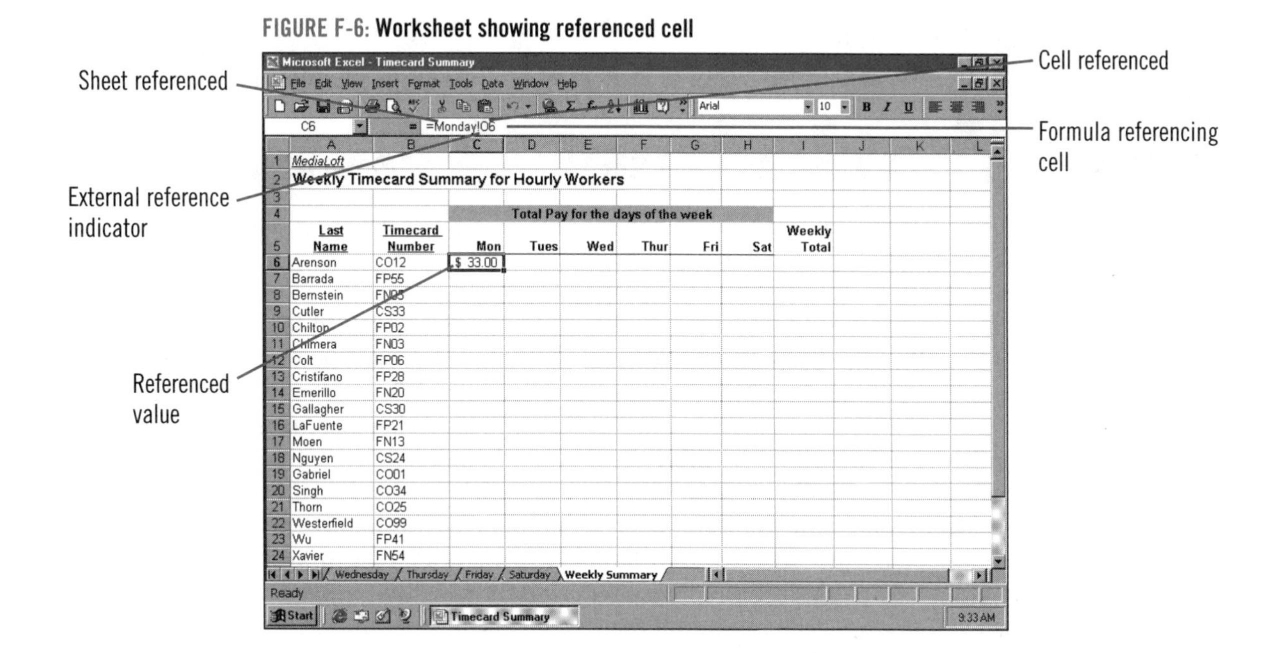

FIGURE F-7: Weekly Summary worksheet with updated reference

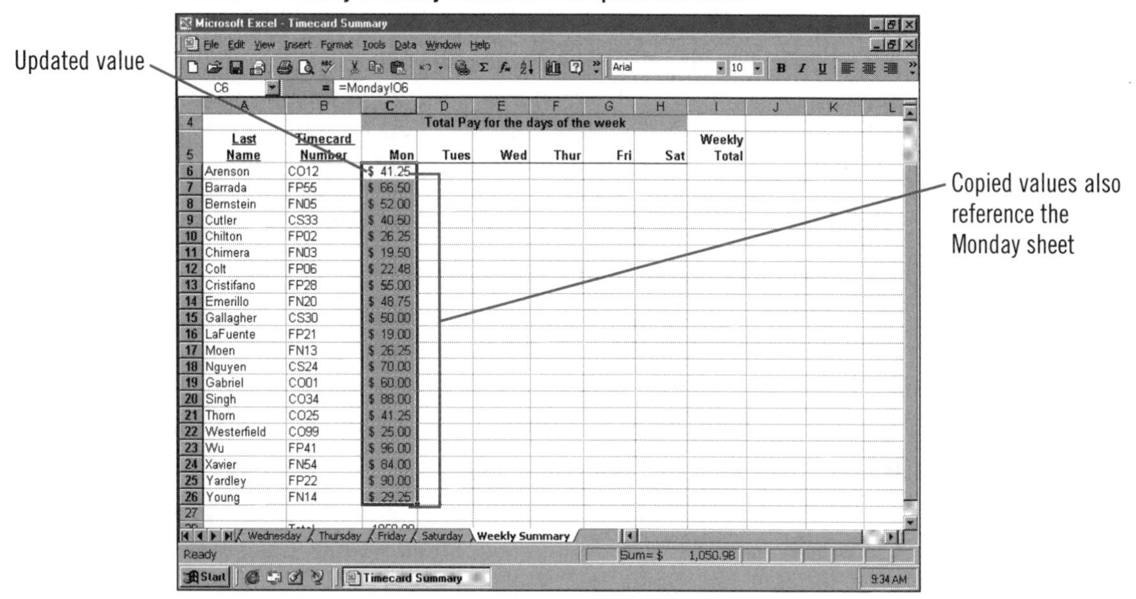

Consolidating data from different workbooks using linking

Just as you can reference data between cells in a worksheet and between sheets, you can reference data between workbooks dynamically so that changes made in referenced cells in one workbook are reflected in the consolidation sheet in the other workbook. This dynamic referencing is called **linking**. To link a single cell between workbooks, open both workbooks, select the cell to receive the linked data, press = (equal sign), select the cell in the other workbook containing the data to be linked, then press [Enter]. Excel automatically inserts the name of the referenced workbook in the cell reference. To perform calculations, enter formulas on the consolidation sheet using cells in the supporting sheets. If you are linking more than one cell, you can copy the linked data to the Clipboard, select in the other workbook the upper-left cell to receive the link, click Edit on the menu bar, click Paste Special, then click Paste Link.

Excel 2000

Hiding and Protecting Worksheet Areas

Worksheets can contain sensitive information that you don't want others to view or alter. To protect such information, Excel gives you two basic options. You can **hide** the formulas in selected cells (or rows, columns, or entire sheets), and you can **lock** selected cells, in which case other people will be able to view the data (values, numbers, labels, formulas, etc.) in those cells but not to alter it in any way. See Table F-1 for a list of options you can use to protect a worksheet. You set the lock and hide options in the Format Cells dialog box. You lock and unlock cells by clicking the Locked check box in the Format Cells dialog box Protection tab, and hide and "unhide" cell formulas by clicking the Hidden check box. The lock and hide options will not function unless an Excel protection feature, which you access via the Tools menu, is also activated. A common worksheet protection strategy is to unlock cells in which data will be changed, sometimes referred to as the **data entry area**, and to lock cells in which the data should not be changed. Then, when you protect the worksheet, the unlocked areas can still be changed. Because Jim will assign someone to enter the sensitive timecard information into the worksheet, he plans to hide and lock selected areas of the worksheet.

Steps

1. **Make sure the Monday sheet is active, select range I6:L27, click Format on the menu bar, click Cells, then click the Protection tab**

   You include row 27, even though it does not contain data, in the event that new data is added to the row later. Notice that the Locked box in the Protection tab is already checked, as shown in Figure F-8. The Locked check box is selected by default, meaning that all the cells in a new workbook start out locked. (Note, however, that cell locking is not applied unless the protection feature is also activated. The protection feature is inactive by default.)

2. **Click the Locked check box to deselect it, then click OK**

   Excel stores time as a fraction of a 24-hour day. In the formula for total pay, hours must be multiplied by 24. This concept might be confusing to the data entry person, so you hide the formulas.

3. **Select range O6:O26, click Format on the menu bar, click Cells, click the Protection tab, click the Hidden check box to select it, then click OK**

   The screen data remains the same (unhidden and unlocked) until you set the protection in the next step.

4. **Click Tools on the menu bar, point to Protection, then click Protect Sheet**

   The Protect Sheet dialog box opens. You choose not to use a password.

5. **Click OK**

   You are ready to test the new worksheet protection.

6. **Click cell O6**

   Notice that the formula bar is empty because of the hidden formula setting.

7. **In cell O6, type T to confirm that locked cells cannot be changed, then click OK**

   When you attempt to change a locked cell, a message box reminds you of the protected cell's read-only status. See Figure F-9.

8. **Click cell I6, type 9, and notice that Excel allows you to begin the entry, press [Esc] to cancel the entry, then save the workbook**

   Because you unlocked the cells in columns I through L before you protected the worksheet, you can make changes to these cells. Jim is satisfied that the Time In and Time Out data can be changed as necessary.

QuickTip

To turn off worksheet protection, click Tools on the menu bar, point to Protection, then click Unprotect Sheet. If prompted for a password, type the password, then click OK. To remove passwords, open the workbook or worksheet using the password, then go to the window where you entered the password, highlight the password, and press [Delete]. Remember that passwords are case sensitive.

FIGURE F-8: Protection tab in Format Cells dialog box

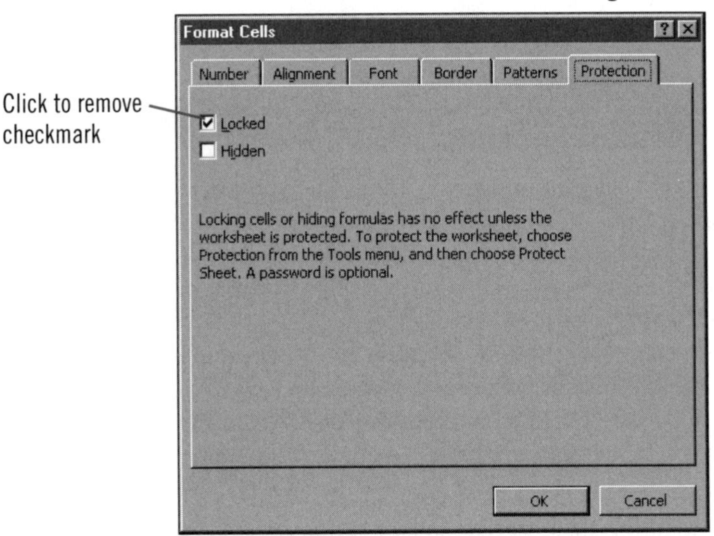

FIGURE F-9: Reminder of protected cell's read-only status

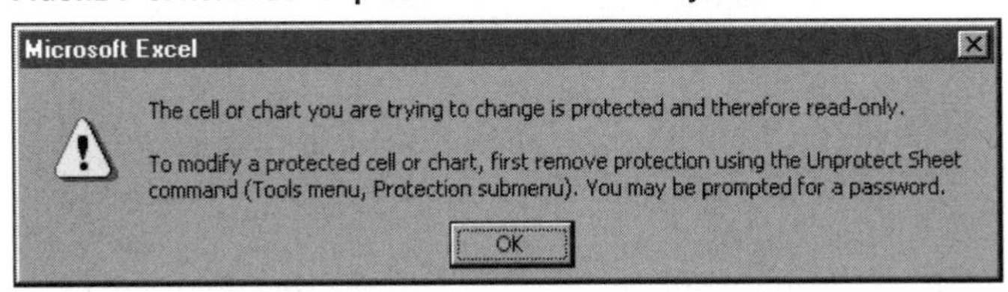

Excel 2000

TABLE F-1: Options for hiding and protecting worksheet elements

task	menu commands
Hide/Unhide a column	Format, Column, Hide or Unhide
Hide/Unhide a formula	Format, Cells, Protection tab, select/deselect Hidden check box
Hide/Unhide a row	Format, Row, Hide or Unhide
Hide/Unhide a sheet	Format, Sheet, Hide or Unhide
Protect workbook	Tools, Protection, Protect Workbook, assign optional password
Protect worksheet	Tools, Protection, Protect Sheet, assign optional password
Unlock/Relock cells	Format, Cells, Protection tab, deselect/select Locked check box
Note: *Some of the hide and protect options do not take effect until protection is enabled.*	

Changing workbook properties

You can also password-protect an entire workbook from being opened or modified by changing its file properties. Click File, click Save As, click Tools, then click General Options. Specify the password(s) for opening or modifying the workbook. You can also use this dialog box to offer users an option to open the workbook in read-only format. To make an entire workbook read-only so that users can open but not change it, click Start on the Taskbar, point to Programs, then click Windows Explorer. Locate and click the filename, click File on the menu bar, click Properties, click the General tab, then, under Attributes, select the Read-only check box.

Excel 2000

Saving Custom Views of a Worksheet

A **view** is a set of display and/or print settings that you can name and save, then access at a later time. By using the Excel Custom Views feature, you can create several different views of a worksheet without having to create separate sheets. For example, if you often switch between portrait and landscape orientations when printing different parts of a worksheet, you can create two views with the appropriate print settings for each view. You set the display and/or print settings first, then name the view. Because Jim will generate several reports from his data, he saves the current print and display settings as a custom view. To better view the data to be printed, he decides to use the Zoom box to display the entire worksheet on one screen. The Zoom box has a default setting of 100% magnification and appears on the Standard toolbar.

Trouble?

If the Zoom box does not appear on your Standard toolbar, click the More Buttons button to view it.

QuickTip

To delete views from the active worksheet, select the view in the Views list box, then click Delete.

Trouble?

If you receive the message, "Some view settings could not be applied," repeat Step 5 to ensure worksheet protection is turned off.

QuickTip

With Report Manager add-in on the View menu, you can group worksheets and their views to be printed in sequence as one large report. If Report Manager is not on your View menu, click Tools/Add-Ins to add it.

1. With the Monday sheet active, select range **A1:O28**, click the **Zoom box list arrow** on the Standard toolbar, click **Selection**, then press **[Ctrl][Home]** to return to cell A1
   Excel automatically adjusts the display magnification so that the data selected fits on one screen. See Figure F-10. After selecting the **Zoom box**, you also can pick a magnification percentage from the list or type the desired percentage.
2. Click **View** on the menu bar, then click **Custom Views**
   The Custom Views dialog box opens. Any previously defined views for the active worksheet appear in the Views box. In this case, Jim had created a custom view named Generic containing default print and display settings. See Figure F-11.
3. Click **Add**
   The Add View dialog box opens, as shown in Figure F-12. Here, you enter a name for the view and decide whether to include print settings and hidden rows, columns, and filter settings. You want to include the selected options.
4. In the Name box, type **Complete Daily Worksheet**, then click **OK**
   After creating a custom view of the worksheet, you return to the worksheet area. You are ready to test the two custom views. In case the views require a change to the worksheet, it's a good idea to turn off worksheet protection.
5. Click **Tools** on the menu bar, point to **Protection**, then click **Unprotect Sheet**
6. Click **View** on the menu bar, then click **Custom Views**
   The Custom Views dialog box opens, listing both the Complete Daily Worksheet and Generic views.
7. Click **Generic** in the Views list box, click **Show**, preview the worksheet, then close the Preview
   The Generic custom view returns the worksheet to the Excel default print and display settings. Now you are ready to test the new custom view.
8. Click **View** on the menu bar, click **Custom Views**, click **Complete Daily Worksheet** in the Views list box, click **Show**
   The entire worksheet fits on the screen.
9. Return to the Generic view, then save your work
   Jim is satisfied with the custom view of the worksheet he created.

FIGURE F-10: Selected data fit to one screen

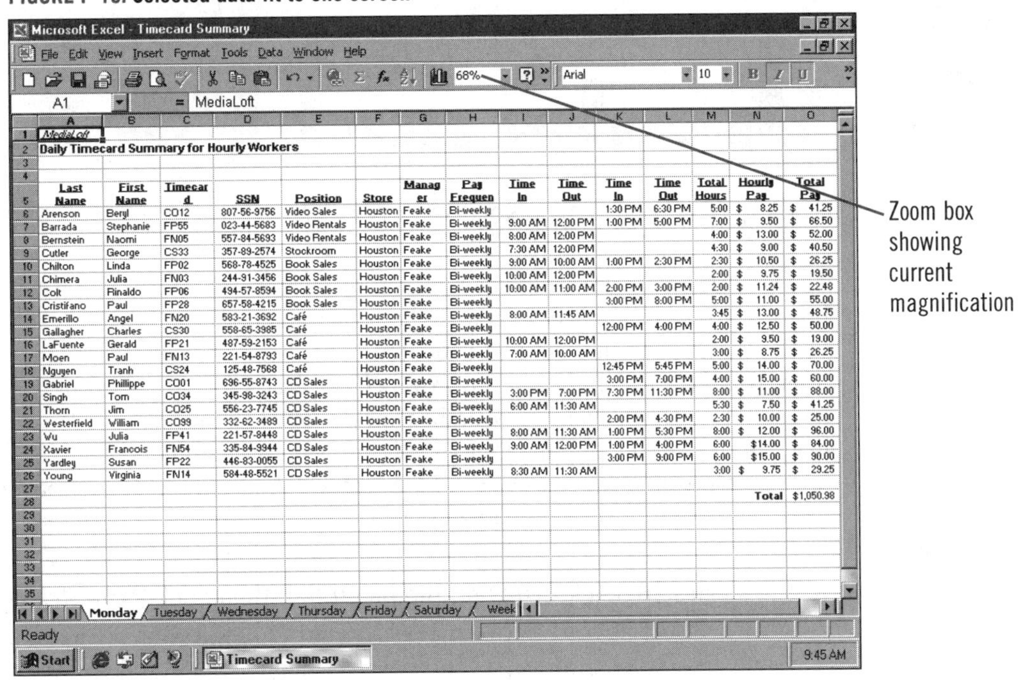

FIGURE F-11: Custom Views dialog box

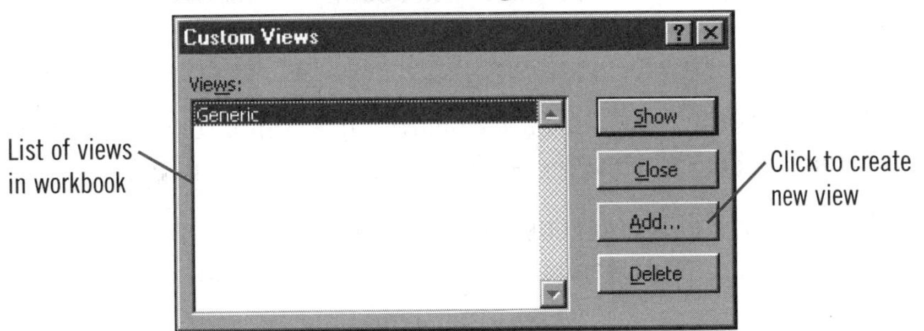

FIGURE F-12: Add View dialog box

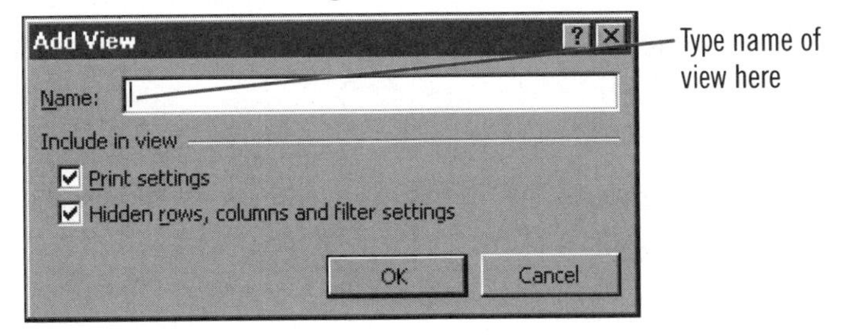

Using a workspace

If you work with several workbooks at a time in a particular arrangement, you can create a **workspace** containing information about their location and window sizes. Then, instead of opening each workbook individually, you can just open the workspace, which will automatically display the workbooks in the sizes and locations saved in the workspace. To create a workspace, open the workbooks and locate and size them as you would like them to appear. Click File on the menu bar, click Save Workspace, then type a name for the workspace file. Then open the workspace file and open the workbooks in their saved locations and sizes. Remember, however, that the workspace file does not contain the workbooks themselves, so you still have to back up the original workbook files. To start the workspace automatically when you turn on your computer, place the workspace file only in your XLStart folder.

Excel 2000

Controlling Page Breaks and Page Numbering

The vertical and horizontal dashed lines in worksheets indicate page breaks. Excel automatically inserts a page break when your worksheet data doesn't fit on one page. These page breaks are **dynamic**, which means they adjust automatically when you insert or delete rows and columns and when you change column widths or row heights. Everything to the left of the first vertical dashed line and above the first horizontal dashed line is printed on the first page. You can override the automatic breaks by choosing the Page Break command on the Insert menu. Table F-2 describes the different types of page breaks you can use. Jim wants another report displaying no more than half the hourly workers on each page. To accomplish this, he must insert a manual page break.

1. Click cell **A16**, click **Insert** on the menu bar, then click **Page Break**
   A dashed line appears between rows 15 and 16, indicating a horizontal page break. See Figure F-13. After you set page breaks, it's a good idea to preview each page.
2. Preview the worksheet, then click **Zoom**
   Notice that the status bar reads "Page 1 of 4" and that the data for the employees up through Charles Gallagher appears on the first page. Jim decides to place the date in the footer.
3. While in the Print Preview window, click **Setup**, click the **Header/Footer tab**, click **Custom Footer**, click the **Right section box**, click the **Date button**
4. Click the **Left section box**, type your name, then click **OK**
   Your name, the page number, and the date appear in the Footer preview area.
5. In the Page Setup dialog box, click **OK**, and, still in Print Preview, check to make sure all the pages show your name and the page numbers, click **Print**, then click **OK**
6. Click **View** on the menu bar, click **Custom Views**, click **Add**, type **Half N Half**, then click **OK**
   Your new custom view has the page breaks and all current print settings.
7. Make sure cell H16 is selected, then click **Insert** on the menu bar and click **Remove Page Break**
8. Save the workbook

QuickTip

To insert the page number in a header or footer section yourself, click the page number button in the Header or Footer dialog box.

QuickTip

To remove a manual page break, select any cell directly below or to the right of the page break, click Insert on the menu bar, then click Remove Page Break.

TABLE F-2: **Page break options**

type of page break	where to position cell pointer
Both horizontal and vertical page breaks	Select the cell below and to the right of the gridline where you want the breaks to occur
Only a horizontal page break	Select the cell in column A that is directly below the gridline where you want the page to break
Only a vertical page break	Select a cell in row 1 that is to the right of the gridline where you want the page to break

FIGURE F-13: Worksheet with horizontal page break

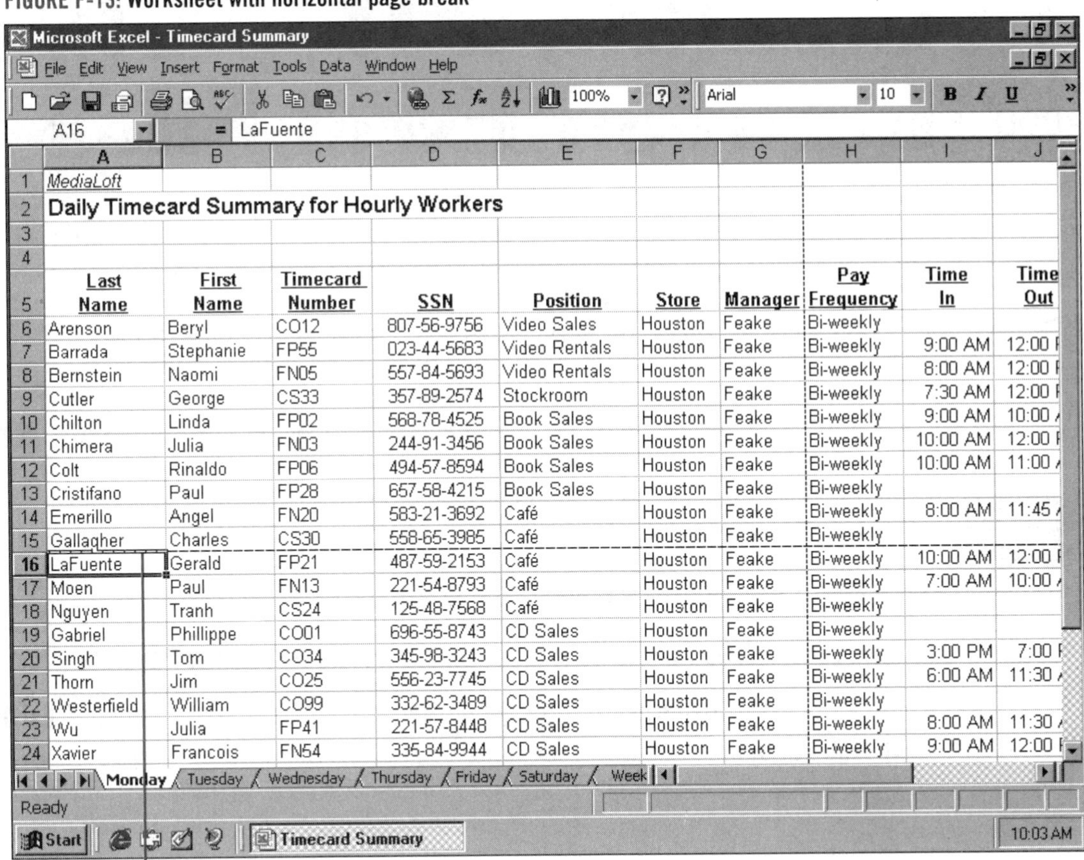

	A	B	C	D	E	F	G	H	I	J
1	MediaLoft									
2	Daily Timecard Summary for Hourly Workers									
3										
4										
5	Last Name	First Name	Timecard Number	SSN	Position	Store	Manager	Pay Frequency	Time In	Time Out
6	Arenson	Beryl	CO12	807-56-9756	Video Sales	Houston	Feake	Bi-weekly		
7	Barrada	Stephanie	FP55	023-44-5683	Video Rentals	Houston	Feake	Bi-weekly	9:00 AM	12:00
8	Bernstein	Naomi	FN05	557-84-5693	Video Rentals	Houston	Feake	Bi-weekly	8:00 AM	12:00
9	Cutler	George	CS33	357-89-2574	Stockroom	Houston	Feake	Bi-weekly	7:30 AM	12:00
10	Chilton	Linda	FP02	568-78-4525	Book Sales	Houston	Feake	Bi-weekly	9:00 AM	10:00
11	Chimera	Julia	FN03	244-91-3456	Book Sales	Houston	Feake	Bi-weekly	10:00 AM	12:00
12	Colt	Rinaldo	FP06	494-57-8594	Book Sales	Houston	Feake	Bi-weekly	10:00 AM	11:00
13	Cristifano	Paul	FP28	657-58-4215	Book Sales	Houston	Feake	Bi-weekly		
14	Emerillo	Angel	FN20	583-21-3692	Café	Houston	Feake	Bi-weekly	8:00 AM	11:45
15	Gallagher	Charles	CS30	558-65-3985	Café	Houston	Feake	Bi-weekly		
16	LaFuente	Gerald	FP21	487-59-2153	Café	Houston	Feake	Bi-weekly	10:00 AM	12:00
17	Moen	Paul	FN13	221-54-8793	Café	Houston	Feake	Bi-weekly	7:00 AM	10:00
18	Nguyen	Tranh	CS24	125-48-7568	Café	Houston	Feake	Bi-weekly		
19	Gabriel	Phillippe	CO01	696-55-8743	CD Sales	Houston	Feake	Bi-weekly		
20	Singh	Tom	CO34	345-98-3243	CD Sales	Houston	Feake	Bi-weekly	3:00 PM	7:00
21	Thorn	Jim	CO25	556-23-7745	CD Sales	Houston	Feake	Bi-weekly	6:00 AM	11:30
22	Westerfield	William	CO99	332-62-3489	CD Sales	Houston	Feake	Bi-weekly		
23	Wu	Julia	FP41	221-57-8448	CD Sales	Houston	Feake	Bi-weekly	8:00 AM	11:30
24	Xavier	Francois	FN54	335-84-9944	CD Sales	Houston	Feake	Bi-weekly	9:00 AM	12:00

Dashed line indicates horizontal break after row 15

Using Page Break Preview

By clicking View on the menu bar, then clicking Page Break Preview, or clicking Page Break Preview in the Print Preview window, you can view and change page breaks manually. (If you see a dialog box asking if you want help, just click OK to close it.) Simply drag the page break lines to the desired location. See Figure F-14. To exit Page Break Preview, click View on the menu bar, then click Normal.

FIGURE F-14: Page Break Preview window

	Last Name	First Name	Timecard	SSN	Position	Store	Manager	Pay Frequency	Time In	Time Out	Time In	Time Out	Total Hours	Hourly Pay	Total Pay
6	Arenson	Beryl	CO12	807-56-9756	Video Sales	Houston	Feake	Bi-weekly			1:30 PM	6:30 PM	5:00	$ 8.25	$ 41.25
7	Barrada	Stephanie	FP55	023-44-5683	Video Rentals	Houston	Feake	Bi-weekly	9:00 AM	######	1:00 PM	5:00 PM	7:00	$ 9.50	$ 66.50
8	Bernstein	Naomi	FN05	557-84-5693	Video Rentals	Houston	Feake	Bi-weekly	8:00 AM	######			4:00	$ 13.00	$ 52.00
9	Cutler	George	CS33	357-89-2574	Stockroom	Houston	Feake	Bi-weekly	7:30 AM	######			4:30	$ 9.00	$ 40.50
10	Chilton	Linda	FP02	568-78-4525	Book Sales	Houston	Feake	Bi-weekly	9:00 AM	######	1:00 PM	2:30 PM	2:30	$ 10.50	$ 26.25
11	Chimera	Julia	FN03	244-91-3456	Book Sales	Houston	Feake	Bi-weekly	######	######			2:00	$ 9.75	$ 19.50
12	Colt	Rinaldo	FP06	494-57-8594	Book Sales	Houston	Feake	Bi-weekly	######	######	2:00 PM	3:00 PM	2:00	$ 11.24	$ 22.48
13	Cristifano	Paul	FP28	657-58-4215	Book Sales	Houston	Feake	Bi-weekly			3:00 PM	8:00 PM	5:00	$ 11.00	$ 55.00
14	Emerillo	Angel	FN20	583-21-3692	Café	Houston	Feake	Bi-weekly	8:00 AM	######			3:45	$ 13.00	$ 48.75
15	Gallagher	Charles	CS30	558-65-3985	Café	Houston	Feake	Bi-weekly			######	4:00 PM	4:00	$ 12.50	$ 50.00
16	LaFuente	Gerald	FP21	487-59-2153	Café	Houston	Feake	Bi-weekly	######	######			2:00	$ 9.50	$ 19.00
17	Moen	Paul	FN13	221-54-8793	Café	Houston	Feake	Bi-weekly	7:00 AM	######			3:00	$ 8.75	$ 26.25
18	Nguyen	Tranh	CS24	125-48-7568	Café	Houston	Feake	Bi-weekly			######	5:45 PM	5:00	$ 14.00	$ 70.00
19	Gabriel	Phillippe	CO01	696-55-8743	CD Sales	Houston	Feake	Bi-weekly			3:00 PM	7:00 PM	4:00	$ 15.00	$ 60.00
20	Singh	Tom	CO34	345-98-3243	CD Sales	Houston	Feake	Bi-weekly	3:00 PM	7:00 PM	7:30 PM	######	8:00	$ 11.00	$ 88.00
21	Thorn	Jim	CO25	556-23-7745	CD Sales	Houston	Feake	Bi-weekly	6:00 AM	######			5:30	$ 7.50	$ 41.25
22	Westerfield	William	CO99	332-62-3489	CD Sales	Houston	Feake	Bi-weekly			2:00 PM	4:30 PM	2:30	$ 10.00	$ 25.00
23	Wu	Julia	FP41	221-57-8448	CD Sales	Houston	Feake	Bi-weekly	8:00 AM	######	1:00 PM	5:30 PM	8:00	$ 12.00	$ 96.00
24	Xavier	Francois	FN54	335-84-9944	CD Sales	Houston	Feake	Bi-weekly	9:00 AM	######	1:00 PM	4:00 PM	6:00	$14.00	$ 84.00
25	Yardley	Susan	FP22	446-83-0055	CD Sales	Houston	Feake	Bi-weekly			3:00 PM	9:00 PM	6:00	$15.00	$ 90.00
26	Young	Virginia	FN14	584-48-5521	CD Sales	Houston	Feake	Bi-weekly	8:30 AM	######			3:00	$ 9.75	$ 29.25
27															
28														Total	#####

Page 1 Page 2 Page 3 Page 4

Cell pointer in cell A16

Drag page break lines to change page breaks

Excel 2000

Creating a Hyperlink between Excel Files

As you manage the content and appearance of your workbooks, you may want the workbook user to have access to information in another workbook. It might be nonessential information or data that is too detailed to place in the workbook itself. In these cases, you can create a **hyperlink**, an object (a filename, a word, a phrase, or a graphic) in a worksheet that, when you click it, will jump to another worksheet, called the **target**. The target can be a document created in another software program or a site on the World Wide Web. For example, in a worksheet that lists customer invoices, at each customer's name, you might create a hyperlink to an Excel file containing payment terms for each customer. You can also use hyperlinks to navigate to other locations in a large worksheet. Jim wants managers who view the Timecard Summary worksheet to be able to view the pay categories for MediaLoft store employees. He creates a hyperlink at the Hourly Pay Rate column heading. Users will click the hyperlink to view the Pay Rate worksheet.

1. Display the Monday worksheet
2. Click **Edit**, click **Go To**, type **N5** (the cell containing **the text Hourly Pay Rate**), then click **OK**
3. Click the **Insert Hyperlink button** on the Standard toolbar, then click **Existing File or Web Page**, if necessary
   The Insert Hyperlink dialog box opens. See Figure F-15. The icons under Link to: on the left side of the dialog box let you specify the type of location you want the link to jump to: an existing file or Web page, a place in the same document, a new document, or an e-mail address. Since Jim wants users to display a document he has created, the first icon, Existing File or Web Page, is correct and is already selected.
4. Click **File** under Browse for, then in the Link to File dialog box, navigate to your Project Disk and double-click **Pay Rate Classifications**
   The Insert Hyperlink dialog box reappears with the filename you selected in the Type the file or Web page name text box. This document appears when users click this hyperlink. You can also specify the ScreenTip that users will see when they hold the pointer over the hyperlink.
5. Click **ScreenTip**, type **Click here to see MediaLoft pay rate classifications**, click **OK**, then click **OK** again
   Cell N5 now contains underlined blue text, indicating that it is a hyperlink. After you create a hyperlink, you should check it to make sure it jumps to the correct destination.
6. Move the pointer over the **Hourly Pay Rate text**, view the ScreenTip, then click once
   Notice that when you move the pointer over the text, the pointer changes to , indicating that it is a hyperlink, and the ScreenTip appears. After you click, the Pay Rate Classifications worksheet appears. See Figure F-16. The Web toolbar appears beneath the Standard and Formatting toolbars.
7. Click the **Back button** on the Web toolbar, then save the workbook

Using hyperlinks to navigate large worksheets

Hyperlinks are useful in navigating large worksheets or workbooks. You can create a hyperlink from any cell to another cell in the same worksheet, a cell in another worksheet, or a defined name anywhere in the workbook. Under Link to in the Insert Hyperlink dialog box, click Place in This Document. Then type the cell reference and indicate the sheet, or select the named location in the scroll box.

FIGURE F-15: Insert Hyperlink dialog box

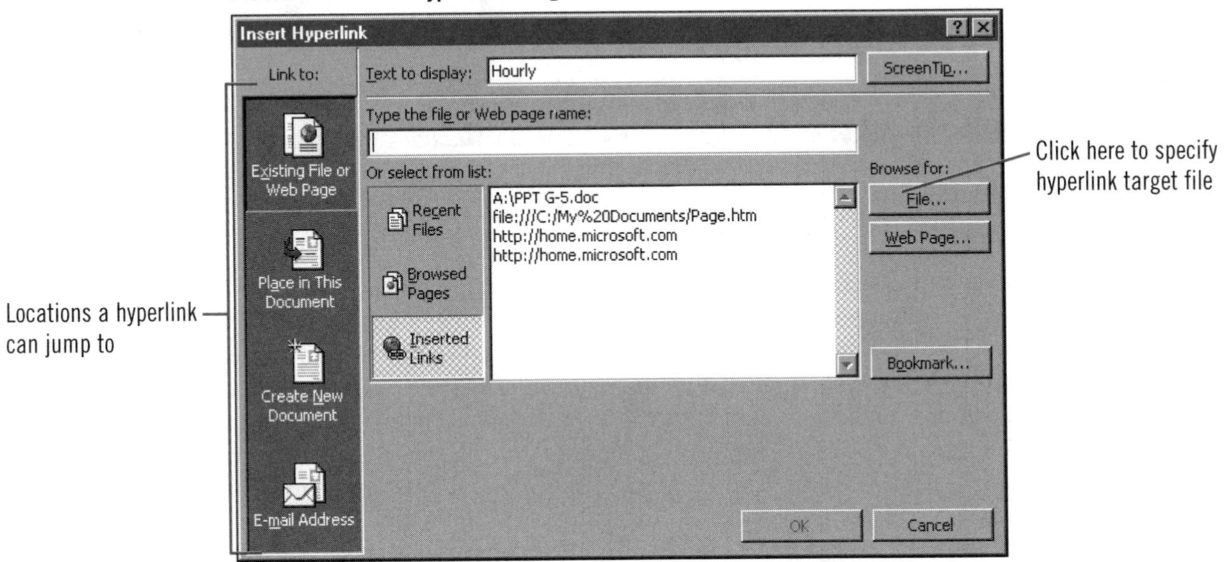

FIGURE F-16: Target document

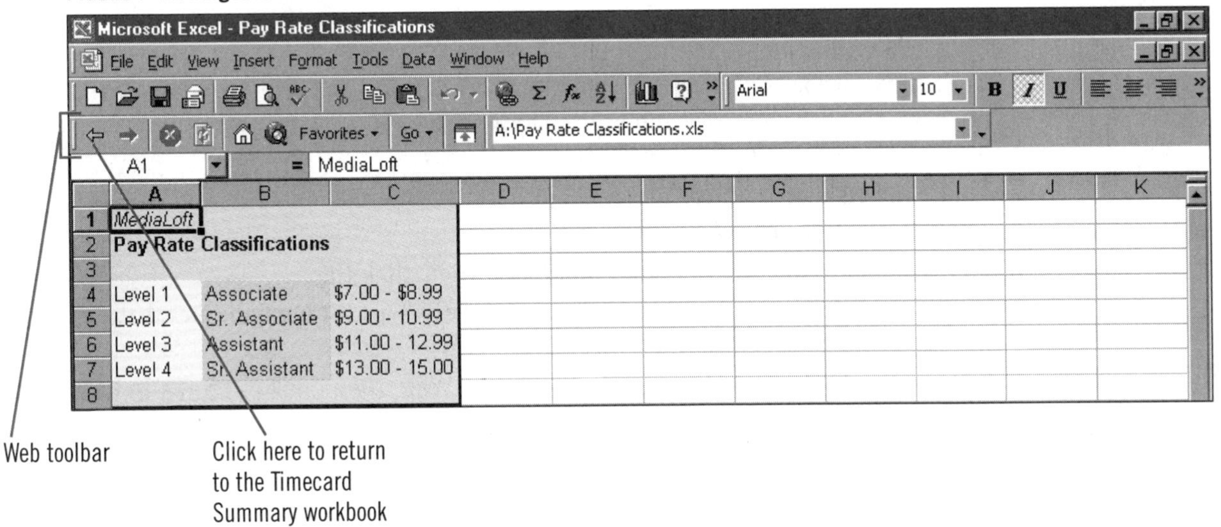

Inserting a picture

As you prepare your workbooks for viewing by others on an intranet or on the Internet, you may want to enhance their appearance by adding pictures. You can easily add your own picture, such as a company logo or a scanned picture, or a picture from the Microsoft Clip Gallery. To insert a Clip Gallery picture on a worksheet, click Insert on the menu bar, point to Picture, then click Clip Art. Click a category, click the image you want to insert, then click the Insert Clip icon. Close the Insert Clip Art window. The picture is an **object** that you can move, resize, or delete. To move a picture, click and then drag it. To resize it, click it once to select it, then drag one of its corners. To delete it, click to select it, then press [Delete].

Saving an Excel file as an HTML Document

One way to share Excel data is to publish, or **post**, it online over a network so that others can access it using their Web browsers. The network can be an **intranet**, which is an internal network site used by a particular group of people who work together, or the World Wide Web. The **World Wide Web** is a structure of documents, or pages, connected electronically over a large computer network called the **Internet**, which is made up of smaller networks and computers. If you save and post an entire workbook, users can click worksheet tabs to view each sheet. If you save a single worksheet, you can make the Web page interactive, meaning that users can enter, format, and calculate worksheet data. To post an Excel document to an intranet or the World Wide Web, you must first save it in **HTML (Hypertext Markup Language)**, which is the format that a Web browser can read. Jim saves the entire Timecard Summary workbook in HTML format so it can be posted on the MediaLoft intranet for managers' use.

Steps

1. Click **File** on the menu bar, then click **Save as Web Page**
   The Save As dialog box opens. See Figure F-17. By default, the Entire Workbook option button is selected, which is what Jim wants. However, he wants the title bar of the Web page to be more descriptive than the filename.
2. Click **Change Title**
   The Set Page Title dialog box opens.
3. Type **MediaLoft Houston Timecard Summary**, then click OK
   The Page title area displays the new title. The Save as type list box indicates that the workbook will be saved as a Web page, which is in HTML format.
4. Change the filename to **Timecard Summary - Web**, then click the **Save in list arrow** and locate your Project Disk
5. Click **Save**
   A dialog box appears, indicating that the custom views you saved earlier will not be part of the HTML file.
6. Click **Yes**
   Excel saves the Web page version as an HTML file in the folder location you specified in the Save As dialog box, and in the same place creates a folder in which it places associated files, such as a file for each worksheet. To make the workbook available to others, you would post all these files on a network server. When the save process is complete, the original XLS file closes and the HTML file opens on your screen.
7. Click **File** on the menu bar, click **Web Page Preview**, then maximize the browser window
   The workbook opens in your default Web browser, which could be Internet Explorer or Netscape, showing you what it would look like if you opened it on an intranet or on the Internet. See Figure F-18. The Monday worksheet appears as it would if it were on a Web site or intranet, with tabs at the bottom of the screen for each daily sheet. If you wanted to use this document online, you would also need to save the target document (Pay Rate Classifications) in HTML format and post it to the Web site.
8. Click the **Weekly Summary tab**
   The Weekly Summary worksheet appears just as it would in Excel.
9. Close the Web browser window, then close the Timecard Summary - Web workbook and the Pay Rate Classifications workbook, then exit Excel

QuickTip

If you want, you can create a folder in the Save As dialog box. Click the Create new folder button and in the Save As dialog box, type the name of the new folder and click OK. The new folder automatically opens and appears in the Save in list. When you click Save, the HTML files will be saved in your new folder.

FIGURE F-17: Save As dialog box

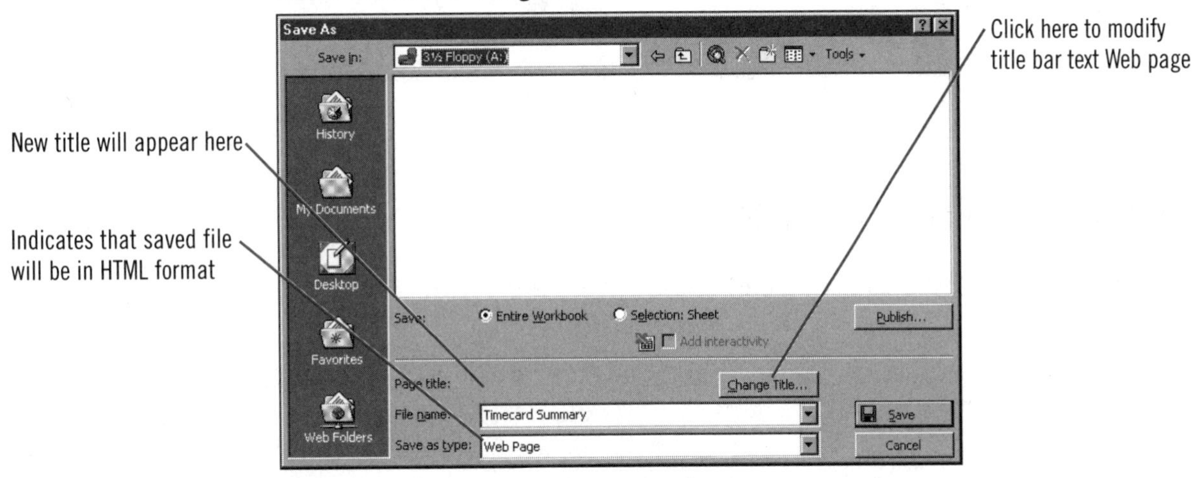

FIGURE F-18: Workbook in Web page preview

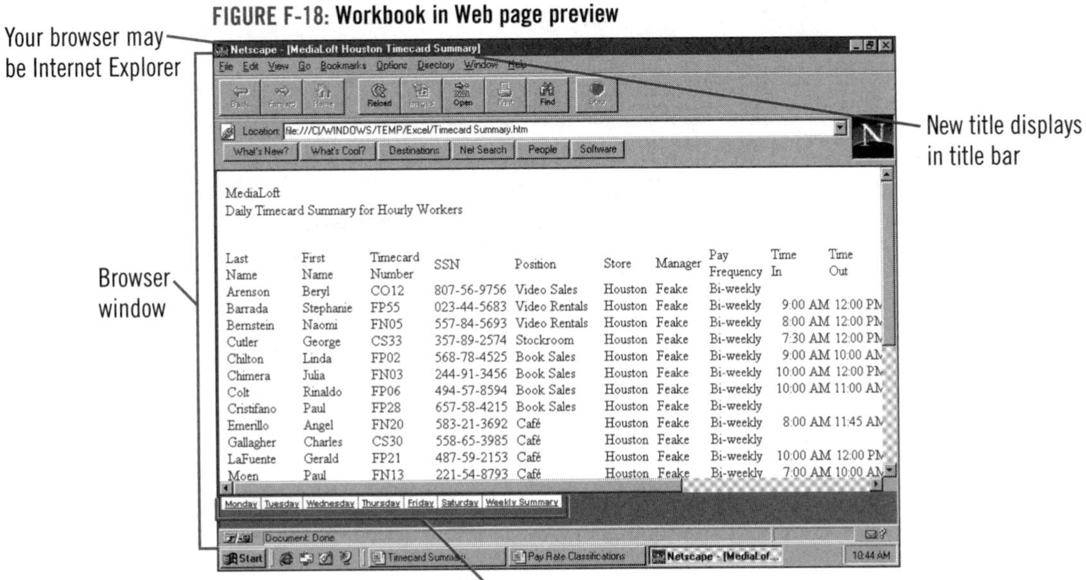

Send a workbook via e-mail

You can send an entire workbook or a worksheet to any e-mail recipient from within Excel. To send a workbook as an attachment to an e-mail message, click File, point to Send to, then click Mail Recipient (as attachment). Fill in the To and Cc information and click Send. See Figure F-19. (If Internet Explorer is not your default Web browser, you may need to respond to additional dialog boxes.) You can also route a workbook to one or more recipients on a routing list that you create. Click File, point to Send to, then click Routing Recipient. Click Create New Contact and enter contact information, then fill in the Routing slip. Depending on your e-mail program, you may have to follow a different procedure. See your instructor or lab resource person for help.

FIGURE F-19: E-mailing an Excel file as an attachment

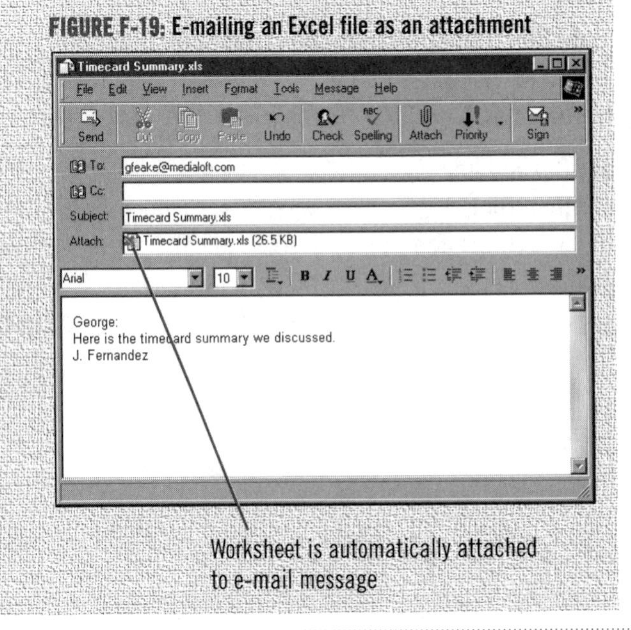

Practice

► Concepts Review

Label each element of the Excel screen shown in Figure F-20.

FIGURE F-20

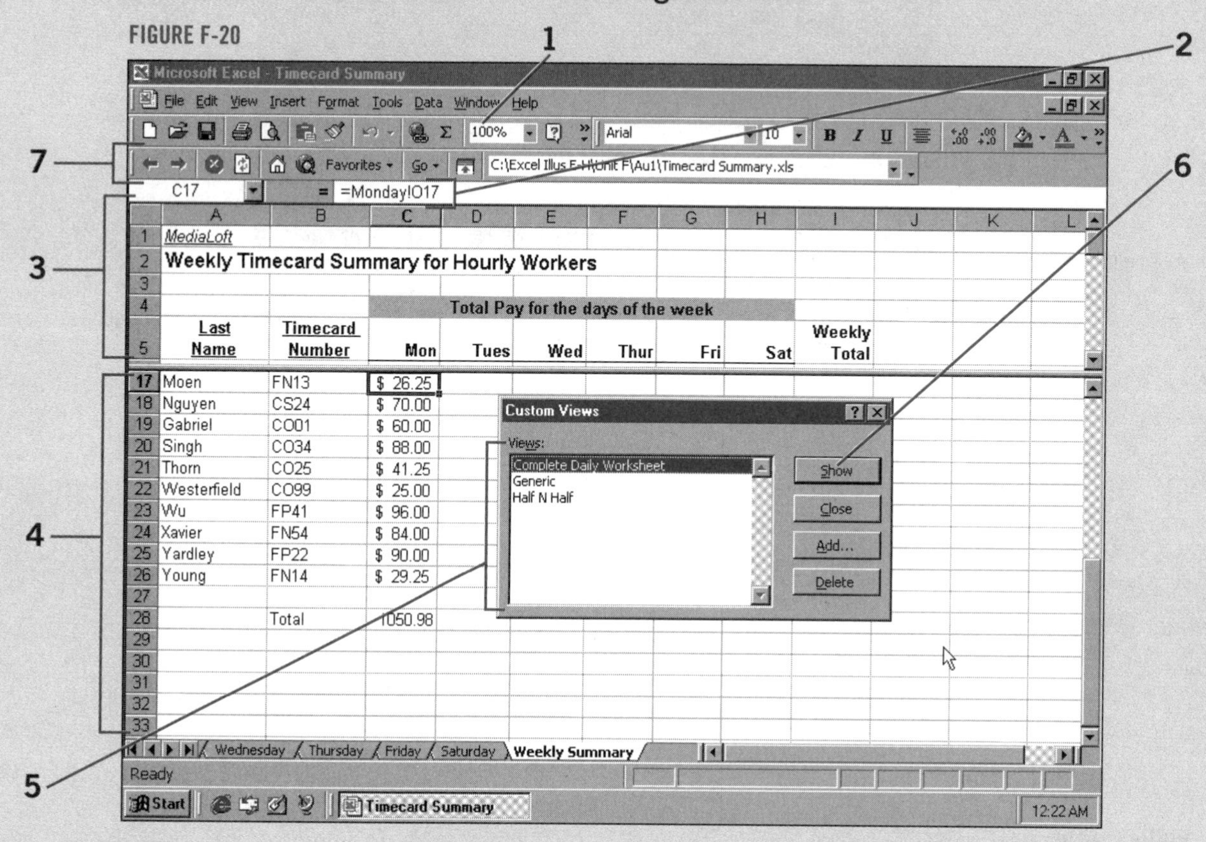

Match each of the terms with the statement that describes its function.

a. **Dashed line**
b. **Hyperlink**
c. **3-D reference**
d.
e.

8. Inserts a code to print the total number of pages
9. Uses values from different workbooks
10. Indicates a page break
11. Inserts a code to print the sheet name in a header or footer
12. An object you click to display a target

Select the best answer from the list of choices.

13. You can save frequently used display and print settings by using the ____________ feature.

a. HTML
b. View menu
c. Custom Views
d. Save command

14. You freeze areas of the worksheet to

a. Freeze data and unlock formulas.
b. Lock column and row headings in place while you scroll through the worksheet.
c. Freeze all data in place so that you can see it.
d. Lock open windows in place.

15. To protect a worksheet, you must first unlock those cells that ____________, and then issue the Protect Sheet command.

a. never change
b. the user will be allowed to change
c. have hidden formulas
d. are locked

► Skills Review

1. Freeze columns and rows.

a. Open the workbook titled EX F-2, then save it as "Quarterly Household Budget".
b. Freeze columns A and B and rows 1 through 3 for improved viewing. (*Hint:* Click cell C4 prior to issuing the Freeze Panes command.)
c. Scroll until columns A and B and F through H are visible.
d. Press [Ctrl][Home] to return to cell C4.
e. Unfreeze the panes.

2. Insert and delete worksheets.

a. With the 2001 sheet active, use the sheet pop-up menu to insert a new Sheet1 to its left.
b. Delete Sheet1.
c. Add a custom footer to the 2001 sheet with your name on the left side and the page number on the right side.
d. Add a custom header with the worksheet name on the left side.
e. Preview and print the worksheet.

3. Consolidate data with 3-D references.

a. In cell C22, enter a reference to cell G7.
b. In cell C23, enter a reference to cell G18.
c. Activate the 2002 worksheet.
d. In cell C4, enter a reference to cell C4 on the 2001 worksheet.
e. In the 2002 worksheet, copy the contents of cell C4 into cells C5:C6.
f. Preview the 2002 worksheet, view the Page Break Preview, and drag the page break so all the data fits on one page.
g. Print the 2002 worksheet and save your work.

4. **Hide and protect worksheet areas.**
   a. On the 2001 sheet, unlock the expense data in the range C10:F17.
   b. Protect the sheet without using a password.
   c. To make sure the other cells are locked, attempt to make an entry in cell D4.
   d. Confirm the message box warning.
   e. Change the first-quarter mortgage expense to $3,400.
   f. Unprotect the worksheet.
   g. Save the workbook.
5. **Save custom views of a worksheet.**
   a. Set the zoom on the 2001 worksheet so all the data fits on your screen.
   b. Make this a new view called "Entire 2001 Budget".
   c. Use the Custom Views dialog box to return to Generic view.
   d. Save the workbook.
6. **Control page breaks and page numbering.**
   a. Insert a page break above cell A9.
   b. Save the view as "Halves".
   c. Preview and print the worksheet, then preview and print the entire workbook.
   d. Save the workbook.
7. **Create a hyperlink between Excel files.**
   a. On the 2001 worksheet, make cell A9 a hyperlink to the file Expense Details, with a ScreenTip that reads "Click here to see expense assumptions".
   b. Test the link, then print the Expense Details worksheet.
   c. Return to the Household Budget worksheet using the Web toolbar.
   d. On the 2002 worksheet, enter the text "Based on 2001 budget" in cell A2.
   e. Make the text in cell A2 a hyperlink to cell A1 in the 2001 worksheet. (*Hint:* Use the Place in this document button.)
   f. Test the hyperlink.
   g. Add any clip art picture to your worksheet, then move and resize it so it doesn't obscure any worksheet information.
8. **Save an Excel file as an HTML document.**
   a. Save the entire budget workbook as a Web page with a title bar that reads "Our Budget" and the file named Quarterly Household Budget - Web.
   b. Preview the Web page in your browser.
   c. Test the worksheet tabs in the browser to make sure they work.
   d. Return to Excel, then close the HTML document.
   e. Close the Expense Details worksheet, then exit Excel.

Independent Challenges

1. You own PC Assist, a software training company. You have added several new entries to the August check register and are ready to enter September's check activity. Because the sheet for August will include much of the same information you need for September, you decide to copy it. Then you will edit the new sheet to fit your needs for September check activity. You will use sheet referencing to enter the beginning balance and beginning check number. Using your own data, you will complete five checks for the September register.

To complete this independent challenge:

a. Open the workbook entitled EX F-3, then save it as "Update to Check Register".
b. Delete Sheet 2 and Sheet 3, then create a worksheet for September by copying the August sheet.
c. With the September sheet active, delete the data in range A6:E24.

d. To update the balance at the beginning of the month, use sheet referencing from the last balance entry in the August sheet.
e. Generate the first check number. (*Hint:* Use a formula that references the last check number in August and adds one.)
f. Enter data for five checks.
g. Add a footer to the September sheet that includes your name left-aligned on the printout and the system date right-aligned on the printout. Add a header that displays the sheet name centered on the printout.
h. Save the workbook.
i. Preview the entire workbook, then close the Preview window.
j. Preview the September worksheet, then print it in landscape orientation on a single page.
k. Save and close the workbook, then exit Excel.

2. You are a new employee for a computer software manufacturer. You are responsible for tracking the sales of different product lines and determining which computer operating system generates the most software sales each month. Although sales figures vary from month to month, the format in which data is entered does not. Use Table F-3 as a guide to create a worksheet tracking sales across personal computer (PC) platforms by month. Use a separate sheet for each month and create data for three months. Use your own data for the number of software packages sold in the Windows and Macintosh columns for each product. Create a summary sheet with all the sales summary information.

To complete this independent challenge:

a. Create a new workbook, then save it as "Software Sales Summary".
b. Enter row and column labels, your own data, and formulas for the totals.
c. Create a summary sheet that totals the information in all three sheets. Customize the header to include your name and the date. Set the footer to (none). In Page Setup, center the page both horizontally and vertically.
d. Save the workbook, then preview and print the four worksheets.

TABLE F-3

	Windows	Macintosh	Total
Games Software			
Space Wars 99			
Safari			
Flight School			
Total			
Business Software			
Word Processing			
Spreadsheet			
Presentation			
Graphics			
Page Layout			
Total			
Utilities Products			
Antivirus			
File recovery			
Total			

3. You are a college student with two roommates. Each month you receive your long-distance telephone bill. Because no one wants to figure out who owes what, you split the bill three ways. You are sure that one of your roommates makes two-thirds of the long-distance calls. To make the situation more equitable, you decide to create a spreadsheet to track the long-distance phone calls each month. Create a workbook with a separate sheet for each roommate. Track the following information for each month's long-distance calls: date of call, time of call (AM or PM), call minutes, location called, state called, area code, phone number, and call charge. Total the charges for each roommate. Create a summary sheet of all three roommates' charges for the month.

To complete this independent challenge:

a. Create a new workbook, then save it as "Monthly Long Distance" to the appropriate folder on your Project Disk.
b. Enter column headings and row labels to track each call.
c. Use your own data, entering at least three long-distance calls for each roommate.
d. Create totals for minutes and charges on each roommate's sheet.
e. Create a summary sheet that shows each name and uses cell references to display the total minutes and total charges for each person.
f. On the summary sheet, create a hyperlink from each person's name to cell A1 of their respective worksheet.
g. Create a workbook with the same type of information for the two people in the apartment next door. Save it as "Next Door".
h. Use linking to create a 3-D reference that displays that information on your summary sheet so your roommates can compare their expenses with the neighbors'.
i. Change the workbook properties to Read only.
j. Save the Monthly Long Distance workbook in HTML format and preview it in your Web browser.

4. Maria Abbott, general sales manager at MediaLoft, has asked you to create a projection of MediaLoft advertising expenditures for 1999–2002 that she can put on the company intranet. She wants managers to review this information for an advertising discussion at the next managers meeting. The categories and 1999 figures are already on the site.

a. Connect to the Internet, go to the MediaLoft intranet site at http://www.course.com/illustrated/MediaLoft, click the Marketing link, then locate and print the Ad Campaign Summary. Close your browser and disconnect from the Internet.
b. Start Excel and create a workbook titled "Ad Campaign Projection". Name Sheet1 "1999", enter the categories and numbers from your printout, and use a formula to calculate the total.
c. Add an appropriate worksheet name in cell A1.
d. Create figures for the years 2000–2002 and put them in the columns to the right of the 1999 figures, then use font and fill colors to make the worksheet attractive.
e. Format all numbers in an appropriate format.
f. Use formulas to create totals for each year and for each ad type. Format the totals so they stand out from the other figures and use cell borders as appropriate.
g. Create a custom view of the worksheet and save the view using a descriptive name.
h. Delete the unused sheets.
i. Add your name to the footer, then save and print the worksheet.
j. Save your workbook as a Web page, using the filename Ad Campaign Projection - Web, adding descriptive text to the title bar.
k. Preview the resulting file in your Web Browser, and test the chart tab.
l. Close your browser and Excel.

Visual Workshop

Create the worksheet shown in Figure F-21. Save the workbook as "Martinez Agency". Preview, then print, the worksheet. (*Hint:* Notice the hyperlink target on the sheet name at the bottom of the figure.)

FIGURE F-21

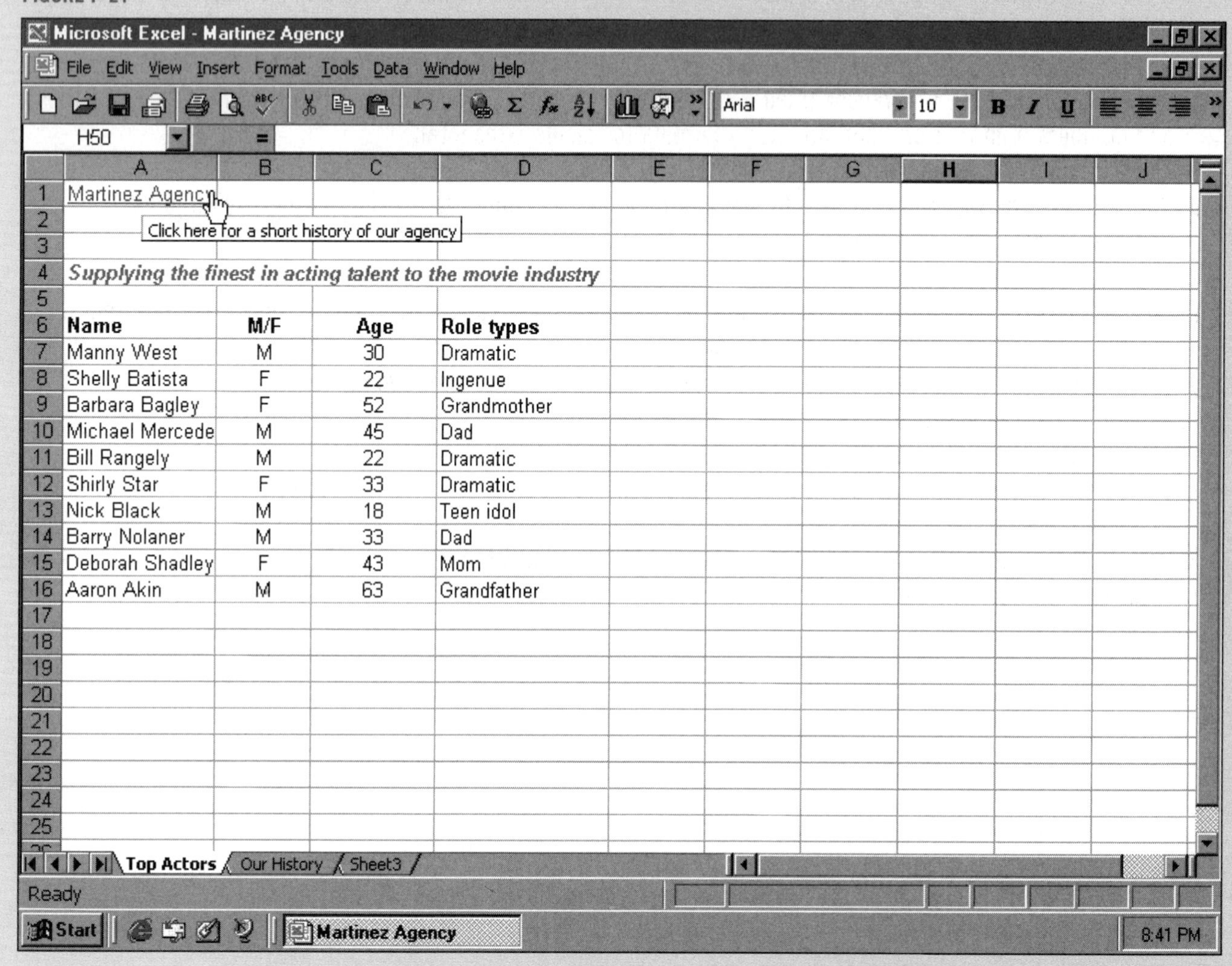

Excel 2000

Automating

Worksheet Tasks

Objectives

- Plan a macro
- MOUS Record a macro
- MOUS Run a macro
- MOUS Edit a macro
- Use shortcut keys with macros
- Use the Personal Macro Workbook
- Add a macro as a menu item
- Create a toolbar for macros

A **macro** is a set of instructions that performs tasks in the order you specify. You create macros to automate frequently performed Excel tasks that require a series of steps. For example, if you usually type your name and date in a worksheet footer, Excel can record the keystrokes in a macro that types the text and inserts the current date automatically. In this unit, you will plan and design a simple macro, then record and run it. Then you will edit the macro. You will also create a macro to run when you use shortcut keys, store a macro in the Personal Macro Workbook, add a macro option to the Tools menu, and create a new toolbar for macros. Jim is creating a macro for the accounting department. The macro will automatically insert text that will identify the worksheet as originating in the accounting department.

Excel 2000

Planning a Macro

You create macros for tasks that you perform on a regular basis. For example, you can create a macro to enter and format text or to save and print a worksheet. To create a macro, you record the series of actions or write the instructions in a special format. Because the sequence of actions is important, you need to plan the macro carefully before you record it. You use commands on the Tools menu to record, run, and modify macros. Jim creates a macro for the accounting department that inserts the text "Accounting Department" in the upper-left corner of any worksheet. He plans the macro using the following guidelines:

Steps

1. **Assign the macro a descriptive name, and write out the steps the macro will perform**
   This planning helps eliminate careless errors. Jim decides to name the macro "DeptStamp". He writes a description of the macro, as shown in Figure G-1. See Table G-1 for a list of macros Jim might create to automate other tasks.

2. **Decide how you will perform the actions you want to record**
   You can use the mouse, the keyboard, or a combination of the two. Jim decides to use both the mouse and keyboard.

3. **Practice the steps you want Excel to record and write them down**
   Jim wrote down the sequence of actions as he performed them, and he is now ready to record and test the macro.

4. **Decide where to locate the description of the macro and the macro itself**
   Macros can be stored in an unused area of the active workbook, in a new workbook, or in the Personal Macro Workbook. Jim stores the macro in a new workbook.

FIGURE G-1: Paper description of planned macro

Macro to create stamp with the department name	
Name:	DeptStamp
Description:	Adds a stamp to the top left of worksheet identifying it as an accounting department worksheet
Steps:	1. Position the cell pointer in cell A1 2. Type Accounting Department, then click the Enter button 3. Click Format on the menu bar, click Cells 4. Click Font tab, under Font style click Bold, under Underline click Single, and under Color click Red, then click OK

TABLE G-1: Possible macros and their descriptive names

description of macro	descriptive name
Enter a frequently used proper name, such as Jim Fernandez	JimFernandez
Enter a frequently used company name, such as MediaLoft	CompanyName
Print the active worksheet on a single page, in landscape orientation	FitToLand
Turn off the header and footer in the active worksheet	HeadFootOff
Show a frequently used custom view, such as a generic view of the worksheet, setting the print and display settings back to the Excel defaults	GenericView

Macros and viruses

When you open an Excel Workbook that has macros, you will see a message asking you if you want to enable or disable macros. This is because macros can contain viruses, destructive software programs that can damage your computer files. If you know your workbook came from a trusted source, click Enable macros. If you are not sure of the workbook's source, click Disable macros. If you disable the macros in a workbook, you will not be able to use them in the workbook. For more information, see the Excel Help topic About Viruses and workbook macros.

Excel 2000

Recording a Macro

The easiest way to create a macro is to record it using the Excel Macro Recorder. You simply turn the Macro Recorder on, enter the keystrokes, select the commands you want the macro to perform, then stop the recorder. As you record the macro, each action is translated into programming code that you can later view and modify. Jim wants to create a macro that enters a department stamp in cell A1 of the active worksheet. He creates this macro by recording his actions.

QuickTip

To return personalized toolbars and menus to a default state, click Tools on the menu bar, click Customize, click Reset my usage data on the Options tab, click Yes, then click Close.

1. **Start Excel if necessary, click the New button on the Standard toolbar, then save the blank workbook as My Excel Macros**
   Now you are ready to start recording the macro.
2. **Click Tools on the menu bar, point to Macro, then click Record New Macro**
   The Record Macro dialog box opens. See Figure G-2. Notice the default name Macro1 is selected. You can either assign this name or type a new name. The first character of a macro name must be a letter; the remaining characters can be letters, numbers, or underscores; (spaces are not allowed in macro names; use underscores in place of spaces). This dialog box also allows you to assign a shortcut key for running the macro and to instruct Excel where to store the macro.
3. **Type DeptStamp in the Macro name box**
4. **If the Store macro in list arrow box does not read "This Workbook", click the list arrow and select This Workbook**
5. **If the Description text box does not contain your name, select the existing name, type your own name, then click OK**
   The dialog box closes. Excel displays the small Stop Recording toolbar containing the Stop Recording button, and the word "Recording" appears on the status bar. Take your time performing the steps below. Excel records every keystroke, menu option, and mouse action that you make.
6. **Press [Ctrl][Home]**
   The cell pointer moves to cell A1. When you begin an Excel session, macros record absolute cell references. By beginning the recording in cell A1, you ensure that the macro includes the instruction to select cell A1 as the first step.
7. **Type Accounting Department in cell A1, then click the Enter button on the formula bar**
8. **Click Format on the menu bar, then click Cells**
9. **Click the Font tab, in the Font style list box click Bold, click the Underline list arrow and click Single, then click the Color list arrow and click red (third row, first color on left)**
   See Figure G-3.
10. **Click OK, click the Stop Recording button on the Stop Recording toolbar, click cell D1 to deselect cell A1, then save the workbook**
    Compare your results with Figure G-4.

QuickTip

If information in a text box is selected, you can simply type new information to replace it. This saves you from having to delete the existing entry before typing the new entry.

Trouble?

If your results differ from Figure G-4, clear the contents of cell A1, then slowly and carefully repeat Steps 2 through 9. When prompted to replace the existing macro at the end of step 5, click Yes.

FIGURE G-2: Record Macro dialog box

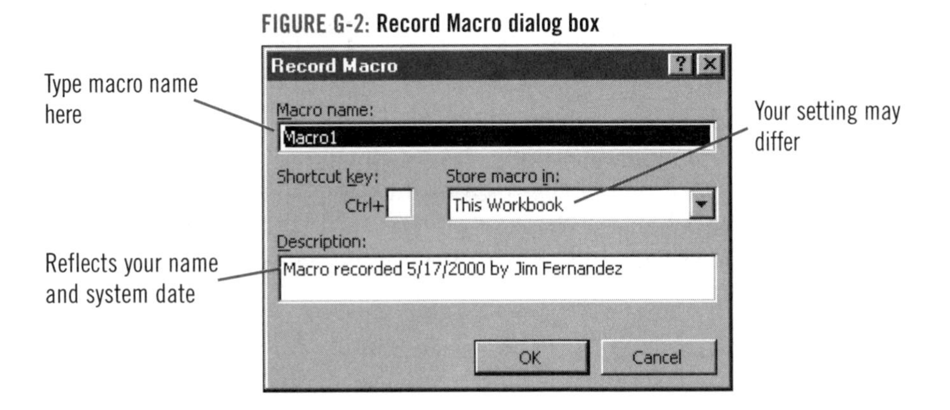

FIGURE G-3: Font tab of the Format Cells dialog box

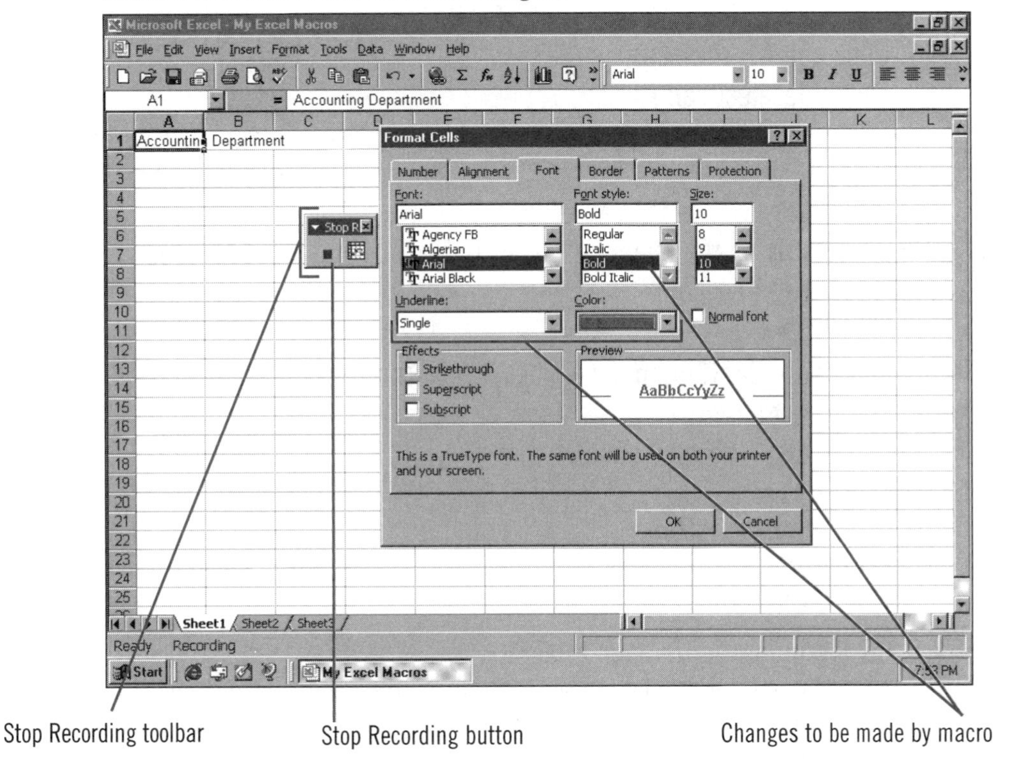

FIGURE G-4: Personalized department stamp

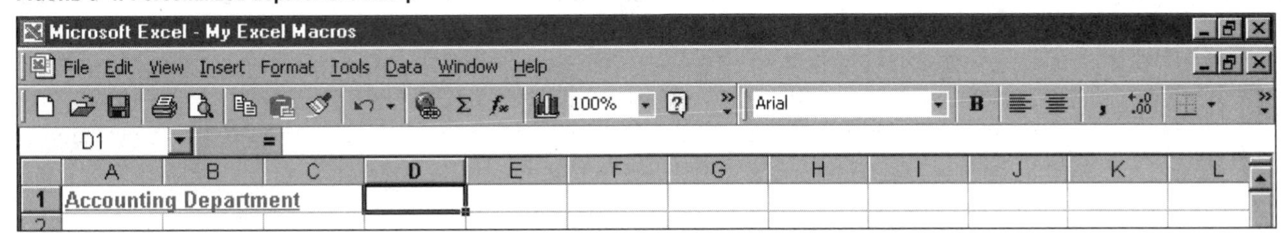

Using templates to create a workbook

You can create a workbook using an Excel **template**, a special-purpose workbook with formatting and formulas, such as an invoice or income statement. Click File on the menu bar, click New, click the Spreadsheet Solutions or Business planner templates tab, then double-click any template. Excel opens a workbook using that template design.

Running a Macro

Once you record a macro, you should test it to make sure that the actions performed are correct. To test a macro, you **run**, or execute, it. One way to run a macro is to select the macro in the Macros dialog box, then click Run. Jim clears the contents of cell A1 and then tests the DeptStamp macro. After he runs the macro from the My Excel Macros workbook, he decides to test the macro once more from a newly opened workbook.

Steps

1. **Click cell A1, click Edit on the menu bar, point to Clear, click All, then click any other cell to deselect cell A1**
   When you delete only the contents of a cell, any formatting still remains in the cell. By using the Clear All option on the Edit menu, you can be sure that the cell is free of contents and formatting.

2. **Click Tools on the menu bar, point to Macro, then click Macros**
   The Macro dialog box, shown in Figure G-5, lists all the macros contained in the open workbooks.

> **QuickTip**
> To delete a macro, select the macro name in the Macro dialog box, click Delete, then click Yes to confirm.

3. **Make sure DeptStamp is selected, click Run, then deselect cell A1**
   Watch your screen as the macro quickly plays back the steps you recorded in the previous lesson. When the macro is finished, your screen should look like Figure G-6. As long as the workbook containing the macro remains open, you can run the macro from any open workbook.

4. **Click the New button on the Standard toolbar**
   Because the new workbook automatically fills the screen, it is difficult to be sure that the My Excel Macros workbook is still open.

5. **Click Window on the menu bar**
   A list of open workbooks appears underneath the menu options. The active workbook name (in this case, Book2) appears with a check mark to its left. The My Excel Macros workbook appears on the menu, so you know it's open. See Figure G-7.

6. **Deselect cell A1 if necessary, click Tools on the menu bar, point to Macro, click Macros, make sure 'My Excel Macros.xls'!DeptStamp is selected, click Run, then deselect cell A1**
   Cell A1 should look like Figure G-6. Notice that when multiple workbooks are open, the macro name includes the workbook name between single quotation marks, followed by an exclamation point, indicating that the macro is outside the active workbook. Since you use this workbook only to test the macro, you don't need to save it.

> **QuickTip**
> To stop a macro while it is running, press [Esc].

7. **Close Book2 without saving changes**
   The My Excel Macros workbook reappears.

FIGURE G-5: Macro dialog box

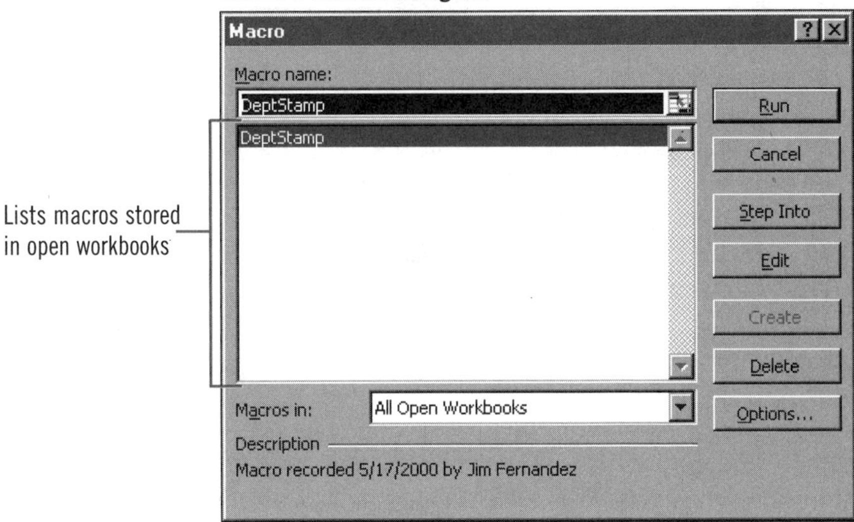

FIGURE G-6: Result of running DeptStamp macro

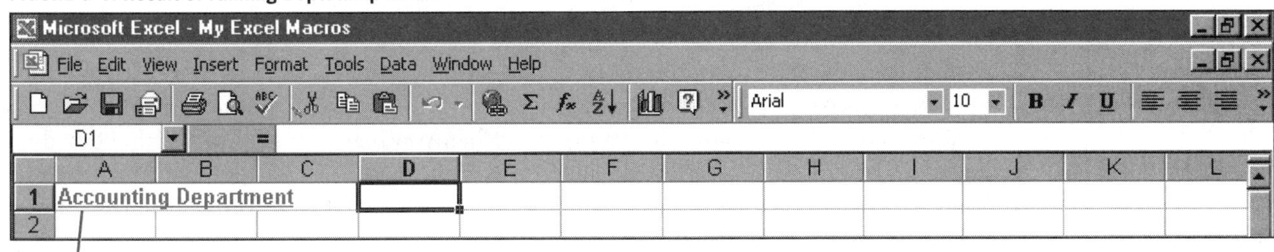

FIGURE G-7: Window menu showing list of open workbooks

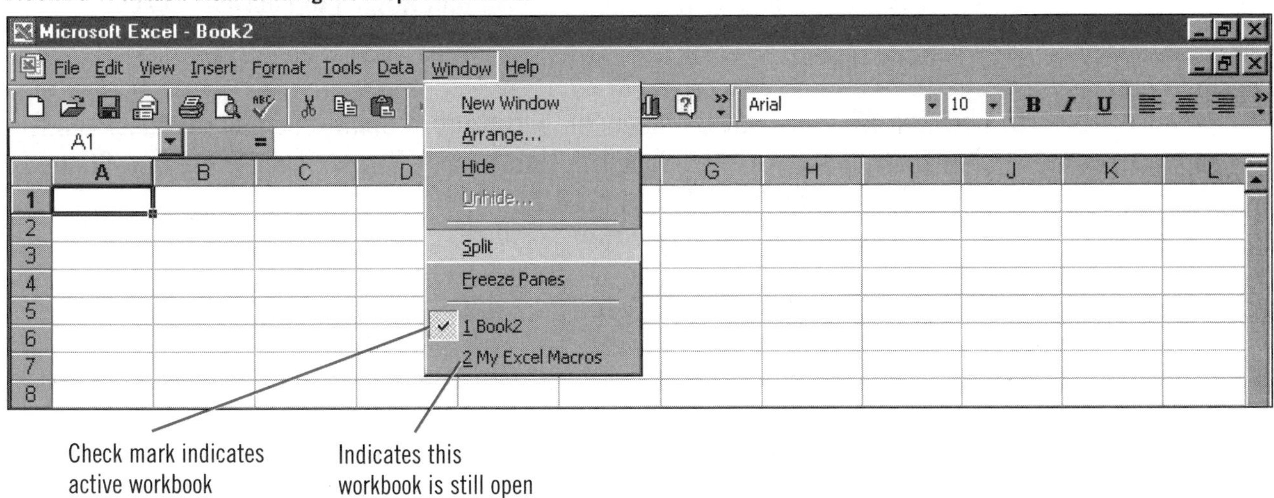

Excel 2000

Editing a Macro

When you use the Macro Recorder to create a macro, the instructions are recorded automatically in Visual Basic for Applications programming language. Each macro is stored as a **module**, or program code container, attached to the workbook. Once you record a macro, you might need to change it. If you have a lot of changes to make, it might be best to re-record the macro. If you need to make only minor adjustments, you can edit the macro code, or program instructions, directly using the Visual Basic Editor. Jim wants to modify his macro to change the point size of the department stamp to 12.

Steps

QuickTip

Another way to start the Visual Basic Editor is to click Tools on the menu bar, point to Macro, then click Visual Basic Editor, or press [Alt][F11].

1. Make sure the My Excel Macros workbook is open, click **Tools** on the menu bar, point to **Macro**, click **Macros**, make sure **DeptStamp** is selected, then click **Edit**
   The Visual Basic Editor starts showing the DeptStamp macro steps in a numbered module window (in this case, Module1).
2. Maximize the window titled **My Excel Macros.xls – [Module1 (Code)]**, then examine the steps in the macro
   See Figure G-8. The name of the macro and the date it was recorded appear at the top of the module window. Notice that Excel translates your keystrokes and commands into words, known as macro code. For example, the line .FontStyle = "Bold" was generated when you clicked Bold in the Format Cells dialog box. When you make changes in a dialog box during macro recording, Excel automatically stores all the dialog box settings in the macro code. You also see lines of code that you didn't generate directly while recording the DeptStamp macro; for example, .Name = "Arial".
3. In the line .Size = 10, double-click **10** to select it, then type **12**
   Because Module1 is attached to the workbook and not stored as a separate file, any changes to the module are saved automatically when the workbook is saved.
4. In the Visual Basic Editor, click **File** on the menu bar, click **Print**, then click **OK** to print the module
   Review the printout of Module1.
5. Click **File** on the menu bar, then click **Close and Return to Microsoft Excel**
   You want to rerun the DeptStamp macro to view the point size edit you made using the Visual Basic Editor.
6. Click cell **A1**, click **Edit** on the menu bar, point to **Clear**, click **All**, deselect cell A1, click **Tools** on the menu bar, point to **Macro**, click **Macros**, make sure **DeptStamp** is selected, click **Run**, then deselect cell A1
   Compare your results with Figure G-9.
7. Save the workbook

FIGURE G-8: Visual Basic Editor showing Module1

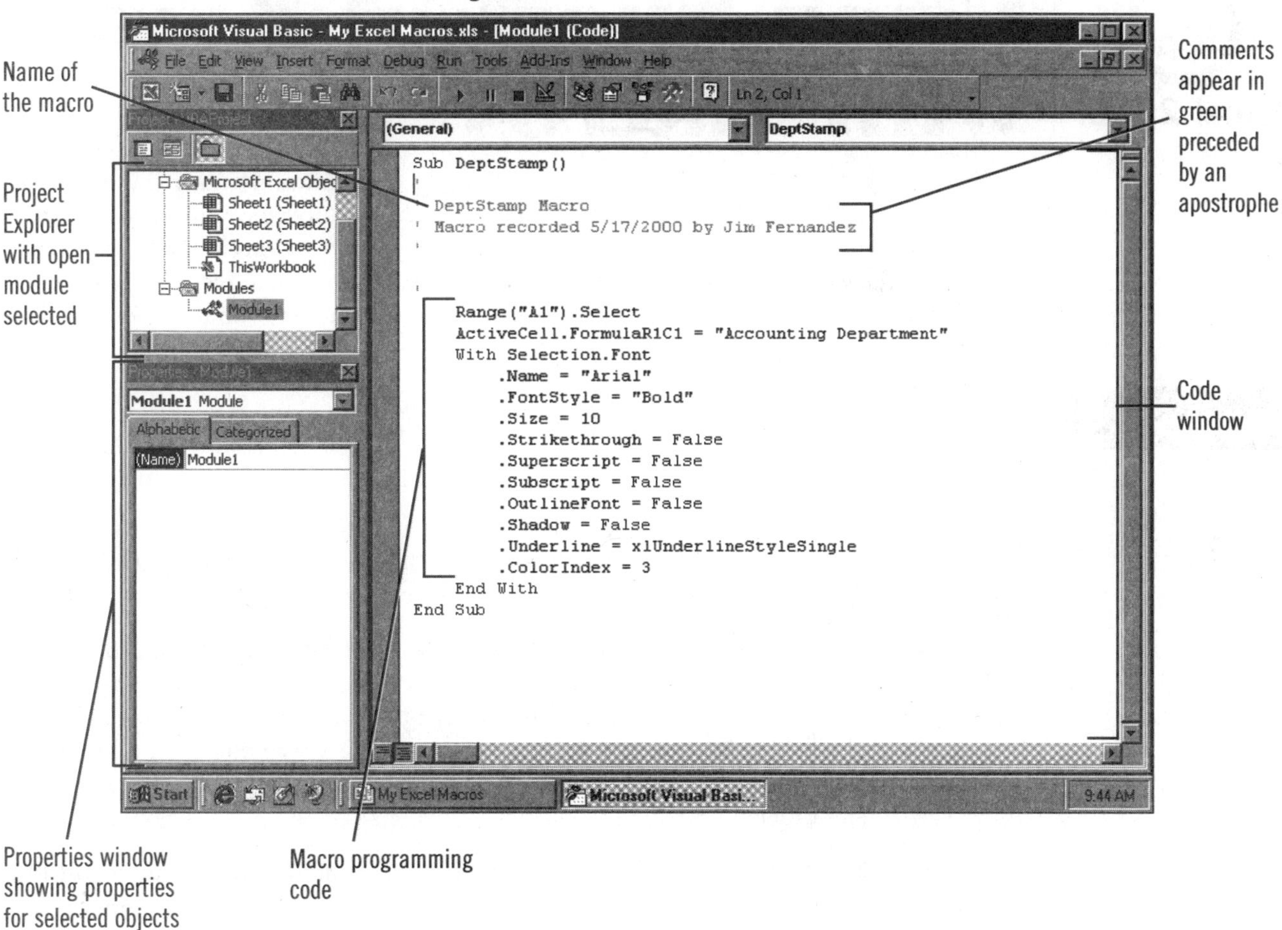

FIGURE G-9: Result of running edited DeptStamp macro

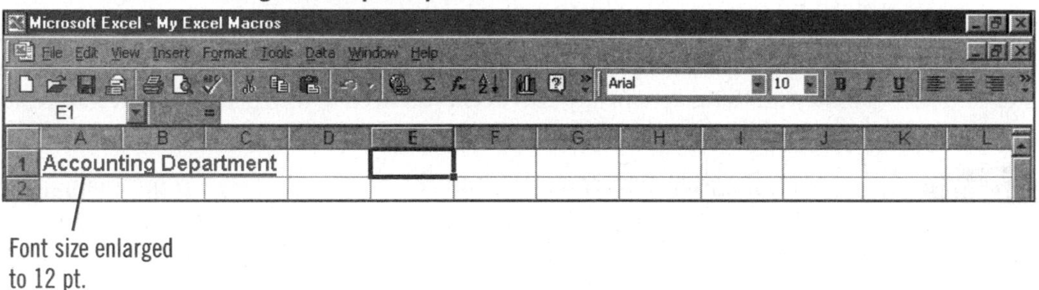

Adding comments to code

With practice, you will be able to interpret the lines of code within your macro. Others who use your macro, however, might want to know the function of a particular line. You can explain the code by adding comments to the macro. Comments are explanatory text added to the lines of code. When you enter a comment, you must type an apostrophe (') before the comment text. Otherwise, Excel thinks you have entered a command. On a color monitor, comments appear in green after you press [Enter]. See Figure G-8. You also can insert blank lines in the macro code to make the code more readable. To do this, type an apostrophe, then press [Enter].

Using Shortcut Keys with Macros

In addition to running a macro from the Macro dialog box, you can run a macro by assigning a shortcut key combination. Using shortcut keys to run macros reduces the number of keystrokes required to begin macro playback. You assign shortcut key combinations in the Record Macro dialog box. Jim also wants to create a macro called CompanyName to enter the company name into a worksheet. He assigns a shortcut key combination to run the macro.

Steps

1. Click **cell B2**
   You will record the macro in cell B2. You want to be able to enter the company name anywhere in a worksheet. Therefore, you will not begin the macro with an instruction to position the cell pointer, as you did in the DeptStamp macro.
2. Click **Tools** on the menu bar, point to **Macro**, then click **Record New Macro**
   The Record Macro dialog box opens. Notice the option Shortcut key: Ctrl+ followed by a blank box. You can type a letter (A-Z) in the Shortcut key box to assign the key combination of [Ctrl] plus that letter to run the macro. You use the key combination [Ctrl][Shift] plus a letter to avoid overriding any of the Excel's assigned [Ctrl] [letter] shortcut keys, such as [Ctrl][C] for Copy.
3. With the default macro name selected, type **CompanyName**, click the **Shortcut key text box**, press and hold **[Shift]**, type **C**, then, if necessary, replace the name in the Description box with your name
   Compare your screen with Figure G-10. You are ready to record the CompanyName macro.
4. Click **OK** to close the dialog box
   By default, Excel records absolute cell references in macros. Beginning the macro in cell B2 causes the macro code to begin with a statement to select cell B2. Because you want to be able to run this macro in any active cell, you need to instruct Excel to record relative cell references while recording the macro.
5. Click the **Relative Reference button** on the Stop Recording toolbar
   The Relative Reference button is now indented to indicate that it is selected. See Figure G-11. This button is a toggle and retains the relative reference setting until you click it again to turn it off.
6. Type **MediaLoft** in cell B2, click the **Enter button** on the formula bar, press **[Ctrl][I]** to italicize the text, click the **Stop Recording button** on the Stop Recording toolbar, then deselect cell B2
   MediaLoft appears in italics in cell B2. You are ready to run the macro in cell A5 using the shortcut key combination.
7. Click cell **A5**, press and hold **[Ctrl][Shift]**, type **C**, then deselect the cell
   The result appears in cell A5. See Figure G-12. Because the macro played back in the selected cell (A5) instead of the cell where it was recorded (B2), Jim is convinced that the macro recorded relative cell references.
8. Save the workbook

QuickTip

When you begin an Excel session, the Relative Reference button is toggled off, indicating that Excel is recording absolute cell references in macros. Once selected, and until it is toggled off again, the Relative Reference setting remains in effect during the current Excel session.

FIGURE G-10: Record Macro dialog box with shortcut key assigned

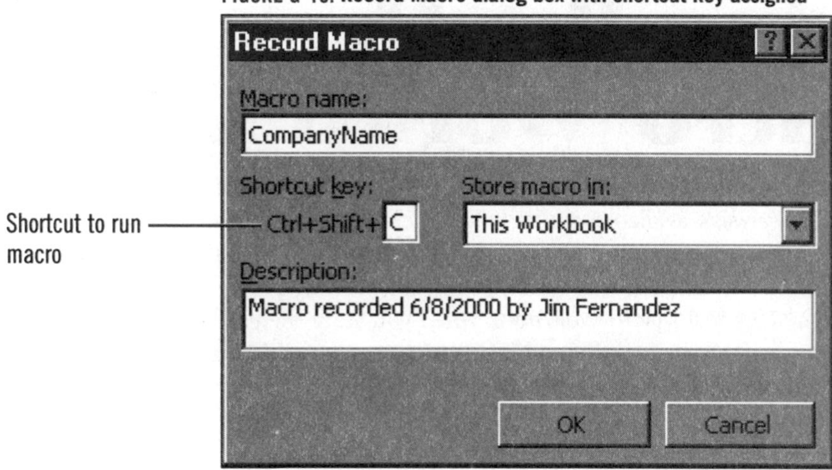

FIGURE G-11: Stop Recording toolbar with Relative Reference button selected

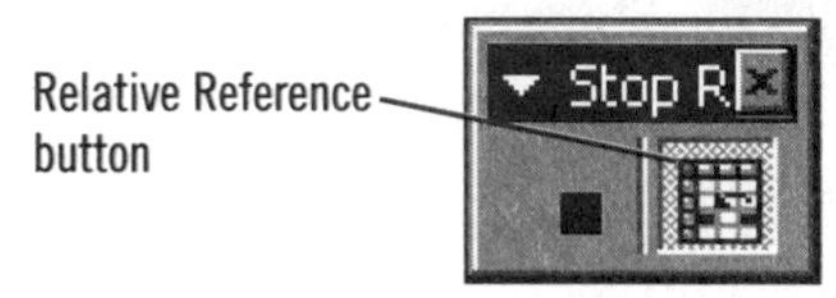

FIGURE G-12: Result of running the CompanyName macro

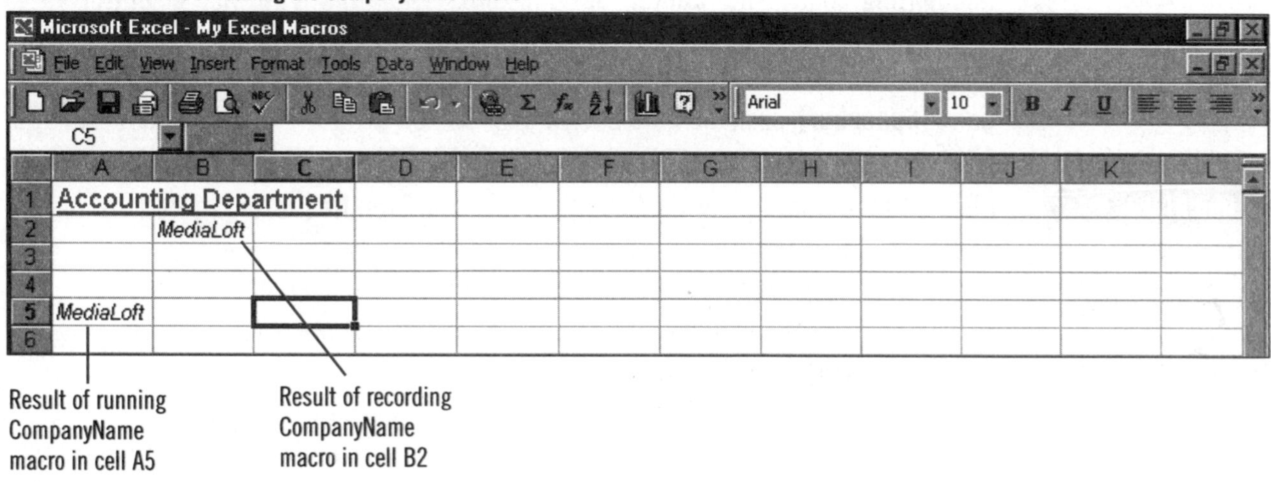

Excel 2000

Excel 2000

Using the Personal Macro Workbook

You can store commonly used macros in a **Personal Macro Workbook**. The Personal Macro Workbook is always available, unless you specify otherwise, and gives you access to all the macros it contains, regardless of which workbooks are open. The Personal Macro Workbook file is created automatically the first time you choose to store a macro in it. Additional macros are added to the Personal Macro Workbook when you store them there. Jim often adds a footer to his worksheets identifying his department, the workbook name, the worksheet name, the page number, and the current date. He saves time by creating a macro that automatically inserts this footer. Because he wants this macro to be available whenever he uses Excel, Jim decides to store this macro in the Personal Macro Workbook.

1. From any cell in the active worksheet, click **Tools** on the menu bar, point to **Macro**, then click **Record New Macro**
   The Record Macro dialog box opens.

Trouble?

If you are prompted to replace an existing macro named FooterStamp, click Yes.

2. Type **FooterStamp** in the Macro name box, click the **Shortcut key box**, press and hold **[Shift]**, type **F**, then click the **Store macro in list arrow**
   You have named the macro FooterStamp and assigned it the shortcut combination [Ctrl][Shift][F]. Notice that This Workbook is selected by default, indicating that Excel automatically stores macros in the active workbook. See Figure G-13. You also can choose to store the macro in a new workbook or in the Personal Macro Workbook.

QuickTip

If you see a message saying that the Personal Macro Workbook needs to be opened, open it, and then begin again from step 1. Once created, the Personal Macro Workbook file is usually stored in the Windows/Application Data/ Microsoft/Excel/XLSTART folder under the name "Personal".

3. Click **Personal Macro Workbook**, replace the existing name in the Description text box with your own name, if necessary, then click **OK**
   The recorder is on, and you are ready to record the macro keystrokes. (If there is already a macro assigned to this shortcut, display the Personal Macro workbook and delete the FooterStamp macro. Then return to the My Excel Macro workbook and begin again from step 1.)
4. Click **File** on the menu bar, click **Page Setup**, click the **Header/Footer tab** (make sure to do this even if it is already active), click **Custom Footer**, in the Left section box, type **Accounting**, click the **Center section box**, click the **File Name button**, press **[Spacebar]**, type /, press **[Spacebar]**, click the **Tab Name button** to insert the sheet name, click the **Right section box**, type your name followed by a comma, press **[Spacebar]**, click the **Date button**, click **OK** to return to the Header/Footer tab
   The footer stamp is set up, as shown in Figure G-14.

QuickTip

You can copy or move macros stored in other workbooks to the Personal Macro Workbook using the Visual Basic Editor.

5. Click **OK** to return to the worksheet, then click the **Stop Recording button** on the Stop Recording toolbar
   You want to ensure that the macro will set the footer stamp in any active worksheet.
6. Activate Sheet2, in cell A1 type **Testing the FooterStamp macro**, press **[Enter]**, press and hold **[Ctrl][Shift]**, then type **F**
   The FooterStamp macro plays back the sequence of commands.
7. Preview the worksheet to verify that the new footer was inserted
8. Print, then save the worksheet
   Jim is satisfied that the FooterStamp macro works in any active worksheet. Next, Jim adds the macro as a menu item on the Tools menu.

FIGURE G-13: **Record Macro dialog box showing Store macro in options**

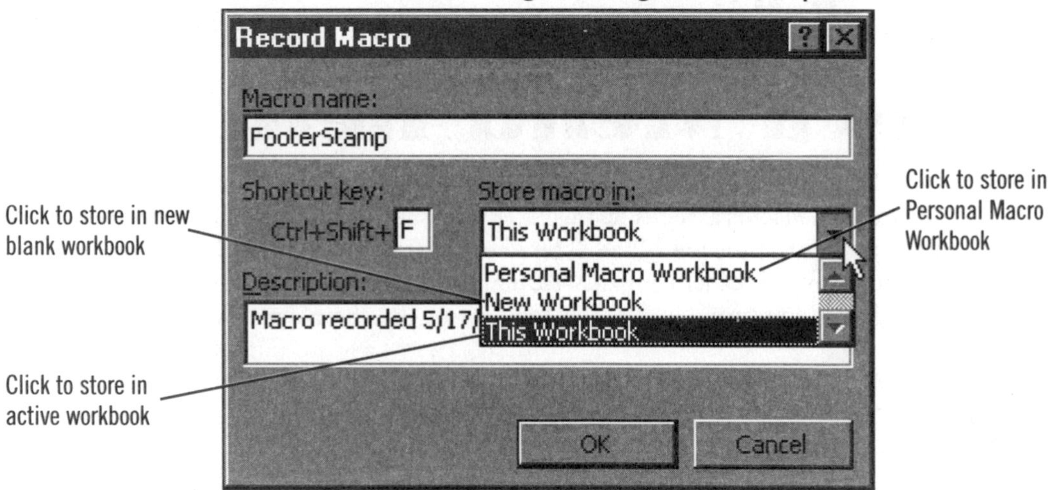

FIGURE G-14: **Header/Footer tab showing custom footer settings**

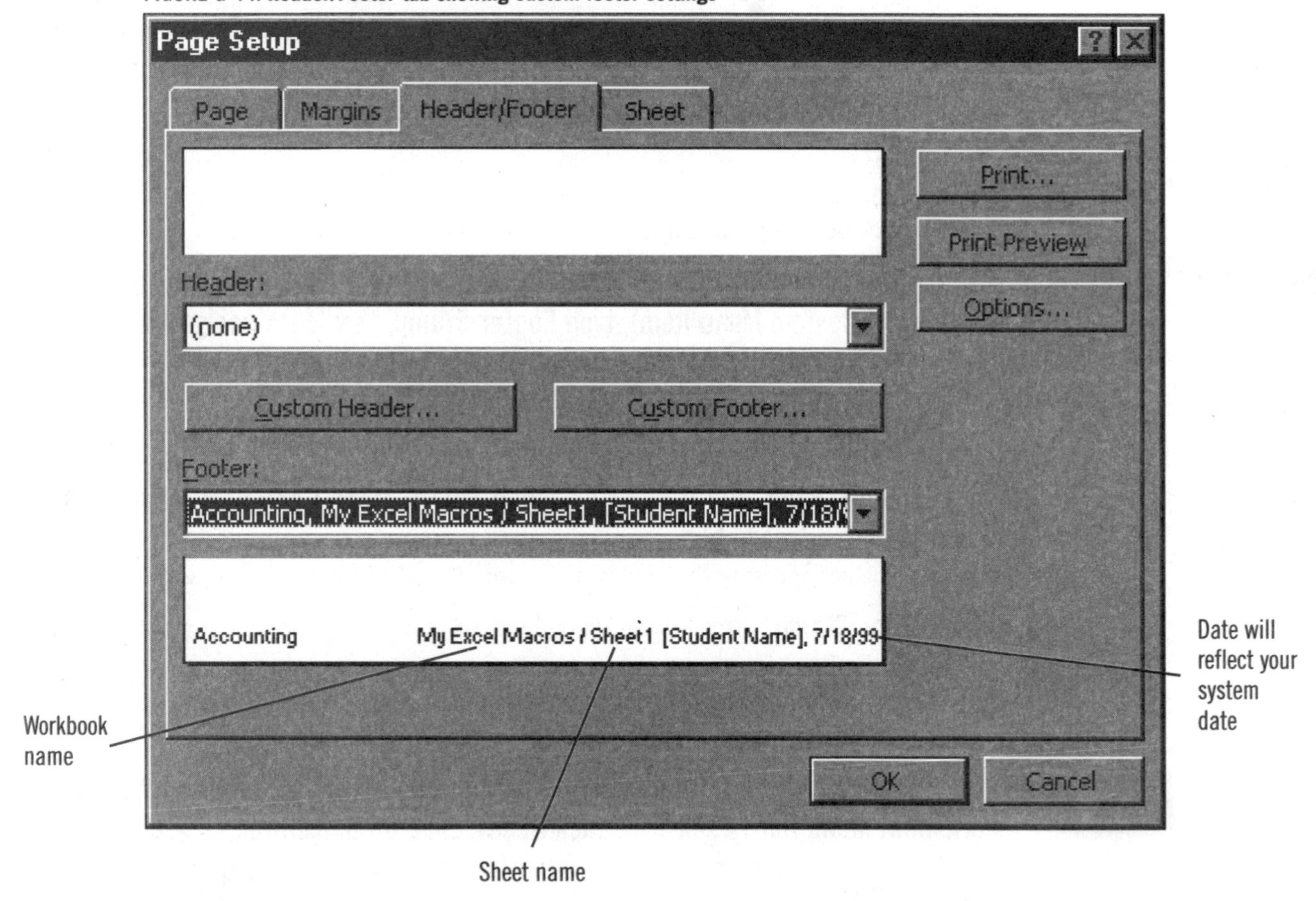

Working with the Personal Macro Workbook

Once created, the Personal Macro Workbook automatically opens each time you start Excel. By default, the Personal Macro Workbook is hidden as a precautionary measure so you don't accidentally add anything to it. When the Personal Macro Workbook is hidden, you can add macros to it but you cannot delete macros from it.

Adding a Macro as a Menu Item

In addition to storing macros in the Personal Macro Workbook so that they are always available, you can add macros as items on the Excel Worksheet menu bar. The **Worksheet menu bar** is a special toolbar at the top of the Excel screen that you can customize. To increase the availability of the FooterStamp macro, Jim decides to add it as an item on the Tools menu. First, he adds a custom menu item to the Tools menu, then he assigns the macro to that menu item.

Steps

QuickTip

If you want to add a command to a menu bar, first display the toolbar containing the menu to which you want to add the command.

1. Click **Tools** on the menu bar, click **Customize**, click the **Commands tab**, then under Categories, click **Macros**
   See Figure G-15.
2. Click **Custom Menu Item** under Commands, drag the selection to **Tools** on the menu bar (the menu opens), then point just under the last menu option, but do not release the mouse button
   Compare your screen to Figure G-16.
3. Release the mouse button
   Now, Custom Menu item is the last item on the Tools menu.
4. With the Tools menu still open, right-click **Custom Menu Item**, select the text in the Name box (&Custom Menu Item), type **Footer Stamp**, then click **Assign Macro**
   Unlike a macro name, the name of a custom menu item can have spaces between words, as do all standard menu items. The Assign Macro dialog box opens.
5. Click **PERSONAL.XLS!FooterStamp** under Macro name, click **OK**, then click **Close**
6. Click the **Sheet3 tab**, in cell A1 type **Testing macro menu item**, press **[Enter]**, then click **Tools** on the menu bar
   The Tools menu appears with the new menu option at the bottom. See Figure G-17.
7. Click **Footer Stamp**, preview the worksheet to verify that the footer was inserted, then close the Print Preview window
   The Print Preview window appears with the footer stamp. Since others using your machine might be confused by the macro on the menu, it's a good idea to remove it.
8. Click **Tools** on the menu bar, click **Customize**, click the **Toolbars tab**, click **Worksheet Menu Bar** to select it, click **Reset**, click **OK** to confirm, click **Close**, then click **Tools** on the menu bar to make sure that the custom item has been deleted
   Because you did not make any changes to your workbook, you don't need to save it. Next, Jim creates a toolbar for macros and adds macros to it.

Trouble?

If you don't see PERSONAL.XLS!FooterStamp under Macro name, try repositioning the Assign Macro dialog box.

FIGURE G-15: Commands tab of the Customize dialog box

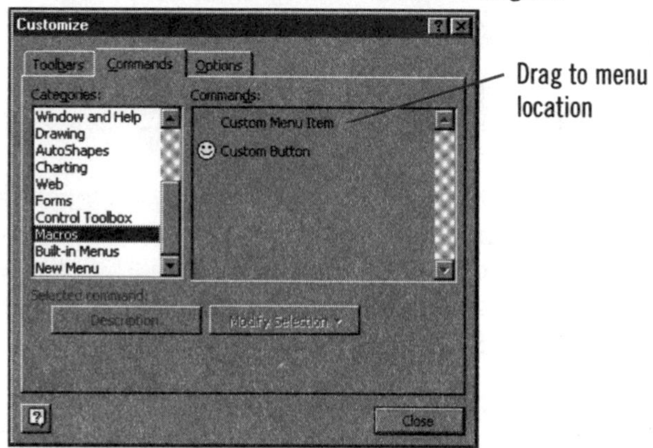

FIGURE G-16: Tools menu showing placement of Custom Menu Item

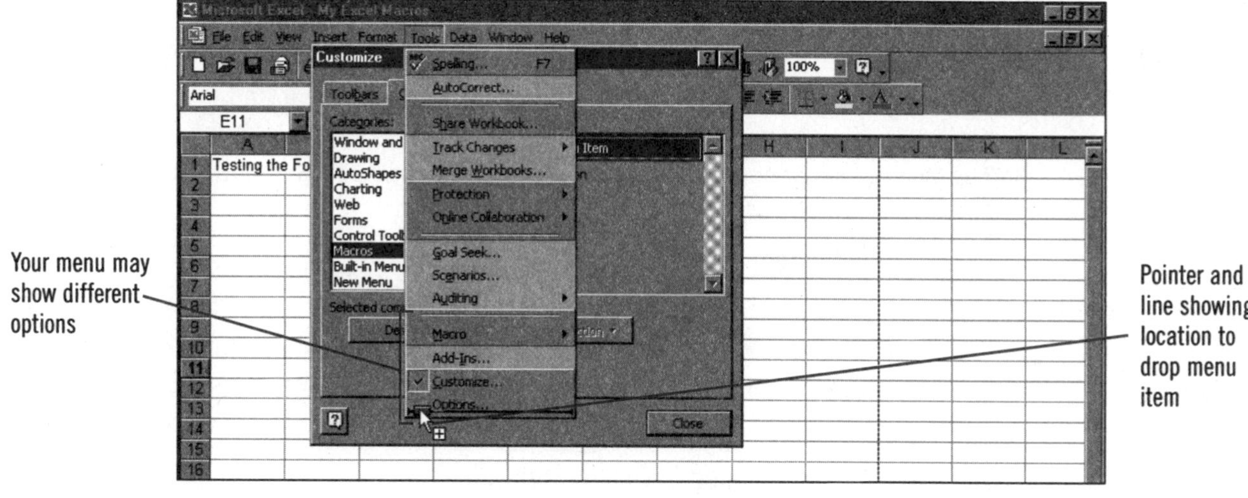

FIGURE G-17: Tools menu with new Footer Stamp item

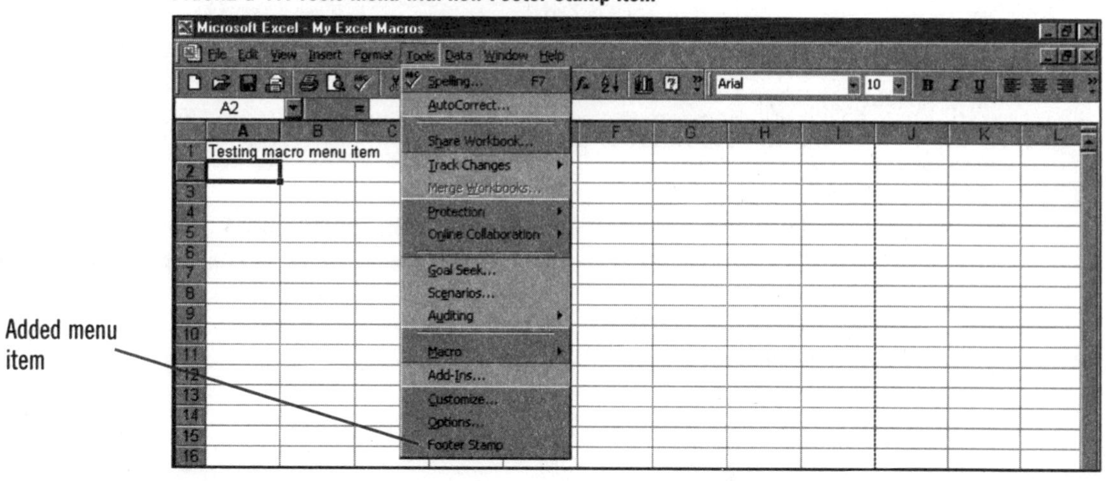

Excel 2000

Creating a Toolbar for Macros

Toolbars contain buttons that allow you to access commonly used commands. You can create your own custom toolbars to organize commands so that you can find and use them quickly. Once you create a toolbar, you then add buttons to access Excel commands such as macros. Jim has decided to create a custom toolbar called Macros that will contain buttons to run two of his macros.

QuickTip

Toolbars you create or customize are available to all workbooks on your PC. You also can ensure that a custom toolbar is available with a specific workbook by attaching the toolbar to the workbook using the Toolbar tab in the Customize dialog box.

1. With Sheet3 active, click **Tools** on the menu bar, click **Customize**, click the **Toolbars tab**, if necessary, then click **New**
   The New Toolbar dialog box opens, as shown in Figure G-18. Under Toolbar name, a default name of Custom1 is selected.
2. Type **Macros**, then click **OK**
   Excel adds the new toolbar named Macros to the bottom of the list and a small, empty toolbar named Macros opens. See Figure G-19. Notice that you cannot see the entire toolbar name. A toolbar starts small and automatically expands to fit the buttons you assign to it.
3. Click the **Commands tab** in the Customize dialog box, click **Macros** under Categories, then drag the **Custom Button** over the new Macros toolbar and release the mouse button
   The Macros toolbar now contains one button. You want the toolbar to contain two macros, so you need to add one more button.
4. Drag the **Custom Button** over the Macros toolbar again
   With the two buttons in place, you customize the buttons and assign macros to them.
5. Right-click the left on the Macros toolbar, select **&Custom Button** in the Name box, type **Department Stamp**, click **Assign Macro**, click **DeptStamp**, then click **OK**
   With the first toolbar button customized, you are ready to customize the second button.
6. With the Customize dialog box open, right-click the right on the Macros toolbar, edit the name to read **Company Name**, click **Change Button Image**, click (bottom row, third from the left), right-click , click **Assign Macro**, click **CompanyName** to select it, click **OK**, then close the Customize dialog box
   The Macros toolbar appears with the two customized macro buttons.
7. Move the mouse pointer over on the Macros toolbar to display the macro name (Department Stamp), then click to run the macro; click **cell B2**, move the mouse pointer over on the Macros toolbar to display the macro name (Company Name), click , then deselect the cell
   Compare your screen with Figure G-20. The DeptStamp macro automatically replaces the contents of cell A1.
8. Click **Tools** on the menu bar, click **Customize**, click the **Toolbars tab**, if necessary, under Toolbars click **Macros** to select it, click **Delete**, click **OK** to confirm the deletion, then click **Close**
9. Save, then close the workbooks

Trouble?

If you are prompted to save the changes to the Personal Macro Workbook, click Yes.

FIGURE G-18: New Toolbar dialog box

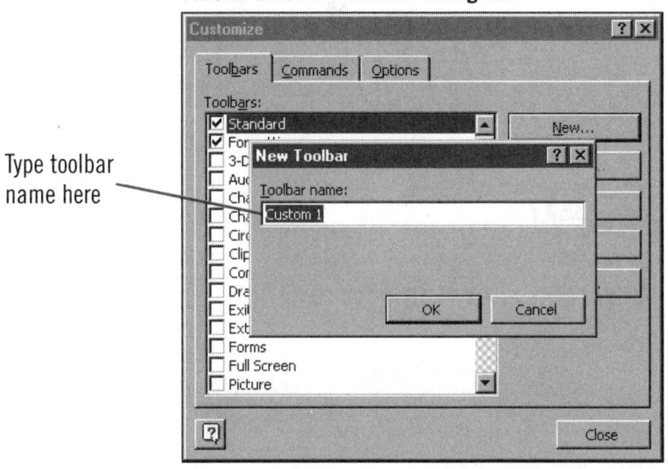

FIGURE G-19: Customize dialog box with new Macros toolbar

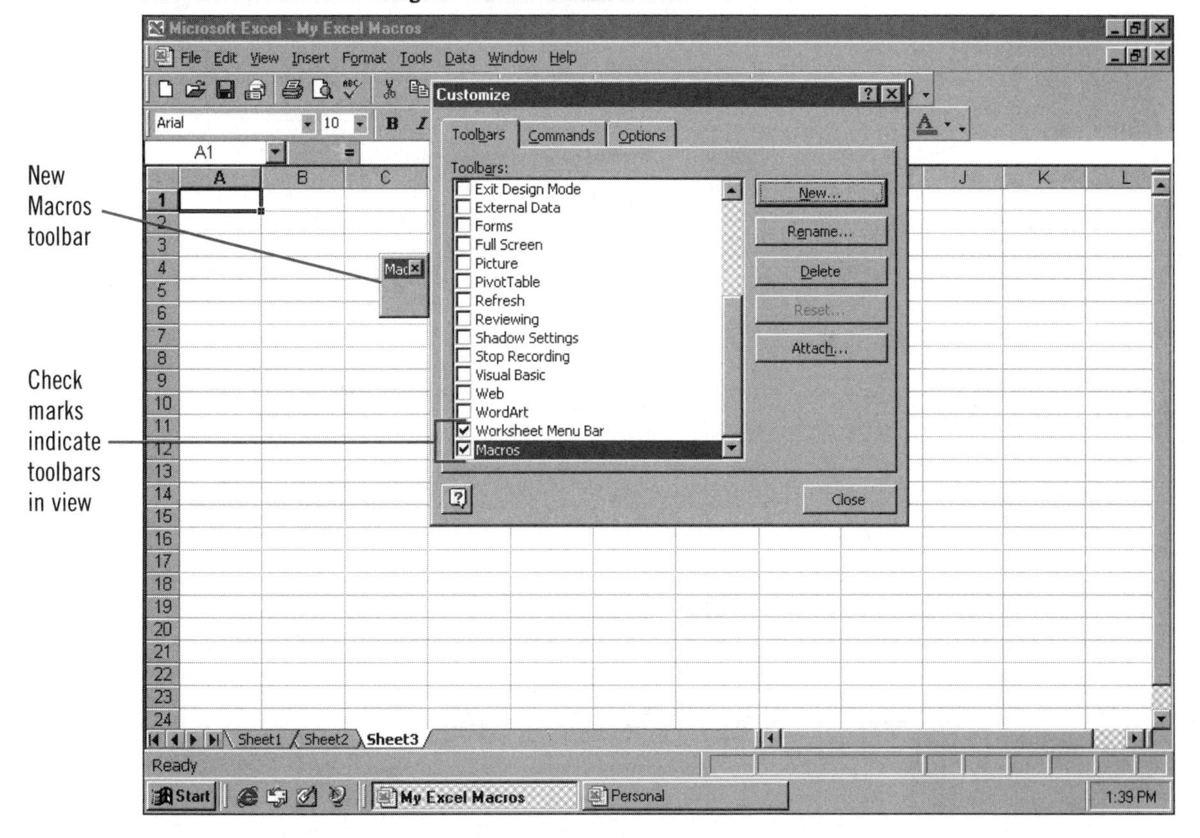

FIGURE G-20: Worksheet showing Macros toolbar with two customized buttons

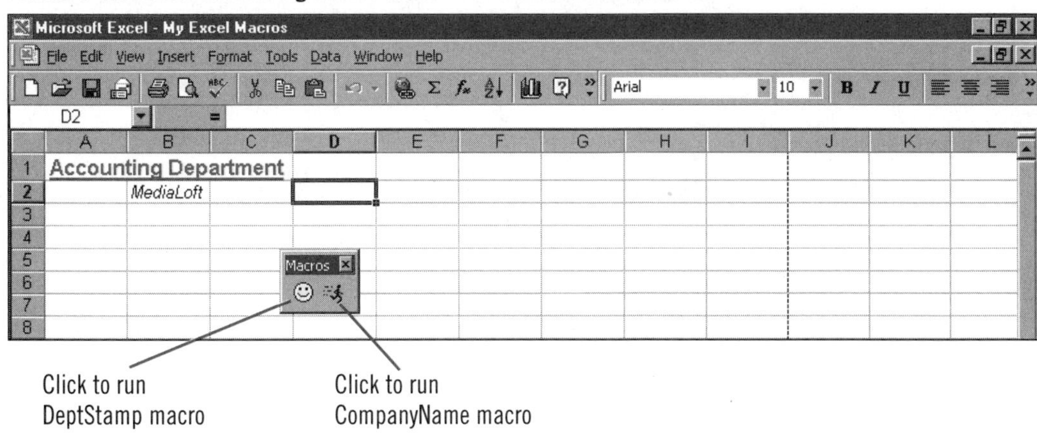

Excel 2000

Practice

► Concepts Review

Label each element of the Excel screen shown in Figure G-21.

FIGURE G-21

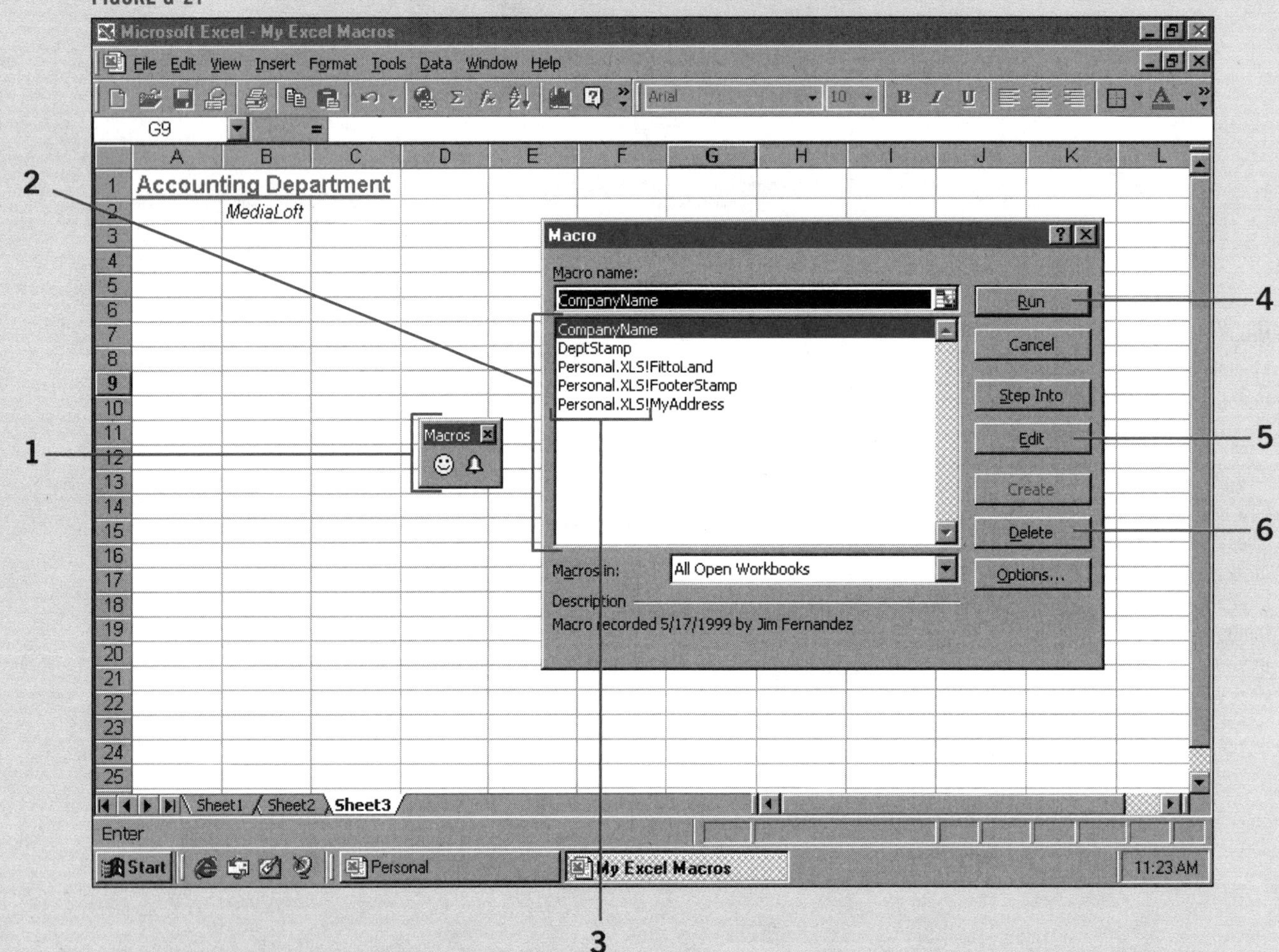

Practice

Select the best answer from the list of choices.

7. Which of the following is the best candidate for a macro?
- **a.** One-button or one-keystroke commands
- **b.** Often-used sequences of commands or actions
- **c.** Seldom-used commands or tasks
- **d.** Nonsequential tasks

8. When you are recording a macro, you can execute commands by using
- **a.** Only the keyboard.
- **b.** Only the mouse.
- **c.** Any combination of the keyboard and the mouse.
- **d.** Only menu commands.

9. A macro is stored in
- **a.** The body of a worksheet used for data.
- **b.** An unused area to the far right or well below the worksheet contents.
- **c.** A module attached to a workbook.
- **d.** A Custom Menu Item.

10. Which of the following is *not* true about editing a macro?
- **a.** You edit macros using the Visual Basic Editor.
- **b.** A macro cannot be edited and must be recorded again.
- **c.** You can type changes directly in the existing macro code.
- **d.** You can make more than one editing change in a macro.

11. Why is it important to plan a macro?
- **a.** Macros won't be stored if they contain errors.
- **b.** Planning helps prevent careless errors from being introduced into the macro.
- **c.** It is very difficult to correct errors you make in a macro.
- **d.** Planning ensures that your macro will not contain errors.

12. Macros are recorded with relative references
- **a.** Only if the Relative Reference button is selected.
- **b.** In all cases.
- **c.** Only if relative references are chosen while recording the macro.
- **d.** Only if the Absolute Reference button is not selected.

13. You can run macros
- **a.** From the Macro dialog box.
- **b.** From shortcut key combinations.
- **c.** As items on menus.
- **d.** Using all of the above.

► Skills Review

1. Record a macro.

- **a.** Create a new workbook, then save it as "Macros". You will record a macro titled "MyAddress" that enters and formats your name, address, and telephone number in a worksheet.
- **b.** Store the macro in the current workbook.
- **c.** Record the macro, entering your name in cell A1, your street address in cell A2, your city, state, and ZIP code in cell A3, and your telephone number in cell A4.
- **d.** Format the information as 14-point Arial bold.
- **e.** Add a border and make the text the color of your choice.
- **f.** Save the workbook.

2. Run a macro.

- **a.** Clear cell entries in the range affected by the macro.
- **b.** Run the MyAddress macro in cell A1.
- **c.** Clear the cell entries generated by running the MyAddress macro.
- **d.** Save the workbook.

3. Edit a macro.

- **a.** Open the MyAddress macro in the Visual Basic Editor.
- **b.** Locate the line of code that defines the font size, then change the size to 18 point.
- **c.** Edit the selected range to A1:E4, which increases it by three columns to accommodate the changed label size. (*Hint*: It is the second Range line in the macro.)
- **d.** Add a comment line that describes this macro.
- **e.** Save and print the module, then return to Excel.
- **f.** Test the macro in Sheet1.
- **g.** Save the workbook.

4. Use shortcut keys with macros.

- **a.** You will record a macro in the current workbook called "MyName" that records your full name in cell G1.
- **b.** Assign your macro the shortcut key combination [Ctrl][Shift][N] and store it in the current workbook.
- **c.** After you record the macro, clear cell G1.
- **d.** Use the shortcut key combination to run the MyName macro.
- **e.** Save the workbook.

5. Use the Personal Macro Workbook.

- **a.** You will record a new macro called "FitToLand" that sets print orientation to landscape, scaled to fit on a page.
- **b.** Store the macro in the Personal Macro Workbook. If you are prompted to replace the existing FitToLand macro, click Yes.
- **c.** After you record the macro, activate Sheet2, and enter some test data in row 1 that exceeds one page width.
- **d.** In the Page Setup dialog box, return the orientation to portrait and adjust the capital A to 100 percent of normal size.
- **e.** Run the macro.
- **f.** Preview Sheet2 and verify that it's in landscape view and fits on one page.

6. Add a macro as a menu item.

- **a.** On the Commands tab in the Customize dialog box, specify that you want to create a Custom Menu Item.
- **b.** Place the Custom Menu Item at the bottom of the Tools menu.
- **c.** Rename the Custom Menu Item "Fit to Landscape".
- **d.** Assign the macro PERSONAL.XLS!FitToLand to the command.
- **e.** Go to Sheet3 and change the orientation to portrait, then enter some test data in column A.
- **f.** Run the Fit to Landscape macro from the Tools menu.
- **g.** Preview the worksheet and verify that it is in landscape view.
- **h.** Using the Tools, Customize menu options, select the Worksheet Menu bar, and reset.
- **i.** Verify that the command has been removed from the Tools menu.
- **j.** Save the workbook.

7. Create a toolbar for macros.

- **a.** With the Macros workbook still open, you will create a new custom toolbar titled "My Info".
- **b.** If necessary, drag the new toolbar onto the worksheet.
- **c.** Display the Macros command category, then drag the Custom Button to the My Info toolbar.
- **d.** Again, drag the Custom Button to the My Info toolbar.
- **e.** Rename the first button "My Address", and assign the MyAddress macro to it.
- **f.** Rename the second button "My Name", and assign the MyName macro to it.
- **g.** Change the second button image to one of your choice.
- **h.** On Sheet3, clear the existing cell data, then test both macro buttons on the My Info toolbar.
- **i.** Use the Toolbars tab of the Customize dialog box to delete the toolbar named My Info.
- **j.** Save and close the workbook, then exit Excel.

Independent Challenges

1. As a computer-support employee of an accounting firm, you need to develop ways to help your fellow employees work more efficiently. Employees have asked for Excel macros that will do the following:

- Delete the current row and insert a blank row
- Delete the current column and insert a blank column
- Format a selected group of cells with a red pattern, in 12-point Times bold italic

To complete this independent challenge:

- **a.** Plan and write the steps necessary for each macro.
- **b.** Create a new workbook, then save it as "Excel Utility Macros".
- **c.** Create a new toolbar called "Helpers".
- **d.** Create a macro for each employee request described above.
- **e.** Add descriptive comment lines to each module.
- **f.** Add each macro to the Tools menu.
- **g.** On the Helpers toolbar, install buttons to run the macros.
- **h.** Test each macro by using the Run command, the menu command, and the new buttons.
- **i.** Save and then print the module for each macro.
- **j.** Delete the new toolbar, and reset the Worksheet menu bar.

2. You are an analyst in the finance department of a large bank. Every quarter, you produce a number of single-page quarterly budget worksheets. Your manager has informed you that certain worksheets need to contain a footer stamp indicating that the worksheet was produced in the finance department. The footer also should show the date, the current page number of the total pages, and the worksheet filename. You decide that the stamp should not include a header. It's tedious to add the footer stamp and to clear the existing header and footer for the numerous worksheets you produce. You will record a macro to do this.

To complete this independent challenge:

a. Plan and write the steps to create the macro.
b. Create a new workbook, then save it as "Header and Footer Stamp".
c. Create the macro described above. Make sure it adds the footer with the department name and other information, and also clears the existing header.
d. Add descriptive comment lines to the macro code.
e. Add the macro to the Tools menu.
f. Create a toolbar titled "Stamp", then install a button on the toolbar to run the macro.
g. Test the macro to make sure it works from the Run command, menu command, and new button.
h. Save and print the module for the macro.
i. Delete the new toolbar, then reset the Worksheet menu bar.

3. You are an administrative assistant to the marketing vice president at Computers, Inc. A major part of your job is to create spreadsheets that project sales results in different markets. It seems that you are constantly changing the print settings so that workbooks print in landscape orientation and are scaled to fit on one page. You have decided that it is time to create a macro to streamline this process.

To complete this independent challenge:

a. Plan and write the steps necessary for the macro.
b. Create a new workbook, then save it as "Computers Inc Macro".
c. Create a macro that changes the page orientation to landscape and scales the worksheet to fit on a page.
d. Test the macro.
e. Save and print the module sheet.
f. Delete any toolbars you created, and reset the Worksheet menu bar.

4. The MediaLoft New York store has recently instituted a budgeting process for its café operation. At the end of every monthly sales report created in Excel, the staff lists the four largest budget items and then fills in what it expects the figures to be for the next month.

Jim Fernandez at MediaLoft corporate headquarters has asked you to use Excel macros and the MediaLoft intranet site to help automate this task. The New York store staff will then distribute the macro to all stores so they can easily add the budget figures to their monthly reports.

a. Connect to the Internet, go to the MediaLoft intranet site at http://www.course.com/illustrated/MediaLoft, click the Accounting link, then click the Cafe Budget link. Examine the information in the NYC Cafe Expenses chart and note the four largest expense categories. Close your browser and disconnect from the Internet.

b. To complete this independent challenge, start Excel, create a new workbook, then save it as "Cafe Budget Macro". Create a macro named "CafeBudget" in the current workbook (activated by the [Shift][Ctrl][B] key combination) that does the following:

- Inserts the names of the four largest expense categories in contiguous cells in a column, starting with the current cell.
- Inserts the word "Total" in the cell below the last category.
- Inserts the words "Next Month's Budget" in the cell just above and to the right of the categories. The managers will insert their budget figures in the four cells below this heading, to the right of each category name.
- Totals the four figures the managers will insert and places the sum to the right of the Total label, just below the four figures.
- Inserts a bottom border on the Next Month's Budget cell and on the cell containing the last of the four figures.
- Boldfaces the Total text and the cell to its right that will contain the total.
- Places a thick box border around all the information, fills the area with a light green color, and autofits the column information where necessary.
- Makes the cell to the right of the first category the active cell.

c. Clear the worksheet of all contents and formats and test the macro. Edit or rerecord the macro as necessary.

d. Make a custom menu item on the Tools menu called "Cafe Budget" that will run the macro you created.

e. Create a custom toolbar named "Budgets" with a button containing the image of a calculator on it, and assign the button to your CafeBudget macro.

f. Test the custom menu item and the custom toolbar button, clearing the worksheet before running each one.

g. Save your workbook, print the results of the macro, then open the macro in the Visual Basic Editor and print the macro code.

h. Return to Excel, save and close the workbook, then exit Excel.

► Visual Workshop

Create the macro shown in Figure G-22. (*Hint:* Save a blank workbook as "File Utility Macros", then create a macro called SaveClose that saves a previously named workbook. Finally, include the line ActiveWorkbook. Close in the module, as shown in the figure.) Print the module. Test the macro. The line "Macro recorded...by..." will reflect your system date and name.

FIGURE G-22

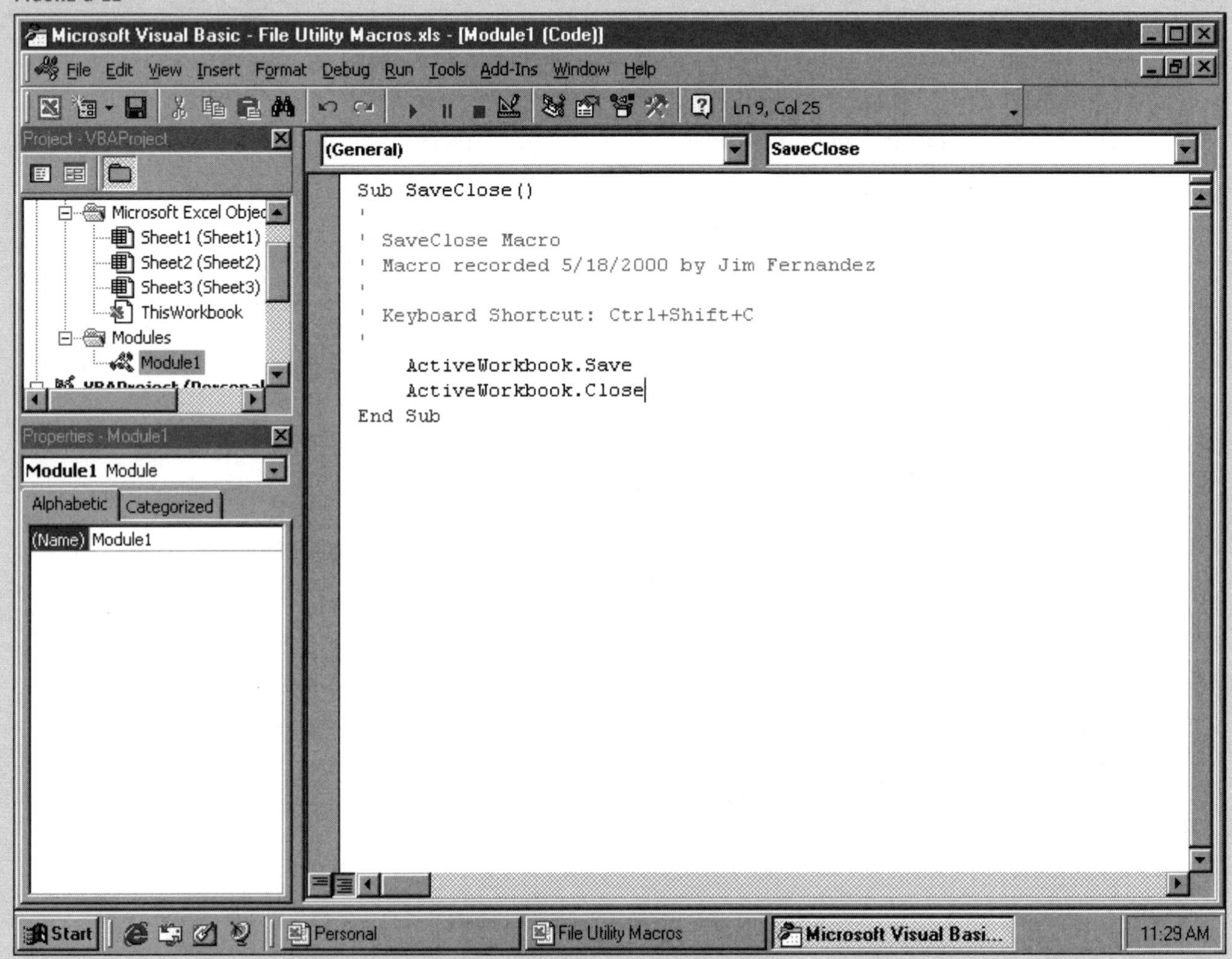

Excel 2000

Unit H

Using Lists

Objectives

- Plan a list
- Create a list
- MOUS Add records with the data form
- MOUS Find records
- MOUS Delete records
- MOUS Sort a list by one field
- MOUS Sort a list by multiple fields
- MOUS Print a list

A **database** is an organized collection of related information. Examples of databases include a telephone book, a card catalog, and a roster of company employees. Excel refers to a database as a **list**. Using an Excel list, you can organize and manage worksheet information so that you can quickly find needed data for projects, reports, and charts. In this unit, you'll learn how to plan and create a list; add, change, find, and delete information in a list; and then sort and print a list.

MediaLoft uses lists to analyze new customer information. Jim Fernandez needs to build and manage a list of new customers as part of the ongoing strategy to focus the company's advertising dollars.

Excel 2000

Planning a List

When planning a list, consider what information the list will contain and how you will work with the data now and in the future. Lists are organized into records. A **record** contains data about an object or person. Records, in turn, are divided into fields. **Fields** are columns in the list; each field describes a characteristic about the record, such as a customer's last name or street address. Each field has a **field name**, a column label that describes the field. See Table H-1 for additional planning guidelines. Jim will compile a list of new customers. Before entering the data into an Excel worksheet, he plans his list using the following guidelines:

Details

Identify the purpose of the list

Determine the kind of information the list should contain. Jim will use the list to identify areas of the country in which new customers live.

Plan the structure of the list

Determine the fields that make up a record. Jim has customer cards that contain information about each new customer. Figure H-1 shows a typical card. Each customer in the list will have a record. The fields in the record correspond to the information on the cards.

Write down the names of the fields

Field names can be up to 255 characters in length (the maximum column width), although shorter names are easier to see in the cells. Field names appear in the first row of a list. Jim writes down field names that describe each piece of information shown in Figure H-1.

Determine any special number formatting required in the list

Most lists contain both text and numbers. When planning a list, consider whether any fields require specific number formatting or prefixes. Jim notes that some Zip codes begin with zero. Because Excel automatically drops a leading zero, Jim must type an apostrophe (') when he enters a Zip code that begins with 0 (zero). The apostrophe tells Excel that the cell contains a label rather than a value. If a column contains both numbers and numbers that contain a text character, such as an apostrophe ('), you should format all the numbers as text. Otherwise, the numbers are sorted first, and the numbers that contain text characters are sorted after that; for example, 11542, 60614, 87105, '01810, '02115. To instruct Excel to sort the Zip codes properly, Jim enters all Zip codes with a leading apostrophe.

FIGURE H-1: Customer record and corresponding field names

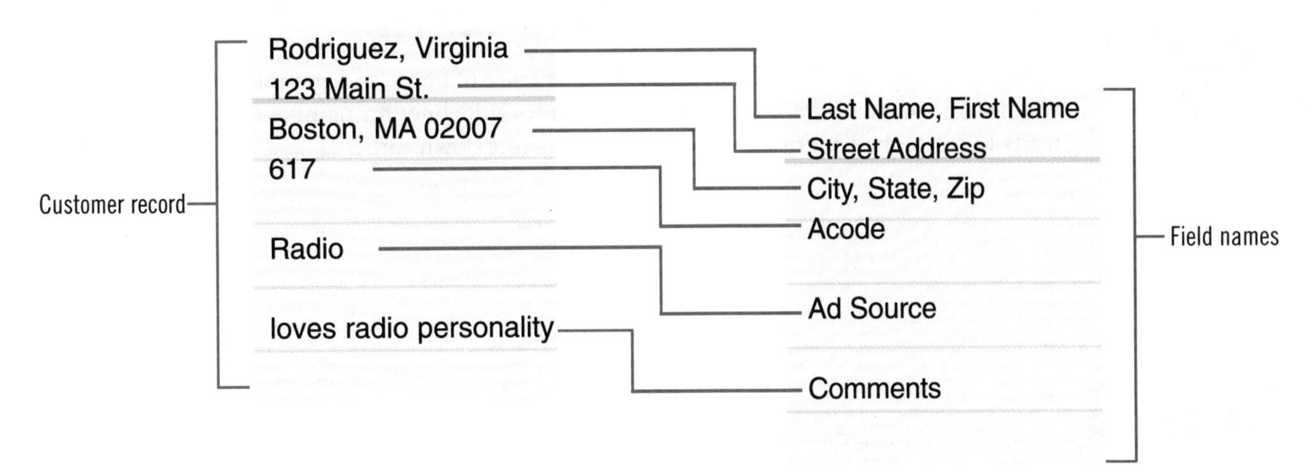

TABLE H-1: Guidelines for planning a list

size and location guidelines	row and column content guidelines
Devote an entire worksheet to your list and list summary information because some list management features can be used on only one list at a time	Plan and design your list so that all rows have similar items in the same column
Leave at least one blank column and one blank row between your list and list summary data. Doing this helps Excel select your list when it performs list management tasks such as sorting	Do not insert extra spaces at the beginning of a cell because that can affect sorting and searching
Avoid placing critical data to the left or right of the list	Use the same format for all cells in a column

Lists versus databases

If your list contains more records than can fit on one worksheet (that is, more than 65,536), you should consider using database software rather than spreadsheet software.

Creating a List

Once you have planned the list structure, the sequence of fields, and any appropriate formatting, you need to create field names. Table H-2 provides guidelines for naming fields. Jim is ready to create the list using the field names he wrote down earlier.

Steps

QuickTip

To return personalized toolbars and menus to their default state, click Tools on the menu bar, click Customize, click the Options tab in the Customize dialog box, click Reset my usage data to restore the default settings, click Yes, click Close, then close the Drawing toolbar if it is displayed.

Trouble?

If the Bold button or Borders button does not appear on your Formatting toolbar, click the More Buttons button to view it.

QuickTip

If the field name you plan to use is wider than the data in the column, you can turn on Wrap Text to stack the heading in the cell. Doing this allows you to use descriptive field names and still keep the columns from being unnecessarily wide. If you prefer a keyboard shortcut, you can press [Alt][Enter] to force a line break while entering field names.

1. Start Excel if necessary, open the workbook titled **EX H-1**, save it as **New Customer List**, rename Sheet1 as **Practice**, then if necessary maximize the Excel window
   It is a good idea to devote an entire worksheet to your list.
2. Beginning in cell A1 and moving horizontally, type each field name in a separate cell, as shown in Figure H-2
   Always put field names in the first row of the list. Don't worry if your field names are wider than the cells; you will fix this later.
3. Select the field headings in range **A1:I1**, then click the **Bold button** on the Formatting toolbar; with range A1:I1 still selected, click the **Borders list arrow**, then click the **thick bottom border** (second item from left in the second row)
4. Enter the information from Figure H-3 in the rows immediately below the field names, using a leading apostrophe (') for all Zip codes; do not leave any blank rows
   If you don't type an apostrophe, Excel deletes the leading zero (0) in the Zip code. The data appears in columns organized by field name.
5. Select the range **A1:I4**, click **Format** on the menu bar, point to **Column**, click **AutoFit Selection**, click anywhere in the worksheet to deselect the range, then save the workbook
   Automatically resizing the column widths this way is faster than double-clicking the column divider lines between each pair of columns. Compare your screen with Figure H-4.

TABLE H-2: **Guidelines for naming fields**

guideline	explanation
Use labels to name fields	Numbers can be interpreted as parts of formulas
Do not use duplicate field names	Duplicate field names can cause information to be incorrectly entered and sorted
Format the field names to stand out from the list data	Use a font, alignment, format, pattern, border, or capitalization style for the column labels that are different from the format of your list data
Use descriptive names	Avoid names that might be confused with cell addresses, such as Q4

FIGURE H-2: Field names entered and formatted in row 1

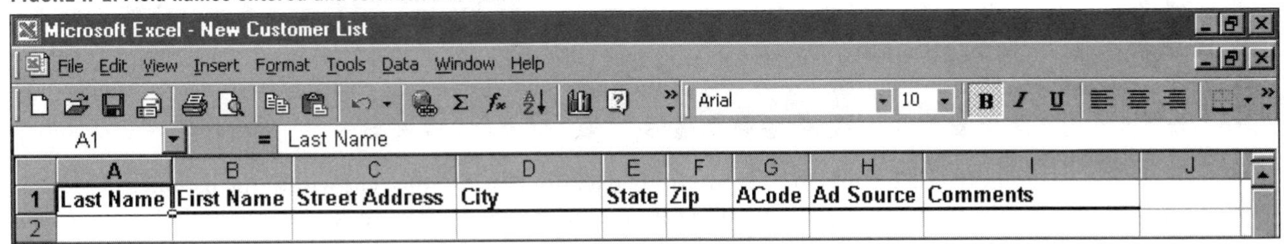

FIGURE H-3: Cards with customer information

Rodriguez, Virginia	Wong, Sam	Smith, Carol
123 Main St.	2120 Central NE.	123 Elm St.
Boston, MA 02007	San Francisco, CA 93772	Watertown, MA 02472
617	415	617
Radio	Newspaper	Newspaper
loves radio personality	graphics caught eye	no comments

FIGURE H-4: List with three records

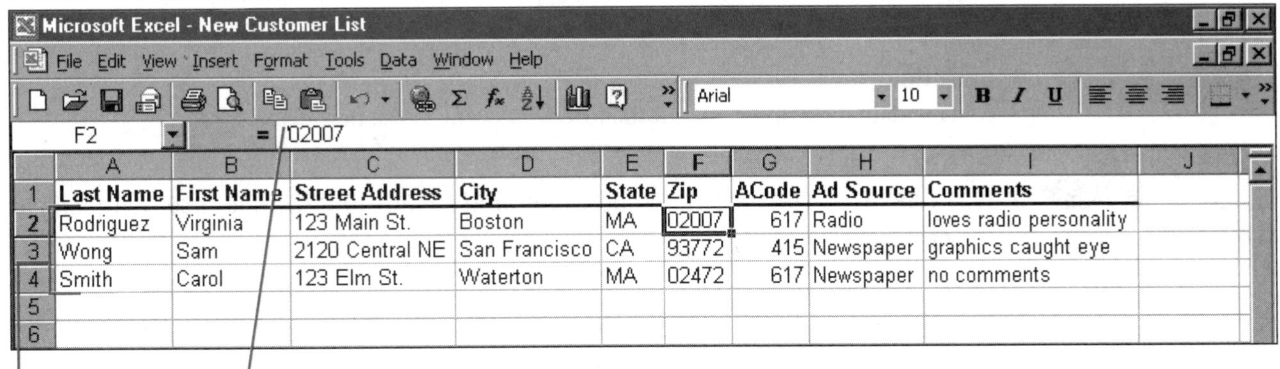

Maintaining the quality of information in a list

To protect the list information, make sure the data is entered in the correct field. Stress care and consistency to all those who enter the list data. Haphazardly entered data can yield invalid results later when it is manipulated.

Excel 2000

Adding Records with the Data Form

You can add records to a list by typing data directly into the cells within the list range. Once the field names are created, you also can use the data form as a quick, easy method of data entry. A **data form** is a dialog box that displays one record at a time. By naming a list range in the name box, you can select the list at any time, and all new records you add to the list will be included in the list range. Jim has entered all the customer records he had on his cards, but he receives the names of two more customers. He decides to use the Excel data form to add the new customer information.

Steps

1. **Make sure the New Customer List file is open, then rename Sheet2 Working List**
   Working List contains the nearly complete customer list. Before using the data form to enter the new data, you must define the list range.

2. **Select the range A1:I45, click the name box to select the reference to cell A1 there, type Database, then press [Enter]**
   The Database list range name appears in the name box. When you assign the name Database to the list, the commands on the Excel Data menu apply to the list named "Database".

3. **While the list is still selected, click Data on the menu bar, then click Form**
   A data form containing the first record appears, as shown in Figure H-5.

4. **Click New**
   A blank data form appears with the insertion point in the first field.

5. **Type Chavez in the Last Name box, then press [Tab] to move the insertion point to the next field**

6. **Enter the rest of the information for Jeffrey Chavez, as shown in Figure H-6**
   Press [Tab] to move the insertion point to the next field, or click in the next field's box to move the insertion point there.

7. **Click New to add Jeffrey Chavez's record and open another blank data form, enter the record for Cathy Relman as shown in Figure H-6, then click Close**
   The list records that you add with the data form are placed at the end of the list and are formatted in the same way as the previous records.

8. **Scroll down the worksheet to bring rows 46 and 47 into view, check both new records, return to cell A1, then save the workbook**

Trouble?

If you accidentally press [↑] or [↓] while in a data form and find yourself positioned in the wrong record, press [↑] or [↓] until you return to the desired record.

QuickTip

Excel 2000 automatically extends formatting and formulas in lists.

FIGURE H-5: Data form showing first record in the list

Working List

Last Name:	Rodriguez
First Name:	Virginia
Street Address:	123 Main St.
City:	Boston
State:	MA
Zip:	02007
ACode:	617
Ad Source:	Radio
Comments on ads:	loves radio personality

1 of 44

New
Delete
Restore
Find Prev
Find Next
Criteria
Close

Total number or records

Click to open a blank data form for adding a record

Current record number

Leading apostrophe not visible in data form after records are inserted

FIGURE H-6: Two data forms with information for two new records

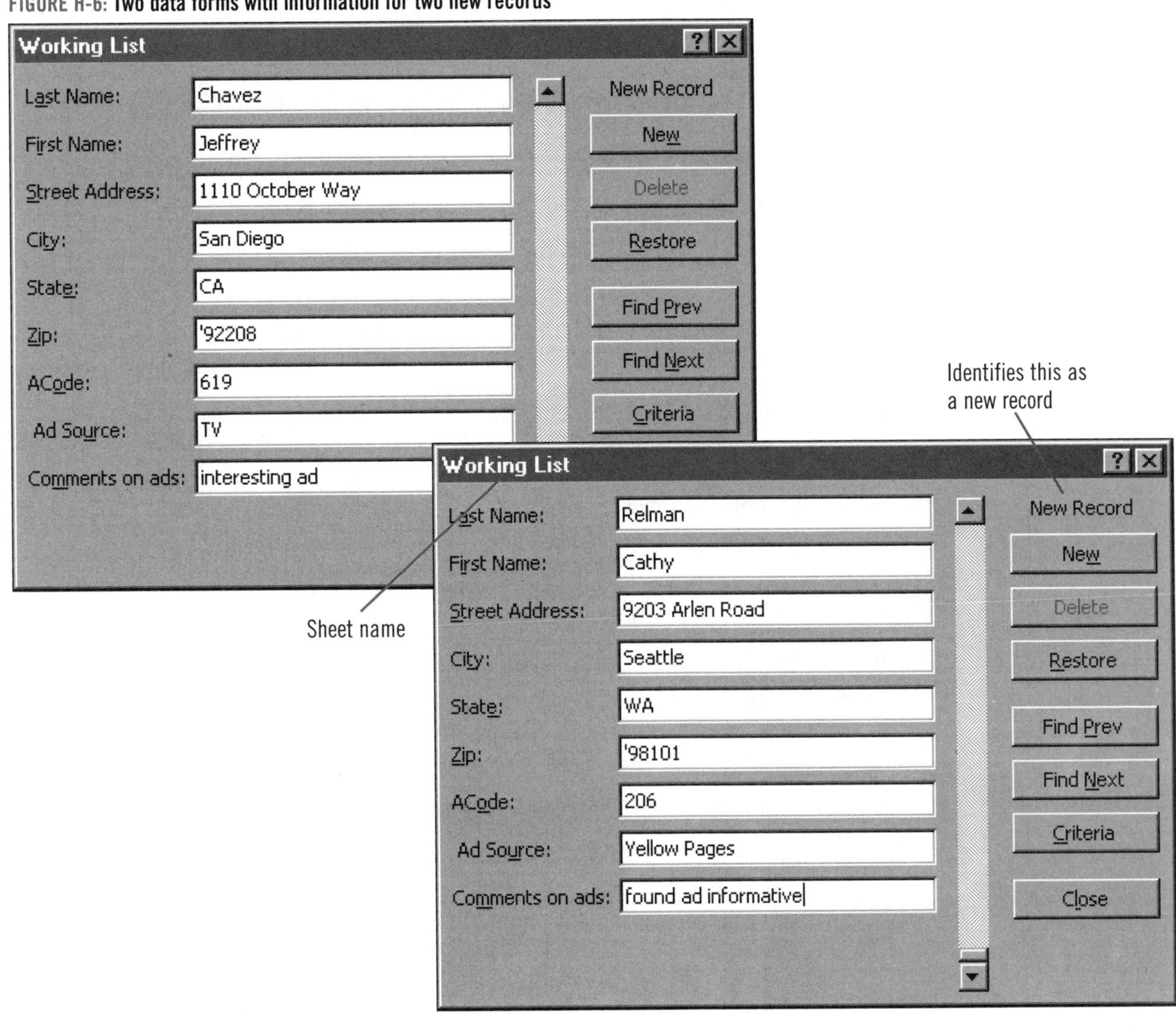

Excel 2000

Excel 2000

Finding Records

From time to time, you need to locate specific records in your list. You can use the Excel Find command on the Edit menu or the data form to search your list. Also, you can use the Replace command on the Edit menu to locate and replace existing entries or portions of entries with specified information. Jim wants to be more specific about the radio ad source, so he replaces "Radio" with "KWIN Radio." He also wants to know how many of the new customers originated from the company's TV ads. Jim begins by searching for those records with the ad source "TV".

Steps

Trouble?

If you receive the message "No list found", select any cell within the list, then repeat Step 1

QuickTip

You can also use comparison operators when performing a search using the data form. For example, you could specify >50,000 in a Salary field box to return those records in the Salary field with a value greater than $50,000.

1. From any cell within the list, click **Data** on the menu bar, click **Form**, then click **Criteria**
   The data form changes so that all fields are blank and "Criteria" appears in the upper-right corner. See Figure H-7. You want to search for records whose Ad Source field contains the label "TV".
2. Press **[Alt][U]** to move to the Ad Source box, type **TV**, then click **Find Next**
   Excel displays the first record for a customer who learned about the company through its TV ads. See Figure H-8.
3. Click **Find Next** until there are no more matching records, then click **Close**
   There are six customers whose ad source is TV. Next, Jim wants to make the radio ad source more specific.
4. Return to cell A1, click **Edit** on the menu bar, then click **Replace**
   The Replace dialog box opens with the insertion point located in the Find what box. See Figure H-9.
5. Type **Radio** in the Find what box, then click the **Replace with box**
   Jim wants to search for entries containing "Radio" and replace them with "KWIN Radio".
6. Type **KWIN Radio** in the Replace with box
   You are about to perform the search and replace option specified. Because you notice that there are other list entries containing the word "radio" with a lowercase "r" (in the Comments column), you need to make sure that only capitalized instances of the word are replaced.
7. Click the **Match case box** to select it, then click **Find Next**
   Excel moves the cell pointer to the first occurrence of "Radio".
8. Click **Replace All**
   The dialog box closes, and you complete the replacement and check to make sure all references to "Radio" in the Ad Source column now read "KWIN Radio". Note that in the Comments column, each instance of the word "radio" remains unchanged.
9. Make sure there are no entries in the Ad Source column that read "Radio", then save the workbook

FIGURE H-7: Criteria data form

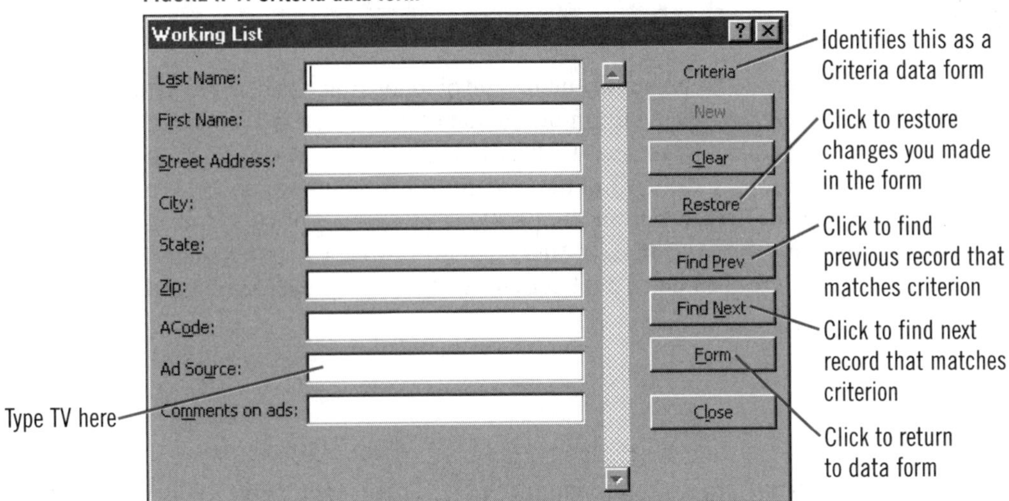

FIGURE H-8: Finding a record using the data form

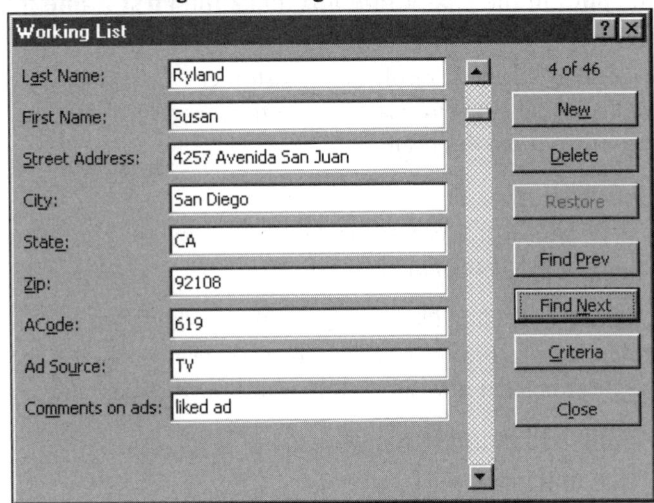

FIGURE H-9: Replace dialog box

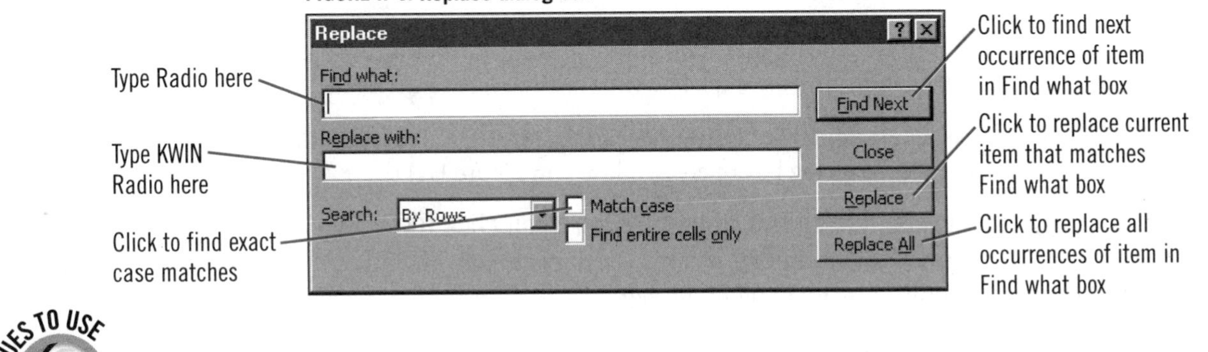

CLUES TO USE

Using wildcards to fine-tune your search

You can use special symbols called **wildcards** when defining search criteria in the data form or Replace dialog box. The question mark (?) wildcard stands for any single character. For example, if you do not know whether a customer's last name is Paulsen or Paulson, you can specify Pauls?n as the search criteria to locate both options. The asterisk (*) wildcard stands for any group of characters. For example, if you specify Jan* as the search criteria in the First Name field, Excel locates all records with first names beginning with Jan (for instance, Jan, Janet, Janice, and so forth).

Deleting Records

You need to keep your list up to date by removing obsolete records. One way to remove records is to use the Delete button on the data form. You can also delete all records that meet certain criteria—that is, records that have something in common. For example, you can specify a criterion for Excel to find the next record containing Zip code 01879, then remove the record using the Delete button. If specifying one criterion does not meet your needs, you can set multiple criteria. After he notices two entries for Carolyn Smith, Jim wants to check the database for additional duplicate entries. He uses the data form to delete the duplicate record.

Steps

1. Click **Data** on the menu bar, click **Form**, then click **Criteria**
   The Criteria data form appears.

QuickTip

You can use the data form to edit records as well as to add, search for, and delete them. Just find the desired record and edit the data directly in the appropriate box.

2. Type **Smith** in the **Last Name box**, click the **First Name box**, type **Carolyn**, then click **Find Next**
   Excel displays the first record for a customer whose name is Carolyn Smith. You decide to leave the initial entry for Carolyn Smith (record 5 of 46) and delete the second one, once you confirm it is a duplicate.
3. Click **Find Next**
   The duplicate record for Carolyn Smith, number 40, appears as shown in Figure H-10. You are ready to delete the duplicate entry.

QuickTip

Clicking Restore on the data form will not restore deleted record(s).

4. Click **Delete**, then click **OK** to confirm the deletion
   The duplicate record for Carolyn Smith is deleted, and all the other records move up one row. The data form now shows the record for Manuel Julio.
5. Click **Close** to return to the worksheet, scroll down until rows 41-46 are visible, then read the entry in row 41
   Notice that the duplicate entry for Carolyn Smith is gone and that Manuel Julio moved up a row and is now in row 41. You also notice a record for K. C. Splint in row 43, which is a duplicate entry.
6. Return to cell A1, and read the record information for K. C. Splint in row 8
   After confirming the duplicate entry, you decide to delete the row.
7. Click cell **A8**, click **Edit** on the menu bar, then click **Delete**
   The Delete dialog box opens, as shown in Figure H-11.

QuickTip

You can also delete selected cells in a row. Highlight the cells to delete, choose Delete from the Edit menu, and, in the dialog box, indicate if the remaining cells should move up or to the left to replace the selection. Use this command with caution in lists, since with lists you usually delete an entire row.

8. Click the **Entire row option button**, then click **OK**
   You have deleted the entire row. The duplicate record for K. C. Splint is deleted and the other records move up to fill in the gap.
9. Save the workbook
   Recall that you can delete a range name by following these steps: click Insert on the menu bar, point to Name, click Define, highlight the range name, and click delete.

FIGURE H-10: Data form showing duplicate record for Carolyn Smith

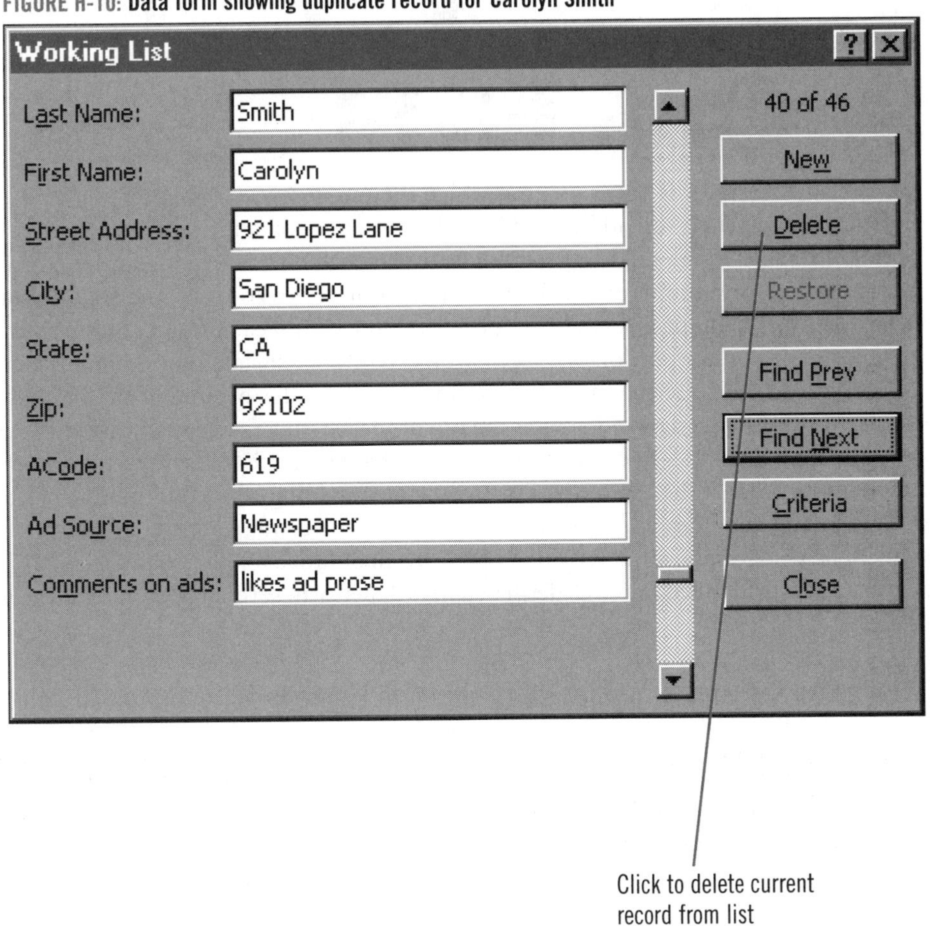

FIGURE H-11: Delete dialog box

Delete

Delete

- Shift cells left
- Shift cells up
- Entire row
- Entire column

OK Cancel

Click to shift remaining cells to fill gap created by deleting cells

Click to delete current row

Click to delete current column

Excel 2000

CLUES TO USE

Advantage of deleting records from the worksheet

When you delete a record using the data form, you cannot undo your deletion. When you delete a record by deleting the row in which it resides inside the worksheet area, however, you can immediately restore the record by using the Undo command on the Edit menu, using the Undo button, or pressing [Ctrl][Z].

Sorting a List by One Field

Usually, you enter records in the order in which they are received, rather than in alphabetical or numerical order. When you add records to a list using the data form, the records are added to the end of the list. Using the Excel sorting feature, you can rearrange the order of the records. You can use the sort buttons on the Standard toolbar to sort records by one field, or you can use the Sort command on the Data menu to perform more complicated sorts. Alternatively, you can sort an entire list or any portion of a list, or you can arrange sorted information in ascending or descending order. In ascending order, the lowest value (the beginning of the alphabet, for instance, or the earliest date) appears at the top of the list. In a field containing labels and numbers, numbers come first. In descending order, the highest value (the end of the alphabet or the latest date) appears at the top of the list. In a field containing labels and numbers, labels come first. Table H-3 provides examples of ascending and descending sorts. Because Jim wants to be able to return the records to their original order following any sorts, he begins by creating a new field called Entry Order. Then he will perform several single field sorts on the list.

Steps

QuickTip

Before you sort records, it is a good idea to make a backup copy of your list or create a field that numbers the records so you can return them to their original order, if necessary.

Trouble?

If your sort does not perform as intended, press [Ctrl][Z] immediately to undo the sort and repeat the step.

1. Enter the text and format in cell J1 shown in Figure H-12, then AutoFit column J

2. Type **1** in cell J2, press **[Enter]**, type **2** in cell J3, press **[Enter]**, select cells **J2:J3**, drag the fill handle to cell **J45**
   With the Entry Order column complete, as shown in Figure H-12, you are ready to sort the list in ascending order by last name. You must position the cell pointer within the column you want to sort prior to issuing the sort command.

3. Return to cell A1, then click the **Sort Ascending button** on the Standard toolbar
   Excel instantly rearranges the records in ascending order by last name, as shown in Figure H-13. You can easily sort the list in descending order by any field.

4. Click cell **G1**, then click the **Sort Descending button** on the Standard toolbar
   Excel sorts the list, placing those records with higher-digit area codes at the top. Jim wants to update the list range to include original entry order.

5. Select the range **A1:J45**, click the **name box**, type **Database**, then press **[Enter]**
   You are now ready to return the list to original entry order.

6. Click cell **J1**, click the **Sort Ascending button** on the Standard toolbar, then save the workbook
   The list is back to its original order, and the workbook is saved.

TABLE H-3: Sort order options and examples

option	alphabetic	numeric	date	alphanumeric
Ascending	A, B, C	7, 8, 9	1/1, 2/1, 3/1	12A, 99B, DX8, QT7
Descending	C, B, A	9, 8, 7	3/1, 2/1, 1/1	QT7, DX8, 99B, 12A

FIGURE H-12: List with Entry Order field added

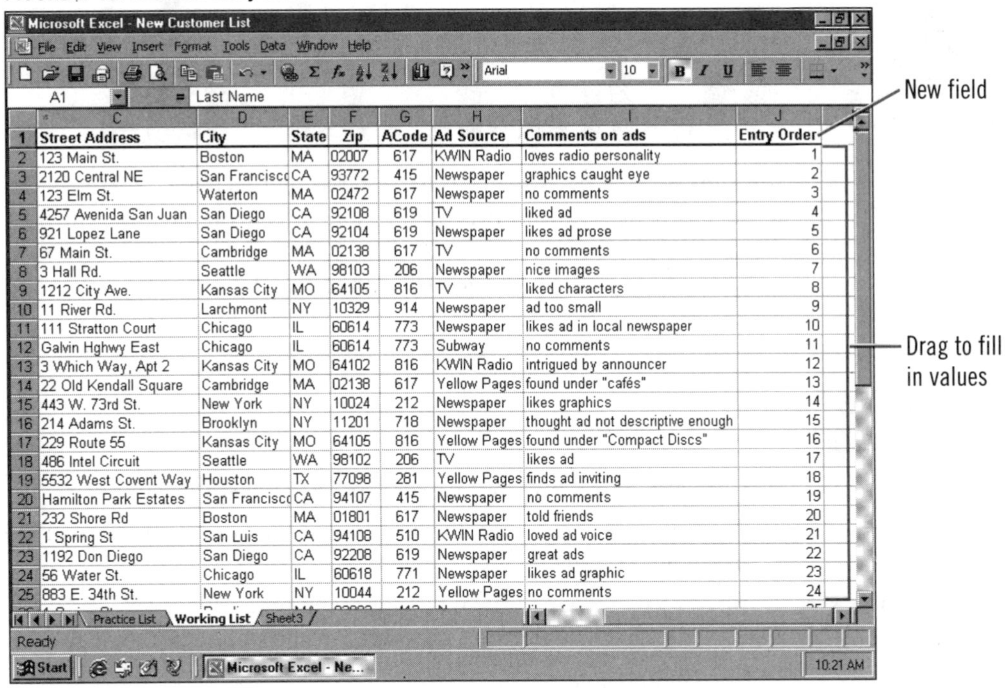

Microsoft Excel - New Customer List

	Street Address	City	State	Zip	ACode	Ad Source	Comments on ads	Entry Order
2	123 Main St.	Boston	MA	02007	617	KWIN Radio	loves radio personality	1
3	2120 Central NE	San Francisco	CA	93772	415	Newspaper	graphics caught eye	2
4	123 Elm St.	Waterton	MA	02472	617	Newspaper	no comments	3
5	4257 Avenida San Juan	San Diego	CA	92108	619	TV	liked ad	4
6	921 Lopez Lane	San Diego	CA	92104	619	Newspaper	likes ad prose	5
7	67 Main St.	Cambridge	MA	02138	617	TV	no comments	6
8	3 Hall Rd.	Seattle	WA	98103	206	Newspaper	nice images	7
9	1212 City Ave.	Kansas City	MO	64105	816	TV	liked characters	8
10	11 River Rd.	Larchmont	NY	10329	914	Newspaper	ad too small	9
11	111 Stratton Court	Chicago	IL	60614	773	Newspaper	likes ad in local newspaper	10
12	Galvin Hghwy East	Chicago	IL	60614	773	Subway	no comments	11
13	3 Which Way, Apt 2	Kansas City	MO	64102	816	KWIN Radio	intrigued by announcer	12
14	22 Old Kendall Square	Cambridge	MA	02138	617	Yellow Pages	found under "cafés"	13
15	443 W. 73rd St.	New York	NY	10024	212	Newspaper	likes graphics	14
16	214 Adams St.	Brooklyn	NY	11201	718	Newspaper	thought ad not descriptive enough	15
17	229 Route 55	Kansas City	MO	64105	816	Yellow Pages	found under "Compact Discs"	16
18	486 Intel Circuit	Seattle	WA	98102	206	TV	likes ad	17
19	5532 West Covent Way	Houston	TX	77098	281	Yellow Pages	finds ad inviting	18
20	Hamilton Park Estates	San Francisco	CA	94107	415	Newspaper	no comments	19
21	232 Shore Rd	Boston	MA	01801	617	Newspaper	told friends	20
22	1 Spring St	San Luis	CA	94108	510	KWIN Radio	loved ad voice	21
23	1192 Don Diego	San Diego	CA	92208	619	Newspaper	great ads	22
24	56 Water St.	Chicago	IL	60618	771	Newspaper	likes ad graphic	23
25	883 E. 34th St.	New York	NY	10044	212	Yellow Pages	no comments	24

FIGURE H-13: List sorted alphabetically by Last Name

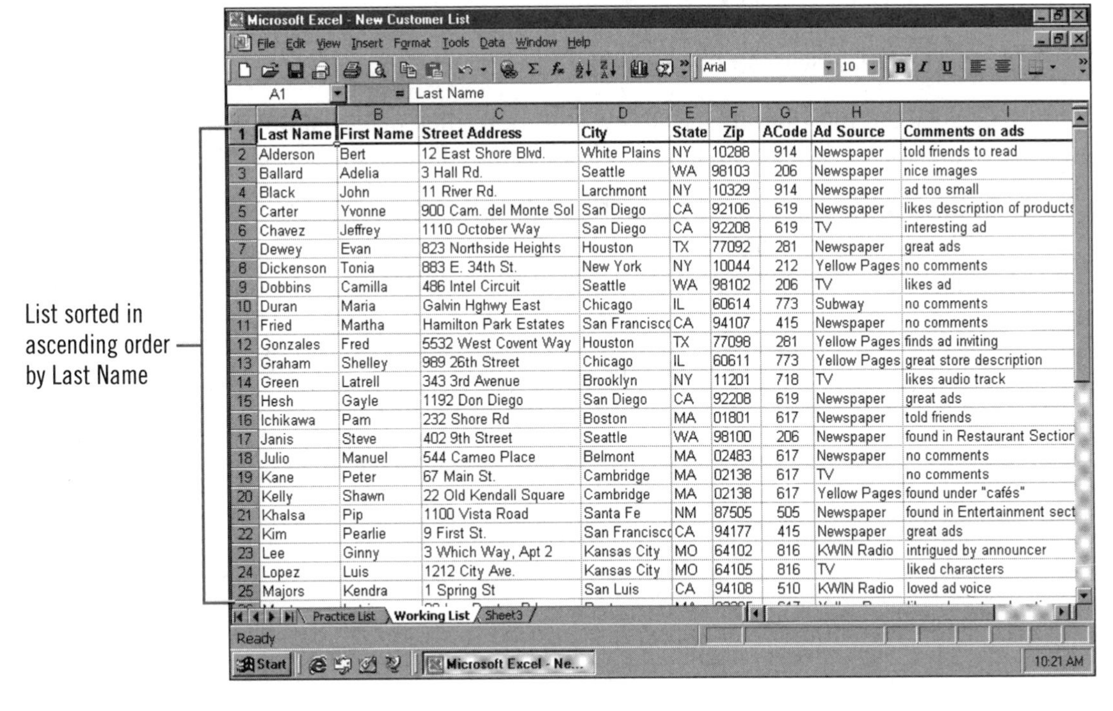

Microsoft Excel - New Customer List

	Last Name	First Name	Street Address	City	State	Zip	ACode	Ad Source	Comments on ads
2	Alderson	Bert	12 East Shore Blvd.	White Plains	NY	10288	914	Newspaper	told friends to read
3	Ballard	Adelia	3 Hall Rd.	Seattle	WA	98103	206	Newspaper	nice images
4	Black	John	11 River Rd.	Larchmont	NY	10329	914	Newspaper	ad too small
5	Carter	Yvonne	900 Cam. del Monte Sol	San Diego	CA	92106	619	Newspaper	likes description of products
6	Chavez	Jeffrey	1110 October Way	San Diego	CA	92208	619	TV	interesting ad
7	Dewey	Evan	823 Northside Heights	Houston	TX	77092	281	Newspaper	great ads
8	Dickenson	Tonia	883 E. 34th St.	New York	NY	10044	212	Yellow Pages	no comments
9	Dobbins	Camilla	486 Intel Circuit	Seattle	WA	98102	206	TV	likes ad
10	Duran	Maria	Galvin Hghwy East	Chicago	IL	60614	773	Subway	no comments
11	Fried	Martha	Hamilton Park Estates	San Francisco	CA	94107	415	Newspaper	no comments
12	Gonzales	Fred	5532 West Covent Way	Houston	TX	77098	281	Yellow Pages	finds ad inviting
13	Graham	Shelley	989 26th Street	Chicago	IL	60611	773	Yellow Pages	great store description
14	Green	Latrell	343 3rd Avenue	Brooklyn	NY	11201	718	TV	likes audio track
15	Hesh	Gayle	1192 Don Diego	San Diego	CA	92208	619	Newspaper	great ads
16	Ichikawa	Pam	232 Shore Rd	Boston	MA	01801	617	Newspaper	told friends
17	Janis	Steve	402 9th Street	Seattle	WA	98100	206	Newspaper	found in Restaurant Section
18	Julio	Manuel	544 Cameo Place	Belmont	MA	02483	617	Newspaper	no comments
19	Kane	Peter	67 Main St.	Cambridge	MA	02138	617	TV	no comments
20	Kelly	Shawn	22 Old Kendall Square	Cambridge	MA	02138	617	Yellow Pages	found under "cafés"
21	Khalsa	Pip	1100 Vista Road	Santa Fe	NM	87505	505	Newspaper	found in Entertainment sect
22	Kim	Pearlie	9 First St.	San Francisco	CA	94177	415	Newspaper	great ads
23	Lee	Ginny	3 Which Way, Apt 2	Kansas City	MO	64102	816	KWIN Radio	intrigued by announcer
24	Lopez	Luis	1212 City Ave.	Kansas City	MO	64105	816	TV	liked characters
25	Majors	Kendra	1 Spring St	San Luis	CA	94108	510	KWIN Radio	loved ad voice

Rotating and indenting to improve label appearance

The column label you added in cell J1 is considerably wider than the data in the column. In cases like this, you can adjust the format of any label or value: Select the cell, click Format on the menu bar, click Cells, and on the Alignment tab drag the red diamond under Orientation to 90 degrees. You can also add space to the left of any label or value by selecting the cells(s) and clicking the Increase Indent button on the Formatting toolbar.

Excel 2000

Sorting a List by Multiple Fields

You can sort lists by as many as three fields by specifying **sort keys**, the criteria on which the sort is based. To perform sorts on multiple fields, you must use the Sort dialog box, which you access through the Sort command on the Data menu. Jim wants to sort the records alphabetically by state first, then within the state by Zip code.

Steps

1. **Click the name box list arrow, then click Database**
   The list is selected. To sort the list by more than one field, you will need to use the Sort command on the Data menu.

2. **Click Data on the menu bar, then click Sort**
   The Sort dialog box opens, as shown in Figure H-14. You want to sort the list by state and then by Zip code.

QuickTip

You can specify a capitalization sort by clicking Options in the Sort dialog box, then clicking the Case sensitive box. When you choose this option, lowercase entries precede uppercase entries.

3. **Click the Sort by list arrow, click State, then click the Ascending option button to select it, if necessary**
   The list will be sorted alphabetically in ascending order (A-Z) by the State field. A second sort criterion will sort the entries within each state grouping.

4. **Click the top Then by list arrow, click Zip, then click the Descending option button**
   You also could sort by a third key by selecting a field in the bottom Then by list box.

5. **Click OK to execute the sort, press [Ctrl][Home], then scroll through the list to see the result of the sort**
   The list is sorted alphabetically by state in ascending order, then within each state by Zip code in descending order. Compare your results with Figure H-15.

6. **Return to cell A1, then save the workbook**

FIGURE H-14: Sort dialog box

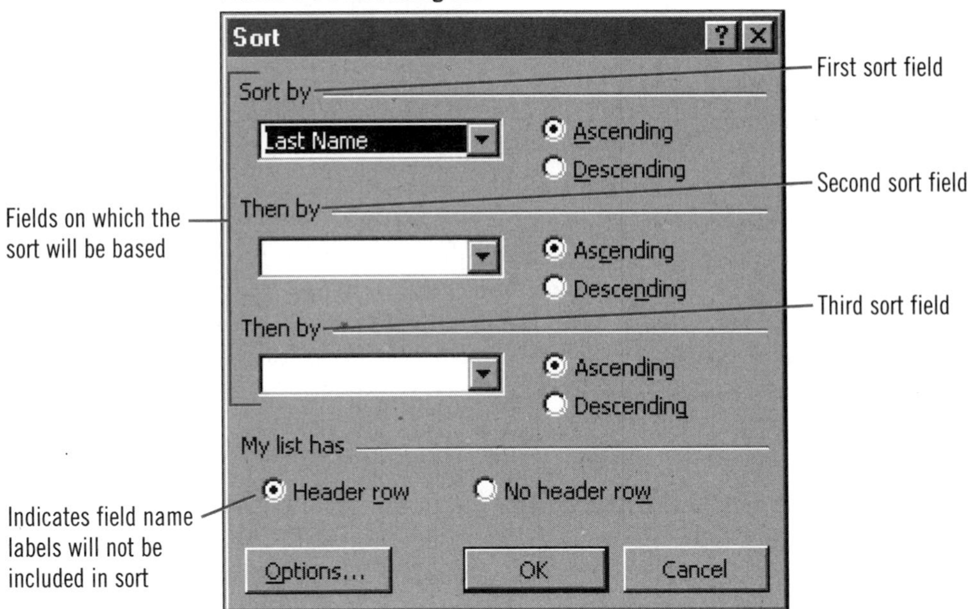

FIGURE H-15: List sorted by multiple fields

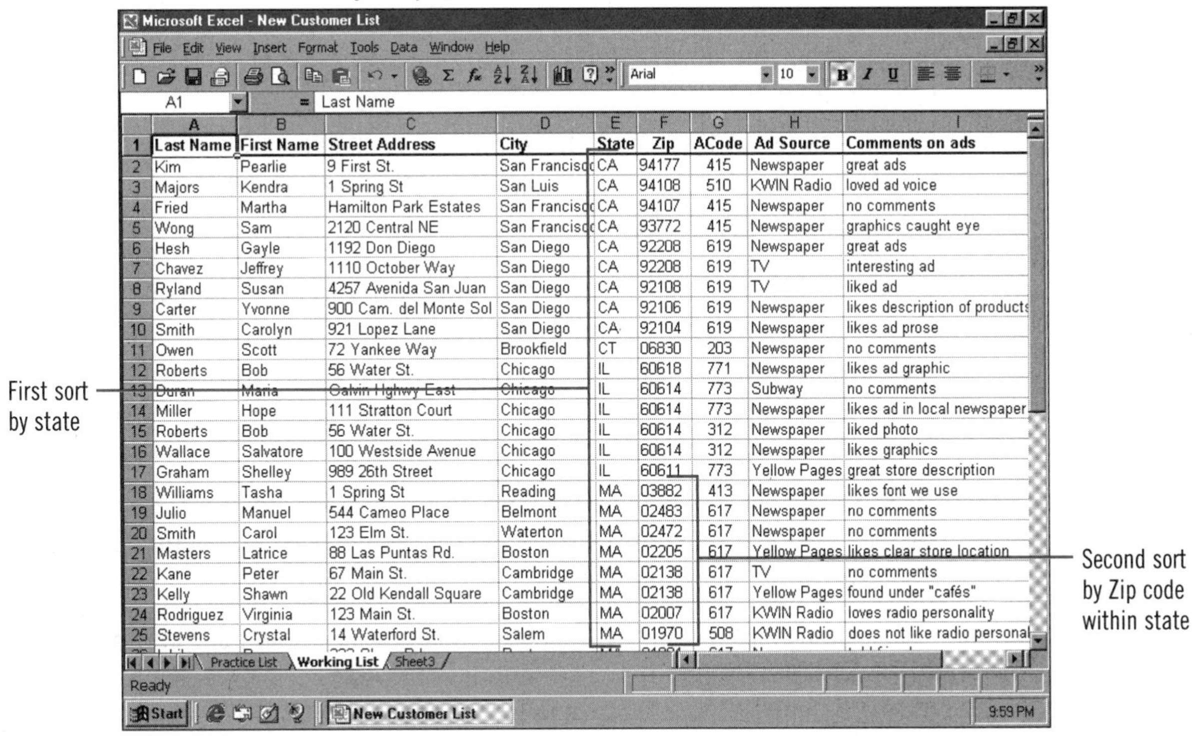

	A	B	C	D	E	F	G	H	I
1	Last Name	First Name	Street Address	City	State	Zip	ACode	Ad Source	Comments on ads
2	Kim	Pearlie	9 First St.	San Francisc	CA	94177	415	Newspaper	great ads
3	Majors	Kendra	1 Spring St	San Luis	CA	94108	510	KWIN Radio	loved ad voice
4	Fried	Martha	Hamilton Park Estates	San Francisc	CA	94107	415	Newspaper	no comments
5	Wong	Sam	2120 Central NE	San Francisc	CA	93772	415	Newspaper	graphics caught eye
6	Hesh	Gayle	1192 Don Diego	San Diego	CA	92208	619	Newspaper	great ads
7	Chavez	Jeffrey	1110 October Way	San Diego	CA	92208	619	TV	interesting ad
8	Ryland	Susan	4257 Avenida San Juan	San Diego	CA	92108	619	TV	liked ad
9	Carter	Yvonne	900 Cam. del Monte Sol	San Diego	CA	92106	619	Newspaper	likes description of products
10	Smith	Carolyn	921 Lopez Lane	San Diego	CA	92104	619	Newspaper	likes ad prose
11	Owen	Scott	72 Yankee Way	Brookfield	CT	06830	203	Newspaper	no comments
12	Roberts	Bob	56 Water St.	Chicago	IL	60618	771	Newspaper	likes ad graphic
13	Duran	Maria	Calvin Hghwy East	Chicago	IL	60614	773	Subway	no comments
14	Miller	Hope	111 Stratton Court	Chicago	IL	60614	773	Newspaper	likes ad in local newspaper
15	Roberts	Bob	56 Water St.	Chicago	IL	60614	312	Newspaper	liked photo
16	Wallace	Salvatore	100 Westside Avenue	Chicago	IL	60614	312	Newspaper	likes graphics
17	Graham	Shelley	989 26th Street	Chicago	IL	60611	773	Yellow Pages	great store description
18	Williams	Tasha	1 Spring St	Reading	MA	03882	413	Newspaper	likes font we use
19	Julio	Manuel	544 Cameo Place	Belmont	MA	02483	617	Newspaper	no comments
20	Smith	Carol	123 Elm St.	Waterton	MA	02472	617	Newspaper	no comments
21	Masters	Latrice	88 Las Puntas Rd.	Boston	MA	02205	617	Yellow Pages	likes clear store location
22	Kane	Peter	67 Main St.	Cambridge	MA	02138	617	TV	no comments
23	Kelly	Shawn	22 Old Kendall Square	Cambridge	MA	02138	617	Yellow Pages	found under "cafés"
24	Rodriguez	Virginia	123 Main St.	Boston	MA	02007	617	KWIN Radio	loves radio personality
25	Stevens	Crystal	14 Waterford St.	Salem	MA	01970	508	KWIN Radio	does not like radio personal

Specifying a custom sort order

You can identify a custom sort order for the field selected in the Sort by box. To do this, click Options in the Sort dialog box, click the First key sort order list arrow, then click the desired custom order.

Commonly used custom sort orders are days of the week (Mon, Tues, Wed, etc.) and months (Jan, Feb, Mar, etc.); alphabetic sorts do not sort these items properly.

Excel 2000

Excel 2000

Printing a List

If a list is small enough to fit on one page, you can print it as you would any other Excel worksheet. If you have more columns than can fit on a portrait-oriented page, try setting the page orientation to landscape. Because lists often have more rows than can fit on a page, you can define the first row of the list (containing the field names) as the **print title**, which prints at the top of every page. Most lists do not have any descriptive information above the field names on the worksheet. To augment the information contained in the field names, you can use headers and footers to add identifying text, such as the list title or report date. If you want to exclude any fields from your list report, you can hide the desired columns from view so that they do not print. Jim has finished updating his list and is ready to print it. He begins by previewing the list.

Steps

1. Click the **Print Preview button** on the Standard toolbar
   Notice that the status bar reads Page 1 of 2. You want all the fields in the list to fit on a single page, but you'll need two pages to fit all the data. The landscape page orientation and the Fit to options will help you do this.

2. From the Print Preview window, click **Setup**, click the **Page tab**, click the **Landscape option button** under Orientation, click the **Fit to option button** under Scaling, double-click the **tall box** and type **2**, click **OK**, then click **Next**
   The list still does not fit on a single page. Because the records on page 2 appear without column headings, you want to set up the first row of the list, containing the field names, as a repeating print title.

3. Click **Close** to exit the Print Preview window, click **File** on the menu bar, click **Page Setup**, click the **Sheet tab**, click the **Rows to repeat at top box** under Print titles, click any cell in row 1, then click OK
   When you select row 1 as a print title, Excel automatically inserts an absolute reference to a beginning row to repeat at the top of each page—in this case, the print title to repeat beginning and ending with row 1. See Figure H-16.

4. Click **Print Preview**, click **Next** to view the second page, then click **Zoom**
   Setting up a print title to repeat row 1 causes the field names to appear at the top of each printed page. You can use the worksheet header to provide information about the list.

5. Click **Setup**, click the **Header/Footer tab**, click **Custom Header**, click the **Left section box** and type your name, then click the **Center section box** and type **MediaLoft–New Customer List**

6. Select the header text in the Center section box, click the **Font button**, change the font size to **14** and the style to **Bold**, click **OK**, click **OK** again to return to the Header/Footer tab, then click **OK** to preview the list
   Page 2 of the report appears as shown in Figure H-17.

7. Click **Print** to print the worksheet, then save and close the workbook
   To print more than one worksheet, select each sheet tab while holding down the [Shift] or [Ctrl] keys, then click the print button on the standard toolbar.

QuickTip

You can print multiple ranges at the same time by clicking the Print area box in the Sheet tab. Then drag to the select areas you wish to print.

QuickTip

You can also use the sheet tab to specify whether you want gridlines, high or low print quality, and row and column headings.

QuickTip

To print a selected area instead of the entire worksheet, select the area, click File, click Print, and, under Print what, click Selection.

FIGURE H-16: Sheet tab of the Page Setup dialog box

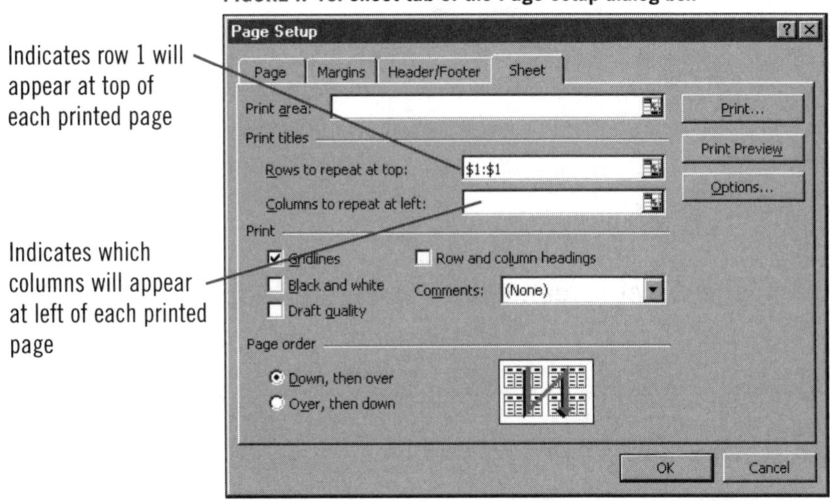

FIGURE H-17: Print Preview window showing page 2 of completed report

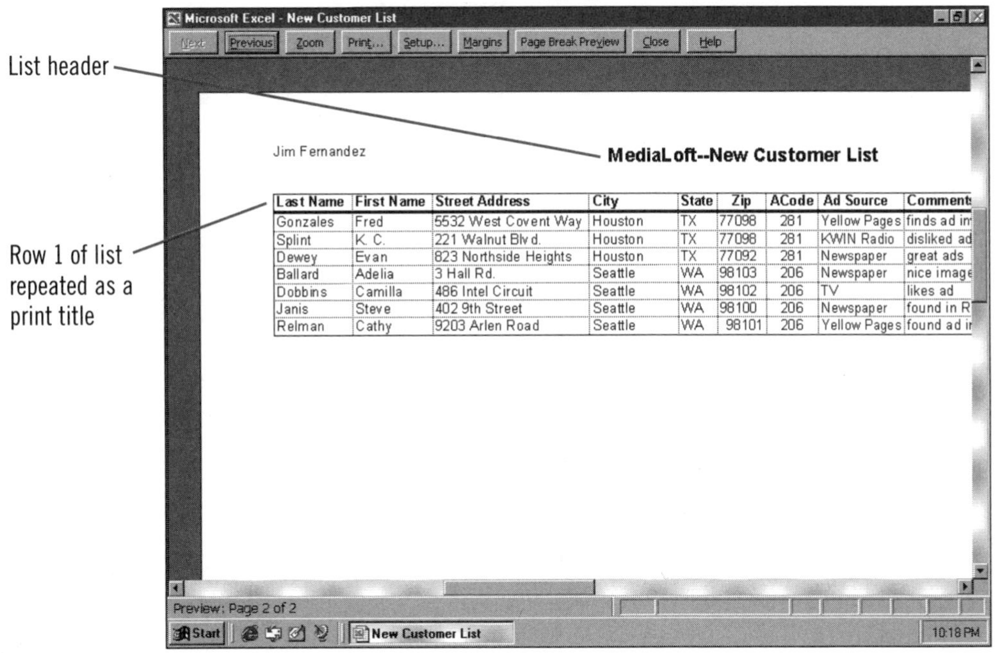

Setting a print area

There are times when you want to print only part of a worksheet. You can do this in the Print dialog box by choosing Selection under Print what. But if you want to print a selected area repeatedly, it's best to define a **print area**, which will print when you click the Print button on the Standard toolbar. To set a print area, click View on the menu bar, then click Page Break Preview. In the preview window, select the area you want to print. Right-click the area, then select Set Print Area. The print area becomes outlined in a blue border. You can drag the border to extend the print area (see Figure H-18) or add nonadjacent cells to it by selecting them, right-clicking them, then selecting Add to Print Area. To clear a print area, click File on the menu bar, point to Print Area, then click Clear Print Area.

FIGURE H-18: Defined print area

Excel 2000

Practice

► Concepts Review

Label each of the elements of the Excel screen shown in Figure H-19.

FIGURE H-19

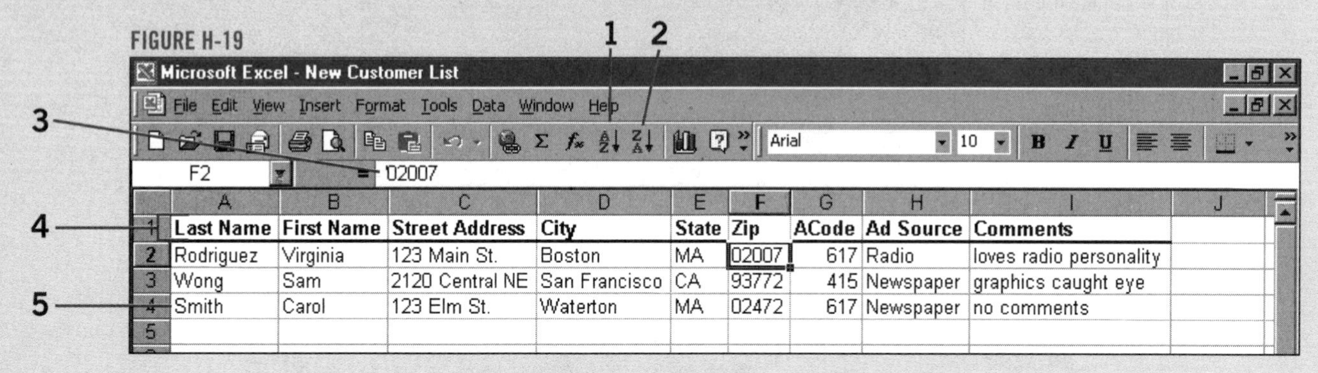

Match each term with the statement that best describes it.

6. List
7. Record
8. Database
9. Sort
10. Field name

a. Arrange records in a particular sequence
b. Organized collection of related information in Excel
c. Row in an Excel list
d. Type of software used for lists containing more than 65,536 records
e. Label positioned at the top of the column identifying data for that field

Select the best answer from the list of choices.

11. Which of the following Excel sorting options do you use to sort a list of employee names in A-to-Z order?
- **a.** Ascending
- **b.** Absolute
- **c.** Alphabetic
- **d.** Descending

12. Which of the following series is in descending order?
- **a.** 4, 5, 6, A, B, C
- **b.** C, B, A, 6, 5, 4
- **c.** 8, 7, 6, 5, 6, 7
- **d.** 8, 6, 4, C, B, A

13. Once the __________ is defined, any new records added to the list using the data form are included in the __________.
- **a.** database, database
- **b.** data form, data form
- **c.** worksheet, worksheet
- **d.** list range, list range

14. When printing a list on multiple pages, you can define a print title containing repeating row(s) to
- **a.** Include appropriate fields in the printout.
- **b.** Include field names at the top of each printed page.
- **c.** Include the header in list reports.
- **d.** Exclude from the printout all rows under the first row.

► Skills Review

1. Create a list.
- **a.** Create a new workbook, then save it as "MediaLoft New York Employee List".
- **b.** In cell A1, type the title "MediaLoft New York Employees".
- **c.** Enter the field names and records using the information in Table H-4.
- **d.** Apply bold formatting to the field names.
- **e.** Center the entries in the Years, Full/Part Time, and Training? fields.
- **f.** Adjust the column widths to make the data readable.
- **g.** Save, then print the list.

TABLE H-4

Last Name	First Name	Years	Position	Full/Part Time	Training?
Lustig	Sarah	3	Book Sales	F	Y
Marino	Donato	2	CD Sales	P	N
Khederian	Jay	4	Video Sales	F	Y
Finney	Carol	1	Stock	F	N
Rabinowicz	Miriam	2	Café Sales	P	Y

2. Add records with the data form.

a. Select all the records in the list, including the field names, then define the range as "Database".

b. Open the data form and add a new record for David Gitano, a one-year employee in Book Sales. David is full time and has not completed the training.

c. Add a new record for George Worley, the café manager. George is full time, has worked there two years, and he has completed the training.

d. Save the list.

3. Find and delete records.

a. Find the record for Carol Finney.

b. Delete the record.

c. Save the list.

4. Sort a list by one field.

a. Select the Database list range.

b. Sort the list alphabetically in ascending order by last name.

c. Save the list.

5. Sort a list by multiple fields.

a. Select the Database list range.

b. Sort the list alphabetically in ascending order, first by whether or not the employees have completed training and then by last name.

c. Save the list.

6. Print a list.

a. Add a header that reads "Employee Information" in the center and that includes your name on the right; format both header items in bold.

b. Set the print area to include the range A1:F9.

c. Delete the database range.

d. Print the list, then save and close the workbook.

e. Exit Excel.

Independent Challenges

1. Your advertising firm, Personalize IT, sells specialty items imprinted with the customer's name and/or logo such as hats, pens, and T-shirts. Plan and build a list of information with a minimum of 10 records using the three items sold. Your list should contain at least five different customers. (Some customers will place more than one order.) Each record should contain the customer's name, item(s) sold, and the individual and extended cost of the item(s). Enter your own data and make sure you include at least the following list fields:

- Item—Describe the item.
- Cost-Ea.—What is the item's individual cost?
- Quantity—How many items did the customer purchase?
- Ext. Cost—What is the total purchase price?
- Customer—Who purchased the item?

To complete this independent challenge:

a. Prepare a list plan that states your goal, outlines the data you'll need, and identifies the list elements.
b. Sketch a sample list on a piece of paper, indicating how the list should be built. What information should go in the columns? In the rows? Which of the data fields will be formatted as labels? As values?
c. Build the list first by entering the field names, then by entering the records. Remember, you will invent your own data. Save the workbook as "Personalize IT".
d. Reformat the list, as needed. For example, you might need to adjust the column widths to make the data more readable. Also, remember to check your spelling.
e. Sort the list in ascending order by item, then by Customer, then by Quantity.
f. Select only the cells with data in the last row. Use the Delete command on the Edit menu to delete those cells, moving the existing cells up to fill the space.
g. Type your name in a blank cell and review the worksheet; adjust any items as needed; then print a copy.
h. Save your work before closing.

2. You are taking a class titled "Television Shows: Past and Present" at a local community college. The instructor has provided you with an Excel list of television programs from the '60s and '70s. She has included fields tracking the following information: the number of years the show was a favorite, favorite character, least favorite character, the show's length in minutes, the show's biggest star, and comments about the show. The instructor has included data for each show in the list. She has asked you to add a field (column label) and two records (shows of your choosing) to the list. Because the list should cover only 30-minute shows, you need to delete any records for shows longer than 30 minutes. Also, your instructor wants you to sort the list by show name and format the list as needed prior to printing. Feel free to change any of the list data to suit your tastes and opinions.

To complete this independent challenge:

a. Open the workbook titled EX H-2, then save it as "Television Shows of the Past".
b. Using your own data, add a field, then use the data form to add two records to the list. Make sure to enter information in every field.
c. Delete any records having show lengths other than 30. (*Hint*: Use the Criteria data form to set the criteria, then find and delete any matching records.)
d. Make any formatting changes to the list as needed and save the list.
e. Sort the list in ascending order by show name.
f. Preview, then print the list. Adjust any items as needed so that the list can be printed on a single page.
g. Sort the list again, this time in descending order by number of years the show was a favorite.
h. Change the header to read "Television Shows of the Past: '60s and '70s".
i. Type your name in a blank cell, then preview and print the list.
j. Save the workbook.

3. You work as a sales clerk at Nite Owl Video. Your roommate and co-worker, Albert Lee, has put together a list of his favorite movie actors and actresses. He has asked you to add several names to the list so he can determine which artists and what kinds of films you enjoy most. He has recorded information in the following fields: artist's first and last name, life span, birthplace, the genre or type of role the artist plays most (for example, dramatic or comedic), the name of a film for which the artist has received or been nominated for an Academy Award, and, finally, two additional films featuring the artist. Using your own data, add at least two artists known for dramatic roles and two artists known for comedic roles.

To complete this independent challenge:

a. Open the workbook titled EX H-3, then add at least four records using the criteria mentioned above. Remember, you are creating and entering your own movie data for all relevant fields.

b. Save the workbook as "Film Star Favorites". Make formatting changes to the list as needed. Remember to check your spelling.

c. Sort the list alphabetically by Genre. Perform a second sort by Last Name.

d. Preview the list, adjust any items as needed, then print a copy of the list sorted by Genre and Last Name.

e. Sort the list again, this time in descending order by the Life Span field, then by Last Name.

f. Enter your name in a blank cell, then print a copy of the list sorted by Life Span and Last Name.

g. Save your work.

4. You work at MediaLoft corporate headquarters, and the Products Department has asked you to create a database to keep track of all CD products that win the People's Choice poll. The poll is new and will be conducted monthly.

To complete this independent challenge:

a. Start Excel, and create a new file with the following list headings: Artist LN, Artist FN, Title, Category, and In Stock, and save the file as "People's Choice". Format the title row with formats of your choice.

b. Connect to the Internet, and go to the MediaLoft intranet site at http://www.course.com/Illustrated/MediaLoft. Click the Products link, and print the page, which contains a table entitled "Results of People's Choice Poll". Disconnect from the Internet.

c. Use the information from the table to create the first six records of your list. For the In Stock column, show the first three products as in stock (Y) and the second three as not in stock (N). AutoFit the columns and save the file.

d. Open the file EX H-4, copy the records, and paste them into your database.

e. Find the CD by Jim Brickman.

f. Find the CD with the title "Mellow".

g. Use the Replace command to find all the records in the Rock category and change the category name to Rock N Roll. Adjust the column widths as necessary.

h. Sort the list by category.

i. Add a new field for Month, indicating the month each recording won the award. Assign a month (January, February, or March) to each winner so that each category has one winner per month.

j. Sort the list by month.

k. Sort the list by category and the artist's last name.

l. Sort by stock status, category, and the artist's last name.

m. Print the list, then save and close the file.

► Visual Workshop

Create the worksheet shown in Figure H-20. Save the workbook as "Famous Jazz Performers". Once you've entered the field names and records, sort the list by Contribution to Jazz and then by Last Name. Change the page setup so that the list is centered on the page horizontally and the header reads "Famous Jazz Performers". Preview and print the list, then save the workbook.

FIGURE H-20

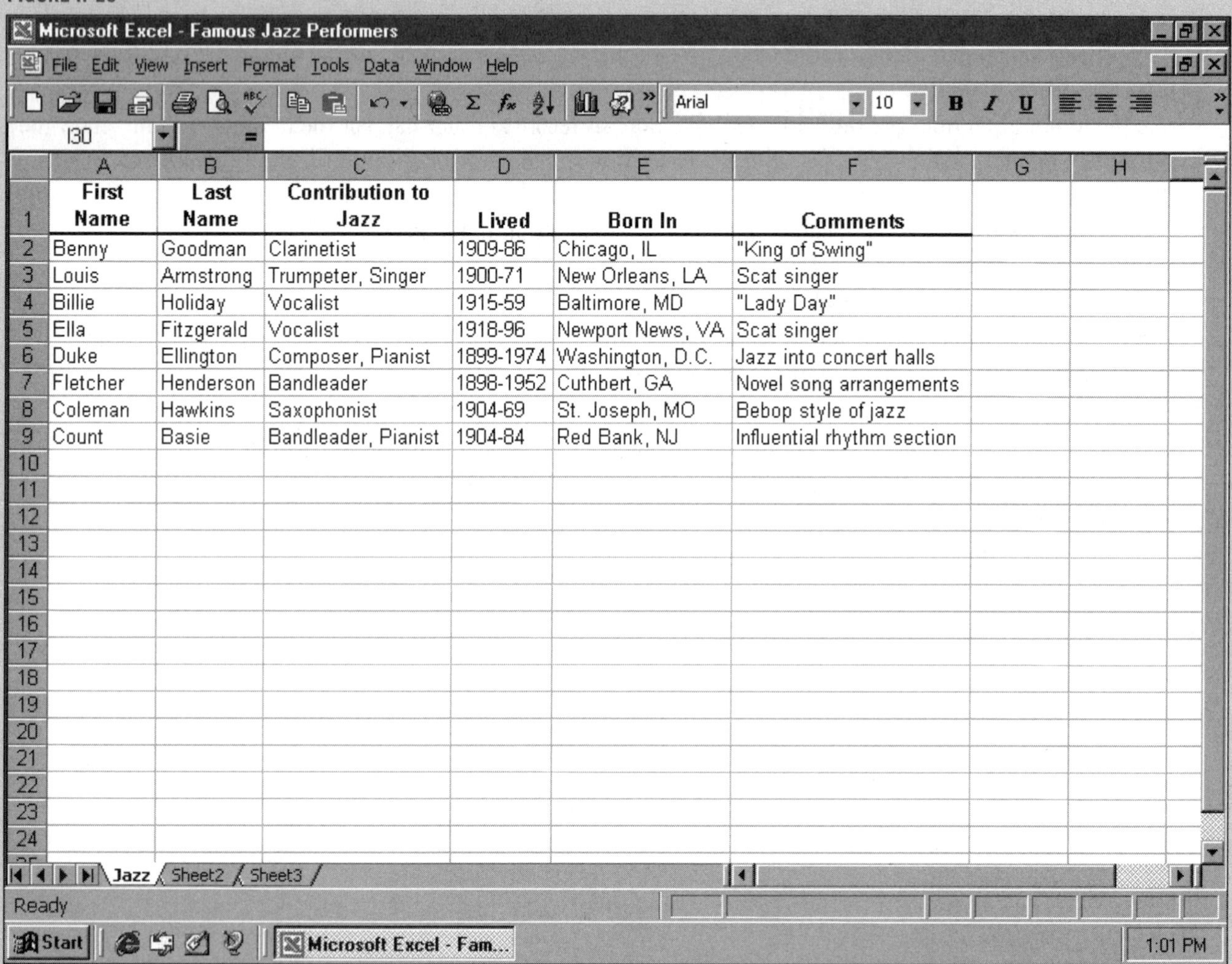

First Name	Last Name	Contribution to Jazz	Lived	Born In	Comments
Benny	Goodman	Clarinetist	1909-86	Chicago, IL	"King of Swing"
Louis	Armstrong	Trumpeter, Singer	1900-71	New Orleans, LA	Scat singer
Billie	Holiday	Vocalist	1915-59	Baltimore, MD	"Lady Day"
Ella	Fitzgerald	Vocalist	1918-96	Newport News, VA	Scat singer
Duke	Ellington	Composer, Pianist	1899-1974	Washington, D.C.	Jazz into concert halls
Fletcher	Henderson	Bandleader	1898-1952	Cuthbert, GA	Novel song arrangements
Coleman	Hawkins	Saxophonist	1904-69	St. Joseph, MO	Bebop style of jazz
Count	Basie	Bandleader, Pianist	1904-84	Red Bank, NJ	Influential rhythm section

Excel 2000

Unit I

Analyzing List Data

Objectives

- MOUS ► **Retrieve records with AutoFilter**
- MOUS ► **Create a custom filter**
- MOUS ► **Filter a list with Advanced Filter**
- MOUS ► **Extract list data**
- MOUS ► **Create subtotals using grouping and outlines**
- MOUS ► **Look up values in a list**
- MOUS ► **Summarize list data**
- MOUS ► **Use data validation for list entries**

There are many ways to **analyze**, or manipulate, list data with Excel. One way is to filter a list so that only the rows that meet certain criteria are retrieved. In this unit you will retrieve records using AutoFilter, create a custom filter, and filter a list using Excel's Advanced Filter feature. In addition, you will learn to insert automatic subtotals, use lookup functions to locate list entries, and apply database functions to summarize list data that meets specific criteria. You'll also learn how to restrict entries in a column using data validation. Jim Fernandez recently conducted a survey for the MediaLoft Marketing department. He mailed questionnaires to a random selection of customers at all stores. After the questionnaires were returned, he entered all the data into Excel, where he will analyze the data and create reports.

Retrieving Records with AutoFilter

The Excel AutoFilter feature searches for records that meet criteria the user specifies, and then lists those matching records. One way is to **filter** out, or hide, data that fails to meet certain criteria. You can filter specific values in a column, use the predefined Top 10 option to filter records based on upper or lower values in a column, or create a custom filter. For example, you can filter a customer list to retrieve names of only those customers residing in Canada. You also can filter records based on a specific field and request that Excel retrieve only those records having an entry (or no entry) in that field. Once you create a filtered list, you can print it or copy it to another part of the worksheet to manipulate it further. Jim is now ready to work on his survey information. He begins by retrieving data on only those customers who live in Chicago, Illinois.

Steps

QuickTip

To return personalized toolbars and menus to their default state, click Tools on the menu bar, click Customize, click the Options tab in the Customize dialog box, click Reset my usage data to restore the default settings, click Yes, click Close, then close the Drawing toolbar if it is displayed.

Trouble?

If the column label in cell A1 covers the column headers, making it difficult to find the appropriate columns, select A2 before scrolling.

1. Open the workbook titled **EX I-1**, then save it as **Survey Data**
   The AutoFilter feature will enable you to retrieve the records for the report.
2. Click **Data** on the menu bar, point to **Filter**, then click **AutoFilter**
   List arrows appear to the right of each field name.
3. Click the **City** list arrow
   An AutoFilter list containing the different city options appears below the field name, as shown in Figure I-1. Because you want to retrieve data for only those customers who live in Chicago, "Chicago" will be your **search criterion.**
4. In the filter list, click **Chicago**
   Only those records containing Chicago in the City field appear, as shown in Figure I-2. The status bar indicates the number of matching records (in this case, 5 of 35), the color of the row numbers changes for the matching records, and the color of the list arrow for the filtered field changes. Next, you want to retrieve information about those customers who purchased the most merchandise. To do so, you must clear the previous filter.
5. Click **Data** on the menu bar, point to **Filter**, then click **Show All**
   All the records reappear.
6. Scroll right until columns G through N are visible, click the **Purchases to Date** list arrow, then click **(Top 10 . . .)**
   The Top 10 AutoFilter dialog box opens. The default is to select the ten records with the highest value. You need to display only the top 2.
7. With **10** selected in the middle box, type **2**, then click **OK**
   The records are retrieved for the two customers who purchased the most merchandise, $3,200 and $2,530. See Figure I-3.
8. Click the **Purchases to Date** list arrow, click **(All)**, press **[Ctrl][Home]**, add your name to the right side of the footer, then print the list
   You have cleared the filter and all the records reappear. Because you didn't make any changes to the list, there is no need to save the file.

FIGURE I-1: Worksheet showing AutoFilter options

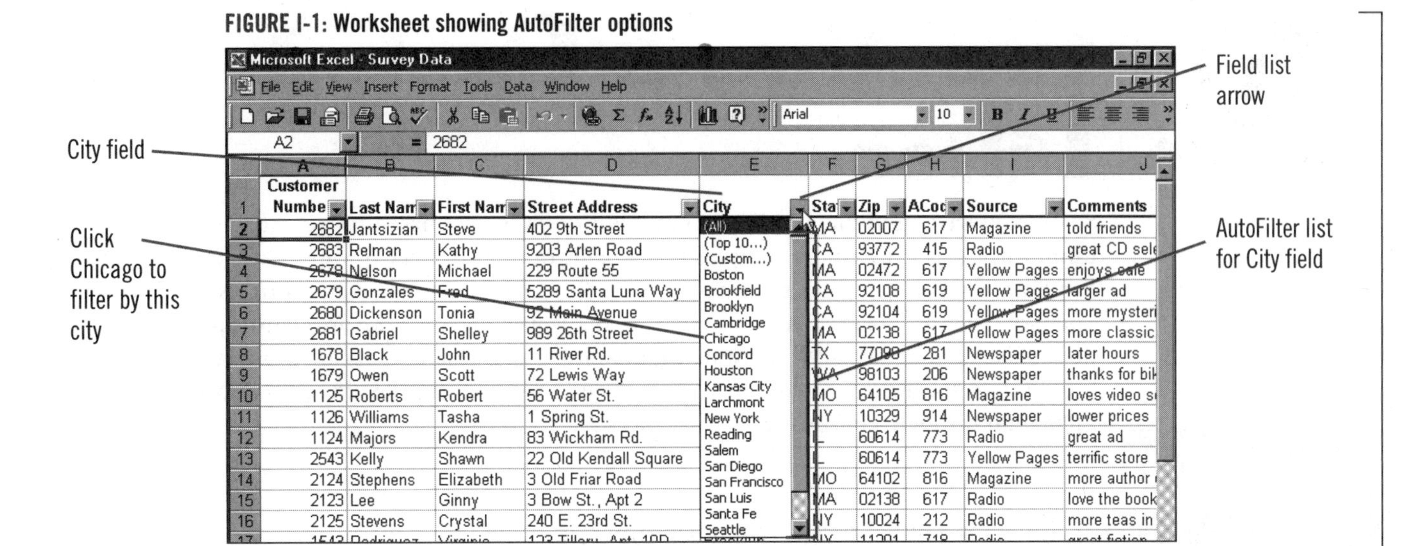

FIGURE I-2: List filtered with AutoFilter

FIGURE I-3: List filtered with Top 2 AutoFilter criteria

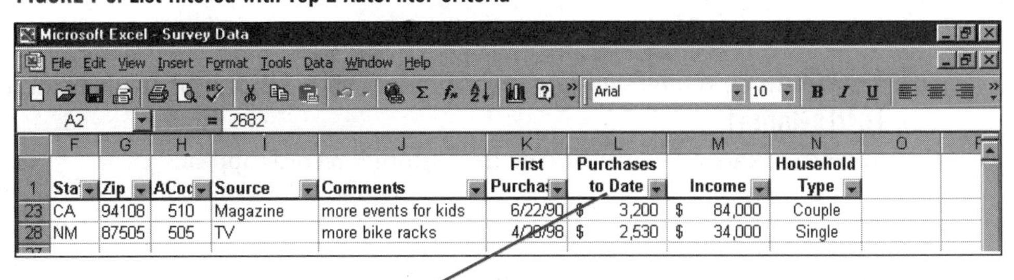

Creating a Custom Filter

So far, you have used the AutoFilter command to filter rows based on an entry in a single column. You can perform more complex filters using options in the Custom AutoFilter dialog box. For example, you can filter rows based on two entries in a single column or use comparison operators such as "greater than" or "less than" to display only those records with amounts greater than $50,000 in a particular column. Jim's next task is to locate those customers who live west of the Rocky Mountains, who live in a "single" household, and who heard about MediaLoft through a magazine advertisement.

Steps 1 2 3 4

QuickTip

When specifying criteria in the Custom AutoFilter dialog box, use the ? wildcard to specify any single character and the * wildcard to specify any series of characters.

Trouble?

If no records are displayed in the worksheet, you may have forgotten to type the apostrophe before the number 81000. Repeat Steps 2 and 3, making sure you include the leading apostrophe.

1. Click the **Zip** list arrow, then click **(Custom . . .)**
   The Custom AutoFilter dialog box opens. Because you know that all residents west of the Rockies have a zip code greater than 81000, you specify this criterion here. Because all the zip codes in the list were originally entered as labels with leading apostrophes, you need to include this apostrophe when entering the zip code value.
2. Click the **Zip** list arrow, click **is greater than**, press **[Tab]**, then type **'81000**
   Your completed Custom AutoFilter dialog box should match Figure I-4.
3. Click **OK**
   The dialog box closes, and only those records having a zip code greater than 81000 appear in the worksheet. Now, you'll narrow the list even further by displaying only those customers who live in a single household.
4. Scroll right until columns G through N are visible, click the **Household Type** list arrow, then click **Single**
   The list of records retrieved has narrowed. Finally, you need to filter out all customers except those who heard about MediaLoft through a magazine advertisement.
5. Click the **Source** list arrow, then click **Magazine**
   Your final filtered list now shows only customers in single households west of the Rocky Mountains who heard about MediaLoft through magazine ads. See Figure I-5.
6. Preview, then print the worksheet
   The worksheet prints using the existing print settings—landscape orientation, scaled to fit on a single page.
7. Click **Data** on the menu bar, point to **Filter**, click **AutoFilter** to deselect it, then press **[Ctrl][Home]**
   You have cleared the filter, and all the customer records appear.

FIGURE I-4: Custom AutoFilter dialog box

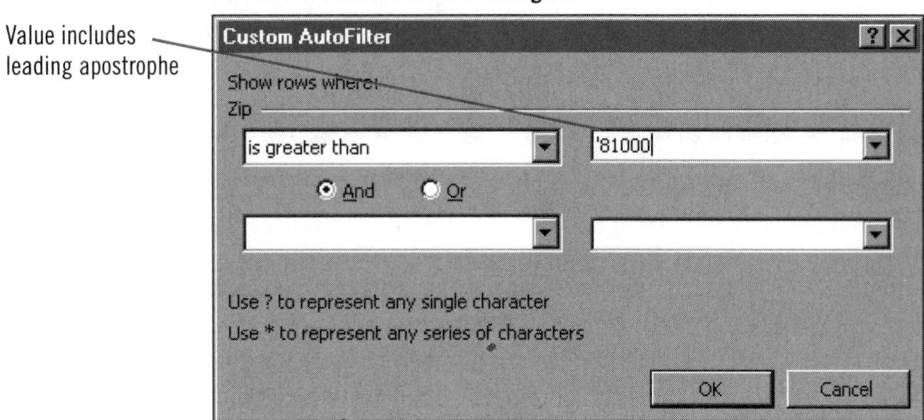

FIGURE I-5: Results of custom filter

Microsoft Excel - Survey Data

File Edit View Insert Format Tools Data Window Help

D3 = 9203 Arlen Road

	F	G	H	I	J	K	L	M	N	O
1	Sta	Zip	ACod	Source	Comments	First Purchas	Purchases to Date	Income	Household Type	
19	WA	98102	206	Magazine	no comments	6/16/96	$ 895	$ 45,000	Single	
30	WA	98100	206	Magazine	more world music	5/14/93	$ 2,100	$ 63,000	Single	
37										

Zip codes greater than 81000

Fields used in custom filter

And and Or logical conditions

CLUES TO USE

You can narrow a search even further by using the And or Or buttons in the Custom AutoFilter dialog box. For example, you can select records for those customers with homes in California *and* Texas as well as select records for customers with homes in California *or* Texas. See Figure I-6. When used in this way, "And" and "Or" are often referred to as logical conditions. When you search for customers with homes in California *and* Texas, you are specifying an And condition. When you search for customers with homes in either California *or* Texas, you are specifying an Or condition.

FIGURE I-6: Using the Custom AutoFilter dialog box

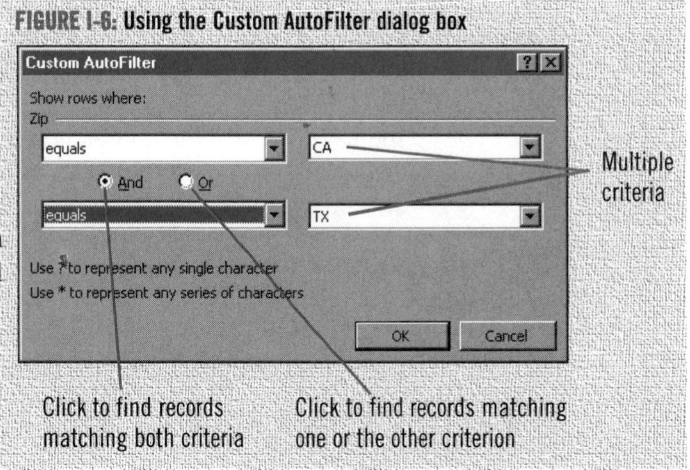

Excel 2000

Filtering a List with Advanced Filter

The Advanced Filter command allows you to search for data that matches complicated criteria in more than one column, using And and Or conditions. To use advanced filtering, you must define a criteria range. A **criteria range** is a cell range containing one row of labels (usually a copy of the column labels) and at least one additional row underneath the row of labels that contains the criteria you want to match. Jim's next task is to identify customers who have been buying at MediaLoft since before May 1, 1999, and whose total purchases are less than or equal to $1,000. He will use the Advanced Filter command to retrieve this data. Jim begins by defining the criteria range.

Steps

1. Select **rows 1 through 6**, click **Insert** on the menu bar, then click **Rows**; click cell **A1**, type **Criteria Range**, click cell **A6**, type **List Range**, then click the **Enter button** on the formula bar
   See Figure I-7. Six blank rows are added above the list. Excel does not require the labels "Criteria Range" and "List Range," but they are useful because they help organize the worksheet. It will be helpful to see the column labels. (In the next step, if the column labels make it difficult for you to drag the pointer to cell N7, try clicking N7 first; then drag the pointer all the way left to cell A7.)

2. Select range **A7:N7**, click the **Copy button** on the Standard toolbar, click cell **A2**, then press **[Enter]**
   Next, you need to specify that you want records for only those customers who have been customers since before May 1 and who have purchased no more than $1,000. In other words, you need records with a date before (less than) May 1, 1999 (<5/1/99) and a Purchases to Date amount that is less than or equal to $1,000 (<=1000).

Trouble?

If the Copy button does not appear on your Standard toolbar, click the More Buttons button to view it.

3. Scroll right until columns H through N are visible, click cell **K3**, type **< 5/1/99**, click cell **L3**, type **<=1000**, then click
   This enters the criteria in the cells directly beneath the Criteria Range labels. See Figure I-8. Placing the criteria in the same row indicates that the records you are searching for must match both criteria; that is, it specifies an And condition.

4. Press **[Ctrl][Home]**, click **Data** on the menu bar, point to **Filter**, then click **Advanced Filter**
   The Advanced Filter dialog box opens, with the list range already entered. (Notice that the default setting under Action is to filter the list in its current location rather than copy it to another location. You will change this setting later.)

5. Click the **Criteria Range box**, select range **A2:N3** in the worksheet (move the dialog box if necessary), then click **OK**
   You have specified the criteria range. The filtered list contains 19 records that match both the criteria—their first purchase was before 5/1/99 and their purchases to date total less than $1,000. You'll filter this list even further in the next lesson.

FIGURE I-7: Using the Advanced Filter command

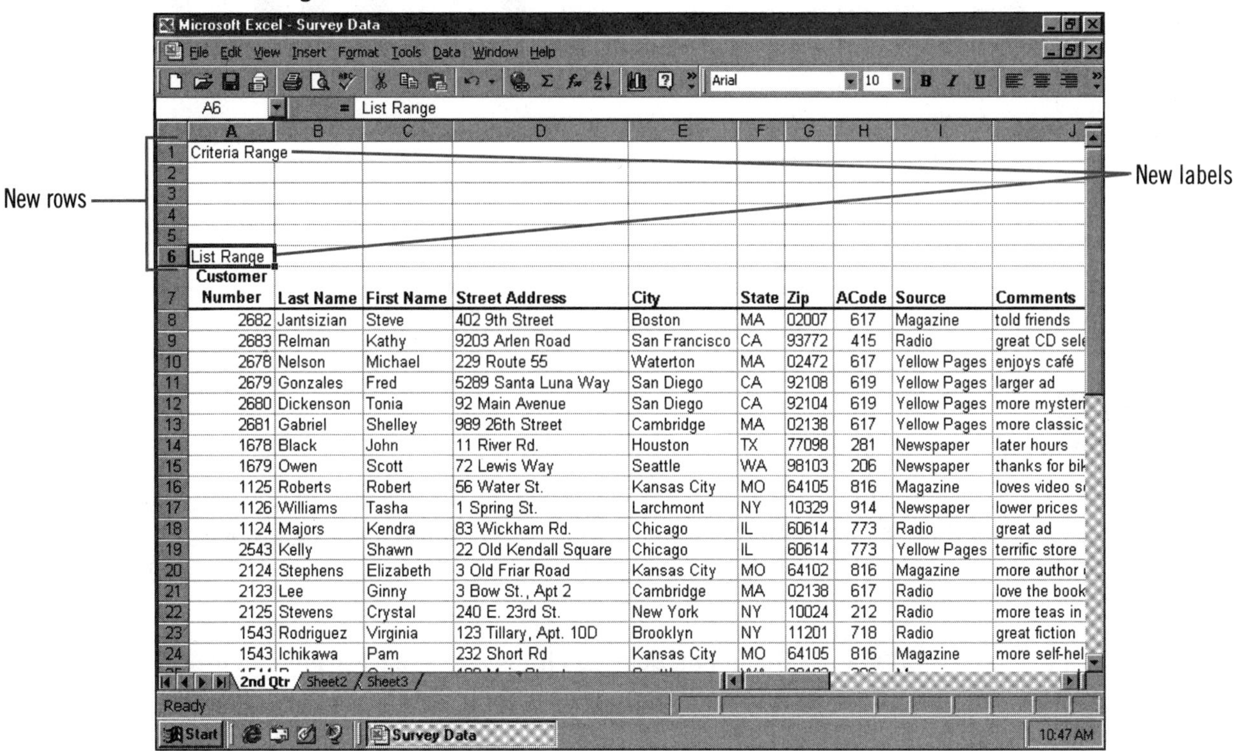

FIGURE I-8: Criteria in the same row

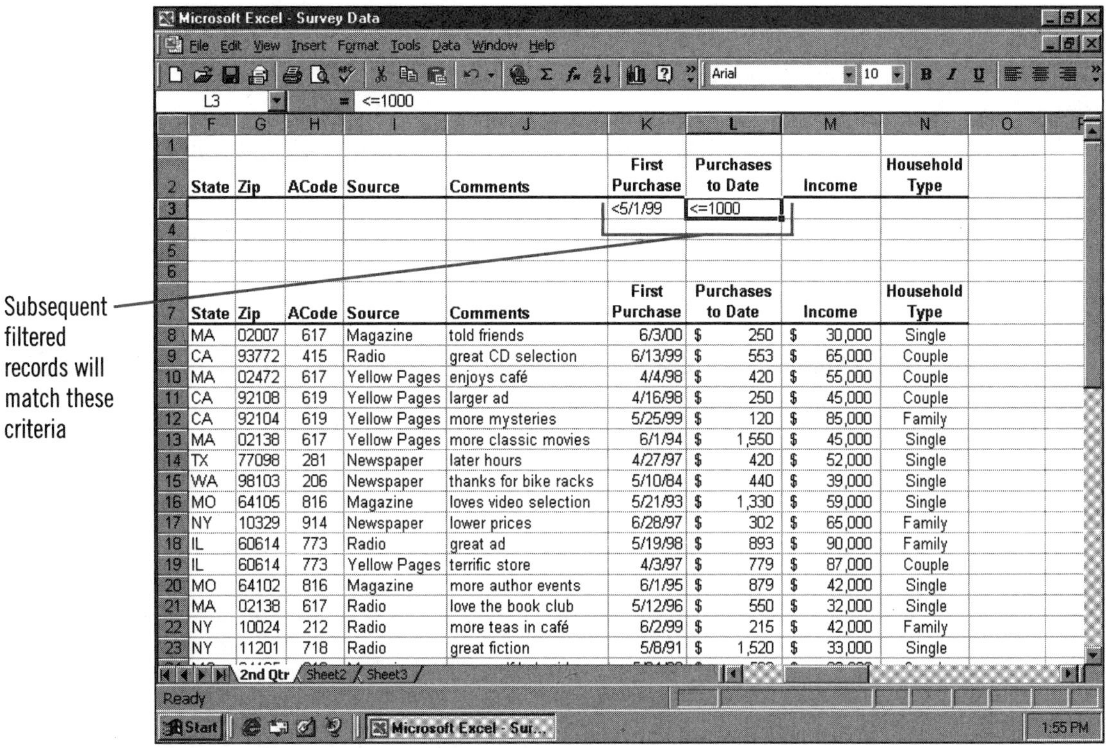

Understanding the criteria range

When you define the criteria range in the Advanced Filter dialog box, Excel automatically creates a name for this range in the worksheet (Criteria). The criteria range includes the field names and any criteria rows underneath the names.

Excel 2000

Excel 2000

Extracting List Data

Whenever you take the time to specify a complicated set of search criteria, it's a good idea to extract the matching records. When you **extract** data, you place a copy of a filtered list in a range you specify in the Advanced Filter dialog box. That way, you won't accidentally clear the filter or lose track of the records you spent time compiling. Jim needs to filter the previous list one step further to reflect only those customers in the current filtered list who heard of MediaLoft through TV or a magazine ad. To complete this filter, he will specify an Or condition by entering two sets of criteria in two separate rows. He decides to save the matching records by extracting them to a different location in the worksheet.

Steps

1. Click cell **I3**, type **TV**, then press **[Enter]**; in cell **I4**, type **Magazine**, click the **Enter button** on the formula bar, then copy the criteria in **K3:L3** to **K4:L4**
   See Figure I-9. This time, you'll indicate that you want to copy the filtered list to a range beginning in cell A50.
2. Click **Data** on the menu bar, point to **Filter**, then click **Advanced Filter**; under Action, click the **Copy to another location option button** to select it, click the **Copy to** box, then type **A50**
   The last time you filtered the list, the criteria range included only rows 2 and 3, and now you have criteria in row 4.
3. In the **Criteria Range box**, edit the current formula to read **$A$2:$N$4**, click **OK**; then scroll down until row 50 is visible
   You have changed the criteria range to include row 4. The matching records are copied to the range beginning in cell A50. The original list (starting in cell A7) contains the records filtered in the previous lesson. See Figure I-10.
4. Select range **A50:N61**, click **File** on the menu bar, click **Print**, under Print what, click the **Selection option button**, click **Preview**, then click **Print**
   The selected area prints.
5. Press **[Ctrl][Home]**, click **Data** on the menu bar, point to **Filter**, then click **Show All**
   All the records in the range reappear. You return to the original list, which starts at its new location in cell A7.
6. Save, then close the workbook

Trouble?

Make sure the criteria range in the Advanced Filter dialog box includes the field names and the number of rows underneath the names that contain criteria. If you leave a blank row in the criteria range, Excel filters nothing and shows all records.

FIGURE I-9: Criteria in separate rows

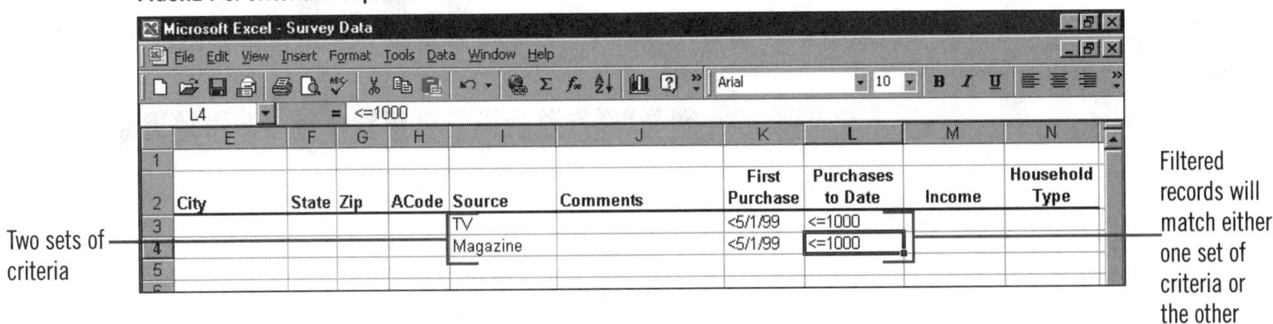

	E	F	G	H	I	J	K	L	M	N
1										
2	City	State	Zip	ACode	Source	Comments	First Purchase	Purchases to Date	Income	Household Type
3					TV		<5/1/99	<=1000		
4					Magazine		<5/1/99	<=1000		
5										

Two sets of criteria

Filtered records will match either one set of criteria or the other

FIGURE I-10: Extracted data records

	Street Address	City	State	Zip	ACode	Source	Comments	First Purchase	Purchases to Date	
50										
51	3 Old Friar Road	Kansas City	MO	64102	816	Magazine	more author events	6/1/95	$ 879	$
52	232 Short Rd	Kansas City	MO	64105	816	Magazine	more self-help videos	5/24/96	$ 530	$
53	100 Main Street	Seattle	WA	98102	206	Magazine	no comments	6/16/96	$ 895	$
54	123 Elm St.	Houston	TX	77098	281	Magazine	salespeople helpful	6/28/98	$ 320	$
55	1110 November Way	Chicago	IL	60618	771	TV	no comments	3/22/99	$ 250	$
56	42 Silver Street	Reading	MA	03882	413	TV	fun store	4/6/87	$ 420	$
57	921 Lopez Lane	Chicago	IL	60611	773	Magazine	add chairs	4/9/93	$ 480	$
58	900 Monument St.	Concord	MA	01742	508	Magazine	love the book club	6/15/97	$ 450	$
59	486 Intel Circuit	Houston	TX	77092	281	TV	very effective ad	5/26/96	$ 990	$
60	2318 Sarah Road	Chicago	IL	60614	312	Magazine	great coffee	4/29/97	$ 640	$
61	2120 Witch Way	Salem	MA	01970	508	Magazine	loves our staff	5/25/97	$ 820	$
62										
63										

2nd Qtr / Sheet2 / Sheet3

Filter Mode

Start | Survey Data | 11:08 AM

Extracted records copied to the range starting at cell A50

Extracted records for customers with first purchase before 5/1/99 or purchases less than $1,000 and who heard about MediaLoft through TV or magazines

Understanding the criteria range and the copy-to location

When you define the criteria range and/or copy-to location in the Advanced Filter dialog box, Excel automatically creates names for these ranges in the worksheet (Criteria and Extract). The criteria range includes the field names and any criteria rows underneath them. The extract range includes just the field names above the extracted list. To extract a different list, simply select Extract as the copy-to location. Excel automatically deletes the old list in the extract area and generates a new list under the field names. Make sure the worksheet has enough blank rows underneath the field names for your data.

Excel 2000

Creating Subtotals Using Grouping and Outlines

The Excel subtotals feature provides a quick, easy way to group and summarize data in a list. Usually, you create subtotals with the SUM function. You also can subtotal groups with functions such as COUNT, AVERAGE, MAX, and MIN. Your list must have field names and be sorted before you can issue the Subtotal command. Jim wants to create a list grouped by advertising source, with subtotals for purchases to date and household income. He starts by sorting the list in ascending order—first by advertising source, then by state, and, finally, by city.

Steps

1. Open the workbook titled **EX I-1**, then save it as **Survey Data 2**
2. Click the **Name Box** list arrow, click **Database**, click **Data** on the menu bar, then click **Sort**; click the **Sort by** list arrow, click **Source**, click the first **Then by** list arrow, click **State**, click the **Ascending option button** to set the Then by sort order; click the second **Then by** list arrow, click **City**, then click **OK**
   You have sorted the list in ascending order, first by advertising source, then by state, and, finally, by city.
3. Press **[Ctrl][Home]**, click **Data** on the menu bar, then click **Subtotals**
   Before you use the Subtotals command, you must position the cell pointer within the list range (in this case, range A1:N36). The Subtotal dialog box opens. Here, you specify the items you want subtotaled, the function you want to apply to the values, and the fields you want to summarize.
4. Click the **At each change in** list arrow, click **Source**, click the **Use function** list arrow, click **Sum**; in the Add subtotal to list, click the **Purchases to Date** and **Income** check boxes to select them; if necessary, click the **Household□Type** check box to deselect it; then, if necessary, click the **Replace current subtotals** and **Summary below data** check boxes to select them
   Your completed Subtotal dialog box should match Figure I-11.
5. Click **OK**, then scroll to and click cell **L41**
   The subtotaled list appears, showing the calculated subtotals and grand total in columns L and M. See Figure I-12. Notice that Excel displays an outline to the left of the worksheet showing the structure of the subtotaled lists.
6. Preview the worksheet, click **Setup** and place your name on the right side of the footer, then print the worksheet using the current settings
7. Press **[Ctrl][Home]**, click **Data** on the menu bar, click **Subtotals**, then click **Remove All**
   You have turned off the Subtotaling feature. The subtotals are removed, and the Outline feature is turned off automatically. Because you did not alter the worksheet data, there's no need to save the file.

Trouble?

You may receive the following message: "No list found. Select a single cell within your list and Microsoft Excel will select the list for you." If you do, this means that you did not select the list before issuing the Subtotals command. Click OK, then repeat Steps 2 and 3.

FIGURE I-11: Completed Subtotal dialog box

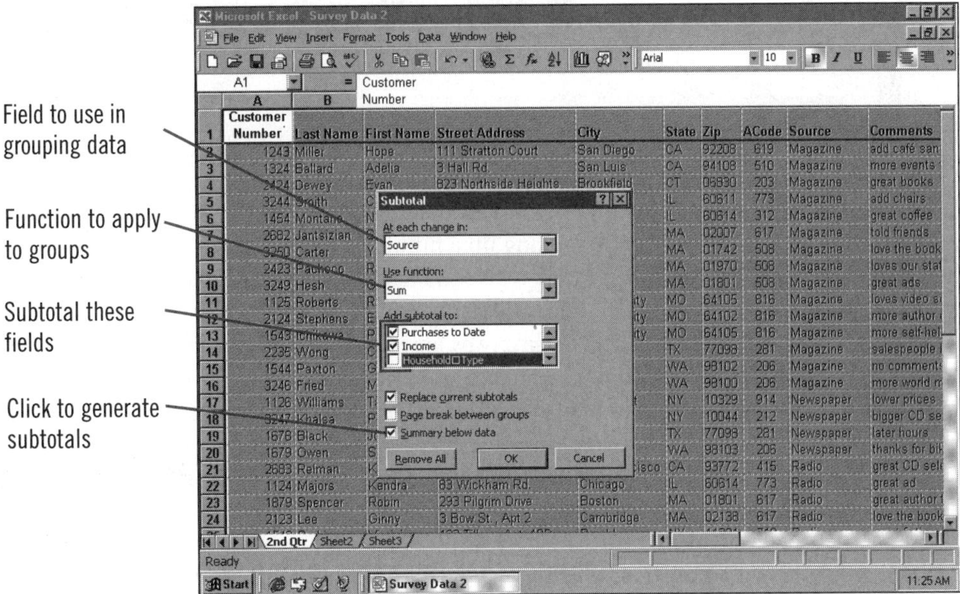

FIGURE I-12: Portion of subtotaled list

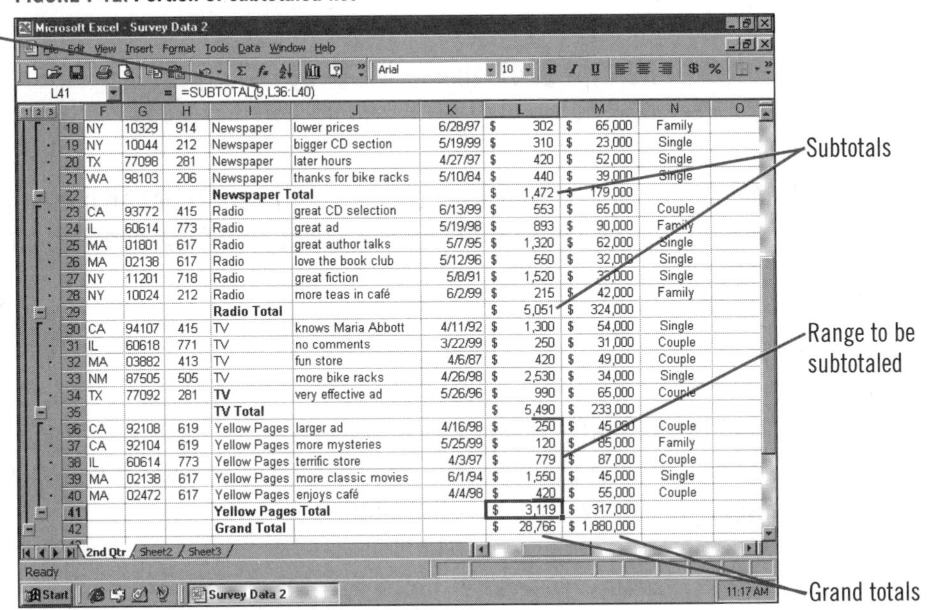

Show or hide details in an Excel outline

Once subtotals have been generated, all detail records are displayed in an outline. See Figure I-13. You can then click the Hide Details button [−] of your choice to hide that group of records, creating a summary report. You can also create a chart that shows the summary data. Any chart you create will be automatically updated as you show or hide data. You can also click the Show Details button [+] for the group of data you want to display. To show a specific level of detail, click the row or column level button for the lowest level you want to display. For example, to display levels 1 through 3, click [3].

FIGURE I-13: Subtotaled list with level 2 details hidden

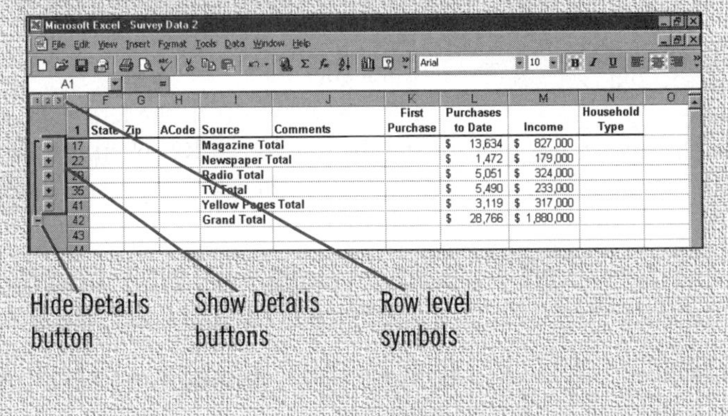

Looking Up Values in a List

The Excel VLOOKUP function helps you locate specific values in a list. The VLOOKUP searches vertically (V) down the leftmost column of a list and then reads across the row to find the value in the column you specify. The process of looking up a number in a phone book uses the same logic as the Excel VLOOKUP function: You locate a person's name and then read across the row to find the phone number you are looking for. At times, Jim wants to be able to find out what type of household a particular customer lives in simply by entering his or her specific customer number. To do this, he uses the VLOOKUP function. He begins by creating a special list, or table, containing the customer numbers he wants to look up. Then he copies names to a separate location.

Steps

QuickTip

Excel also has a Lookup Wizard to help you perform lookups. It is an Excel add-in (or extra) program. Open the Tools menu, point to Wizards, then click Lookup. If you don't see Wizards on the Tools menu, install the add-in from the Microsoft Office CD.

Trouble?

If the Office Assistant activates for this task, select the "No" option to indicate you don't want to learn more about this function at the present time. Continue with Step 5.

Trouble?

If an exact match is not returned, make sure the Range_lookup is set to FALSE.

1. Click cell **C2**, click **Window** on the menu bar, then click **Freeze Panes**; scroll right until columns N through T and rows 1 through 15 are visible
2. Click cell **P1**, type **VLOOKUP Function**, click the **Enter button** on the formula bar; copy the contents of cell **A1** to cell **R1**, copy the contents of cell **N1** to cell **S1**, widen the columns as necessary to display the text, then click any blank cell
   See Figure I-14. Jim wants to know the household type for customer number 3247.
3. Click cell **R2**, type **3247**, then press **[→]**
   The VLOOKUP function in the Paste Function dialog box will let Jim find the household type for customer number 3247.
4. Make sure cell S2 is still selected, click the **Paste Function button** on the Standard toolbar, under Function category click **Lookup & Reference**, under Function name click **VLOOKUP**, then click **OK**
   The VLOOKUP dialog box opens. Because the value you want to find is in cell R2, that will be the Lookup_value. The list you want to search is the customer list, so its name ("Database") will be the Table_array.
5. Drag the **VLOOKUP dialog box** down so that at least rows 1 and 2 of the worksheet are visible; with the insertion point in the Lookup_value box, click cell **R2**, click the **Table_array box**, then type **DATABASE**
   The column you want to search (Household Type) is the fourteenth column from the left, so the Col_index_num will be 14. Because you want to find an exact match for the value in cell R2, the Range_lookup argument will be FALSE. (If you want to find only the closest match for a value, you enter TRUE in the Range_lookup box, as indicated in the bottom of the VLOOKUP dialog box.)
6. Click the **Col_index_num box**, type **14**, click the **Range_lookup box**, then type **FALSE**
   Your completed VLOOKUP dialog box should match Figure I-15.
7. Click **OK**
   Excel searches down the leftmost column of the customer list until it finds a value matching the one in cell R2. Then it finds the household type for that record ("Single") and displays it in cell S2. Now, you'll use this function to determine the household type for one other customer.
8. Click cell **R2**, type **2125**, then click
   The VLOOKUP function returns the value Family in cell S2.
9. Press **[Ctrl][Home]**, then save the workbook.

FIGURE I-14: Worksheet with headings for VLOOKUP

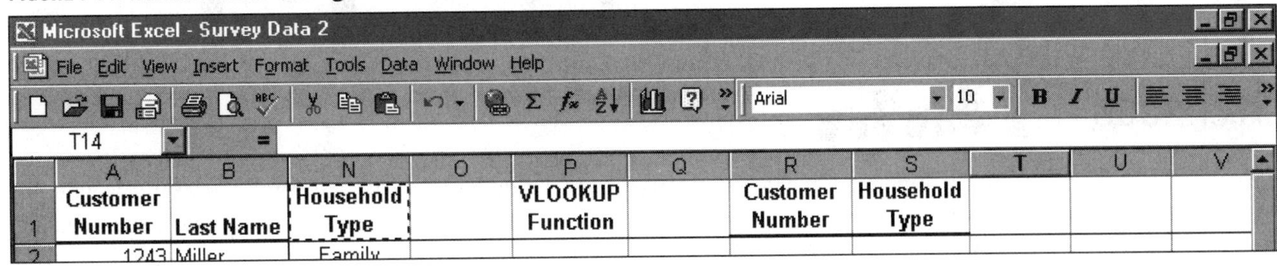

FIGURE I-15: Completed VLOOKUP dialog box

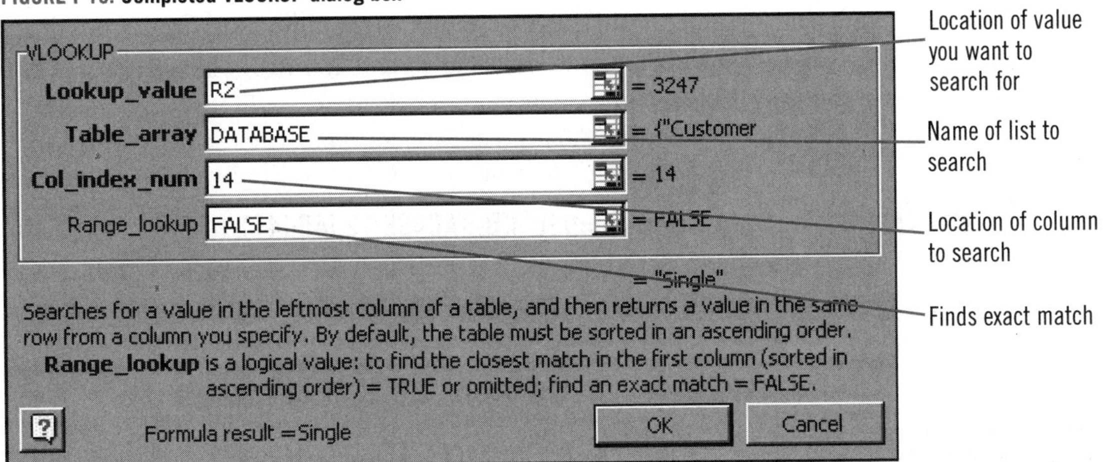

Excel 2000

Using the HLOOKUP function

The VLOOKUP (Vertical Lookup) function is useful when your data is arranged vertically in columns. The HLOOKUP (Horizontal Lookup) function is useful when your data is arranged horizontally in rows. HLOOKUP searches horizontally across the topmost row of a list until the matching value is found, then looks down the number of rows you specify. The arguments for this function are identical to those for the VLOOKUP function, with one exception. Instead of a Col_index_number, HLOOKUP uses a Row_index_number, which indicates the location of the row you want to search. For example, if you want to search the fourth row from the top, the Row_index_number should be 4.

Excel 2000

Summarizing List Data

Database functions allow you to summarize list data in a variety of ways. For example, you can use them to count, average, or total values in a field for only those records that meet specified criteria. When working with a sales activity list, for instance, you can use Excel to count the number of client contacts by sales representative or to total the amount sold to specific accounts by month. The format for database functions is explained in Figure I-16. Jim wants to summarize the information in his list in two ways. First, he wants to find the total purchases to date for each advertising source. He also wants to count the number of records for each advertising source. Jim begins by creating a criteria range that includes a copy of the column label for the column he wants to summarize, as well as the criterion itself.

Steps

1. With the panes still frozen, scroll down until row 31 is the top row underneath the frozen headings, then enter and format the five labels shown in Figure I-17 in the range: **I39:K41**
   The criteria range in I40:I41 tells Excel to summarize records with the entry "Yellow Pages" in the Source column. The functions will be in cells L39 and L41.
2. Click cell **L39**, type **=DSUM(DATABASE,12,I40:I41)**, then click the **Enter button** on the formula bar
   The result in cell L39 is 3119. For the range named Database, Excel totaled the information in column 12 (Purchases to Date) for those records that meet the criteria of Source = Yellow Pages. The DCOUNTA function will help you determine the number of nonblank records meeting the criteria Source = Yellow Pages.
3. Click cell **L41**, type **=DCOUNTA(DATABASE,1,I40:I41)**, then click
   The result in cell L41 is 5, meaning that there are five customers who heard about MediaLoft through the Yellow Pages. This function uses the first field in the list, Customer Number, to check for nonblank cells within the criteria range Source = Yellow Pages. Jim also wants to see total purchases and a count for the magazine ads.
4. Click cell **I41**, type **Magazine**, then click
   With total purchases of $13,634, it's clear that magazine advertising is the most effective way of attracting MediaLoft customers. Compare your results with Figure I-18.
5. Press **[Ctrl][Home]**, then save and close the workbook

QuickTip

You can use a column label, such as "City", in place of a column number. Type the text exactly as it is entered in the list and enclose it in double quotation marks.

Trouble?

If the result you receive is incorrect, make sure you entered the formula correctly, using the letter "I" in the criteria range address, and the number one (1) for the column number.

FIGURE I-16: Format of database function

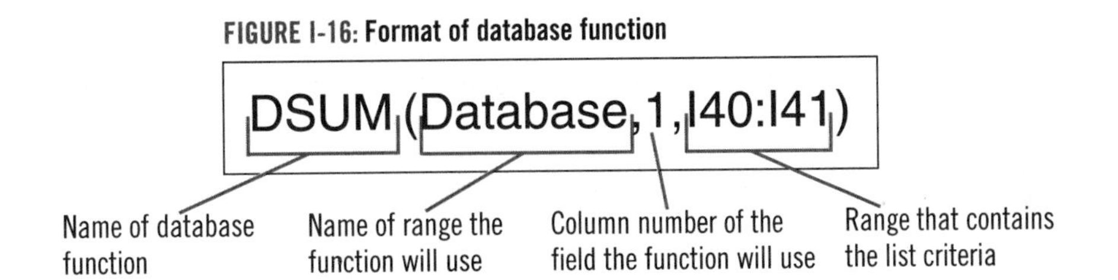

FIGURE I-17: Portion of worksheet showing summary area

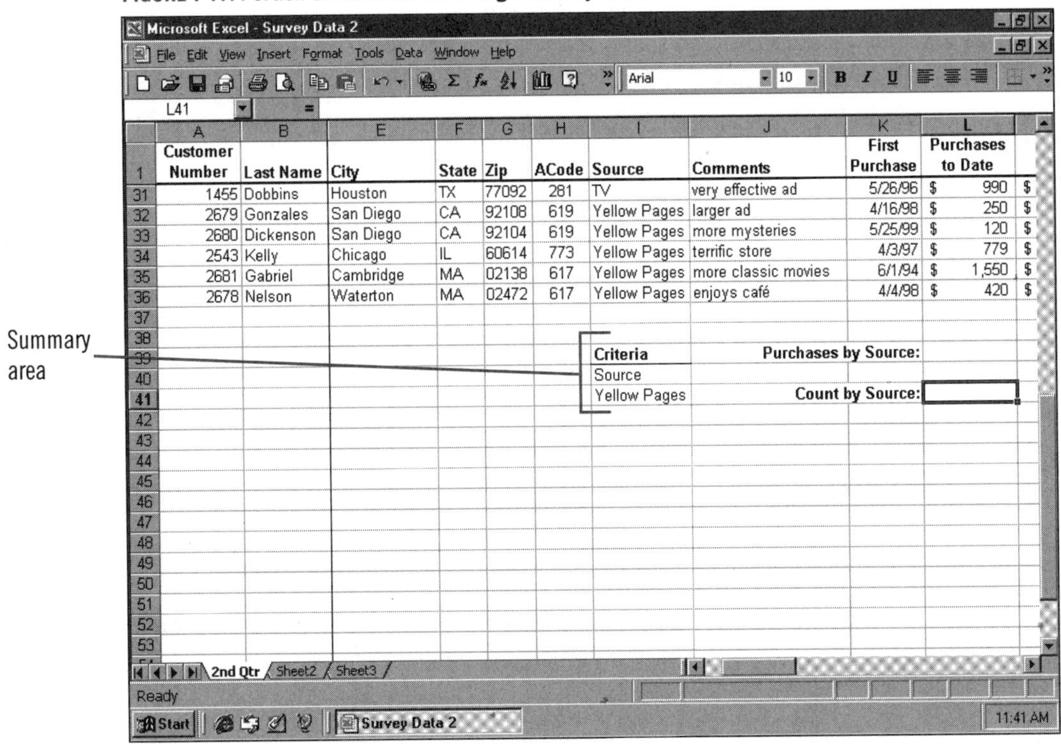

FIGURE I-18: Result generated by database function

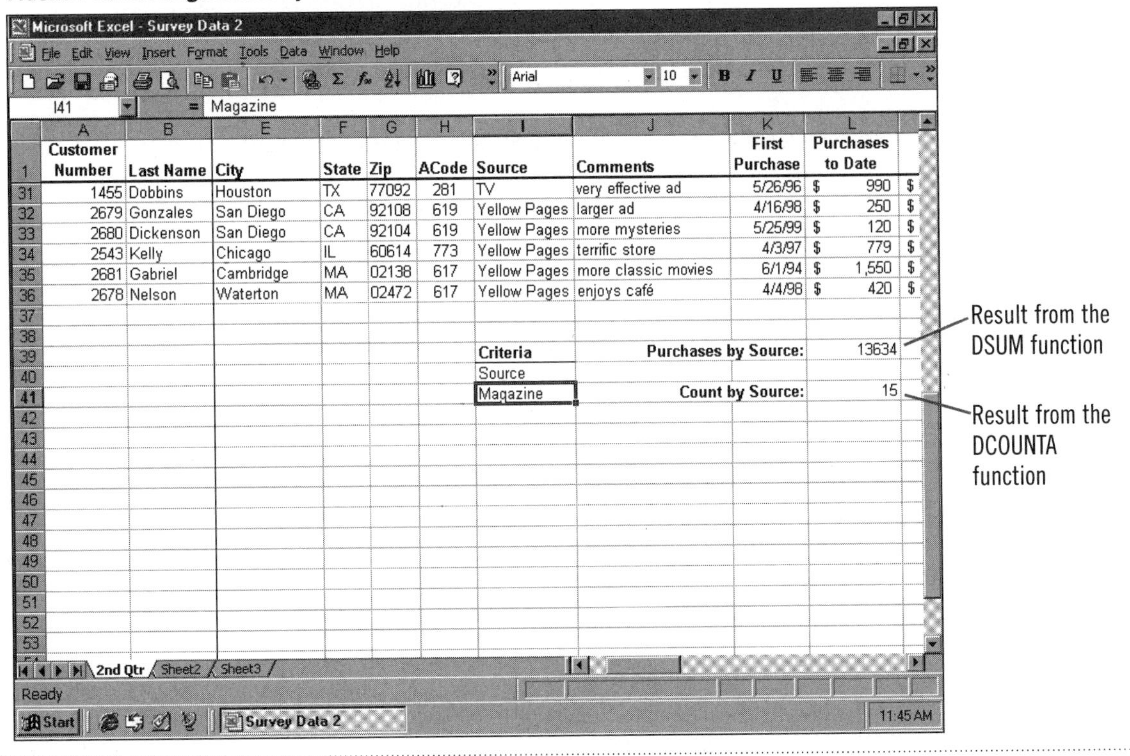

Excel 2000

Using Data Validation for List Entries

The Excel Data Validation feature allows you to specify what data is valid for a range of cells. You can restrict data to whole numbers, decimal numbers, or text, or you can set limits on entries. You can also specify a list of acceptable entries. Once you've specified what data is considered valid, Excel prevents users from entering any other data (considered invalid) except your specified choices. Jim wants to make sure that information in the Household Type column is entered consistently in the future. He decides to restrict the entries in that column to three options: Couple, Single, and Family. First, he selects the column he wants to restrict.

Steps

1. **Open the workbook titled EX I-1, then save it as Survey Data 3**
2. **Scroll right until column N is displayed, then click the Column N column header**
   The entire column is selected.
3. **Click Data on the menu bar, click Validation, click the Settings tab if necessary, click the Allow list arrow, then click List**
   Selecting the List option enables you to type a list of specific options.
4. **Click the Source box, then type Couple, Single, Family**
   You have entered the list of acceptable entries, separated by commas. See Figure I-19. Jim wants the data entry person to be able to select a valid entry from a drop-down list.
5. **Click the In-cell Drop-down check box to select it if necessary, then click OK**
   The dialog box closes, and you return to the worksheet. The new data restrictions will apply only to new entries in the Household Type column.
6. **Click cell N37, then click the list arrow to display the list of valid entries**
   See Figure I-20. You could click an item in the list to have it entered in the cell, but Jim first wants to know what happens if you enter an invalid entry.
7. **Click the list arrow to close the list, type Individual, then press [Enter]**
   A warning dialog box appears to prevent you from entering the invalid data. See Figure I-21.
8. **Click Cancel, click the list arrow, then click Single**
   The cell accepts the valid entry. The data restriction ensures that new records will contain only one of the three correct entries in the Household Type column. The customer list is finished and ready for future data entry.
9. **Save and close the workbook**

QuickTip

To restrict entries to decimal or whole numbers, dates, or times, select the appropriate option in the Allow list. To specify a long list of valid entries, type the list in a column elsewhere in the worksheet, then type the address of the list in the Source box.

FIGURE I-19: Creating data restrictions

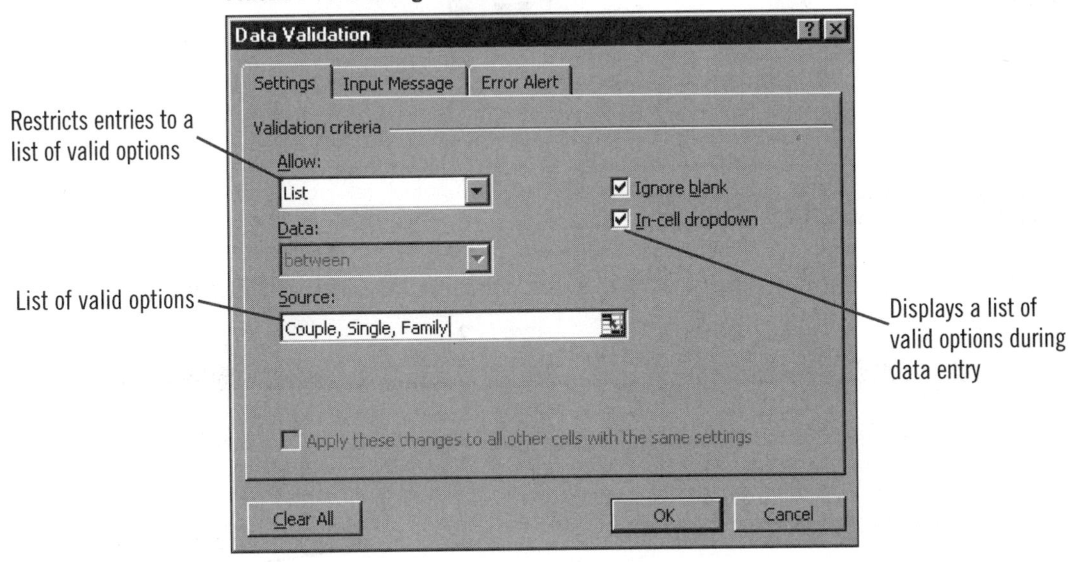

FIGURE I-20: Entering data in restricted cells

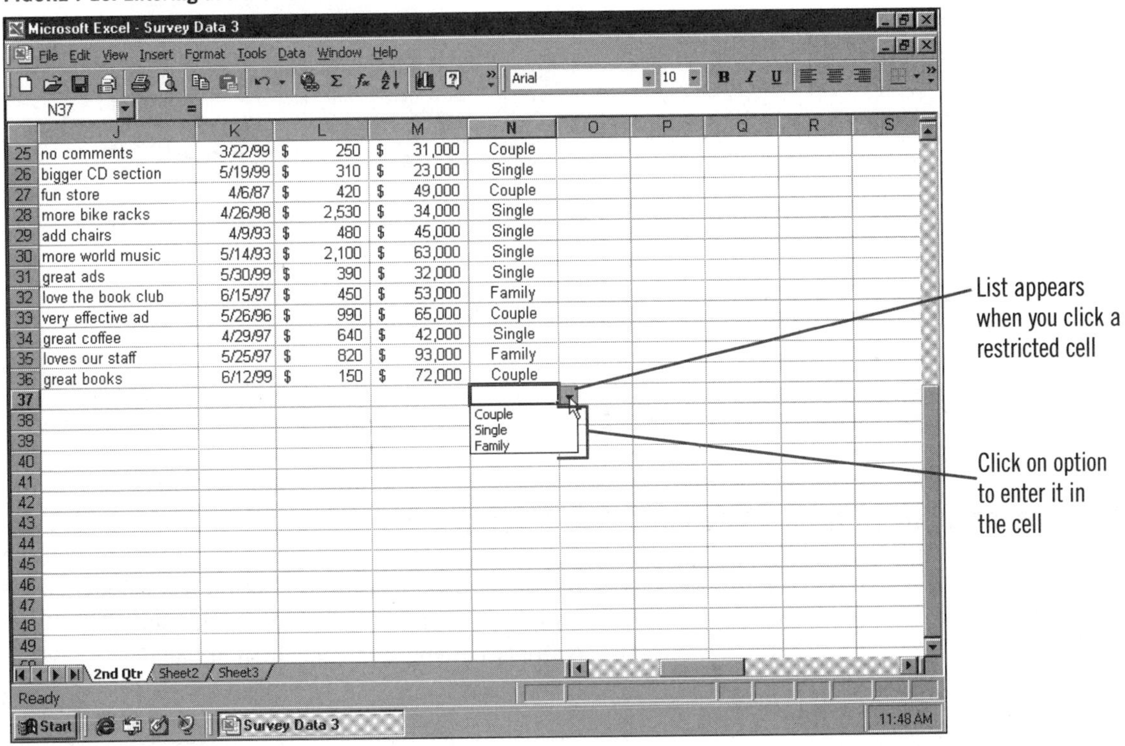

FIGURE I-21: Validation message

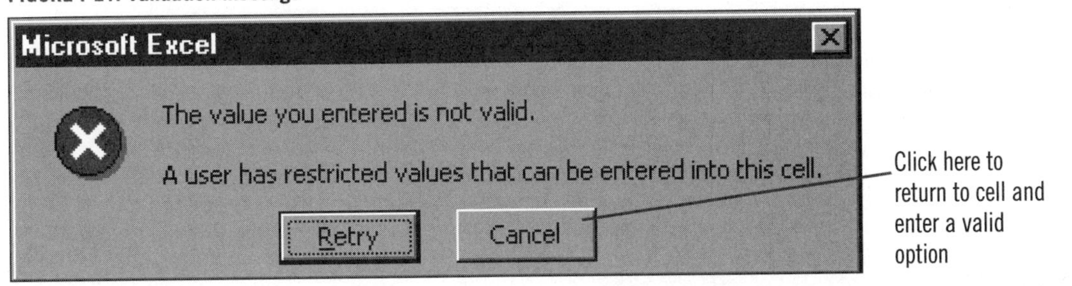

Practice

► Concepts Review

Explain the function of each element of the Excel screen labeled in Figure I-22.

FIGURE I-22

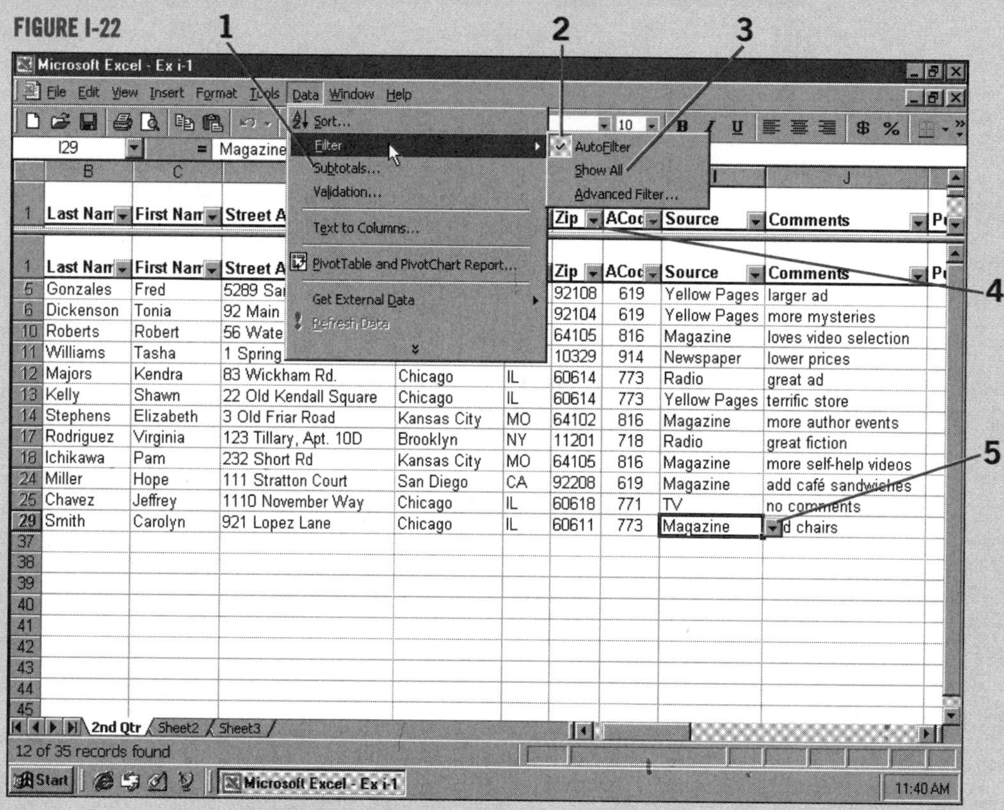

Match each term with the statement that describes it.

6. **HLOOKUP**
7. **Extracted list**
8. **Data validation**
9. **Criteria range**
10. **List range**

a. Cell range when advanced filter results are copied to another location
b. Range in which search conditions are set
c. Restricts list entries to specified options
d. Range used to specify a database in database functions
e. Function to use when data is arranged horizontally in rows

Select the best answer from the list of choices.

11. **You might perform an AutoFilter and search for nonblank entries in order to**
    a. Identify missing data.
    b. Find records with data in a particular field.
    c. Sum records with data in a particular field.
    d. b and c.

12. What does it mean when you select the Or option when creating a custom filter?
- **a.** Neither criterion has to be 100% true.
- **b.** Either criterion can be true to find a match.
- **c.** Both criteria must be true to find a match.
- **d.** Custom filter requires a criteria range.

13. What must a list have before automatic subtotals can be inserted?
- **a.** Enough records to show multiple subtotals
- **b.** Grand totals
- **c.** Column or field headings
- **d.** Formatted cells

► Skills Review

1. Retrieve records with AutoFilter.
- **a.** Open the workbook titled EX I-2, then save it as "Compensation Summary".
- **b.** Use AutoFilter to list records for employees in the Accounting department.
- **c.** Redisplay all employees, then use AutoFilter to show the three employees with the highest annual salary.
- **d.** Redisplay all the records.

2. Create a custom filter.
- **a.** Create a custom filter showing employees hired prior to 1/1/90 or after 1/1/94.
- **b.** Preview, then print the list in A1:J11.
- **c.** Redisplay all records.
- **d.** Turn off AutoFilter.

3. Filter and extract a list with Advanced Filter.
- **a.** You will retrieve a list of employees who were hired prior to 1/1/90 and earn more than $60,000 a year. Define a criteria range by copying the field names in range A1:J1 to cell A14.
- **b.** In cell D15, enter the criterion < 1/1/90, then in cell G15 enter >60000.
- **c.** Return to cell A1.
- **d.** Open the Advanced Filter dialog box.
- **e.** Indicate that you want to copy to another location, enter the criteria range A14:J15, then indicate that you want to copy to cell A18.
- **f.** If necessary, scroll so that rows 18 through 20 are visible to confirm that the retrieved list meets the criteria.
- **g.** Change the page setup to landscape orientation, then select and print only the extracted list in range A18:J20.
- **h.** Use the Edit menu to clear data and formats from the range A14:J20.

4. Creating subtotals using grouping and outlines.
- **a.** Move to cell A1. Sort the list in ascending order by department, then in descending order by monthly salary.
- **b.** Group and create subtotals by department, using the Sum function; select Monthly Salary in the Add Subtotal to list box, deselect Annual Comp., then click OK.
- **c.** AutoFit column E.
- **d.** Use the outline to display only the subtotals, preview, then print only the subtotaled list in landscape orientation fitting the data to one page.
- **e.** Remove the subtotals.

5. Look up values in a list.

- **a.** You will locate annual compensation information by entering a social security number. Scroll so that columns I through Q are visible.
- **b.** In cell N2, enter 556-53-7589.
- **c.** In cell O2, enter the following function: =VLOOKUP(N2,A2:J11,10,FALSE), then view the results.
- **d.** Enter another social security number, 356-93-2123, in cell N2 and view the annual compensation for that employee.
- **e.** Save your worksheet.

6. Summarize list data.

- **a.** You'll enter a database function to average the annual salaries by department, using the Marketing department as the initial criterion.
- **b.** Define the criteria area: In cell C14, enter "Criteria"; in cell C15, enter "Dept." (make sure you type the period); then in cell C16, enter "Marketing".
- **c.** In cell E14, enter "Average Annual Salary by Department:".
- **d.** In cell H14, enter the following database function: =DAVERAGE(Database,7,C15:C16).
- **e.** Test the function further by entering the text "Accounting" in cell C16. When the criterion is entered, cell H14 should display 58650 as the result.
- **f.** Save the workbook, then close it.

7. Use data validation for list entries.

- **a.** Open the workbook titled EX I-2 again, then save it as "Compensation Summary 2".
- **b.** Select column E.
- **c.** For the validation criteria, specify that you want to allow a list of valid options.
- **d.** Enter a list of valid options that restricts the entries to "Accounting", "Information Systems", and "Marketing". Remember to use a comma between each item in the list.
- **e.** Indicate that you want the options to appear in an in-cell dropdown list, then close the dialog box.
- **f.** Go to cell E12, then select "Accounting" in the dropdown list.
- **g.** Select column F.
- **h.** Indicate that you want to restrict the data entered to be only whole numbers.
- **i.** In the minimum box, enter 1000. In the Maximum box, enter 20000. Close the dialog box.
- **j.** Click cell F12, enter 25000, then press [Enter].
- **k.** Click Cancel, then enter 19000.50.
- **l.** Click Cancel, then enter 19000.
- **m.** Save, then close the workbook and exit Excel.

► Independent Challenges

1. Your neighbor, Phillipe, brought over his wine cellar inventory workbook file on disk and asked you to help him manipulate the data in Excel. Phillipe would like to filter the list to show two subsets: all wines with a 1985 vintage and Chardonnay wines with a vintage prior to 1985. He would also like to subtotal the list and show the total dollar value by type of wine as well as restrict entries in the Type of Wine column to eight possibilities.

To complete this independent challenge:

a. Open the workbook titled EX I-3, then save it as "Wine Cellar Inventory".
b. Use AutoFilter to generate a list of wines with a 1985 vintage. Preview, then print the list.
c. Use Advanced Filter to extract a list of Chardonnay wines with a vintage in or prior to 1985. Preview, then print the list.
d. Clear the filter, and insert subtotals for Total $ according to type of wine. (*Hint:* Make sure to sort the list by type of wine prior to creating the subtotals.) Print the subtotaled list. Turn off subtotaling.
e. Beginning in cell H1, type the list of eight wine types in column H. The list should include Cabernet, Champagne, Chardonnay, Muscat, Pinot Noir, Riesling, Sauvignon Blanc, and Zinfandel.
f. Select column B. Open the Data Validation dialog box, then click List in the Allow box. Enter the range address for the list of wine types in the Source box. Make sure the In-cell dropdown check box is selected. Close the dialog box.
g. Test the data validation by entering valid and invalid data in cell B31.
h. Type your name in the worksheet footer, then save, print, and close the workbook.

2. Your neighbor, Phillipe, was pleased when you delivered his filtered and subtotaled wine inventory list. After viewing your printouts, he asks you to help him with a few more tasks. He wants the list to be sorted by wine label. In addition, he wants to be able to type in the vintage year (starting with 1985) and get a total bottle count and average cost per bottle for that vintage. (*Hint:* You need to define a criteria area outside the list to contain the two database functions.) Finally, Phillipe wants you to provide him with some form of documentation on how to accomplish the summaries.

To complete this independent challenge:

a. Open the workbook titled EX I-3, then save it as "Wine Cellar Inventory 2".
b. Sort the list alphabetically by wine label.
c. Define an area either above or below the list with the label "Criteria". Add appropriate column labels and criteria. Use 1985 as the vintage year for the criterion.
d. Near the criteria area, type labels for the two database functions.
e. Enter the database functions to find total bottle count and average price per bottle for a particular vintage.
f. Save your work. Preview and then print the list. Display the worksheet formulas, add your name to the worksheet footer, then preview and print the criteria area. Hide the formulas again.
g. Create a separate worksheet that documents the functions you used: Format the two cells containing the database functions as text by adding leading apostrophes. Widen any columns as necessary. Print a second copy of the list with the two database functions. Change the page setup so that the gridlines and row and column headings are printed. Leave a valid entry in the cell.
h. Save, then close the workbook.

3. A few months ago, you started your own business, called Books 4 You. You create and sell personalized books for special occasions. You bought a distributorship from an established book company and the rights to use several of the company's titles. Using your personal computer, specialized software, and preprinted book pages, you create personalized books on your laser printer. All you need from a customer is the name of the book's "star," his or her special date if appropriate (usually a birth or anniversary date), and the desired book title. Using the software, you enter the data and generate book pages, which you later bind together. After several months of struggle, you are starting to make a profit. You decided to put together an invoice list to track sales, starting in October. Now that you have this list, you would like to manipulate it in several ways. First, you want to filter the list to retrieve only children's books ordered during the first half of the month (prior to 10/16). Next, you want to subtotal the unit price, sales tax, and total cost columns by book title. Finally, you want to restrict entries in the Order Date column.

To complete this independent challenge:

a. Open the workbook titled EX I-4, then save it as "Books 4 You, Invoice Database".
b. Filter the list to show children's books ordered prior to 10/16/00. Print the filtered list on a single page with gridlines and row and column headings. Clear the filter, then save your work.
c. Create subtotals in the Unit Price, Sales Tax, and Total Cost columns by book title. Print the subtotaled list on a single page without gridlines, row, or column headings. Clear the subtotals.
d. Use the Data Validation dialog box to restrict entries to those with order dates between 12/31/99 and 1/1/01. Select "Date" In the Allow list, then enter the appropriate dates in the Start date and End date boxes. Test the data restrictions by attempting to enter an invalid date.
e. Add your name to the worksheet footer, then save, print, and close the workbook.
f. Open the workbook titled EX I-4, then save it as "Books 4 You, Lookup".
g. Enter a VLOOKUP function to retrieve a customer's book title based on its invoice number. Enter a second VLOOKUP function to look up the order date. Format the cell displaying the date in a date format, then save your work.
h. Below the VLOOKUP area, and to the right of the invoice list, define an area in which to count the number of birthday books ordered on any given date. Save your work.
i. Add your name to the worksheet footer, then print the list on a single page, if possible.
j. Provide documentation for any functions used, then add your name to the range and print the worksheet functions with gridlines and row and column headings on a single page, if possible.
k. Save, then close the workbook.

4. Each month, the MediaLoft Product department lists the top-selling book, video, and CD products on the MediaLoft intranet site. The department also keeps track of these products in an Excel list. As a new employee of the MediaLoft Corporate Headquarters, you have been asked to update the Excel list with the latest information on the intranet site and to then analyze the information using Excel.

To complete this independent challenge:

a. Connect to the Internet, then go to the MediaLoft intranet site at http://www.course.com/Illustrated/MediaLoft. Click the Products link, then click the Bestsellers of the month link. Print the page and disconnect from the Internet.
b. Open the file EX I-5 on your Project Disk, save it as "Bestsellers", and, referring to your printout, add the three top-selling items. (If there is more than one author/performer, choose only the first one.) Enter the date as 12/30/00.
c. Use AutoFilter to display only books.
d. Further filter the list to display only books that were on the bestseller list before 7/30/00.
e. Enter your name in the worksheet footer, then print the filtered list.
f. Clear the filter.
g. Create an advanced filter that retrieves, to its current location, records whose dates were before 9/1/2000 and whose dollar sales were greater than $2,000. Print only the cells containing the filtered list, then clear the filter and redisplay all the records.
h. Create another advanced filter that extracts products whose sales were $3,000 or more and places them in another area of the worksheet.
i. Print the range containing only the extracted list, centered horizontally on the page, with row and column headings.
j. Save and close the Bestsellers workbook.
k. Open the file EX I-5 and save it as "Bestsellers 2".
l. Subtotal the sales by category.
m. Use the outline to display only category names and totals. Enter your name in the worksheet footer and print the worksheet.
n. Redisplay the records and remove the subtotals.
o. Freeze the column headings and scroll to display several blank lines below the last line.
p. Use the DSUM function to let worksheet users find the total sales by category. Format the cell containing the function appropriately.
q. Use data validation to restrict category entries to CD, Book, or Video, then test an entry with valid and invalid entries.
r. Print, save, and close the worksheet.

Visual Workshop

Create the worksheet shown in Figure I-23. Save the workbook as "Commission Lookup" on your Project disk. (*Hints:* The formula in cell D5 accesses the commission from the table. Calculate the commission by multiplying the Amount of Sale by the Commission Rate. If an exact amount for the Amount of Sale does not exist, the next highest or lowest dollar value is used.) Add your name to the worksheet footer, then preview and print the worksheet.

FIGURE I-23

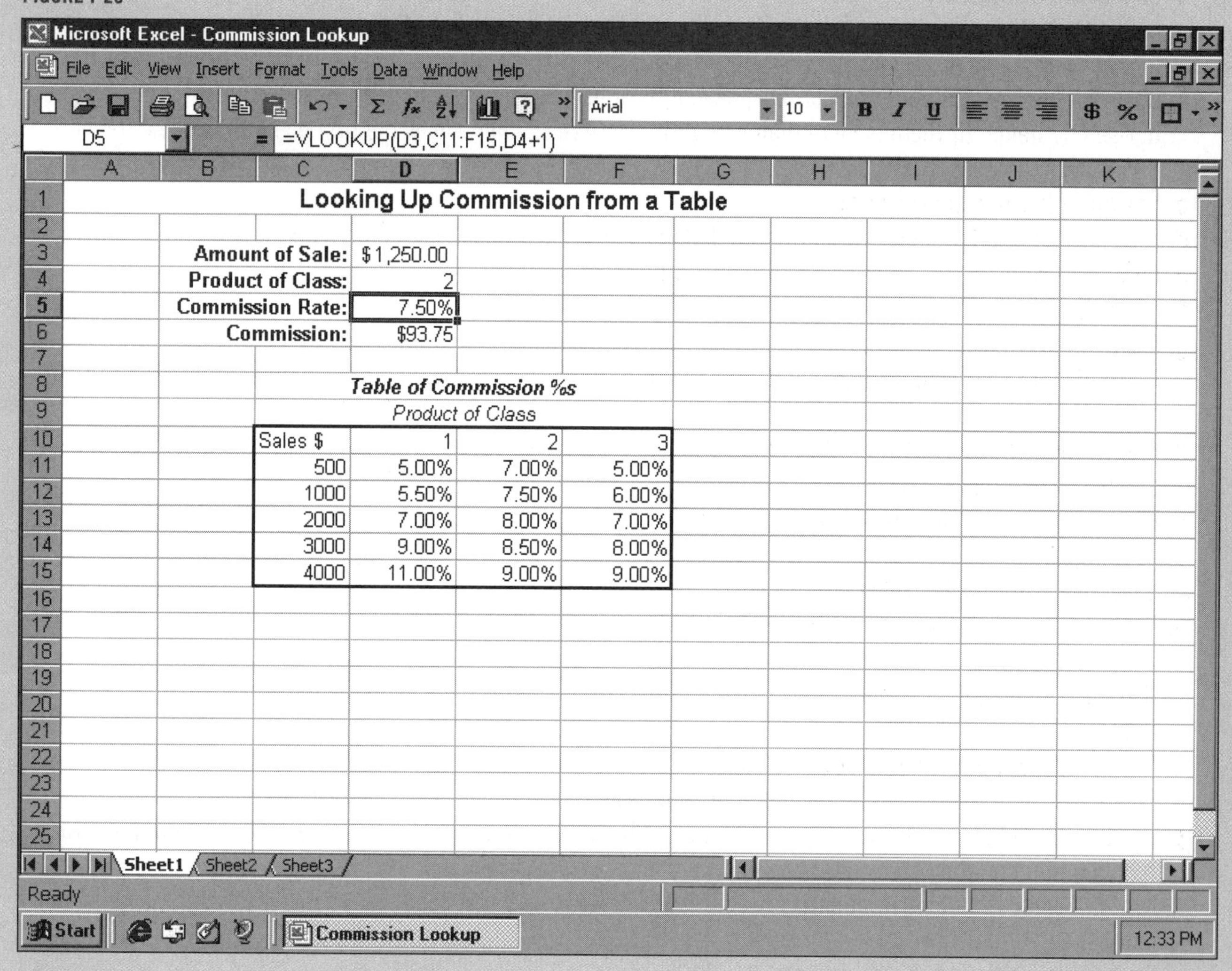

Excel 2000

Enhancing

Charts and Worksheets

Objectives

- ► Select a custom chart type
- ► Customize a data series
- ► Format a chart axis
- ► Add a data table to a chart
- ► Rotate a chart
- ► Enhance a chart with WordArt
- ► Rotate text
- ► Map data

There are many ways to revise a chart or a worksheet to present its data with greater impact. In this unit, you enhance both charts and worksheets by selecting a custom chart type, customizing a data series, formatting axes, adding a data table, and rotating a chart. You also add special text effects and rotate text. Finally, you increase the impact of geographical data by plotting it on a map. Keep in mind that your goal in enhancing charts or worksheets is to communicate your data more clearly. Avoid excessive customization, which can be visually distracting. MediaLoft's director of café operations, Jeff Shimada, has asked Jim Fernandez to produce two charts showing the sales of café pastry products in the first two quarters. He encourages Jim to enhance the charts and the worksheet data to improve their appearance and make the data more accessible. Finally, he asks Jim to create a map illustrating pastry sales by state.

Excel 2000

Selecting a Custom Chart Type

The Excel Chart Wizard offers a choice between standard and custom chart types. A **standard chart type** is a commonly used column, bar, pie, or area chart with several variations. For each standard chart type, you can choose from several subtypes, such as clustered column or stacked column. You can use the Wizard to add display options, and can later modify the formatting of any chart element. Excel supplies 20 built-in **custom chart types**, with special formatting already applied. You can also define your own custom chart type by modifying any of the existing Excel chart types. For example, you could define a company chart type that has the same title and then distribute it to other users in your office. Jim's first task is to create a chart showing the amount of each pastry type sold for the first quarter. To save time, he decides to use an Excel built-in custom chart.

Steps

QuickTip

To return personalized toolbars and menus to their default state, click Tools on the menu bar, click Customize, click the Options tab in the Customize dialog box, click Reset my usage data to restore the default settings, click Yes, click Close, then close the Drawing toolbar if it is displayed.

1. **Open the workbook titled EX J-1, then save it as Pastry Sales**
   The first step is to select the data you want to appear in the chart. In this case, you want the row labels in cells A6:A10 and the data for January and February in cells B5:C10.
2. **Select the range A5:C10**
3. **Click the Chart Wizard button on the Standard toolbar, click the Custom Types tab in the Step 1 Chart Wizard dialog box, then under Select from, click the Built-in option button to select it if necessary**
   See Figure J-1. When the built-in option button in the Custom Types tab is selected, all of the Excel custom chart types are displayed in the Chart type box, and a sample of the default chart appears in the Sample box. Once you make a selection in the Chart type box, the default chart disappears and a preview of the selected chart type appears in the Sample box. If the Chart Wizard button does not appear on your Standard toolbar, click the More Buttons button to view it.
4. **Click Columns with Depth in the Chart type box**
   A preview of the chart appears in the Sample box. Notice that this custom chart type, with its 3-D bars and white background, has a more elegant appearance than the default chart shown in Figure J-1. Unlike the previous default chart, this chart doesn't have gridlines.
5. **Click Next**
6. **Make sure = 'TotalSales'!A$5:$C$10 appears as the data range in the Data range box in the Step 2 Chart Wizard dialog box, then click Next**
7. **In the Step 3 Chart Wizard dialog box, click Next; if necessary, click the As object in option button in the Step 4 Chart Wizard dialog box to select it; then click Finish**
   The completed chart appears, covering part of the worksheet data, along with the Chart toolbar. The Chart toolbar can appear anywhere within the worksheet window. As you complete the following steps, you may need to drag the toolbar to a new location.
8. **Scroll down the worksheet until rows 13 through 28 are visible, click the chart border and drag the chart left and down until its upper-left corner is in cell A13, drag the middle right sizing handle right to the border between column H and column I, then check that its bottom border is between rows 25 and 26**
   The new chart fills the range A13:H25, as shown in Figure J-2.
9. **Save the workbook**

Trouble?

If the Chart toolbar does not open, right-click any toolbar and click Chart.

Trouble?

Remember to drag the Chart toolbar out of the way if it blocks your view of the chart.

FIGURE J-1: Custom Types tab settings

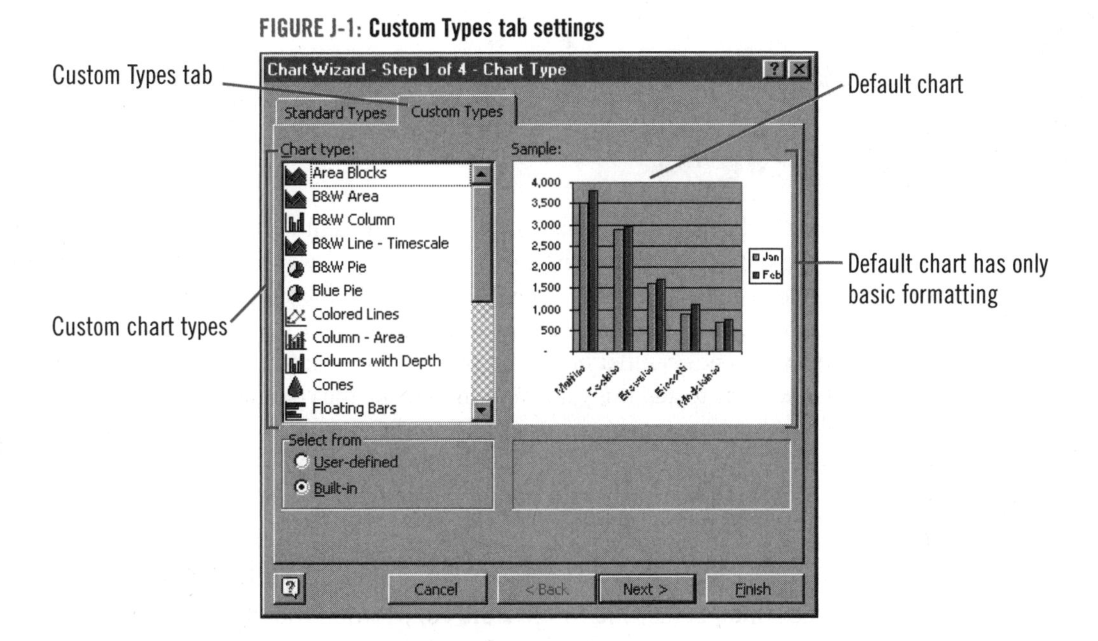

FIGURE J-2: New chart

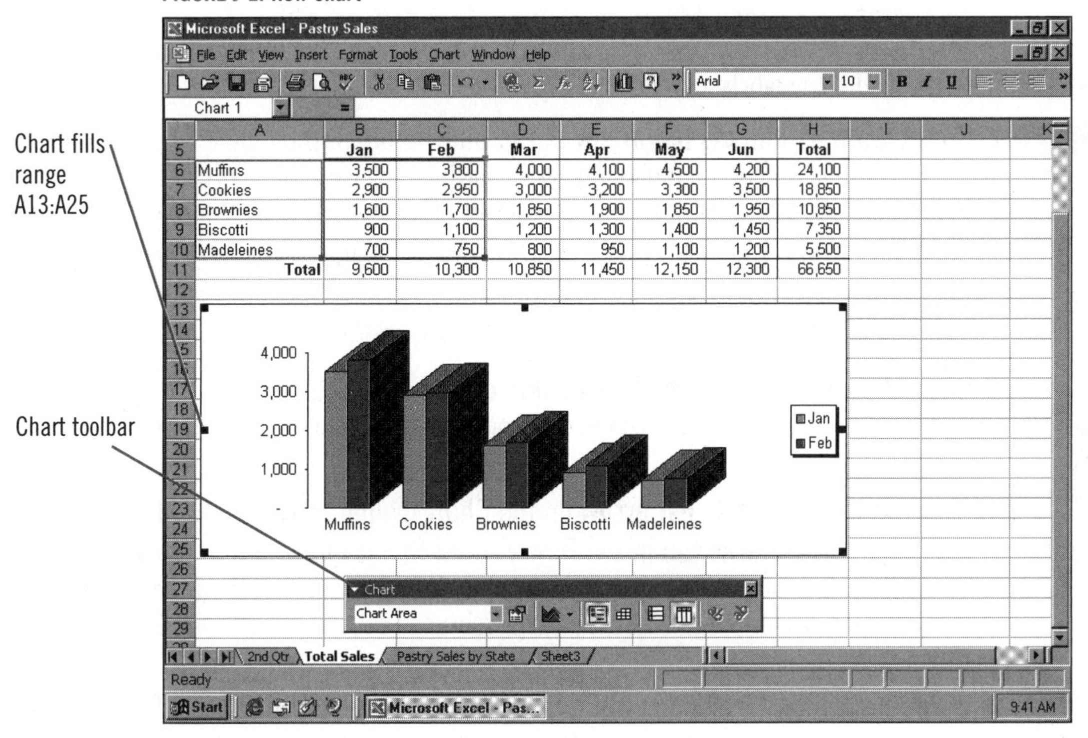

Creating a custom chart type

You can create your own custom chart type by starting with a standard chart and then adding elements (such as a legend, color, or gridlines) that suit your needs. After you've finished creating the chart, click it to activate the Chart menu on the menu bar, click Chart, click Chart type, click the Custom Types tab, then click User-defined. Click Add, then type a name for your chart type in the Name box. To use your custom chart type when creating additional charts, open the Chart Wizard dialog box, then click the User-defined button in the Custom Types tab.

Excel 2000

Customizing a Data Series

A **data series** is the information, usually numbers or values, that Excel plots on a chart. You can customize the data series in a chart easily by altering the spreadsheet range that contains the chart data *or* by entering descriptive text, called a **data label**, that appears above a data marker in a chart. As with other Excel elements, you can change the borders, patterns, or colors of a data series. Jim notices that he omitted the data for March when he created his first-quarter sales chart. He needs to add this information to make the chart accurately reflect the entire first-quarter sales. Also, he wants to customize the updated chart by adding data labels to one of the data series to make it more specific. Then he'll change the color of another data series so its respective column figures will stand out more. He starts by adding the March data.

1. If necessary, click the **chart** to select it, scroll up until **row 5** is the top row in the worksheet area, select the range **D5:D10**, position the pointer over the lower border of cell D10 until it changes to , then drag the selected range anywhere within the chart area
   The chart now includes data for the entire first quarter: January, February, and March. Next, you will add data labels to the March data series.
2. Click the **Chart Objects list arrow** in the Chart toolbar, then click **Series "Mar"**
   See Figure J-3. Selection handles appear on each of the columns representing the data for March. Now that the data series is selected, you can format it by adding labels.
3. Click the **Format Object button** on the Chart toolbar, then click the **Data Labels tab** in the Format Data Series dialog box
   The Data Labels tab opens. You want the value to appear on top of each selected data marker.
4. Under Data labels, click the **Show value option button** to select it, then click **OK**
   The data labels appear on the data markers, as shown in Figure J-4. The February data series could stand out more.
5. Click the **Chart Objects list arrow** on the Chart toolbar, click **Series "Feb"**, click , then click the **Patterns tab** in the Format Data Series dialog box
   The Patterns tab opens. See Figure J-5. The maroon color in the Sample box matches the current color displayed in the chart for the February data series. You decide that the series would show up better in a brighter shade of red.
6. Under Area, click the **red box** (third row, first color from the left), click **OK**, press **[Esc]** to deselect the data series, press **[Esc]** again to deselect the entire chart, then save the workbook
   The February data series now appears in a brighter shade of red.

QuickTip

If you have difficulty identifying the Chart Objects list arrow, rest your pointer on the first list arrow to the left on the Chart toolbar until the name "Chart Objects" appears.

QuickTip

The ToolTip name for the Format Data Series button changes, depending on what is selected. In this book it is called the Format Object button.

QuickTip

You also can click outside the chart to deselect it.

FIGURE J-3: **Selected data series**

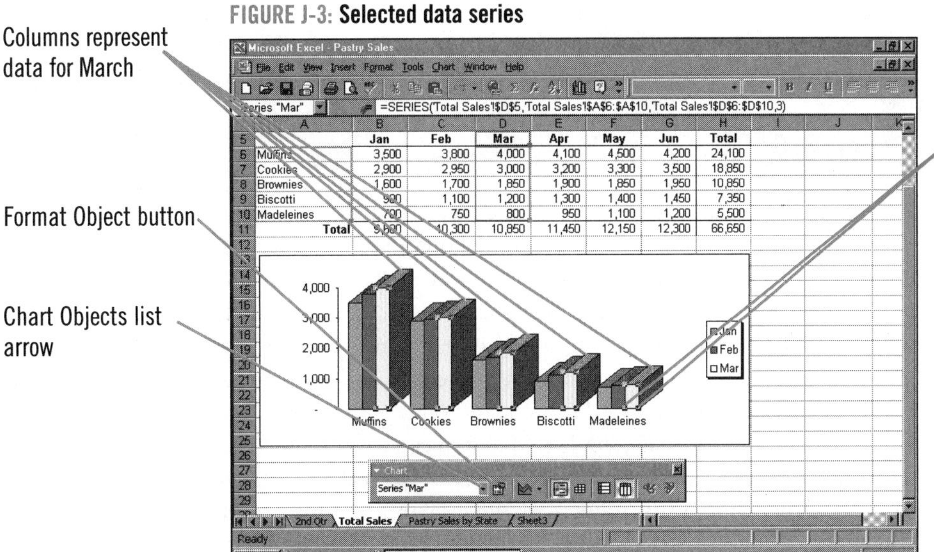

FIGURE J-4: **Chart with data labels**

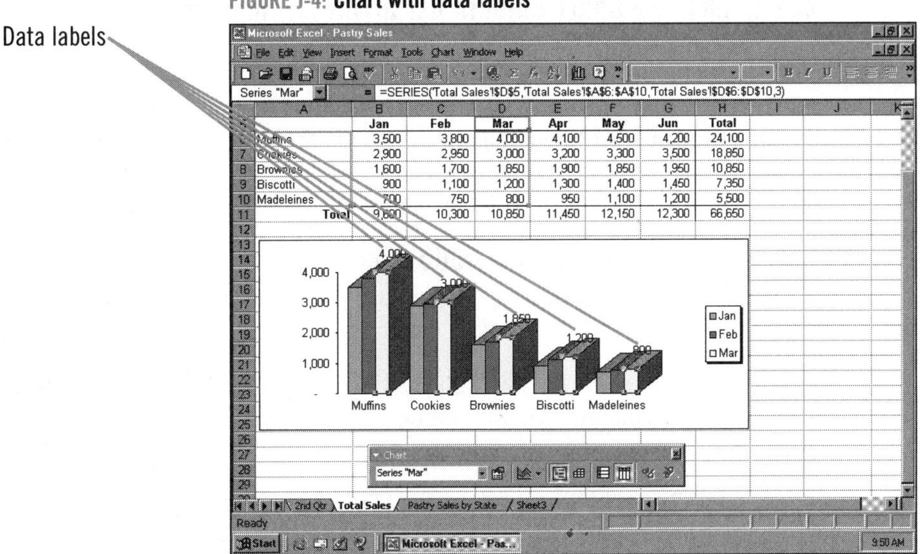

FIGURE J-5: **Patterns tab settings**

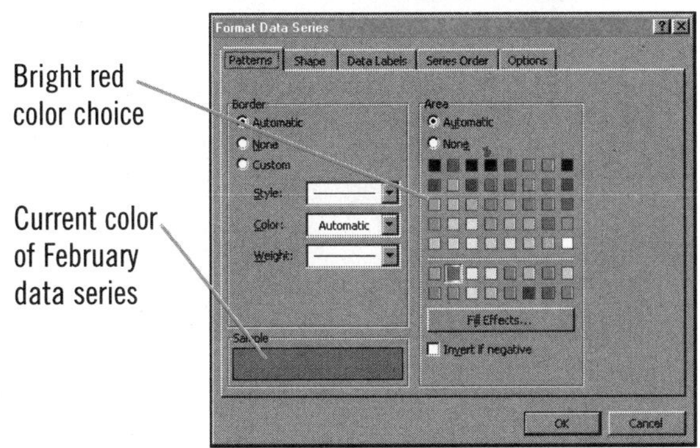

Excel 2000

Removing, inserting, and formatting legends

To insert or remove a legend, click the Legend button on the Chart toolbar to toggle the legend on or off. To format legend text, click Legend in the Chart Objects list box of the Chart toolbar. Then click the Format Object button on the Chart toolbar and choose the options you want in the Font tab.

Excel 2000

Formatting a Chart Axis

Excel automatically plots and formats all chart data and places chart axes within the chart's **plot area**. Data values in two-dimensional charts are plotted on the value (y) axis and categories are plotted on the category (x) axis. Excel creates a scale for the value (y) axis that is based on the highest and lowest values in the data series. Then Excel determines the intervals in which the values occur along the scale. In three-dimensional charts, like the one in Figure J-6, Excel generates three axes, where x remains the category axis but z becomes the value axis and y becomes the measure for the third dimension on the chart, depth. In 3-D charts, the value (z) axis usually contains the scale. For a list of the axes Excel uses to plot data, see Table J-1. You can override the Excel default formats for chart axes at any time by using the Format Axis dialog box. Because the highest column is so close to the top of the chart, Jim wants to increase the maximum number on the value axis, which in this case is the y-axis, and change its number format. To begin, he selects the object he wants to format.

Steps 1 2 3 4

1. Click the **chart**, click the **Chart Objects list arrow** on the Chart toolbar, then click **Value Axis**
   The vertical axis becomes selected.
2. Click the **Format Object button** on the Chart toolbar, then click the **Scale tab**
   The Scale tab of the Format Axis dialog box opens. The check marks under Auto indicate the default scale settings. You can override any of these settings by entering a new value.
3. In the Maximum box select **4000**, type **5000**, then click **OK**
   The chart adjusts so that 5000 appears as the maximum value on the value axis. Next, you want the minimum value to appear as a zero (0) and not as a hyphen (-).
4. With the Value Axis still selected, click on the Chart toolbar, then click the **Number tab**
   The Number tab of the Format Axis dialog box opens. Currently, a custom format is selected under Category, which instructs Excel to use a hyphen instead of 0 as the lowest value.
5. Under Category click **General**, click **OK**, press **[Esc]** twice, then save the workbook
   The chart now shows 0 as the minimum value, as shown in Figure J-7.

FIGURE J-6: Chart elements in a 3-D chart

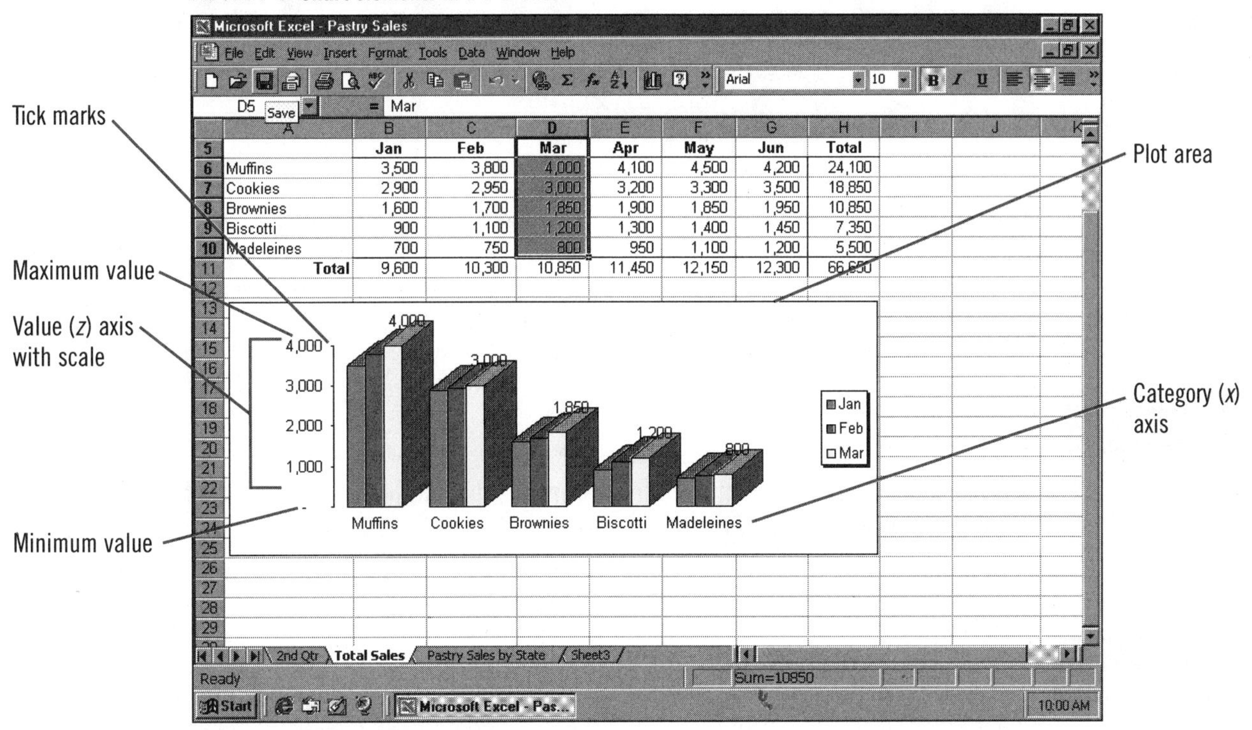

FIGURE J-7: Chart with formatted axis

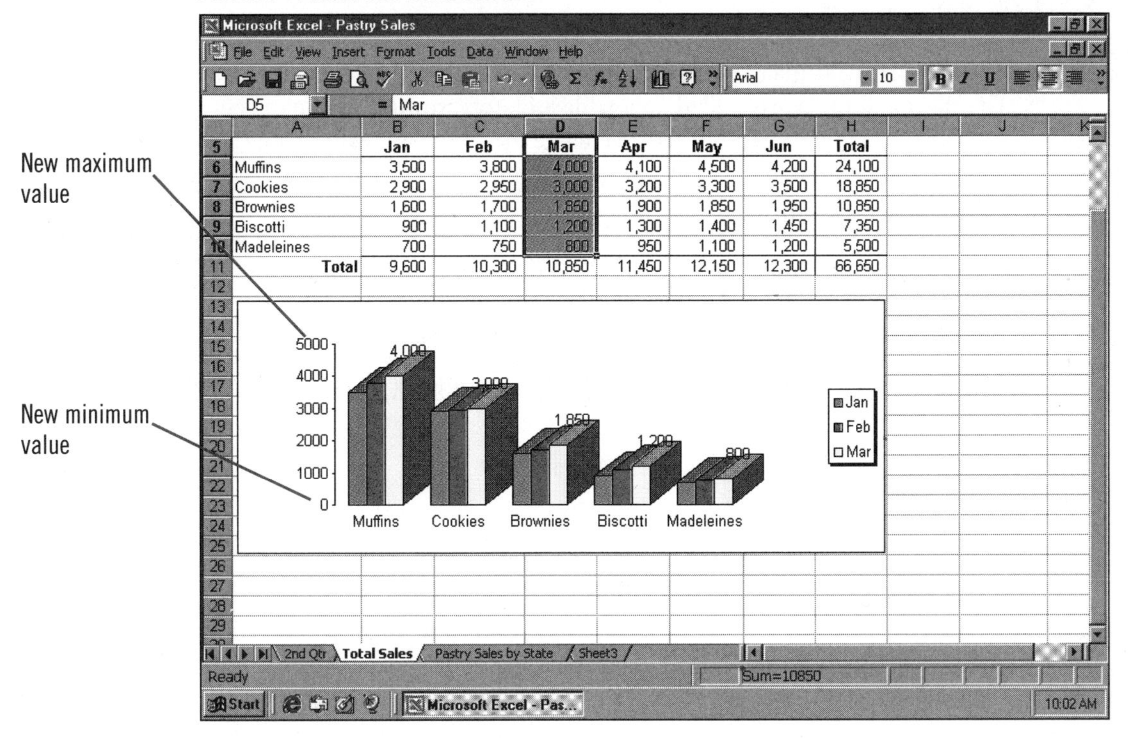

TABLE J-1: Axes used by Excel for chart formatting

axes in a two-dimensional chart	axes in a three-dimensional chart
Category (*x*) axis (horizontal)	Category (*x*) axis (horizontal)
Value (*y*) axis (vertical)	Series (*y*) axis (depth)
	Value (*z*) axis (vertical)

Adding a Data Table to a Chart

A **data table**, attached to the bottom of a chart, is a grid containing the chart data. Data tables are useful because they highlight the data used to generate a chart, which might otherwise be difficult to find. Data tables can be displayed in line, area, column, and bar charts, and print automatically along with a chart. It's good practice to add data tables to charts stored separately from worksheet data. Jim wants to emphasize the first-quarter data used to generate his chart. He decides to add a data table.

Steps

1. Click the **chart** to select it, click **Chart** on the menu bar, click **Chart Options**, then click the **Data Table tab**
   The Data Table tab in the Chart Options dialog box opens, as shown in Figure J-8. The preview window displays the selected chart.

QuickTip

You also do this when creating a chart in the Step 3 Chart Wizard dialog box.

2. Click the **Show data table check box** to select it
   The chart in the preview window changes to show what the chart will look like with a data table added to the bottom. See Figure J-9. The data table crowds the chart labels, making them hard to read. (Your chart may look slightly different.) You'll fix this problem after you close the Chart Options dialog box.

QuickTip

To hide a data table, open the Data Table tab in the Chart Options dialog box, then clear the Show data table check box.

3. Click **OK**, then, if necessary, scroll down to display the chart
   The chart and the newly added data table look too crowded inside the current chart area. If you were to drag the chart borders to enlarge the chart, you wouldn't be able to see the entire chart displayed on the screen. It's more convenient to move the chart to its own sheet.
4. If necessary, click the **chart** to select it, click **Chart** on the menu bar, click **Location**, click the **As new sheet option button** under Place chart, click **OK**
   The chart is now located on a new sheet, where it is fully displayed in the worksheet window. See Figure J-10.
5. Put your name in the sheet footer, save the workbook, then print the chart sheet

FIGURE J-8: Data Table tab settings

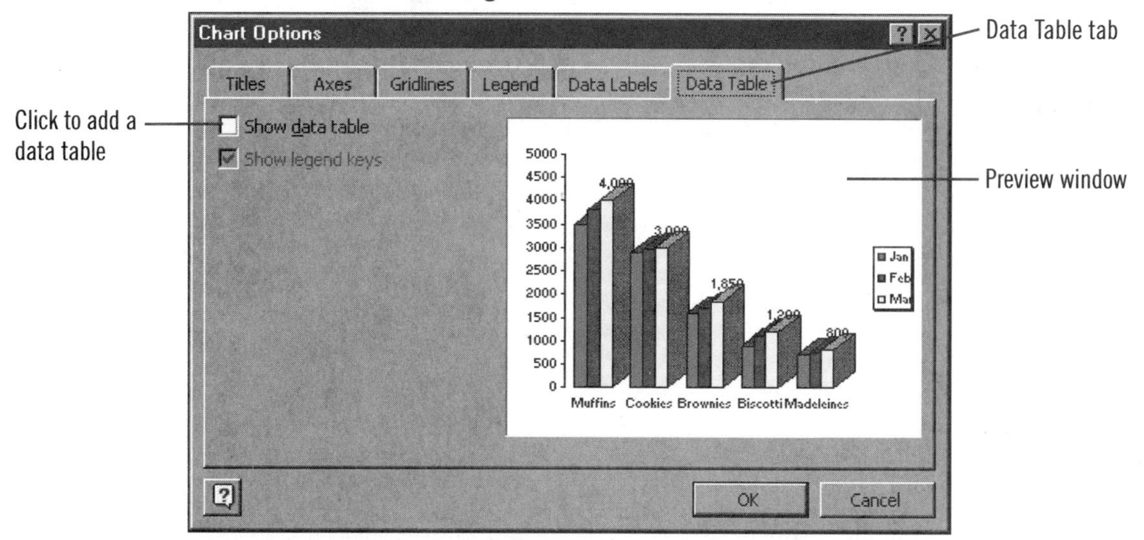

FIGURE J-9: Show Data Table box selected

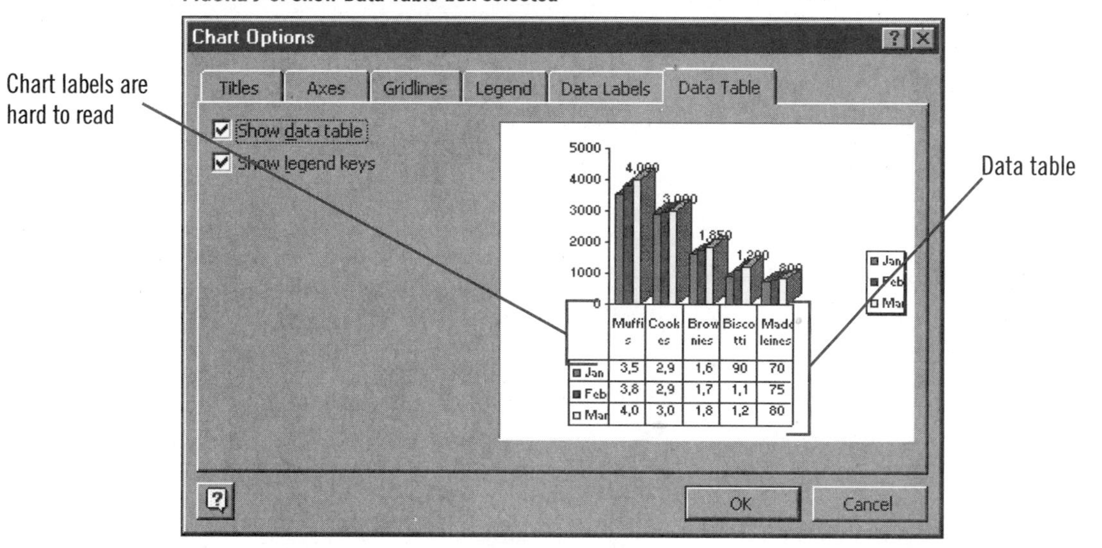

FIGURE J-10: Chart moved to chart sheet

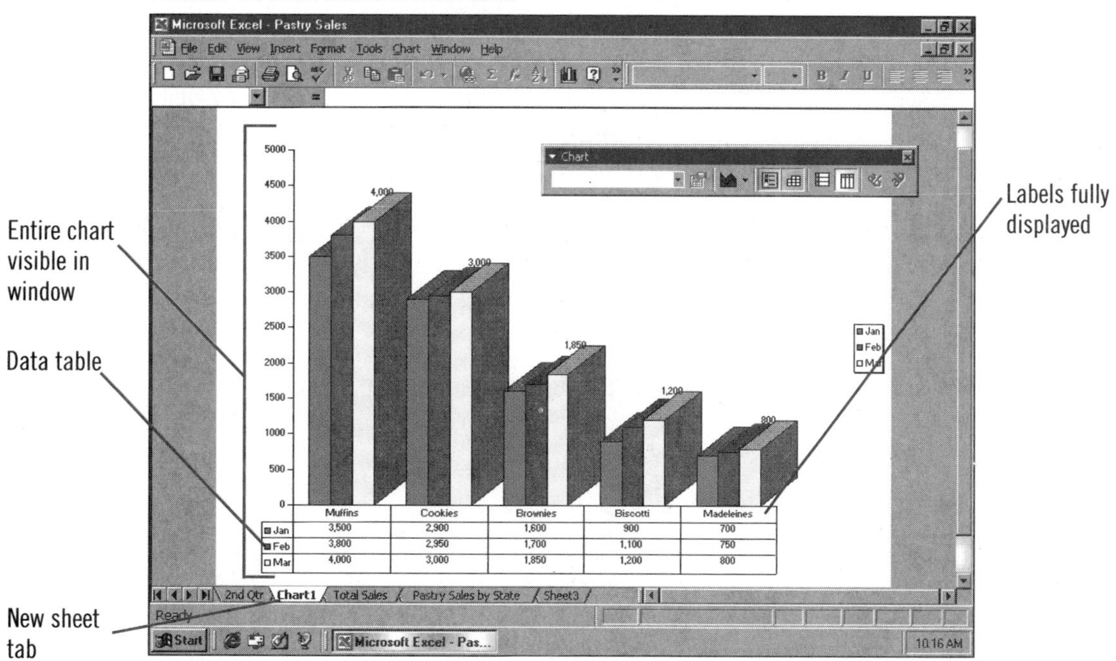

Rotating a Chart

Three-dimensional (3-D) charts do not always display data in the most effective way. In many cases, data in these charts can be obscured by one or more of the chart's data markers. By rotating and/or elevating the axes, you can improve the visibility of the chart's data. With Excel, you can adjust the rotation and elevation of a 3-D chart by dragging it with the mouse or using the 3-D View command on the Chart menu. Jim's workbook already contains a 3-D chart illustrating the sales data for the second quarter. He will display that chart, then rotate it so that the June columns are easier to see.

Steps

1. Click the **2nd Qtr sheet tab**, click the **Chart Objects list arrow** on the Chart toolbar, then click **Corners**
   Selection handles appear on the corners of the chart, as shown in Figure J-11.
2. Click the **lower-right corner handle** of the chart, press and hold the left mouse button, then drag the chart left approximately 2" until it looks like the object shown in Figure J-12, then release the mouse button
   The June columns are still not clearly visible. When using the dragging method to rotate a three-dimensional chart, you might need to make several attempts before you're satisfied with the view. It's usually more efficient to use the 3-D View option on the Chart menu.
3. Click **Chart** on the menu bar, click **3-D View**, then drag the **3-D View dialog box** to the upper-right corner of the screen
   See Figure J-13. The preview box in the 3-D View dialog box allows you to preview changes to the chart's orientation in the worksheet.
4. Click **Default**
   The chart returns to its original position. Next, Jim decreases the chart's elevation, the height from which the chart is viewed.
5. To the left of the preview box, click the **Decrease Elevation button**
   Notice how the preview image of the chart changes when you change the elevation.
6. Click **Apply**
   As the number in the Elevation box decreases, the viewpoint shifts downward. Note that the chart gains some vertical tick marks. Next, you'll change the rotation and **perspective**, or depth, of the chart.
7. In the Rotation box, select the current value, then type **55**; in the Perspective box, select the current value, type **0**, then click **Apply**
   The chart is reformatted. You notice, however, that the columns appear crowded. To correct this problem, you change the height as a percent of the chart base.
8. In the Height box, select the current value, type **70**, click **Apply**, then click **OK**
   The 3-D View dialog box closes. The chart columns now appear less crowded, making the chart easier to read.
9. Save your work

Trouble?

Don't worry if your 3-D View dialog box settings are different from the ones shown in Figure J-13.

Trouble?

If you have difficulty locating the Decrease Elevation button, refer to Figure J-13.

FIGURE J-11: Chart corners selected

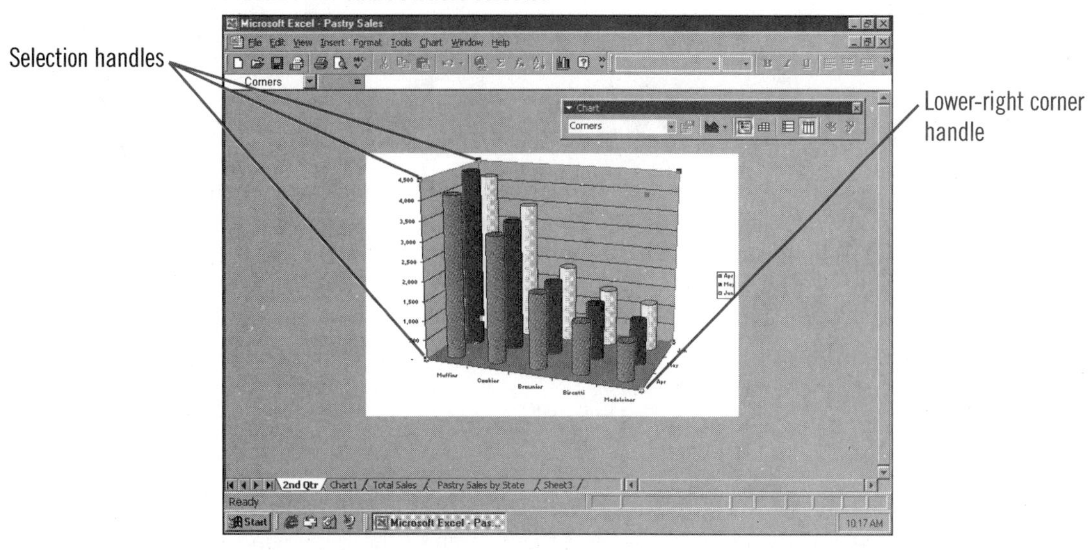

FIGURE J-12: Chart rotation in progress

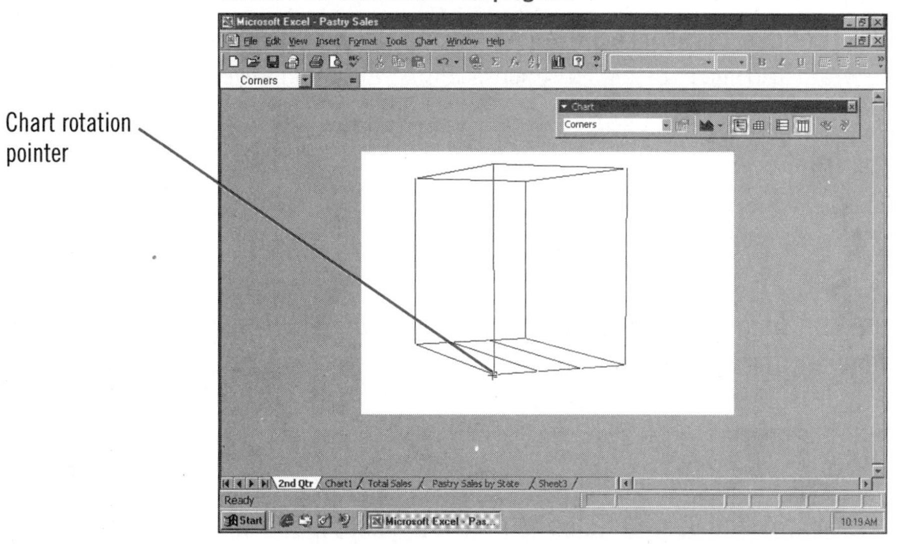

FIGURE J-13: Screen with chart and 3-D View dialog box

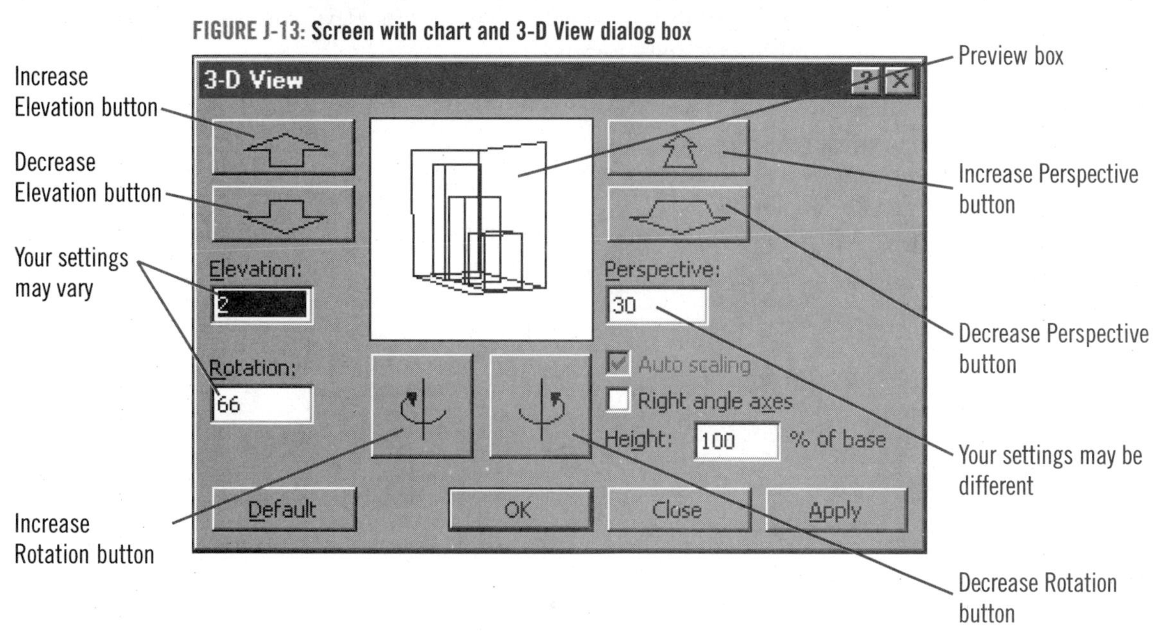

Excel 2000

Excel 2000

Enhancing a Chart with WordArt

You can enhance your chart or worksheet by adding specially formatted text using the WordArt tool on the Drawing toolbar. Once you've added a piece of WordArt to your workbook, you can edit or format it using the tools on the WordArt toolbar. Text formatted as WordArt is considered a drawing object rather than text. This means that WordArt objects cannot be treated as if they were labels entered in a cell; that is, you cannot sort, spell check, or use their cell references in formulas. Jim decides to add a WordArt title to the second-quarter chart. He begins by displaying the Drawing toolbar.

1. Click the **Drawing button** on the Standard toolbar
   The Drawing toolbar appears at the bottom of the Excel window. The WordArt text will be your chart title.
2. Click the **Insert WordArt button** on the Drawing toolbar
   The WordArt Gallery dialog box opens. This is where you select the style for your text.
3. In the second row, click the **second style from the left**, as shown in Figure J-14; then click **OK**
   The Edit WordArt Text dialog box opens, as shown in Figure J-15. This is where you enter the text you want to format as WordArt. You also can adjust the point size or font of the text or select bold or italic styles.
4. Type **2nd Quarter Sales**, click the **Bold button**, if necessary select **Times New Roman** in the Font list box and **36** in the Size list box, then click **OK**
   The Edit WordArt Text dialog box closes, and the chart reappears with the new title in the middle of the chart.

QuickTip

To delete a piece of WordArt, click it to make sure it is selected, then press [Delete].

5. Place the pointer over 2nd Quarter Sales (the WordArt title) until the pointer changes to ✥, then drag **2nd Quarter Sales** up until it appears in the upper-right corner of the chart
   The title is repositioned as shown in Figure J-16. Next, you decide to edit the WordArt to change "2nd" to the word "Second."
6. Click **Edit Text** on the WordArt toolbar, double-click **2nd** in the Edit WordArt Text box, type **Second**, then click **OK**
   The Edit WordArt Text dialog box closes, and the edited title appears over the chart.
7. Press **[Esc]** to deselect the WordArt, click , put your name in the chart sheet footer, save the workbook, then print the sheet

QuickTip

To change the style of a piece of WordArt, click the WordArt Gallery button on the WordArt toolbar and select a new style.

FIGURE J-14: Selecting a WordArt style

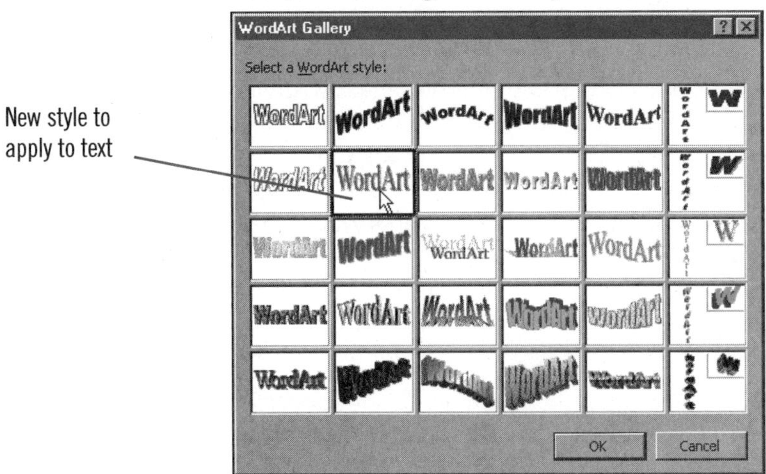

FIGURE J-15: Entering the WordArt text

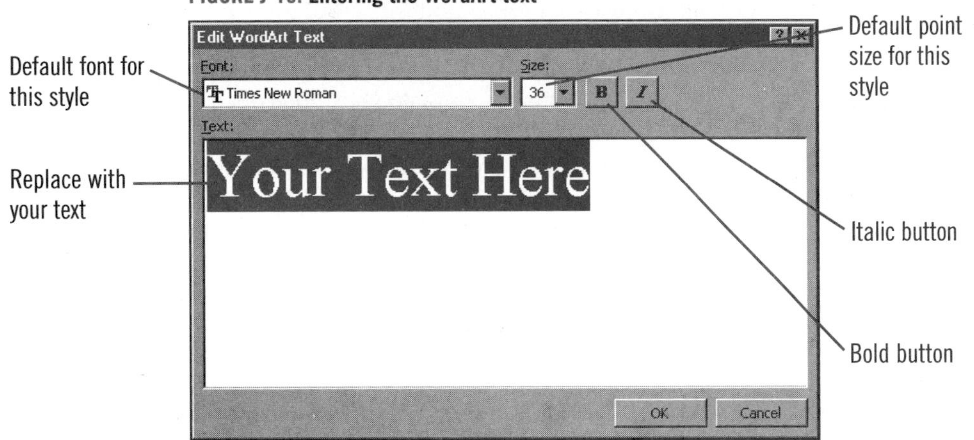

FIGURE J-16: Positioning the WordArt

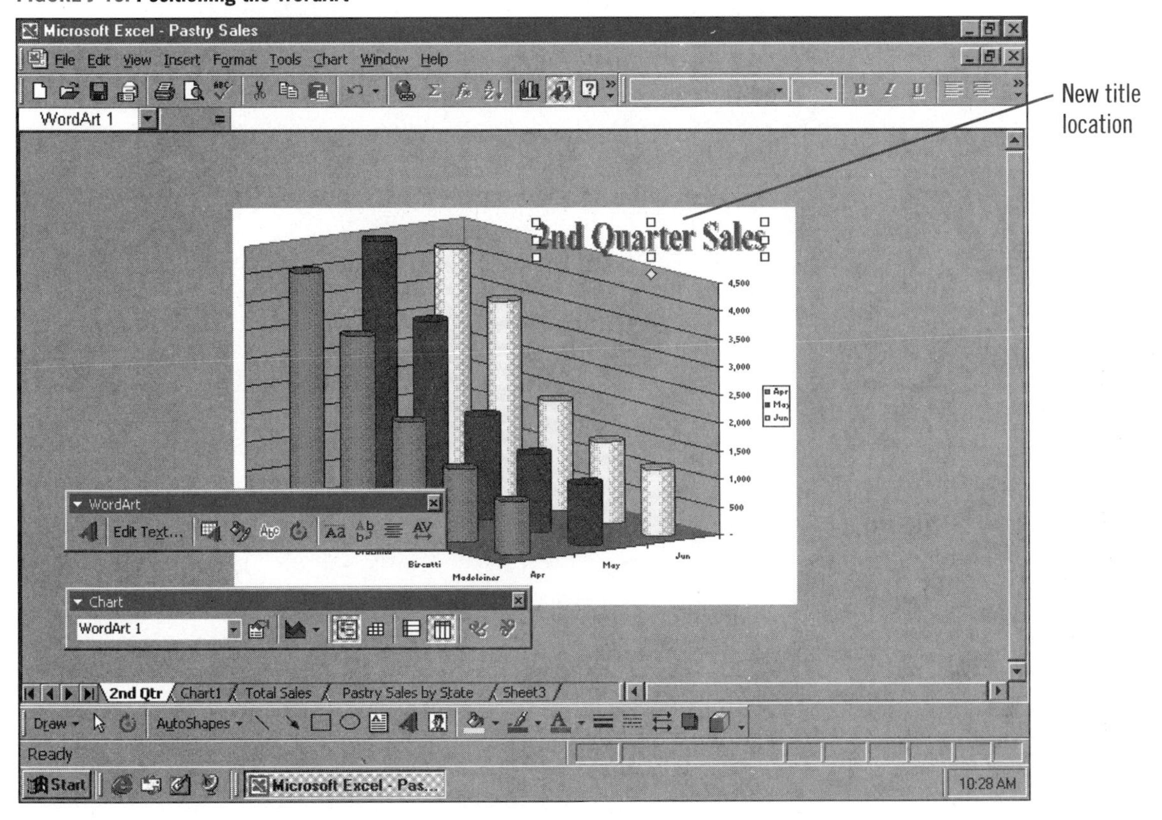

Excel 2000

Excel 2000

Rotating Text

By rotating text within a worksheet cell, you can draw attention to column labels or titles without turning the text into a drawing object (as in WordArt). Unlike WordArt, rotated text retains its usefulness as a worksheet entry, which means you can still sort it, spell check it, and use its cell reference in formulas. Now that he's finished enhancing the two charts in his workbook, Jim wants to improve the worksheet's appearance. He decides to rotate the column labels in cells B5 through G5.

Steps

1. **Click the Total Sales sheet tab, make sure row 5 is the top row in the worksheet area, then select cells B5:G5**
2. **Click Format on the menu bar, click Cells, then click the Alignment tab**
   The Alignment tab of the Format Cells dialog box opens. See Figure J-17. The settings under Orientation enable you to change the rotation of cell entries. Clicking the Vertical Text box on the left (the narrow one) allows you to display text vertically in the cell. To rotate the text to another angle, drag the rotation indicator in the Right Text box to the angle you want, or type the degree of angle you want in the Degrees box. You'll use the Degrees box to rotate the text entries.
3. **Double-click the Degrees box, type 45, then click OK**
   The Format Cells dialog box closes.
4. **If necessary, scroll up until row 1 is the top row in the worksheet area, then click cell A1**
   The column labels for January through June now appear at a 45-degree angle in their cells, as shown in Figure J-18. The worksheet is now finished.
5. **Put your name in the sheet footer, then save and print the worksheet**

FIGURE J-17: Alignment tab settings

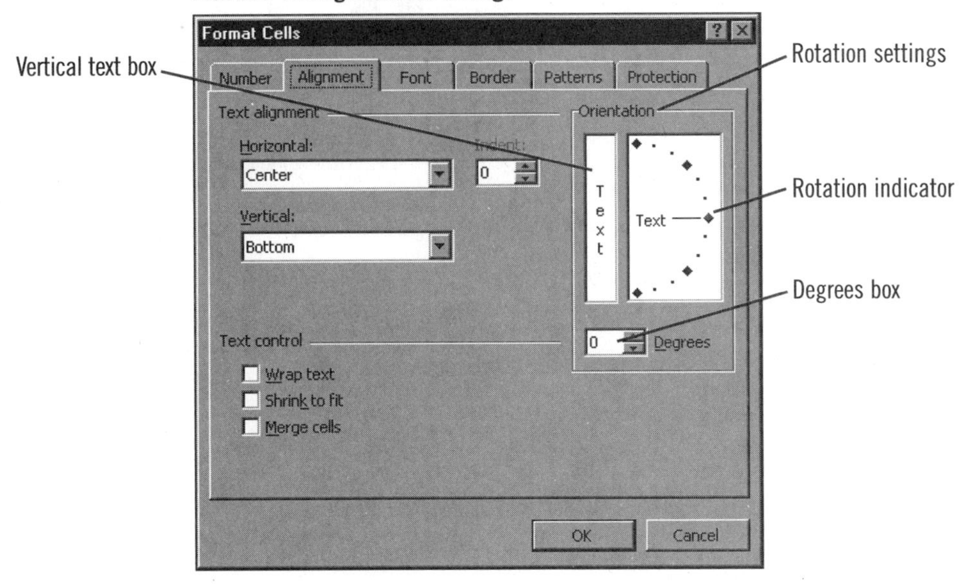

FIGURE J-18: Rotated column labels

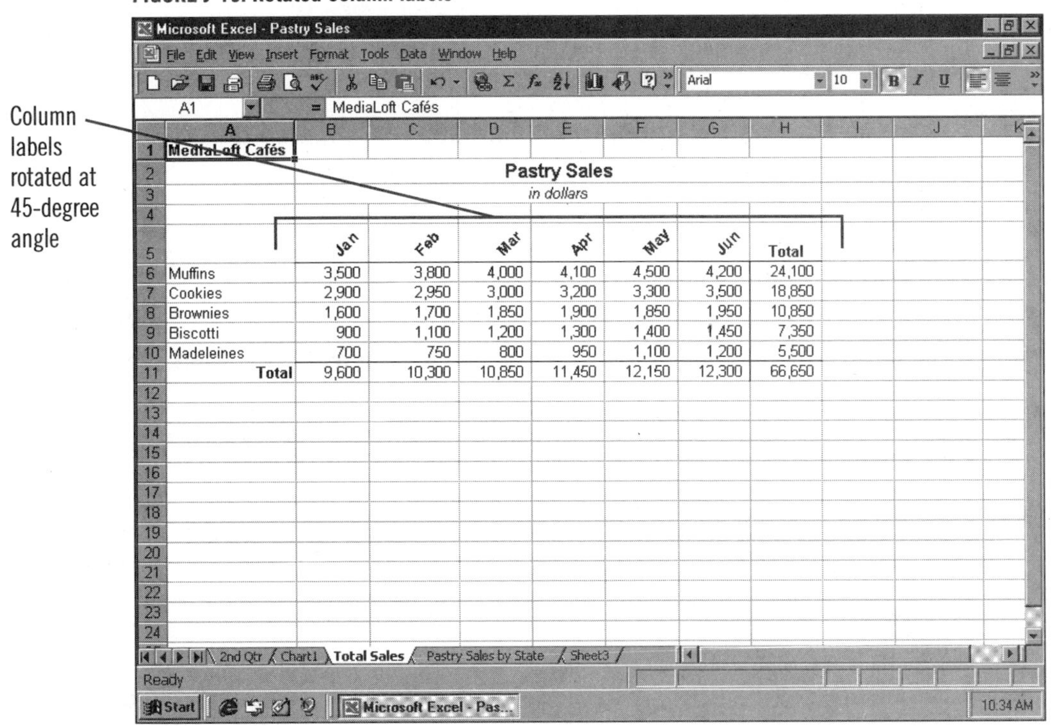

Rotating chart labels

You can easily rotate the category labels on a chart by using the buttons on the Chart toolbar. First, you select the Category Axis in the Chart Objects list box. Then you click either the Angle Text Downward button or the Angle Text Upward button on the Chart toolbar.

Excel 2000

Mapping Data

A **data map** shows geographic features and their associated data. To create a simple data map, arrange your worksheet data in two columns—with the first containing geographic data, such as the names of countries or states, and the second column containing the related data. Jim has compiled detailed sales figures for pastry by state. Now, he wants to create a map that clearly illustrates which states have the highest sales. He begins by selecting the data he wants to map.

Steps 1 2 3 4

1. **Click the Pastry Sales by State sheet tab, then select the range A4:B11**
   The first column of data contains the state names and the second contains the sales figures for each state. The column labels in row 4 (which you also selected) will be used in the legend title.

2. **Click the Map button on the Standard toolbar, drag the crosshair pointer from the middle of cell C4 to the lower-right corner of cell H23, then release the mouse button**
   The map range is outlined on the worksheet, and the Multiple Maps Available dialog box opens on top.

3. **Click United States (AK & HI Inset) if necessary, then click OK**
   The map and the Microsoft Map Control dialog boxes appear.

4. **Drag the Microsoft Map Control dialog box to the lower-left corner of the screen, then scroll up until most of the map is visible on your screen**
   See Figure J-19. Excel automatically divides the sales data into intervals and assigns a different shade of gray to each interval, as the map legend indicates. The rectangular border indicates that the map is in Edit mode.

5. **Double-click the United States (AK & HI Inset) map title, select the default text in the Edit Text Object dialog box, type MediaLoft Pastry Sales, then click OK**
   The new title replaces the default map title. Next, to highlight the sales data more dramatically, you'll change the way values are represented using the Microsoft Map Control dialog box, shown in Figure J-20. You adjust the way data is represented on the map by dragging format buttons into the Format box. You want to change the format from shading to dots of varying density.

6. **Click the Dot Density button in the Microsoft Map Control dialog box, then drag it over the top of the Value Shading button in the Format box**
   When you release the mouse button, the map display changes from shading to dots, with one dot equal to $6,000 in pastry sales.

7. **Click Map on the Menu bar, click Features, under Fill Color click the Custom option button, click the Custom list arrow, click the turquoise square, then click OK**
   The map's background color changes to turquoise, as shown in Figure J-21. The legend could be more descriptive.

8. **Double-click the map legend; click the Legend Options tab in the Format Properties dialog box if necessary; select the default text in the Title box, type 1st and 2nd Quarter, then click OK**

9. **Press [Esc] three times to deselect the map, put your name in the sheet footer, save the workbook, print the worksheet, and exit Excel**

Trouble?
If you don't see the Map button, click Tools on the menu bar, click Command, and click Insert. Then under Commands, scroll to the Map icon and drag it to the Standard toolbar.

QuickTip
Click the Map Refresh button to incorporate any changes to the data range into an existing map.

Trouble?
If your map doesn't print, your printer may not have enough memory. Try using another printer.

FIGURE J-19: Newly created map

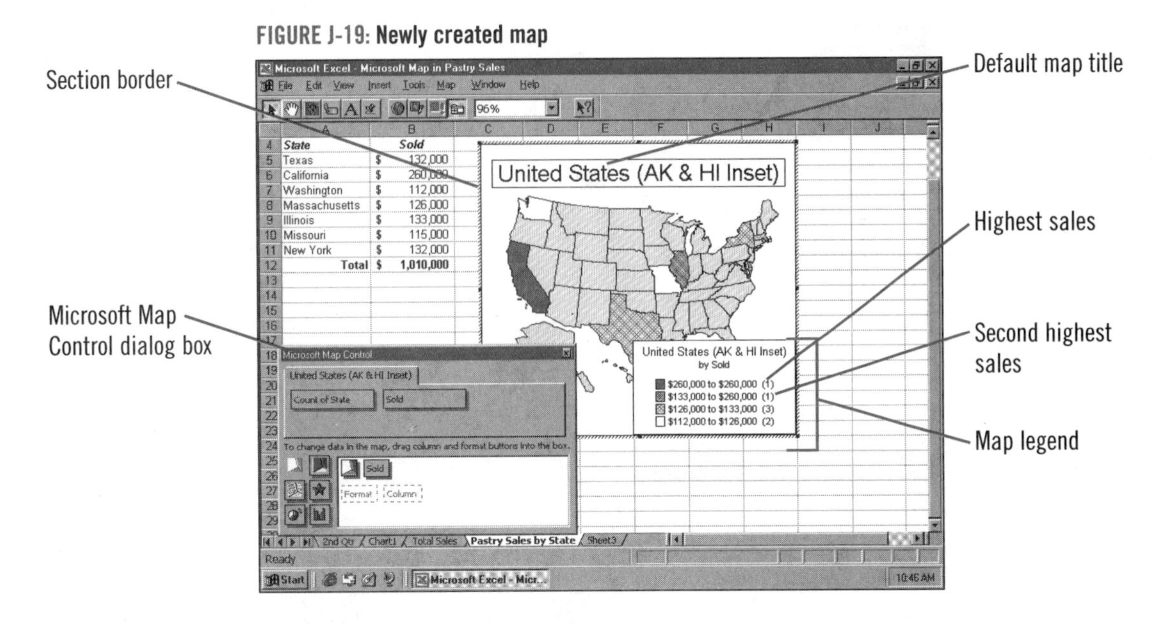

FIGURE J-20: Microsoft Map Control dialog box

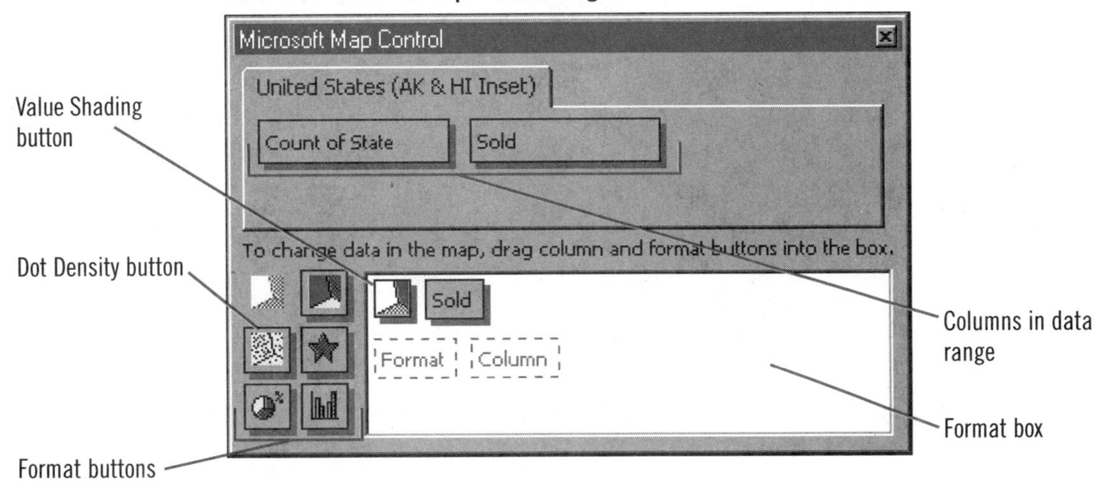

FIGURE J-21: Values formatted as dots

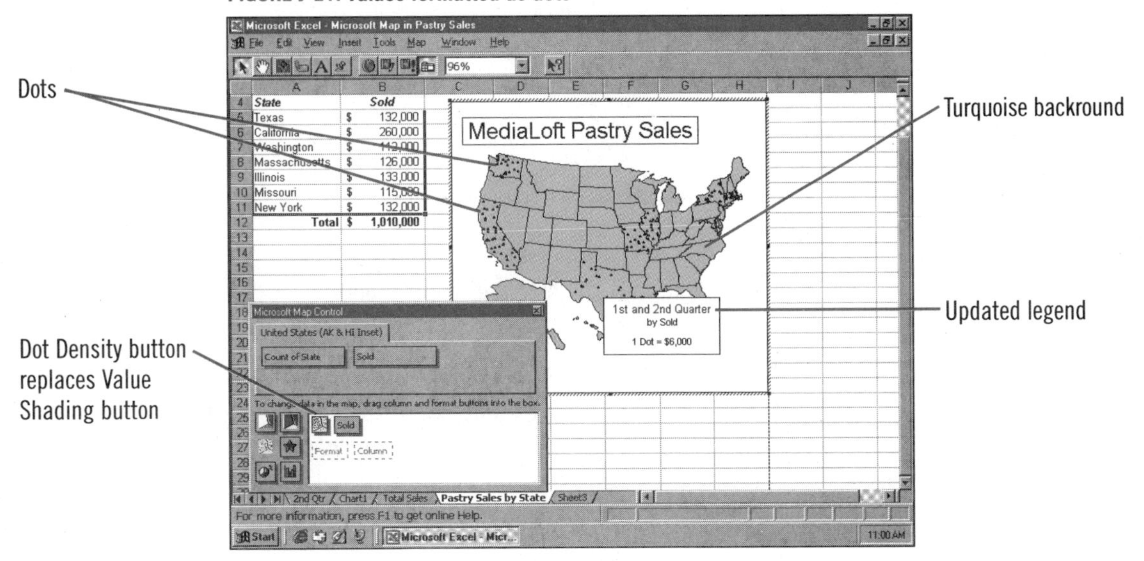

Practice

► Concepts Review

Label each element of the Excel screen shown in Figure J-22.

FIGURE J-22

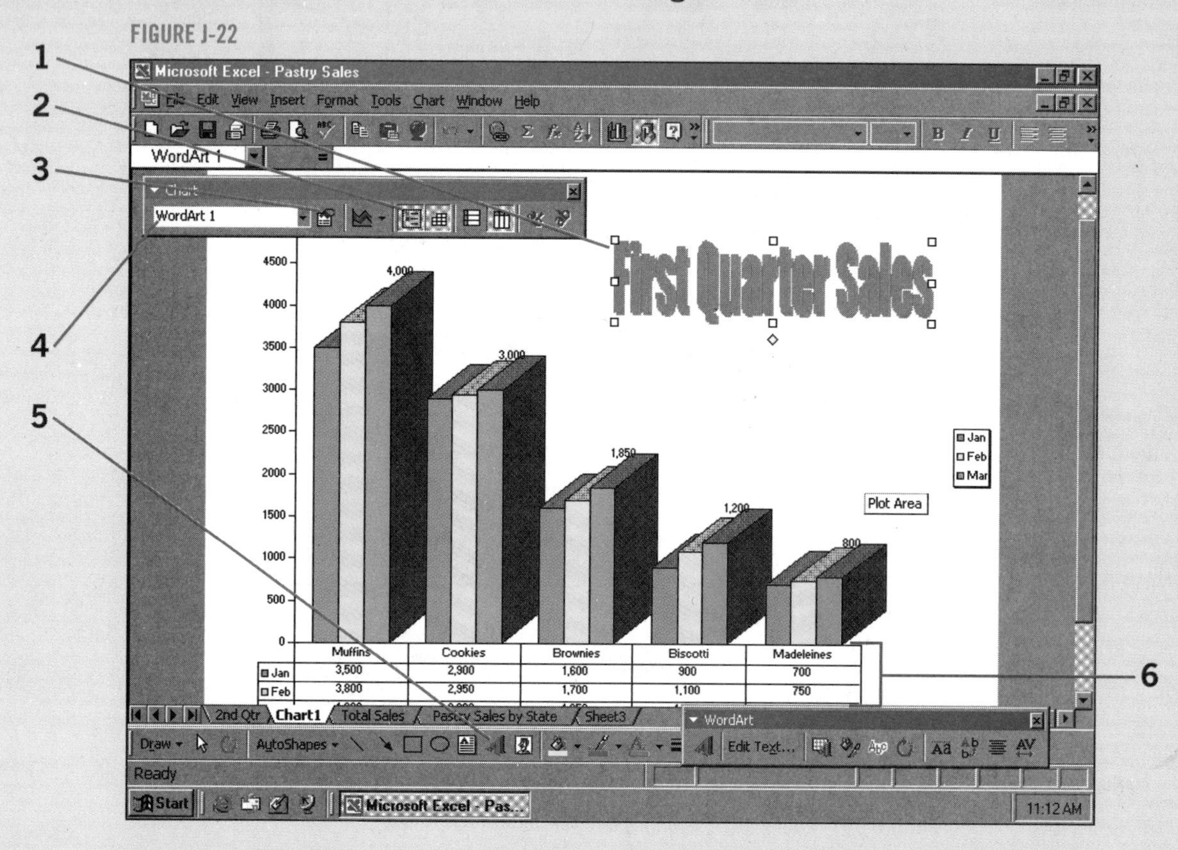

Match each button with the statement that describes it.

7.
8.
9.
10.
11.

a. Opens the WordArt dialog boxes
b. Use to format the selected chart object
c. Use to create a data map
d. Use to change the style of a piece of WordArt
e. Use to display the Drawing toolbar

Select the best answer from the list of choices.

12. A chart's scale
- **a.** Appears on the category (*x*) axis.
- **b.** Displays values on the value (*y*) axis or the value (*z*) axis.
- **c.** Always appears on the value (*y*) axis.
- **d.** Cannot be modified.

13. What is the most efficient method of rotating a 3-D chart?
- **a.** Click Edit on the menu bar, then click Default.
- **b.** Adjust settings in the 3-D View dialog box.
- **c.** Select the chart corners, then drag a corner.
- **d.** Delete the chart, and start over with a new one.

14. How can you change the way data is represented on a map?
- **a.** Drag format buttons in the Microsoft Data Control dialog box.
- **b.** Click Map, then click Data Representation.
- **c.** Click the Map Refresh button.
- **d.** None of the above.

15. Which statement best describes the difference between two- and three-dimensional column charts?
- **a.** Two-dimensional charts have category (*x*) and value (*y*) axes; three-dimensional charts have category (*x*), series (*y*), and value (*z*) axes.
- **b.** Two-dimensional charts show the data in three dimensions.
- **c.** Three-dimensional charts show the data in four dimensions.
- **d.** Two-dimensional charts have a value scale on the *x*-axis, and three-dimensional charts have a value scale on the *z*-axis.

16. What is a data table?
- **a.** A three-dimensional arrangement of data on the *y*-axis.
- **b.** Worksheet data arranged geographically.
- **c.** A customized data series.
- **d.** The data used to create a chart displayed in a grid.

17. A custom chart type
- **a.** Is supplied only by Excel.
- **b.** Can be supplied by Excel or the user.
- **c.** Cannot be saved.
- **d.** All of the above.

18. To rotate text in a worksheet cell,
- **a.** Adjust settings on the Alignment tab of the Format cells dialog box.
- **b.** Click the Rotate button on the Standard toolbar.
- **c.** Select the text, then drag to rotate it the desired number of degrees.
- **d.** Format the text as WordArt, then drag the WordArt.

▶ Skills Review

1. Select a custom chart type.
- **a.** Open the workbook titled EX J-2, then save it as "MediaLoft Coffee Sales".
- **b.** On the 1st Quarter sheet, select the range A4:B7.
- **c.** Open the Chart Wizard, and on the Custom Types tab in the Chart Wizard dialog box, make sure the Built-in option button is selected.
- **d.** Select Blue Pie in the Chart type box.
- **e.** Go to the Step 2 Chart Wizard dialog box.
- **f.** Make sure the data range is correct, then go to the Step 3 Chart Wizard dialog box, read the contents, then go to the Step 4 Chart Wizard dialog box.
- **g.** Make sure the As Object In button is selected, then finish the Wizard.
- **h.** Drag the chart to a better location in the worksheet.
- **i.** Put your name in the sheet footer, then save, preview, and print the worksheet data and chart.

2. Customize a data series.
- **a.** On the 2nd Quarter sheet, move the June data in D4:D7 into the chart area.
- **b.** Select the April data series and display its data labels.
- **c.** Use the Format Data Series dialog box to change the color of the May data series to the green color of your choice.
- **d.** Save the workbook.

3. Format a chart axis.
- **a.** Select the value axis.
- **b.** Set its maximum to 10000 and its minimum to 0.
- **c.** On the Number tab in the Format Axis dialog box under Category, use the Currency format to add a dollar sign and two decimal places to the values, then close the dialog box.
- **d.** Save the workbook.

4. Add a data table to a chart.
- **a.** Show the data table.
- **b.** Use the Location command on the Chart menu to move the chart to its own sheet.
- **c.** Display the 3rd Quarter sheet tab.
- **d.** Use the Data Table tab in the Chart Options dialog box to hide the data table.
- **e.** Remove the chart legend.
- **f.** Save the workbook.

5. Rotate a chart.
- **a.** On the Chart1 sheet, use the Chart Objects list arrow to select the chart corners.
- **b.** Drag a chart corner to rotate the chart.
- **c.** Return the chart to its default rotation using the 3-D View command on the Chart menu.
- **d.** Change the rotation to 315.
- **e.** Change the elevation to 13.
- **f.** Deselect the chart corners.
- **g.** Save the workbook.

6. Enhance a chart with WordArt.

- **a.** Display the Drawing toolbar.
- **b.** Open WordArt and select the second style from the right in the second row.
- **c.** In the Edit WordArt Text dialog box, enter the text "Second Quarter Sales" and format it in italic.
- **d.** Position the new title above the chart.
- **e.** Make sure the WordArt is still selected, then use the WordArt Gallery button on the WordArt toolbar to select a new style for the title.
- **f.** Save the workbook.
- **g.** Close the Drawing toolbar.

7. Rotate text.

- **a.** On the 1st Quarter sheet tab, select cells B4:D4.
- **b.** Change the alignment to 45 degrees.
- **c.** On the 2nd Quarter sheet tab, select the range B4:D4.
- **d.** Use the rotation indicator on the Alignment tab in the Format Cells dialog box to change the rotation to 45 degrees.
- **e.** On the 3rd Quarter sheet tab, rotate the Category Axis labels downward.
- **f.** Save the workbook.

8. Map worksheet data.

- **a.** Make the Mail Order Contacts sheet active.
- **b.** Select the range A4:B16.
- **c.** Start Microsoft Map.
- **d.** Position the map in the range C4:H23, and use the United States (AK & HI Inset) map.
- **e.** Change the map title to "Western Region Contacts".
- **f.** Change the map's background color to bright pink.
- **g.** Change the data formatting to dot density.
- **h.** Change the legend title to "Mail Order".
- **i.** In cell B9, change the data for California to 25.
- **j.** Double-click the map to put it in Edit mode, then click the Map Refresh button on the Map toolbar to update the map.
- **k.** Put your name in the sheet footer, save the workbook, then select, preview, and print each sheet in the workbook.

► Independent Challenges

1. You are the owner of Sandwich Express, a metropolitan delicatessen. Each week, you order several pounds of cheese: Cheddar, Monterey Jack, Swiss, Provolone, and American. Last month was especially busy, and you ordered an increasing amount of cheese each week in every category except American, which is declining in popularity. Recently, your spouse has joined you in the business and wants to develop a more efficient forecast of the amount of cheese to order each week. To help your spouse analyze last month's cheese orders, you developed a worksheet with a three-dimensional stacked bar chart. Now, you want to enhance the chart by adding data labels, reformatting the value (*z*) axis, increasing the elevation, and adding several titles.

To complete this independent challenge:

- **a.** Open the workbook titled EX J-3, then save it as "Cheese Order Tracking".
- **b.** Customize the data series. Add the data for 8/22 and 8/29 to the chart. Then add data labels to all data markers.
- **c.** Reformat the value (*z*) axis to show values every 40 pounds instead of every 50 pounds.

d. Increase the chart's elevation.
e. Add a WordArt title that reads "Cheese Ordered in August".
f. Move the chart to a chart sheet and add a data table.
g. Put your name in the footer of each sheet, preview and print the worksheet and chart together, then save the workbook.

2. As the owner of Sandwich Express, you meet quarterly with your dairy product salesman, James Snyder, to discuss trends in dairy product usage at your delicatessen. These quarterly meetings seem to take longer than necessary, and you are not always sure he has retained all the information discussed. You decide to use charts to communicate during these meetings. As part of your presentation at the end of the third quarter, you decide to generate an additional chart showing what percentage of the total cheese orders for each month each cheese type represents, starting with August. Because this chart will compare parts of a whole, you create a three-dimensional pie chart. Also, to ensure the intended messages are communicated effectively, you add a few enhancements to the chart and worksheet. First, you need to add totals to the worksheet.

To complete this independent challenge:

a. Open the workbook titled EX J-3, then save it as "Cheese Order Pie".
b. Select and delete the current 3-D bar chart from the worksheet.
c. Add monthly totals in column G that total each cheese type across all five weeks. Then calculate a grand total for the month. (*Hint*: To double-check your monthly total, add totals for each week in row 10. Then insert totals for each week, select the totals in B10:F10, and note the sum in the AutoCalculate box in the Status bar.)
d. Use the Chart Wizard to create a custom chart showing what percentage of the total cheese ordered in August (1,745 pounds) each type of cheese represents. (*Hint*: Use the Control key to select nonadjacent ranges of cheese types and totals to be charted before you open the Chart Wizard.) Place the chart on its own sheet.
e. Add the WordArt title "Sandwich Express—August Cheese Orders".
f. Add an italicized WordArt subtitle that reads "(% of total pounds ordered)".
g. In the August worksheet, rotate the dates in row 4 to a 45-degree angle.
h. Put your name in the footer of each sheet, review and save the workbook, then print the worksheet and the chart.

3. You are a real estate agent for Galaxy Properties, which specializes in residential real estate. In September, you were voted salesperson of the month. Your sales manager has asked you to assemble a brief presentation on your sales activity during September to show to the new agents in the office. You decide to include a chart showing how many properties you closed and their respective dollar amounts in each of three areas: single-family homes, condominiums, and townhouses. Using your own data, create a worksheet and accompanying chart to present the data. Enhance the chart as outlined in the following.

To complete this independent challenge:

a. Create a new workbook, then save it as "September Sales, Galaxy Properties".
b. Enter your own worksheet labels, data, and formulas.
c. Create a custom bar chart showing your September sales activity.
d. Include data labels on the condominium data series.
e. Add a WordArt title.
f. Add new data to the worksheet for rental properties, then add the data series to the chart.
g. Move the chart to a chart sheet and add a data table.
h. Rotate the column labels in the worksheet.
i. Put your name in the sheet footers, preview and print the worksheet and chart, then save the workbook.

4. Maria Abbott of the MediaLoft Sales department has asked you to chart some information from a recent survey of MediaLoft book customers.

To complete this independent challenge:

a. Connect to the Internet, and go to the MediaLoft intranet site at http://www.course.com/Illustrated/MediaLoft. Click the Marketing link, then click the Book Survey Results link. Print the results of the survey. Disconnect from the Internet.

b. Open a new Excel worksheet and save it as "Book Survey". Enter the occupation information in question 5 of the survey, and chart it using a pie chart of your choice on the same sheet. Enlarge the chart to be as large as possible while still fitting on the screen.

c. Move the chart to a separate sheet; name the sheet "Occupation".

d. Reformat one of the pie slices by single-clicking the chart, then single-clicking a slice. Format the area with a new color.

e. Chart the # of children data in question 9 as a horizontal bar chart. Do not add a legend or a title. Place it on a sheet named "Children".

f. Add a WordArt Title to each chart.

g. Rotate the category axis labels on the Children sheet so they point downward and to the right.

h. Put your name in the sheet footers, save the workbook, print all three sheets, then exit Excel.

▶ Visual Workshop

Create the worksheet and accompanying custom chart shown in Figure J-23. Save the workbook as "The Dutch Garden". Study the chart and worksheet carefully to make sure you start with the most appropriate chart type, and then make all the modifications shown. Put your name in the sheet footer, preview, and then print the worksheet and chart together in landscape orientation.

FIGURE J-23

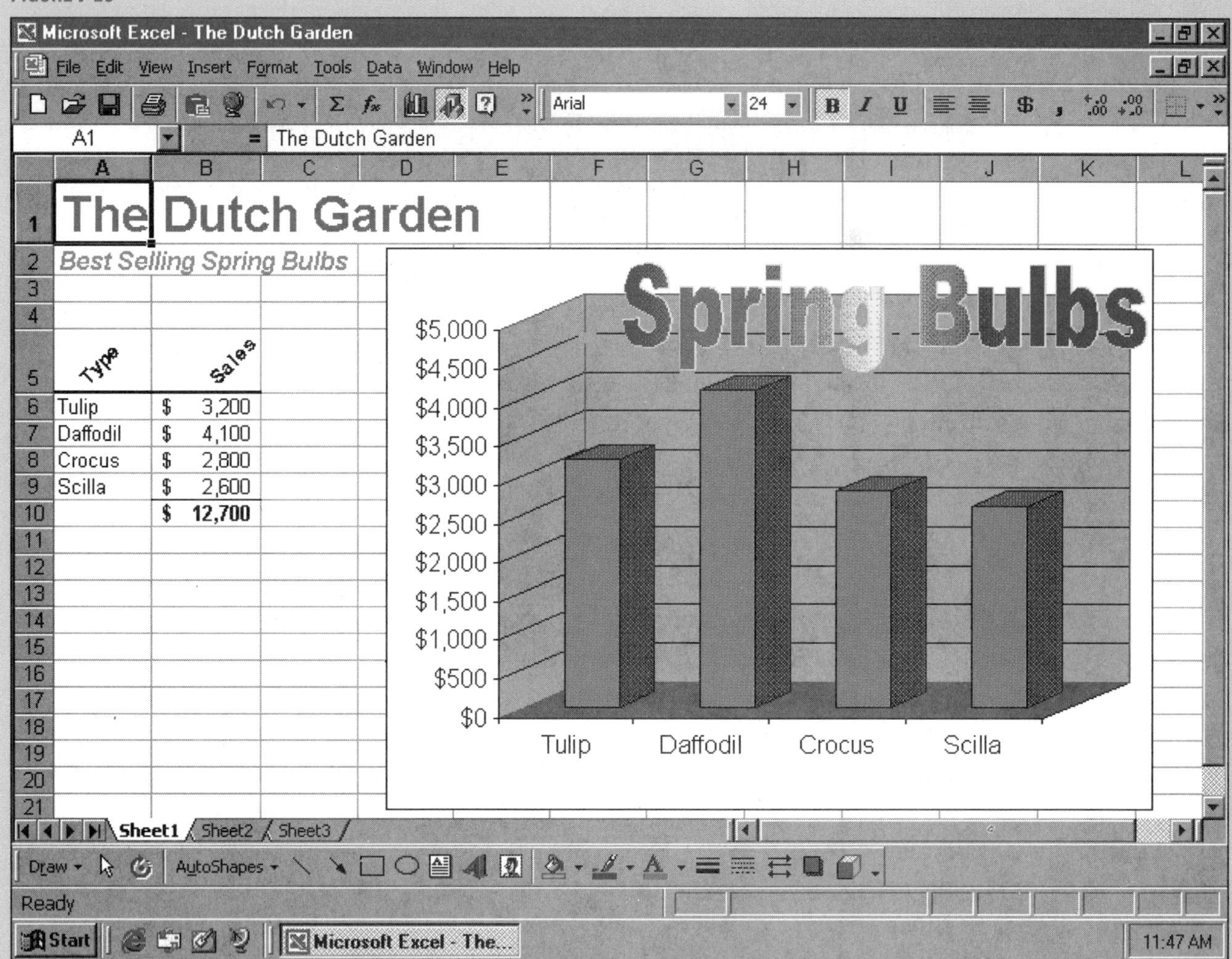

Excel 2000

Using a What-If Analysis

Objectives

- ► Define a what-if analysis
- MOUS ► Track a what-if analysis with Scenario Manager
- MOUS ► Generate a scenario summary
- ► Project figures using a data table
- ► Create a two-input data table
- MOUS ► Use Goal Seek
- MOUS ► Set up a complex what-if analysis with Solver
- MOUS ► Run Solver and generate an Answer Report

Each time you use a worksheet to answer the question "what if?" you are performing a **what-if analysis**. For example, what would happen to a firm's overall expense budget if company travel expenses decreased by 30%? Using Excel, you can perform a what-if analysis in many ways. In this unit, you will learn to track what-if scenarios and generate summary reports using the Excel Scenario Manager. You will design and manipulate one-input and two-input data tables to project multiple outcomes. Also, you will use the Excel Goal Seek feature to solve a what-if analysis. Finally, you will use Solver to perform a complex what-if analysis involving multiple variables. The MediaLoft corporate office is considering the purchase of several pieces of capital equipment, as well as several vehicles.

Excel 2000

Defining a What-If Analysis

By performing a what-if analysis in a worksheet, you can get immediate answers to questions such as "What happens if we sell 30% more of a certain product?" or "What happens if interest rates rise 2 points?" A worksheet used to produce a what-if analysis is often referred to as a **model** because it acts as the basis for multiple outcomes. To perform a what-if analysis in a worksheet, you change the value in one or more **input cells** (cells that contain data rather than formulas) and then observe the effects on dependent cells. A **dependent cell** is a cell—usually containing a formula—whose value changes depending on the values in the input cells. A dependent cell can be located either in the same worksheet as the changing value or in another worksheet. Jim has created a worksheet model to perform an initial what-if analysis of equipment loan payments. See Figure K-1. Jim follows the guidelines below to perform a what-if analysis.

Understand and state the purpose of the worksheet model

The worksheet model is designed to calculate a fixed-rate, monthly equipment loan payment.

Determine the data input value(s) that, if changed, affect the dependent cell results

The model contains three data input values (labeled Loan Amount, Annual Interest Rate, and Term in months), in cells B4, B5, and B6, respectively.

Identify the dependent cell(s), usually containing formulas, that will contain adjusted results once different data values are entered

There are three dependent cell formulas (labeled Monthly Payment, Total Payments, and Total Interest). The results appear in cells B9, B10, and B11, respectively.

Formulate questions you want the what-if analysis to answer

Jim wants to answer the following questions with his model: (1) What happens to the monthly payments if the interest rate is 10%? (2) What happens to the monthly payments if the loan term is 60 months (5 years) instead of 48 months (4 years)? (3) What happens to the monthly payments if a less-expensive car with a lower loan amount is purchased?

Perform the what-if analysis and explore the exact relationships between the input values and the dependent cell formulas, which depend on the input values

Jim wants to see what effect a 10% interest rate has on the dependent cell formulas. Because the interest rate is located in cell B5, any formula that references cell B5 will be directly affected by a change in interest rate—in this case, the Monthly Payment formula in cell B9. Because the formula in cell B10 references cell B9 and the formula in cell B11 references cell B10, however, a change in the interest rate in cell B5 affects these other two formulas as well. Figure K-2 shows the result of the what-if analysis described in this example.

FIGURE K-1: Worksheet model for a what-if analysis

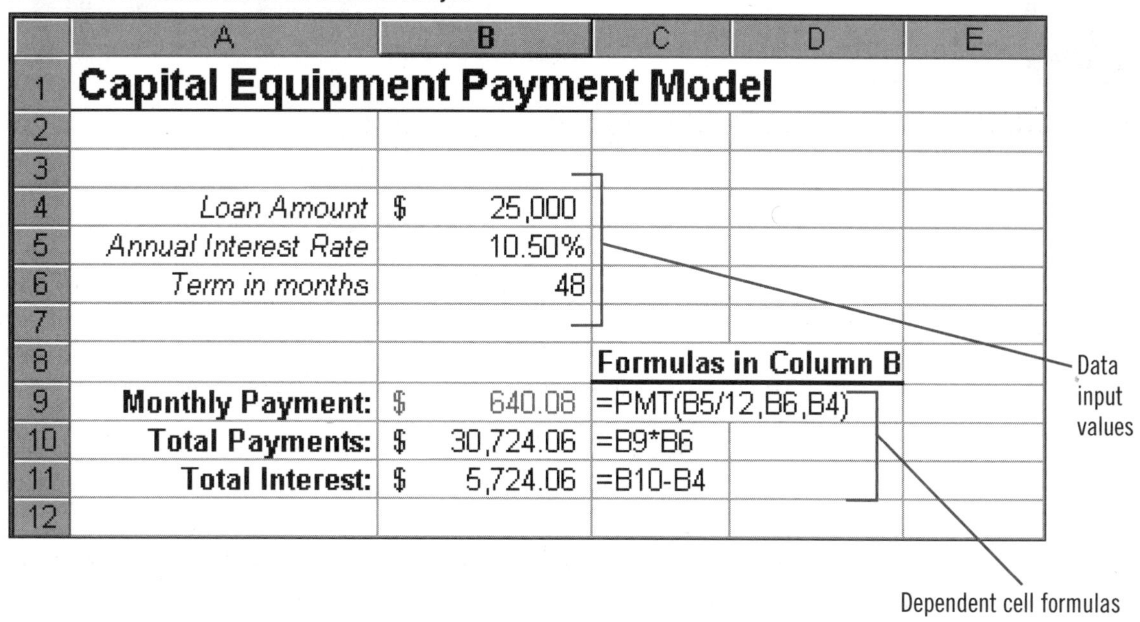

FIGURE K-2: What-if analysis with changed input value and dependent formula results

	A	B	C	D	E
1	**Capital Equipment Payment Model**				
2					
3					
4	*Loan Amount*	$ 25,000			
5	*Annual Interest Rate*	10.00%			
6	*Term in months*	48			
7					
8					
9	**Monthly Payment:**	$ 634.06			
10	**Total Payments:**	$ 30,435.10			
11	**Total Interest:**	$ 5,435.10			
12					

Changed input value

Dependent cell values affected by changed input value

Excel 2000

Tracking a What-If Analysis with Scenario Manager

A **scenario** is a set of values you use to forecast worksheet results. The Excel Scenario Manager simplifies the process of what-if analysis by allowing you to name and save different scenarios with the worksheet. Scenarios are particularly useful when you work with uncertain or changing variables. If you plan to create a budget, for example, but are uncertain of your revenue, you can assign several different values to the revenue and then switch between the scenarios to perform a what-if analysis. Jim uses Scenario Manager to consider three equipment loan scenarios: (1) the original loan quote, (2) a longer-term loan, and (3) a reduced loan amount.

Steps

QuickTip

To return personalized toolbars and menus to their default state, click Tools on the menu bar, click Customize, click the Options tab in the Customize dialog box, click Reset my usage data to restore the default settings, click Yes, click Close, then close the Drawing toolbar if it is displayed.

1. Open the workbook titled **EX K-1**, then save it as **Capital Equipment Payment Model**
   The first step in defining a scenario is choosing the cells that will vary in the different scenarios; these are known as **changing cells**.
2. Select range **B4:B6**, click **Tools** on the menu bar, then click **Scenarios**
   The Scenario Manager dialog box opens with the following message: "No Scenarios defined. Choose Add to add scenarios."
3. Click **Add** if necessary, drag the Add Scenario dialog box to the right until columns **A** and **B** are visible, then type **Original loan quote** in the Scenario name box
   The range in the Changing cells box reflects your initial selection, as shown in Figure K-3.
4. Click **OK** to confirm the Add Scenario settings
   The Scenario Values dialog box opens, as shown in Figure K-4. Notice that the existing values appear in the changing cell boxes. Because this first scenario reflects the original loan quote input values ($25,000 at 10.5% for 48 months), these values are correct.
5. Click **OK**
   The Scenario Manager dialog box reappears with the new scenario listed in the Scenarios box. Jim wants to examine a second scenario, this one with a loan term of 60 months.
6. Click **Add**; in the Scenario name box type **Longer term loan**, click **OK**; in the Scenario Values dialog box, select **48** in the third changing cell box, type **60**, then click **Add**
   Jim also wants to examine a scenario that uses $21,000 as the loan amount.
7. In the Scenario name box type **Reduced loan amount**, click **OK**; in the Scenario Values dialog box, change the **25000** in the first changing cell box to **21000**, then click **OK**
   The Scenario Manager dialog box reappears. See Figure K-5. All three scenarios are listed, with the most recent—Reduced loan amount—selected. Now that you have defined the three scenarios, you can apply them and see what effect they will have on the monthly payment.
8. Make sure Reduced loan amount is still selected, click **Show**, notice that the monthly payment in the worksheet changes from $640.08 to $537.67; click **Longer term loan**, click **Show**, notice that the monthly payment is now $537.35; click **Original loan quote**, click **Show** to return to the original values, then click **Close**
9. Save the workbook

Merging scenarios

To bring scenarios from another workbook into the current workbook, click the Merge button in the Scenario Manager dialog box. The Merge Scenarios dialog box opens, letting you select scenarios from other workbooks.

FIGURE K-3: Add Scenario dialog box

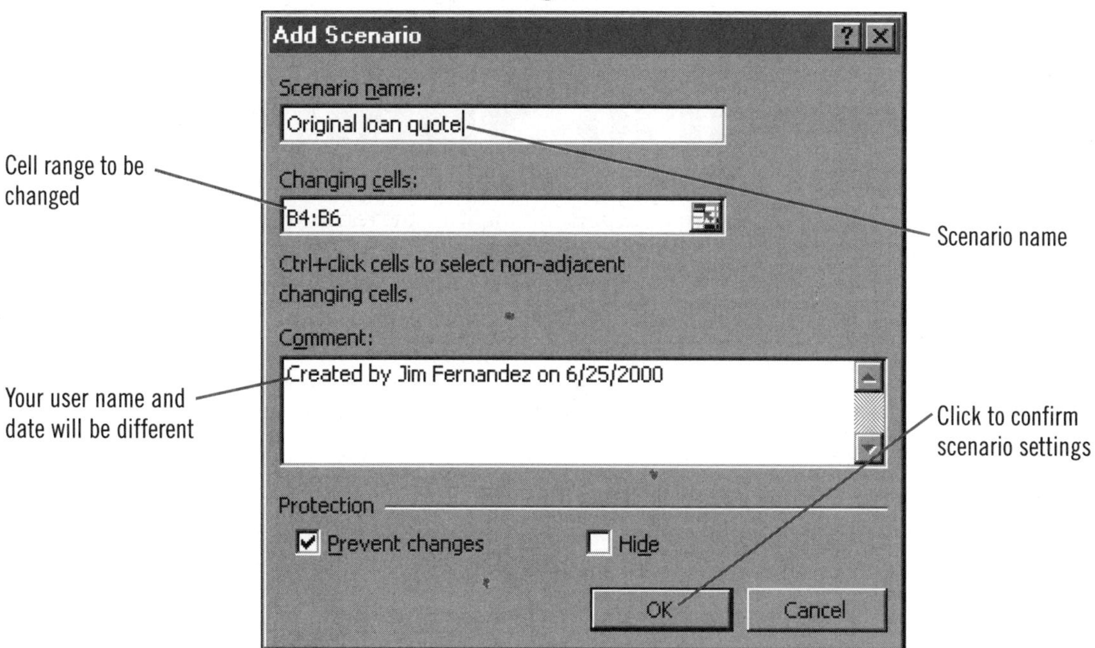

FIGURE K-4: Scenario Values dialog box

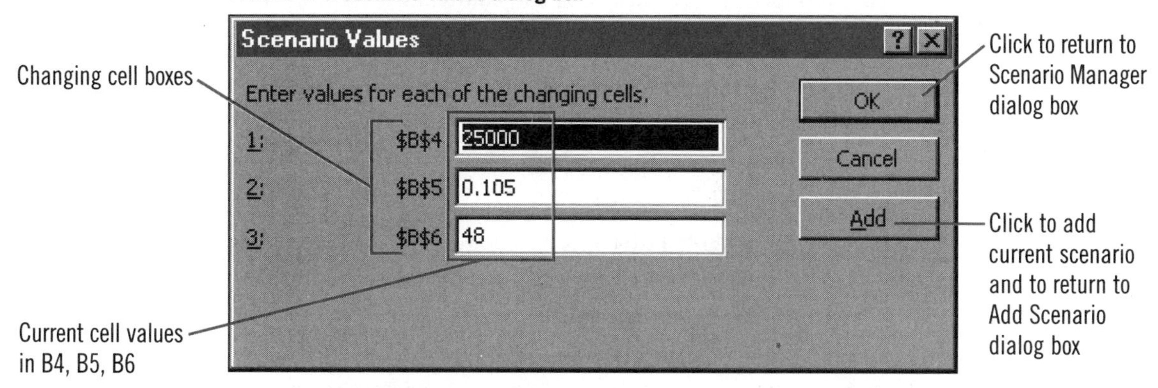

FIGURE K-5: Scenario Manager dialog box with three scenarios listed

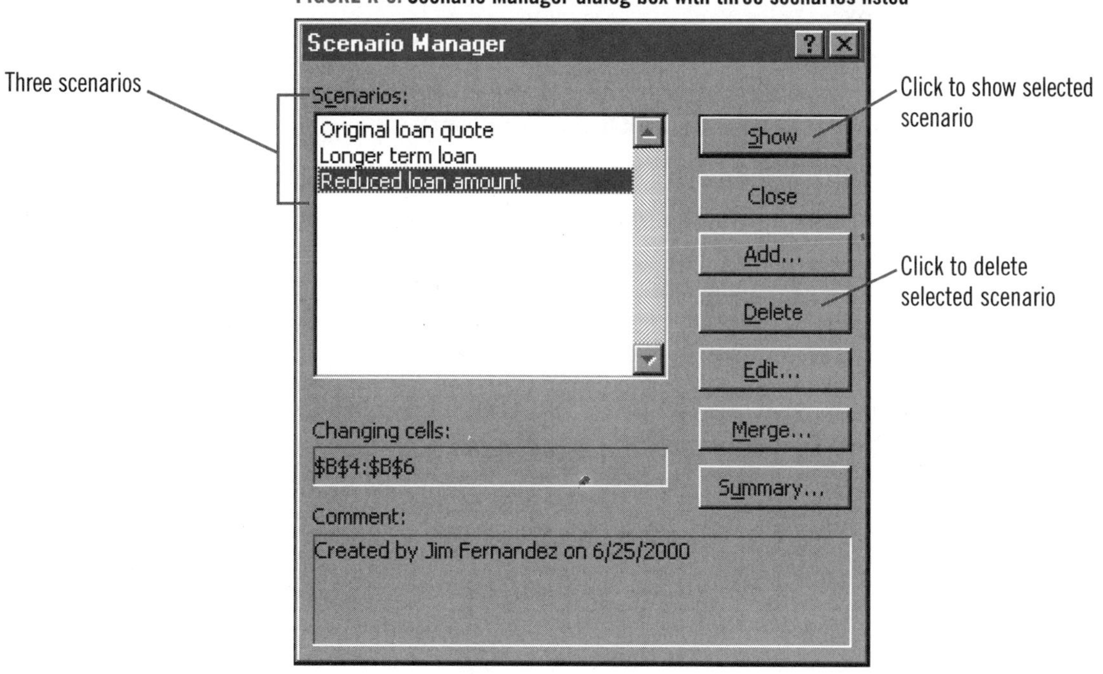

Excel 2000

Generating a Scenario Summary

Although it may be useful to switch between different scenarios when analyzing data, in most cases you will want to refer to a single report summarizing the results of the scenarios in a worksheet. A **scenario summary** is an Excel table that compiles data from the changing cells and corresponding result cells for each scenario. You can use a scenario summary to illustrate the best, worst, and most likely scenarios for a particular set of circumstances. Now that he's defined his scenarios, Jim needs to generate and print a scenario summary report. Naming the cells makes the summary easier to read because the names, not the cell references, are listed in the report. Jim begins by creating cell names in column B based on the labels in column A (the left column).

QuickTip

To delete a range, click Insert on the menu bar, click Define, click the range name, then click Delete.

1. Select range **A4:B11**, click **Insert** on the menu bar, point to **Name**, click **Create**, click the **Left column check box** to select it if necessary, then click **OK**
   Excel creates the names based on the cell contents.
2. Click cell **B4** to make sure Loan_Amount appears in the name box, then click the **name box list arrow**
   All six labels appear in the name box list, confirming that they were created. See Figure K-6. Now you are ready to generate the scenario summary report.
3. Press **[Esc]**, click **Tools** on the menu bar, click **Scenarios**, then click **Summary** in the Scenario Manager dialog box
   The Scenario Summary dialog box opens. Notice that Scenario summary is selected, indicating that it is the default report type.
4. Double-click the **Result cells box** to select it if necessary, then select range **B9:B11** in the worksheet
   The references in the Result cells box adjust to reflect those cells affected by the changing cells (that is, the references now refer to the result cells). See Figure K-7. With the report type and result cells specified, you are now ready to generate the report.

QuickTip

Scroll right to see all three scenarios included in the report. The scenario summary is not linked to the worksheet. If you change cells in the worksheet, you must generate a new scenario summary.

5. Click **OK**
   The summary of the worksheet's scenarios appears on a new sheet. The report appears in outline format so that you can hide or show report details. Because the Current Values column shows the same values as the Original loan quote column, Jim wants to delete column D.
6. Press **[Ctrl][Home]**, click the **Current Values column header** for column D, click the **right mouse button**, then click **Delete** in the pop-up menu
   The column containing the current values is deleted and the Original loan quote column data shifts left to fill column D. Next, Jim wants to delete the notes at the bottom of the report because they refer to the column that no longer exists. He also wants to make the report title more descriptive.
7. Select range **B13:B15**, press **[Delete]**, select cell **B2**, edit its contents to read **Scenario Summary for Equipment Loan**, then click cell **A1**
   The completed scenario summary is shown in Figure K-8.
8. Add your name to the report footer, save your work, then print the report in landscape orientation

FIGURE K-6: List box containing newly created names

Name box list arrow

Names match labels in column A

FIGURE K-7: Scenario Summary dialog box

Default report type

Cells to be recalculated when a new scenario is applied

FIGURE K-8: Completed Scenario Summary report

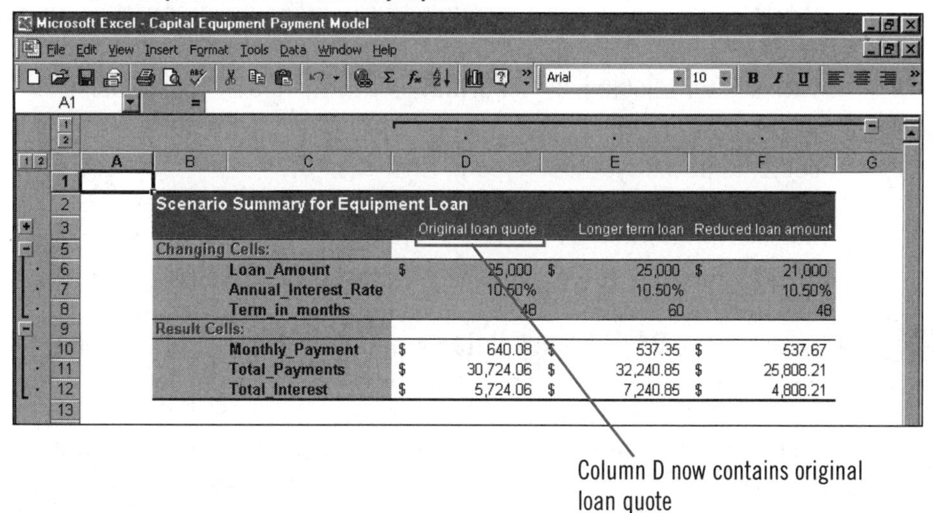

Scenario Summary for Equipment Loan

	Original loan quote	Longer term loan	Reduced loan amount
Changing Cells:			
Loan_Amount	$ 25,000	$ 25,000	$ 21,000
Annual_Interest_Rate	10.50%	10.50%	10.50%
Term_in_months	48	60	48
Result Cells:			
Monthly_Payment	$ 640.08	$ 537.35	$ 537.67
Total_Payments	$ 30,724.06	$ 32,240.85	$ 25,808.21
Total_Interest	$ 5,724.06	$ 7,240.85	$ 4,808.21

Excel 2000

Using Report Manager

You can create customized, printed reports using the Excel Report Manager, an extra Excel program called an "add-in." A report can contain worksheets, views, or scenarios that you want to print repeatedly in a given order. To create a report, click View on the menu bar, click Report Manager, then click Add. In the Add Report dialog box, type a report name, select the sheets, views, or scenarios you want to include, then click Add. Repeat until you've added all the sections you need, click OK, select the report name, then click Print. The sections of the report print in the order in which you've listed them.

Excel 2000

Projecting Figures Using a Data Table

Another way to answer what-if questions in a worksheet is by using a data table. A **data table**, sometimes referred to as a **one-input data table**, is a range of cells that shows the resulting values when one input value is varied in a formula. For example, you could use a data table to calculate your monthly mortgage payment based on several different interest rates. Now that he's completed his analysis, Jim wants to find out how the monthly equipment payments would change as interest rates increase by increments of 0.25%. He estimates that the lowest interest rate would be about 9.75% and the highest 11.25%. To project these figures, Jim will generate a one-input data table. First, he creates a table structure, with the varying interest rates listed in the left column.

Steps

1. **Click the Single Loan sheet tab, select cell D4, type Interest, select cell D5, type 9.75%, select cell D6, type 10.00%; select range D5:D6, drag the fill handle to select range D7:D11, then release the mouse button**
   With the varying interest rates (that is, the input values) listed in column D, you need to enter a formula reference to cell B9. This tells Excel to use the formula in cell B9 to calculate multiple results in column E, based on the changing interest rates in column D.
2. **Click cell E4, type =B9, then click the Enter button on the formula bar**
   Notice that the value in cell B9, $640.08, now appears in cell E4, and the formula reference (=B9) appears in the formula bar. See Figure K-9. Because the value in cell E4 isn't a part of the data table (Excel uses it only to calculate the values in the table), Jim wants to hide the contents of cell E4 from view using a custom number format.
3. **With cell E4 selected, click Format on the menu bar, click Cells, click the Number tab in the Format Cells dialog box if necessary; click Custom under Category, select the contents of the Type box, type ;;, then click OK**
   Because custom number formats usually specify the formats for positive and then negative numbers, with semicolons in between, the two semicolons actually specify no format, so the cell will remain blank. With the table structure in place, you can now generate monthly payment values for the varying interest rates.
4. **Select range D4:E11, click Data on the menu bar, then click Table**
   You have highlighted the range that makes up the table structure. The Table dialog box opens, as shown in Figure K-10. This is where you indicate in which worksheet cell you want the varying input values (the interest rates in column D) to be substituted. Because the monthly payments formula in cell B9 (which you just referenced in cell E4) uses the annual interest rate in cell B5, you'll enter a reference to cell B5. You'll place this reference in the Column input cell box, rather than the Row input cell box, because the varying input values are arranged in a column.
5. **Click the Column input cell box, click cell B5, then click OK**
   Excel generates monthly payments for each interest rate. The monthly payment values are displayed next to the interest rates in column E. The new data and the heading in cell D4 need formatting.
6. **Click cell D4, click the Bold button, then click the Align Right button (both on the Formatting toolbar)**
7. **Select range E5:E11, click the Currency Style button on the Formatting toolbar, deselect the range, add your name to the footer, then save and print the worksheet**
   The completed data table appears as shown in Figure K-11. Notice that the monthly payment amount for a 10.50% interest rate is the same as the original loan quote in cell B9 and the reference to it in cell E4. You can use this information to cross-check the values Excel generates in data tables.

Trouble?

If you receive the message "Selection not valid", repeat Step 4, taking care to select the entire range D4:E11.

QuickTip

You cannot delete individual values in a data table; you must clear all values.

Trouble?

If the Bold button does not appear on your Formatting toolbar, click the More Buttons button to view it.

FIGURE K-9: One-input data table structure

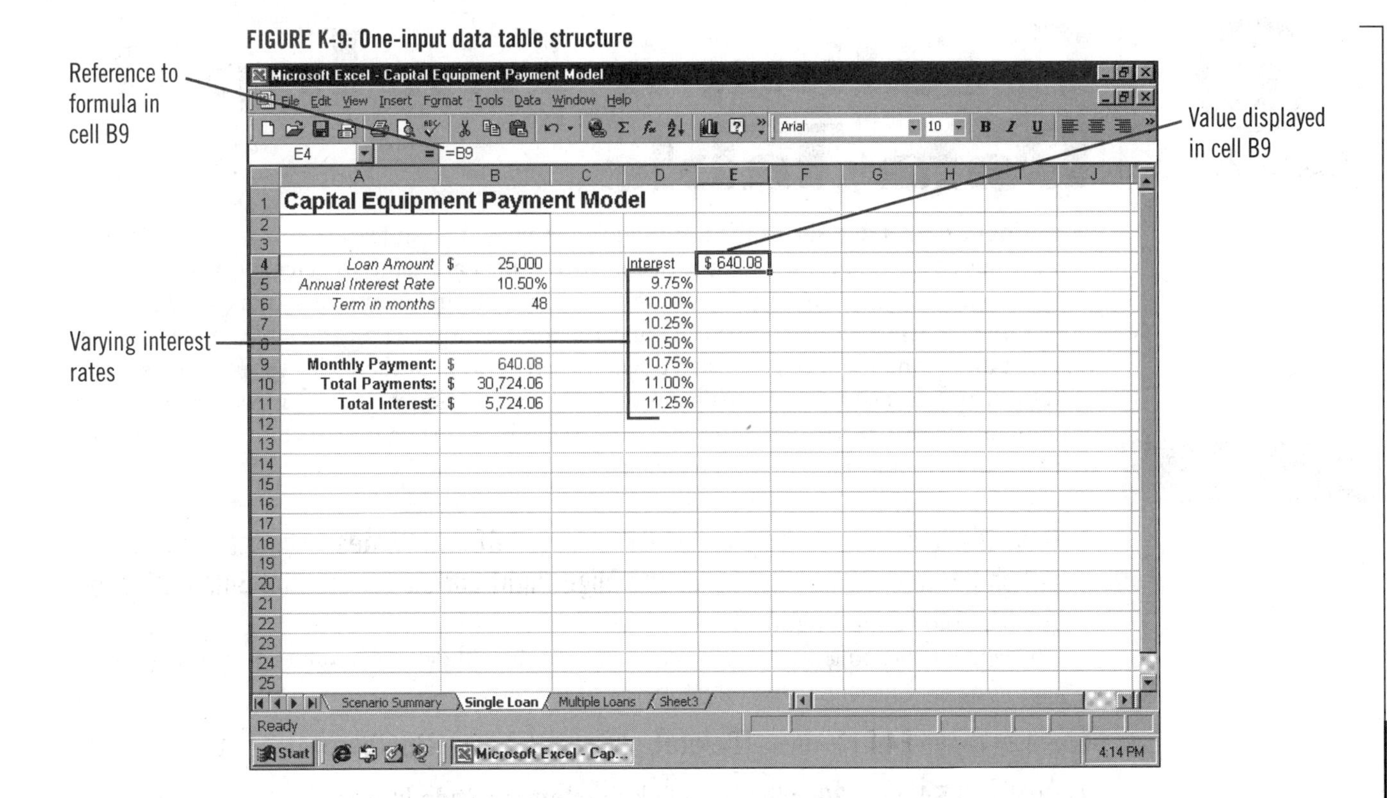

FIGURE K-10: Table dialog box

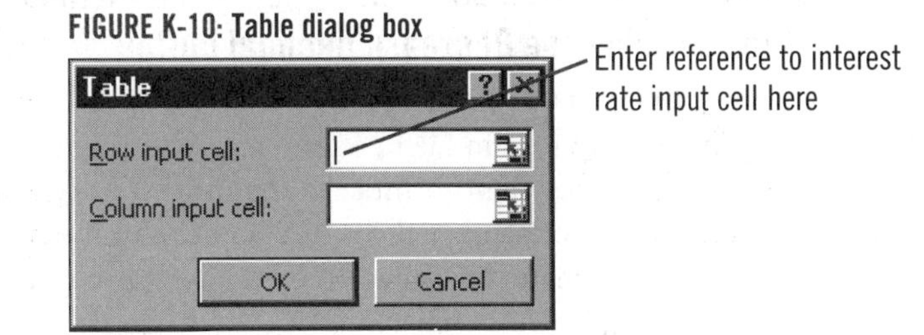

FIGURE K-11: Completed data table with resulting values

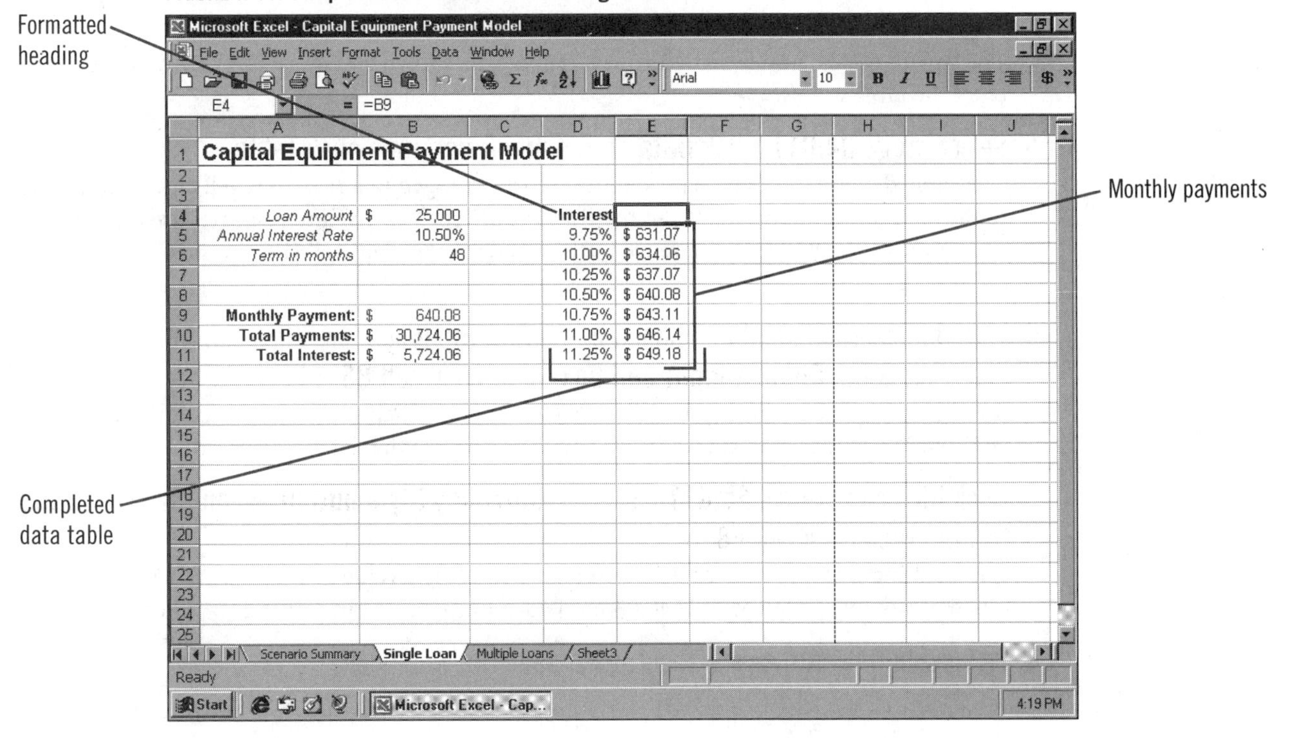

Creating a Two-Input Data Table

A **two-input data table** shows the resulting values when two different input values are varied in a formula. You could, for example, use a two-input data table to calculate your monthly mortgage payment based on varying interest rates and varying loan terms. In a two-input data table, different values of one input cell appear across the top row of the table, while different values of the second input cell are listed down the left column of the table. Jim wants to use a two-input data table to see what happens if the various interest rates are applied across several different loan terms, such as 3, 4, and 5 years. He begins by changing the structure of the one-input data table to accommodate a two-input data table.

Steps

1. Move the contents of cell **D4** to cell **C7**; click cell **C8**, type **Rates**, click the **Enter button** on the formula bar, then click the **Align Right button** and the **Bold button** (both on the Formatting toolbar)
   The left table heading is in place. You don't need the old data table values, but you will need a heading for the values along the top row of the table.
2. Select range **E4:E11**, press **[Delete]**, click cell **F3**, type **Months**, click , then click
3. Click cell **E4**, type **36**, click , click the **Comma Style button** on the Formatting toolbar, click the **Decrease decimal button** twice on the Formatting toolbar, press [→], in cell F4 type **48**, press [→], in cell G4 type **60**, then click
   With both top row and left column values and headings in place, you are ready to reference the monthly payment formula in the upper-left cell of the table. Again, this is the formula Excel will use to calculate the values in the table. Because it is not part of the table (Excel uses it only to calculate the values in the table), it is best to hide the cell contents from view.
4. Click cell **D4**, type **=B9**, click , click **Format** on the menu bar, click **Cells**, in the Format Cells dialog box click the **Number tab** if necessary, click **Custom**, select the contents of the Type box, type ;;, then click **OK**
   The two-input data table structure is complete, as shown in Figure K-12. You are ready to enter the table values.
5. Select range **D4:G11**, click **Data** on the menu bar, then click **Table**
   The Table dialog box opens. The loan terms are arranged in a row, so you'll enter a reference to the loan term input cell (B6) in the Row input cell box. The interest rates are arranged in a column, so you'll enter a reference to the interest rate input cell (B5) in the Column input cell box.
6. With the insertion point positioned in the Row input cell box, click cell **B6** in the worksheet, click the **Column input cell box**, then click cell **B5**
   See Figure K-13. The row input cell (B6) references the loan term, and the column input cell (B5) references the interest rate. Now, you can generate the data table values.
7. Click **OK**, select range **F5:G11**, click the **Currency Style button** on the Formatting toolbar, then click cell **F8**
   The resulting values appear, as shown in Figure K-14. The value in cell F8 matches the original quote: a monthly payment of $640.08 for a 48-month loan term at a 10.50% interest rate.
8. Preview and print the worksheet, then save the workbook

FIGURE K-12: Two-input data table structure

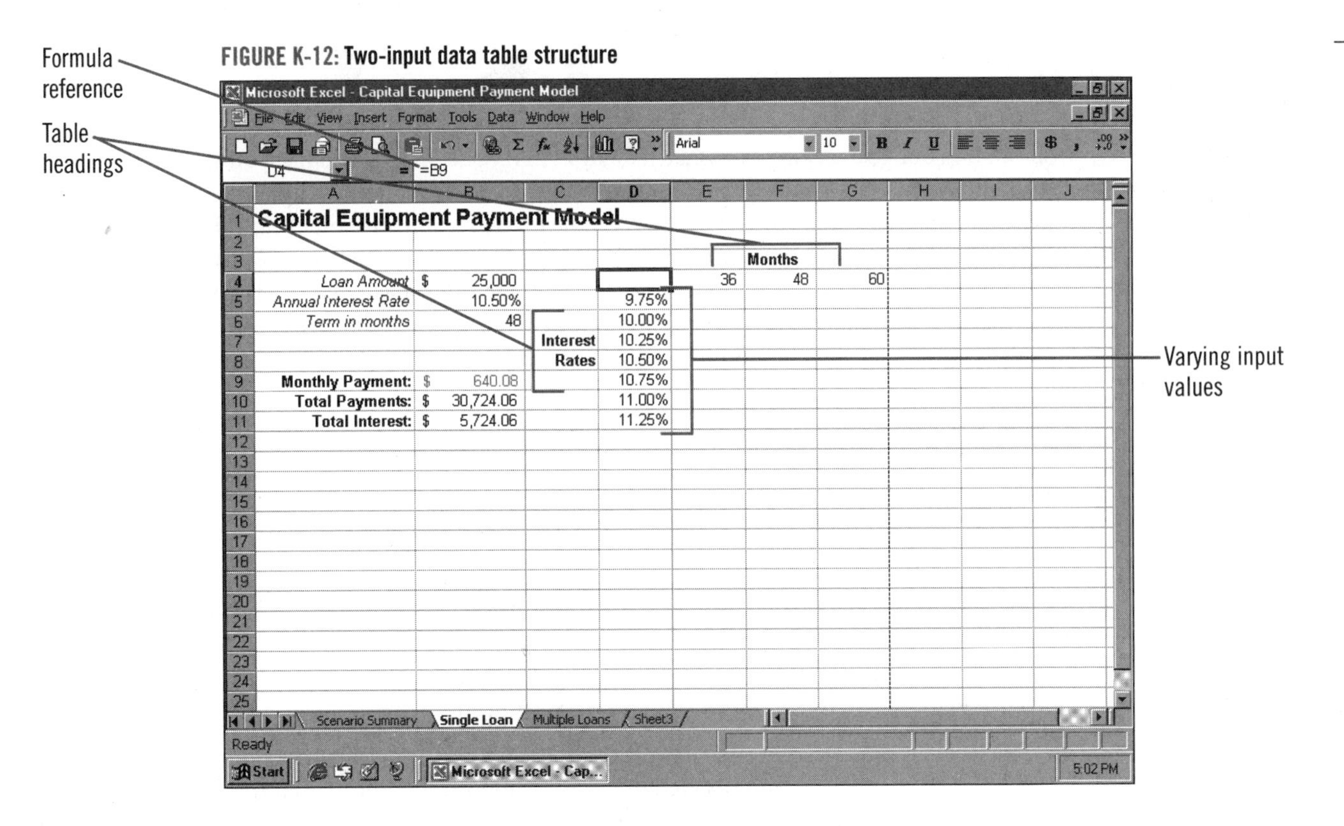

FIGURE K-13: Table dialog box

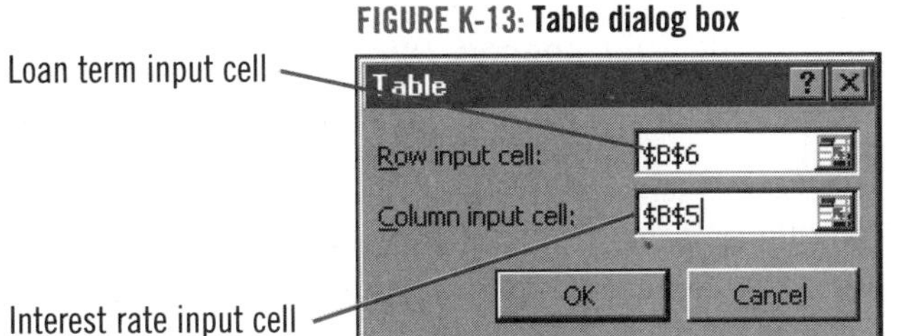

FIGURE K-14: Completed two-input data table

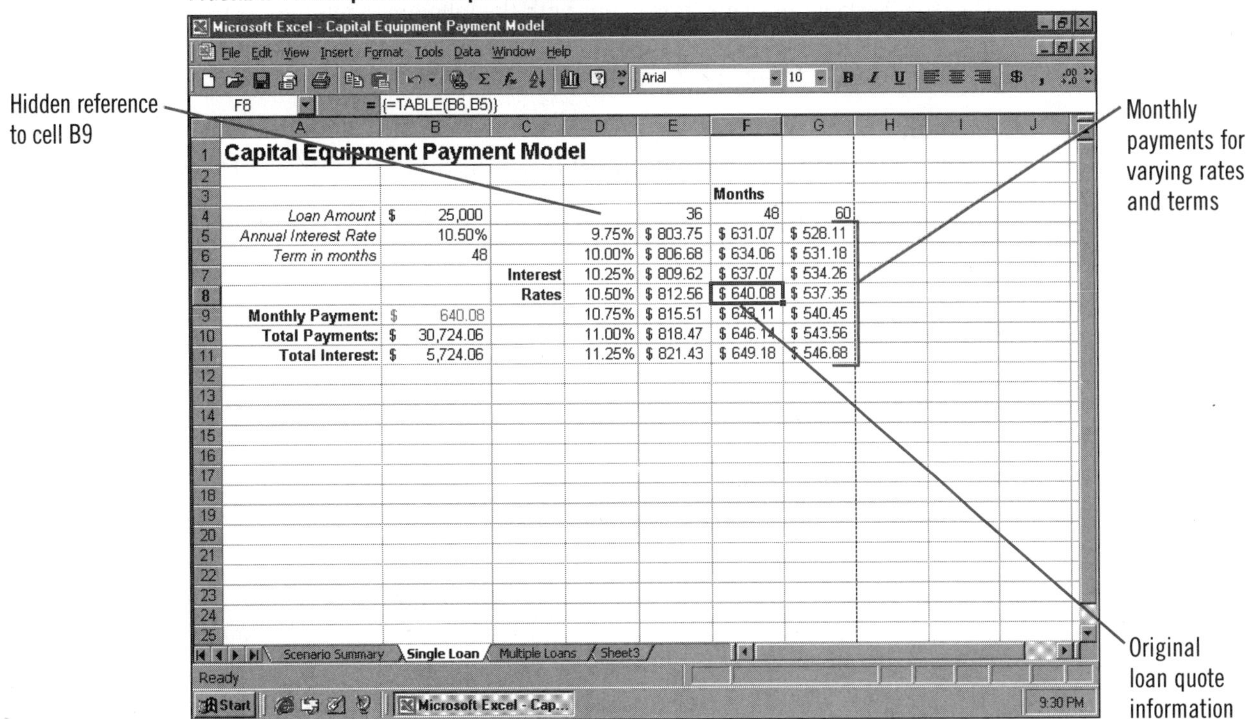

Excel 2000

Excel 2000

Using Goal Seek

You can think of goal seeking as a what-if analysis in reverse. In goal seeking, you specify a solution and then find the input value that produces the answer you want. Backing into a solution in this way, sometimes referred to as **backsolving**, can save a significant amount of time. For example, you can use Goal Seek to determine how many units must be sold to reach a particular sales goal or to determine the expenses that must be cut to meet a budget. After reviewing his data table, Jim has a follow-up question: How much money could MediaLoft borrow if the company wanted to keep the total payment amount of all the equipment to $28,000? Jim uses Goal Seek to answer this question.

Steps

1. **Click cell B10**
   The first step in using Goal Seek is to select a goal cell. A **goal cell** contains a formula in which you can substitute values to find a specific value, or goal. You use cell B10 as the goal cell because it contains the formula for total payments.
2. **Click Tools on the menu bar, then click Goal Seek**
   The Goal Seek dialog box opens. Notice that the Set cell box contains a reference to cell B10, the Total Payments cell you selected in Step 1. You need to indicate that the figure in cell B10 should not exceed 28000.
3. **Click the To value box, then type 28000**
   The 28000 figure represents the desired solution that will be reached by substituting different values in the goal cell.
4. **Click the By changing cell box, then click cell B4**
   You have specified that cell B4 will be changed to reach the 28000 solution. See Figure K-15. With the target value in the target cell specified, you can begin the Goal Seek.
5. **Click OK, then move the dialog box as needed so that column B is visible**
   The Goal Seek Status dialog box opens with the following message: "Goal Seeking with Cell B10 found a solution". Notice that by changing the Loan Amount figure in cell B4 from $25,000 to $22,783, Goal Seek achieves a Total Payments result of $28,000.
6. **Click OK**
   Changing the loan amount value in cell B4 affects the entire worksheet. See Figure K-16.
7. **Save, then print the workbook**

QuickTip

Before you select another command, you can return the worksheet to its status prior to the Goal Seek by pressing [Ctrl][Z].

FIGURE K-15: **Completed Goal Seek dialog box**

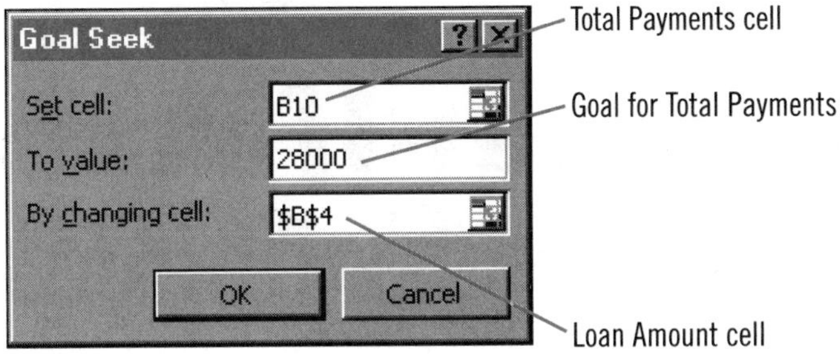

Goal Seek
Set cell:
B10
To value:
28000
By changing cell:
$B$4
OK
Cancel
Total Payments cell
Goal for Total Payments
Loan Amount cell

FIGURE K-16: **Worksheet with new values**

Microsoft Excel - Capital Equipment Payment Model
=B9*B6
Capital Equipment Payment Model
Months
Loan Amount $ 22,783
Annual Interest Rate 10.50%
Term in months 48
Interest Rates
Monthly Payment: $ 583.33
Total Payments: $ 28,000.00
Total Interest: $ 5,216.55
Scenario Summary
Single Loan
Multiple Loans
Sheet3
Ready
Goal amount
Monthly payment and total interest also changed along with loan amount
New loan amount
Table values change to reflect new loan amount

Excel 2000

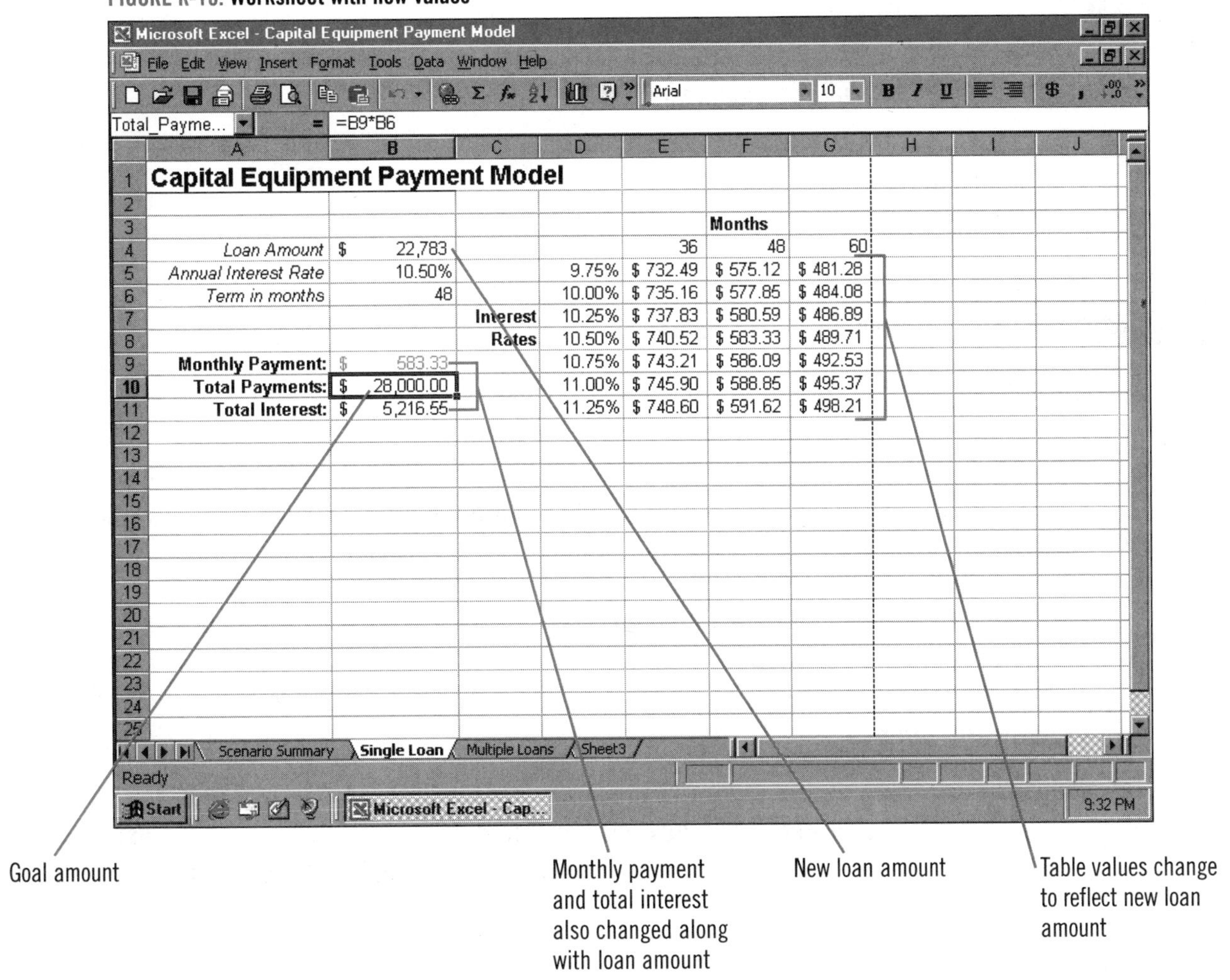

Excel 2000

Setting Up a Complex What-If Analysis with Solver

The Excel Solver finds the most appropriate value for a formula by changing the input values in the worksheet. The cell containing the formula is called the **target cell**. Cells containing the values that change are called **changing cells**. Solver is helpful when you need to perform a complex what-if analysis involving multiple input values or when the input values must conform to specific constraints. After seeing his analysis of interest rates and payments, Jim now addresses the vehicle purchase for the MediaLoft shuttle service. He decides that the best plan is to purchase a combination of vans, sedans, and compact cars that will accommodate a total of 44 passengers, the number of people Jim has estimated the company will need to transport to and from the stores for special events. In addition, the total monthly payments for the vehicles should not exceed $3,700. Jim uses Solver to find the best possible combination of vehicles.

Trouble?

If Solver is not an option on your Tools menu, you need to install the Solver add-in. See your instructor or technical support person for assistance.

Trouble?

If your Solver Parameters dialog box has entries in the By Changing Cells box or in the Subject to the Constraints box, click Reset All, then click OK, and continue with Step 3.

1. Click the **Multiple Loans sheet tab**
   See Figure K-17. This worksheet is designed to calculate total loans, payments, and passengers for a combination of vans, sedans, and compact cars. It assumes an annual interest rate of 10% and a loan term of 48 months. You will use Solver to change the purchase quantities in cells B7:D7 (the changing cells) to achieve your target of 44 passengers in cell B15 (the target cell). Your solution will include a constraint on cell C14, specifying that the total monthly payments must be less than or equal to $3,700.
2. Click **Tools**, then click **Solver**
   The Solver Parameters dialog box opens. This is where you indicate the target cell, the changing cells, and the constraints under which you want Solver to work. You begin by changing the value in the target cell.
3. With the Set Target Cell box selected in the Solver Parameters dialog box, click cell **B15** in the worksheet, click the **Value of option button**, double-click the **Value of box**, then type **44**
   $B$15 appears in the Set Target Cell box, and 44 appears in the Value of box.
4. Click the **By Changing Cells box**, then select cells **B7:D7** in the worksheet
   $B$7:$D$7 appears in the By Changing Cells box. You need to specify the constraints on the worksheet values, the values you don't want them to exceed.
5. Click **Add**
   The Add Constraint dialog box opens. This is where you specify the total monthly payment amount—in this case, no higher than $3,700.
6. Click the **Cell Reference box**, click cell **B14** in the worksheet, click the **list arrow** in the Add Constraint dialog box, select **<=**, click the **Constraint text box**, then type **3700**
   See Figure K-18.The Change Constraint dialog box specifies that cell B14 should contain a value that is less than or equal to 3700. Next, you need to specify that the purchase quantities should be as close as possible to integers. They should also be greater than or equal to zero.
7. Click **Add**, click the **Cell Reference box**, select range **B7:D7**, click the **list arrow** in the Add constraint dialog box, then select **int**
8. Make sure "integer" appears in the Constraint box, click **Add**, click the **Cell Reference box**, select cells **B7:D7** in the worksheet, in the Add Constraint dialog box select **>=**, click the **Constraint box**, type **0**, then click **OK**
   The Solver Parameters dialog box reappears, with the constraints listed as shown in Figure K-19. In the next lesson, you will run Solver and generate an answer report.

FIGURE K-17: Worksheet setup for complex what-if analysis

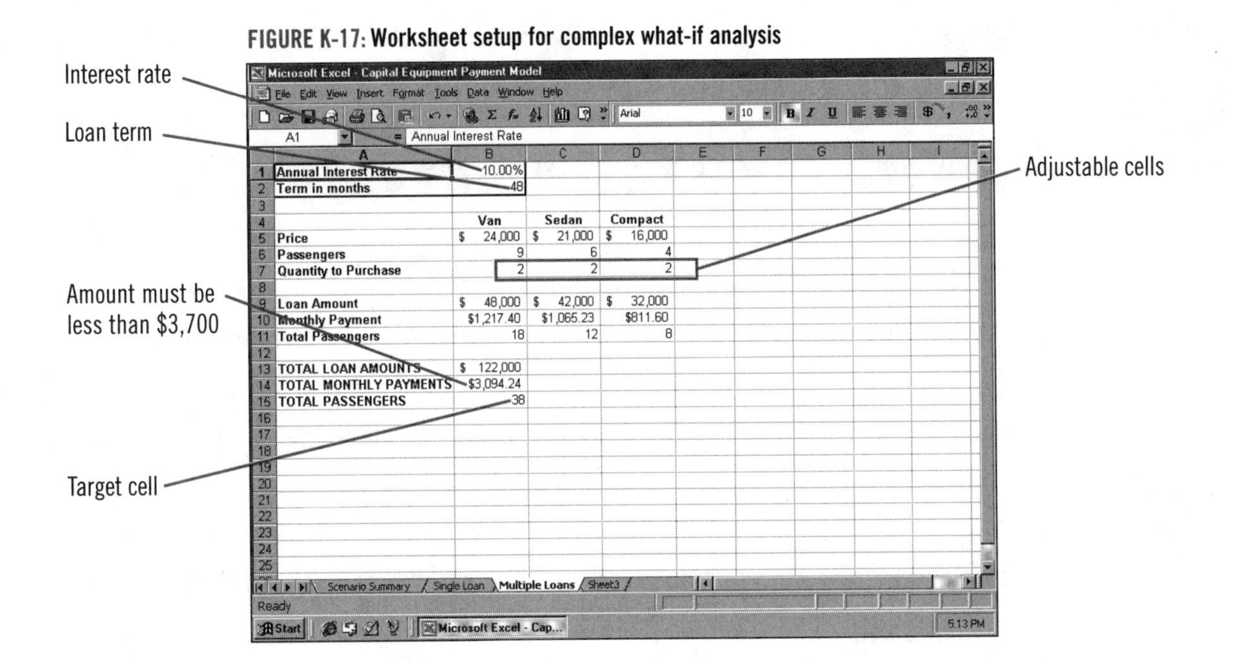

FIGURE K-18: Adding constraints

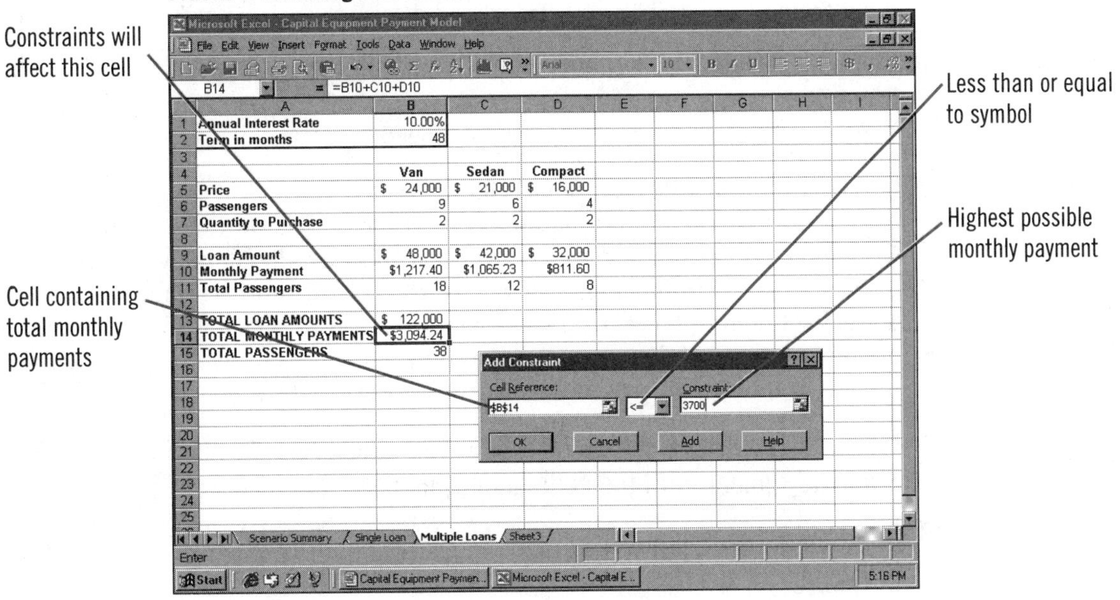

FIGURE K-19: Completed Solver Parameters dialog box

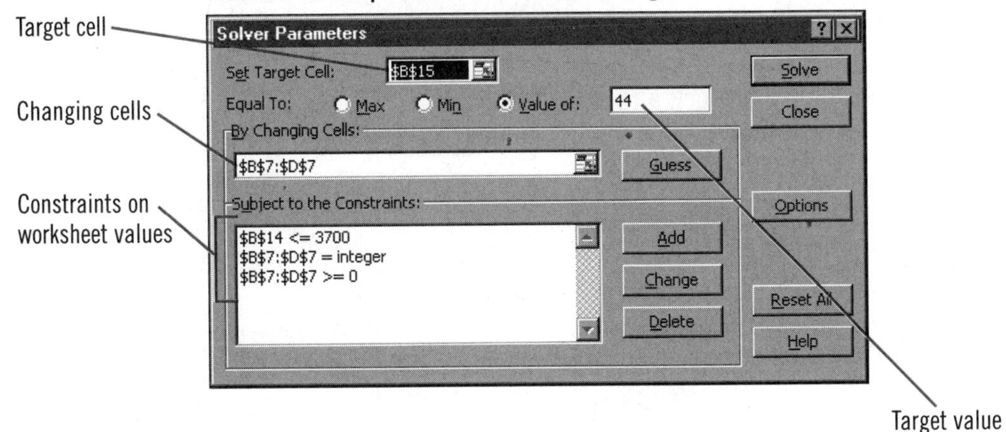

Excel 2000

Excel 2000

Running Solver and Generating an Answer Report

After entering all the parameters in the Solver Parameters dialog box, you can run Solver to find an answer. In some cases, Solver may not be able to find a solution that meets all of your constraints; then you would need to enter new constraints and try again. Once Solver finds a solution, you can choose to create a special report explaining the solution. Jim has finished entering his parameters in the Solver Parameters dialog box. Now he's ready to run Solver and create an answer report.

1. Make sure your Solver Parameter dialog box matches Figure K-19 in the previous lesson
2. Click **Solve**
   After a moment, the Solver Results dialog box opens, indicating that Solver has found a solution. See Figure K-20. The solution values appear in the worksheet, but you decide to move them to a special Answer Report and display the original values in the worksheet.
3. Click **Restore Original Values**, click **Answer** in the Reports list box, then click **OK**
   The Solver Results dialog box closes, and the original values are displayed in the worksheet. The Answer Report appears on a separate sheet.
4. Click the **Answer Report 1 sheet tab**
   The Answer Report displays the solution to the vehicle-purchase problem, as shown in Figure K-21. To accommodate 44 passengers and keep the monthly payments to less than $3,700, you need to purchase two vans, three sedans, and two compact cars. Notice that Solver's solution includes two long decimals that are so small as to be insignificant. You'll now format the worksheet cells to display only integers. Also, because the Original Value column doesn't contain any useful information, you'll delete it.
5. Press **[Ctrl]**, click cell **E8** and cell **E14**, click the **Decrease Decimal button** on the Standard toolbar until the cells display no decimal places
6. Right-click the **column D column header**, click **Delete** in the pop-up menu, press **[Ctrl][Home]**, then put your name in the worksheet footer, save the workbook, and print the worksheet
   You've successfully found the best combination of vehicles using Solver. The settings you specified in the Solver Parameters for the Multiple Loans worksheet are saved along with the workbook.
7. Close the workbook and exit Excel

FIGURE K-20: **Solver Results dialog box**

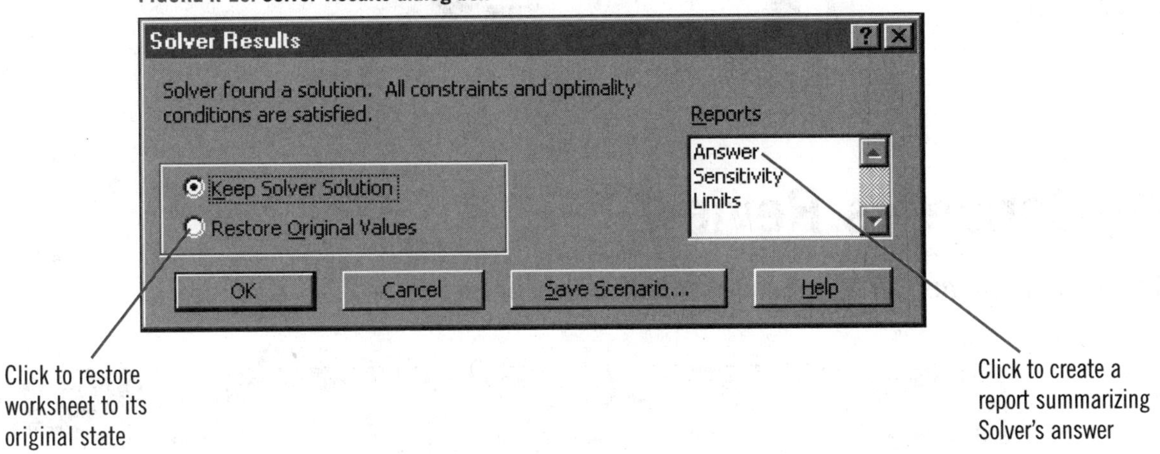

FIGURE K-21: **Answer Report**

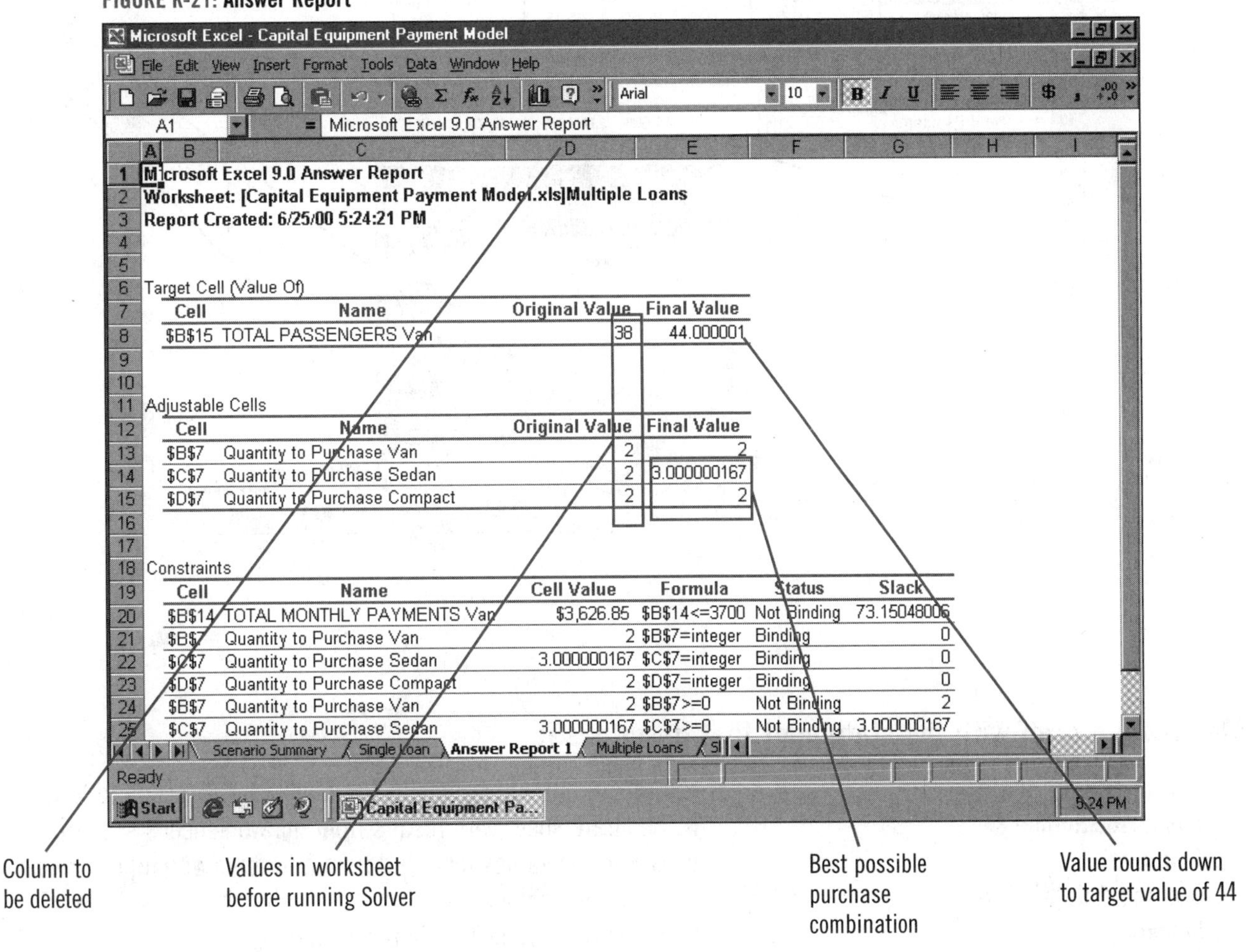

Practice

► Concepts Review

Label each element of the Excel screen shown in Figure K-22.

FIGURE K-22

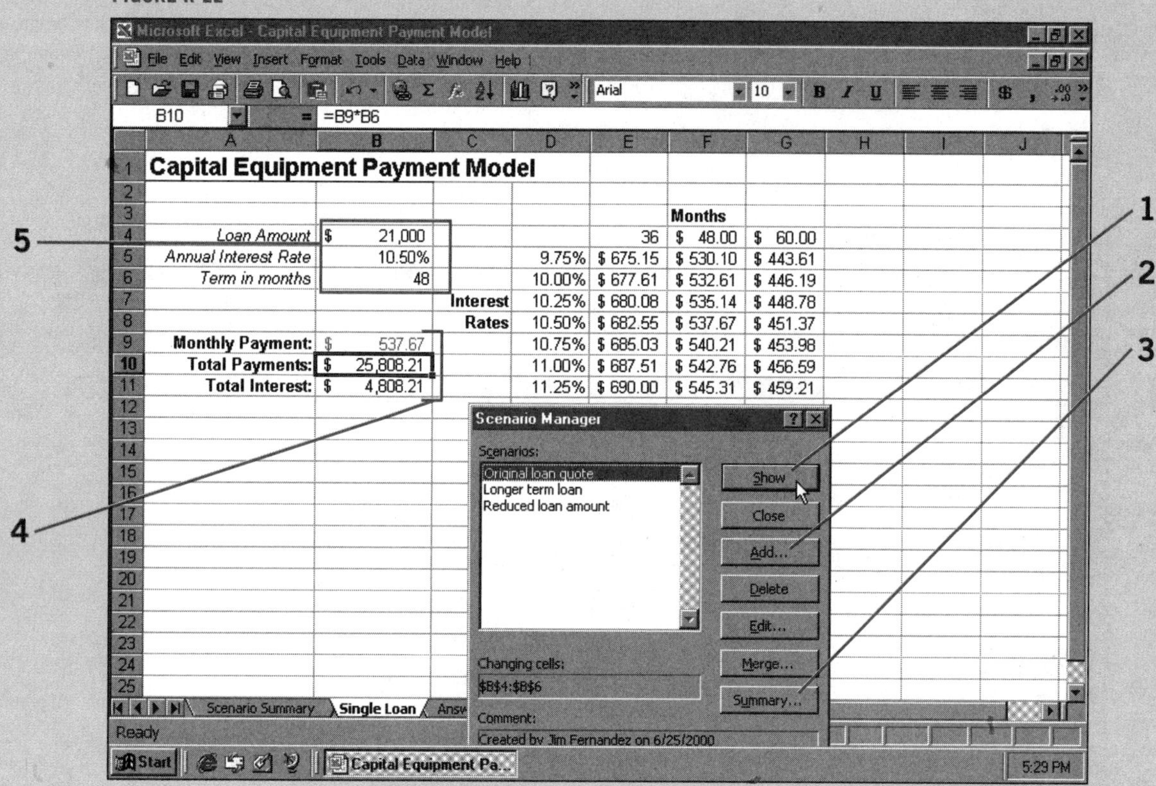

Match each term with the statement that describes it.

6. **Two-input data table**
7. **Scenario summary**
8. **Goal Seek**
9. **One-input data table**
10. **Solver**

a. Add-in that helps you solve complex what-if scenarios
b. Separate sheet with results from the worksheet's scenarios
c. Generates values resulting from a formula and input values variations across the top row and left column
d. Helps you backsolve what-if scenarios
e. Generates values resulting from a formula and input values variations across the top row or left column

Select the best answer from the list of choices.

11. A scenario is
- **a.** A worksheet model.
- **b.** A set of values used to forecast worksheet results.
- **c.** The same as a changing cell.
- **d.** The same as a dependent cell.

12. What are changing cells?
- **a.** Input cells that change, depending on their formulas.
- **b.** Formulas that change, depending on their input cells.
- **c.** Input cells whose values can be changed in a scenario.
- **d.** Cells that change positions during a what-if analysis.

13. Dependent cells are usually
- **a.** Formula cells that depend on input from other cells.
- **b.** Data cells that depend on their formulas.
- **c.** Input cells that depend on the results of a data table.
- **d.** Formula cells that depend on the results of a scenario.

14. In Solver, the cell containing the formula is called the
- **a.** Changing cell.
- **b.** Input cell.
- **c.** Output cell.
- **d.** Target cell.

Skills Review

1. Define a what-if analysis.
- **a.** Open the workbook titled EX K-2, then save it as "Capital Equipment Repair Models" and make sure the Cappuccino Machine Repair sheet is active.
- **b.** State the purpose of the worksheet model.
- **c.** Locate the data input cells.
- **d.** Locate any dependent cells.
- **e.** Write three questions this what-if analysis model could answer.

2. Track a what-if analysis with Scenario Manager.
- **a.** Set up the most likely scenario with the current data input values. Select range B3:B5, then create a scenario called Most Likely.
- **b.** Add a scenario called Best Case using the same changing cells, but change the $B$3 value to 50, change $B$4 value to 45, then change the $B$5 value to .75. Add the scenario to the list.
- **c.** Add a scenario called Worst Case. Change the $B$3 value to 75, change the $B$4 value to 70, then change the $B$5 value to 2.
- **d.** If necessary, drag the Scenario Manager dialog box to the right until columns A and B are visible.
- **e.** Show the Worst Case scenario results.
- **f.** Show the Best Case scenario results. Finally, display the Most Likely scenario results.
- **g.** Close the Scenario Manager dialog box.
- **h.** Save your work.

3. **Generate a scenario summary.**
   a. Create names for the input value cells and the dependent cell in the range A3:B7 (based on the left column).
   b. Verify that the names were created.
   c. Create a Scenario Summary report in the result cell B7.
   d. Edit cell B2 to read "Scenario Summary for Cappuccino Machine Repair".
   e. Delete the Current Values column.
   f. Delete the notes beginning in cell B11.
   g. Return to cell A1, add your name to the sheet footer, then print the Scenario Summary report in landscape orientation and save your work.
4. **Project figures using a data table.**
   a. Click the Cappuccino Machine Repair sheet tab.
   b. Enter the label "Labor $" in cell D3.
   c. Adjust the formatting of the label so that it is boldfaced and right-aligned.
   d. In cell D4, enter 50; then in cell D5, enter 55.
   e. Select range D4:D5, then use the fill handle to extend the series to cell D9.
   f. Reference the job cost formula in the upper-right corner of the table structure: In cell E3, enter =B7.
   g. Format the contents of cell E3 as hidden, using the ;; Custom formatting type on the Number tab of the Format Cells dialog box.
   h. Generate the new job costs based on the varying labor costs: Select range D3:E9 and create a data table. In the Table dialog box, make cell B3 the Column Input Cell.
   i. Format range E3:E9 as currency.
   j. Add your name to the footer, save the workbook, then preview and print the worksheet.
5. **Create a two-input data table.**
   a. Move the contents of cell D3 to cell C6.
   b. Delete the contents of range E4:E9.
   c. Format cell E3 using the Currency Style button, then move the contents of cell E3 to cell D3.
   d. Format the contents of cell D3 as hidden, using the ;; Custom formatting type on the Number tab of the Format Cells dialog box.
   e. Enter "Hrs. per job" in cell F2, and format it so it is boldfaced.
   f. Enter "1" in cell E3, enter 1.5 in cell F3, then enter 2 in cell G3.
   g. Select range D3:G9 and make it a data table, making cell B5 the row input cell and cell B3 the column input cell.
   h. Format range F4:G9 as currency.
   i. Save the workbook, preview, then print the worksheet.
6. **Use Goal Seek.**
   a. Determine what the parts would have to cost so that the cost to complete the job is $125: Click cell B7, and open the Goal Seek dialog box.
   b. Enter 125 as the To value, and B4 as the By changing cell.
   c. Return to the worksheet and note the cost of the parts.
   d. Save the workbook.
   e. Determine what the labor would have to cost so that the cost to complete the job is $100. Note the result.
   f. Save the workbook.
   g. Determine what the number of hours would have to be for the cost to complete the job to equal $90. Note the result.
   h. On a blank area of the worksheet, enter the results you obtained when the job cost equaled $125, the labor costs when the job cost equaled $100, and the hours when the job cost equaled $90.
   i. Save the workbook, then preview and print the worksheet.

7. Perform a complex what-if analysis with Solver and generate an Answer Report.
  a. Click the Vehicle Repair sheet tab to make it active, then open the Solver dialog box.
  b. Make B16 the target cell, with a target value of 146.
  c. Use cells B6:D6 as the changing cells.
  d. Specify that cell B14 must be greater than or equal to 4000.
  e. Specify that cell B15 must be greater than or equal to 6000.
  f. Use Solver to find a solution.
  g. Generate an Answer Report and restore the original values to the worksheet.
  h. Edit the Answer Report to delete the original values column.
  i. Add your name to the footer, save the workbook, preview and print the Answer Report, then close the workbook.

Independent Challenges

1. You are an independent mortgage broker and have been working on your own for several years. One of your clients is a couple who wants to buy their first home and has qualified for a $150,000 loan. You have created a preliminary worksheet model to determine their monthly payment based on several different interest rates and loan terms. Although they are still saving for a down payment, the couple predicts they will be ready to buy in about six months. Interest rates are on the rise, and you want to show your clients a few different mortgage payment scenarios. The couple wants to secure either a 15-year or a 30-year fixed loan. Using Scenario Manager, create the following three scenarios: the original quote, a 30-year loan at 8%; a 30-year loan at 10%; and a 15-year loan at 7.75%. Then create a Scenario Summary report showing the details.

To complete this independent challenge:

  a. Open the workbook titled EX K-3, then save it as "Fixed-Rate Mortgage Loan Payment Model".
  b. Using Scenario Manager and assuming a constant loan amount of $150,000, create the following three scenarios: one with the current input values called 30-year loan at 8%; a 30-year loan at 10%; and a 15-year loan at 7.75%. Use cells B4:B6 as the changing cells for each scenario, and create range names as necessary.
  c. Show each scenario to make sure it performs as intended.
  d. Generate a scenario summary titled "Scenario Summary for Fixed-Rate Mortgage Loan Payment". Eliminate any references to current values in the report.
  e. Add your name to the footer, preview, then print the scenario summary.
  f. Save the worksheet, return to Sheet1 and delete the range names, then close the workbook.

2. Your real-estate clients are grateful for the information you provided in the what-if scenarios. The couple asks if you can show them what the monthly payments would be for a $150,000 loan, over 15- and 30-year terms, with interest rates ranging in 0.25% increments. Using the workbook provided, create a two-input data table that shows the results of varying loan term and interest rates.

To complete this independent challenge:

  a. If you completed Independent Challenge 1, open and use the workbook titled "Fixed-Rate Mortgage Loan Payment Model". Otherwise, open the workbook titled EX K-3, then save it as "Fixed-Rate Mortgage Loan Payment Model".
  b. Create a data table structure with varying interest rates for 15- and 30-year terms. Use 7% as the lowest possible rate. Make the highest possible interest rate 3% greater than the lowest, and vary the rates in-between by 0.25%.
  c. Reference the appropriate cell in the table.
  d. Generate the two-input data table.
  e. Add your name to the footer, then preview and print the scenario summary.
  f. Save the worksheet, then close the workbook.

3. As the owner of Micros Unlimited, a small personal computer (PC) store, you assemble your own PCs to sell to the home and business markets. You have created a PC production financial model to determine the costs and profits associated with your three models: PC-1, PC-2, and PC-3. You want to show how the hourly cost affects total profit for each PC model your company produces. To do this, you decide to use a one-input data table. Use the workbook provided to create the table.

In addition to the data table, you need to do a what-if analysis regarding the effect of hours per unit on total profit. Specifically, you want to find out by how much you must reduce hours per unit to increase total profits to a specific target value. You decide to solve the problem by changing the hours only for PC-3, using Goal Seek. If that doesn't work, you'll specify more complicated parameters using Solver.

To complete this independent challenge:

a. Open the workbook titled EX K-4, then save it as "PC Production Model".
b. Create a data table structure with varying hourly costs, in $5 increments, from $15 to $45. Reference multiple profit formulas across the top of the table. (*Hint:* Although this is a one-input data table, you will have multiple columns, one for each model's profit formula.)
c. Generate the one-input data table that shows the effect of varying hourly cost on the profitability of each machine.
d. Boldface the table values that are the same as the total profit figures in the table (the current values).
e. Preview, then print the worksheet.
f. Open the Goal Seek dialog box and set cell H9 to 25000 by changing cell B8. Click OK to find a solution.
g. Save the workbook, then print the worksheet.
h. Open the Solver dialog box. Set cell H8 as the target cell, with a value of 10000. Use cells B6:B8 as the changing cells. Specify that cells B6:B8 must be greater than or equal to 0 (zero) and less than or equal to 4.
i. Generate an Answer Report and restore the original values to the worksheet.
j. Add your name to the footer, save the workbook, preview and print the Answer Report, then close the workbook.

4. Jim Fernandez has asked you to help him explore ways to increase MediaLoft's profitability. He asks you to start with the profitability figures for the New York store's café.

To complete this independent challenge:

a. Connect to the Internet, and go to the MediaLoft intranet site at http://www.course.com/Illustrated/MediaLoft. Click the Accounting link, then click the Café Budget link. Print the page and disconnect from the Internet.

b. Open a new Excel worksheet and save it as "Cafe Profitability". Enter the sales and expense information for the fourth quarter, then enter formulas that calculate total expenses and net profit.

c. Jim is negotiating a new lease for the New York store and wants to know the effect of a reduced rent on fourth-quarter profitability. Use a data table to calculate profitability for the quarter for varying levels of rent from $2,700 to $3,500 in $100 increments.

d. Jim also wants to find a way to increase profitability for the fourth quarter to $40,000. He feels that marketing could be persuaded to reduce advertising expenses to help accomplish this. To what level would advertising have to be reduced for Jim to achieve his goal?

e. Jim feels he could increase profitability by taking out a loan to buy more inventory and rent more warehouse space. He wants to investigate taking out a $50,000 loan for five years at a variable rate. He feels the rate would vary between 6.5% and 8.5%, at .5% increments. He wants to forecast the amount by which MediaLoft's payments would vary for each possible level of interest rate within this range. Display a blank worksheet and use the appropriate Excel feature to find the answer.

f. Jim now tells you he would also consider varying the term of the loan for 5, 10, or 15 years. Use a blank part of the worksheet to calculate MediaLoft's payments in each of these situations, using the same interest rate assumptions. Format and label the figures appropriately, add your name to the footer, then save and print the worksheet.

Visual Workshop

Create the worksheet shown in Figure K-23. Make sure to generate the table on the right as a data table. Save the workbook as "Color Laptop Loan Payment Model". Add your name to the footer, then preview and print the worksheet. Print the worksheet again with the formulas displayed.

FIGURE K-23

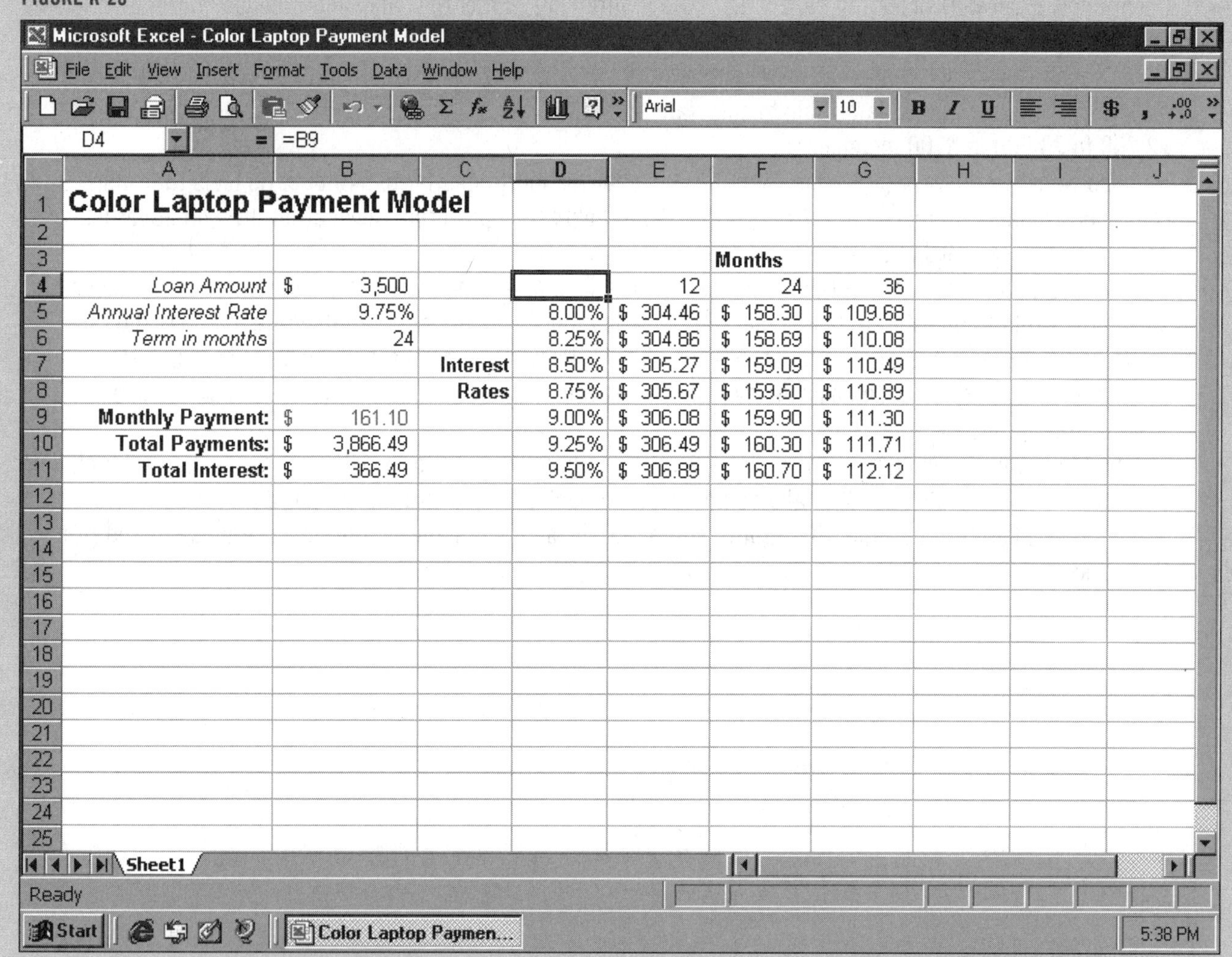

Excel 2000

Unit L

Summarizing Data with PivotTables

Objectives

- Plan and design a PivotTable report
- MOUS Create a PivotTable report
- MOUS Change the summary function of a PivotTable report
- MOUS Analyze three-dimensional data
- Update a PivotTable report
- MOUS Change the structure and format of a PivotTable report
- MOUS Create a PivotChart report
- Use the GETPIVOTDATA function

With the Excel PivotTable feature, you can summarize selected data in a worksheet, then list and display that data in a table format. The interactive quality of a PivotTable allows you to freely rearrange, or "pivot," parts of the table structure around the data and summarize any data values within the table. You also can designate a PivotTable page field that lets you view list items three-dimensionally, as if they were arranged in a stack of pages. There are two PivotTable features in Excel: PivotTable reports and PivotChart reports. In this unit, you will plan, design, create, update, and change the layout and format of a PivotTable report. You will also add a page field to a PivotTable report, then create a PivotChart report. It's nearing the end of the fiscal year and the Accounting department has asked Jim Fernandez to develop a departmental salary analysis for selected corporate and management positions. Jim uses a PivotTable report to do this.

Excel 2000

Planning and Designing a PivotTable Report

Creating a PivotTable report (often called a PivotTable) involves only a few steps. Before you begin, however, you need to review the data and consider how a PivotTable can best summarize it. Jim plans and designs his PivotTable using the following guidelines:

Details

Review the list information

Before you can effectively summarize list data in a PivotTable, you need to know what information each field contains and understand the list's scope. Jim is working with a list of corporate and managerial staff that he received from Karen Rosen, MediaLoft's human resource manager. This list is shown in Figure L-1.

Determine the purpose of the PivotTable, then write down the names of the fields you want to include

The purpose of Jim's PivotTable is to summarize corporate salary information by position across various departments. Jim will include the following fields in the PivotTable: department, position, and annual salary.

Determine which field contains the data you want summarized and which summary function will be used

Jim intends to summarize salary information by averaging the salary field for each department and position. He'll do this by using the Excel Average function.

Decide how you want to arrange the data

The layout of a PivotTable is crucial in delivering its intended message. Jim will define department as a column field, position as a row field, and annual salary as a data summary field. See Figure L-2.

Determine the location of the PivotTable

You can place a PivotTable in any worksheet of any workbook. Placing a PivotTable on a separate worksheet makes it easier to locate, however, and prevents you from accidentally overwriting parts of an existing sheet. Jim decides to create the PivotTable as a new worksheet in the current workbook.

FIGURE L-1: Management salary worksheet

	A	B	C	D	E	F	G	H	I	J
1	First Name	Last Name	Hire Date	Department	Position	Mgmt Level	Annual Salary	Perf Rating		
2	Maria	Abbott	10/18/93	Corporate Manager	General Sales Manager	2	70,000	2		
3	Tyler	Amodo	9/5/94	Corporate Staff	Division Manager	3	65,000	3		
4	Michael	Cole	2/6/97	Management Staff	Accounting Staff	2	42,000	3		
5	Katherine	DeNiro	4/29/99	Corporate Staff	Accounting Staff	3	55,000	2		
6	David	Dumont	4/7/86	Section Manager	Director of Training	3	53,500	4		
7	Catherine	Favreau	3/19/99	Corporate Manager	Director of Advertising	2	55,500	3		
8	George	Feake	8/1/94	Store	Store Manager	3	46,000	3		
9	Jim	Fernandez	1/2/96	Corporate Manager	Office Manager	2	58,000	5		
10	Louis	Grazio	5/24/96	Management Staff	Payroll Manager	3	45,000	3		
11	Lois	Greenwood	5/2/94	Store	Store Manager	3	42,000	4		
12	Patrick	Ikutu	3/12/98	Corporate Staff	Division Manager	3	48,000	4		
13	Robert	Jaworski	3/1/98	Corporate Staff	Accounting Staff	2	42,000	4		
14	John	Kim	3/3/99	Section Manager	Dir. Of Shipping	3	57,500	1		
15	Mike	MacDowell	2/8/99	Management Staff	Web Manager	3	55,000	2		
16	Goran	Manchevski	4/5/95	Store	Store Manager	3	47,500	2		
17	Michael	Martin	2/15/98	Store	Store Manager	3	48,000	3		
18	Eileen	Murphy	2/10/94	Corporate Staff	Ad Copy Writer	4	45,000	3		
19	Patricia	Fabel	6/21/96	Management Staff	Accounting Staff	3	48,000	3		
20	Elizabeth	Reed	2/1/96	Corporate Manager	Vice President	1	85,000	5		
21	Evelyn	Storey	1/10/92	Corporate Staff	Circulation Manager	3	55,000	4		
22	Alice	Wegman	1/5/97	Corporate Manager	Marketing Manager	2	65,000	4		
23										
24										

Manager List

Ready

Start | Microsoft Excel - Ex l-1 | 10:45 PM

FIGURE L-2: Example of a PivotTable report

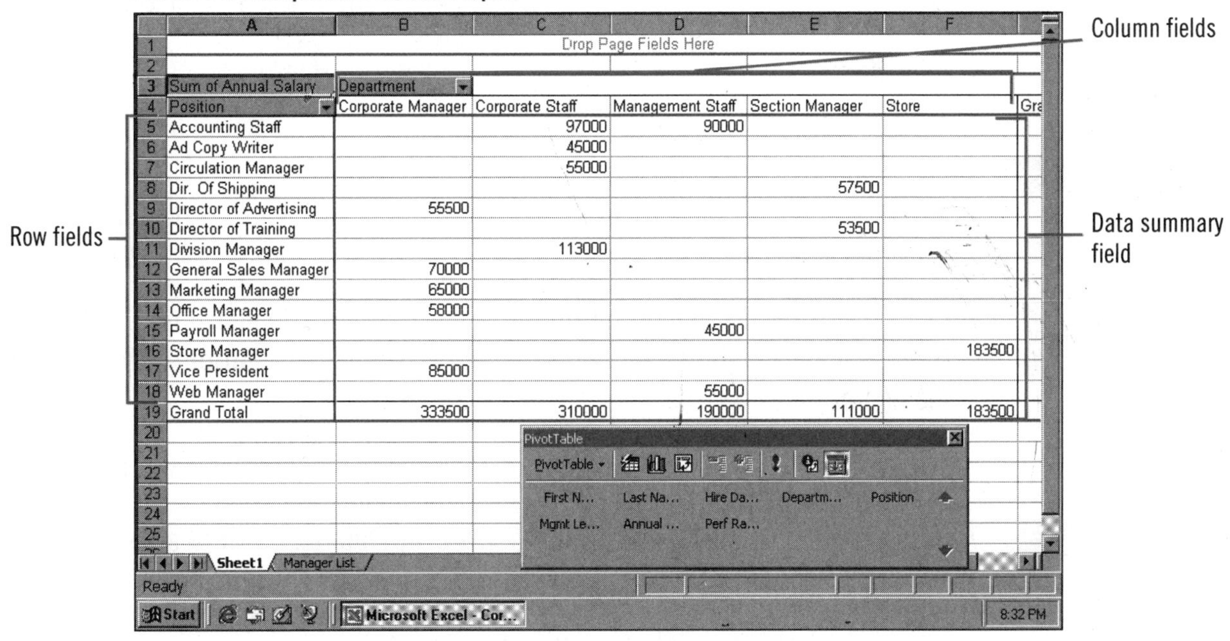

	A	B	C	D	E	F
3	Sum of Annual Salary	Department				
4	Position	Corporate Manager	Corporate Staff	Management Staff	Section Manager	Store
5	Accounting Staff		97000	90000		
6	Ad Copy Writer		45000			
7	Circulation Manager		55000			
8	Dir. Of Shipping				57500	
9	Director of Advertising	55500				
10	Director of Training				53500	
11	Division Manager		113000			
12	General Sales Manager	70000				
13	Marketing Manager	65000				
14	Office Manager	58000				
15	Payroll Manager			45000		
16	Store Manager					183500
17	Vice President	85000				
18	Web Manager			55000		
19	Grand Total	333500	310000	190000	111000	183500

Creating a PivotTable Report

Once you've planned and designed your PivotTable, you can create it. The PivotTable Wizard takes you through the process step-by-step. With the planning and design stage complete, Jim is ready to create a PivotTable that summarizes corporate salary information. After they add the remaining salary information, the Accounting and Human Resources departments will use this information to budget salaries for the coming year.

Steps

QuickTip

To return personalized toolbars and menus to their default state, click Tools on the menu bar, click Customize, click the Options tab in the Customize dialog box, click Reset my usage data to restore the default settings, click Yes, click Close, then close the Drawing toolbar if it is displayed.

1. Open the workbook titled **EX L-1**, then save it as **Corporate Salaries**
   This worksheet contains information about some of MediaLoft's corporate employees and managers, including hire date, department, position, management level, salary, and performance rating. Notice that the records are sorted alphabetically by last name.
2. Click cell **A1** if necessary, click **Data** on the menu bar, then click **PivotTable and PivotChart report**
   The first PivotTable and PivotChart Wizard dialog box opens, as shown in Figure L-3. This is where you specify the type of data source you want to use for your PivotTable: an Excel list or database, an external data source (for example, a Microsoft Access file), or multiple consolidation ranges (another term for worksheet ranges). You also have the option of choosing a PivotTable or PivotChart report.
3. Make sure the **Microsoft Excel list or database option button** is selected, make sure **PivotTable** is selected, then click **Next**
   The second PivotTable and PivotChart Wizard dialog box opens. Because the cell pointer was located within the list before you opened the PivotTable Wizard, Excel automatically completes the Range box with the table range that includes the selected cell—in this case, $A$1:$H$22. You can either type a new range in the Range box or confirm that the PivotTable will be created from the existing range.
4. Click **Next**
   The third PivotTable Wizard dialog box opens. You use this dialog box to specify the location of the PivotTable.

Trouble?

If your PivotTable toolbar does not appear, click View on the menu bar, click Toolbars, then click PivotTable to select it. If the PivotTable toolbar blocks your view of the worksheet, drag it to the bottom of the worksheet window.

5. Make sure **New Worksheet** is selected, then click **Finish**
   A worksheet appears with an empty PivotTable, as shown in Figure L-4. The PivotTable toolbar also appears. It contains buttons that allow you to manipulate data as well as field names that you can drag into various "drop areas" of the PivotTable to analyze your data.
6. Drag the **Department field button** from the PivotTable toolbar to the area marked **Drop Column Fields here**, then drag the **Position field button** to the **Drop Row Fields Here** area
   This format will create a PivotTable with the departments as column headers and the management positions as row labels. To display the entire field name in a ToolTip in the PivotTable toolbar, place the pointer over the field button.

QuickTip

You can use more than one summary function in a PivotTable by simply dragging multiple field buttons to the data area.

7. Drag the **Annual Salary field button** to the **Drop Data Items Here** area
   Because SUM is the Excel default function for data fields containing numbers, Excel automatically calculates the sum of the salaries by department and by position. See Figure L-5. Notice that the position titles now appear as row labels in the left column, and the department names are listed across the columns as field names.

FIGURE L-3: First PivotTable Wizard dialog box

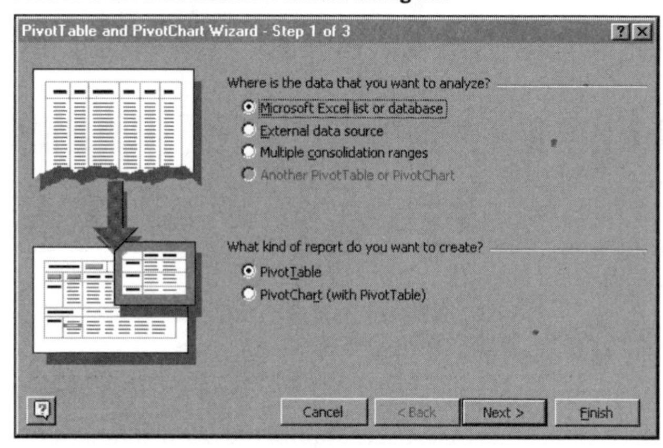

FIGURE L-4: New PivotTable ready to receive field data

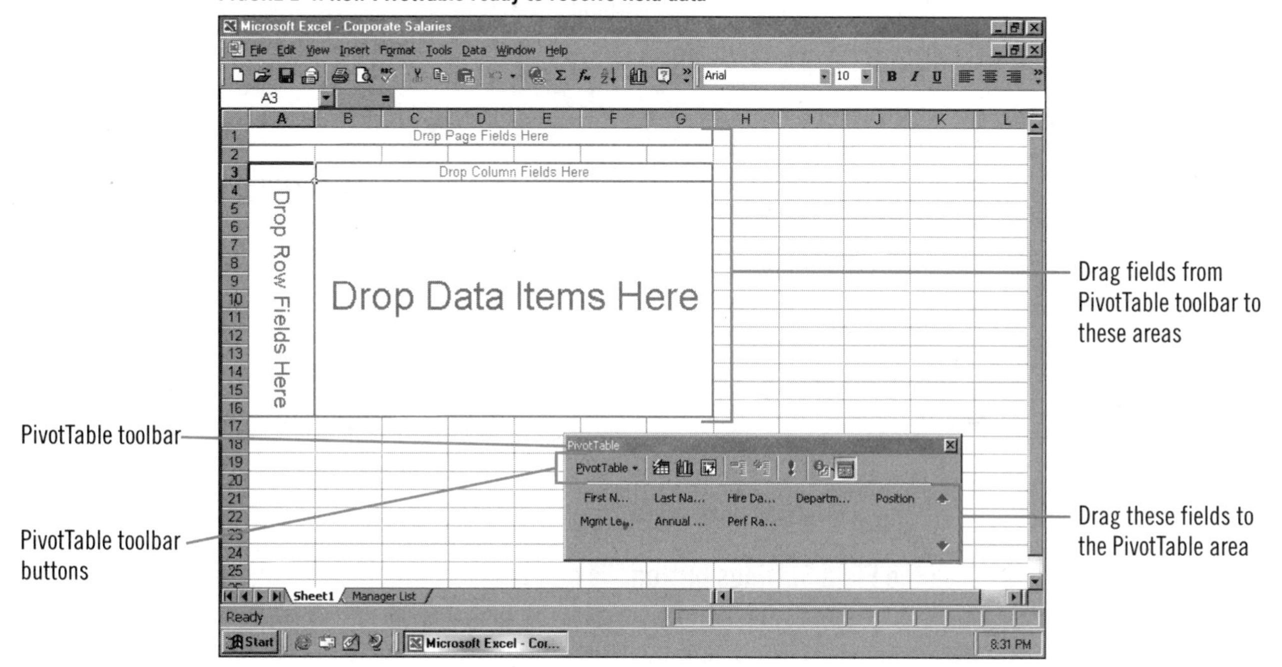

FIGURE L-5: New PivotTable with fields in place

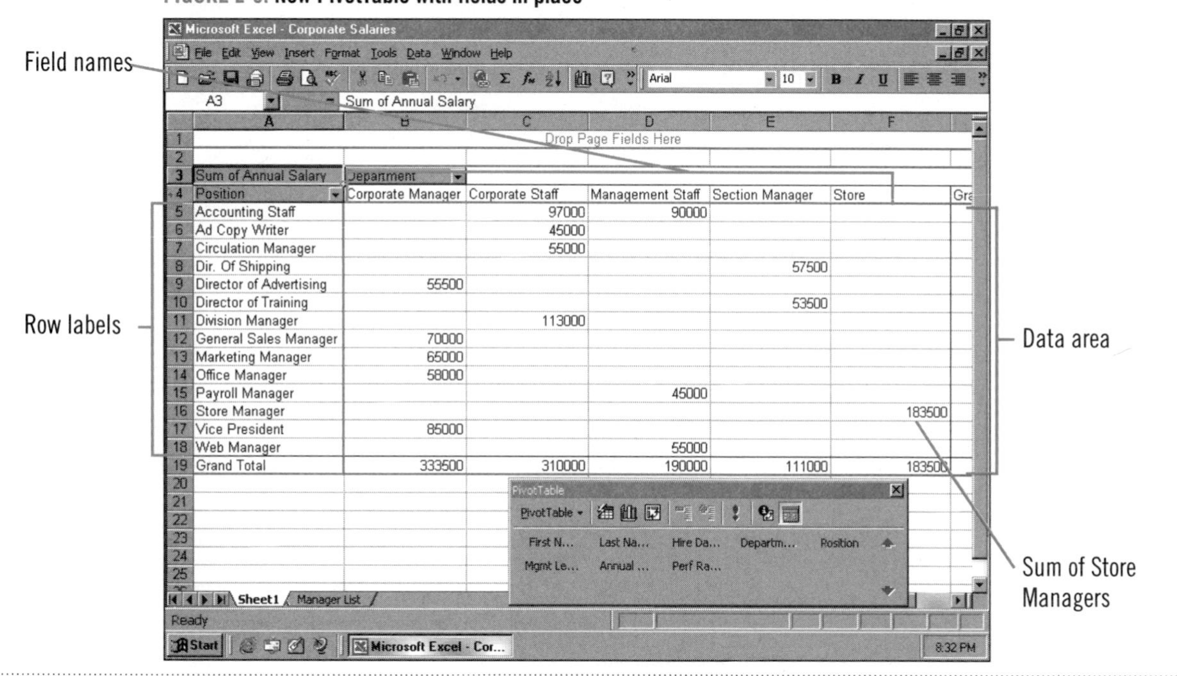

Excel 2000

Changing the Summary Function of a PivotTable Report

A PivotTable's **summary function** controls what type of calculation is applied to the table data. Unless you specify otherwise, Excel applies the SUM function to numeric data and the COUNT function to data fields containing text. However, you can easily change the SUM function in the PivotTable Wizard dialog box to a different function, such as AVERAGE (which calculates the average of all values in the field), PRODUCT (which multiplies all the values in a field), or MAX (which finds the highest value in a field). Jim wants to calculate the average salary for the managers using the AVERAGE function.

Steps 1 2 3 4

1. **Click any cell in the data area, then click the Field Settings button on the PivotTable toolbar**
   The PivotTable Field dialog box opens. The functions listed in the Summarize by list box designate how the data will be calculated. Other buttons on the PivotTable toolbar are described in Table L-1.
2. **In the Summarize by list box, click Average, then click OK**
   The PivotTable Field dialog box closes. The data area of the PivotTable shows the average salary for each position by department. See Figure L-6. The numbers representing sums in the last column and row now represent averages of annual salary. After reviewing the data, you decide that it would be more useful to sum the salary information than to average it.
3. **Click the Field Settings button on the PivotTable toolbar; in the Summarize by list box, click Sum, then click OK**
   The PivotTable Field dialog box closes and Excel recalculates the PivotTable—this time, summing the salary data instead of averaging it.
4. **Rename Sheet1 PivotTable, add your name to the worksheet footer, save the workbook, then preview and print the worksheet in landscape orientation**

FIGURE L-6: PivotTable showing averages

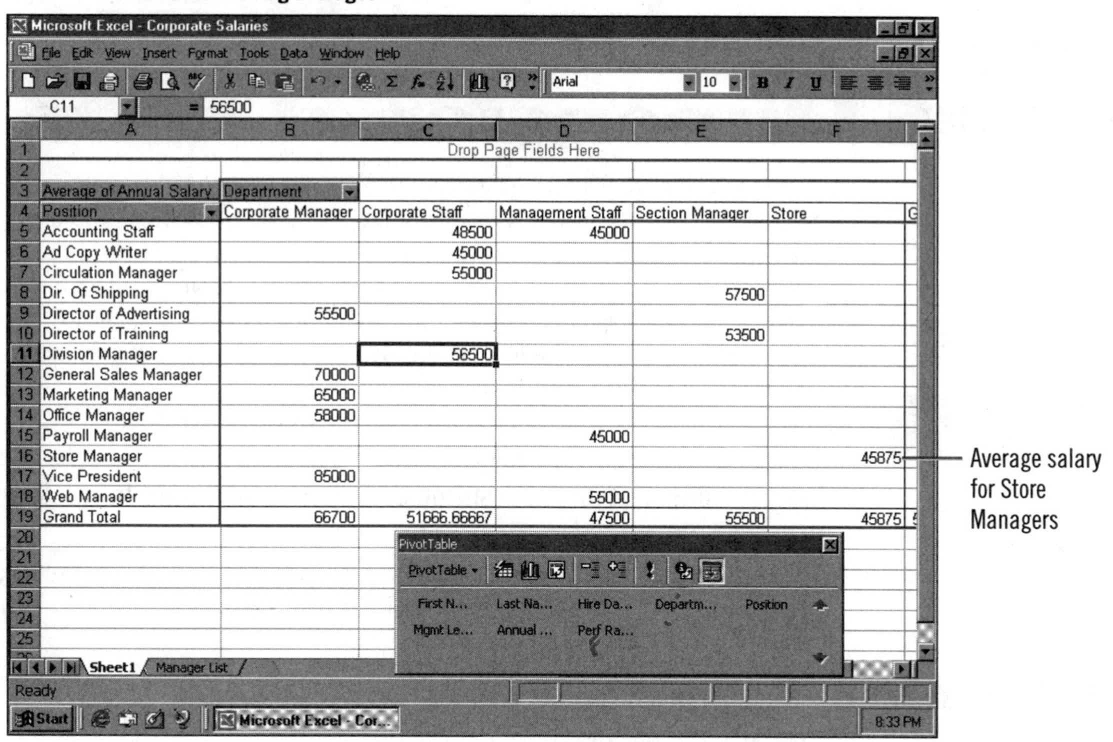

TABLE L-1: PivotTable toolbar buttons

button	name	description
PivotTable ▾	**PivotTable Menu**	Displays menu of PivotTable commands
	Format Report	Displays a list of PivotTable formats
	Chart Wizard	Creates a PivotChart report
	PivotTable Wizard	Starts PivotTable Wizard
	Hide Detail	Hides detail in table groupings
	Show Detail	Shows detail in table groupings
	Refresh Data	Updates list changes within the table
	Field Settings	Displays a list of field settings
	Show/Hide Fields	Displays/hides PivotTable fields on toolbar; in a chart, displays or hides outlines and labels

Excel 2000

Analyzing Three-Dimensional Data

When row and column field positions are established in a PivotTable, you are working with two-dimensional data. You can convert a PivotTable to a three-dimensional data analysis tool by adding a **page field**. Page fields make the data appear as if it is stacked in pages, thus adding a third dimension to the analysis. When using a page field, you are in effect filtering data through that field. To add the page field, you simply drag it to the Drop Page Fields Here area. Jim wants to filter the PivotTable so that only one department's data is visible at one time. He uses the PivotTable Wizard to add the Department page field.

Steps

1. Drag the **Department field button** from the column area to the **Drop Page Fields Here** area
   The PivotTable is re-created with a page field showing data for each department. See Figure L-7. You can select and view the data for each department, page by page, by clicking the Department list arrow and selecting the page you want to view.
2. Click the **Department list arrow**
3. Click **Management Staff**, then click **OK**
   The PivotTable displays the salary data for the management staff only, as shown in Figure L-8.
4. Click the **Department list arrow**, click **Corporate Staff**, then click **OK**
   The salaries for the corporate staff appear.
5. Save the workbook, then print the worksheet

QuickTip

To display each page of the page field on a separate worksheet, click PivotTable on the PivotTable toolbar, then click Show Pages, then click OK.

FIGURE L-7: PivotTable with Department as page field

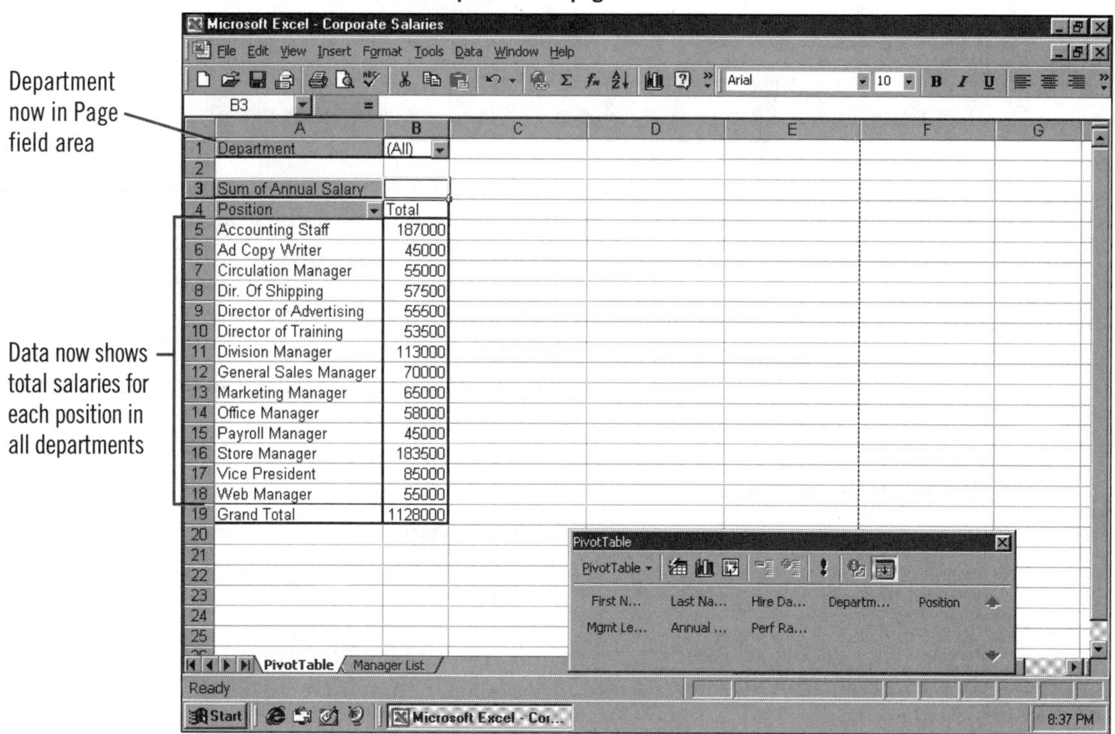

FIGURE L-8: PivotTable filtered to show only salaries for management staff

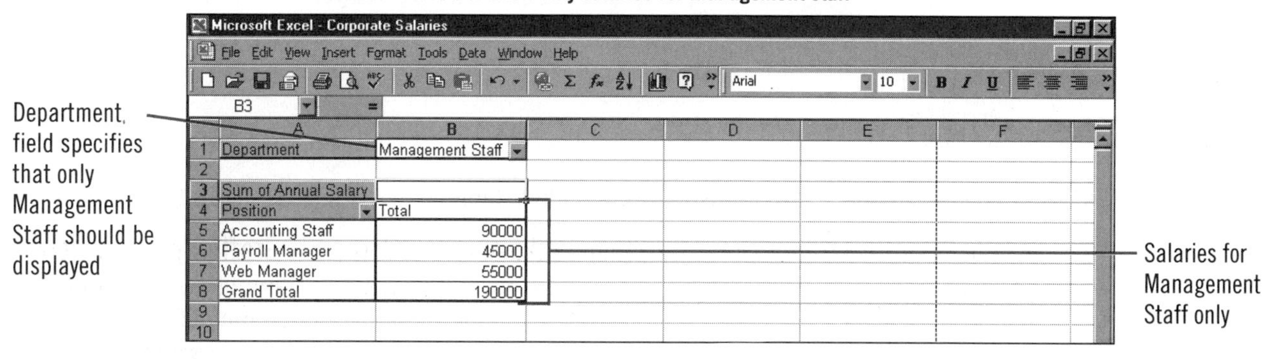

Excel 2000

Excel 2000

Updating a PivotTable Report

The data displayed in a PivotTable looks like typical worksheet data. Because the PivotTable data is linked to a source list, however, the values and results in the PivotTable are read-only values. That means you cannot move or modify part of a PivotTable by inserting or deleting rows, editing results, or moving cells. To change PivotTable data, you must edit the items directly in the list you used to create the table, called the **source list**, and then update, or **refresh**, the PivotTable to reflect the changes. Jim just learned that the training manager, Howard Freeberg, was never entered into the workbook. Jim needs to add information about this manager to the current list; he starts by inserting a row for Freeberg's information.

1. **Click the Manager List sheet tab**
   By inserting the new row in the correct position alphabetically, you will not need to sort the list again. Also, by adding the new manager within the named range, Database, the new row data will be included automatically in the named range.
2. Right-click the **row 10 header**; then on the pop-up menu, click **Insert**
   A blank row appears as the new row 10, and the data in the old row 10 moves down to row 11. You'll enter the data on Freeberg in the new row 10.
3. Enter the data for the new manager based on the following information

field name	new data item
First Name	Howard
Last Name	Freeberg
Hire Date	10/29/98
Department	Corporate Staff
Position	Training Manager
Mgmt Level	2
Annual Salary	59,000
Perf Rating	2

   After you add data, you must refresh the PivotTable so that it reflects the additional data.
4. Click the **PivotTable sheet tab**, then make sure the Corporate Staff page is in view
   Notice that the Corporate Staff list does not currently include a training manager and that the grand total is $310,000. Before you select the Refresh Data command to refresh the PivotTable, you need to make sure the cell pointer is located within the current table range.
5. Click anywhere within the table range (A3:B9), then click the **Refresh Data button** on the PivotTable toolbar
   A message dialog box opens with the message "The Refresh Data operation changed the PivotTable report" to confirm that the update was successful.
6. Click **OK**
   The PivotTable now includes the training manager in row 9, and the grand total has increased by the amount of his salary (59,000) to $369,000. See Figure L-9.
7. Save the workbook and print the worksheet

QuickTip

Clicking a row label in a PivotTable selects the entire row. Clicking a data cell selects only that cell.

FIGURE L-9: Refreshed PivotTable

Microsoft Excel - Corporate Salaries

	A	B
1	Department	Corporate Staff
2		
3	Sum of Annual Salary	
4	Position	Total
5	Accounting Staff	97000
6	Ad Copy Writer	45000
7	Circulation Manager	55000
8	Division Manager	113000
9	Training Manager	59000
10	Grand Total	369000

New record for Training Manager now appears in Corporate Staff salaries

Total reflects new record for Training Manager

Maintaining original table data

Once you select the Refresh Data command, you cannot undo the operation. If you want the PivotTable to display the original source data, you must change the source data list, then re-select the Refresh Data command. If you're concerned about the effect refreshing the PivotTable might have on your work, save a second (working) copy of the workbook so that your original data remains intact.

Excel 2000

Excel 2000

Changing the Structure and Format of a PivotTable Report

Although you cannot change the actual data in a PivotTable, you can alter its structure and format at any time. You might, for example, want to rename a PivotTable field button, add another column field, or switch the positions of existing fields. You can quickly change the way data is displayed in a PivotTable by dragging field buttons in the worksheet from a row position to a column position, or vice versa. Alternatively, you may want to enhance the appearance of a PivotTable by changing the way the text or values are formatted. It's a good idea to format a PivotTable using AutoFormat, because once you refresh a PivotTable any formatting that has not been applied to the cells through AutoFormat is removed. Jim wants to add the performance ratings to the PivotTable in order to supply the Accounting department with additional data needed for salary budgeting. Once the new field is added, Jim will format the PivotTable.

Steps

1. Make sure that the **PivotTable sheet** is active, that the Corporate Staff page is in view, and that the cell pointer is located anywhere inside the PivotTable (range A3:B10)
   When you move fields in a PivotTable, you can drag them as you did when you moved the Department field into the page area. Sometimes, however, you may want to drag fields while looking only at the PivotTable structure, without the data. You can do this by using the PivotTable Wizard Layout dialog box.
2. Click the **PivotTable Wizard button** on the PivotTable toolbar
3. Click **Layout**, drag the **Perf Rating button** to the **COLUMN** area and compare your screen with Figure L-10
4. Click **OK**, then click **Finish**
   The PivotTable is re-created, and the new field is added. In addition to displaying the manager's position and annual salary on each department page, each manager's last performance rating on a scale from 1 to 5 appears as a column label. Now you are ready to format the PivotTable.
5. Click cell **B5**, click the **Field Settings button** on the PivotTable toolbar, then in the PivotTable Field dialog box, click **Number**
6. Under Category in the Format Cells dialog box, click **Accounting**, edit the Decimal Places box to read **0**, click **OK**, then click **OK** again
   The PivotTable Field dialog box closes, and the annual salaries are formatted with commas and dollar signs.
7. Click cell **A3**; click the **Format Report button** on the PivotTable toolbar bar; in the AutoFormat dialog box, scroll down and then click **Table 2**, click **OK**, then click outside the range to deselect it
   The PivotTable appears as shown in Figure L-11. The AutoFormat is applied to all pages of the PivotTable.
8. Click the **Department list arrow**, click **Management Staff**, then click **OK**
   The Management Staff page has the same formatting.
9. Save the workbook, then preview and print the active sheet

QuickTip

Report formats 1–10 are indented formats, like a banded database report. Tables 1–10 are not indented. Indented reports contain only row fields, not column fields.

FIGURE L-10: Revised PivotTable structure

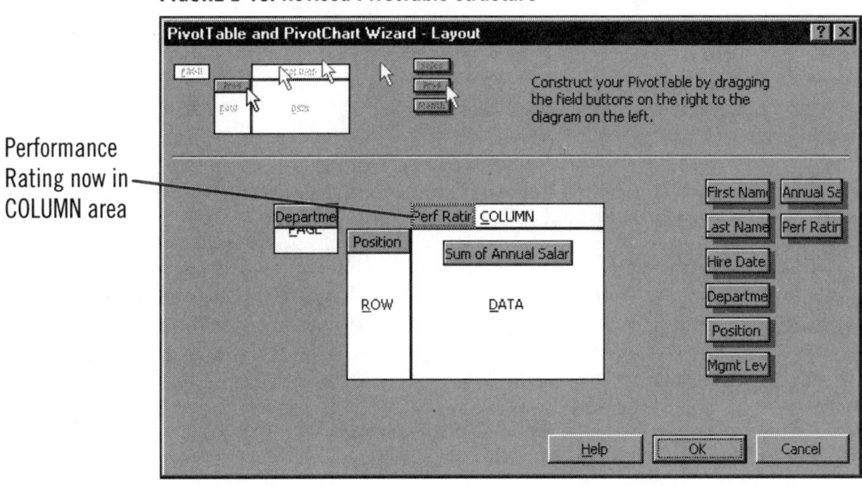

FIGURE L-11: Corporate Staff page with AutoFormat applied

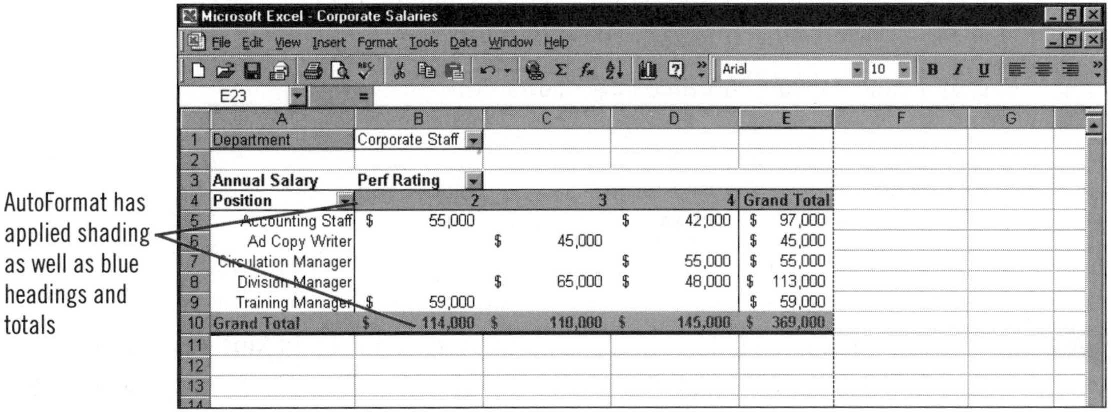

	A	B	C	D	E
1	Department	Corporate Staff			
2					
3	Annual Salary	Perf Rating			
4	Position	2	3	4	Grand Total
5	Accounting Staff	$ 55,000		$ 42,000	$ 97,000
6	Ad Copy Writer		$ 45,000		$ 45,000
7	Circulation Manager			$ 55,000	$ 55,000
8	Division Manager		$ 65,000	$ 48,000	$ 113,000
9	Training Manager	$ 59,000			$ 59,000
10	Grand Total	$ 114,000	$ 110,000	$ 145,000	$ 369,000

Excel 2000

Creating a PivotChart Report

A PivotChart report is a chart that you create from data or from a PivotTable report. Like a PivotTable report, a PivotChart report has fields that you can drag to explore new data relationships. Table L-2 describes how the elements in a PivotTable report correspond to the elements in a PivotChart report. When you create a PivotChart directly from data, Excel automatically creates a corresponding PivotTable report. When you change a PivotChart report by dragging fields, Excel updates the corresponding PivotTable report to show the new layout. You can create a PivotChart report from any PivotTable report to reflect that view of your data, but if you use an indented PivotTable report format, your chart will not have series fields; indented PivotTable report formats do not include column fields. Jim wants to chart the annual salary and performance rating information for the Corporate Manager department. He uses the PivotTable and PivotChart Wizard to create a column chart from the PivotTable data.

Steps

1. Click the **Manager List tab**, click anywhere in the data range, click **Data**, then click **PivotTable and PivotChart Report**
   The PivotTable and PivotChart Wizard opens.
2. Make sure Excel list or database is selected, then click to select **PivotChart (with PivotTable)** as shown in Figure L-12, click **Next**, then click **Next** again
   A message tells you that your existing PivotTable was created from the same source data and recommends using the same data to save memory.
3. Click **Yes**, click **Next**, then click **Finish**
   A new chart sheet opens, shown in Figure L-13. Jim wants to explore salary levels as they relate to performance ratings and management level.
4. Drag fields to PivotChart areas as follows:

Field	Area
Department	Page Fields
Management Level	Category Fields
Performance Rating	Series Fields
Annual Salary	Data

   The chart representing your data appears in the chart area.
5. Click **Sum of Annual Salary** on the PivotChart, click the **Field Settings button** on the PivotTable toolbar, click **Average** in the PivotTable Field dialog box, then click **OK**
   The PivotChart report is recalculated, as shown in Figure L-14.
6. Click the **Department list arrow**, click **Corporate Manager**, click **OK**, then drag the **Position field** from the PivotTable toolbar to the Series fields area (the legend).
   The positions and ratings appear in the legend. Jim now has more detail on which to base his discussions with Human Resources and upper management.
7. Save the workbook, place your name in the chart sheet footer, then preview and print the PivotChart report

Trouble?

If the Chart toolbar does not appear on your screen, open it: Click View on the menu bar, point to Toolbars, then click Chart.

FIGURE L-12: PivotTable and PivotChart Wizard

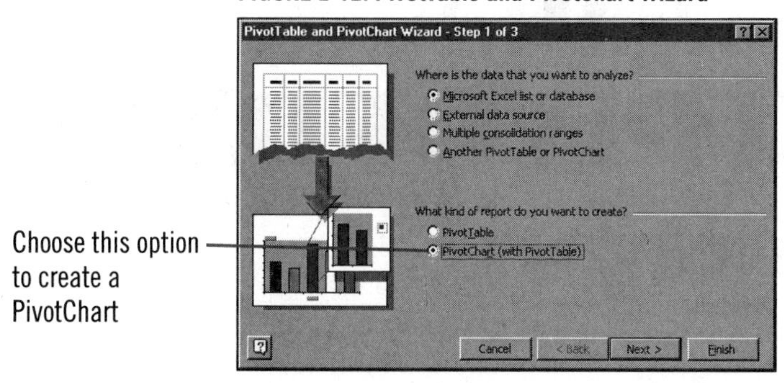

FIGURE L-13: New chart sheet, ready to receive fields

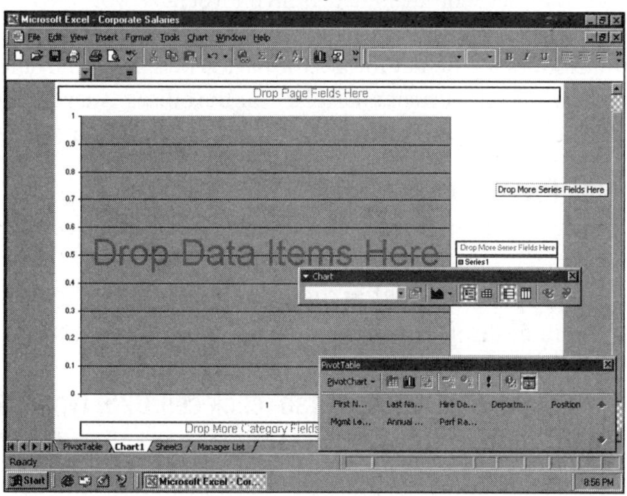

FIGURE L-14: PivotChart report recalculated to show averages

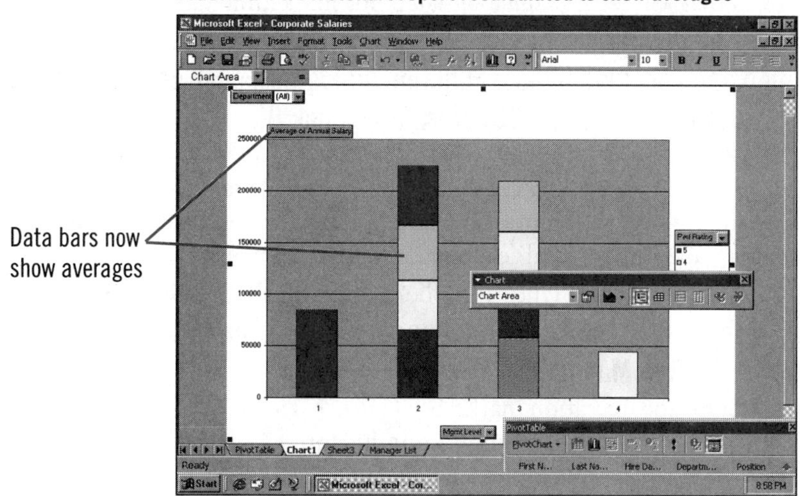

TABLE L-2: PivotTable and PivotChart elements

PivotTable items	become	PivotChart items
row fields		category fields
column fields		series fields
page fields		page fields

Excel 2000

Using the GETPIVOTDATA Function

Because a PivotTable is rearranged so easily, you can't use an ordinary cell reference when you want to reference a PivotTable cell in another worksheet. If you change the way data is displayed in a PivotTable (for example, by displaying a different page), the data moves, rendering an ordinary cell reference incorrect. Instead, to retrieve summary data from a PivotTable, you need to use the Excel GETPIVOTDATA function. Its syntax is displayed in Figure L-15. In creating next year's budget, the Accounting department is allocating money toward the payroll budget for the office manager. The department has asked Jim to include the current total salary for the office manager on the Manager List sheet. Jim uses the GETPIVOTDATA function to retrieve this information from the PivotTable.

1. Click the **PivotTable sheet tab**
   The Management Staff page is currently visible. You need the salary information for marketing managers in all departments.
2. Click the **Department list arrow**, click **(All)**, then click **OK**
   The PivotTable displays the salary data for all positions. Next, you will reference the total for marketing managers in the Manager List sheet.
3. Click the **Manager List sheet tab**, click cell **D25**, type **Office Manager Salary:**, click the **Enter button** on the formula bar, click the **Align Right button** on the Formatting toolbar, then click the **Bold button** on the Formatting toolbar
   The new label appears formatted in cell D25. Now, you'll enter a GETPIVOTDATA function in cell E25 that will retrieve the total salary for marketing managers from the PivotTable.
4. Click cell **E25**, click the **Paste Function button** on the Standard toolbar; under Function category in the Paste Function dialog box, click **Lookup & Reference**; under Function name, click **GETPIVOTDATA**; then click **OK**
   The GETPIVOTDATA formula palette opens. The function's first argument, Pivot_table, can contain a reference to any cell within the PivotTable range. The second argument, Name, can contain the row or column label for the summary information you want (in this case, the column label Grand Total) enclosed in quotation marks.
5. With the pointer in the Pivot_table box, click the **PivotTable sheet tab**; click cell **F14** (or any other cell in the PivotTable range); in the formula palette, click the **Name box**; then type **"Office Manager"**
   Be sure to type the quotation marks. See Figure L-16.
6. Click **OK**, then click the **Currency Style button** on the Formatting toolbar
   The current total salary for Office Manager is $58,000, as shown in Figure L-17. This is the same value displayed in cell F14 of the PivotTable. The GETPIVOTDATA function will work correctly only when the salary for all departments is displayed in the PivotTable. You can verify this by displaying a different page in the PivotTable and viewing the effect on the Manager List worksheet.
7. Click the **PivotTable sheet tab**, click the **Department list arrow**, click **Corporate Manager**, click **OK**, then click the **Manager List sheet tab**
   The error message in cell E25 will disappear when you redisplay the (All) page.
8. Click the **PivotTable sheet tab**, click the **Department list arrow**, click **(All)**, click **OK**, then click the **Manager List sheet tab**
   Note that the correct value—$58,000.00—is once again displayed in cell E25.
9. Put your name in the footer, save the workbook, print the Manager List worksheet, then close the file and exit Excel

Trouble?

If the Align Right button does not appear on your Formatting toolbar, click the More Buttons button to view it.

FIGURE L-15: Syntax of GETPIVOTDATA function

GETPIVOTDATA(pivot_table,name)

- pivot_table: Reference to any page in the PivotTable that shows the data you want to retrieve.
- name: The row or column label (enclosed in quotation marks) describing the summary value you want to retrieve. For example, "January 2000" for the grand total for January 2000.

FIGURE L-16: Completed GETPIVOTDATA formula palette

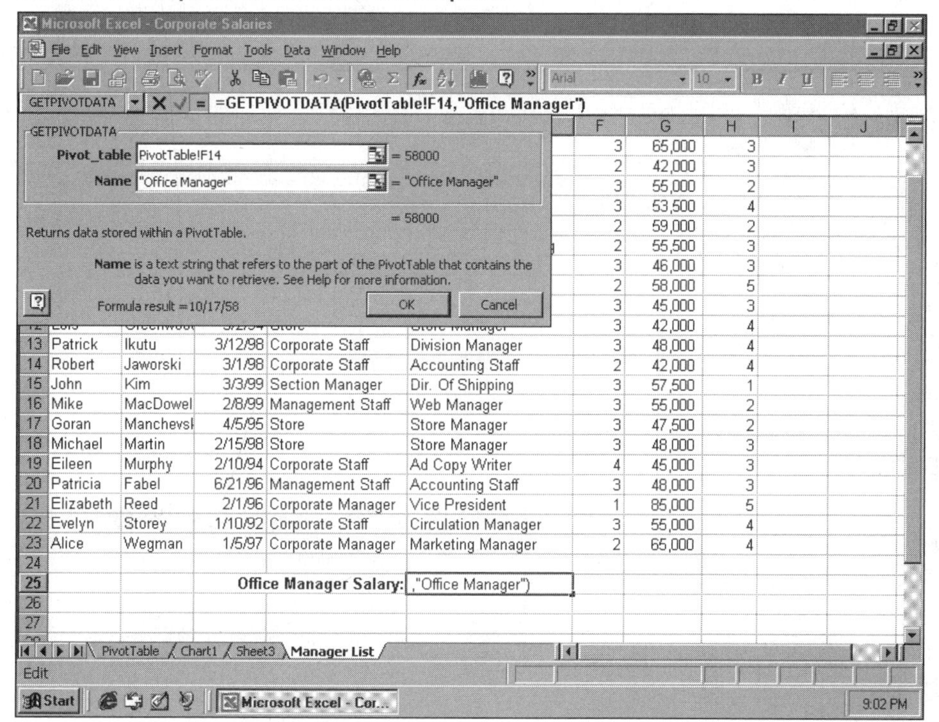

	A	B	C	D	E	F	G	H
13	Patrick	Ikutu	3/12/98	Corporate Staff	Division Manager	3	48,000	4
14	Robert	Jaworski	3/1/98	Corporate Staff	Accounting Staff	2	42,000	4
15	John	Kim	3/3/99	Section Manager	Dir. Of Shipping	3	57,500	1
16	Mike	MacDowel	2/8/99	Management Staff	Web Manager	3	55,000	2
17	Goran	Manchevsl	4/5/95	Store	Store Manager	3	47,500	2
18	Michael	Martin	2/15/98	Store	Store Manager	3	48,000	3
19	Eileen	Murphy	2/10/94	Corporate Staff	Ad Copy Writer	4	45,000	3
20	Patricia	Fabel	6/21/96	Management Staff	Accounting Staff	3	48,000	3
21	Elizabeth	Reed	2/1/96	Corporate Manager	Vice President	1	85,000	5
22	Evelyn	Storey	1/10/92	Corporate Staff	Circulation Manager	3	55,000	4
23	Alice	Wegman	1/5/97	Corporate Manager	Marketing Manager	2	65,000	4

FIGURE L-17: Results of GETPIVOTDATA function

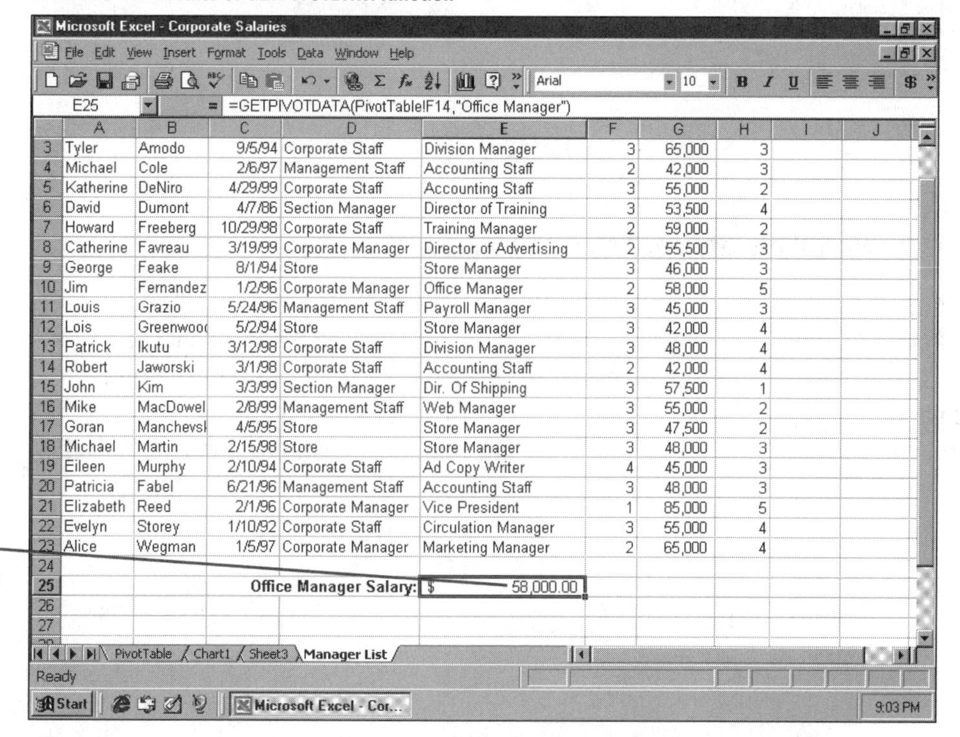

	A	B	C	D	E	F	G	H
3	Tyler	Amodo	9/5/94	Corporate Staff	Division Manager	3	65,000	3
4	Michael	Cole	2/6/97	Management Staff	Accounting Staff	2	42,000	3
5	Katherine	DeNiro	4/29/99	Corporate Staff	Accounting Staff	3	55,000	2
6	David	Dumont	4/7/86	Section Manager	Director of Training	3	53,500	4
7	Howard	Freeberg	10/29/98	Corporate Staff	Training Manager	2	59,000	2
8	Catherine	Favreau	3/19/99	Corporate Manager	Director of Advertising	2	55,500	3
9	George	Feake	8/1/94	Store	Store Manager	3	46,000	3
10	Jim	Fernandez	1/2/96	Corporate Manager	Office Manager	2	58,000	5
11	Louis	Grazio	5/24/96	Management Staff	Payroll Manager	3	45,000	3
12	Lois	Greenwoo	5/2/94	Store	Store Manager	3	42,000	4
13	Patrick	Ikutu	3/12/98	Corporate Staff	Division Manager	3	48,000	4
14	Robert	Jaworski	3/1/98	Corporate Staff	Accounting Staff	2	42,000	4
15	John	Kim	3/3/99	Section Manager	Dir. Of Shipping	3	57,500	1
16	Mike	MacDowel	2/8/99	Management Staff	Web Manager	3	55,000	2
17	Goran	Manchevsl	4/5/95	Store	Store Manager	3	47,500	2
18	Michael	Martin	2/15/98	Store	Store Manager	3	48,000	3
19	Eileen	Murphy	2/10/94	Corporate Staff	Ad Copy Writer	4	45,000	3
20	Patricia	Fabel	6/21/96	Management Staff	Accounting Staff	3	48,000	3
21	Elizabeth	Reed	2/1/96	Corporate Manager	Vice President	1	85,000	5
22	Evelyn	Storey	1/10/92	Corporate Staff	Circulation Manager	3	55,000	4
23	Alice	Wegman	1/5/97	Corporate Manager	Marketing Manager	2	65,000	4

Excel 2000

Practice

► Concepts Review

Label each element of the Excel screen shown in Figure L-18.

FIGURE L-18

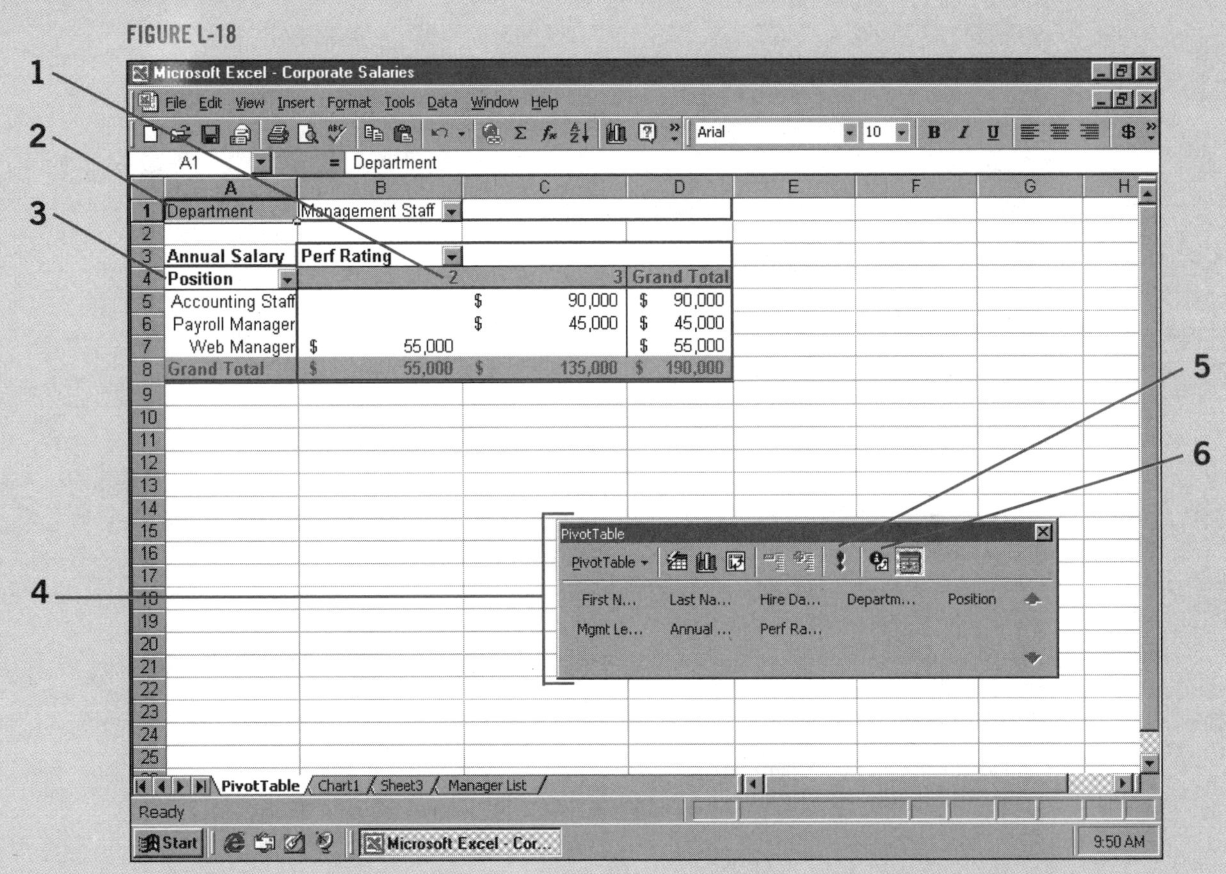

Match each term with the statement that describes it.

7. **COLUMN area**
8. **GETPIVOTDATA function**
9. **DATA area**
10. **PivotTable page**
11. **Summary function**

a. Determines how data will be calculated
b. Displays fields as column labels
c. Shows data for one item at a time in a table
d. Displays summarized values
e. Retrieves information from a PivotTable

Select the best answer from the list of choices.

12. A PivotTable report is best described as an Excel feature that

a. Displays columns and rows of data.
b. "Stacks" pages of data.
c. Allows you to display, summarize, and analyze list data.
d. Requires a source list.

13. Which PivotTable report field allows you to average values?

a. Row field
b. Data field
c. Page field
d. Column field

14. To make changes to PivotTable data, you must

a. Create a page field.
b. Edit cells in the source list and then refresh the PivotTable.
c. Edit cells in the PivotTable and then refresh the source list.
d. Drag a column header to the column area.

Skills Review

1. Plan and design a PivotTable.

a. Open the workbook titled EX L-2, then save it as "October CDs".
b. You'll create a PivotTable to show the sum of sales across products and regions. Study the list, then write down the field names you think should be included in the PivotTable. Determine which fields you think should be column fields, row fields, and data fields, then sketch a draft PivotTable.

2. Create a PivotTable report

a. Using the data on the Sales List, generate a PivotTable report on a new worksheet, and arrange the data fields as follows: (*Hint:* In the Row area, place the Store field to the left of the Sales Rep field.):

Field	Area
Store	Row
Sales Rep	Row
Product	Column
Sales $	Data

3. Change the summary function of a PivotTable report.

a. Change the PivotTable summary function to Average, then change it back to Sum.
b. Rename the new sheet "Oct. 99 PivotTable".
c. Save your work.

4. **Analyze three-dimensional data.**
   a. Place the Region field in the page area.
   b. Display sales for only the East region.
   c. Add your name to the worksheet footer, then print the worksheet in landscape orientation.
   d. Save your work.

5. **Update a PivotTable.**
   a. On the PivotTable, note the Boston total for The Sunset Trio.
   b. Go to the Sales List sheet.
   c. Create a new blank row 8 and enter the following data:

field name	new data item
Period	Oct-99
Product	The Sunset Trio
Region	East
Store	Boston
Sales $	4,900
Sales Rep	L. Smith

   d. Refresh the PivotTable so it reflects the new data item.
   e. Note the Boston total for The Sunset Trio and verify that it increased by $4,900.
   f. Add your name to the worksheet footer then print the PivotTable.
   g. Save your work.

6. **Change the structure and format of a PivotTable.**
   a. In the PivotTable, redisplay data for all regions and return the summary function to Sum of sales.
   b. Drag fields so that the following areas contain the following fields: (*Hint:* To remove fields from an area, drag them back over to the field area in the PivotTable toolbar.)

Field	**Area**
Product	Row
Sales Rep	Column
Store	Page

   c. Change the numbers to Currency format with 0 decimal places.
   d. Apply the Report 6 AutoFormat and print the PivotTable.
   e. Apply the Table 4 AutoFormat and print the PivotTable in landscape orientation, fitting the information on one page.
   f. Save your work.

7. **Create a PivotChart report.**
   a. Go to the Sales List sheet.
   b. Create a PivotChart report (with PivotTable), using the existing PivotTable data on a new worksheet.
   c. Place fields in the PivotChart report areas as follows:

Field	**Area**
Product	Series
Region	Category
Store	Category
Sales$	Data

   d. Change the Summary function to Average.
   e. Add your name to the chart sheet, then preview and print the chart.
   f. Save the workbook.

8. **Use the GETPIVOTDATA function.**
   a. In cell E27 of the Sales List, create a function to retrieve the grand total for S. Gupta from the October 99 PivotTable.
   b. Format the figure in E27 as currency with no decimal places.
   c. Save the workbook, then preview and print the worksheet.
   d. Close the workbook and exit Excel.

Independent Challenges

1. You are the bookkeeper for the small accounting firm called Chavez, Long, and Doyle. Until recently, the partners had been tracking their hours manually in a log. Recently, you created an Excel list to track basic information: billing date, partner name, client name, nature of work, and hours spent. You used abbreviated field names to simplify the reports. It is your responsibility to generate a table summarizing this billing information by client. You will create a PivotTable that sums the hours by accountant and date for each project. Once the table is completed, you will print the PivotTable for the partners and the summary page for the managing partner, Maria Chavez, for approval.

To complete this independent challenge:

a. Open the workbook titled EX L-3, then save it as "Partner Billing Report".
b. Create a PivotTable that sums hours by partner and dates according to client. Use Figure L-19 as a guide.
c. Name the new sheet "PivotTable", and format the PivotTable using the AutoFormat of your choice.
d. Add your name to the worksheet footer, then preview and print three copies of the PivotTable, one for each of the three partners. Then preview and print the (All) page.
e. Save the worksheet, then close the workbook.

FIGURE L-19

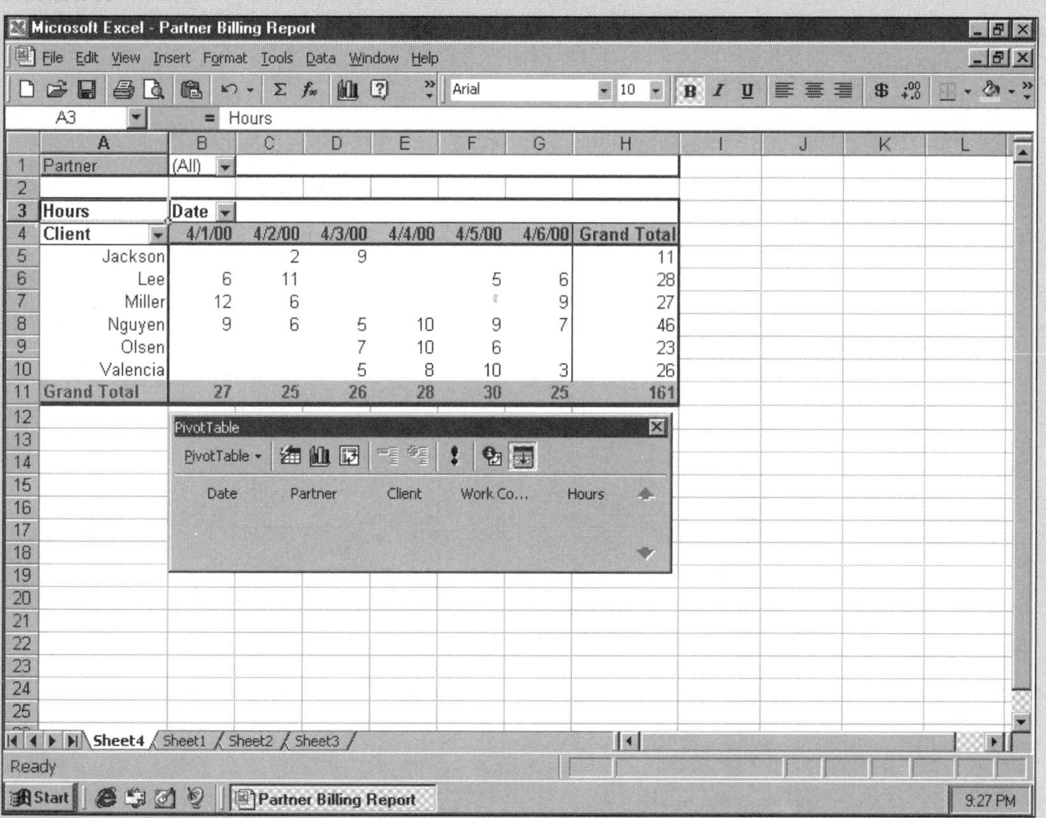

Hours	Date						
Client	4/1/00	4/2/00	4/3/00	4/4/00	4/5/00	4/6/00	Grand Total
Jackson		2	9				11
Lee	6	11			5	6	28
Miller	12	6				9	27
Nguyen	9	6	5	10	9	7	46
Olsen			7	10	6		23
Valencia			5	8	10	3	26
Grand Total	27	25	26	28	30	25	161

Excel 2000

2. You are the owner of three midsized computer stores called PC Assist. One is located downtown, one is in the Plaza Mall, and one is in the Sun Center shopping center. You have been using Excel to maintain a sales summary list for the first-quarter sales in the following three areas: hardware, software, and miscellaneous items. You want to create a PivotTable to analyze and graph the sales in each category by month and store.

To complete this independent challenge:

a. Open the workbook titled EX L-4, then save it as "PC Assist - First Qtr Sales".
b. Create a PivotTable that sums the sales amount for each store across the rows and each category of sales down the columns. Add a page field for month.
c. Change the summary function to Average to show the average sales amount in each category.
d. Format the PivotTable using the Table 6 AutoFormat.
e. Format the amounts as Currency with no decimal places.
f. On a separate sheet, create a PivotChart report for the January sales data in all three stores. (*Hint*: Display the January sales page and click the ChartWizard button on the PivotTable toolbar.) Remember to add a descriptive title to your chart, using the same technique you would on any Excel chart.
g. Add your name to the worksheet footers, then print the PivotTable and the chart.
h. Save, then close the workbook.

3. You manage a group of sales offices in the Western region for a cellular phone company called Digital Ear. Management has asked you to provide a summary table showing information on your sales staff, their locations, and their titles. You will create a PivotTable summarizing this information.

To complete this independent challenge:

a. Open the workbook titled EX L-5, then save it as "Western Sales Employees".
b. Create a PivotTable that lists the number of employees in each city, with the names of the cities listed across the columns and the titles listed down the rows. (*Hint:* Remember that the default summary function for cells containing text is Count.)
c. Name the new sheet "PivotTable".
d. Add and format the label "Total Seattle Staff:" in cell C19 of the Employee List sheet.
e. Create a formula in cell D19 that retrieves the total number of employees located in Seattle.
f. Create a PivotChart that shows the number of employees in each store by position.
g. Drag the State field into the Series area.
h. Add your name to the worksheet footer, then preview and print the PivotTable and the Staff List.
i. Save the worksheet, then close the workbook.

4. Jim Fernandez has asked you to analyze MediaLoft's 1999 Sales and produce a PivotTable report and a PivotChart report that he can manipulate to explore relationships within the data. He gives you an Excel file, but it is missing the data for the Houston store. He asks you to get that information from the company intranet site.

To complete this independent challenge:

a. Connect to the Internet, and go to the MediaLoft intranet site at http://www.course.com/Illustrated/MediaLoft. Click the Sales link, then click the Sales Report link. Print the page and disconnect from the Internet.
b. Open the file EX L-6, save it as "1999 Sales", then insert a blank row just under the headings and enter the data from the Houston store, which is in the West region. Format the data so that it looks like the data in the other rows. Make sure that the totals are updated.
c. Create a PivotTable report from the 1999 Sales data. Experiment with different arrangements of data to determine which layout produces the most useful information. Try filtering by Region and by Store. Name the PivotTable sheet appropriately.
d. Format the sales figures appropriately, apply an AutoFormat, add your name to the worksheet footer, then print the sheet.
e. Create a PivotChart report from your data on a separate sheet. Move at least one field to obtain a different view of the data, format the chart appropriately, add your name to the chart sheet footer, and print the sheet.
f. Use the GETPIVOTDATA function to bring a figure from the PivotTable to the 1999 Sales sheet and label it.
g. Save the file, print your chart, then close the workbook.

► Visual Workshop

Open the workbook titled EX L-7, then save it as "Corner Fruit Stand". Using the data in the workbook provided, create the PivotTable shown in Figure L-20. (*Hint:* There are two data summary fields.) Add your name to the worksheet footer, then preview and print the PivotTable. Save the worksheet, then close the workbook.

FIGURE L-20

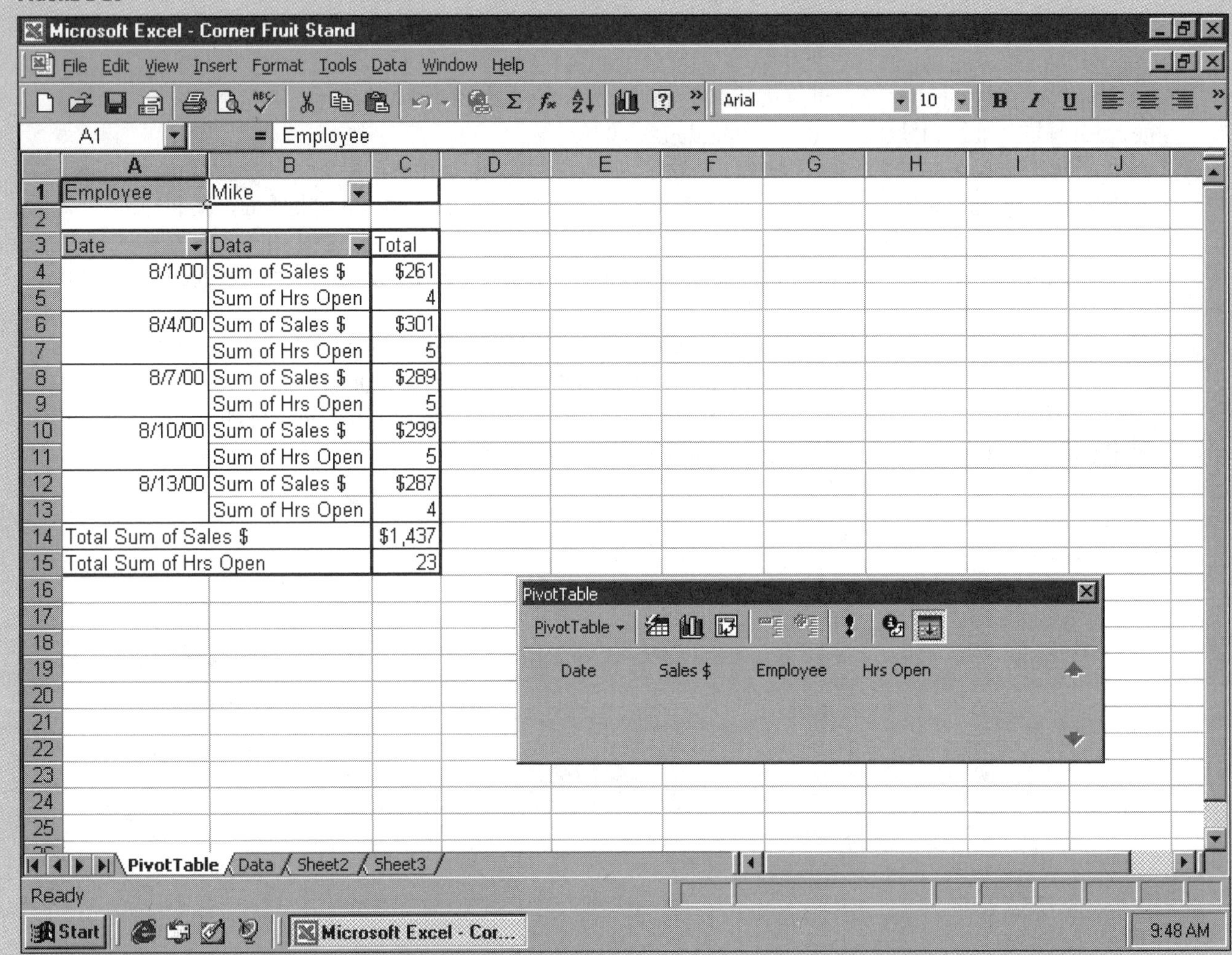

Excel 2000

Unit M

Exchanging

Data with Other Programs

Objectives

- Plan a data exchange
- MOUS Import a text file
- MOUS Import a database table
- MOUS Insert a graphic file in a worksheet
- MOUS Embed a worksheet
- MOUS Link a worksheet to another program
- MOUS Embed an Excel chart into a PowerPoint slide
- Convert a list to an Access table

In a Windows environment, you can freely exchange data between Excel and most other Windows programs. In this unit, you will plan a data exchange with Excel. MediaLoft's upper management has asked MediaLoft office manager Jim Fernandez to research the possible purchase of CafeCorp, a small company that operates cafés in large businesses, hospitals, and, more recently, drug stores. Jim is reviewing the broker's paper documents and electronic files and developing a presentation on the feasibility of acquiring this company. To complete this project, Jim will exchange data between Excel and other programs.

Planning a Data Exchange

Because the tools available in Windows and Windows-supported programs are so flexible, exchanging data between Excel and other programs is easy. The first step involves planning what you want to accomplish with each data exchange. Jim uses the following guidelines to plan data exchanges between Excel and other programs in order to complete the business analysis project.

Steps

1. **Identify the data you want to exchange, its file type, and, if possible, the program used to create it**
   Whether the data you want to exchange is contained in a graphic file or a worksheet or consists only of text, it is important to identify the data's **source program**, the file type, and the program used to create it. Once the source program has been identified, you can determine options for exchanging that data with Excel. Jim has been asked to analyze a text file containing the CafeCorp product data. Although he does not know the source program, Jim knows that the file contains unformatted text. A file that consists of text but no formatting is sometimes referred to as an **ASCII file**. Because an ASCII file is a universally accepted text file format, Jim can easily import it into Excel.
2. **Determine the program with which you want to exchange the specified data**
   You might want to insert a graphic object into an Excel worksheet or add a spreadsheet to a WordPad document. Data exchange rules vary from program to program. Besides knowing which program created the data to be exchanged, you must also identify which program will receive the data (that is, the **destination program**). Jim received a database table of CafeCorp's corporate customers created with the dBASE IV program. After determining that Excel can import dBASE IV tables, he plans to import that database file into Excel to perform his analysis.
3. **Determine the goal of your data exchange**
   Although it is convenient to use the Clipboard to cut, copy, and paste data within and between programs, you cannot retain a connection with the source program or document using this method. However, there are two ways to transfer data within and between programs that allow you to retain some connection with the source document and/or the source program. These data-transfer options involve using a Windows technology known as object linking and embedding, or **OLE**. The data to be exchanged, called an **object**, may consist of text, a worksheet, or any other type of data. You use **embedding** to insert a copy of the original object in the destination document and, if necessary, to subsequently edit this data separately from the source document. This process is illustrated in Figure M-1. You use **linking** when you want the information you inserted to be updated automatically when the data in the source document changes. This process is illustrated in Figure M-2. Embedding and linking are discussed in more detail later in this unit. Jim has determined that he needs to use both object embedding and object linking for his analysis and presentation project.
4. **Set up the data exchange**
   When you exchange data between two programs, it is best to start both programs prior to initiating the exchange. You might also want to tile the programs on the screen either horizontally or vertically so that you can see both while the data is exchanged. See Table M-1 for a list of file formats that Excel can import. Jim will work with Excel and WordPad when exchanging data for this project.
5. **Execute the data exchange**
   The steps you use will vary, depending on the type of data exchanged. Jim is eager to attempt the data exchanges to complete his business analysis of CafeCorp.

FIGURE M-1: Embedded object

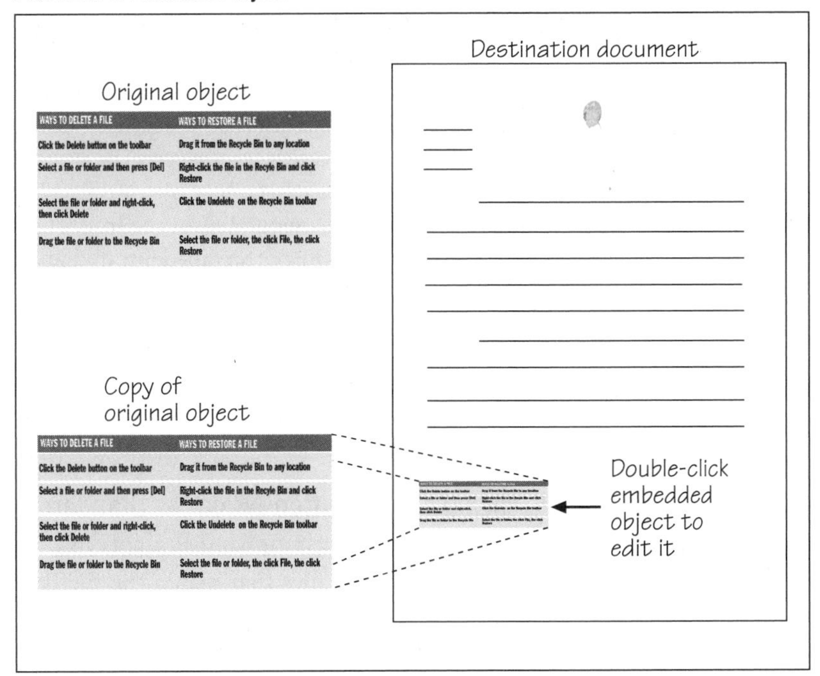

FIGURE M-2: Linked object

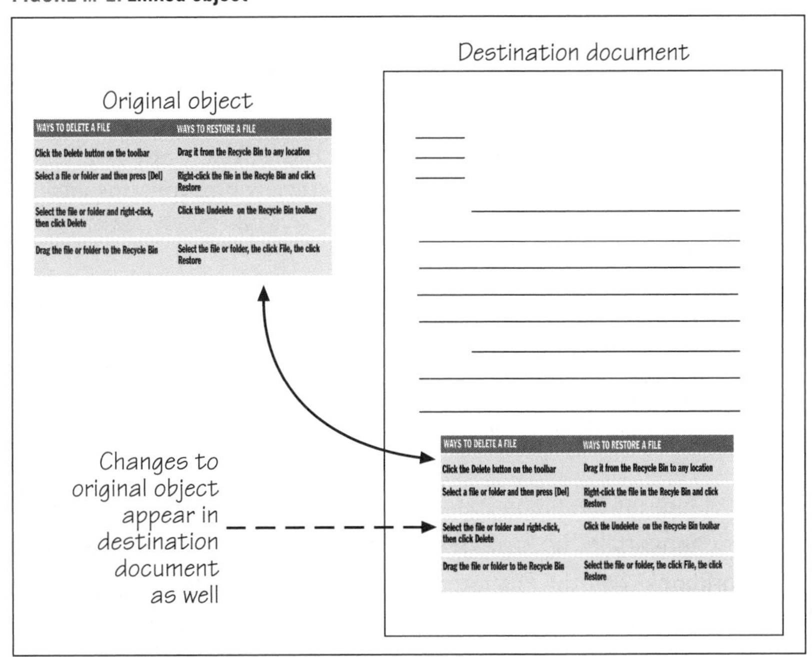

TABLE M-1: Importable file formats and extensions

file format	file extension(s)	file format	file extensions
dBASE II, III, IV	DBF	**CSV (Comma Separated Values)**	CSV
Excel 4.0	XLS, XLW, XLC, XLM	**DIF (Data Interchange Format, i.e., VisiCalc)**	DIF
Excel 5.0/7.0	XLS, XLT	**Formatted Text (Space or column delimited)**	TXT, PRN
Lotus 1-2-3	WKS, WK1, WK3, ALL, FMT, WK3, FM3, WK4	**Text (Tab delimited)**	TXT
Quattro/Quattro Pro	WQ1, WBI	**SYLK (Symbolic Link: Multiplan, Microsoft Works)**	SLK

Excel 2000

Importing a Text File

You can import data stored in other programs into Excel by simply opening the file, so long as Excel can read the file type. After importing the file, use the Save As command on the File menu to save the data in Excel format. Text files use a tab or space as the **delimiter**, or column separator, to separate columns of data. When you import a text file into Excel, the Text Import Wizard automatically opens and describes how text is separated in the imported file. Now that he's planned his data exchange, Jim wants to import a tab-delimited text file containing product cost and pricing data from CafeCorp.

Steps

1. In a blank workbook, click the **Open button** on the Standard toolbar, click the **Look in list arrow**, then click the drive containing your Project Disk
   The Open dialog box shows only those files that match the file types listed in the Files of type box—usually Microsoft Excel files. In this case, however, you're importing a text file.
2. Click the **Files of type list arrow**, click **Text Files,** click **EX M-1** if necessary, then click **Open**
   The first Text Import Wizard dialog box opens. See Figure M-3. Notice that under Original data type, the Delimited option button is selected. In the Preview of file box, line 1 indicates that the file contains three columns of data: Item, Cost, and Price. No changes are necessary in this dialog box.
3. Click **Next**
   The second Text Import Wizard dialog box opens. Under Delimiters, the tab character is selected as the delimiter, and the Data preview box contains an image showing where the delimiters divide the data into columns.
4. Click **Next**
   The third Text Import Wizard dialog box opens with options for formatting the three columns of data. Notice that under Column data format, the General option button is selected. This is the best formatting option for text mixed with numbers.
5. Click **Finish**
   Excel imports the text file into the blank worksheet as three columns of data: Item, Cost, and Price.
6. Click **File** on the menu bar, click **Save As**, make sure the drive containing your Project Disk appears in the Save in box, click the **Save as type list arrow**, click **Microsoft Excel Workbook**, edit the File name box to read **CafeCorp - Product Info**, then click **Save**
   The file is saved as a workbook, and the new name appears in the title bar. The worksheet is automatically named after the imported file, EX M-1. The worksheet information would be easier to read if it were formatted and if it showed the profit for each item.
7. Double-click the border between the headers in **Columns A** and **B**, click cell **D1**, type **Profit**, click cell **D2**, type **=C2-B2**, click the **Enter button** on the Formula bar, copy the contents of cell D2 to range **D3:D18**, then center the column labels, apply bold formatting to them, and format the data in columns B, C, and D with two decimal places using the Number style
   The completed worksheet, which analyzes the text file imported into Excel, is shown in Figure M-4.
8. Add your name to the worksheet footer, preview and print the list in portrait orientation, then save and close the workbook

Trouble?

If the Preview window in the Text Import Wizard dialog box contains odd-looking characters, make sure you selected the correct original data type.

QuickTip

To format numbers with dollar signs, use the Currency or Accounting format on the Numbers tab of the Format Cells dialog box.

FIGURE M-3: First Text Import Wizard dialog box

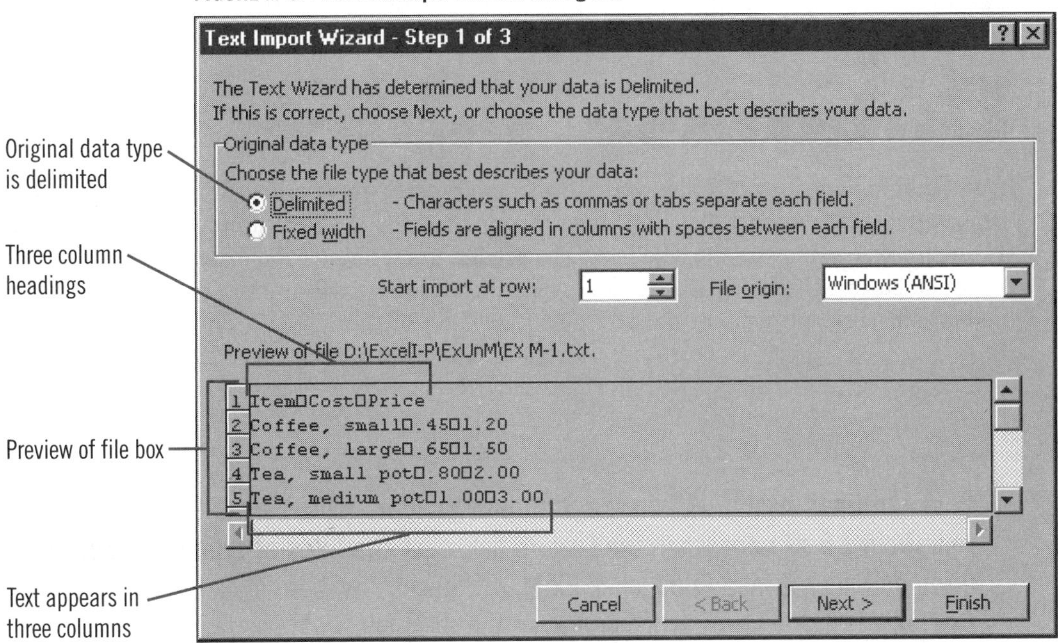

FIGURE M-4: Completed worksheet with imported text file

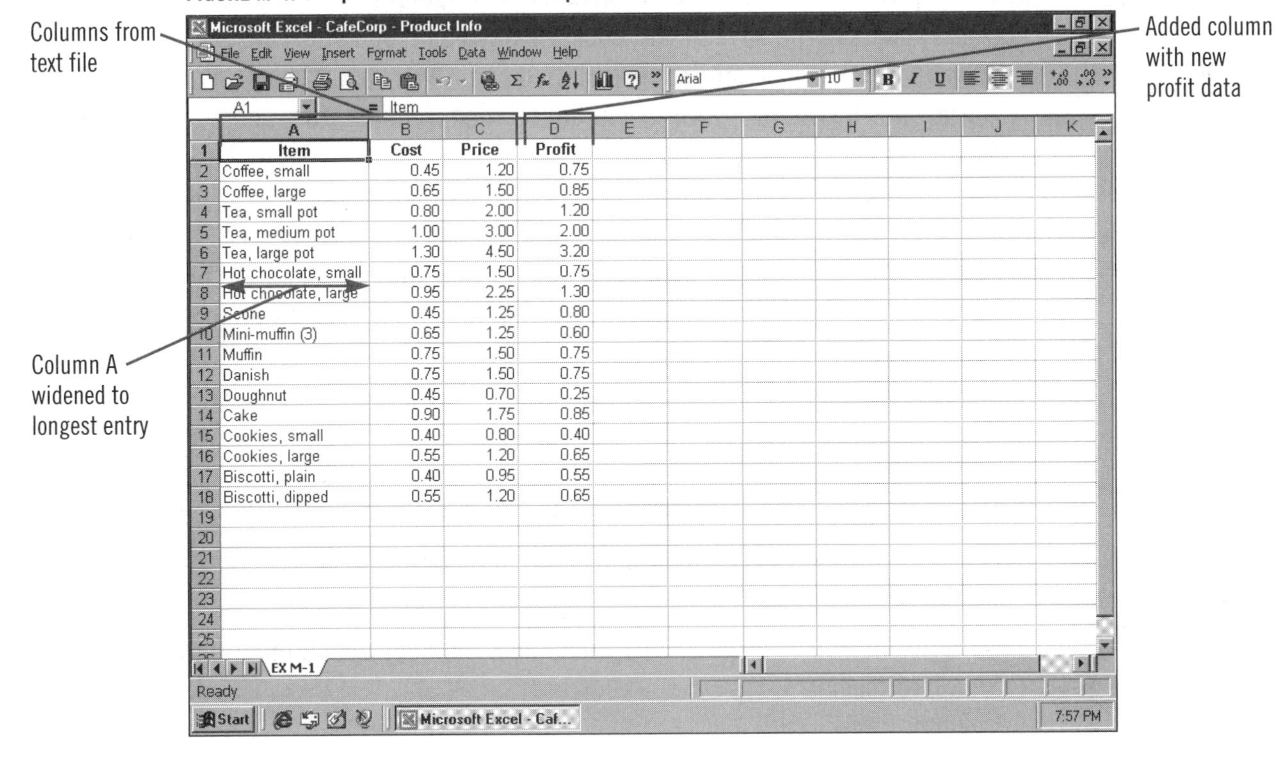

Item	Cost	Price	Profit
Coffee, small	0.45	1.20	0.75
Coffee, large	0.65	1.50	0.85
Tea, small pot	0.80	2.00	1.20
Tea, medium pot	1.00	3.00	2.00
Tea, large pot	1.30	4.50	3.20
Hot chocolate, small	0.75	1.50	0.75
Hot chocolate, large	0.95	2.25	1.30
Scone	0.45	1.25	0.80
Mini-muffin (3)	0.65	1.25	0.60
Muffin	0.75	1.50	0.75
Danish	0.75	1.50	0.75
Doughnut	0.45	0.70	0.25
Cake	0.90	1.75	0.85
Cookies, small	0.40	0.80	0.40
Cookies, large	0.55	1.20	0.65
Biscotti, plain	0.40	0.95	0.55
Biscotti, dipped	0.55	1.20	0.65

CLUES TO USE

Other ways to import text files

Although the Text Import Wizard gives you the most flexibility, there are other ways to import text files. On the Windows desktop, drag your text file over the Excel program icon. Excel opens your text file. You can also click Insert on the menu bar, click Object, click Create from File, click the Browse button and locate the text file, click Insert, then click OK. The text file is inserted as an icon on your worksheet. Double-click the icon to open the text file in WordPad. You can then copy it into your worksheet.

Excel 2000

Importing a Database Table

In addition to importing text files, you can also use Excel to import files from other programs or database tables. To import files that contain supported file formats, simply open the file, then you are ready to work with the data in Excel. Jim received a database table of CafeCorp's corporate customers, which was created with dBASE IV. He will import this table into Excel, then format, sort, and total the data.

Steps

QuickTip

You can also import information from a database outside Excel using the Excel Query Wizard. Click Data on the menu bar, point to Get External Data, then click New Database Query. Open the database with the information you want to retrieve. See the Excel help topic "Get external data by using Microsoft Query."

1. Click the **Open button** on the Standard toolbar, make sure the drive containing your Project Disk appears in the Look in box, click the **Files of type list arrow**, scroll down and click **dBase Files**, click **EX M-2**, if necessary, then click **Open**
   Excel opens the database table and names the sheet tab EX M-2. See Figure M-5. Before manipulating the data, you should save the table as an Excel workbook.
2. Click **File** on the menu bar; click **Save As**; make sure the drive containing your Project Disk appears in the Save in box; click the **Save as type list arrow**; scroll up, if necessary, and click **Microsoft Excel Workbook**; edit the File name box to read **CafeCorp - Corporate Customer Info**; click **Save**; then rename the sheet tab **Corporate Customer Info**
   The truncated column labels in row 1 are not very readable; they would look better if the text wrapped to two lines.
3. Edit cell A1 to read **COMPANY NAME** (no underscore), click cell **F1**, type **1994**, press **[Alt][Enter]** to force a new line, type **ORDER**, press **Tab**, type **1995**, press **[Alt][Enter]**, type **ORDER**, then press **[Enter]**
   Pressing [Alt][Enter] as you create cell entries forces the text to wrap to the next line. Columns F and G could be wider, and the column labels would look better if they were formatted.
4. Format the numbers in **columns F** and **G** using the Comma style with no decimal places, center and apply bold formatting to all the column labels, then widen the columns as necessary

QuickTip

If the Sort Descending button does not appear on the Standard toolbar, click the More Buttons button to view it.

5. Save the workbook, click cell **G2**, then click the **Sort Descending button** on the Standard toolbar
   Columns F and G need totals.
6. Select range **F19:G19**, click the **AutoSum button** on the Standard toolbar, then format the range F19:G19 with the Comma style and no decimal places, add a border around it, then click cell A1
   Your completed worksheet should match Figure M-6.
7. Add your name to the worksheet footer, preview and print the list in landscape orientation, fit the list to one page if necessary, then save the workbook

FIGURE M-5: Imported dBASE table

Excel substitutes underscores in place of spaces

Truncated column label

Microsoft Excel - EX M-2.dbf

A1 = COMPANY_NA

	A	B	C	D	E	F	G	H
1	COMPANY_NA	CITY	STATE	CONTACT	PHONE	1994_OR	1995_ORDER	
2	Gelco Electronics	Denver	CO	Lee Jones	303-334-4388	3433	3676	
3	PC Computer Supply	Boulder	CO	Maria Lopez	303-335-9934	1250	1893	
4	Heritage Insurance	Denver	CO	Sam Winston	303-334-4421	2212	2544	
5	Cornerstone Construction	Colorado Springs	CO	Jack Wilcox	719-356-9943	895	1544	
6	Dee & Kline Law Office	Colorado Springs	CO	Amy Fong	719-356-4595	0	1211	
7	Aspen Mutual Mortgage	Aspen	CO	Nick Albert	303-332-3393	1299	1633	
8	Symphonic Stereo	Orem	UT	Jenny Garcia	801-434-2232	0	1543	
9	Tigeroga Minerals	Salt Lake City	UT	Priscilla Gomez	801-538-7789	839	1322	
10	NationBuilder Bank	Ogden	UT	Alex Hart	801-733-9877	534	1699	
11	Earthwise Paper Co	Ogden	UT	Mary Tyler	801-733-9987	0	1234	
12	Sunny Pool Products	Albuquerque	NM	Corey Olsen	505-233-4432	254	1123	
13	Myers Investments	Santa Fe	NM	Jeff Punatar	505-233-9939	456	1088	
14	WorldWide Art	Denver	CO	Gilbert Hahn	303-334-2203	734	1409	
15	Earthly Foods	Orem	UT	Lisa Sanchez	801-434-4432	893	1233	
16	Attaboy Toys	Colorado Springs	CO	Harry Yang	719-356-9987	190	1433	
17	Miller Office Products	Denver	CO	Pam Miller	303-334-6785	334	2011	
18	Bumble Bee Nurseries	Salt Lake City	UT	Willy McFee	801-538-4493	0	1688	

EX M-2

Ready

3:52 PM

FIGURE M-6: Completed worksheet containing imported data

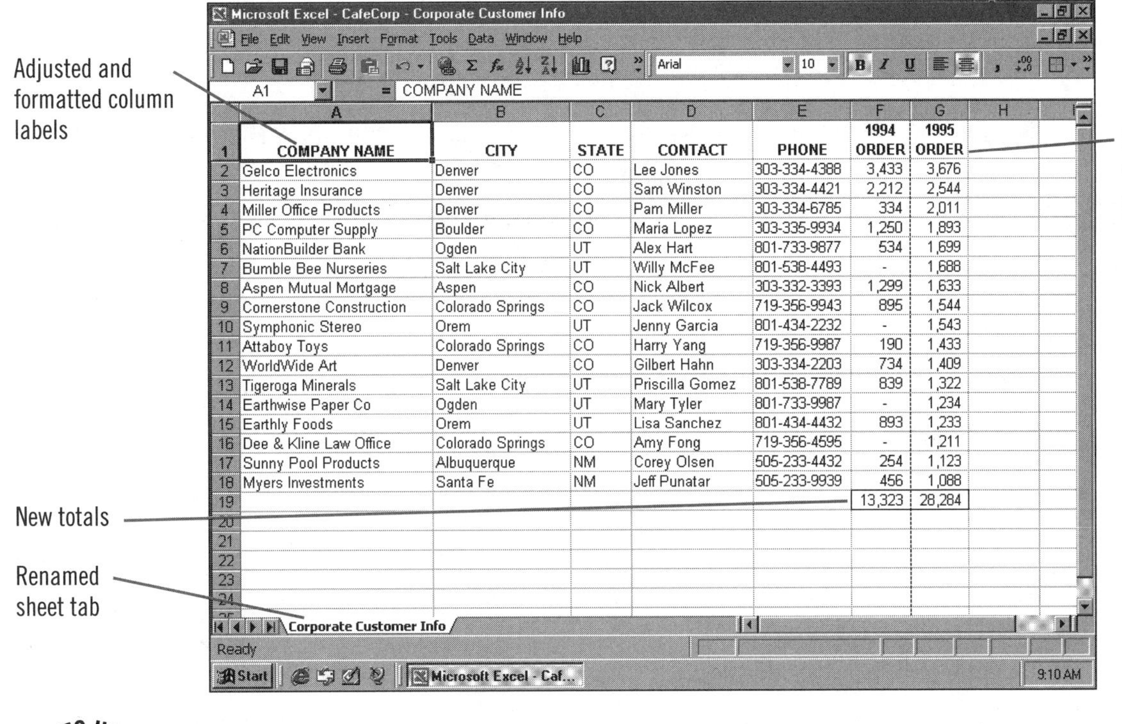
Microsoft Excel - CafeCorp - Corporate Customer Info

A1 = COMPANY NAME

	A	B	C	D	E	F	G	H
1	COMPANY NAME	CITY	STATE	CONTACT	PHONE	1994 ORDER	1995 ORDER	
2	Gelco Electronics	Denver	CO	Lee Jones	303-334-4388	3,433	3,676	
3	Heritage Insurance	Denver	CO	Sam Winston	303-334-4421	2,212	2,544	
4	Miller Office Products	Denver	CO	Pam Miller	303-334-6785	334	2,011	
5	PC Computer Supply	Boulder	CO	Maria Lopez	303-335-9934	1,250	1,893	
6	NationBuilder Bank	Ogden	UT	Alex Hart	801-733-9877	534	1,699	
7	Bumble Bee Nurseries	Salt Lake City	UT	Willy McFee	801-538-4493	-	1,688	
8	Aspen Mutual Mortgage	Aspen	CO	Nick Albert	303-332-3393	1,299	1,633	
9	Cornerstone Construction	Colorado Springs	CO	Jack Wilcox	719-356-9943	895	1,544	
10	Symphonic Stereo	Orem	UT	Jenny Garcia	801-434-2232	-	1,543	
11	Attaboy Toys	Colorado Springs	CO	Harry Yang	719-356-9987	190	1,433	
12	WorldWide Art	Denver	CO	Gilbert Hahn	303-334-2203	734	1,409	
13	Tigeroga Minerals	Salt Lake City	UT	Priscilla Gomez	801-538-7789	839	1,322	
14	Earthwise Paper Co	Ogden	UT	Mary Tyler	801-733-9987	-	1,234	
15	Earthly Foods	Orem	UT	Lisa Sanchez	801-434-4432	893	1,233	
16	Dee & Kline Law Office	Colorado Springs	CO	Amy Fong	719-356-4595	-	1,211	
17	Sunny Pool Products	Albuquerque	NM	Corey Olsen	505-233-4432	254	1,123	
18	Myers Investments	Santa Fe	NM	Jeff Punatar	505-233-9939	456	1,088	
19						13,323	28,284	

Corporate Customer Info

Ready

9:10 AM

Adjusted and formatted column labels

Figures for 1995 arranged in descending order

New totals

Renamed sheet tab

Exporting Excel data

Most of the file types that Excel can import (listed in Table M-1) are also the file types to which Excel can **export**, or deliver data. Excel can also export Text and CSV formats for Macintosh and OS/2. To export an Excel worksheet, use the Save As command on the File menu, click the Save as type list arrow, then select the desired format. Saving to a non-Excel format might result in the loss of formatting that is unique to Excel.

Inserting a Graphic File in a Worksheet

A graphic object (such as a drawing, logo, or photograph) can greatly enhance a worksheet's visual impact. The Picture options on the Insert menu make it easy to insert graphics into an Excel worksheet. Once you've inserted a picture, you can edit it using the tools available on the Picture toolbar. Jim wants to insert a copy of the MediaLoft logo at the top of his corporate customer database table. He has a copy of the logo, previously created by the company's Marketing department, saved as a graphics file on a disk. He starts by creating a space for it.

Steps

QuickTip

You can insert shapes, clip art, scanned pictures, and special text effects into your worksheet. You can use a graphic as a hyperlink to another file or as a way to start a macro. Search the keyword "text graphics" in Excel help to find "About using graphics in Microsoft Excel."

1. Select **rows 1** through **5**, click **Insert** on the menu bar, then click **Rows**
   Five blank rows appear above the header row. To insert a picture, you start with the Insert menu.
2. Click cell **A1**, click **Insert** on the menu bar, then point to **Picture**
   The Picture menu opens. See Figure M-7. This menu offers several options for inserting graphics. You will insert a picture that you already have in a file.
3. Click **From File**; in the Insert Picture dialog box, make sure the drive containing your Project Disk appears in the Look in box; then click **EX M-3**, if necessary, to select it
   A preview of the selected graphic displays on the right side of the Insert Picture dialog box. See Figure M-8.
4. Click **Insert**
   Excel inserts the graphic and opens the Picture toolbar.
5. Drag the lower-right corner up and to the left so the logo fits within rows 1–5
   See Figure M-9. To improve the look of the graphic, you'll add a border.
6. With the graphic still selected, click the **Line Style button** on the Picture toolbar and click the **1½ pt** line style, then press **[Esc]** to deselect the graphic and close the Picture toolbar
   The Drawing toolbar closes and the graphic is displayed with a border.
7. Preview and print the worksheet, save the workbook, then close the workbook and exit Excel

QuickTip

You can also use the Line Style button on the Drawing toolbar to add a border for a selected object.

FIGURE M-7: Picture menu

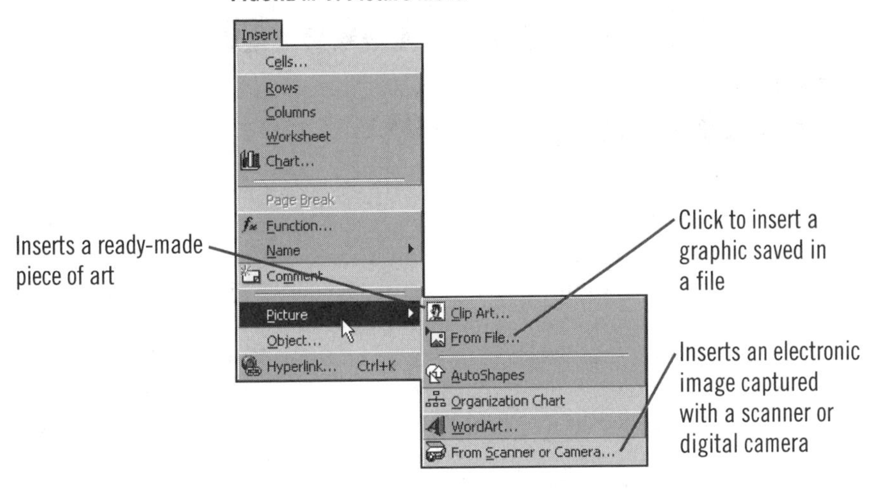

FIGURE M-8: Insert Picture dialog box

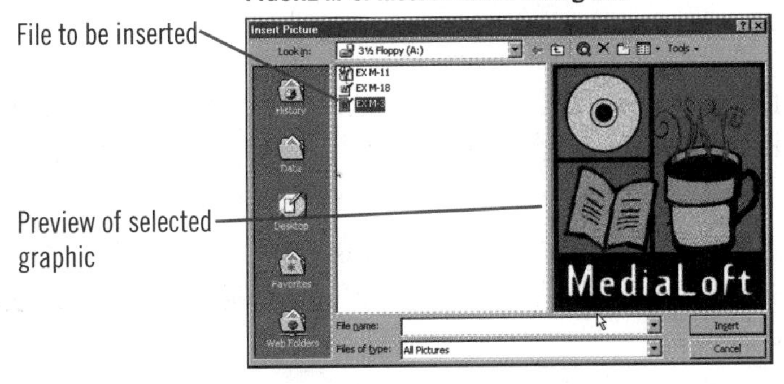

FIGURE M-9: Worksheet with inserted picture

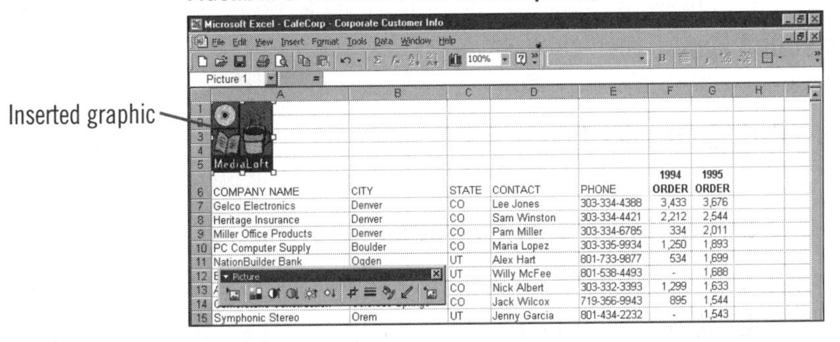

Importing data from HTML files

You can easily import information from HTML files and Web pages into Excel by using drag and drop or the Insert Object command. To use drag and drop, open Internet Explorer, then open the HTML file or Web page that contains the data you want to import. Resize the Explorer window so it covers only half of the screen, then open the Excel file to which you want to import the data and resize the Excel window so it covers the other half of the screen. In the Explorer window, highlight the table or information you want to import, then drag it over to the Excel window. When the pointer changes to a white arrow with a plus sign, release the mouse button. The table will appear in your Excel document, ready for analysis. You can use this method to update worksheets you have published on the Web. You can also open an HTML file from your intranet or a Web site in Excel and modify it, which is known as HTML round tripping. To use the Object command on the Insert menu to embed an HTML file in an Excel worksheet, click Insert on the menu bar, click Object, click the Create from File tab, click Browse, then navigate to the HTML file you want to Import and click OK. The page appears as an icon in your Excel document. Double-click the icon to view the file. To retrieve data from a particular Web page on a regular basis, use a Web query, which you'll learn about in the next unit.

Excel 2000

Embedding a Worksheet

Microsoft Office programs work together to make it easy to copy an object (such as text, data, or a graphic) in a source program and then insert it into a document in a different program (the destination program). If you insert the object using a simple Paste command, however, you retain no connection to the source program. That's why it is often more useful to embed objects rather than simply paste them. **Embedding** allows you to edit an Excel workbook from within a different program using Excel commands and tools. You can embed a worksheet so the data is visible in the destination program or so it appears as an icon in the destination document. To access data embedded as an icon, you simply double-click the icon. Jim decides to update Maria on the project status. He uses a WordPad memo, which includes the projected sales revenue worksheet embedded as an icon. First, he starts the WordPad program and opens the memo.

Steps

1. Press **[Ctrl][Esc]** to open the Windows Start menu; point to **Programs**; point to **Accessories**; click **WordPad**; then, if necessary, maximize the WordPad window
   The WordPad program opens, with a blank document displayed in the WordPad window.
2. Click **File** on the WordPad menu bar, click **Open**, make sure the drive containing your Project Disk appears in the Look in box, click **EX M-4**, then click **Open**
   The memo opens.
3. Click **File** on the menu bar, click **Save As**, make sure the Save in box contains the drive containing your Project Disk, edit the File name box to read **CafeCorp - Sales Projection Memo**, then click **Save**
   You want to embed the worksheet below the last line of the document.
4. Press **[Ctrl][End]**, click **Insert** on the menu bar, then click **Object**
   After a moment, the Insert Object dialog box opens. You are embedding an existing file.
5. Click the **Create from File option button**
6. Click **Browse**, make sure the drive containing your Project Disk appears in the Look in box, click **EX M-5**, click **Insert**; then in the Insert Object dialog box, select the **Display As Icon check box**
   The Insert Object dialog box now shows the file to be embedded. See Figure M-10. You are now ready to embed the object.
7. Click **OK**, then click outside the object to deselect it
   The memo now contains an embedded copy of the sales projection worksheet, displayed as an icon. See Figure M-11.
8. Double-click the **Microsoft Excel Worksheet icon**
   The Excel program starts and displays the embedded worksheet. See Figure M-12.
9. Click **File** on the Excel menu bar, click **Close & Return to CafeCorp - Sales Projection**, then save the memo

Trouble?

If the entire worksheet appears, not just the icon, you might not have checked the Display As Icon box.

QuickTip

To edit an embedded object, double-click the object to open the source program, then make the desired changes. When you save and exit the source program, the embedded object reflects the changes.

FIGURE M-10: Insert Object dialog box

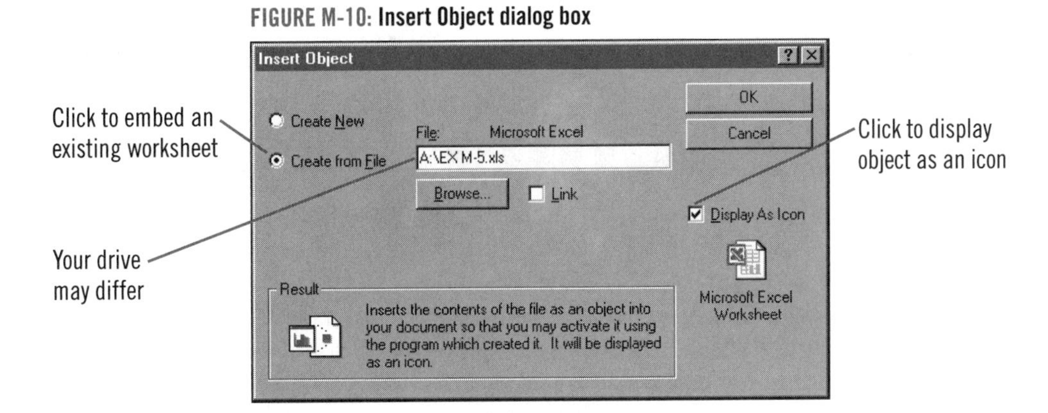

FIGURE M-11: Memo with embedded worksheet

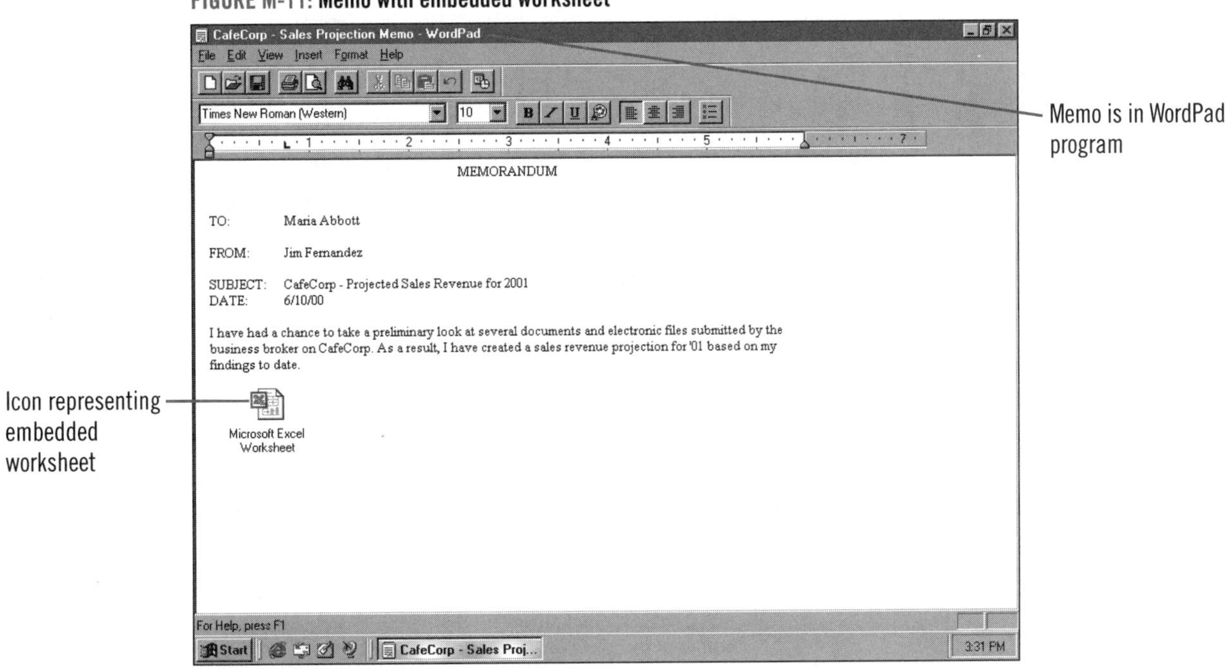

FIGURE M-12: Embedded worksheet opened in Excel

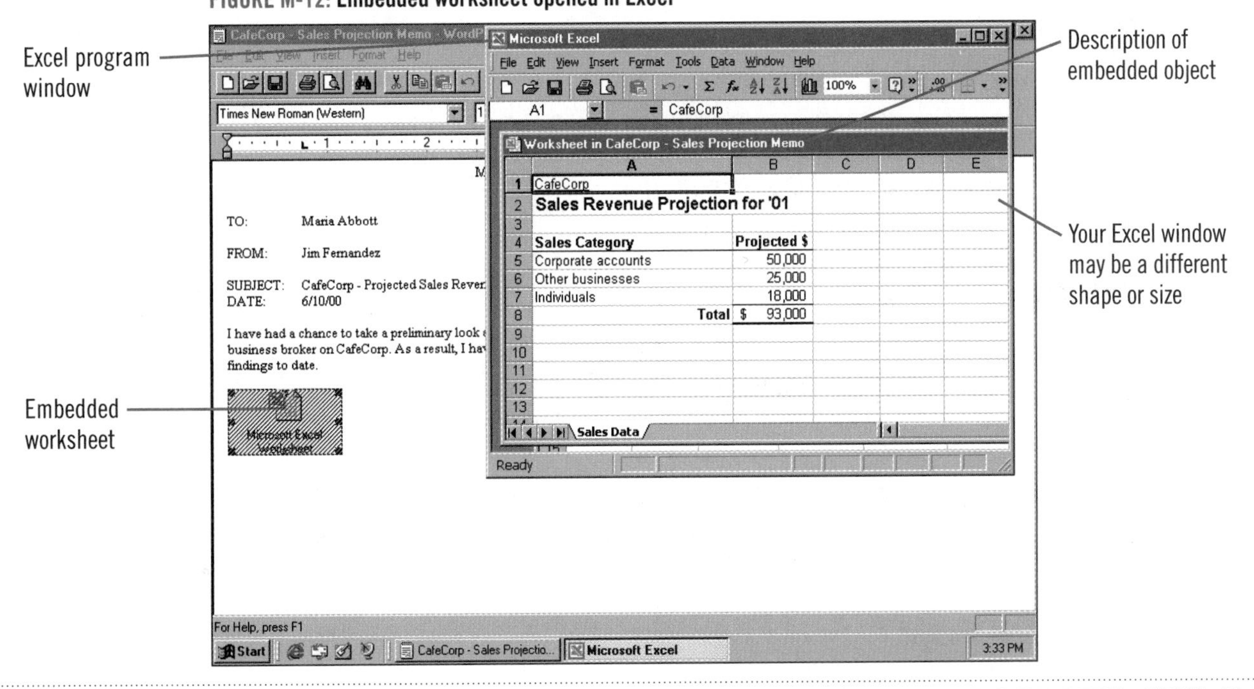

Excel 2000

Linking a Worksheet to Another Program

You use **linking** when you want to insert a worksheet into another program and retain a connection with the original document as well as the original program. When you link a worksheet to another program, the link contains a pointer to the source document so that, when you double-click it, the source document opens for editing. Once you link a worksheet to another program, any changes you make to the original worksheet document are reflected in the linked object. Jim realizes he may be making some changes to the workbook he embedded in the memo to Maria. To ensure that these changes will be reflected in the memo, he decides to link a copy of the worksheet to the source document rather than simply embed it. First, he deletes the embedded worksheet icon; he then replaces it with a linked version of the same worksheet.

1. With the WordPad memo still displayed in your window, click the Microsoft Excel Worksheet icon to select it if necessary, then press **[Delete]**
   The embedded worksheet is removed. Now, you will link the same worksheet to the memo.
2. Make sure the insertion point is below the last line of the memo, click **Insert** on the WordPad menu bar, click **Object**, then click the **Create from File option button** in the Insert Object dialog box
3. Click **Browse**, make sure the drive containing your Project Disk appears in the Look in box, click **EX M-5**, click **Insert**, then select the **Link check box**
   With the file containing the worksheet object selected, you are ready to link the worksheet object to the memo.
4. Click **OK**; drag the worksheet's **lower-right selection handle** to the right margin to enlarge the window, then click outside the worksheet to deselect it
   The memo now displays a linked copy of the sales projection worksheet. See Figure M-13. In the future, any changes made to the source file (EX M-5) will also be made to the linked copy in the WordPad memo. In the next step, you'll verify this by making a change to the source file and viewing its effect on the WordPad memo.
5. Click the **Save button** on the WordPad Standard toolbar, click **File** on the WordPad menu bar, then click **Exit**; start Excel if necessary, then open the file **EX M-5**
   The worksheet appears in the Excel window. You will test the link by changing the sales projection for other businesses to $20,000.
6. Click cell **B6**, type **20,000**, then press **[Enter]**
   Now you will open the WordPad memo to verify that the same change was made automatically to the linked copy of the worksheet.
7. Press **[Ctrl][Esc]** to open the Windows Start menu, point to **Programs**, point to **Accessories**, click **WordPad**; click **File** on the WordPad menu bar, then click **1 CafeCorp - Sales Projection Memo**
   After a message about updating the link appears briefly, the memo re-displays on your screen with the new amount automatically inserted. See Figure M-14.
8. Click **File** on the WordPad menu bar, click **Exit**, click **No** if you are asked if you want to save changes; click **File** on the Excel menu bar, click **Exit**, then click **No** to close the workbook without saving changes

QuickTip

When you open an Excel workbook containing a linked object, a dialog box will appear asking if you want to update the links.

Trouble?

If you can't read the worksheet clearly, select it, then drag the lower-right selection handle to enlarge it. Continue with Step 8.

FIGURE M-13: Memo with linked worksheet

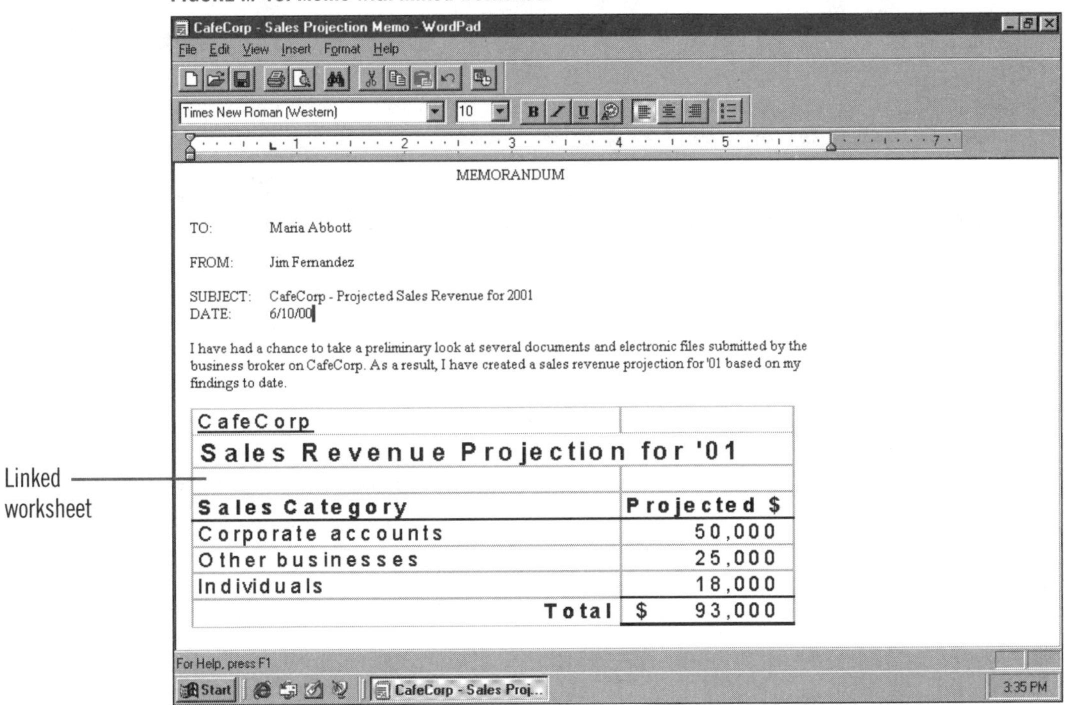

FIGURE M-14: Viewing updated WordPad memo

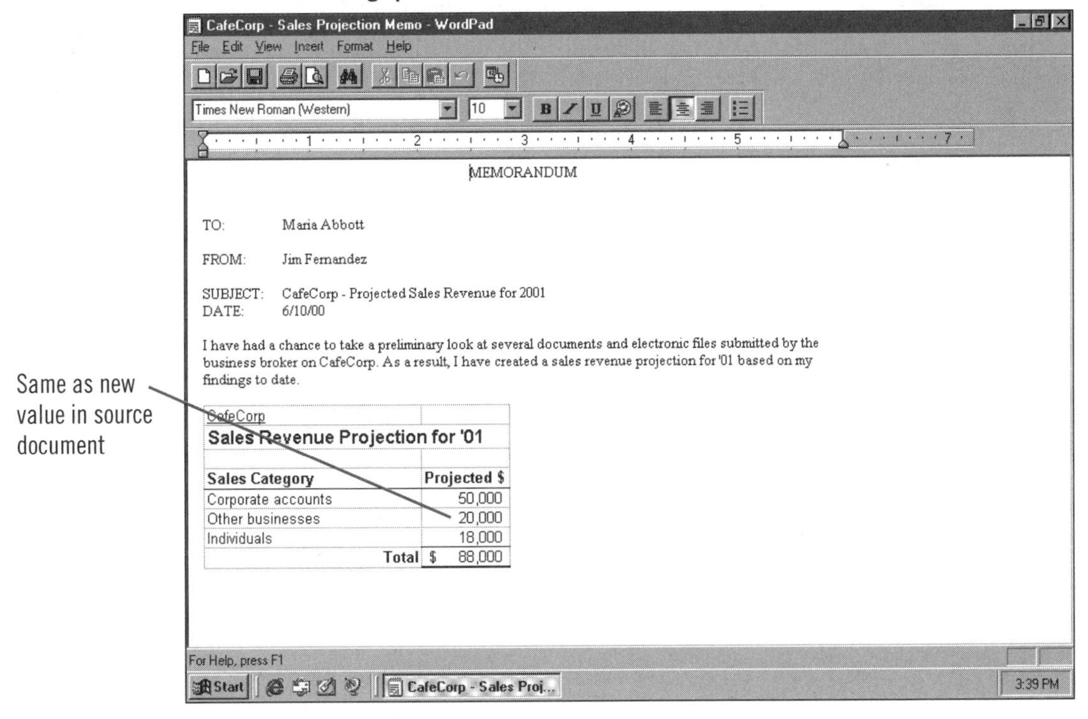

Managing links

When you make changes to a source file, the link is updated automatically each time you open the destination document. You can manage linked objects further by choosing Links on the Edit menu. This opens the Links dialog box, which allows you to update a link or to change the source file of a link. You can also **break**, or delete, a link by selecting the linked object in the Links dialog box, then pressing [Delete].

Excel 2000

Embedding an Excel Chart into a PowerPoint Slide

Microsoft PowerPoint is a presentation graphics program that you can use to create slide show presentations. For example, you can create a slide show to present a sales plan to management or to inform potential clients about a new service. PowerPoint slides can include a mix of text, data, and graphics. Adding an Excel chart to a slide helps to illustrate complicated data, which gives your presentation more visual appeal. Based on his analysis thus far, upper management asks Jim to brief the Marketing department on the possible acquisition of CafeCorp. Jim will make his presentation using PowerPoint slides. He decides to add an Excel chart to one of the presentation slides illustrating the 2001 sales projection data. He begins by starting PowerPoint.

Trouble?

If you don't see Microsoft PowerPoint on your Programs menu, look for something with a similar name somewhere on the Programs menu or the Start menu. If you still can't find it, Microsoft PowerPoint may not be installed on your computer. See your instructor or technical support person for assistance. If the Office Assistant opens when you start PowerPoint, click close and continue with Step 2.

QuickTip

The Insert Chart button on the Standard toolbar allows you to create a new chart using a limited spreadsheet program called Microsoft Graph. Experienced Excel users will find it easier to create a chart in Excel.

QuickTip

The Excel worksheet you see in the PowerPoint slide is the one that was active when the workbook was last saved.

1. Press **[Ctrl][Esc]** to open the Windows Start menu, point to **Programs**, then click **Microsoft PowerPoint**

   The PowerPoint dialog box opens within the Microsoft PowerPoint window. This is where you indicate whether you want to create a new presentation or open a previously created one. You want to open a previously created presentation.

2. Click the **Open an existing presentation option button** if necessary; click **OK**; make sure the drive containing your Project Disk appears in the Look in box; click **EX M-6** if necessary; then click **Open**, then save the presentation as **Marketing Department Presentation**

   The presentation appears in Normal view and contains three panes, as shown in Figure M-15. Notice that the outline of the presentation in the outline pane on the left shows the title and text included on each slide. You will add an Excel chart to slide 2, "2001 Sales Projections". To add the chart, you first need to select the slide, then display it in Slide view.

3. Click the **slide 2 icon** in the outline pane

   The slide appears in the slide pane on the right.

4. Click **Insert** on the PowerPoint menu bar, then click **Object**

   The Insert Object dialog box opens. You want to insert an object (the Excel chart) that has already been saved in a file.

5. Click the **Create from file option button**, click **Browse**, make sure the drive containing your Project Disk appears in the Look in box, click **EX M-7**, click **OK**; in the Insert Object dialog box click **OK** again, then press **[Esc]** to select the object

   After a moment, a pie chart illustrating the 2001 sales projections appears in the slide. The chart is difficult to read in Normal view, so you'll switch to Slide Show view to display the slide on the full screen.

6. Click **View** on the PowerPoint menu bar, then click **Slide Show**

   After a pause, the first slide appears on the screen. You need to display slide 2, which contains your graphic.

7. Press **[Enter]**

   The finished sales projection slide appears, as shown in Figure M-16. The presentation for the Marketing department is complete.

8. Press **[Esc]**, click the **Save button** on the PowerPoint Standard toolbar, click **File** on the menu bar, then click **Exit**

FIGURE M-15: Presentation in Normal view

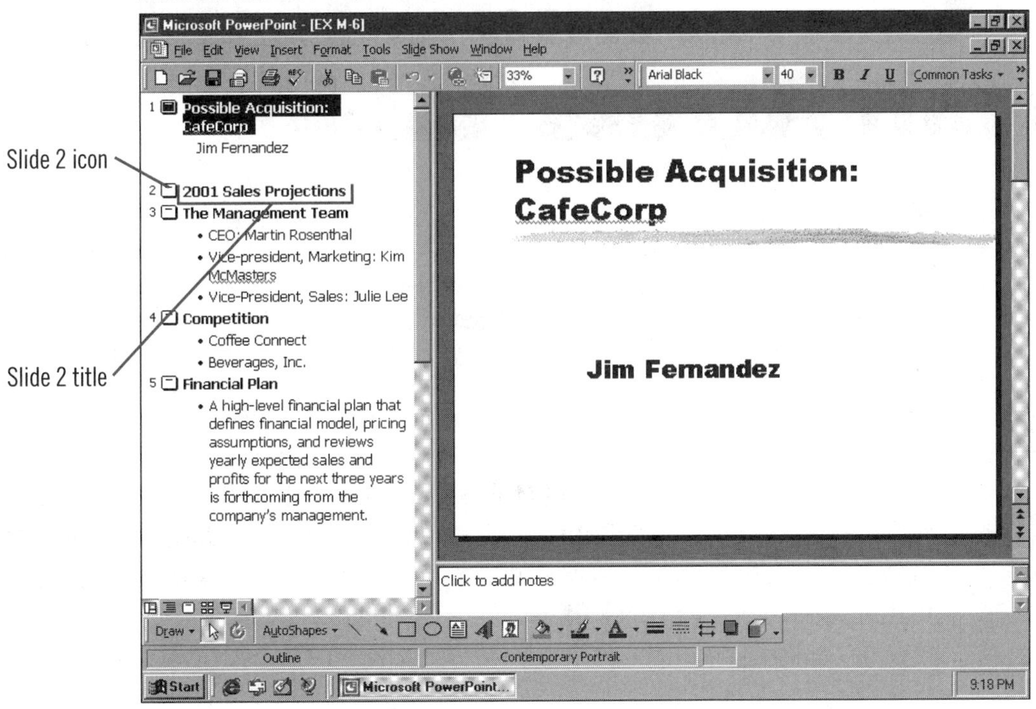

FIGURE M-16: Completed Sales Projections slide in Slide Show view

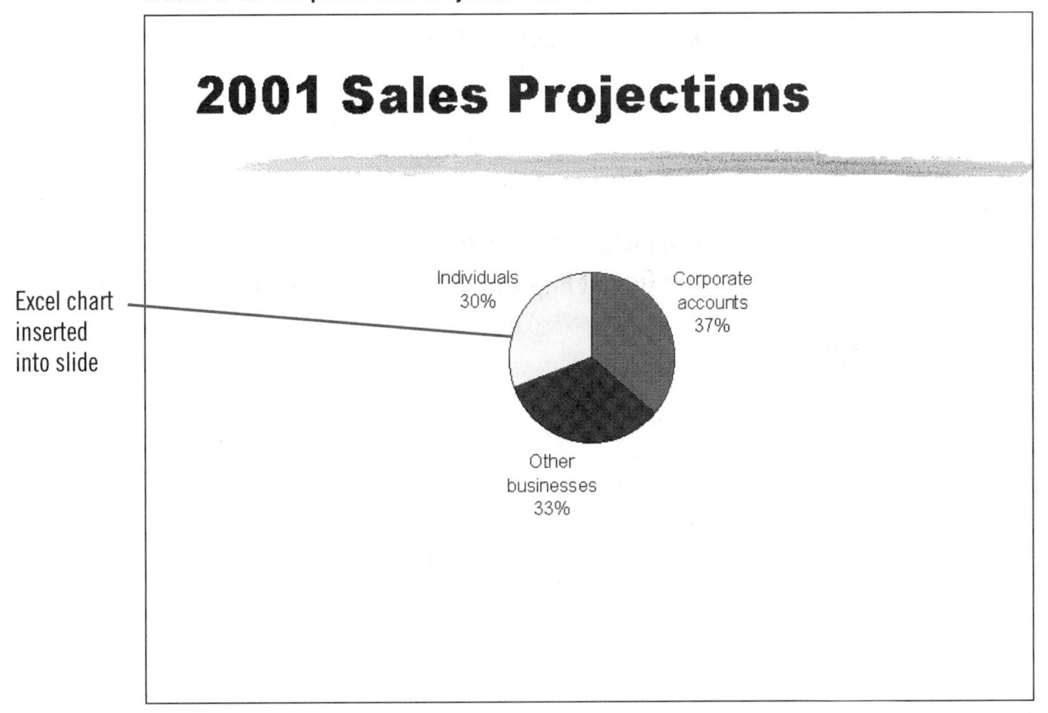

Excel 2000

Converting a List to an Access Table

An Excel data list can be easily converted for use in Microsoft Access, a sophisticated database program. You need to make sure, however, that the list's column labels don't contain spaces between words or any of the following special characters: a period (.), an exclamation point (!), an accent mark (\`), or brackets ([ ]) so that Access can interpret the labels correctly. Once converted to Access format, a data list is called a **table.** Upper management has just received a workbook containing salary information for the managers at CafeCorp. One of the managers asks Jim to convert the list to a Microsoft Access table so that it can be added to MediaLoft's database of compensation information for all employees. Jim begins by opening the list in Excel.

Steps

Trouble?

If you don't see the Convert to MS Access command on the Excel Data menu, you need to install the Microsoft AccessLinks Add-in program. See your instructor or technical support person for assistance.

QuickTip

If Access chooses your primary key, it will select a field with unique data or create a new field that assigns a unique number.

1. Start Excel, open the workbook **EX M-8**, then save it as **CafeCorp Management**
2. With cell A1 selected, click **Data** on the menu bar, then click **Convert to MS Access**; in the Convert to Microsoft Access dialog box, make sure the **New database option button** is selected, then click **OK**

   The Microsoft Access window opens, followed by the First Import Spreadsheet Wizard dialog box. See Figure M-17. In the next step, you'll indicate that you want to use the column headings in the Excel list as the field names in the Access database.
3. Select the **First Row Contains Column Headings check box** if necessary, then click **Next**

   In the next Import Spreadsheet Wizard dialog box, you specify whether you want to store the Excel data in a new or an existing table. In this case, you want to store it in a new table.
4. Make sure the **In a New Table option button** is selected, then click **Next**

   The next Import Spreadsheet Wizard dialog box opens. This is where you specify information about the fields (the Excel columns) you are converting. Notice that the column headings from the Excel list are used as the field names. You can also indicate which columns from the Excel list you do not want to import. In this case, you do not want to import the Annual Salary column.
5. Scroll right until the **Annual Salary column** is in view; click anywhere in the column to select it, then select the **Do not import field (Skip) check box** under Field Options

   Your completed Import Spreadsheet Wizard dialog box should match Figure M-18.
6. Click **Next**

   The next Import Spreadsheet Wizard dialog box opens. This is where you specify the table's primary key. A **primary key** is the field that contains unique information for each record (or row) of information. Specifying a primary key allows you to retrieve data more quickly in the future. In this case, you use the Social Security field as the primary key because the Social Security number for each person in the list is unique.
7. Click the **Choose my own primary key option button**; make sure Social Security appears in the list box next to the selected option button; click **Next**; in the next Import Spreadsheet Wizard dialog box, click **Finish**; click **OK**; then click the **Maximize button** on the Microsoft Access window

   The icon and name representing the new Access table are shown in the new database. See Figure M-19. Next, you'll open the table to make sure it was imported correctly.
8. Make sure **Compensation** is selected, then click **Open**

   The data from the Excel workbook is displayed in the new Access table. When you click the Save button on the Access toolbar, Access automatically saves the database to the same location as the original Excel workbook.
9. Click the **Save button** on the Access toolbar, click **File** on the Access menu bar, then click **Exit**; in the Excel window, save the workbook, then exit Excel

FIGURE M-17: First Import Spreadsheet Wizard dialog box

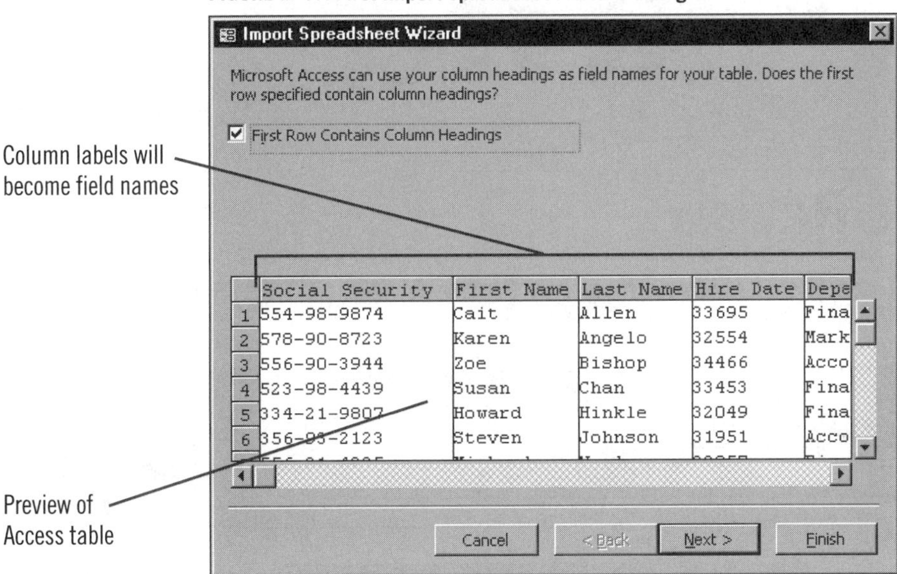

FIGURE M-18: Completed Input Spreadsheet Wizard dialog box

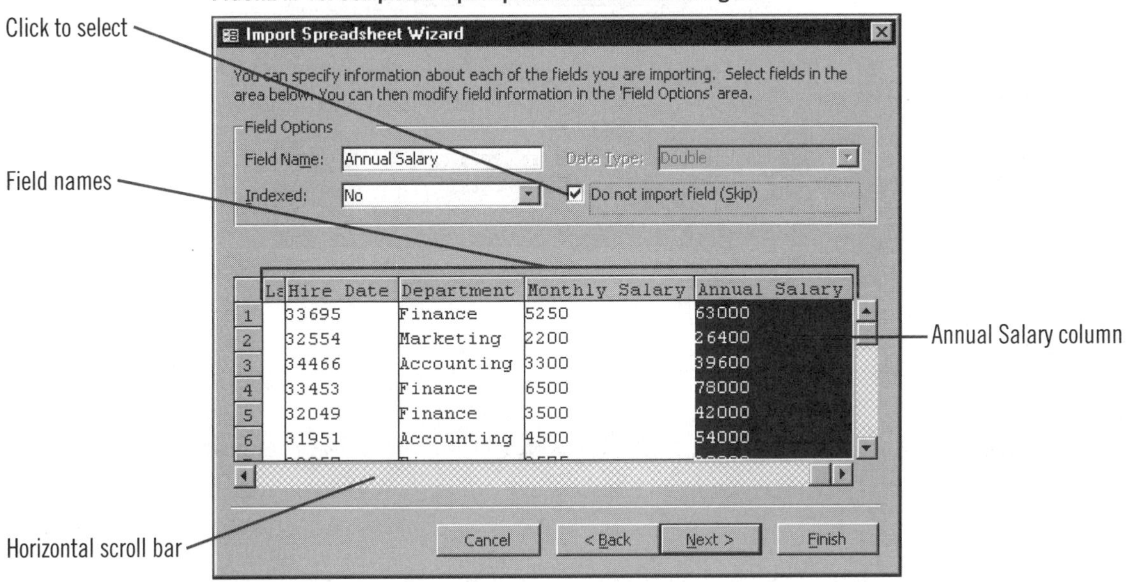

FIGURE M-19: Maximized Microsoft Access window

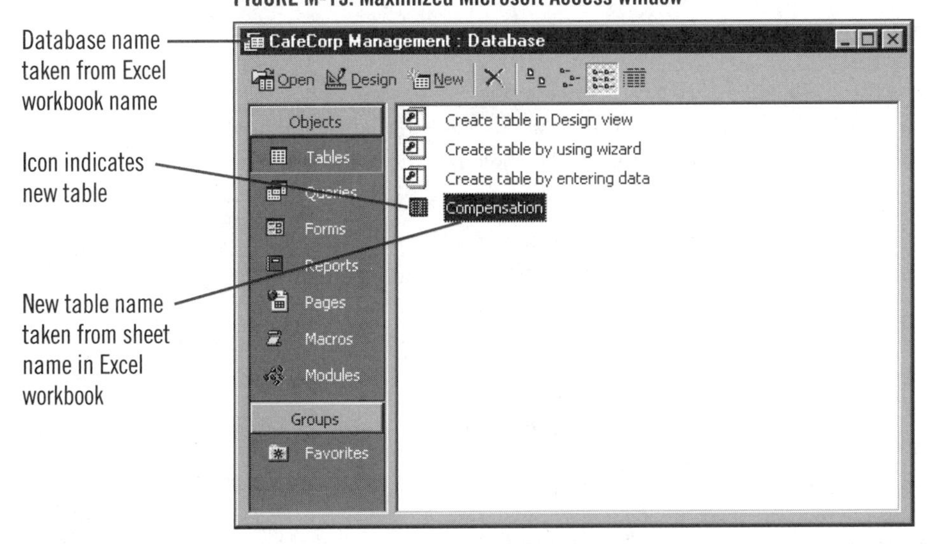

Excel 2000

Practice

► Concepts Review

Label each element of the Excel screen shown in Figure M-20.

FIGURE M-20

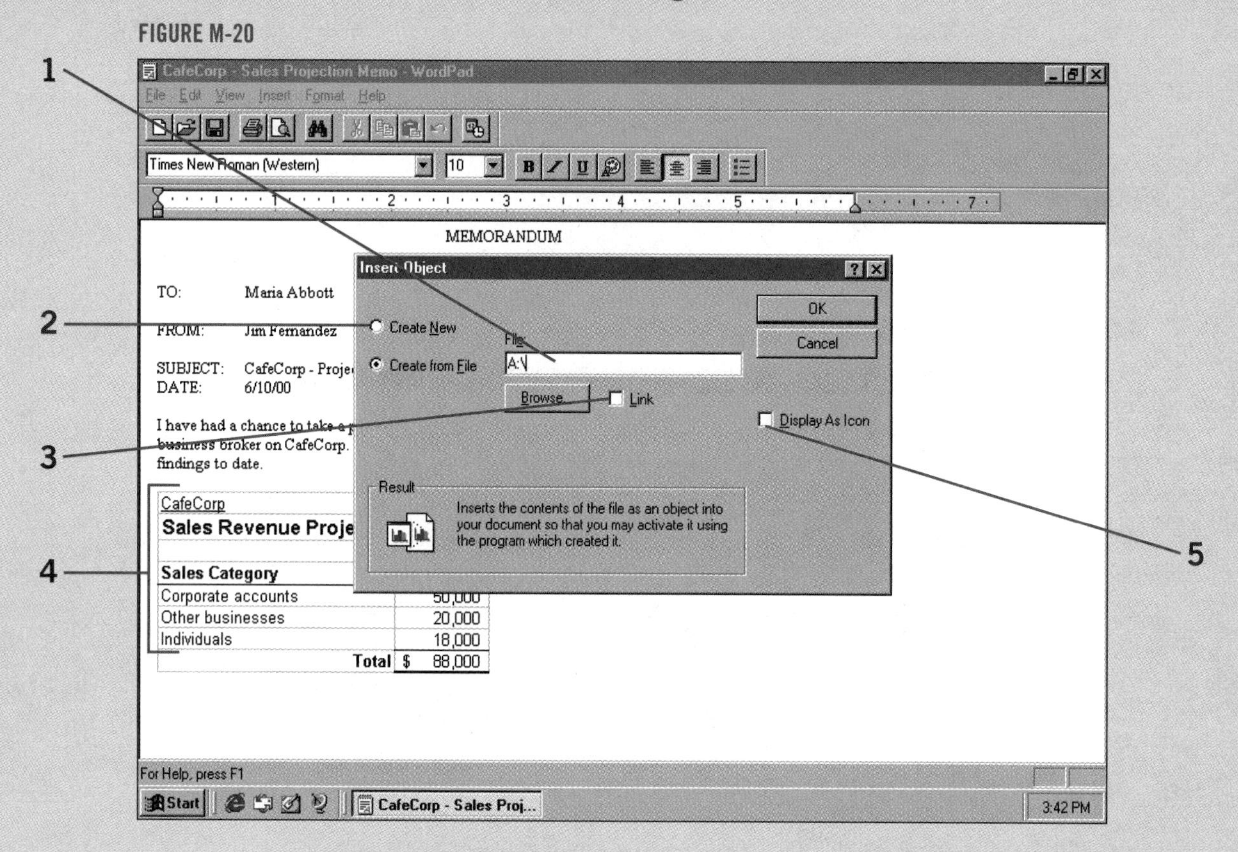

Match each term with the statement that describes it.

6. Source document	**a.** Used to create slide shows
7. Linking	**b.** Copies and retains a connection with the source program and source document
8. Destination document	**c.** Document receiving the object to be embedded or linked
9. Embedding	**d.** An Excel list converted to Access format
10. Presentation program	**e.** Copies and retains a connection with the source program
11. Table	**f.** File from which the object to be embedded or linked originates

Select the best answer from the list of choices.

12. An ASCII file
- **a.** Contains formatting but no text.
- **b.** Contains an unformatted worksheet.
- **c.** Contains text but no formatting.
- **d.** Contains a PowerPoint presentation.

13. An object consists of
- **a.** Text only.
- **b.** Text, a worksheet, or any other type of data.
- **c.** A worksheet only.
- **d.** Database data only.

14. Which of the following is true about converting an Excel list to an Access table?
- **a.** The column labels cannot contain spaces.
- **b.** You must convert all the columns in the list to an Access table.
- **c.** The column headings cannot be used as the table's field names.
- **d.** All of the above.

15. To view a worksheet that has been embedded as an icon in a WordPad document, you need to
- **a.** Click View, then click Worksheet.
- **b.** Drag the icon.
- **c.** Click File, then click Open.
- **d.** Double-click the worksheet icon.

16. To diplay numbers with a dollar sign you can use the following format:
- **a.** Accounting
- **b.** Currency
- **c.** Number
- **d.** a and b

Skills Review

1. Import a text file.
- **a.** Start Excel, then open the tab-delimited text file EX M-9.
- **b.** Save the file as an Excel workbook with the name "Sunshine Temporary - Income Summary".
- **c.** Widen the columns so that all the data is visible.
- **d.** Center the column labels and apply bold formatting.
- **e.** Add your name to the worksheet footer, preview and print your work, then save and close the workbook and close Excel.
- **f.** At the Windows desktop, drag the text file EX M-9 over the Excel program icon. When the file opens, save it as an Excel file named "Sunshine Temporary - Income Summary 2", then close the file.
- **g.** Use the Object command on the Insert menu to insert the text file EX M-9 into a blank worksheet as an icon. Double-click the icon to open the file in Notepad, then copy the data into the worksheet below the icon.
- **h.** Save the file as "Sunshine Temporary - Income Summary 3", then close the file.

2. Import a database table.

a. In Excel, open the dBase file EX M-10.
b. Save the file as an Excel workbook with the name "Sunshine Temporary - Company Budget".
c. Rename the sheet tab "Company Budget".
d. Change the column labels so they read as follows: BUDGET CATEGORY, BUDGET ITEM, MONTH, and AMOUNT BUDGETED.
e. Use AutoSum to calculate a total in cell D26, then add a top and bottom border to the cell.
f. Format range D2:D26 using the Accounting style with no decimal places.
g. Add bold formatting to the column labels, then wrap the text on two lines.
h. Center the column labels and manually adjust the column widths as necessary.
i. Save your work.

3. Embed a graphic file in a worksheet.

a. Add four rows above row 1 to create space for the graphic file.
b. Insert the picture file EX M-11 in the space.
c. Make the graphic smaller so it doesn't cover up any column headings.
d. Open the Drawing toolbar, if necessary.
e. Use the Line style button to add a 1-point border around the graphic.
f. Adjust the size and position as necessary, using [Ctrl] with the arrow keys to move it in small increments.
g. Press [Esc] to deselect the graphic, then close the Drawing toolbar, if necessary.
h. Add your name to the worksheet footer, preview and print the worksheet, then save your work.

4. Embed a worksheet in another program.

a. In cell A33, type "For details on Green Hills salaries, click this icon:".
b. In cell D33, embed the worksheet object EX M-12 and display it as an icon.
c. Double-click the icon to verify that the worksheet opens, then close it.
d. Preview, then print the Sunshine Temporary - Company Budget worksheet.
e. Save your work.

5. Link a worksheet.

a. Delete the embedded object icon.
b. Link the spreadsheet object EX M-12 to cell D33, displaying the worksheet, not an icon.
c. Save, then close the Sunshine Temporary - Company Budget worksheet.
d. Open the EX M-12 workbook, change the Manager salary to 5,000, correct the first and last name order of employees Smith and Hargrove, then open the Sunshine Temporary - Company Budget worksheet; click Yes when you are asked if you want to update links, then verify that the manager salary has changed to 5,000 and that the name order is correct in the linked workbook.
e. Preview, then print the worksheet with the linked object on one page.
f. Close both workbooks without saving changes, then exit Excel.

6. Paste an Excel chart into a PowerPoint slide.

a. Open the Microsoft PowerPoint program.
b. Open the PowerPoint presentation file EX M-13.
c. Save the presentation as "Monthly Budget Meeting".
d. Display Slide 2, January Expenditures.
e. Embed the Excel file EX M-14, then drag the chart until it is centered in the blank area of the slide.

f. View the slide with the chart in Slide Show view.
g. Press [Esc] to return to Normal view, save the file, and exit PowerPoint.

7. Converting an Excel list to an Access database.

a. Start Excel, open the workbook EX M-15, then save it as Budget List.
b. Convert the worksheet into a new Access database table, using the first row as column headings. Do not import the month column, and let Access add the primary key.
c. Open the January Budget table in the Budget List in Access and drag the column borders as necessary to fully display the field names.
d. Save the database file and exit Access.
e. In the Excel window, add your name to the worksheet footer, print the worksheet (along with the conversion notice), then save the workbook and exit Excel.

Independent Challenges

1. You are opening a new store, called Bridge Blades, that rents in-line skates. The store is located right outside Golden Gate Park in San Francisco, California. Recently, you heard that Tim Botano, the owner of Gateway In-line, a similar store, is planning to retire. You ask him for a list of his suppliers, and he agrees to sell it to you for a nominal fee. Because you have a personal computer (PC) running Excel, you ask him if he can put the list on a disk. The next day, you stop by his store and he sells you the text file containing the supplier information. You need to import this file and convert it to a workbook so that you can manipulate it in Excel. Then you will convert the file to an Access table, so that you can share it with your partner, who has Access, but not Excel, on her PC.

To complete this independent challenge:

a. Open the file titled EX M-16 (a text file). (*Hint*: The data type of the original file is tab delimited.)
b. Save the file as an Excel workbook titled "In-line Skate Supplier List".
c. Adjust the column labels and widths so that all the data is visible. Add any formatting you feel is appropriate.
d. Sort the list in ascending order, first by item purchased, then by supplier.
e. Add your name to the worksheet footer, preview and print your work on a single page, then save your work.
f. Save the workbook with the new name "Supplier List Converted to Access", then convert the worksheet to an Access table in a new database. Use the column labels as the field names, store the data in a new table, import all columns in the list, then let Access add the primary key.
g. Open the Access table and autofit the columns, then save the table and exit Access.
h. In the Excel window, save the open worksheet, print it (along with the conversion notice) on one page, then close the workbook.

2. You are the newly hired manager at Burger Pit, the local burger joint in your small town. A past employee, Roberta Carlson, has filed a grievance that she was underpaid in January 1996. The files containing the payroll information for early 1996 are in Lotus 1-2-3 (WK1) format. In June 1996, the owner switched the business records to Microsoft Excel. You have located the files containing the payroll information you need. You import the Lotus 1-2-3 file, convert it to an Excel workbook, and correct the formatting in order to verify the values and formulas, especially those for Roberta Carlson, to determine if she was indeed underpaid.

To complete this independent challenge:

a. Open the Lotus 1-2-3 file titled EX M-17.
b. Save the file as an Excel workbook titled "Burger Pit Payroll Info".
c. Click Tools on the menu bar, click Options, click the View tab, then select the Gridlines check box to turn on the worksheet gridlines and click OK.

d. Check all values and formulas for discrepancies. If you find any, open the Drawing toolbar and note the discrepancy: Click AutoShape on the Drawing toolbar, point to callouts, choose one of the callout AutoShapes to draw a line to the discrepancy, then describe the discrepancy by typing in the callout box. Do *not* change any spreadsheet formulas or values.
e. Correct the formatting. Delete any row(s) containing dashes or equal signs and add appropriate borders. Format all dollar values using the Number style with two decimal places. Add or delete any other formatting you feel is appropriate.
f. Add your name to the worksheet footer, preview and then print your work on a single page.
g. Save the worksheet, then close the workbook.

3. You are a loan officer for a local bank. You have been asked to give a talk about the banking industry to a local high school economics class. As part of your talk, you decide to give a presentation explaining the most popular consumer loans. To illustrate your comments, you will add an Excel chart to one of your slides showing the most popular loan types and the number of applications received yearly for each.

To complete this independent challenge:

a. Create a worksheet containing popular loan types, then save it as "Most Popular Consumer Loans". Include the loans and the corresponding number of applications shown in Table M-2.
b. Create a pie chart from the loan data on a new sheet. Add an appropriate title to your chart.
c. Save the workbook, print the chart, then (with the chart sheet the active sheet) close the workbook.
d. Start PowerPoint, click the Blank presentation option button, then click OK.
e. In the New Slide dialog box, click the layout on the far right in the bottom row (Blank), then click OK.
f. Make sure the slide is displayed in Normal view, then insert the Excel chart into the blank slide.
g. Double-click the chart on slide 1 and observe how Excel tools appear in the toolbar, and how the Chart toolbar appears. Use the Chart toolbar to change the title to 28 point bold and the legend to 22-point type.
h. Click outside the chart to return to PowerPoint.
i. View the slide in Slide Show view, then press [Esc] to end the show.
j. Click File on the PowerPoint menu bar, click Save As, then save the presentation as "Banking Industry Presentation".
k. Close the presentation, then exit PowerPoint and Excel.

TABLE M-2

loan type	number of applications
Fixed home loans	1456
New-car loans	5400
Used-car loans	3452
Adjustable home loans	760
Boat loans	250

4. The MediaLoft Product department wants to create a handout listing out-of-stock products that it can give to customers who ask for it. You know that this information exists on the MediaLoft intranet site, but you would like to reformat it, and Mike MacDowell, the MediaLoft Web manager, has the original .xls and .htm files for the intranet site and he is out of town. You decide to e-mail Mike to obtain the files when he returns. In the meantime, you download the data into an Excel worksheet, reformat it, and print it. Several days later, Mike e-mails you the HTML file, which you then decide to embed in a workbook.

To complete this independent challenge:

a. Open a blank Excel workbook and save it as "Out of Stock".

b. Use Internet Explorer to connect to the Internet, and go to the MediaLoft intranet site at http://www.course.com/Illustrated/MediaLoft. Click the Products link, then click the Out of Stock items link.

c. Select the table of out-of-stock items, then use drag and drop to place the information in the Excel worksheet starting in cell A1.

d. Reformat the sheet as follows:

- Change the blue cells to a light green. (*Hint*: Remember that you can use the F4 function key to repeat your previous action.)
- Use the Alignment tab in the Format Cells dialog box to unwrap the text within cells.
- Sort the café items by the "Expected" date. (*Hint*: In the Sort dialog box, sort on column C.)
- Delete any blank columns if necessary.
- Add any other formatting you think would make the handout attractive.

e. Place your name in the workbook footer, save your changes, then print the workbook. Republish it in HTML format as "Out of Stock - Web". You have now received the HTML file from Mike MacDowell. Create a new workbook called Out of Stock File, and use the Insert Object command to insert an icon representing the file "Out of Stock - Web".

f. Save the file, then double-click the icon to verify that the HTML file appears.

g. Close Internet Explorer, then close the Excel file and exit Excel.

Visual Workshop

Create the worksheet shown in Figure M-21. Insert the graphic file EX M-18, resizing it as necessary. (*Hint*: Drag the resize handles as necessary to enlarge the art to the proper size.) Save the workbook as "Atlantic Price List". Preview, add your name to the worksheet footer, then print the worksheet.

FIGURE M-21

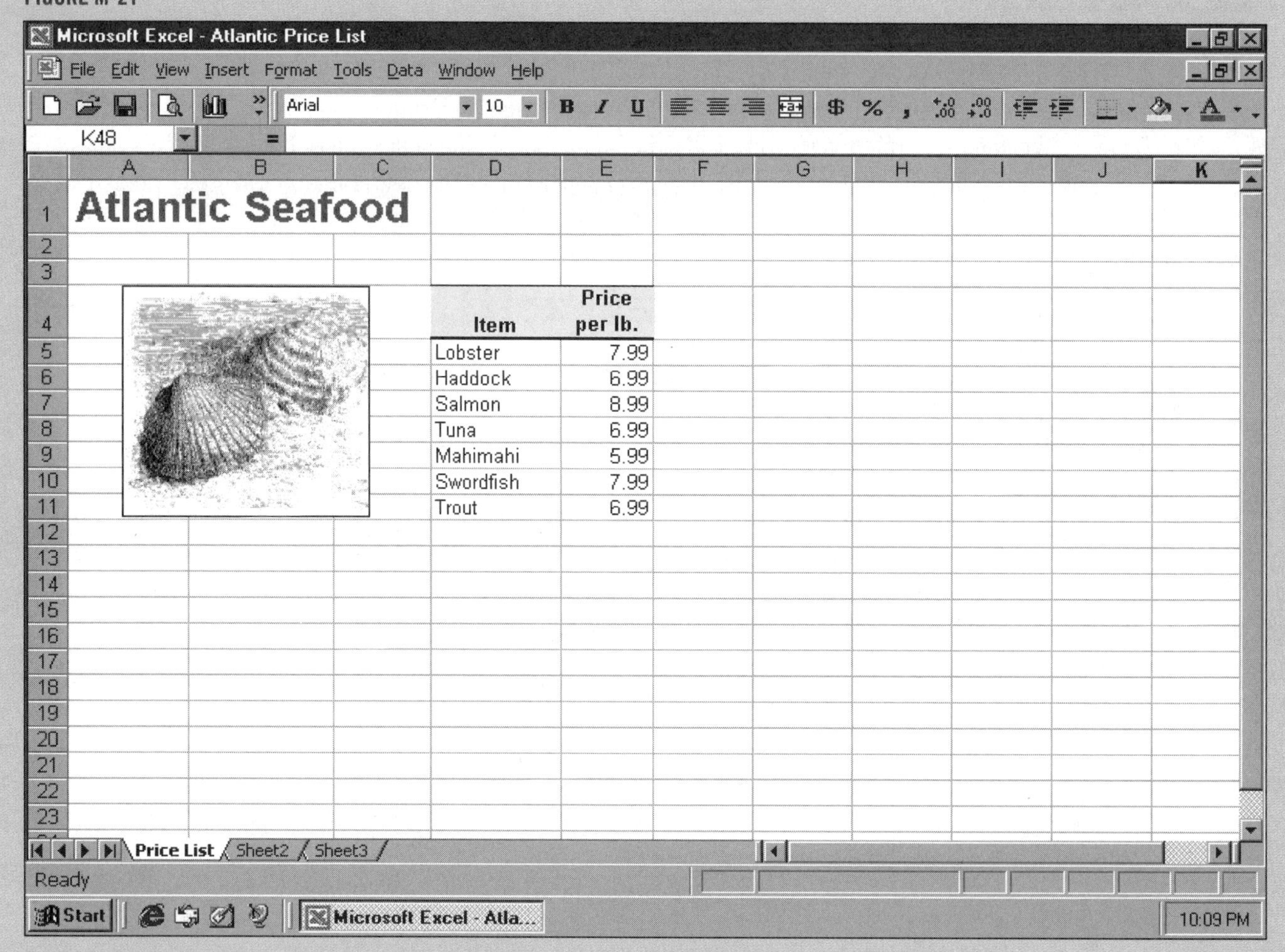

Excel 2000

Unit N

Sharing
Excel Files and Incorporating Web Information

Objectives

- Share Excel Files
- Set up a shared workbook
- Track changes in a shared workbook
- Apply and remove passwords
- Create an interactive worksheet for an intranet or the Web
- Create an interactive PivotTable for an intranet or the Web
- Create hyperlinks between Excel files and the Web
- Run queries to retrieve data on the Web

With the recent growth of networks, company intranets, and the World Wide Web, people are increasingly sharing electronic spreadsheet files with others for review, revision, and feedback. They are also incorporating information from intranets and the World Wide Web into their worksheets. Jim Fernandez has some MediaLoft corporate information he wants to share with corporate office employees and store managers. He also wants to track information on MediaLoft's competitors.

Excel 2000

Sharing Excel Files

Microsoft Excel provides many different ways to share spreadsheets electronically with people in your office, company, or anywhere on the World Wide Web. Users can not only retrieve and review your workbooks and worksheets, but they can modify them electronically and return their revisions to you for incorporation with others' changes. When you share workbooks, you also have to consider how you will protect information that you don't want everyone to see. You can post workbooks, worksheets, or other parts of workbooks for users to interact with on a company intranet or on the World Wide Web. You can also use Excel workbooks to run queries to retrieve data from the Web. Jim considers the best way to share his Excel workbooks with corporate employees and store managers. He also thinks about how to get Web data for use in his workbooks. He considers the following issues:

Details

Allowing others to use a workbook

When you pass on Excel files to others, you could just have them write their comments on a printed copy. But it's easier to set up your workbook so that several users can simultaneously open the workbook from a network server and modify it. Then you can view each user's name and the date the change was made. Jim wants to get feedback on selected store sales and customer information from MediaLoft corporate staff and store managers.

Controlling access to workbooks on a server

When you set up a workbook on a network server, you may want to control who can open and make changes to it. You can do this easily with Excel passwords. Jim assigns a password to his workbook and gives it to the corporate staff and store managers, so only they will be able to open it and make changes.

Distributing workbooks to others

There are several ways of making workbook information available to others. You can send it to recipients simultaneously as an e-mail attachment or as the body of an e-mail message; you can **route** it, or send it sequentially to each user, who then forwards it on to the next user using a **routing slip**, or list of recipients. You can also save the file in HTML format and post it on a company intranet server or on the Web, where people can view it with their Web browsers. Jim decides to make an Excel workbook available to others by putting it on a central company server.

Publishing a worksheet for use on an intranet or the World Wide Web

When you save a workbook in HTML format, you can save the entire workbook or just part of it—a worksheet, a chart, a filtered list, a cell range, or a print area. When you save only part of a workbook, you can specify that you want to make that particular part, or object, **interactive**, meaning that users can make changes to it when they view it in their browsers. They do not have to have the Excel program on their machines. See Figure N-1. The changes remain in effect until users close their browsers. Jim decides to publish part of a worksheet about MediaLoft café pastry sales.

Interactive PivotTables

You can save a PivotTable in HTML format so people can only view it, but the data is much more useful if people can interact with it from their browsers, just as they would in Excel. To make an Excel PivotTable interactive, you need to save it as a PivotTable list. Jim wants corporate staff to explore some sales data using their browsers just as he would with Excel.

Creating hyperlinks to the Web

You can make Web information available to users by creating hyperlinks to any site on the Web. Jim decides to include a hyperlink to a competitor's Web site.

Using an Excel query to retrieve data from the Web

By using Microsoft Query from Excel, you can get data from the Web that you can bring into your workbooks, and then organize and manipulate it with Excel spreadsheet and graphics tools. See Figure N-2. Jim uses a query to get stock information about one of MediaLoft's competitors.

FIGURE N-1: Interactive worksheet in Web browser

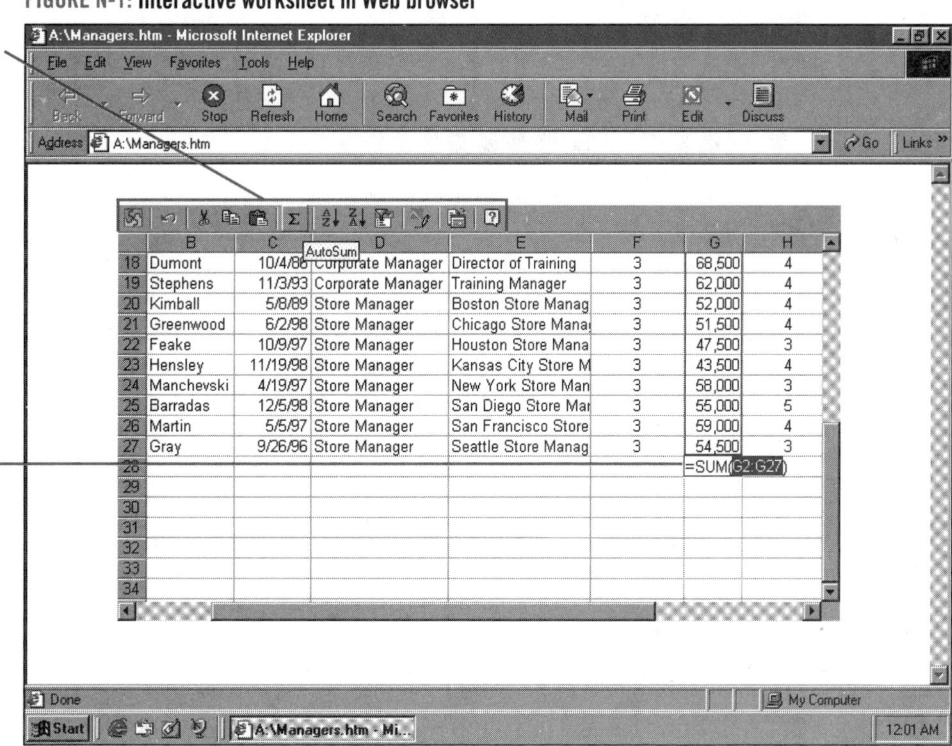

FIGURE N-2: Retrieving data from the World Wide Web using a Web query

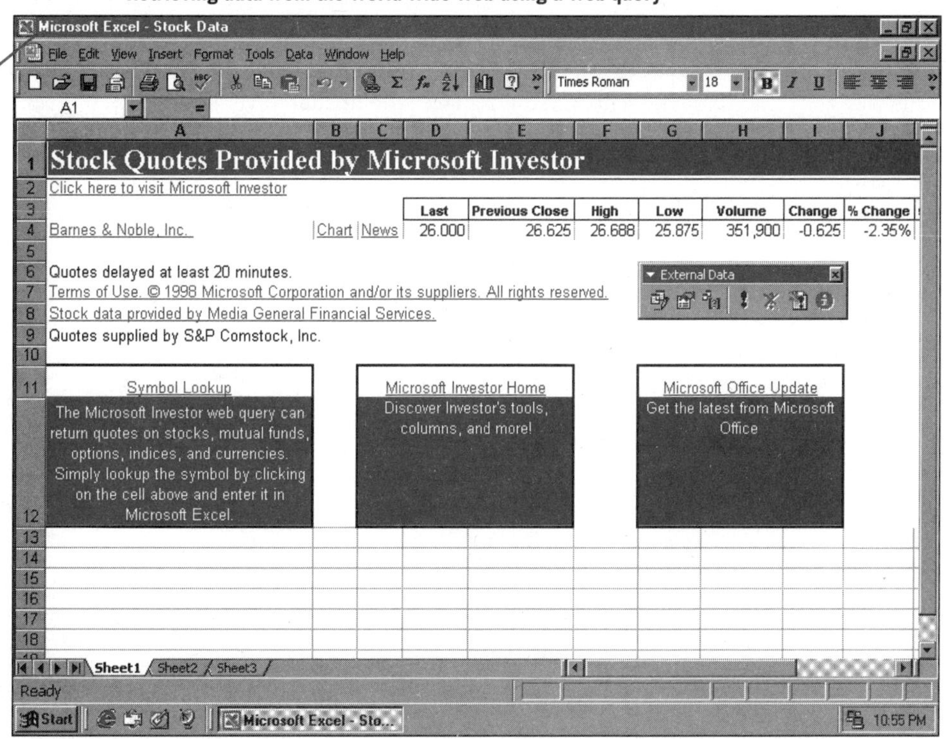

Excel 2000

Setting Up a Shared Workbook

You can make an Excel file a **shared workbook** so that several users can open and modify it at the same time. This is very useful for workbooks that you want others to review on a network server. The workbook is equally accessible to all users who have access to that location on the network. When you share a workbook, you can have Excel keep a list of all changes to the workbook, called a **change history**, that you can view and print at any time. Users must have Excel 97 or later to modify the workbook. Jim makes his workbook containing customer and sales data a shared workbook. He will later put it on a network server and ask for feedback from selected corporate staff and store managers before using the information in a presentation at the next corporate staff meeting.

QuickTip

To return personalized toolbars and menus to their default state, click Tools on the menu bar, click Customize, click the Options tab in the Customize dialog box, click Reset my usage data to restore the default settings, click Yes, click Close, then close the Drawing toolbar if it is displayed.

QuickTip

You can remove users from the list by clicking their names and clicking Remove User.

QuickTip

You can easily return the workbook to unshared status. Click Tools, click Share Workbook, and on the Editing tab click to deselect the Allow changes… option.

1. **Open the workbook titled EX N-1, then save it as Sales Info**
   The workbook with the sales information opens. It contains three worksheets. The first is the chart of café pastry sales for the first quarter, the second contains the worksheet and map of pastry sales by state, and the third contains a listing of sales for selected stores and sales representatives for the last four quarters.
2. **Click Tools on the menu bar, then click Share Workbook**
   The Share Workbook dialog box opens, similar to Figure N-3.
3. **If necessary, click the Editing tab**
   The lower part of the dialog box lists the names of people who are currently using the workbook. You are the only user, so your name (or the name of the person entered as the machine user) appears, along with the date and time.
4. **Click to select the check box next to Allow changes by more than one user at the same time, then click OK**
   A dialog box appears, asking if you want to save the workbook. This will resave it as a shared workbook.
5. **Click OK**
   Excel saves the file as a shared workbook. The toolbar now reads Sales Info [Shared]. See Figure N-4. This version replaces the unshared version.

FIGURE N-3: Share Workbook dialog box

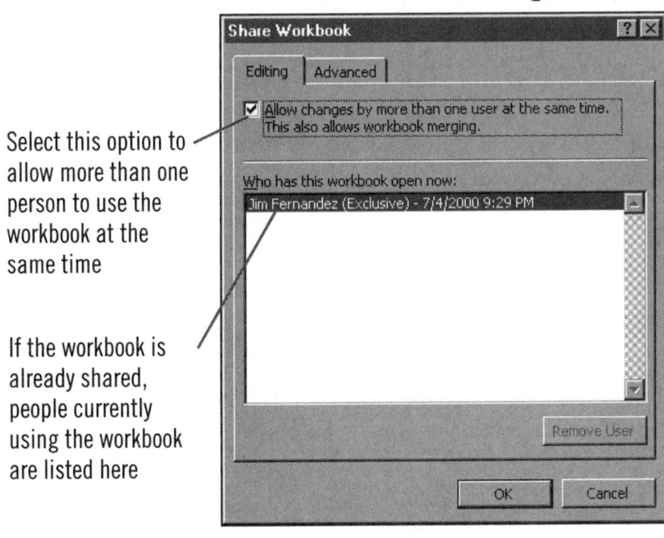

FIGURE N-4: Shared workbook

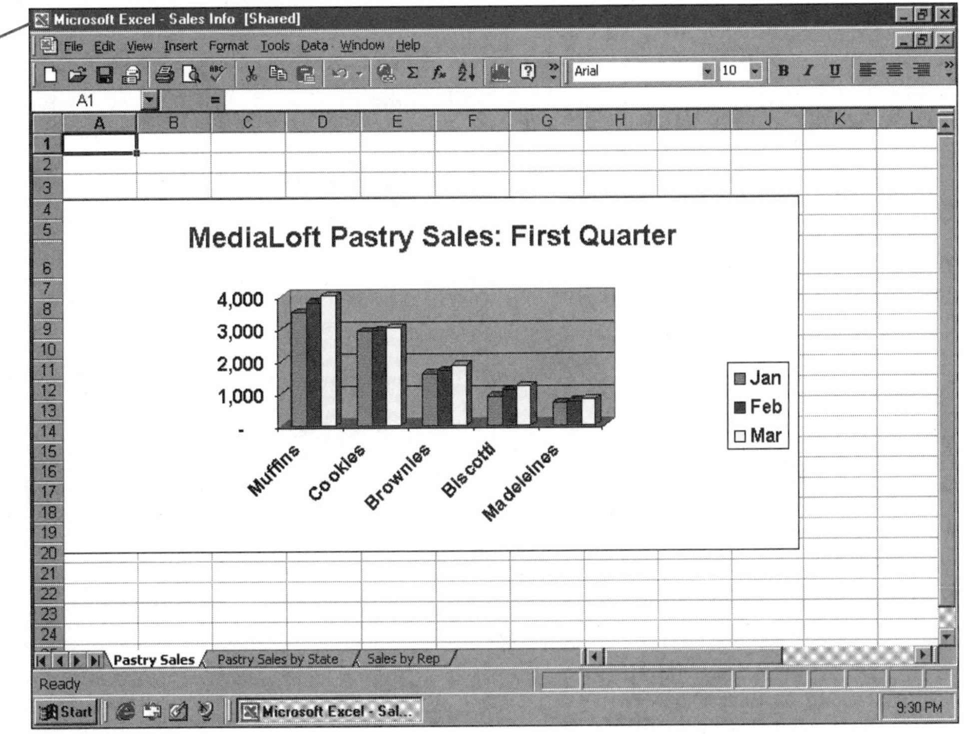

Excel 2000

Tracking Changes in a Shared Workbook

When you share workbooks, it is often helpful to **track** modifications, or identify who made which changes. If you disagree with any of the changes, you can reject them. When the Excel change tracking feature is activated, changes are highlighted in a different color for each user. Each change is identified with the user name and date. In addition to highlighting changes, Excel keeps track of all changes in a **change history**, a list of all changes that you can place on a separate worksheet so you can review them all at once. Jim sets up the shared Sales Info workbook so that all future changes will be tracked. He then opens another workbook that has been on the server and reviews the changes and the change history.

1. Click **Tools** on the menu bar, point to **Track Changes**, click **Highlight Changes**
   The Highlight Changes dialog box opens, allowing you to turn on change tracking, to specify which changes to highlight, and to display changes on the screen or save the change history in a separate worksheet.
2. Click to select **Track changes while editing**, remove check marks from all other boxes except for Highlight changes on screen, compare your screen to Figure N-5, click **OK**, then click **OK** in the dialog box that informs you that you have yet to make changes
   To track all changes, you can leave the When, Who, and Where check boxes blank.
3. Click the **Pastry Sales by State tab**, then change the sales figure for Texas to **133,000**
   A border with a small triangle in the upper-left corner appears around the figure you changed.
4. After you enter the change, move the **mouse pointer** over the cell you just changed, but do not click
   A screen tip appears with your name, the date, the time, and a phrase describing the change. See Figure N-6. Cells that other users change will appear in different colors.
5. Save and close the workbook
   Alice Wegman and Maria Abbott have made changes to a version of this workbook.
6. Open the workbook **EX N-2** and save it as **Sales Info Edits**
7. Click **Tools** on the menu bar, point to **Track Changes**, click **Highlight Changes**, in the Highlight Changes dialog box click the **When** check box to deselect it, click to select **List changes on a new sheet**, then click **OK**
   The History tab appears, as shown in Figure N-7, with a record of each change in the form of a filtered list. Notice that you could, for example, click the Who list arrow in row 1 and show a list of Maria Abbott's changes only.
8. Examine the three sheets, holding the pointer over each change, then click the **History sheet tab**
9. Put your name in the History sheet footer, preview and print the History sheet on one page, then save the workbook, which closes the History worksheet, and close the workbook
   The change history prints, showing who has made which changes to the workbook.

FIGURE N-5: Highlight changes dialog box

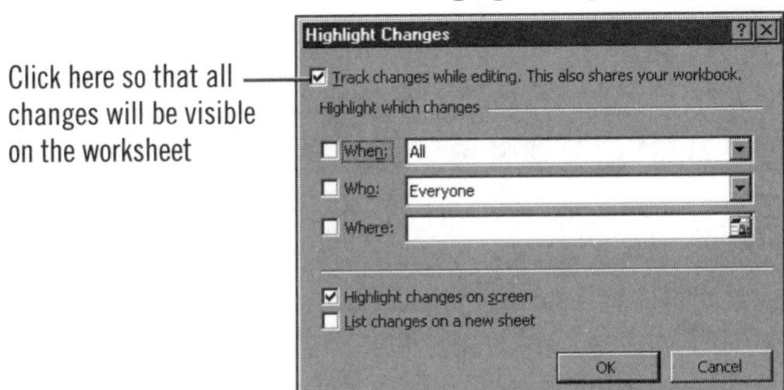

FIGURE N-6: Tracked change

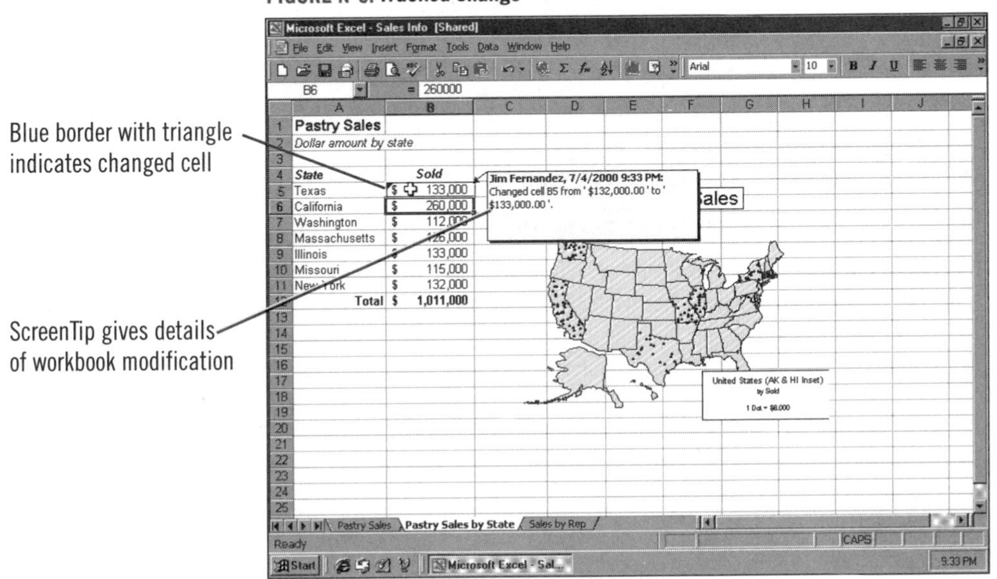

FIGURE N-7: History sheet tab with change history

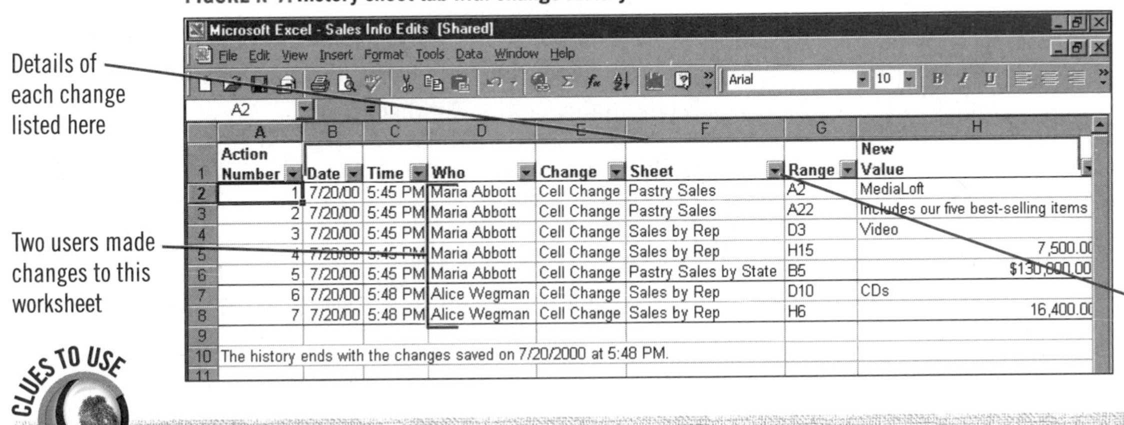

Action Number	Date	Time	Who	Change	Sheet	Range	New Value
1	7/20/00	5:45 PM	Maria Abbott	Cell Change	Pastry Sales	A2	MediaLoft
2	7/20/00	5:45 PM	Maria Abbott	Cell Change	Pastry Sales	A22	Includes our five best-selling items
3	7/20/00	5:45 PM	Maria Abbott	Cell Change	Sales by Rep	D3	Video
4	7/20/00	5:45 PM	Maria Abbott	Cell Change	Sales by Rep	H15	7,500.00
5	7/20/00	5:45 PM	Maria Abbott	Cell Change	Pastry Sales by State	B5	$130,000.00
6	7/20/00	5:48 PM	Alice Wegman	Cell Change	Sales by Rep	D10	CDs
7	7/20/00	5:48 PM	Alice Wegman	Cell Change	Sales by Rep	H6	16,400.00

The history ends with the changes saved on 7/20/2000 at 5:48 PM.

CLUES TO USE

Merging workbooks

Instead of putting the shared workbook on a server, you may want to distribute copies to your reviewers, perhaps via e-mail. Once everyone has entered their changes, you can merge the changed copies into one workbook that will contain all the changes. Each copy you distribute must be designated as shared, and the Change History feature must be activated. Once you get the changed copies back, open your master copy of the workbook, click Tools on the menu bar, click Merge Workbooks, then save when prompted. The Select Files to Merge Into Current Workbook dialog box opens. Click the name of the workbook you want to merge, then click OK. Repeat for all shared workbooks. It's important that you specify that each copy of the shared workbook keep a change history from the date you copy them to the merge date. In the Advanced tab in the Share Workbooks dialog box, set Keep change history for a large number, such as 1,000 days.

Excel 2000

Applying and Removing Passwords

When you place a shared workbook on a server, you may want to use a password so that only certain people will be able to open it or make changes to it. If you do assign a password, it's very important that you write it down and keep it in a secure place where you can access it, in case you forget it. *If you lose your password, you will not be able to open or change the workbook.* Remember also that all passwords are case sensitive, so you must type them exactly as you want users to type them, with the same spacing and upper- and lowercase letters. For example, if your password to open a workbook is Stardot, and a user enters stardot, star dot, or StarDot, the workbook will not open. Jim wants to put the Sales Info 2 workbook on a server, so he decides to save a copy with two passwords: one that users will need to open it, and another to make changes to it.

Steps 1 2 3 4

1. Open the workbook **EX N-1**, click **File** on the menu bar, then click **Save As**
2. In the Save As dialog box, click **Tools**, then click **General Options**
   The Save Options dialog box opens, with two password boxes: one to open the workbook, and one to allow changes to the workbook, similar to Figure N-8.
3. In the Password to open box, type **Saturn**
   Be sure to type the capital S and the rest of the letters lowercase. This is the password users will have to type to open the workbook. Whenever you type passwords, they appear as asterisks (***) so that no one nearby will be able to see them.
4. Press **[Tab]**, then in the Password to modify box type **Atlas**, compare your screen to Figure N-8, then click **OK**
   This is the password users will have to type to make changes to the workbook. A dialog box asks you to verify the password by re-entering it.
5. In the first Confirm Password dialog box, type **Saturn**, then click **OK;** in the second Confirm Password dialog box, type **Atlas**, click **OK**, edit the workbook name so it reads **Sales Info PW**, then click **Save** and close the workbook
6. Reopen the workbook **Sales Info PW**, enter the password **Saturn** when prompted in order to open the workbook as shown in Figure N-9, click **OK**, then type **Atlas** to obtain write access and click **OK**
7. In the Pastry Sales by State worksheet, click cell A-14 and enter **One-year totals**
   You have confirmed that you can make changes to the workbook.
8. Save and close the workbook

FIGURE N-8: Save options dialog box

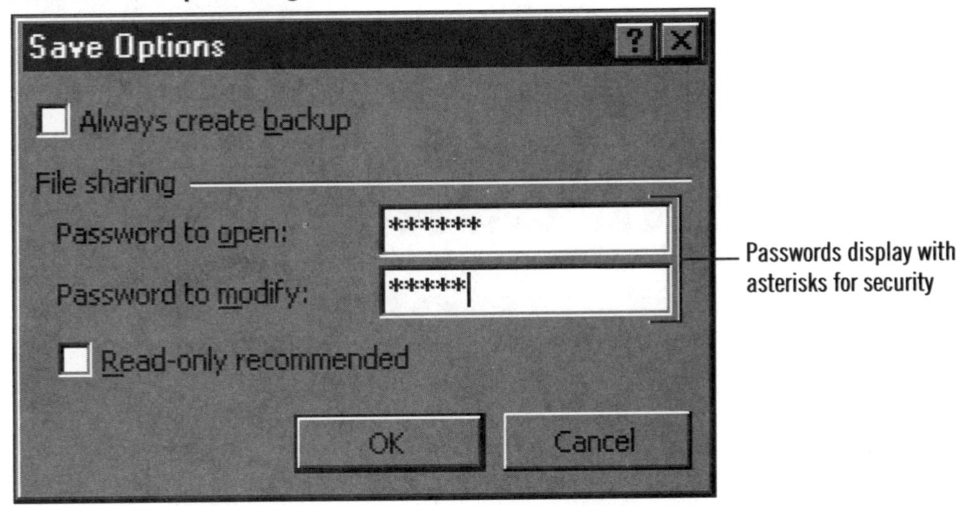

FIGURE N-9: Password entry prompt

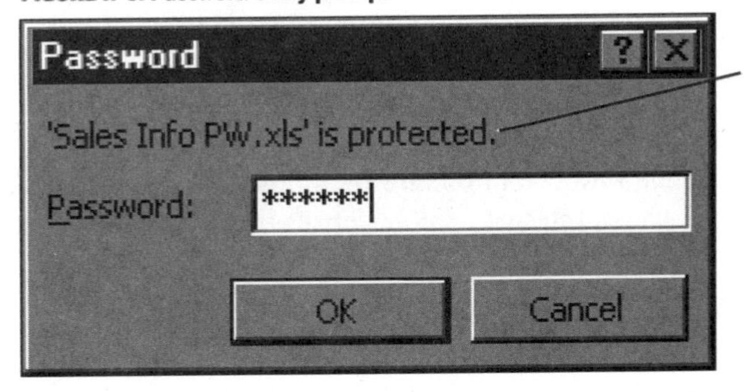

Removing passwords

You must know a workbook's password in order to change or delete it. Open the workbook, click File on the menu bar, then click Save As. In the Save As dialog box, click Tools, then click General Options. Double-click the symbols for the existing passwords in the Password to open or Password to modify boxes, and press [Delete]. Change the filename if you wish, then click Save.

Excel 2000

Creating an Interactive Worksheet for an Intranet or the Web

You can save an entire workbook in HTML format for users to view. But you can also save part of a workbook—a worksheet, chart, or PivotTable—in HTML format and make it interactive. You cannot save an entire workbook in interactive format. To work with interactive data, users must have installed Internet Explorer version 4.01 or later as well as the Office Web Components. Anyone with Office 2000 will have these. Users do not need to have Excel. Jim decides to save the Pastry Sales by State sheet as an interactive Web page.

Steps

QuickTip

Internet Explorer 4.01 or later must be your default browser or you will not be able to use interactive features.

1. Open **EX N-1**, save it as **Sales Info 2**, then click the **Pastry Sales by State sheet**
2. Click **File** on the menu bar, click **Save as Web Page**, then click **Publish**
   The Publish as Web Page dialog box opens.
3. Click the **Choose list arrow** and choose **Items on Pastry Sales by State**, then under Viewing options click to select **Add interactivity with**
4. In the Publish as section, click **Change** and type **Pastry Sales by State**, click **OK**, click **Browse**, make sure your project disk name appears as the Save in location, type the filename **Pastry Sales Web**, then click **OK**

QuickTip

See the Microsoft Excel Help topic "Limitations of putting interactive data on a Web page" for more information about which features might not work or might appear differently on your Web page.

5. If necessary, click to select **Open published Web page in browser** at the bottom of the dialog box, click **Publish**, then maximize your browser window
   After a pause, Internet Explorer opens the HTML version of your data. See Figure N-10. Notice that only the worksheet appears, not the map.
6. Change the Sold number for Washington in cell B7 to **115,000**, press **Enter**, and observe the total update automatically to 1,013,000
   You know the interactive feature is working. Changes you make to the HTML file in your browser remain in effect until you close your browser.
7. Select the range **A5:B11**, click the **Sort Ascending button** on the toolbar above the worksheet, then click **State**
   The data is sorted in a new order according to state name.
8. Select the range **A4:B11**, click the **AutoFilter button** , click the **State list arrow**, click the **Total check mark** to remove it, click **OK**, then click the **Property Toolbox button**
   The total is no longer visible on the worksheet. The Spreadsheet Property Toolbox opens and should look similar to that shown in Figure N-11.
9. Click the **Fill Color list arrow** after Cell format, click the **light green color** in the bottom row, then click the Spreadsheet **Property Toolbox close button** and click outside the selected range
   The range fills with the light green color.
10. Enter your name in any worksheet cell, click **File** on the menu bar, click **Print**, click **OK**, then close your browser

FIGURE N-10: Pastry Sales worksheet as Web page in Internet Explorer

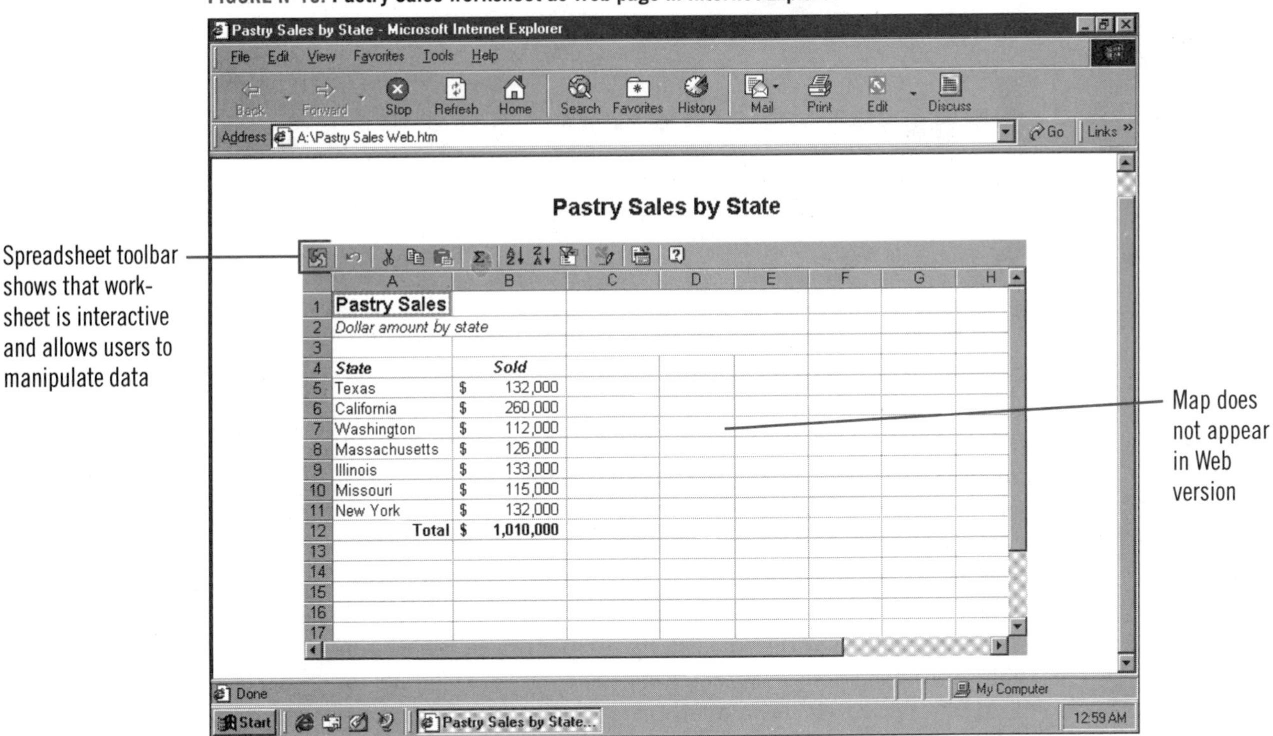

FIGURE N-11: Spreadsheet Property Toolbox

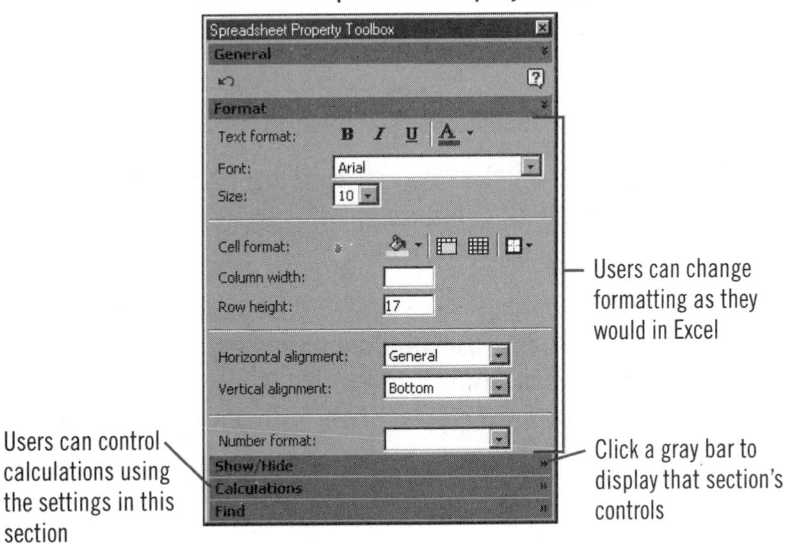

Managing HTML files on an intranet or Web site

Once you save your Excel file or item in HTML format, determine the best location for saving your file: an HTTP site, an FTP (File Transfer Protocol) site, or a network server. Check with your system administrator or Internet Service Provider (ISP) to see how your files should be organized—whether they should all be in one folder, whether graphics and other supporting files should be in a separate folder, and the like.

Excel 2000

Creating an Interactive PivotTable for an Intranet or the Web

Not only can you create interactive worksheets that users can modify in their Web browsers, but you can also create interactive PivotTables that users can analyze by dragging fields to get different views of the data. An interactive PivotTable for the Web is called a **PivotTable list**. Users cannot enter new values to the list, but they can filter and sort data, add calculations, and rearrange data to get a different perspective on the information. As the PivotTable list creator, you have complete control over what information is included from the source data, which could be an Excel worksheet, a PivotTable, or external data (for example, an Access database). You can include only selected columns of information if you wish. You can also include charts with your PivotTable data. As with spreadsheets you publish in HTML format, users view PivotTable lists in their browsers, and changes they make to them are retained for only that browser session. The HTML file remains in its original form. Jim has compiled some sales information about sales representatives at selected stores for the last four quarters. He saves it as a PivotTable list so he and selected corporate staff and store managers can review it using their Web browsers.

Steps

QuickTip

As with saving spreadsheets in interactive format, you need Office Web Tools and Internet Explorer 4.01 or later to create and use PivotTable lists.

1. **In the Sales Info 2 workbook, click the Sales by Rep tab**
   Jim will create the PivotTable list directly from the data rather then creating an Excel PivotTable first.
2. **Click File on the menu bar, click Save as Web Page, then click Publish**
3. **Click the Choose list arrow, click Items on Sales by Rep, then in the Choose list make sure Sheet All contents of Sales by Rep is selected**
   This will select all the items on the selected PivotTable sheet.
4. **Under Viewing options, click Add interactivity with, click the Add interactivity with list arrow, and click PivotTable functionality**
   PivotTable functionality will give users the option to move list items around on the PivotTable list as they would move data items on a PivotTable in Excel.
5. **Click Browse, type Sales Info PT List, make sure your Project Disk is selected, click OK, make sure Open published web page in browser is checked, and compare your screen to Figure N-12**
6. **Click Publish, then maximize the Internet Explorer window if necessary**
   The new PivotTable list opens in Internet Explorer. Its layout looks similar to a PivotTable report in Excel, with row and column fields and field drop-down arrows. As with an Excel PivotTable, you can change the layout to view the data in different ways. In this case, however, there is no PivotTable toolbar; you simply drag the field headings to the desired drop areas.
7. **Drag the Store field to the Row area, then drag the Department field to the Column area**
   The layout of the PivotTable list changes, and you now see the data rearranged by region, department, and store. See Figure N-13.
8. **Click File on the menu bar, click Print, then close your browser**

QuickTip

To retain the PivotTable in its original state, click the Address box containing the URL and press [Return]

FIGURE N-12: Publish as Web Page dialog box

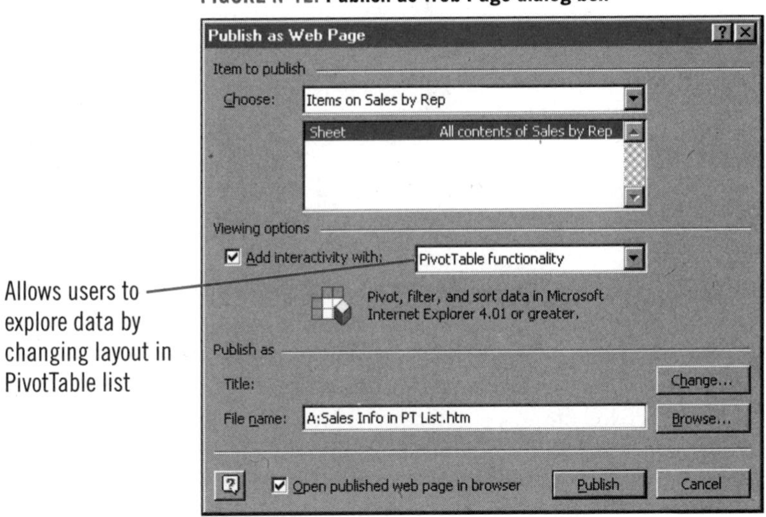

FIGURE N-13: PivotTable list with new layout in Internet Explorer

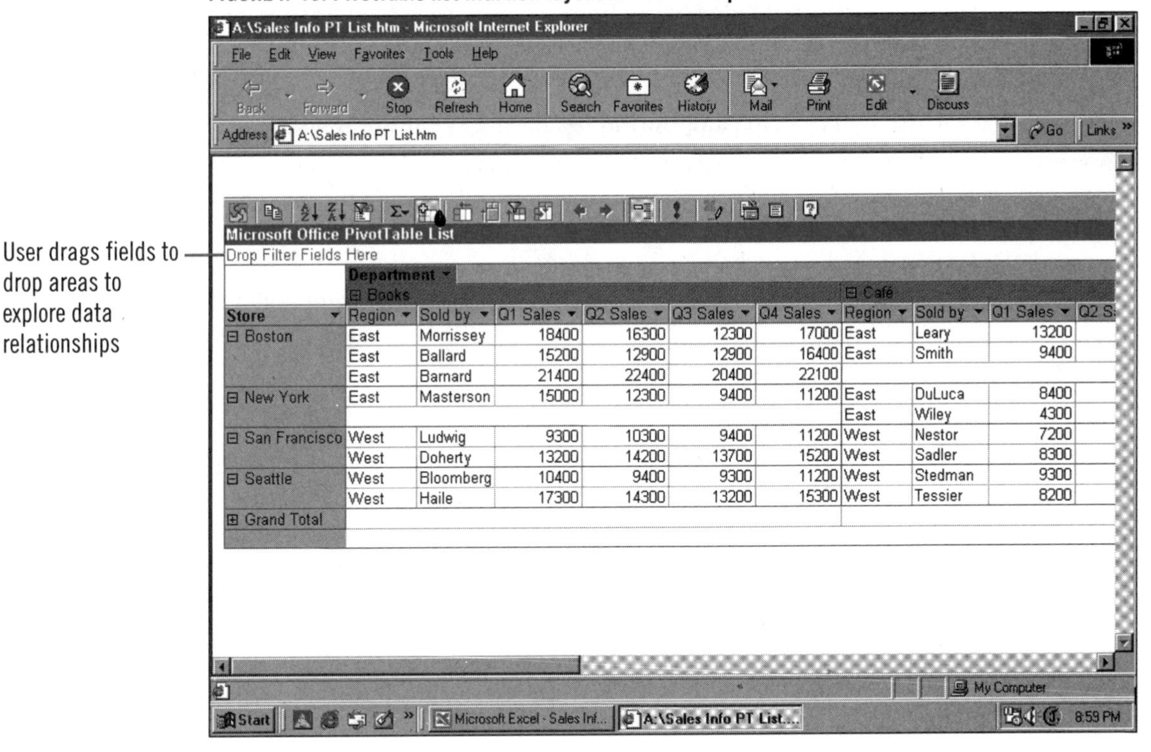

Store	Region	Sold by	Q1 Sales	Q2 Sales	Q3 Sales	Q4 Sales	Region	Sold by	Q1 Sales	Q2 S
⊟ Boston	East	Morrissey	18400	16300	12300	17000	East	Leary	13200	
	East	Ballard	15200	12900	12900	16400	East	Smith	9400	
	East	Barnard	21400	22400	20400	22100				
⊟ New York	East	Masterson	15000	12300	9400	11200	East	DuLuca	8400	
							East	Wiley	4300	
⊟ San Francisco	West	Ludwig	9300	10300	9400	11200	West	Nestor	7200	
	West	Doherty	13200	14200	13700	15200	West	Sadler	8300	
⊟ Seattle	West	Bloomberg	10400	9400	9300	11200	West	Stedman	9300	
	West	Haile	17300	14300	13200	15300	West	Tessier	8200	
⊞ Grand Total										

CLUES TO USE

Adding fields to a PivotTable list using the Web browser

You can add filter, data, or detail fields to the PivotTable list to display data. On the toolbar above the PivotTable list, click the Field List button . In the PivotTable Field List dialog box locate the name of the field you want to add. Click the field, and in the lower-right corner of the box, click the area list arrow, then click the section to which you want to add the field: Filter Area, Data Area, or Detail Data. If Add to is not available, the PivotTable creator may have restricted access to it.

Creating Hyperlinks between Excel Files and the Web

In addition to using hyperlinks to connect related Excel files, you can also create hyperlinks between files created in other Windows programs. You can even use hyperlinks to move between Excel files and information stored on the Web. Every Web page is identified by a unique address called a **Uniform Resource Locator (URL)**. You create a hyperlink to a Web page in the same way you create a hyperlink to another Excel file—by specifying the location of the Web page (its URL) in the Link to File or URL text box in the Insert Hyperlink dialog box. You enter a URL for an intranet site or a site on the World Wide Web using the same method. Jim decides that users of the Pastry Sales worksheet would find it helpful to view competitive information. He decides to include a hyperlink to the URL of one of MediaLoft's competitors, Barnes and Noble, which is also a café bookstore.

1. Activate the **Pastry Sales worksheet**, click cell **A2**, type **Barnes and Noble**, then click the **Enter button** on the Formula bar

2. Click the **Insert Hyperlink button** on the Standard toolbar
   The Insert Hyperlink dialog box opens. This is where you specify the target for the hyperlink, the Barnes and Noble Web site, by entering its URL in the Link to file or URL section of the Insert Hyperlink dialog box.

Trouble?

If this button does not appear on your Standard toolbar, click the More Buttons button to view it.

3. Under Link to, click **Existing File or Web Page**, click in the Type the file or Web page name text box, and type the URL for the Barnes and Noble Web site: **http://www.barnesandnoble.com**
   Your completed Insert Hyperlink dialog box should match Figure N-14. The program will automatically add a slash after the URL, as shown in Figure N-14, if you return to the dialog box and enter a Web address that you've entered previously.

QuickTip

Make sure the URL address appears in the text box exactly as shown in Figure N-14. Every Web page URL begins with "http://". This acronym stands for HyperText Transfer Protocol, the method all intranet and Web page data use to travel over the Internet to your computer.

4. Click **OK**
   The Barnes and Noble text is blue and underlined, indicating that it is a hyperlink. You should always test new hyperlinks to make sure they link to the correct destination. To test this hyperlink, you must have a modem, a Web browser installed on your computer, and access to an Internet Service Provider (ISP).

5. Click the **Barnes and Noble** hyperlink in cell A2
   After a moment, the Web browser installed on your computer starts and displays the Barnes and Noble Web page in your browser window.

6. If necessary, click the **Maximize button** on the browser title bar to maximize the browser window

7. Click **File** on the menu bar, click **Print**, click **OK**, then click the **Back button** on the Web toolbar
   Now that you know the hyperlink works correctly, you return to the Sales Info 2 worksheet.

8. Save and close the workbook, then if necessary close your browser, but stay connected to the Internet

FIGURE N-14: Insert Hyperlink dialog box

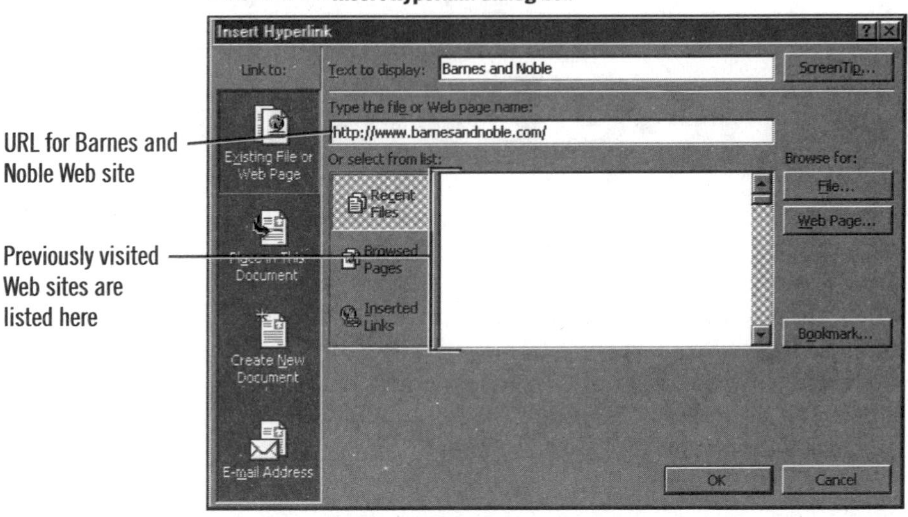

FIGURE N-15: Barnes and Noble Web site in Internet Explorer

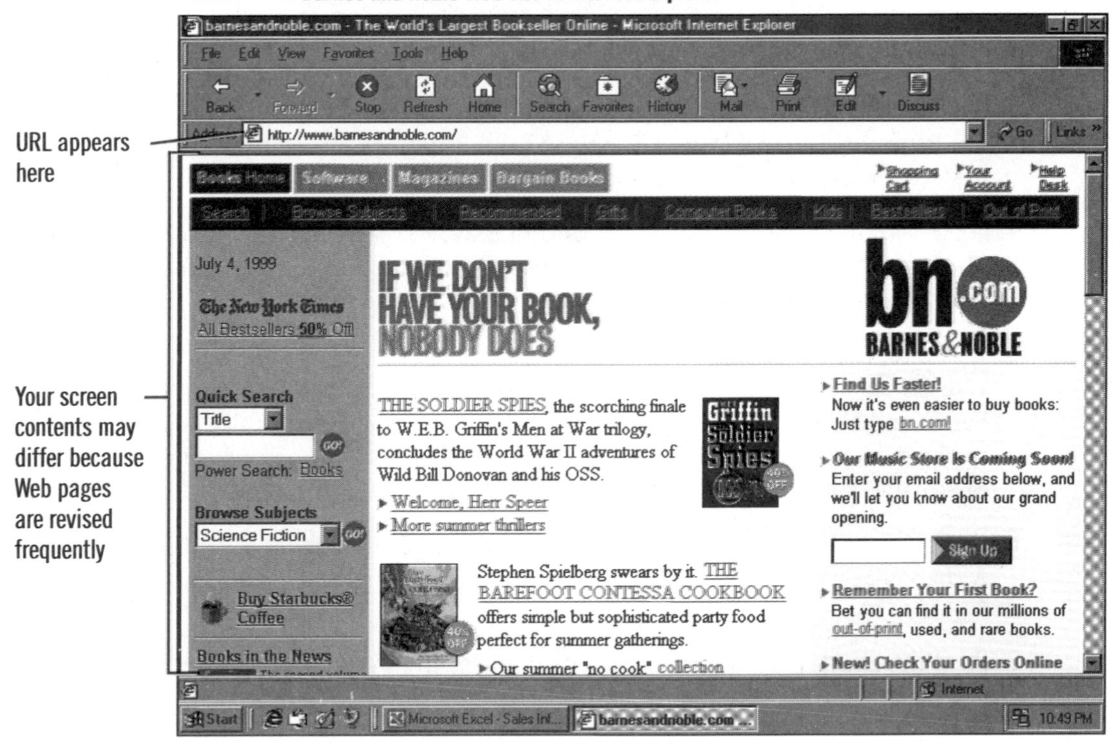

Using hyperlinks to navigate large worksheets

Previously, when you needed to locate and view different sections of a particularly large worksheet, you used the scroll bars, or, if there were range names associated with the different worksheet sections, the name box. You can also use hyperlinks to more easily navigate a large worksheet. To insert a hyperlink that targets a cell or a range of cells at another location in the worksheet or another sheet in the workbook, click the cell where you want the hyperlink to appear, then click the Insert Hyperlink button on the Standard toolbar. In the Insert Hyperlink dialog box, click Place in This Document. Enter the cell address or range name of the hyperlink target in the Type the cell reference text box, or select a sheet or a defined name from the list box below it, then click OK.

Excel 2000

Running Queries to Retrieve Data on the Web

Often you'll want to access information on the Web or the Internet to incorporate into an Excel worksheet. Using Excel, you can obtain data from a Web, Internet, or intranet site by running a **Web query**. You can then save the information as an Excel workbook and manipulate it in any way you choose. As part of a special project for Leilani Ho, Jim needs to obtain stock information on MediaLoft's competitors. He will run a Web query to obtain the most current stock information from the World Wide Web.

Steps 1 2 3 4

1. Open a new workbook, then save it as **Stock Data**
2. Click **Data** on the menu bar, point to **Get External Data**, then click **Run Saved Query**
   The Run Query dialog box opens, similar to Figure N-16. This is where you select the Web query you want to run from a list of predefined queries.
3. Click **Microsoft Investor Stock Quotes**, then click **Get Data**
   The Returning External Data to Microsoft Excel dialog box opens. This is where you specify the location to place the incoming data.
4. Make sure the **Existing worksheet option button** is selected, then click **OK**
   The Enter Parameter Value dialog box opens, prompting you to enter a stock symbol. The stock symbol for Barnes and Noble is BKS.
5. Type **BKS**, then click **OK**
   Your Internet Service Provider connects to the Web. The Microsoft Investor stock quote for Barnes and Noble appears on the screen. The External Data toolbar also appears, as shown in Figure N-17. Now you have the stock information that Jim can use to research one of MediaLoft's competitor's stock values.
6. Click **File** on the menu bar, click **Print**, then click **Chartlink** on the stock quote page
   A chart appears, showing the stock price and company income for the last year, similar to Figure N-18.
7. Print the chart, close your browser, disconnect from the Internet, save and close the workbook, then exit Excel and your browser

Trouble?

If you don't have a modem and access to the Web through an ISP, check with your instructor or technical support person. If your ISP's connection dialog box opens, follow your standard procedure for getting online, then continue with Step 6.

Finding stock symbols

If you want to check on a stock but don't know its symbol, click the Symbol Lookup hyperlink on the Stock Data worksheet. You may need to download the Microsoft Investor software, which takes about five minutes.

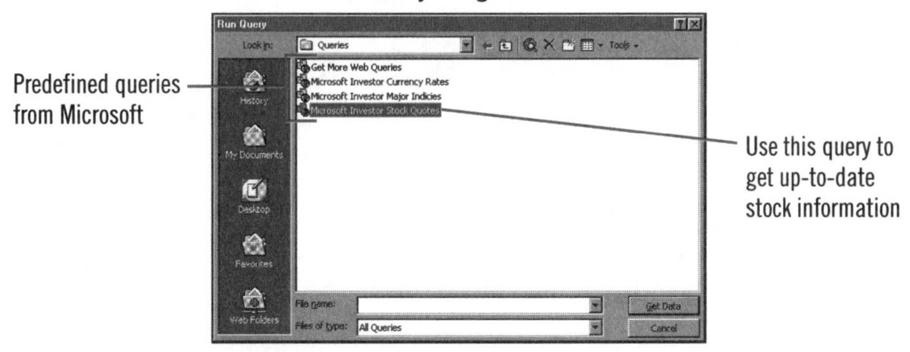

FIGURE N-16: Run Query dialog box

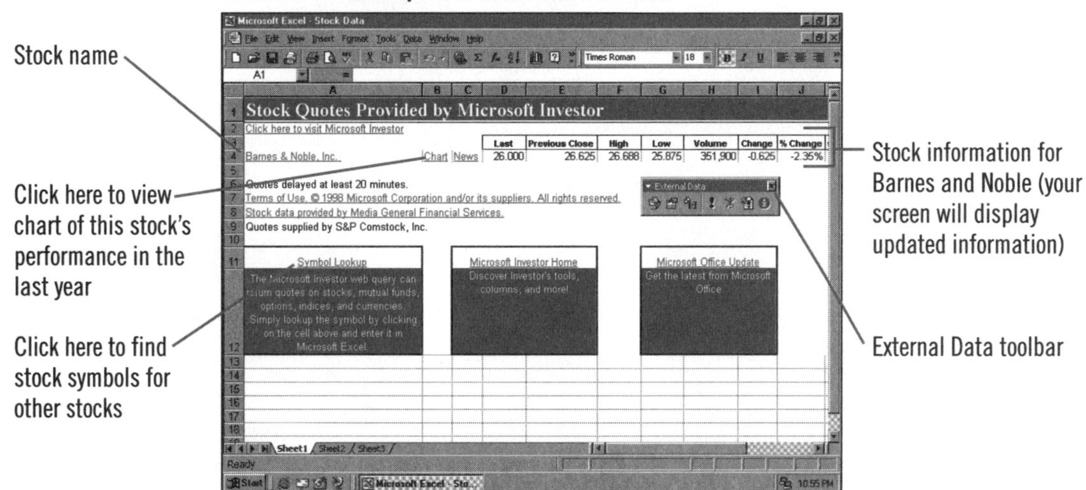

FIGURE N-17: Stock quote in Stock Data worksheet

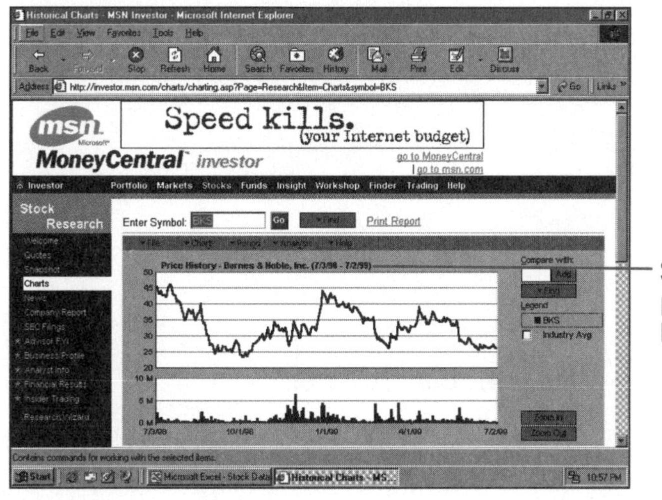

FIGURE N-18: Stock chart for Barnes and Noble

Creating a new query to retrieve Web page data

To retrieve data from a particular Web page on a regular basis, it's easiest to create a customized Web query. Click Data on the menu bar, point to Get External Data, then click New Web Query. In the New Web Query dialog box, click Browse Web to start your browser, go to the Web page from which you want to retrieve data, click the Web page, then return to the dialog box; the address of the Web page will appear in the address text box. Specify which part of the Web page you want to retrieve (for example, only the tables) and how much formatting you want to keep. Click Save Query to save the query for future use with the Run Saved Query command. Then click OK. Specify the location in the worksheet where you want the data, then click OK. The data from the Web page appears in the open Excel worksheet.

Practice

▶ Concepts Review

Label each of the elements shown in Figure N-19

FIGURE N-19

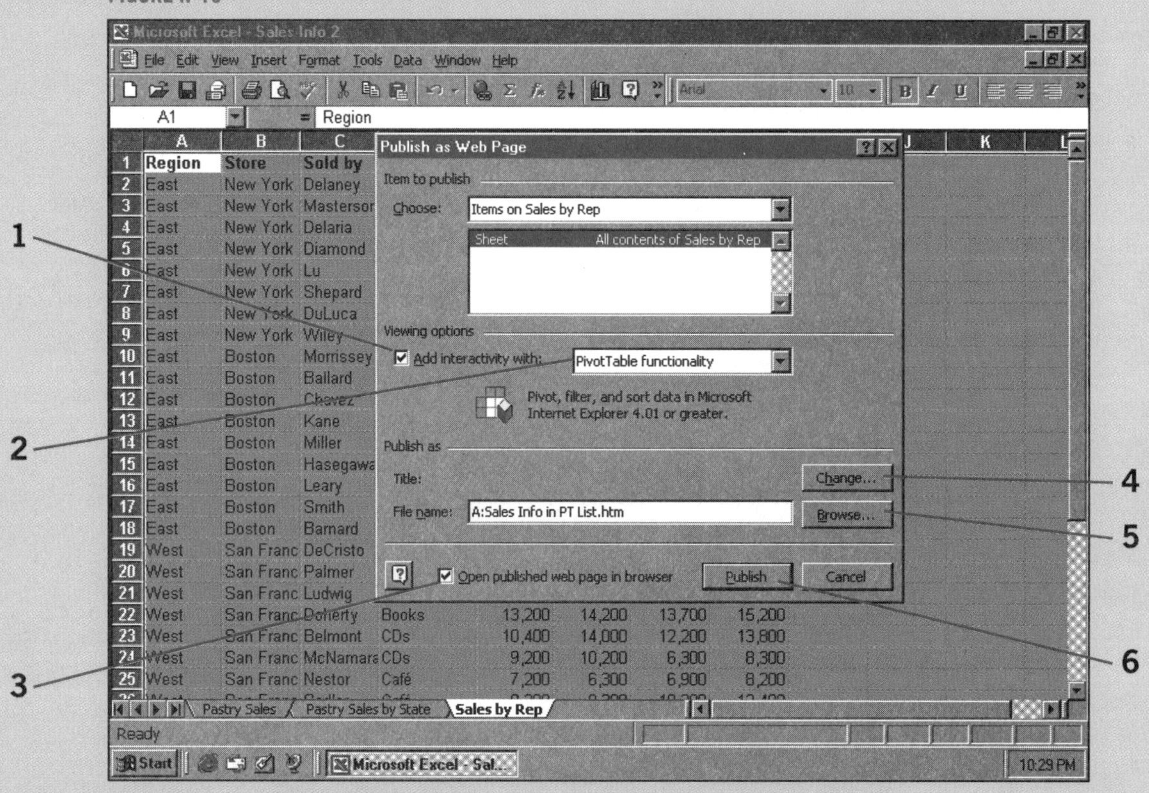

Match each item with the statement that describes it.

7. **Web query**
8. **Change history**
9. **Shared workbook**
10. **Interactive worksheet or PivotTable**
11. **URL**

a. A unique address on the World Wide Web
b. Used by many people on a network
c. Can be manipulated using a Web browser
d. Starts the installed Web browser to search the WWW
e. A record of edits others have made to a worksheet

12. A ____________ is a list of recipients to whom you are sending a workbook sequentially.
    a. PivotTable
    b. Hypertext document
    c. Routing slip
    d. Shared workbook

13. Which of the following can be saved in HTML format, placed on a server, and then manipulated on an intranet or Internet using a Web browser?
    a. A worksheet
    b. A PivotTable
    c. A workbook
    d. a and b only

14. Which of the following allows you to obtain data from a Web or intranet site?
    a. Web Wizard
    b. PivotTable
    c. Data query
    d. Web query

15. A shared workbook is a workbook that
    a. Has hyperlinks to the Web.
    b. Is on the World Wide Web.
    c. Several people can use at the same time.
    d. Requires a password to open.

16. In an interactive worksheet or PivotTable,
    a. You can make changes and they are saved to the HTML file.
    b. You can make changes but they are not saved to the HTML file.
    c. You can change formatting but not perform calculations.
    d. You can perform calculations but not change formatting.

Skills Review

1. **Set up a shared workbook**
    a. Open the file EX N-3 and save it as Ad Campaigns.
    b. Set up the workbook so that more than one person can use it at one time.
    c. On the Advanced tab, specify that the change history should be maintained for 1,000 days.

2. **Track changes in a shared workbook**
    a. Specify that all changes should be highlighted. Changes should be both highlighted on the screen and listed in a new sheet.
    b. In the Ads Q1 All Stores worksheet, change the Billboards totals to $600 for each month.
    c. Save the file.
    d. Display and print the History sheet. (If the History worksheet does not appear, reopen the Highlight Changes dialog box and reselect the options for All and List changes on a new sheet.)
    e. Save and close the workbook.

3. **Apply and remove passwords**
   a. Open the file EX N-3, open the Save As dialog box, then open the General Options dialog box.
   b. Set the password to open as Marsten and the password to modify as Spring.
   c. Resave the password-protected file as Ad Campaigns PW.
   d. Close the workbook.
   e. Reopen the workbook and verify that you can change it, using passwords where necessary.

4. **Create an interactive worksheet for an intranet or the Web.**
   a. Save the Ads Q1 All Stores worksheet as an interactive Web page, with spreadsheet functionality.
   b. Set the title bar to read Ad Campaign Forecast, automatically preview it in Internet Explorer, if that is your Web browser, and save it to your Project Disk using the filename Ad Campaigns. If you use a different Web browser, don't use the automatic preview option.
   c. If you can open the HTML file in Internet Explorer, do so.
   d. In Internet Explorer, add totals for each month in B11:D11, then add a grand total to cell E11.
   e. In F3, enter a formula that calculates the percentage newspaper ads are of the grand total. (*Hint:* You will need to type in the formula instead of clicking cells, and use the Property Toolbox to change the number format to a percent.)
   f. Use the Property Toolbox to fill the range B11:E11 with yellow.
   g. Sort the list in ascending order by ad type. You might need to reenter the percentage formula.
   h. Print the worksheet from Internet Explorer, then close Internet Explorer.

5. **Create an interactive PivotTable for an intranet or the Web.**
   a. In the Ad Campaigns PW workbook, save the worksheet Ad Detail as an interactive PivotTable with PivotTable functionality. Make the title Ad Forecast 4 Stores, and save it as Ads4Stores. Open the file in Internet Explorer.
   b. Drag fields to analyze the data by Region, Ad Piece, Store, and Department.
   c. Print the page showing changed data.

6. **Create Hyperlinks between Excel files and the Web.**
   a. On the Ads Q1 All Stores worksheet, enter the text "American Ad Foundation" and make it a hyperlink to the American Ad Foundation at http://www.aaf.org in cell A13.
   b. Test the hyperlink and print the Web page.
   c. Save and close the workbook.

7. **Run queries to retrieve data on the Web.**
   a. Open a new workbook and save it as Stock Quotes.
   b. Use the Run Saved Query command to locate Microsoft Investor Major Indices.
   c. Specify that you want to return the data to cell A1 of the current worksheet.
   d. After the stock quotes appear, click one of the stock indices listed and print the results.
   e. Display a chart for one of the indices, then print the chart. (*Hint:* If you are prompted to download MSN Money Central and you are unable to download software at your site, continue with step f.)
   f. Preview and print the Stock Quotes sheet, then save and close the workbook.
   g. Open a new workbook and save it as MediaLoft Products.
   h. Create a new Web query that retrieves the following page from the MediaLoft intranet site: www.course.com/illustrated/MediaLoft/Product.html. Import the entire page with full HTML formatting, and save the query as MediaLoft Products on your project disk.
   i. Test the hyperlinks on the imported Web page, use the Back arrow to return to the workbook, then save and close the workbook.

▶ Independent Challenges

1. Blantyre Consulting helps small businesses attain and maintain profitability by monitoring their sales and expense information. The company makes it a practice to hold a monthly phone conference with clients to discuss strategy. There are 10 consultants in the organization, and they share information via the company intranet. They have adopted a team approach to their accounts, so five consultants work on each account. You are setting up the information for a new client, Boston Touring Company, which specializes in giving trolley and bus tours in Boston, Massachusetts, and the surrounding area. You are preparing the workbook to be placed on the company intranet so that only the consultant group for that account can view the information.

To complete this independent challenge:

a. Open the file EX N-4 and save it as Boston Touring.
b. Format the workbook so it is more attractive and the information is easy to read.
c. Make the workbook shared so that all consultants can access it.
d. Set up the workbook so that all changes will be tracked. Make two changes to the worksheets as a test and print the change history.
e. Password protect the workbook for both opening and editing, and write down the passwords you have chosen.
f. Save and close the workbook, then reopen it, using passwords as necessary.
g. Save the Q1 Sales worksheet as an interactive worksheet with spreadsheet functionality. Make the browser title bar read "Boston Touring Company" using the filename Boston Touring - Web.
h. Open the worksheet in Internet Explorer, then calculate the percentage that half-day tours of Cambridge are of the total.
i. Add the heading Total over the column of totals and format it in a different text color.
j. Print the interactive worksheet, then close the browser.
k. Save and close the Boston Touring worksheet.

2. The First Southern Bank has a Web page containing information about its current rates and procedures for opening an account. The bank would like to expand the site in order to help customers find answers to more of the questions the Customer Service line receives. Customers frequently call in asking for the bank's Mortgage Calculator, a printed table that shows various mortgage amounts and interest rates, and lets customers look up what their monthly payments would be. John Barnes, the Customer Service Manager, has asked you to set up an Excel worksheet for their Web site that will allow customers to enter various mortgage amounts and interest rates, and automatically see what their monthly payments, total payments, and total interest would be. He wants you to make the worksheet both attractive and easy to use.

To complete this independent challenge:

a. Open the file EX N-5 and save it as Mortgage Calculator.
b. Add the bank's name and any other marketing-oriented information that will identify what the worksheet is and how to use it.
c. Format the worksheet with colors, fonts, or other formats to make it attractive for public use.
d. Save the worksheet in HTML format with interactive spreadsheet functionality and an appropriate title in the title bar.
e. Open the HTML file in Internet Explorer, then test the calculator. Enter various mortgage amounts and interest rates and make sure the payment information changes appropriately.
f. Close Internet Explorer, the Mortgage Calculator worksheet, and Excel, saving as necessary.

3. Tuckerman Teas is a tea import and export firm with offices in Tokyo and London that distributes teas to shops in the United States and Canada. Tuckerman wants the officers in both offices to be able to analyze sales data, but because of incompatible software, they must rely on their Web browsers. They have asked you to help them set up a file that they will all be able to access on their intranet site.

To complete this independent challenge:

- **a.** Open the file EX N-6 and save it as Tuckerman Teas.
- **b.** Format the worksheet using fonts and colors to make it more attractive.
- **c.** Save the file as a Web page with PivotTable functionality. Assign the title bar an appropriate title.
- **d.** Open the file in Internet Explorer and manipulate the data to determine the following:
  - How do shipments of the flavored afternoon blends compare to the flavored breakfast blends?
  - Considering only blends, flavored, and Japanese teas, what is the total kilos shipped for afternoon and breakfast teas?
  - Which category consistently did better than the others during the quarter?
- **e.** Explore any other data relationships you wish.
- **f.** Return to the Tuckerman Teas worksheet, and on a blank sheet, write three or four sentences summarizing your conclusions.

4. Jim Fernandez, MediaLoft's office manager, has been asked by the Accounting department to examine CD sales trends. Assuming that a higher stock price reflects higher sales, he has decided to compare MediaLoft CD sales patterns to the stock price of Amazon.com, which also sells CDs, to see if both display seasonal trends, particularly the higher sales at the end of the calendar year. You will get sales information from the MediaLoft intranet site, retrieve stock data on Amazon.com, then create charts that illustrate trends of each one for easy comparison.

To complete this independent challenge:

- **a.** Connect to the Internet, and go to the MediaLoft intranet site at http://www.course.com/Illustrated/MediaLoft. Click the Accounting link, then click the CD Sales Analysis link. Print the page and disconnect from the Internet.
- **b.** Open a new workbook, then enter the total figures for CD sales for each of the four quarters. Save the workbook as Trend Analysis.
- **c.** Create a line chart of the figures on the same worksheet as the sales figures, assigning the chart an appropriate title.
- **d.** Name the sheet Trends.
- **e.** Run a Microsoft Investor Stock Quote Web query to obtain a stock quote for Amazon.com, stock symbol AMZN, placing the data in a new worksheet.
- **f.** Display the chart of this data by clicking Chart.
- **g.** On the File menu above the chart, select Export Data. The data will appear in Excel in a separate workbook called AMZN.
- **h.** In the new workbook, delete all the rows of data except the row representing the earliest date for each month. Generally, this will be the first of the month, unless that falls on a weekend, in which case it might be the second or third of the month. You should end up with one row of data for each month, showing the High, Low, Close, and Volume. If any line is blank, use the date nearest to it that has data.
- **i.** Delete the columns for High, Low, and Volume, leaving the Date and Close columns.
- **j.** Sort the rows in ascending order by date, then copy the data into the Trends sheet in the Trend Analysis workbook.

k. Create a line chart of the Amazon data, and assign it an appropriate title. Place it on the same sheet as the MediaLoft chart. Use any Excel features to point out similarities or differences you see. Do both rise toward the end of the year?
l. On the chart sheet, create a hyperlink to Amazon.com.
m. Save and close the Trend Analysis workbook, close the AMZN workbook without saving, then close Internet Explorer.

▶ Visual Workshop

Create the interactive Web page shown in Figure N-20. Use Excel to create the company name, product listing, and the sales figures for each quarter, all in black text. Save and print the worksheet. Save the worksheet in interactive HTML format, using the title bar text shown. Use Internet Explorer to obtain totals for each quarter and to apply formatting to totals, column headings, and the company name. (*Hint:* If you have any trouble with AutoSum, try formatting the figures using the Number format.) Print the HTML worksheet with your modifications applied.

FIGURE N-20

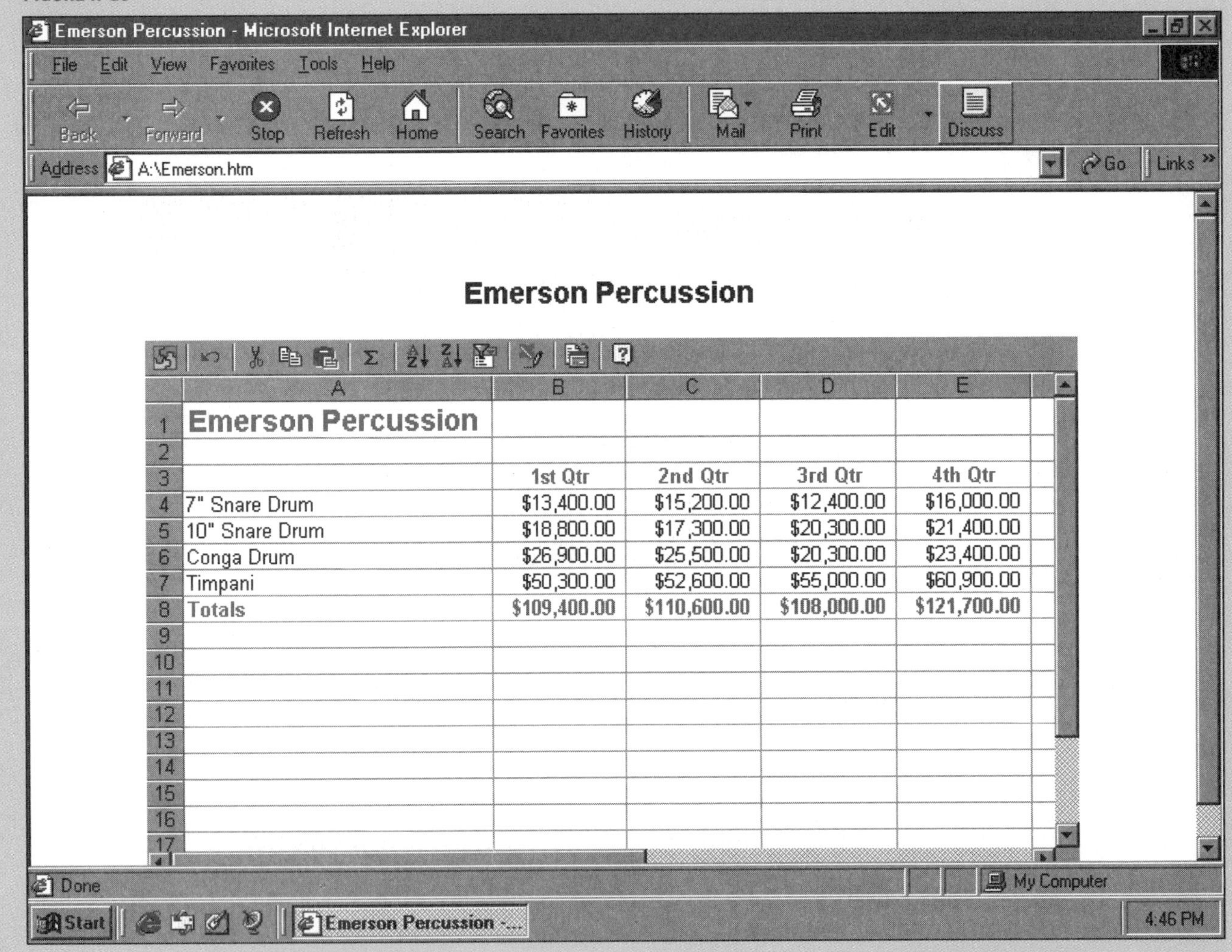

	A	B	C	D	E
1	Emerson Percussion				
2					
3		1st Qtr	2nd Qtr	3rd Qtr	4th Qtr
4	7" Snare Drum	$13,400.00	$15,200.00	$12,400.00	$16,000.00
5	10" Snare Drum	$18,800.00	$17,300.00	$20,300.00	$21,400.00
6	Conga Drum	$26,900.00	$25,500.00	$20,300.00	$23,400.00
7	Timpani	$50,300.00	$52,600.00	$55,000.00	$60,900.00
8	Totals	$109,400.00	$110,600.00	$108,000.00	$121,700.00

Excel 2000

Gaining Control over Your Work

Objectives

- ► Find files
- MOUS ► Audit a worksheet
- ► Outline a worksheet
- ► Control worksheet calculations
- ► Create custom AutoFill lists
- ► Customize Excel
- MOUS ► Add a comment to a cell
- MOUS ► Save a workbook as a template

Excel includes numerous tools and options designed to help you work as efficiently as possible. In this unit, you will learn how to use some of these elements to find errors and hide unnecessary detail. You'll also find out how to eliminate repetitive typing chores, save calculation time when using a large worksheet, and customize basic Excel features. Finally, you'll learn how to document your workbook and save it in a format that makes it easy to reuse. MediaLoft's assistant controller, Lisa Wong, routinely asks Jim Fernandez to help with a variety of spreadsheet-related tasks. The numerous options available in Excel help Jim perform his work quickly and efficiently.

Finding Files

The Open dialog box in Excel contains powerful searching tools that make it easy for you to find files. You can search for a file in several ways, such as by name or according to specific text located within a particular file. Recently, Jim created a workbook that tracks the number of overtime hours worked in each MediaLoft store. He can't remember the exact name of the file, so he searches for it by the first few letters of the filename.

Steps

1. **Start Excel, then click the Open button on the Standard toolbar**

   At the top of the Open dialog box, there are two menus: the Views menu (represented by the Views icon and the Tools menu. The Views menu controls the amount of information displayed about each file and folder. See Table O-1 for a description of Views menu selections. The amount of detail currently on your screen depends on the view option that you clicked the last time you opened this dialog box. The Tools menu helps you find, delete, and print files, as well as perform other file management tasks. First you'll display files so they match the figures in this lesson.

2. **Click the Views list arrow, click each of the views to observe the results, then click Details**

   Your files display with the filename, size, type, and date modified.

3. **Click Tools, then click Find**

   The Find dialog box opens, similar to Figure O-1. You can find files by specifying one or more criteria, or conditions that must be met, to find your file. For example, you can specify that Excel should find only files that have the word "Inventory" in the filename and that were created after 6/15/2000. The criteria list in the "Find files that match these criteria" list is already set to find only Excel files. You'll specify another criterion. Jim thinks his filename starts with the prefix EX O but he's not sure of the number.

4. **In the Define more criteria area, under Property, select File name if necessary, then under Condition select includes if necessary**

5. **Click in the Value box, then type EX O***

   Be sure you type the letter "O" and not a zero. Because you know only the first few letters of the filename, you'll use the wildcard symbol * (an asterisk) to substitute for the remaining unknown characters. Next, you need to specify where you want Excel to search for the file. This saves you time if you have access to several disks and you want to limit the search to one or two of them.

6. **Click the Look in list arrow, click the drive that contains your Project Disk, then click the Search subfolders check box to select it**

7. **Click Find Now, then click Yes to add your search criterion to the criteria list**

   After a moment, Excel displays five files that begin with "EX O", along with detailed information about the files. See Figure O-2. You can check to see if the criterion was added.

8. **Click Tools, then click Find**

   The criterion "Filename **begins with** EX O." appears in the criteria list.

9. **Click Cancel, double-click the file EX O-1 in the Open dialog box, then save the workbook as Overtime Hours**

QuickTip

You can cycle through the four available views by clicking the Views button repeatedly.

QuickTip

You can also search for text within Excel files. For example, if you know your worksheet contains the text "Overtime hours", you can specify Contents under property, and then specify the appropriate "include" condition and value. To use this feature you may need to install the Find Fast utility from your Office 2000 CD.

Trouble?

If Excel doesn't find the files you're looking for, you may have typed zero instead of the letter "O" or you may not have selected the Search subfolders check box. Repeat the steps from Step 4, being sure to use the letter "O".

FIGURE O-1: Find dialog box

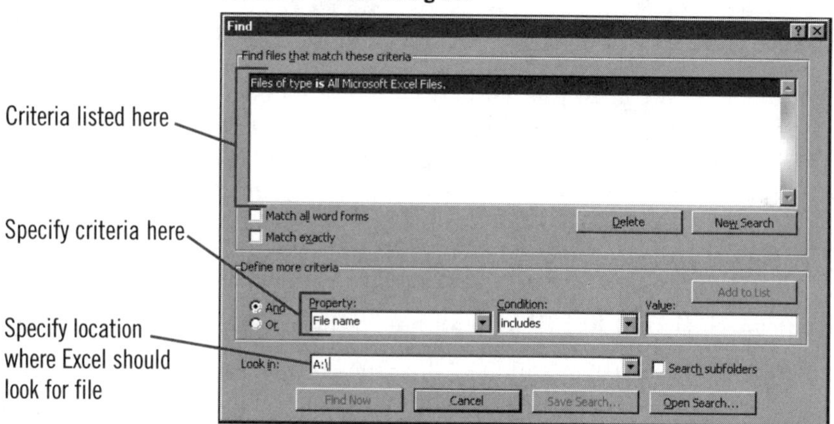

FIGURE O-2: Search results

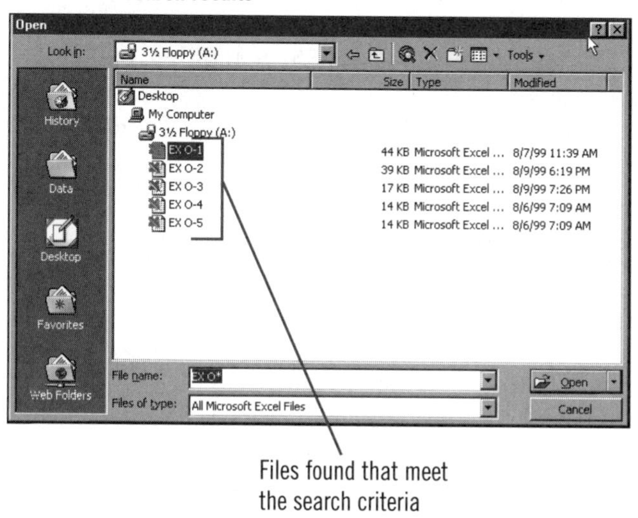

FIGURE O-3: Properties dialog box

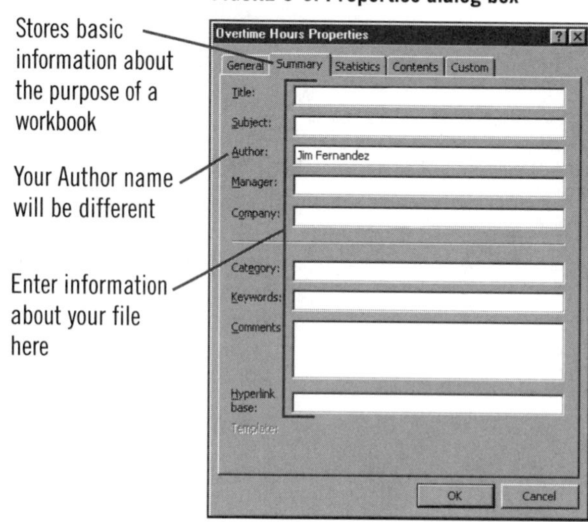

TABLE O-1: Views menu selections

button	name	description
	List	Displays file and folder names
	Details	Displays file and folder names, along with the file type and the date last modified
	Properties	Displays information about the highlighted file, such as subject and keywords
	Preview	Displays the upper-left corner of the first sheet in a workbook
Arrange Icons	**Arrange icons**	Lets you rearrange your file icons by name, type, size, and date

File properties

Excel automatically tracks specific file properties, such as author name, file size, and file type, and displays them when you display file details. You can also enter additional file properties, such as a descriptive title or a subject. Right-click the file in the Open dialog box, click Properties to open the [Filename] Properties dialog box, click the Summary tab, then add any information you want. See Figure O-3. To search for a file by a specific property, in the Open dialog box, click Tools, then click Find. In the Find dialog box select Text or property in the Property list, then enter the property text in the Value box.

Excel 2000

Auditing a Worksheet

The Excel auditing feature helps you track errors and determine worksheet logic—that is, how a worksheet is set up. Because errors and faulty logic can be introduced at any stage of worksheet development, it is important to include auditing as part of your workbook-building process. Jim audits the worksheet that tracks the number of overtime hours at each store to verify the accuracy of the year-end totals. Before beginning the auditing process, Jim adds a vertical pane to the window so he can view the first and last columns of the worksheet at the same time.

1. **Drag the vertical split box (the small box to the right of the horizontal scroll arrow) to the left until the vertical window pane divider is situated between columns A and B, then scroll the worksheet to the right until columns P through S are visible in the right pane**
   See Figure O-4.

2. **Click Tools on the menu bar, point to Auditing, then click Show Auditing Toolbar**
   You use the buttons on the Auditing toolbar, shown in Figure O-5, to identify any errors in your worksheet. Notice the #DIV/0! error in cell S6. These symbols indicate a **divide-by-zero error**, which occurs when you divide a value by zero. The Trace Error button on the Auditing toolbar helps locate the source of this problem.

3. **Click cell S6, then click the Trace Error button on the Auditing toolbar**
   The formula bar reads =R6/$R$16, indicating that the value in cell R6 will be divided by the value in cell R16. Tracer arrows, or **tracers**, point from cells that might have caused the error to the active cell containing the error, as shown in Figure O-5. The tracers extend from cells R6 and R16 to cell S6. Note that cell R6 contains a value, whereas cell R16 is blank. In Excel formulas, blank cells have a value of zero. That means the value in cell R6 cannot be divided by the value in cell R16 (zero) because division by zero is impossible. To correct the error, you must edit the formula so that it references cell R15, the grand total of overtime hours, not R16.

4. **Press [F2] to switch to Edit mode, edit the formula to read =R6/$R$15, then click the Enter button on the formula bar**
   The error message and trace arrows disappear, and the formula produces the correct result, 9%, in cell S6. Next, notice that the total for the Boston store in cell R5 is unusually high compared with the totals of the other stores. You can investigate this value by tracing the cell's precedents—the cells on which cell R5 depends.

5. **Click cell R5, click the Trace Precedents button on the Auditing toolbar, then scroll left until you identify the tracer's starting point**
   The tracer arrow runs between cells B5 and R5, indicating that the formula in cell R5 reflects the quarterly *and* monthly totals of overtime hours. Because both the quarterly totals and monthly totals are summed in this formula, the resulting figure is twice what it should be. Only the quarterly totals should be reflected in cell R5.

6. **If necessary, click cell R5, click the AutoSum button on the Standard toolbar, then press [Enter]**
   The tracer arrow disappears, the formula changes to include only the quarterly totals, and the correct result, 490, appears in cell R5. Correcting the formula in cell R5 also adjusts the Grand Total percentage in cell S5 to 13%. Now that all the errors in the worksheet have been identified and corrected, you are finished auditing.

7. **Click Window on the menu bar, click Remove Split, then close the Auditing toolbar and save the workbook**

Trouble?

If the Auditing toolbar blocks your view of the worksheet, drag it to another place on the worksheet.

QuickTip

To find cells with formulas that refer to a specific cell, click the cell, then click the Trace Dependents button on the Auditing toolbar.

Trouble?

If the AutoSum button does not appear on your Standard toolbar, click the More Buttons button to view it.

QuickTip

You can also double-click the split to remove it.

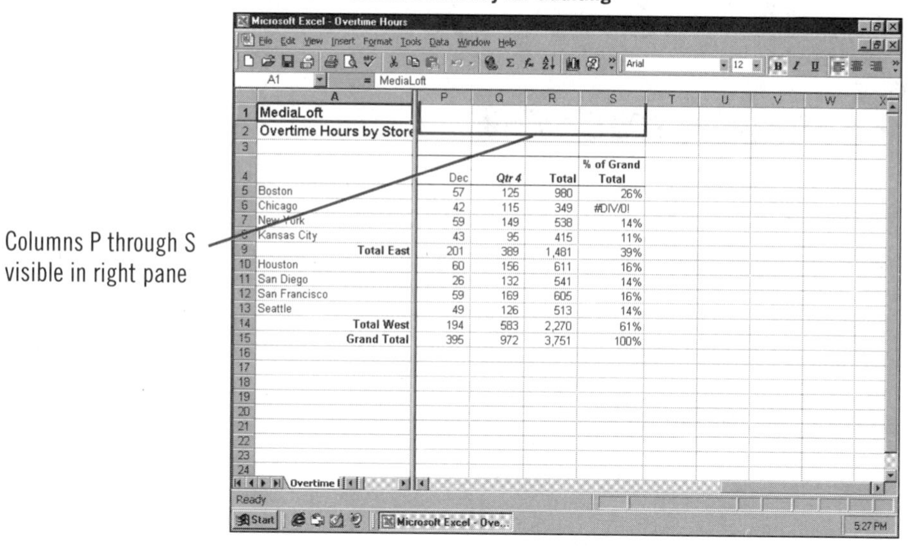

FIGURE O-4: Worksheet ready for auditing

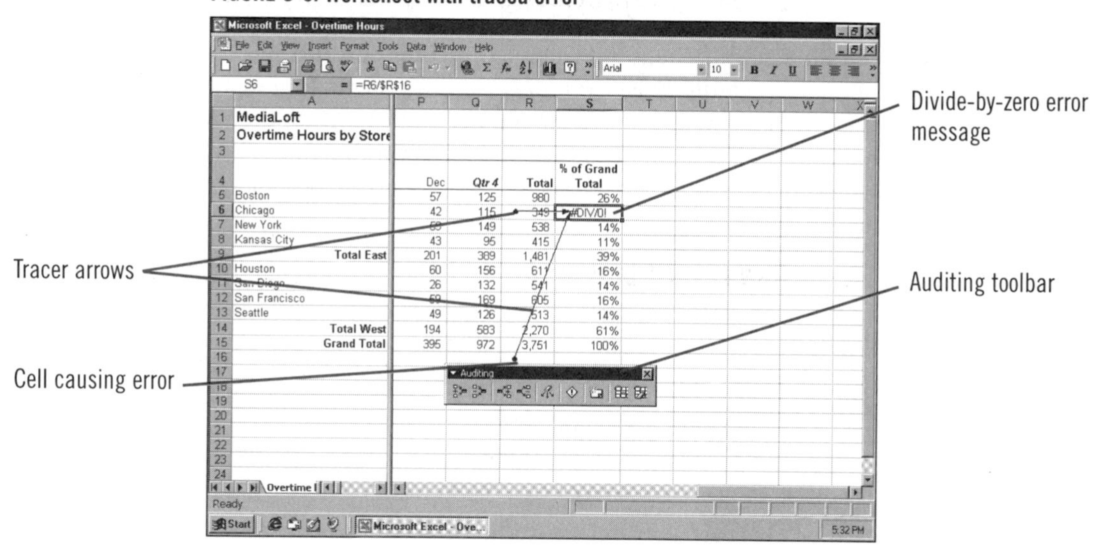

FIGURE O-5: Worksheet with traced error

Excel 2000

Circular references

A cell with a **circular reference** contains a formula that refers to its own cell location. If you accidentally enter a formula with a circular reference, a warning box will open, alerting you to the problem, and the Circular Reference toolbar appears. Click OK to open a Help window explaining how to find the circular reference using the Circular Reference toolbar. In simple formulas, a circular reference is easy to spot. To correct it, simply edit the formula to remove any reference to the cell where the formula is located.

Hiding and displaying toolbars

You display the Auditing toolbar using the Tools menu, however, to display other toolbars, right-click the Standard or Formatting toolbar, then click the name of the toolbar you want to display. To hide the toolbar, right-click it and select its name from the pop-up menu.

Outlining a Worksheet

The Excel Outline command displays a worksheet with buttons that allow you to adjust the display of the worksheet to show only the critical rows and columns. For outlining to function properly, worksheet formulas must point consistently in the same direction: Summary rows, such as subtotal rows, must be located below related data, whereas summary columns, such as grand total columns, must be located to the right of related data. (If you're not sure which way your formulas point, click the Trace Precedents button on the Auditing toolbar.) Jim needs to give Lisa Wong, the MediaLoft assistant controller, the updated year-end totals. To emphasize the subtotals for both East and West regions, as well as the grand total of overtime hours, he decides to outline the worksheet first.

Steps

1. If necessary, press **[Ctrl][Home]** to display the upper-left corner of the worksheet
2. Click **Data** on the menu bar, point to **Group and Outline**, then click **Auto Outline**
   The worksheet is displayed in Outline view, as shown in Figure O-6. There are several ways to change the amount of detail in an outlined worksheet, but the easiest is by using the Column Level and Row Level buttons, which hide a varying amount of detail. The Row Level 1 button hides everything in the worksheet except the most important row or rows—in this case, the Grand Total row.
3. Click the **Row Level 1 button** 1
   This selection doesn't display enough information, so you'll try the Row Level 2 button, which hides everything except the second most important rows—in this case, the subtotal rows and the Grand Total row.
4. Click the **Row Level 2 button** 2
   Now you can see the rows you want. Next, you'll display only the columns you choose—in this case, the Qtr 1–Qtr 4 columns, the Total column, and the % of Grand Total column. Like the Row Level 2 button, the Column Level 2 button displays the Grand Total column, along with its corresponding subtotals.
5. Click the **Column Level 2 button** 2
   The quarterly totals appear and the monthly figures are no longer visible. Jim needs to give a printed copy of the worksheet outline to Lisa.
6. Place your name in the worksheet footer, then print the worksheet
   Your printed worksheet should look like the one shown in Figure O-7. You're finished using the outlining feature.
7. Click the **Row Level 3 button** 3, then click the **Column Level 3 button** 3
   The monthly figures for each store reappear.
8. Click **Data** on the menu bar, point to **Group and Outline**, then click **Clear Outline**

FIGURE O-6: Worksheet in Outline view

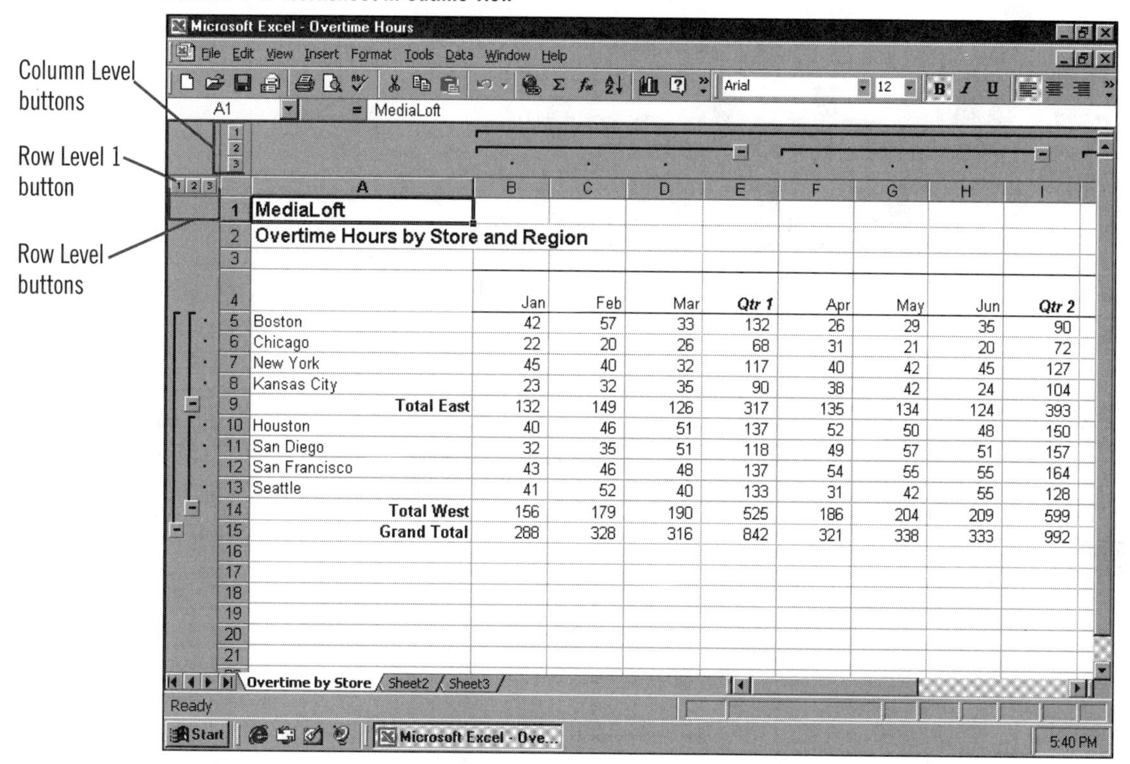

FIGURE O-7: Printed worksheet outline

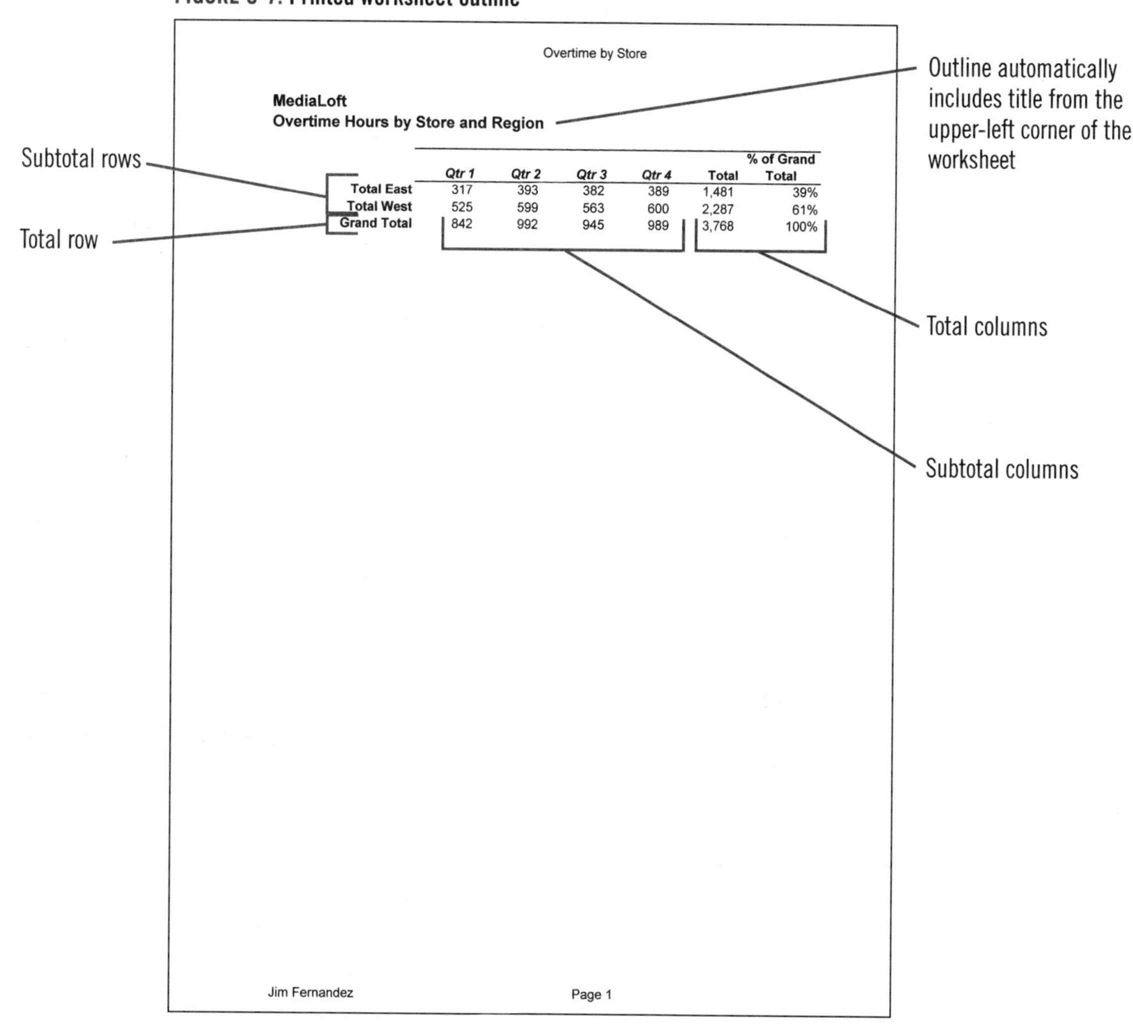

	Qtr 1	Qtr 2	Qtr 3	Qtr 4	Total	% of Grand Total
Total East	317	393	382	389	1,481	39%
Total West	525	599	563	600	2,287	61%
Grand Total	842	992	945	989	3,768	100%

Excel 2000

Controlling Worksheet Calculations

Whenever you change a value in a cell, Excel automatically recalculates all the formulas in the worksheet based on that cell. This automatic calculation is efficient until you create a worksheet so large that the recalculation process slows down data entry and screen updating. Worksheets with many formulas, data tables, or functions may also recalculate slowly. In these cases, you might want to selectively determine if and when you want Excel to perform calculations automatically. You do this by applying the manual calculation option. Once you change the calculation mode to manual, the manual mode is applied to all open worksheets. Because Jim knows that using specific Excel calculation options can help make worksheet building more efficient, he decides to change from automatic to manual calculation.

Steps

1. **Click Tools on the menu bar, click Options, then click the Calculation tab**
   The Calculation tab of the Options dialog box opens, as shown in Figure O-8.

2. **Under Calculation, click the Manual option button**
   The Recalculate before save box automatically becomes active and contains a checkmark when you select the Manual option. Because the workbook will not recalculate until you save or close and reopen the workbook, make sure to recalculate your worksheet before you print and after you make changes.

QuickTip

To automatically recalculate all worksheet formulas except one- and two-input data tables, under Calculation, click Automatic except tables.

3. **Click OK**
   Jim just received word that the December total for the San Francisco store is incorrect. You'll adjust the entry in cell P12 accordingly.

4. **Click cell B5, click Window on the menu bar, click Freeze Panes, then scroll right to bring columns P through S into view**

5. **Click cell P12, type 76, then click the Enter button on the formula bar**
   See Figure O-9. Notice that the formula results in the worksheet are *not* updated. (For example, the percentage in cell S12 is still 16%.) The word "Calculate" appears in the status bar to indicate that a specific value in the worksheet did indeed change and must be recalculated. You can press [F9] at any time to calculate all the open worksheets manually or [Shift][F9] to calculate just the active worksheet.

6. **Press [Shift][F9], then save the workbook**
   See Figure O-10. The percentage in cell S12 is now 17% instead of 16%. The other formulas in the worksheet affected by the value in cell P12 changed as well. Because this is a relatively small worksheet that recalculates quickly, you will return to automatic calculation.

QuickTip

If a worksheet formula is linked to a worksheet that you have not recalculated and you update that link, you will see a message informing you of the situation. To update the link using the current value, click OK. To use the previous value, click Cancel.

7. **Click Tools on the menu bar, click Options if necessary, click the Calculation tab if necessary, under Calculation click the Automatic option button, then click OK**
   Now any additional changes you make to the worksheet will again be recalculated automatically.

FIGURE O-8: Calculation tab of the Options dialog box

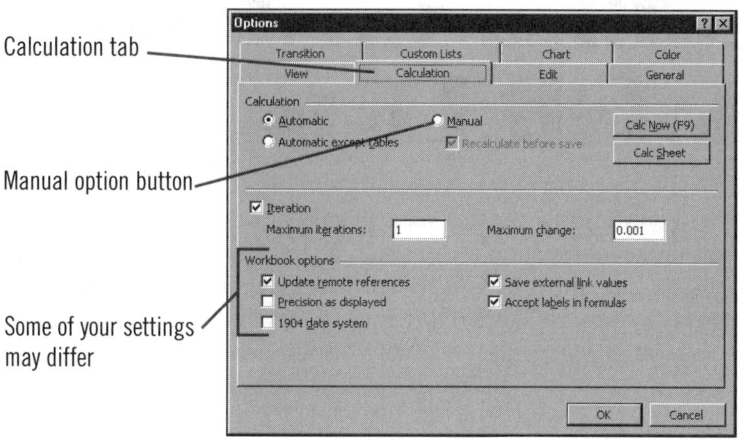

FIGURE O-9: Worksheet in manual calculation mode

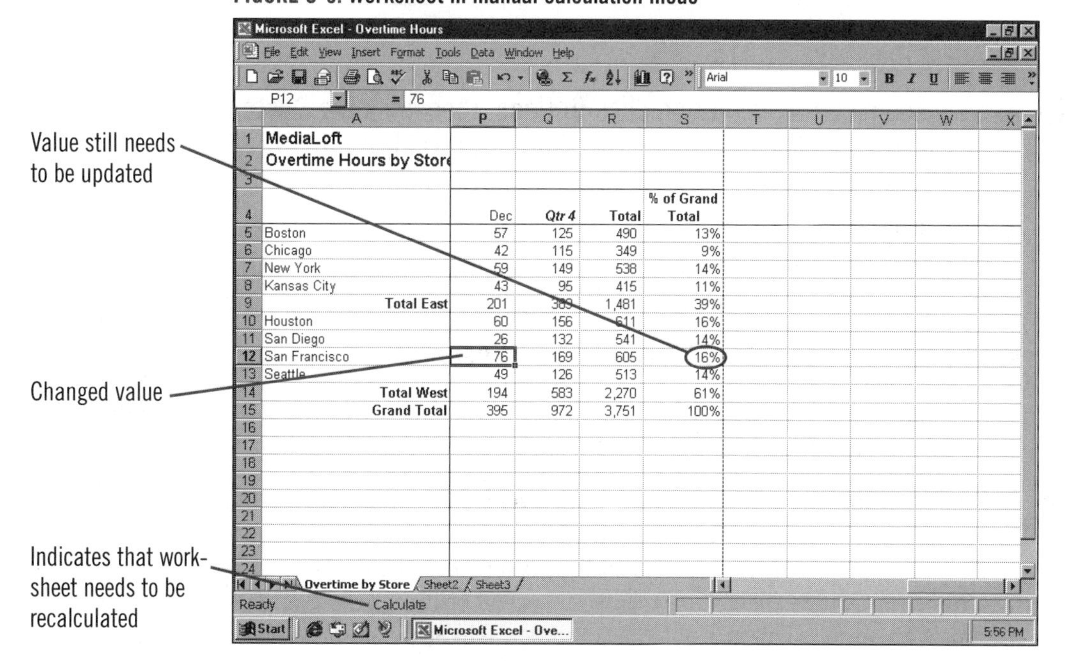

FIGURE O-10: Worksheet with updated values

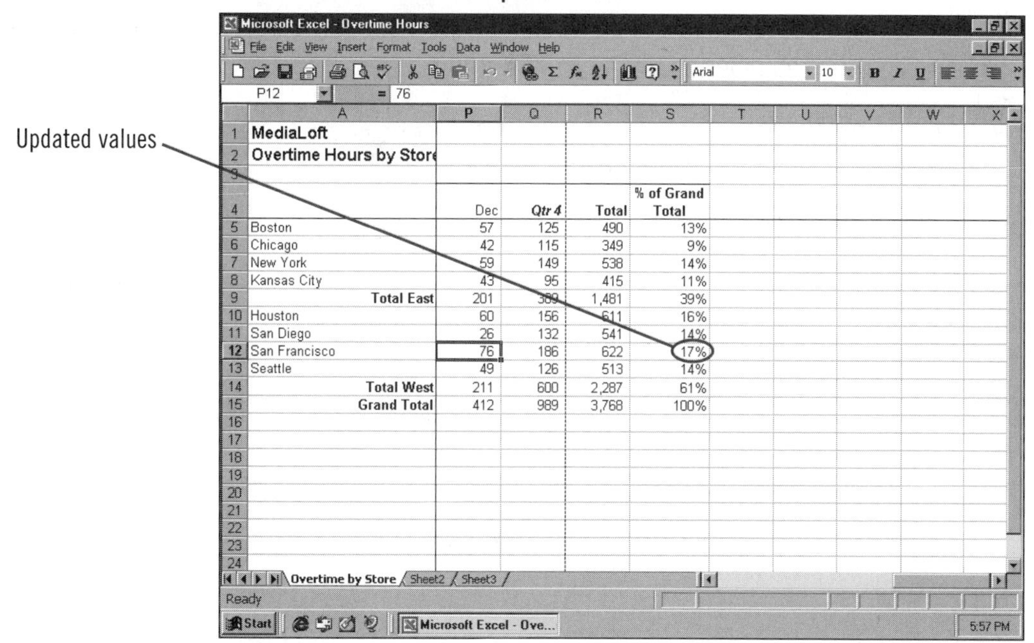

Excel 2000

Excel 2000

Creating Custom AutoFill Lists

Whenever you need to type a list of words regularly, you can save time by creating a custom AutoFill list. Then you need only to enter the first value in a blank cell and drag the AutoFill handle. Excel will enter the rest of the information for you automatically. Figure O-11 shows some examples of AutoFill lists. Jim often has to repeatedly enter MediaLoft store names and regional total labels in various worksheets. He decides to create an AutoFill list to save time in performing this task. He begins by selecting the names and total labels in the worksheet.

Steps

1. Select the range **A5:A15**
2. Click **Tools** on the menu bar, click **Options**, then click the **Custom Lists** tab
   See Figure O-12. The Custom Lists tab shows the existing AutoFill lists. The Import list from cells box contains the range you selected in Step 1.
3. Click **Import**
   The list of names is highlighted in the Custom lists box and displays in the List entries box. Jim wants to test the custom AutoFill list by placing it in a blank worksheet.
4. Click **OK**, click the **Sheet2 tab**, then type **Boston** in cell A1
5. Position the pointer over the AutoFill handle in the lower-right corner of cell A1
   Notice that the pointer changes to +, as shown in Figure O-13.
6. Click and drag the pointer down to cell **A11**, then release the mouse button
   The highlighted range now contains the custom list of store names and total rows you created. Now that you've finished creating and applying your custom AutoFill list, you need to delete it from the Options dialog box in case others will be using your computer to complete the lesson. If no one else will be using the computer, skip Step 7 and proceed to the next lesson.
7. Click **Tools** on the menu bar, click **Options** if necessary, click the **Custom Lists tab**, click the list of store and region names in the Custom lists box, click **Delete**, click **OK** to confirm the deletion, then click **OK** again
8. Save the workbook

Trouble?

If a list of store names already appears in the Custom lists box, the person using the computer before you forgot to delete it. Click the list, click [Delete], and proceed with Step 3. You cannot delete the four default lists for days and months.

QuickTip

You also can drag the AutoFill handle down or to the right to repeat the AutoFill in other rows or columns.

FIGURE O-11: Sample AutoFill list

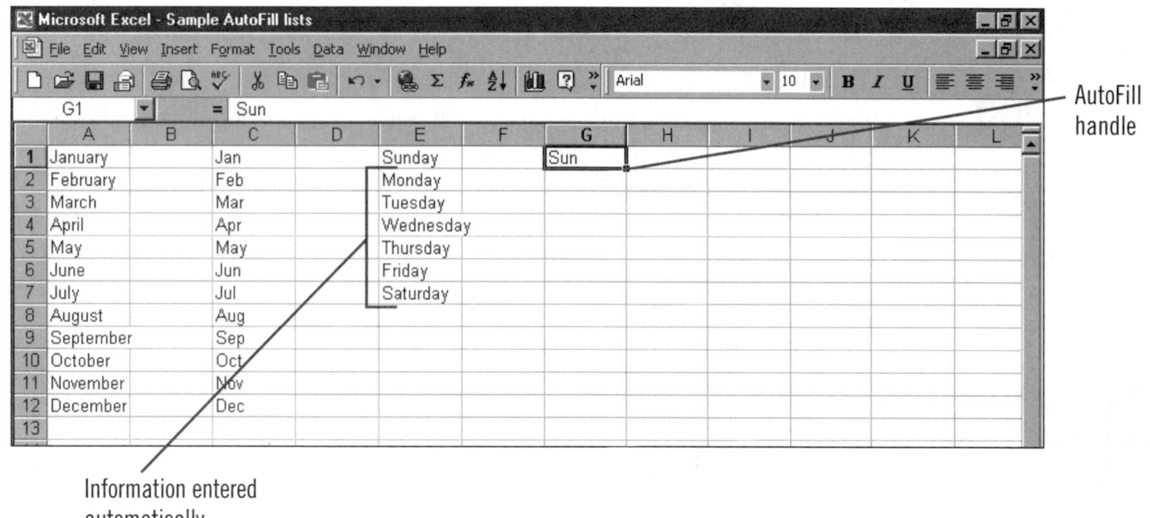

FIGURE O-12: Custom Lists tab

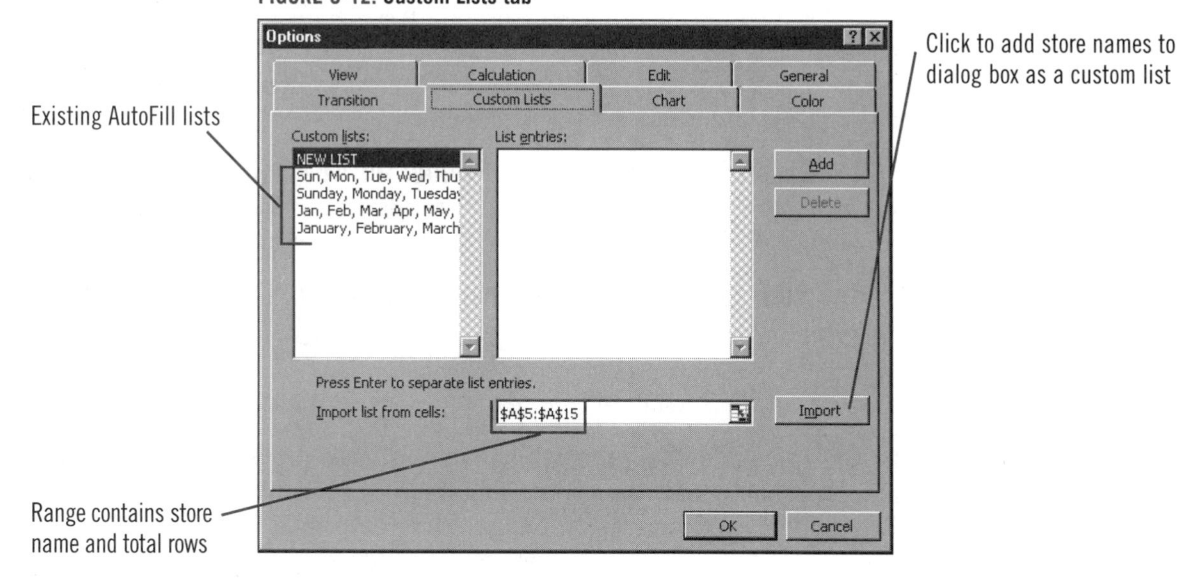

FIGURE O-13: Applying a custom AutoFill list

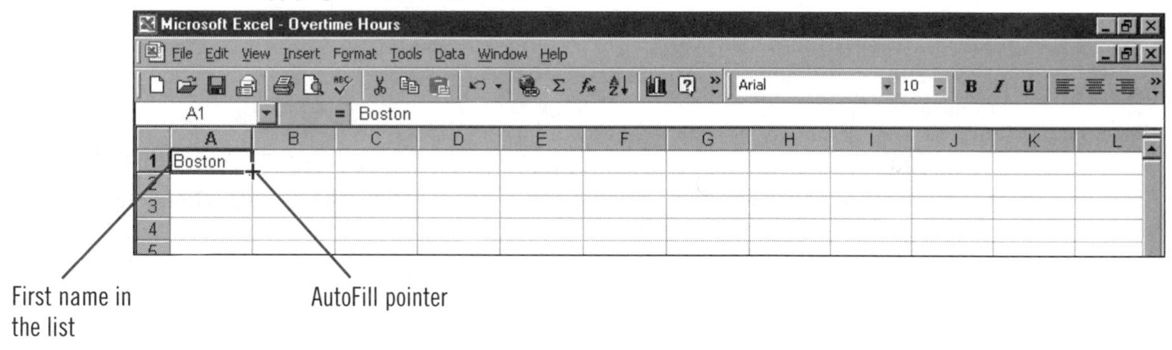

Customizing Excel

The Excel default settings for editing and viewing the worksheet are designed with user convenience in mind. You may find, however, that a particular setting doesn't always fit your needs (for example, where the cell selector moves after you press [Enter]). The eight tabs of the Options dialog box allow you to customize Excel to suit your work habits and needs. You've already used the Calculation tab to switch to manual calculation and the Custom Lists tab to create your own AutoFill list. The most commonly used functions of the Options dialog box tabs are explained in more detail in Table O-2. It's especially important not to permanently change any other General tab settings if you're sharing a computer. Jim is curious about how he can customize Excel to allow him to work more efficiently. He decides to use a blank workbook to explore some of the features of Excel accessed through the Options dialog box.

Steps

QuickTip

Do not change any settings in the Options dialog box other than those covered in this lesson.

1. Click the **New button** on the Standard toolbar, click **Tools** on the menu bar, click **Options**, then click the **Edit tab**

   In some worksheets, it's more convenient to have the cell selector automatically move right one cell, rather than down one cell, after you press [Enter].

2. Click the **Direction list arrow**, then click **Right**

   See Figure O-14. Now when you press [Enter] the selector will move to the right. You can enter detailed information (or properties) to document your workbook in the Properties dialog box. This documentation may be useful to co-workers because it allows them to read a summary of your workbook without actually having to open it; they can right-click the file in the Open dialog box, then click Properties.

3. Click the **General tab**, then click the **Prompt for workbook properties check box**

   Now, when you save a workbook, Excel will open a dialog box asking you to enter file properties. Finally, Jim thinks the workbook would look better without gridlines.

4. Click the **View tab**, then under Window options click the **Gridlines check box** to deselect it

   This setting, as well as the others under "Window options", affects only the active worksheet. Next you'll check the results of your new workbook settings.

5. Click **OK**, type **Accounts Receivable** in cell A1, then press **[Enter]**

   The information in your new worksheet is displayed without any gridlines. In addition, the cell selector moved to the right of cell A1 when you pressed [Enter]. Next, as you save the workbook, you'll enter some information in the Properties dialog box.

QuickTip

For more information about file properties, see the Clues to Use in the "Finding Files" lesson earlier in this unit.

6. Save the workbook as **Accounts** to your Project Disk, in the Accounts Properties dialog box click the **Summary tab** if necessary, then in the Comments text box type **Sample workbook used to practice customizing Excel**

   See Figure O-15.

7. Click **OK**

   Now that you're finished exploring the Options dialog box, you need to reestablish the original Excel settings. You don't need to adjust the Gridlines setting because that change applied only to the active worksheet.

8. Click **Tools** on the menu bar, click **Options**, click the **Edit tab**, click the **Direction list arrow**, click **Down**, click the **General tab**, click the **Prompt for workbook properties check box** to deselect it, click **OK**, then close the workbook

   The Overtime Hours workbook reappears.

FIGURE O-14: Edit tab in the Options dialog box

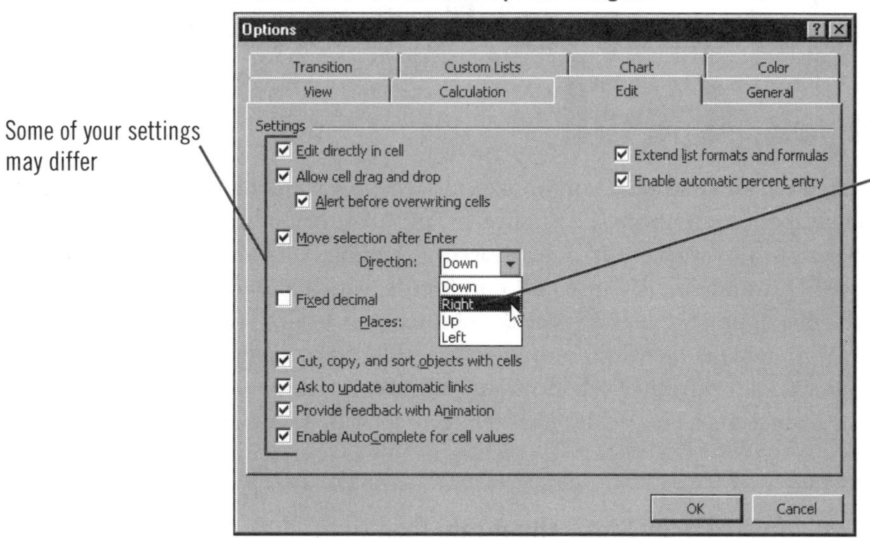

FIGURE O-15: Properties dialog box

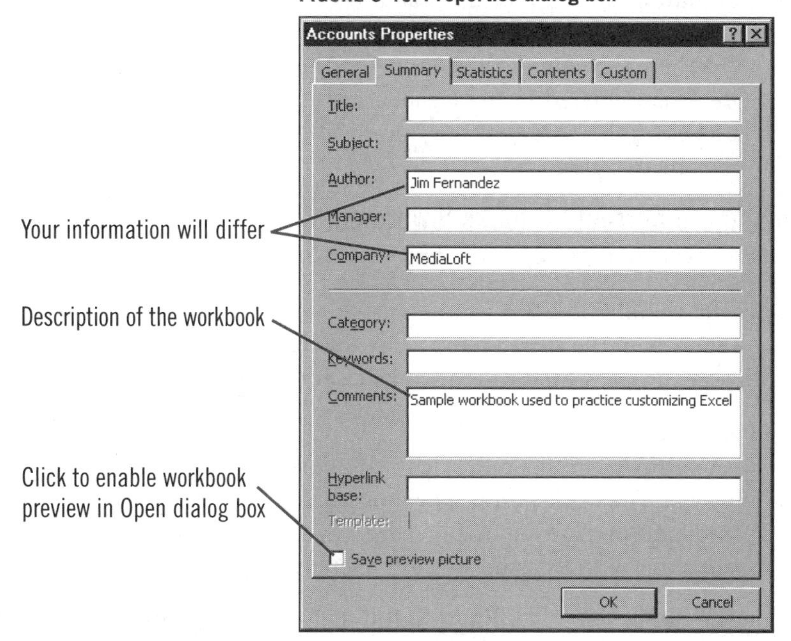

TABLE O-2: Options dialog box tabs

tab	description
Calculation	Controls how the worksheet is calculated; choices include automatic versus manual
Chart	Controls how empty cells are treated in a chart and whether chart tips are displayed
Color	Allows you to copy a customized color palette from one workbook to another
Custom Lists	Allows you to add or delete custom AutoFill lists
Edit	Controls the direction in which the cell selector moves after you press [Enter] and the ability to edit directly in cells
General	Controls the option to display the Properties dialog box after saving a workbook, the number of sheets in a new workbook, and the drive and folder used in the Save dialog box by default; User name is also listed here
Transition	Provides options useful for users familiar with Lotus 1-2-3
View	Controls the visibility of the formula bar, status bar, gridlines, row and column headers, and scroll bars; also controls the option to display formulas in a worksheet

Excel 2000

Adding a Comment to a Cell

Whenever you'll be sharing a workbook with others, it's a good idea to **document**, or make notes about, basic assumptions, complicated formulas, or questionable data. By reading your documentation, a co-worker can quickly become familiar with your workbook. The easiest way to document a workbook is to use **cell comments**, which are notes you've written about your workbook that appear when you place the pointer over a cell. When you sort or copy and paste cells, any comments in them will move to the new location. In PivotTable reports, however, the comments stay in the original cell locations. Jim thinks one of the figures in the worksheet may be incorrect. He decides to add a comment for Lisa, pointing out the possible error.

QuickTip

You can also insert a comment by clicking the New Comment button on the Auditing or Reviewing toolbar.

QuickTip

To edit an existing comment, select the cell to which the comment is attached, click Insert on the menu bar, then click Edit Comment. To copy only comments, copy the cell contents, right-click the destination cell, select Paste Special, then click Comments.

1. Click the **Overtime by Store sheet tab**, then right-click cell **P11**
2. Click **Insert Comment** on the pop-up menu
   The Comment box opens, as shown in Figure O-16. Notice that Excel automatically includes the user name at the beginning of the comment. The user name data was collected from information previously entered in the General tab of the Options dialog box. Notice the white sizing handles on the border of the Comment box. You use these handles to change the size of the box by dragging.
3. Type **Is this figure correct? It looks low to me.**
   Notice how the text automatically wraps to the next line as necessary.
4. Click outside the Comment box
   A red triangle appears in the upper-right corner of cell P11, indicating that a comment is attached to the cell. People who use your worksheet can easily display comments.
5. Place the pointer over cell P11
   The comment appears next to the cell. When you move the pointer outside of cell P11, the comment disappears. The worksheet is now finished and ready for printing. You'll print the worksheet in landscape orientation on one page. On a second printed page, you print only the cell comment along with its associated cell reference.
6. Click **File** on the menu bar, click **Page Setup**, click the **Page tab** if necessary, under Orientation click the **Landscape option button**, under Scaling click the **Fit to option button**, click the **Sheet tab**, under Print click the **Comments list arrow**, click **At end of sheet**, click the **Row and column headings check box** to select it, click **Print**, then click **OK**
   Excel prints two pages.
7. Save the workbook

FIGURE O-16: Comment box

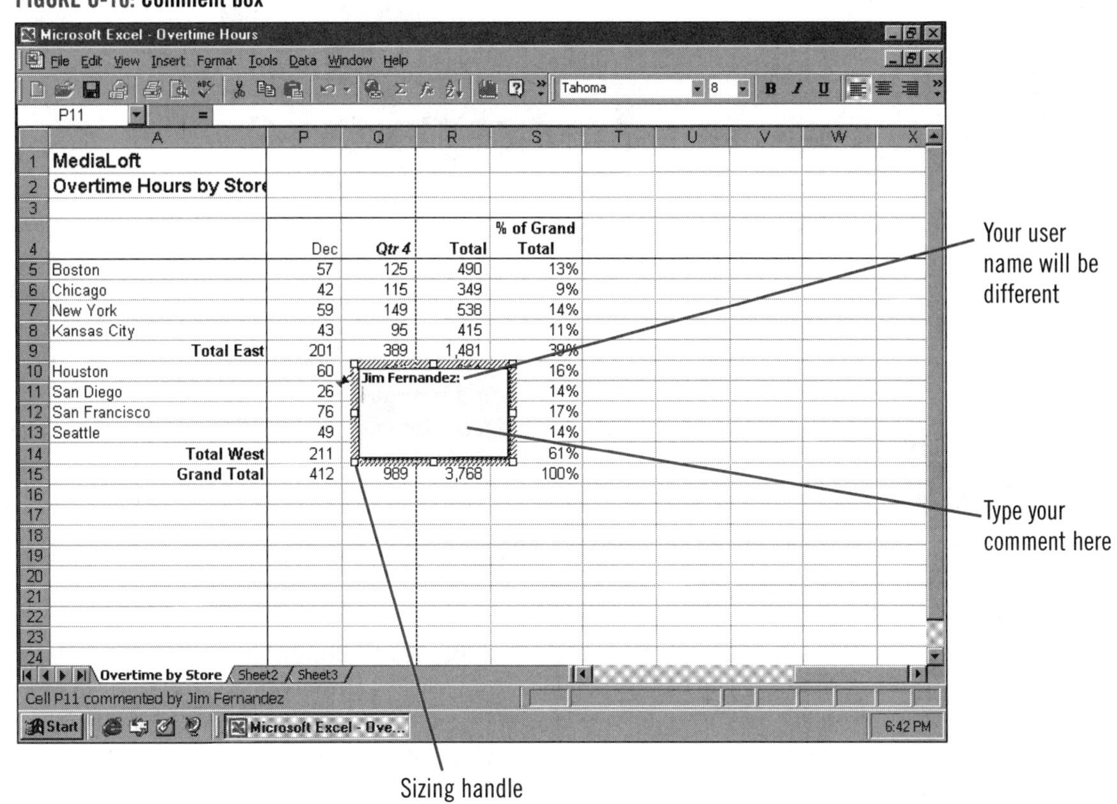

Preview and print multiple worksheets

To preview and print multiple worksheets, press and hold down [Ctrl] and click the tabs for the sheets you want to print, then click the Preview or Print button. In Page Preview, the multiple worksheets will appear as separate pages in the Preview window, which you can display by clicking Next and Previous.

Excel 2000

Saving a Workbook as a Template

A **template** is a workbook that contains text (such as column and row labels), formulas, macros, and formatting you use repeatedly. Once you save a workbook as a template, it provides a model for creating a new workbook without your having to reenter standard data. Excel provides several templates on the Spreadsheet Solutions tab of the New dialog box. In most cases, though, you'll probably want to create your own template from a worksheet you use regularly. When you save a file as a template, the original workbook remains unchanged. Jim plans to use the same formulas, titles, frozen panes, and row and column labels from the Overtime Hours worksheet for subsequent yearly worksheets. He will delete the extra sheets, the comments, and the data for each month, then save the workbook as a template.

Steps

1. Click the **Sheet2 tab**, press **[Ctrl]**, click the **Sheet3 tab**, right-click the **Sheet3 tab**, click **Delete**, then click **OK**
2. Right-click cell **P11**, then click **Delete Comment**
   Now that you've removed the extra sheets and the comment, you'll delete the data on overtime hours. You'll leave the formulas in rows 9, 14, and 15, and in columns E, I, M, Q, R, and S, however, so that another user can simply begin entering data without having to re-create the formulas.
3. Press **[Ctrl]**, select the ranges **B5:D8**, **B10:D13**, **F5:H8**, **F10:H13**, **J5:L8**, **J10:L13**, **N5:P8**, **N10:P13**, press **[Delete]**, then click anywhere to deselect the ranges
   See Figure O-17. The hyphens in the subtotal and total rows and columns indicate that the current value of these cells is zero. The divide by zero error messages in column S are only temporary and will disappear as soon as you open the template, save it as a workbook, and begin to enter next year's data. To make subsequent template use easier, it's best to have the first data entry cell selected when you save it.
4. Scroll left to bring columns B through G into view, then click cell **B5**
5. Click **File**, click Save As, click the **Save as type list arrow**, then click **Template (.xlt)**
   Excel adds the .xlt extension to the filename (although you will not see it if your file extensions are turned off) and automatically switches to the Templates folder, as shown in Figure O-18. If you are using a computer on a network, you may not have permission to save to the Templates folder. You'll save your template to your Project Disk instead.
6. Click the **Save in list arrow**, click the drive and folder containing your Project Disk, click **Save**, close the workbook, then exit Excel
   Jim would save the template to one of his template folders. Next year, when he needs to compile the information for overtime hours, he can simply open a document based on the Overtime Hours template and begin entering data. When this new work is saved for the first time, Excel will automatically save the template as a regular workbook. The original template will remain intact.

Trouble?

If you accidentally delete a formula, insert a copy from the appropriate adjoining cell or click the Undo button and repeat Step 3.

FIGURE O-17: Preparing the template

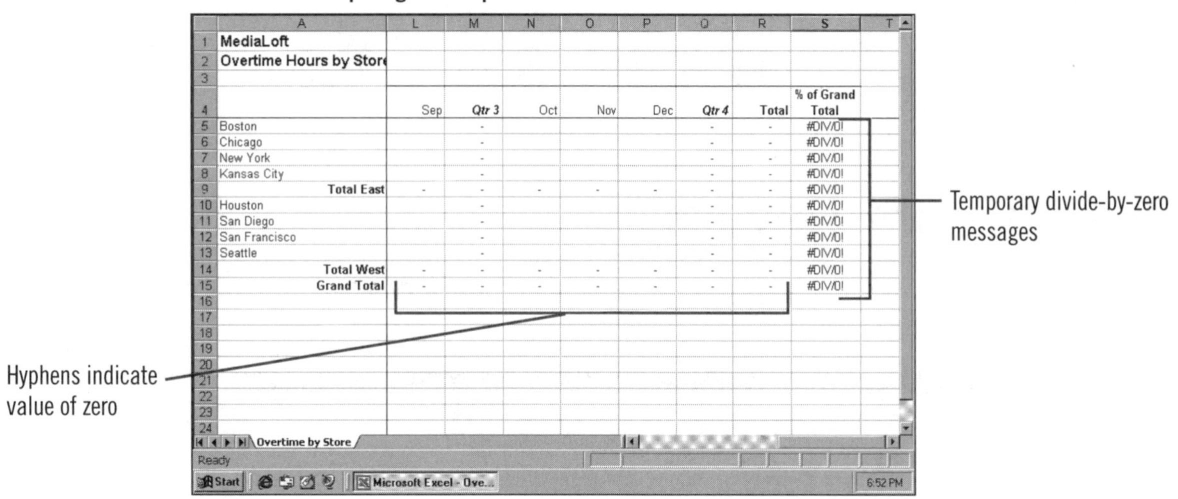

FIGURE O-18: Saving a template

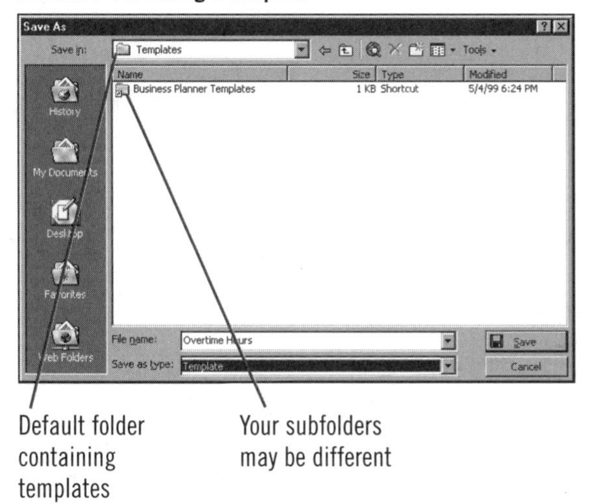

FIGURE O-19: New dialog box

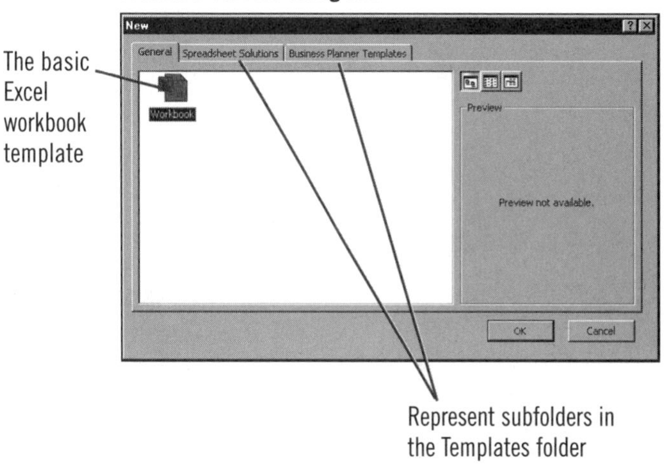

Storing, applying, and modifying templates

If you're using your own computer, you may want to save your templates in one of the Templates subfolders, such as the one shown in Figure O-18. Then you can quickly open a document based on your template (that is, apply a template to a document) from the New dialog box by clicking File, clicking New, then selecting the template.

The New dialog box contains tabs containing icons for workbook templates, as shown in Figure O-19. The Spreadsheet Solutions tab in the New dialog box contains several ready-made templates you can use for business-related tasks, such as creating invoices or purchase orders. The other tabs in the New dialog box depend on which subfolders of the Templates folder you used to save your templates. For instance, if you saved a template named "Personnel" in the Other Documents subfolder, then you would see an Other Documents tab in the New dialog box, with the Personnel template as an option. To open a document based on this template, you would click it, then click OK.

To edit a template, you must use the Open command to open the template itself, change it, then save it under the same name. The changes will be applied only to new documents you create; it does not change documents you've already created using the template.

Practice

► Concepts Review

Label each element of the Excel screen shown in Figure O-20.

FIGURE O-20

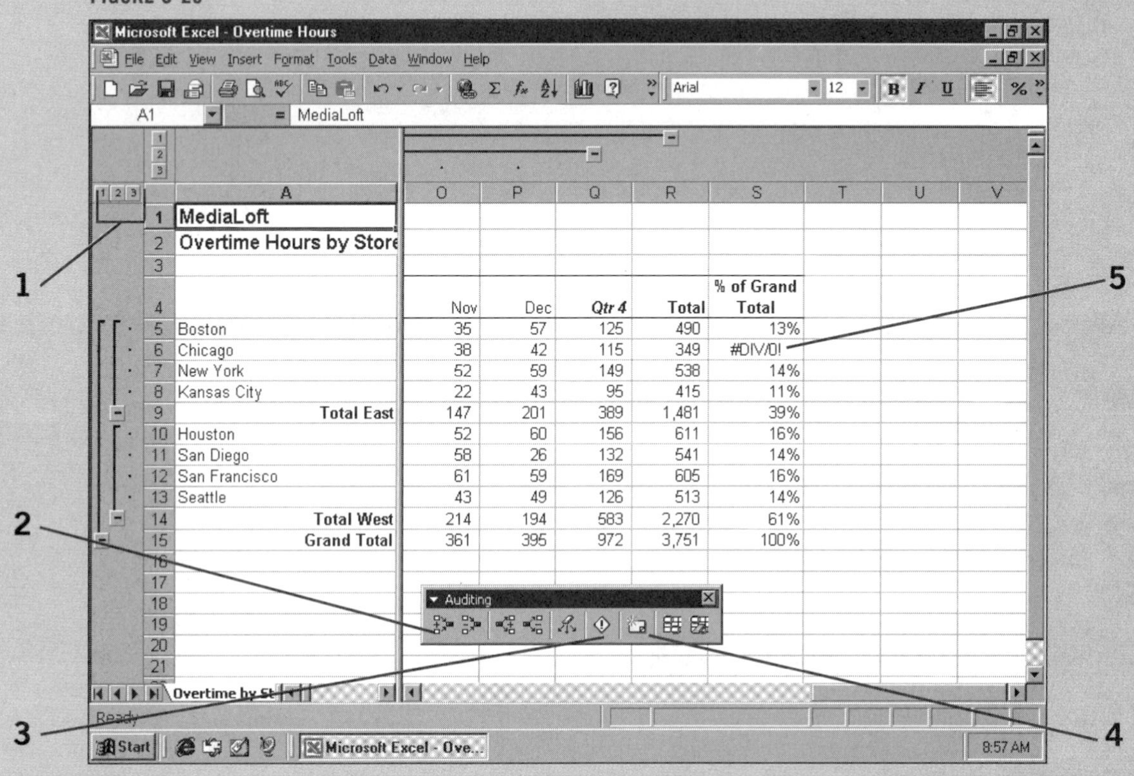

Match each term with the statement that describes it.

a. **Find dialog box**
b. **Options dialog box**
c. **Auditing toolbar**
d. **Outlining a worksheet**
e. **Circular reference**
f. **[Shift][F9]**
g. **AutoFill**
h. **Comment**

6. Contains settings for customizing Excel
7. Note that appears when you place the pointer over a cell
8. Occurs in a formula that refers to its own cell location
9. Calculates the worksheet manually
10. Automatically enters a list in a worksheet
11. Used to track errors and determine worksheet logic
12. A powerful searching tool that makes it easy to locate files
13. Allows you to display the most important columns and rows

Select the best answer from the list of choices.

14. When searching for a file, which of these characters can substitute for unknown characters in a filename?
- **a.** #
- **b.** &
- **c.** *
- **d.** !

15. You can search for a file by
- **a.** Name.
- **b.** Text within the file.
- **c.** Property.
- **d.** All of the above.

16. The ____________ button locates the cells used in the active cell's formula.
- **a.** Trace Precedents
- **b.** Trace Antecedents
- **c.** Function
- **d.** Validation Circle

17. The ____________ automatically hides everything in the worksheet except the most important row or rows.
- **a.** Column Level 1 button
- **b.** Row Level 1 button
- **c.** Trace Precedents button
- **d.** Outline feature

18. To create a custom AutoFill list you should first
- **a.** Press [Shift][F9].
- **b.** Click the AutoFill tab in the Edit dialog box.
- **c.** Drag the AutoFill handle.
- **d.** Select the list in the worksheet.

19. The ____________ tab in the Options dialog box controls whether the Properties dialog box is displayed when you save a workbook.
- **a.** General
- **b.** Edit
- **c.** Properties
- **d.** View

► Skills Review

1. Find files.

- **a.** In the Open dialog box, locate the drive that contains your Project Disk, and, if necessary, the folder where you store your Project Files.
- **b.** If necessary, display detailed information about each file.
- **c.** Display the files' properties.
- **d.** Display only filenames.
- **e.** Search for all files that begin with EX O, adding the search criterion to the criteria list.
- **f.** Open the workbook EX O-2.
- **g.** Save the workbook as "Cafe Budget".

2. Audit a worksheet.

- **a.** Display the Auditing toolbar and drag it to the bottom of the worksheet.
- **b.** Select cell E10, then use the New Comment button on the Auditing toolbar to add the comment "Does this include temporary holiday staff?" Close the Comments box, then use the pointer to redisplay the comment.
- **c.** Select cell B10, then use the Trace Dependents button to locate all the cells that depend on this cell. (*Hint:* Click the button three times.)
- **d.** Clear the arrows from the worksheet using the Remove All Arrows button on the Auditing toolbar.
- **e.** Select cell B19, use the Trace Precedents button on the Auditing toolbar to find the cells on which that figure is based, then correct the formula in cell B19.
- **f.** Select cell G6, trace the error it contains, then correct the formula.
- **g.** Hide the Auditing toolbar, then save the workbook.
- **h.** Practice opening and hiding the Picture toolbar.

3. Outline a worksheet.

- **a.** Display the worksheet in outline view.
- **b.** Use the Row Level buttons to display only the most important rows in the budget.
- **c.** Use the Row Level buttons to display the second most important rows in the budget.
- **d.** Add your name to the footer, then print the outlined worksheet in Landscape orientation.
- **e.** Use the Row Level buttons to display all the rows in the budget.
- **f.** Clear the outline from the worksheet.

4. Control worksheet calculations.

- **a.** Open the Options dialog box and switch to manual calculation.
- **b.** Change the figure in cell B6 to 30000.
- **c.** Recalculate the worksheet manually using the appropriate key combination.
- **d.** Turn off manual calculation and save the workbook.

5. Create a custom AutoFill list.

- **a.** Select the range A4:A19.
- **b.** Open the Custom Lists tab in the Options dialog box. Delete any custom lists except the four default day and month lists.
- **c.** Import the selected text into the dialog box.
- **d.** Close the dialog box.
- **e.** On Sheet2, enter "Income" in cell A1.
- **f.** Drag the fill handle to cell A15.

g. Select cell A1 again, and drag its fill handle to cell O1.
h. Open the Options dialog box again, and delete the list you just created.
i. Save the workbook.

6. **Customize Excel.**
   a. Open the Options dialog box.
   b. In the Edit tab, change the direction of the cell selector to "Up".
   c. In the General tab, indicate that you want the Properties dialog box to appear when you save a workbook for the first time.
   d. In the View tab, turn off the worksheet gridlines.
   e. Close the dialog box and return to Sheet2, which is now displayed without gridlines.
   f. Click the Budget tab, and notice that this worksheet is displayed with gridlines.
   g. Open a new workbook.
   h. Type your name in cell C5, then press Enter. Check to make sure the cell selector moves up.
   i. Save the workbook to your Project Disk as "Customizing Excel", adding your name if necessary, and the comment "Sample workbook" to the Properties dialog box, then close the workbook.
   j. Open the Options dialog box and change the cell selector direction back to "Down". Then turn off the Prompt for workbook properties option and close the Options dialog box.

7. **Add a comment to a cell.**
   a. In the Budget sheet, select cell E12.
   b. Open the Comment box by using the Comment command on the Insert menu.
   c. Type "Does this include TV and radio spots, or only newspaper and magazine advertising? It is very important to include these."
   d. Drag the resize handles on the borders of the Comment box until you can see the entire note.
   e. Click anywhere outside the Comment box to close it.
   f. Display the comment, and check it for errors.
   g. Edit the comment in cell E12 so it ends after the word "spots", with a question mark at the end.
   h. Delete the comment you added earlier in cell E10.
   i. Print the worksheet and your comment in landscape orientation.
   j. Change the orientation of Sheet2 to landscape and fit it to one page.
   k. Preview and print both the Budget worksheet and Sheet2 at the same time.
   l. Save the workbook.

8. **Save a workbook as a template.**
   a. Delete Sheet2 and Sheet3.
   b. Delete the comment in cell E12.
   c. Delete the budget data for all four quarters. Leave the worksheet formulas intact.
   d. Save the workbook to your Project Disk as a template, using the filename Budget Template.
   e. Select cell B4 and close the template.
   f. Copy the template into your Business Planner directory. (If you do not have access to the Business Planner directory, skip to Step 1.)
   g. Open a document based on the template using the New command on the File menu.
   h. Enter your own data for all four quarters and in every budget category.
   i. Save the workbook as Cafe Budget 2.
   j. Open the template using the Open command on the File menu, reformat it any way you wish, then save it.
   k. Delete the copy of the template from the Business Planner directory.
   l. Print and close the workbook, then exit Excel.

Independent Challenges

1. You are a manager at Life Skills, a nonprofit agency devoted to helping people with severe learning disabilities become proficient computer users. Your department specializes in hands-on instruction for popular personal computer (PC) programs. During the month of October, you created a check register in Excel for department expenses. Before you begin generating a November register, however, you want to check the October register for errors. In your worksheet audit, you will look for missing check numbers, miscalculated totals, and faulty formula logic. Also, you want to add comments to document the worksheet.

To complete this independent challenge:

a. Open the workbook titled EX O-3, then save it as "2000 Monthly Check Register".
b. Open the Auditing toolbar.
c. The balance in cell F16 does not reflect the RAM upgrade on 10/15/00. Use the Trace Precedents button to show the logic of the formula in F16. Once you identify the error in cell F16, edit the formula in cell F16 to subtract the RAM expense from the previous balance.
d. Due to illness, your Excel instructor taught only three hours of a six-hour course. Create a comment indicating this in cell C19.
e. Use the Trace Error button to determine the source of the problem in cell E24. Edit the formula to solve the problem, then format the cell to display a percentage with no decimal places.
f. Add your name to the worksheet footer, then save the workbook. Preview, then print the worksheet on one page and the comment on another.
g. Close the Auditing toolbar, then close the workbook, saving changes, if necessary.

2. As a manager at Life Skills, a nonprofit agency devoted to helping people with severe learning disabilities become proficient computer users, you need to keep track of your department's regular monthly expenses. Your assistant has compiled a list of fixed expenses in an Excel workbook but forgot the filename. Once you find the file using the Search tools in the Open dialog box, you want to create a custom AutoFill list containing each expense item to save time in preparing similar worksheets in the future. Finally, you will practice using manual calculation, then turn off the worksheet gridlines to make the expense data easier to read.

To complete this independent challenge:

Note: If you have access to the Microsoft Office 2000 installation disks, begin from Step a; if not, open the file EX O-4 and begin with Step b.

a. Search your Project Disk for a file with the text "printer paper" in the workbook. Search again for a file with the text "Fixed Monthly Expenses" in the workbook. Open the workbook.
b. Save the workbook as "Monthly Budget".
c. Select the cells containing the list of expense items. Then open the Options dialog box and import the list into the Custom Lists tab.
d. Close the Options dialog box and practice using the AutoFill handle to insert your list in a column in Sheet2. Insert the list a second time in a row in Sheet2.
e. Add your name to the worksheet footer, save the workbook, then preview and print Sheet2 on a single page.
f. Return to the Fixed Expenses sheet, then delete your custom list from the Options dialog box.
g. Use the Options dialog box to switch to manual calculation and to turn off the gridlines in the Fixed Expenses sheet.
h. Change the expense for printer paper to 25.00. Calculate the worksheet manually.
i. Turn on automatic calculation again, add your name to the footer, then print the Fixed Expenses worksheet.
j. Save and close the workbook.

3. Your business, Babies, Inc., helps parents find high-quality in-home childcare. In exchange for a one-time fee, you recruit and interview potential nannies, confirm references, and conduct thorough background checks. In addition, once a nanny has been hired, you provide training in child development and infant CPR. Currently, you are preparing your budget for the next four quarters. After you enter the data for each expense and income category, you will create a condensed version of the worksheet using Excel outlining tools.

To complete this independent challenge:

a. Open a new workbook, then save it as "Babies Budget".
b. Enter a title, then the following column labels: Description, 1st Qtr, 2nd Qtr, 3rd Qtr, 4th Qtr, and Total.
c. Enter the following income items: Nanny Fee, Child Development Course, and CPR Course. Subtotal the income items, then enter at least six office-expense items.
d. Subtotal the expenses. Enter expenses and income data for each quarter. Create formulas for the total column and a cash flow row (income - expenses). Format the worksheet appropriately.
e. Display the worksheet in Outline view.
f. Contract the outline to display only the subtotal and total rows, add your name to the footer, then print the outline.
g. Redisplay all the rows, then contract the outline again to eliminate the data for each quarter. Print the outline.
h. Clear the outline, then print the entire worksheet.
i. Save the workbook, and close it.

4. The MediaLoft Accounting department has asked Jim Fernandez to analyze the CD sales for the New York store for the next year. The department wants him to use the format that is currently used on the Accounting page of the MediaLoft intranet site. Jim wants to begin the analysis right away, so he decides to copy the table containing the information categories he needs directly from the site. He will then add information and a comment, then save the worksheet as a template that he can use again in the future.

To complete this independent challenge:

a. Connect to the Internet, and use Internet Explorer to go to the MediaLoft intranet site at http://www.course.com/Illustrated/MediaLoft. Click the Accounting link, then scroll until you see the table under New York Q2 Book Sales. Minimize the Internet Explorer window.
b. Open a new Excel workbook, minimize the Excel window, and arrange the Internet Explorer and Excel windows so they are next to each other.
c. Select the Sales by Category at MediaLoft New York table and drag it to cell A1 of the blank worksheet, then save the worksheet as New York Q2 Book Sales.
d. Close Internet Explorer and disconnect from the Internet.
e. Use formulas to add totals for each month and each book category, then put the totals in boldface.
f. Format the numbers in Comma format with no decimal places.
g. Change the workbook calculation from automatic to manual.
h. Change the children's book figure for April to 13,000, print the worksheet, circle the incorrect totals, then manually update the totals and return calculation to automatic.
i. On Sheet2, create a custom AutoFill list containing the book categories on Sheet1.
j. On Sheet1, add a comment to any cell, then print both Sheet1 and the comment.
k. Clear the data, the comment, and the month names from the worksheet, leaving the formulas intact, and save the workbook as a template called "New York Book Sales Template" on your Project Disk.
l. With the template still open, format the template using colors or other formatting to make it more attractive, then save your changes.
m. Close the workbook template and exit Excel.

► Visual Workshop

Open the workbook titled EX O-5, then click Cancel to close the dialog box warning you of a circular reference. Save the workbook as "City Zoo Animal Count" to your Project Disk. Use the auditing techniques you have learned so far to correct any errors so that the worksheet entries and formulas match Figure O-21. Make sure to include the cell comment in cell F11. Add your name to the footer, then preview and print the worksheet and comment in landscape orientation, showing row and column headings. In addition to printing the worksheet, also print the worksheet formulas on a separate sheet, showing row and column headings.

FIGURE O-21

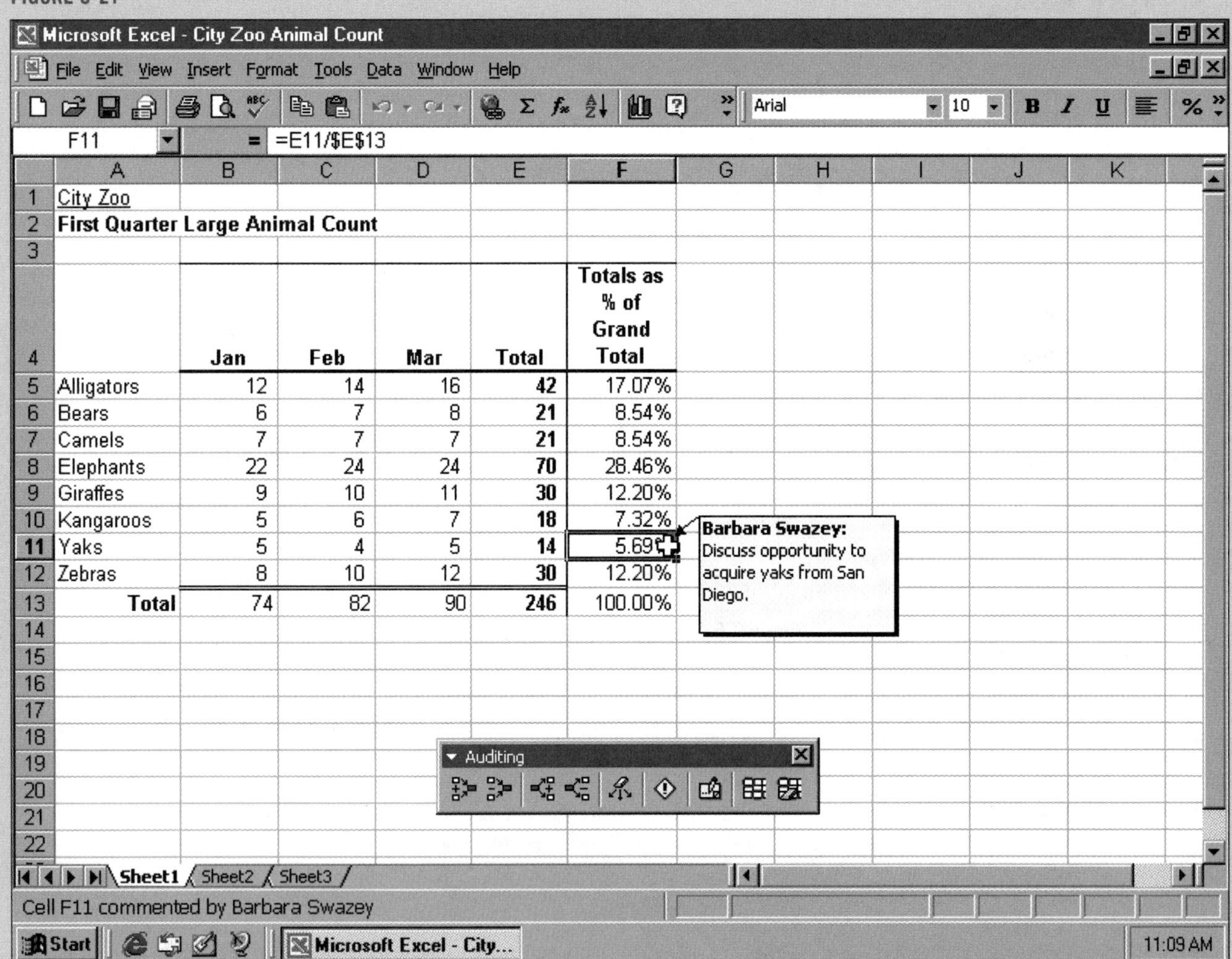

	A	B	C	D	E	F
1	City Zoo					
2	First Quarter Large Animal Count					
3						
4		Jan	Feb	Mar	Total	Totals as % of Grand Total
5	Alligators	12	14	16	42	17.07%
6	Bears	6	7	8	21	8.54%
7	Camels	7	7	7	21	8.54%
8	Elephants	22	24	24	70	28.46%
9	Giraffes	9	10	11	30	12.20%
10	Kangaroos	5	6	7	18	7.32%
11	Yaks	5	4	5	14	5.69%
12	Zebras	8	10	12	30	12.20%
13	Total	74	82	90	246	100.00%

Excel 2000

Unit P

Programming with Excel

Objectives

- View VBA code
- Analyze VBA code
- Write VBA code
- Add a conditional statement
- Prompt the user for data
- Debug a macro
- Create a main procedure
- Run a main procedure

All Excel macros are written in a programming language called Visual Basic for Applications or, simply, **VBA**. When you create a macro with the Excel macro recorder, the recorder writes the required VBA instructions for you. You can also create an Excel macro by entering the appropriate VBA instructions manually. The sequence of VBA statements contained in a macro is called a **procedure**. In this unit, you will view and analyze existing VBA code. Then you will write some VBA code on your own. You will learn how to add a conditional statement to a procedure, as well as how to prompt the user for information while the macro is running. You will also find out how to locate any errors, or bugs, in a macro. Finally, you will combine several macros into one. Alice Wegman, MediaLoft's marketing manager, has asked Jim Fernandez to create five macros to automate some of the division's time-consuming tasks.

Viewing VBA Code

Before you can write Excel macro procedures, you must become familiar with the VBA (Visual Basic for Applications) programming language. A common method of learning any programming language is to view existing code. To view VBA, you open the Visual Basic Editor, which contains a Project window, a Properties window, and a Code window. The VBA code for macro procedures appears in the Code window. The first line of a procedure, called the **procedure header**, defines the procedure's type, name, and arguments. Items displayed in blue are **keywords**, which are words recognized as part of the VBA programming language. **Comments**, which are notes explaining the code, are shown in green, and the remaining code is shown in black. You use the Editor to view or edit an existing macro procedure as well as to create a new macro procedure. Each week, MediaLoft receives a text file from the KHOT radio station containing information about weekly radio ads. Alice has already imported the text file into a worksheet but still needs to format it. Jim has begun work on a macro to automate the process of formatting this imported text file.

Steps

Trouble?

If the Virus warning dialog box shown in Figure P-1 appears, click Enable Macros. If a macro information dialog box opens informing you that Visual Basic macro modules are now edited in the Visual Basic Editor, click OK, then continue with Step 2.

QuickTip

If you only see the Code window, click Tools on the menu bar, click Options, click the Docking tab, and make sure the Project Explorer and Properties options are selected.

1. Open the workbook titled **EX P-1**, save it as **KHOT Procedures**, then reset personalized toolbars and menus to their default state
   The KHOT Procedures workbook displays a blank worksheet. It is in this workbook that you will create and store all the procedures for this lesson.
2. Click **Tools** on the menu bar, point to **Macro**, then click **Macros**
   The Macro dialog box appears with the FormatFile macro procedure selected in the list box.
3. Click **Edit**
   The Visual Basic Editor opens and displays the FormatFile procedure in the Code window. See Figure P-2.
4. Make sure both the Visual Basic window and the Code window are maximized to match Figure P-2. If the Properties or Project Explorer window is not displayed, click the **Properties Window button**, then click the **Project Explorer button** on the toolbar
5. Examine the top three lines of comments and the first line of code beginning with Sub FormatFile ( )
   Notice that the different parts of the procedure appear in various colors. The third line of comments explains that the keyboard shortcut for this macro procedure is Ctrl+F. The keyword *Sub* in the procedure header indicates that this is a **Sub procedure**, or a series of Visual Basic statements that perform an action but do not return a value. In the next lesson, you will analyze the procedure code to see what each line does.

FIGURE P-1: Virus warning dialog box

Click here to open workbook with the ability to run macros

Microsoft Excel

A:\KHOT Procedures.xls contains macros.

Macros may contain viruses. It is always safe to disable macros, but if the macros are legitimate, you might lose some functionality.

Disable Macros | Enable Macros | More Info

FIGURE P-2: Procedure displayed in the Visual Basic Editor

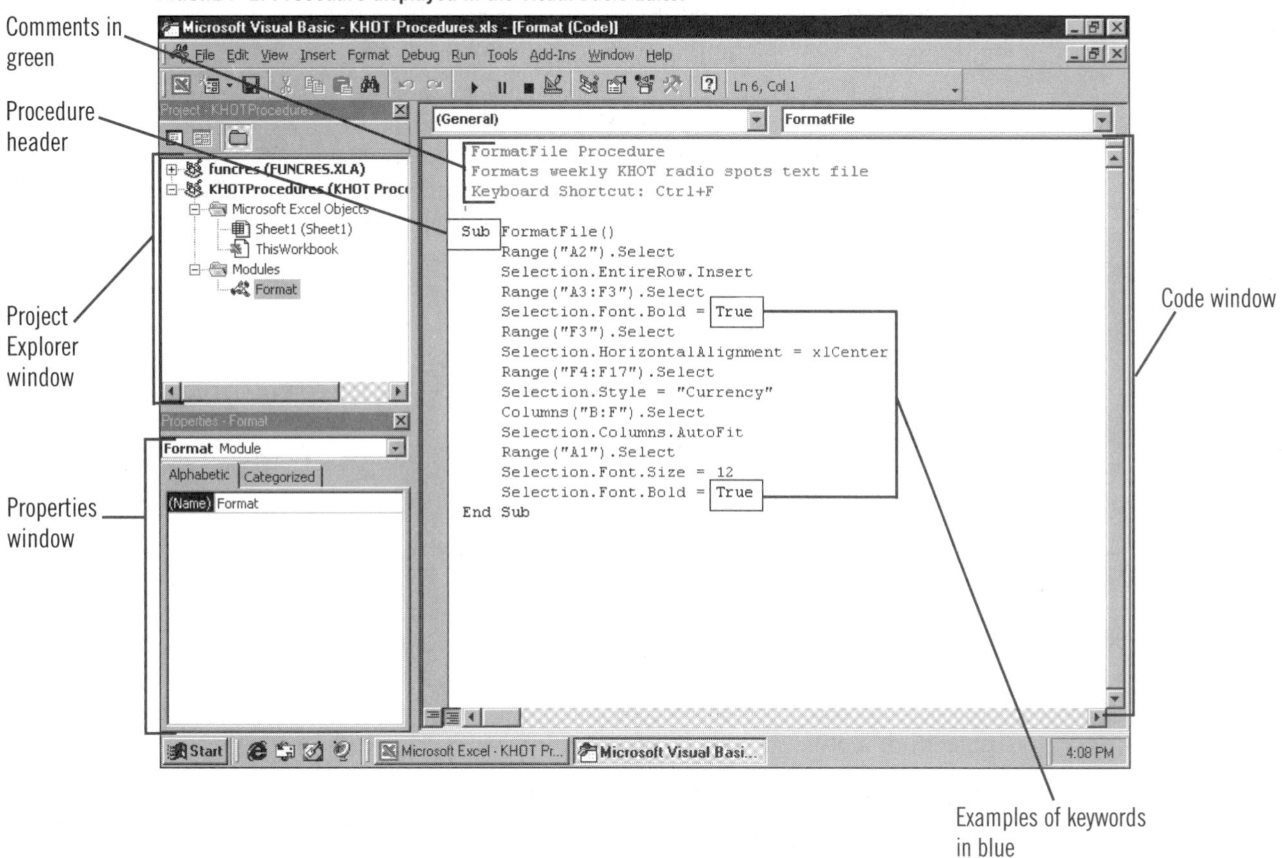

Understanding the Visual Basic Editor

A **module** is the Visual Basic equivalent of a worksheet. In it, you store macro procedures, just as you store data in worksheets. Modules, in turn, are stored in workbooks (or **projects**), along with worksheets. You view and edit modules in the Visual Basic Editor, which is made up of three windows, the Project Explorer (also called the Project window), the Code window, and the Properties window. The **Project Explorer** displays a list of all open projects (or workbooks) and the worksheets and modules they contain. To view the procedures stored in a module, you must first select the module in the Project Explorer (just as you would select a file in the Windows Explorer). The **Code window** then displays the selected module's procedures. The **Properties window** displays a list of characteristics (or **properties**) associated with the module. A newly inserted module has only one property, its name.

Analyzing VBA Code

You can learn a lot about the VBA language simply by analyzing the code generated by the Excel macro recorder. The more VBA code you analyze, the easier it will be for you to write your own programming code. Before writing any new procedures, Jim analyzes the procedure he's already written, then opens a worksheet to which he wants to apply the formatting macro and runs the macro.

Steps

1. **With the FormatFile procedure still displayed in the Code window, examine the next four lines of code, beginning with Range("A2").Select**
   See Figure P-3. Every element of Excel, including a range, is considered an **object**. A **range object** represents a cell or a range of cells. The statement *Range("A2").Select* selects the range object cell A2. Notice that several times in the procedure a line of code (or **statement**) selects a range, and then subsequent lines act on that selection. The next statement, *Selection.EntireRow.Insert*, inserts a row above the selection, which is currently cell A2. The next two lines of code select range A3:F3 and apply bold formatting to that selection. In VBA terminology, whether bold formatting is enabled is a value of an object's Bold property. A **property** is an attribute of an object that defines one of the object's characteristics (such as size) or an aspect of its behavior (such as whether it is enabled). The properties of an object are listed in the Properties window. To change the characteristics of an object, you simply change the values of its properties. For example, to apply bold formatting to a selected range, you assign the value True to the range's Bold property. To remove bold formatting, assign the value False.
2. **Examine the remaining lines of code, beginning with Range ("F3").Select**
   The next two statements select the range object cell F3 and center its contents, then the following two statements select the F4:F17 range object and format it as currency. Column objects B through F are then selected and their widths set to AutoFit. Finally, the range object cell A1 is selected, its font size is changed to 12, and its Bold property is set to True. The last line, *End Sub*, indicates the end of the Sub procedure and is also referred to as the **procedure footer**.
3. **Click the View Microsoft Excel button on the Visual Basic Editor Standard toolbar to return to Excel**
   The macro is stored in the KHOT Procedures workbook. This way Jim can use it repeatedly each week after he receives that week's data. You will open the workbook containing data for January 1–7 and run the macro to format that data. You must leave the KHOT Procedures workbook open to use the macro stored there.
4. **Open the workbook titled EX P-2, maximize if necessary, then save it as KHOT Advertising Jan 1-7**
   This is the workbook containing data you want to format.
5. **Press [Ctrl][F] to run the procedure**
   The FormatFile procedure formats the text, as shown in Figure P-4.
6. **Place your name in the worksheet footer, print the worksheet, then save the workbook**
   Now that you've successfully viewed and analyzed code and run the macro, you will learn how to write your own code.

FIGURE P-3: VBA code for the FormatFile procedure

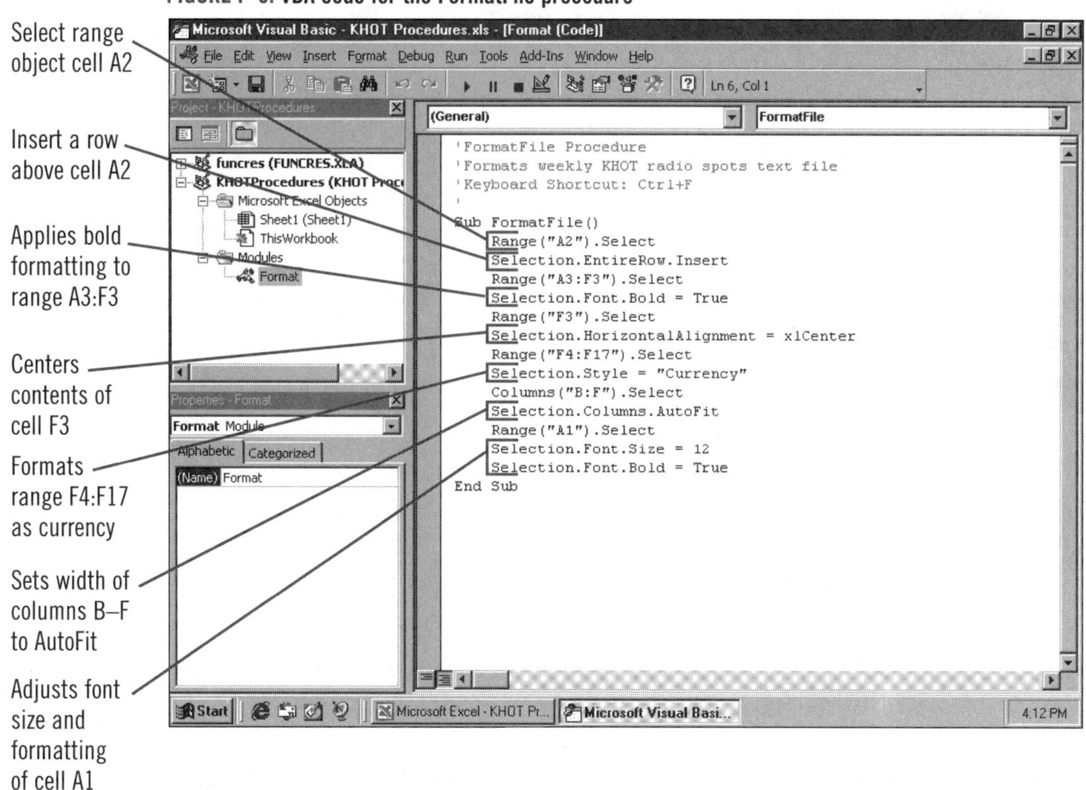

FIGURE P-4: Worksheet formatted using FormatFile procedure

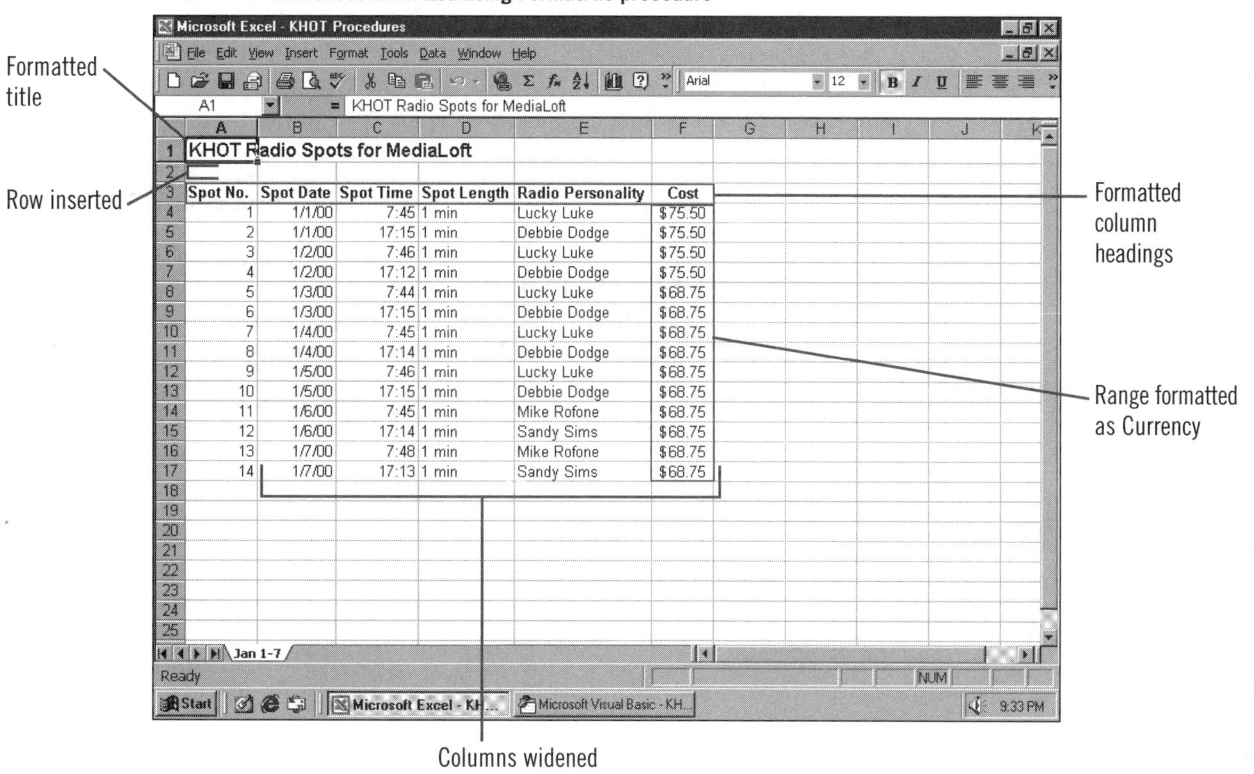

Excel 2000

Writing VBA Code

To write your own code, you first need to open the Visual Basic Editor and add a module to the workbook. You can then begin entering the procedure code. In the first few lines of a procedure, you typically include comments indicating the name of the procedure, a brief description of the procedure, and shortcut keys, if applicable. When writing Visual Basic code for Excel, you must follow the formatting rules, or **syntax**, of the VBA programming language exactly. Even an extra space or a period could cause a procedure to fail. It is important to review the procedure based on the code you've written before you actually run it. Each week, Alice asks Jim to total the cost of the radio ads. Jim decides to write a procedure that will automate this routine task.

Trouble?

If the Code window is empty, verify that the workbook that contains your procedures (KHOT Procedures) is open.

QuickTip

As you type, you may see lists of words in dropdown menus. For now, just continue to type.

Trouble?

If an error message appears, click Debug. Click the Reset button on the Visual Basic Editor Standard toolbar to leave debug mode, correct the error by referring to Figure P-5, then repeat Steps 6–8.

1. **With the Jan 1-7 worksheet still displayed, click Tools on the menu bar, point to Macro, then click Visual Basic Editor**

   Two projects are displayed in the Project Explorer window, KHOT Procedures and KHOT Advertising Jan 1-7. KHOT Procedures is the active project; the Visual Basic title bar confirms this. The FormatFile procedure is again displayed in the Visual Basic Editor.

2. **Click the Modules folder in the KHOT Procedures project**

   You will store all of the procedures in the KHOT Procedures project.

3. **Click Insert on the Visual Basic Editor menu bar, then click Module**

   A new, blank module, with the default name Module1, is inserted in the KHOT Procedures workbook.

4. **Click (Name) in the Properties window, type Total, then press [Enter]**

   This changes the default name to a more descriptive one. The module name ("Total") should not be the same as the procedure name (which will be "AddTotal"). Look at the code shown in Figure P-5. Notice that comments begin with an opening apostrophe and that the lines of code under "Sub AddTotal ( )" have been indented using the Tab key. When you enter the code in the next step, after you type *Sub AddTotal( )* (the procedure header) and press [Enter], the Visual Basic Editor will automatically enter *End Sub* (the procedure footer) in the Code window.

5. **Click in the Code window, then type the procedure code exactly as shown in Figure P-5**

   The lines that begin with *ActiveCell.Formula* insert the information enclosed in quotation marks into the active cell. For example, *ActiveCell.Formula = "Weekly Total:"* inserts the words "Weekly Total:" into cell E18, the active cell. The *With* clause near the bottom of the procedure is used to repeat several operations on the same object.

6. **Compare the procedure code you entered in the Code window with Figure P-5; if necessary, make any corrections; then click the Save KHOT Procedures.xls button on the Visual Basic Editor Standard toolbar**

7. **Click the View Microsoft Excel button on the Visual Basic Editor Standard toolbar, use the Windows menu to display the KHOT Advertising Jan 1-7 workbook, click Tools on the Excel menu bar, point to Macro, then click Macros**

   The Macro dialog box opens. This is where you select the macro procedure you want to run. Notice that the names of the macros have two parts. The first part ('KHOT Procedures.xls'!) indicates the workbook where the macro is stored. The second part (AddTotal or FormatFile) is the name of the procedure, taken from the procedure header.

8. **Click 'KHOT Procedures.xls'!AddTotal if necessary, then click Run**

   The AddTotal procedure inserts and formats the ad expenditure total in cell F18, as shown in Figure P-6.

9. **Save the workbook**

FIGURE P-5: VBA code for the AddTotal procedure

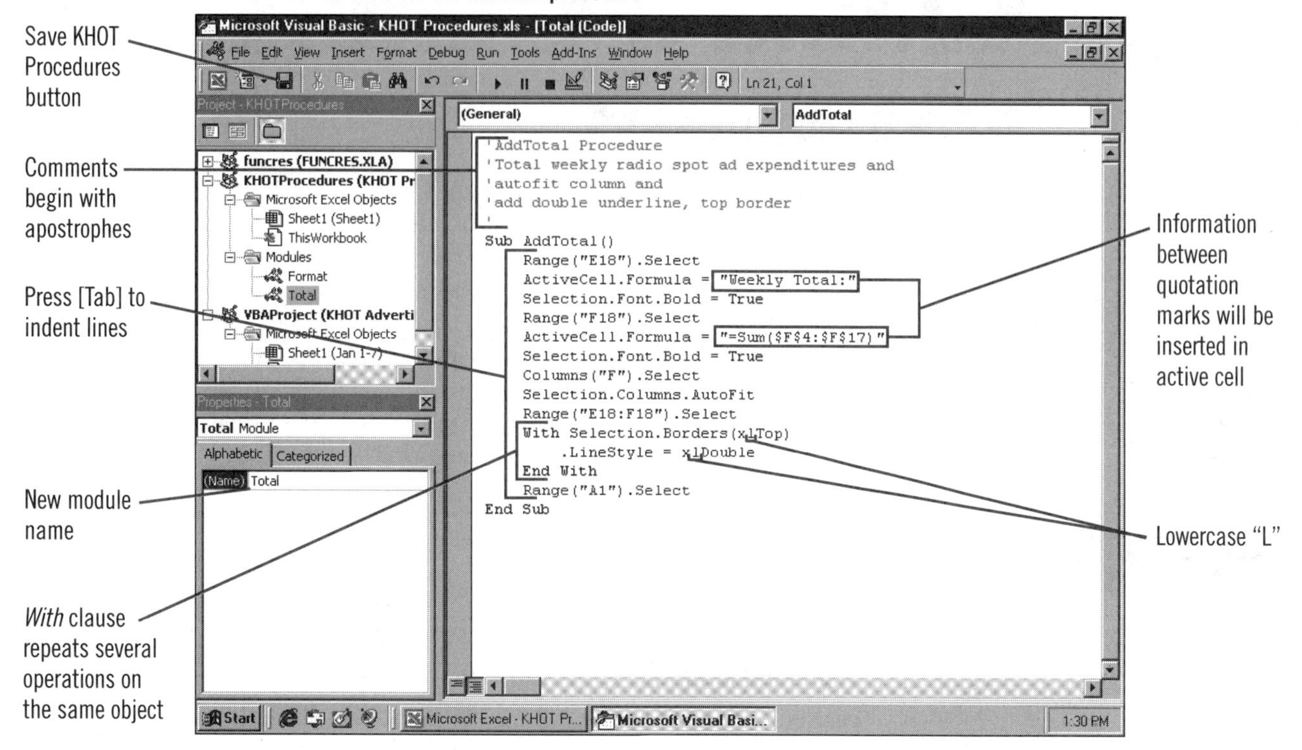

FIGURE P-6: Worksheet after running the AddTotal procedure

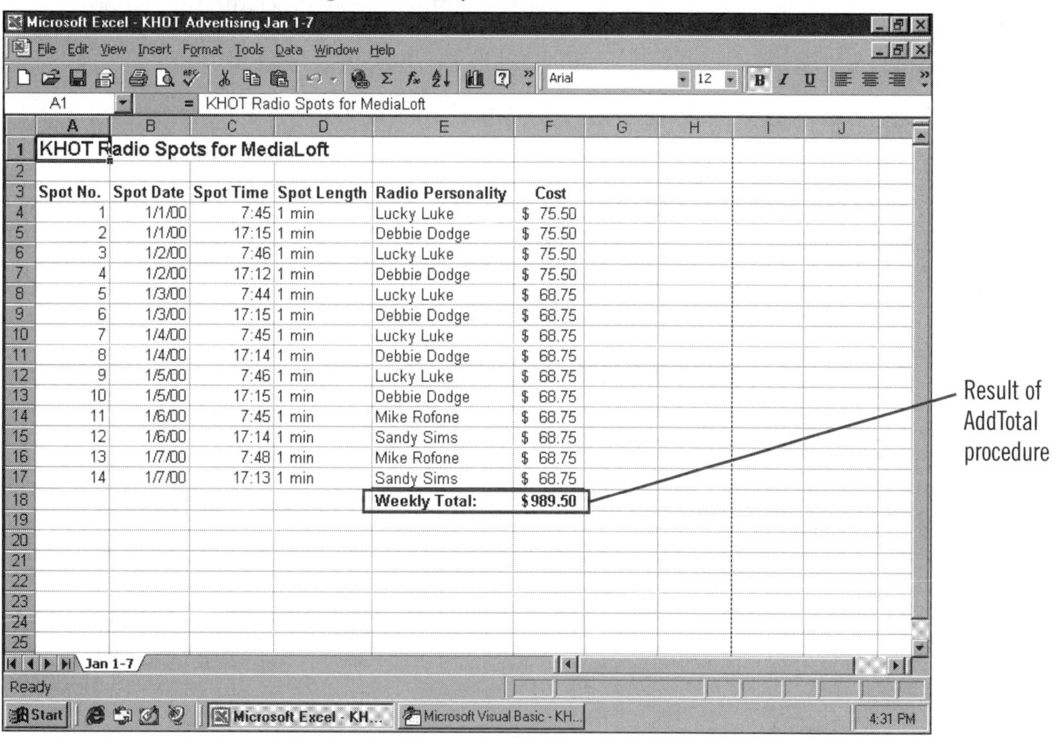

Spot No.	Spot Date	Spot Time	Spot Length	Radio Personality	Cost
1	1/1/00	7:45	1 min	Lucky Luke	$ 75.50
2	1/1/00	17:15	1 min	Debbie Dodge	$ 75.50
3	1/2/00	7:46	1 min	Lucky Luke	$ 75.50
4	1/2/00	17:12	1 min	Debbie Dodge	$ 75.50
5	1/3/00	7:44	1 min	Lucky Luke	$ 68.75
6	1/3/00	17:15	1 min	Debbie Dodge	$ 68.75
7	1/4/00	7:45	1 min	Lucky Luke	$ 68.75
8	1/4/00	17:14	1 min	Debbie Dodge	$ 68.75
9	1/5/00	7:46	1 min	Lucky Luke	$ 68.75
10	1/5/00	17:15	1 min	Debbie Dodge	$ 68.75
11	1/6/00	7:45	1 min	Mike Rofone	$ 68.75
12	1/6/00	17:14	1 min	Sandy Sims	$ 68.75
13	1/7/00	7:48	1 min	Mike Rofone	$ 68.75
14	1/7/00	17:13	1 min	Sandy Sims	$ 68.75
				Weekly Total:	**$989.50**

Entering code

To assist you in entering the macro code, the Editor often displays a list of words that can be used in the macro statement. Typically, the list appears after you press the . (period). To include a word from the list in the macro statement, select the word in the list, then press [Tab]. For example, to enter the *Range("E12").Select* instruction, type *Range(" E12"),* then press the . (period). Type *s* to select the Select command in the list, then press [Tab] to enter the word "Select" in the macro statement.

Excel 2000

Adding a Conditional Statement

Sometimes, you may want a procedure to take an action based on a certain condition or set of conditions. For example, *if* a salesperson's performance rating is a 5 (top rating), *then* calculate a 10% bonus; otherwise (*else*), there is no bonus. One way of adding this type of conditional statement in Visual Basic is by using an **If...Then...Else statement**. The syntax for this statement is: "If *condition* Then *statements* Else [*elsestatements*]." The brackets indicate that the Else part of the statement is optional. Alice wants to find out if the amount spent on radio ads stays within or exceeds the $1,000 budgeted amount. Jim will use Excel to add a conditional statement that indicates this information. He starts by returning to the Visual Basic Editor and inserting a new module in the KHOT Procedures workbook.

Steps

1. With the Jan 1-7 worksheet still displayed, click **Tools** on the menu bar, point to **Macro**, click **Visual Basic Editor**, verify that KHOT Procedures is the active project in the Project Explorer window, click **Insert** on the Visual Basic Editor menu bar, then click **Module**
   A new, blank module is inserted in the KHOT Procedures workbook.
2. In the Properties window click **(Name)**, then type **Budget**
3. Click in the Code window, then type the code exactly as shown in Figure P-7
   Notice the additional comment lines (in green) in the middle of the code. These extra lines help explain the procedure.
4. Compare the procedure you entered with Figure P-7; if necessary, make any corrections; then click the **Save KHOT Procedures.xls button** on the Visual Basic Editor Standard toolbar
5. Click the **View Microsoft Excel button** on the Visual Basic Editor toolbar; click **Tools** on the menu bar; point to **Macro**; click **Macros**; in the Macro dialog box, click **'KHOT Procedures.xls'!BudgetStatus**; then click **Run**
   The BudgetStatus procedure indicates the status—within budget—as shown in Figure P-8.
6. Save your work

QuickTip

The If...Then...Else statement is similar to Excel's IF function.

FIGURE P-7: VBA code for the BudgetStatus procedure

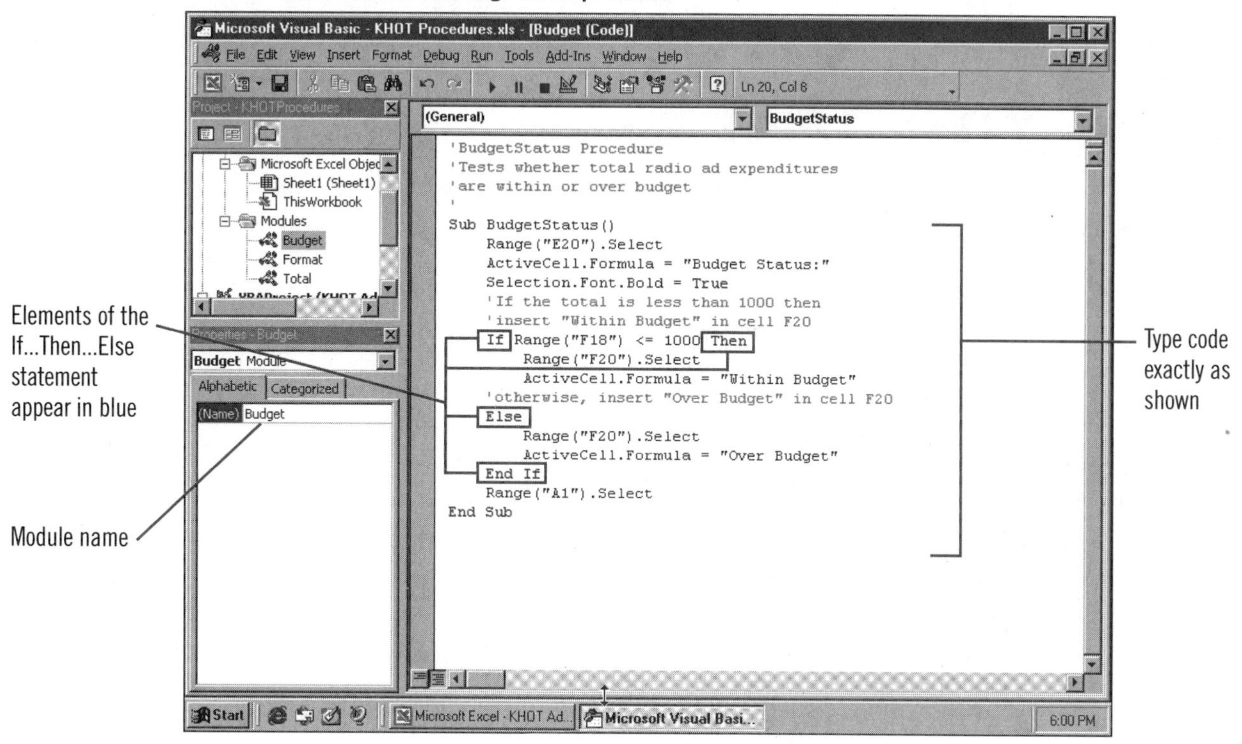

FIGURE P-8: Result of running BudgetStatus procedure

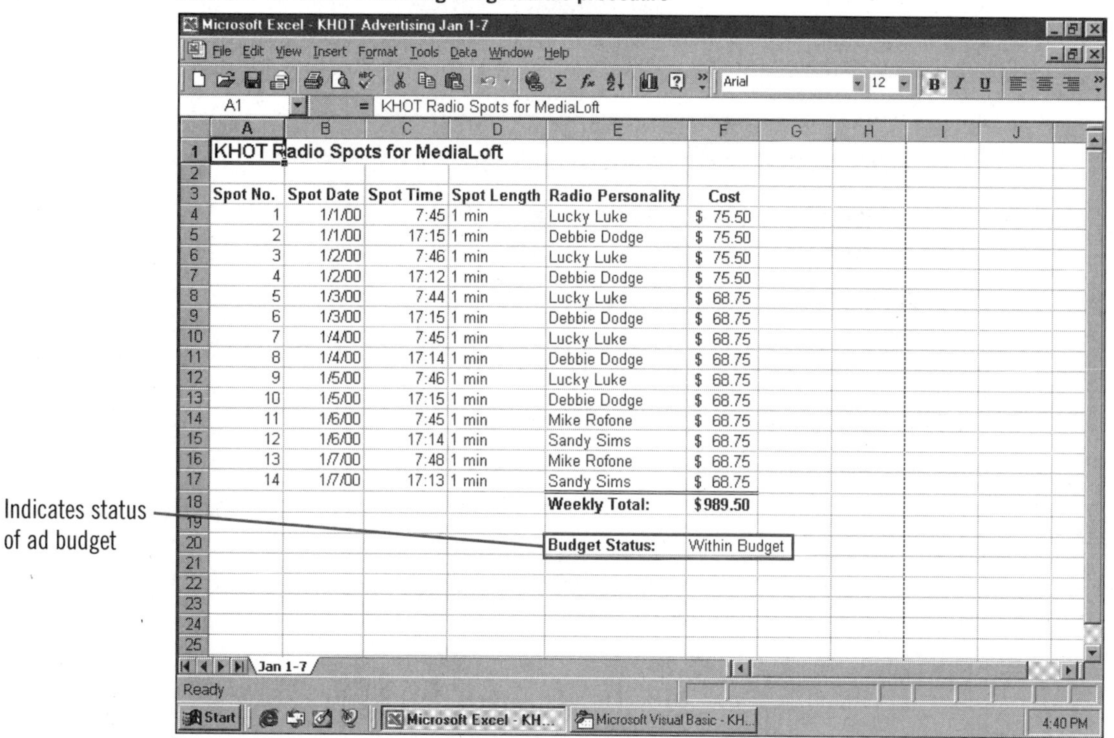

Spot No.	Spot Date	Spot Time	Spot Length	Radio Personality	Cost
1	1/1/00	7:45	1 min	Lucky Luke	$ 75.50
2	1/1/00	17:15	1 min	Debbie Dodge	$ 75.50
3	1/2/00	7:46	1 min	Lucky Luke	$ 75.50
4	1/2/00	17:12	1 min	Debbie Dodge	$ 75.50
5	1/3/00	7:44	1 min	Lucky Luke	$ 68.75
6	1/3/00	17:15	1 min	Debbie Dodge	$ 68.75
7	1/4/00	7:45	1 min	Lucky Luke	$ 68.75
8	1/4/00	17:14	1 min	Debbie Dodge	$ 68.75
9	1/5/00	7:46	1 min	Lucky Luke	$ 68.75
10	1/5/00	17:15	1 min	Debbie Dodge	$ 68.75
11	1/6/00	7:45	1 min	Mike Rofone	$ 68.75
12	1/6/00	17:14	1 min	Sandy Sims	$ 68.75
13	1/7/00	7:48	1 min	Mike Rofone	$ 68.75
14	1/7/00	17:13	1 min	Sandy Sims	$ 68.75
				Weekly Total:	$989.50
				Budget Status:	Within Budget

Excel 2000

Prompting the User for Data

When automating routine tasks, you sometimes need to pause a macro to allow user input. You use VBA's InputBox function to display a dialog box that prompts the user for information. A **function** is a predefined procedure that returns a value; in this case the value returned is the information the user enters. The required elements of an InputBox function are as follows: *object*.InputBox("*prompt*"), where "*prompt*" is the message that appears in the dialog box. For a detailed description of the InputBox function, use the Visual Basic Editor's Help menu. Jim decides to create a procedure that will insert the user's name in the left footer area of the workbook. He'll use the InputBox function to display a dialog box in which the user can enter his or her name.

Steps

1. **With the Jan 1-7 worksheet still displayed, click Tools on the menu bar, point to Macro, click Visual Basic Editor, click Insert on the Visual Basic Editor menu bar, then click Module**
   A new, blank module is inserted in the KHOT Procedures workbook.
2. **In the Properties window, click (Name), then type Footer**
3. **Click in the Code window, then type the procedure code exactly as shown in Figure P-9**
   Like the Budget procedure, this procedure also contains comments that explain the code. The first part of the code, *Dim LeftFooterText As String,* **declares**, or defines, *LeftFooterText* as a text string variable. In Visual Basic, a **variable** is a slot in memory in which you can temporarily store one item of information. Dim statements are used to declare variables and must be entered in the following format: Dim *variablename* As *datatype*. The datatype here is "string." In this case, you plan to store the information received from the input box in the temporary memory slot called LeftFooterText. Then you can place this text in the left footer area. The remaining statements in the procedure are explained in the comment line directly above each statement.
4. **Review your code for errors, make any changes if necessary, then click the Save KHOT Procedures.xls button on the Visual Basic Editor Standard toolbar**
5. **Click the View Microsoft Excel button on the Visual Basic Editor toolbar, click Tools on the menu bar, point to Macro, click Macros, in the Macro dialog box click 'KHOT Procedures.xls'!FooterInput, then click Run**
   The procedure begins, and a dialog box generated by the InputBox function appears, prompting you to enter your name. See Figure P-10.
6. **With the cursor in the text box, type your name, then click OK**
7. **Click the Print Preview button on the Standard toolbar**
   Although the customized footer is inserted on the sheet, notice that, due to an error, your name does *not* appear in the left section of the footer. In the next lesson, you will learn how to step through a procedure's code, line by line. This will help you locate the error in the Footer procedure.
8. **Click Close**
   This closes the Print Preview window and returns you to the Jan 1-7 worksheet.

QuickTip

To enlarge your Code window, place the mouse pointer on the left border of the Code window until it turns into ⟺, then drag the border to the left until the Code window is the desired size.

QuickTip

If your macro doesn't run correctly, it may contain a spelling or syntax error. You'll learn how to correct such macro errors in the next lesson.

FIGURE P-9: VBA code for the FooterInput procedure

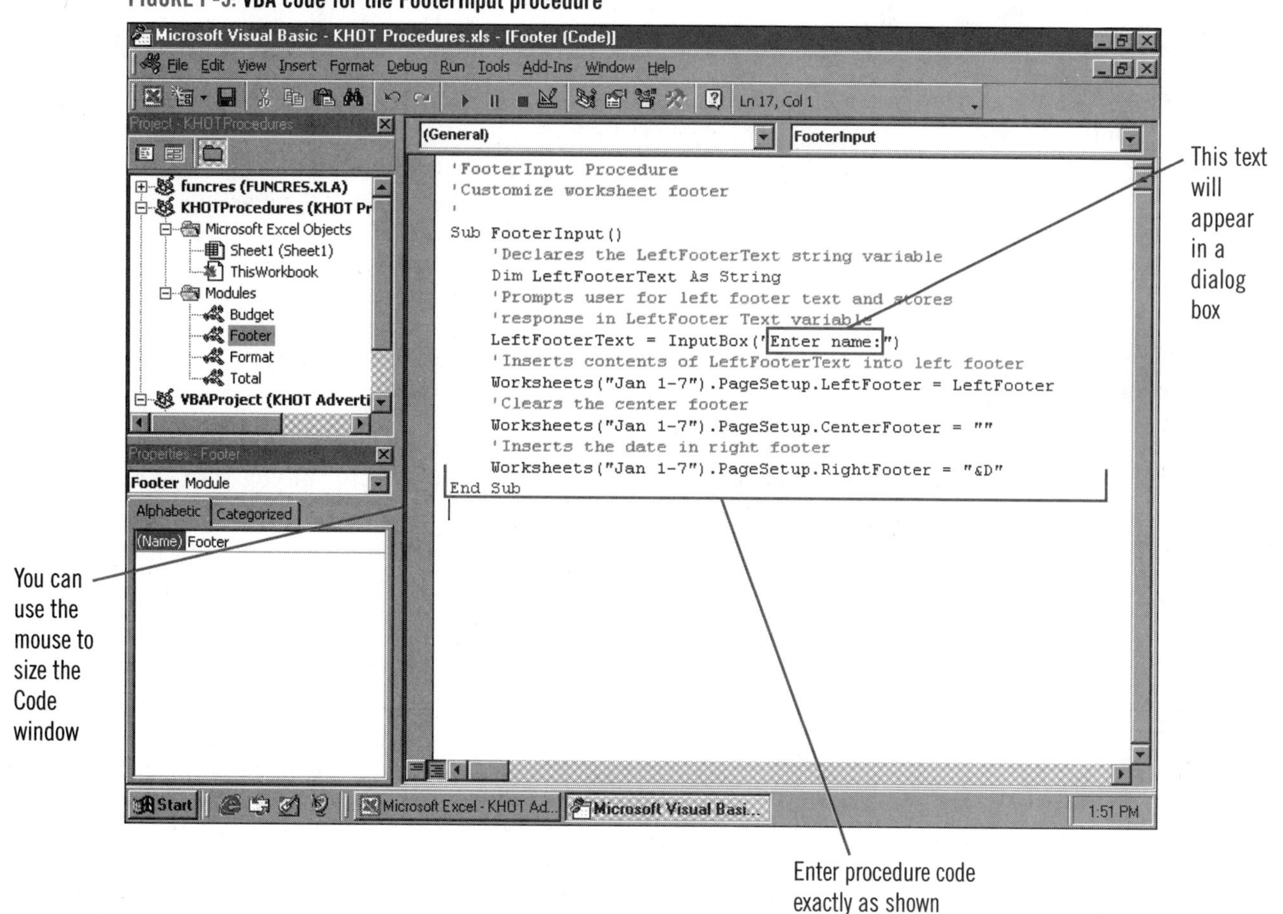

FIGURE P-10: InputBox function's dialog box

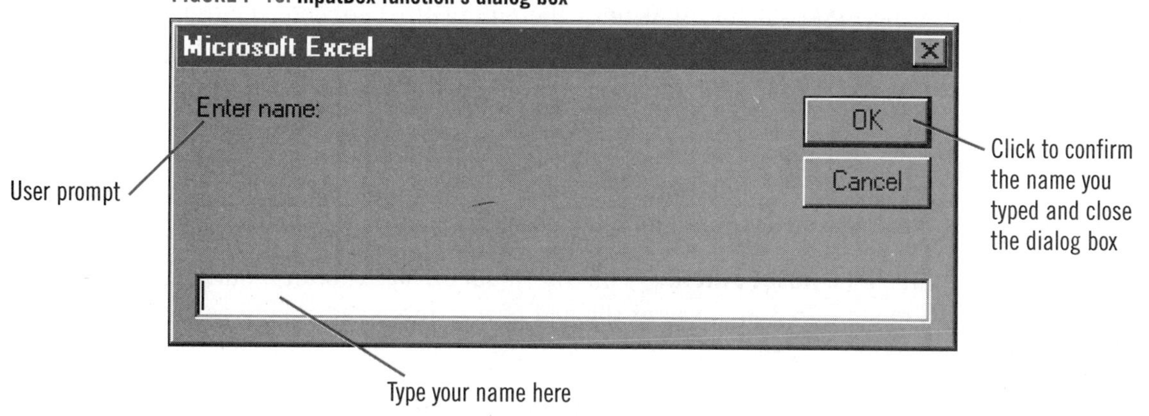

Excel 2000

Excel 2000

Debugging a Macro

When a macro procedure does not run properly, it can be due to an error, referred to as a **bug**, in the code. To assist you in finding the bug(s) in a procedure, you can use the Visual Basic Editor to step through the procedure's code, one line at a time. When you locate the error (bug), you can then correct, or **debug**, it. Jim decides to debug the macro procedure to find out why it failed to insert his name in the worksheet's footer.

Steps

1. With the KHOT Advertising Jan 1-7 workbook still displayed, click **Tools** on the menu bar; point to **Macro**; click **Macros**; in the Macro dialog box, click **'KHOT Procedures.xls'!FooterInput**; then click **Step Into**
   The Visual Basic Editor appears with the statement selector positioned on the first statement of the procedure. See Figure P-11.
2. Press **[F8]** to step through the code
   The statement selector skips over the comments and the line of code beginning with Dim. The Dim statement indicates that the procedure will store your name in a variable named LeftFooterText. Because Dim is a declaration of a variable and not a procedure statement, the statement selector skips it and moves to the line containing the InputBox function.
3. Press **[F8]** again; with the cursor in the text box in the InputBox function dialog box, type your name, then click **OK**
   The Visual Basic Editor reappears. The statement selector is now positioned on the statement that reads *Worksheets ("Jan 1-7").PageSetup.LeftFooter = LeftFooter*. This statement inserts your name (which you just typed in the Input Box) in the left section of the footer. This is the instruction that does not appear to be working correctly.
4. If necessary, scroll right until the end of the LeftFooter instruction is visible, then place the mouse pointer on **LeftFooter**, as shown in Figure P-12
   The last part of the InputBox function should be the variable (LeftFooterText) where the procedure stored your name. Rather than containing your name, however, the variable at the end of the procedure is empty. That's because the InputBox function assigned your name to the LeftFooterText variable, not to the LeftFooter variable. Before you can correct this bug, you need to turn off the Step Into feature.
5. Click the **Reset button** on the Visual Basic Editor Standard toolbar to turn off the Step Into feature, click at the end of the statement, then type **Text**
   The revised statement now reads *Worksheets("Jan 1-7").PageSetup.LeftFooter = LeftFooterText.*
6. Click the **Save KHOT Procedures.xls button** on the Visual Basic Editor Standard toolbar, then click the **View Microsoft Excel button** on the Visual Basic Editor toolbar
7. Click **Tools** on the menu bar, point to **Macro**, click **Macros**; in the Macro dialog box, click **'KHOT Procedures.xls'!FooterInput**; click **Run** to rerun the procedure; when prompted, type your name; then click **OK**
8. Click the **Print Preview button** on the Standard toolbar
   Your name now appears in the bottom-left section of the footer.
9. Click **Close**, save the workbook, then print your work

FIGURE P-11: Statement selector positioned on first procedure statement

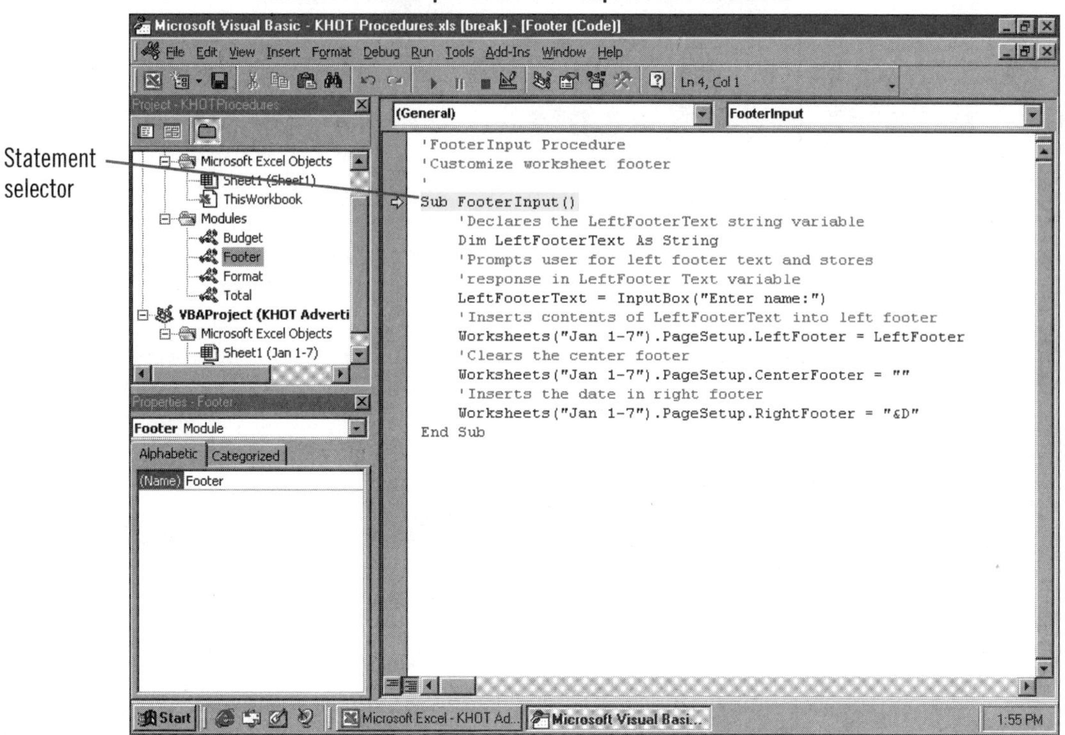

FIGURE P-12: Value contained in LeftFooter variable

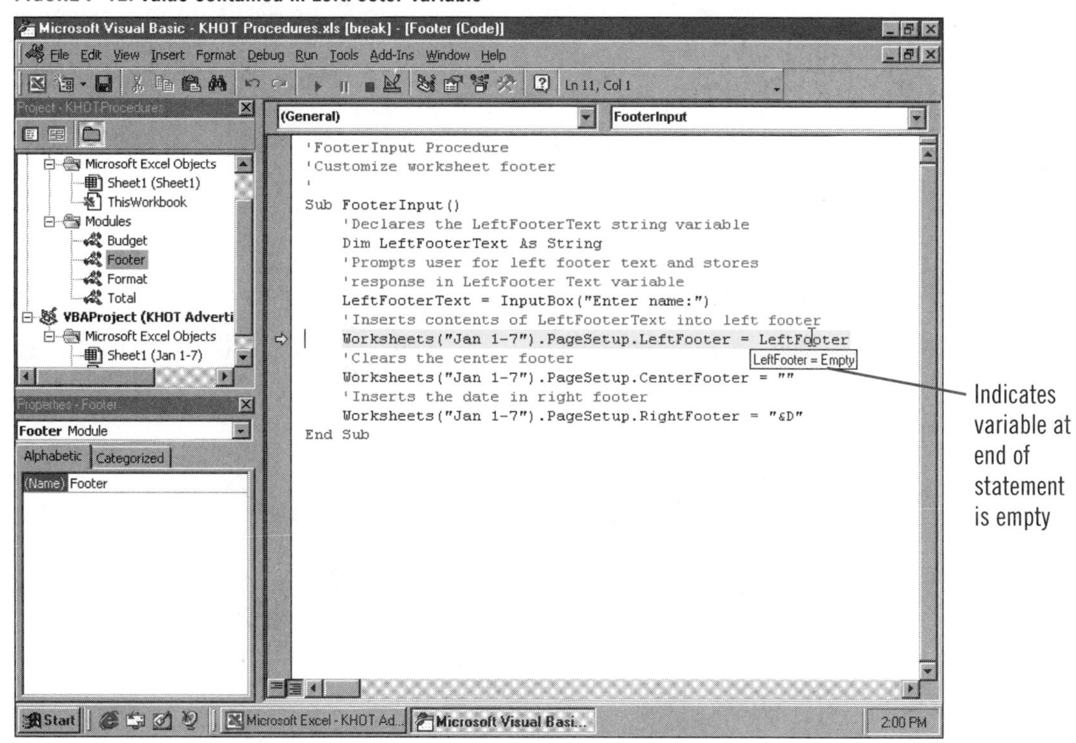

Creating a Main Procedure

When you routinely need to run several macros one after another, you can save time by combining them into one procedure. The resulting procedure, which processes (or runs) multiple procedures in sequence, is referred to as the **main procedure**. To create a main procedure, you type a Call statement for each procedure you want to run. The syntax of the Call statement is Call *procedurename*, where *procedurename* is the name of the procedure you want to run. To avoid having to run his macros one after another every month, Jim decides to create a main procedure that will run (or call) each of the procedures in the KHOT Procedures workbook in sequence.

Steps

1. With the Jan 1-7 worksheet displayed, click **Tools** on the menu bar, point to **Macro**, then click **Visual Basic Editor**
2. Verify that KHOT Procedures is the active project, Click **Insert** on the menu bar, then click **Module**
   A new, blank module is inserted in the KHOT Procedures workbook.
3. In the Properties window, click **(Name)**, then type **MainProc**
4. In the Code window, enter the procedure code exactly as shown in Figure P-13
5. Compare your main procedure code with Figure P-13, correct any errors if necessary, then click the **Save KHOT Procedures.xls button** on the Visual Basic Editor Standard toolbar
   To test the new main procedure you need an unformatted version of the KHOT radio spot workbook.
6. Click the **View Microsoft Excel button** on the Visual Basic Editor Standard toolbar, then close the KHOT Advertising Jan 1-7 workbook, saving your changes
   The KHOT Procedures workbook remains open.
7. Open the workbook titled EX P-2, then save it as **KHOT Advertising Jan 1-7 Version 2**
   In the next lesson, you'll run the main procedure.

FIGURE P-13: VBA code for the MainProcedure procedure

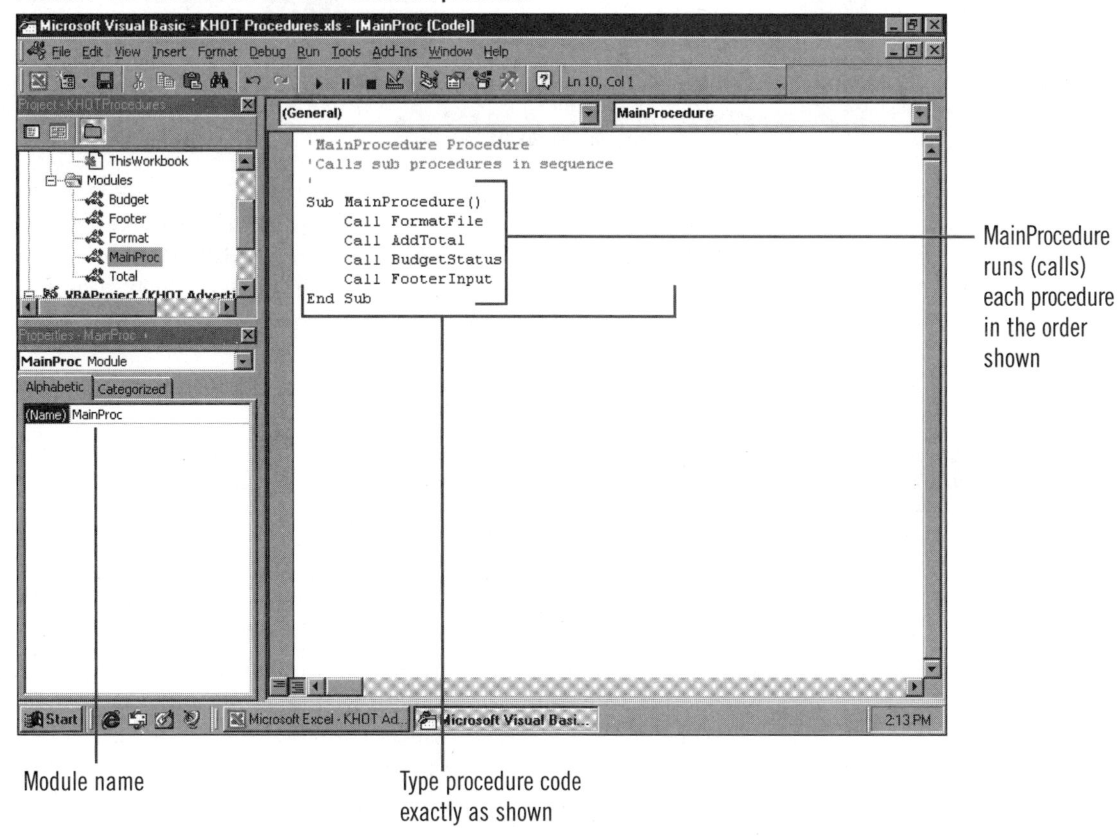

Excel 2000

Running a Main Procedure

Running a main procedure allows you to instantly run several macros in sequence. You can run a main procedure just as you would any other macro procedure—by selecting it in the Macro dialog box, then clicking Run. Jim has finished creating his main procedure and is now ready to run it. If the main procedure works correctly, it should format the worksheet, insert a budget status message, insert the ad expenditure total, and add Jim's name to the worksheet footer.

Steps

1. With the Jan 1-7 Version 2 worksheet displayed, click **Tools** on the menu bar, point to **Macro**, and click **Macros**; in the Macro dialog box click **'KHOT Procedures.xls'! MainProcedure**; click **Run**; when prompted type your name, then click **OK**
   The MainProcedure runs the FormatFile, AddTotal, BudgetStatus, and FooterInput procedures in sequence. See Figure P-14. You can see the results of the FormatFile, AddTotal, and BudgetStatus procedures in the worksheet window. To view the results of the FooterInput procedure, you need to switch to the Preview window.
2. Click the **Print Preview button** on the Standard toolbar, verify that your name appears in the left footer area, then click **Close**
   You could print each procedure separately, but it's faster to print all the procedures in the workbook at one time.
3. Click **Tools** on the menu bar, point to **Macro**, then click **Visual Basic Editor**
4. In the Project Explorer window, double-click each procedure and add a comment line after the procedure name that reads "Written by [your name]"
5. Click **File** on the Visual Basic Editor menu bar, then click **Print**
   The Print - KHOTProcedures dialog box opens, as shown in Figure P-15. Collectively, all procedures in a workbook are known as a project, as mentioned earlier in the unit.
6. In the Print - KHOTProcedures dialog box, select the **Current Project option button** if necessary, then click **OK**
   Each procedure prints on a separate page.
7. Click the **View Microsoft Excel button** on the Visual Basic Editor Standard toolbar
8. Save the workbook and close it, close the KHOT Procedures workbook, then exit Excel

FIGURE P-14: Result of running MainProcedure procedure

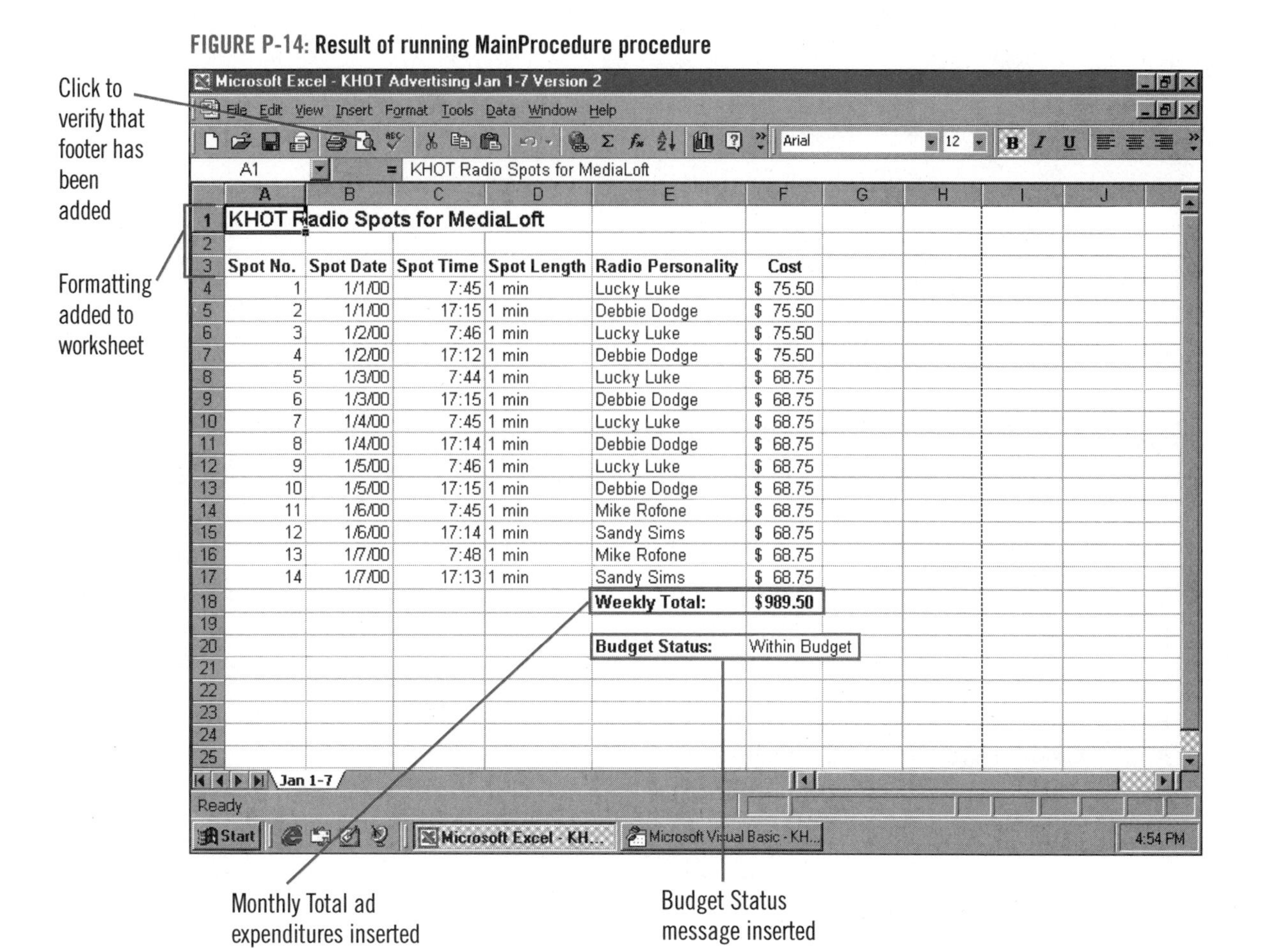

FIGURE P-15: Printing the macro procedures

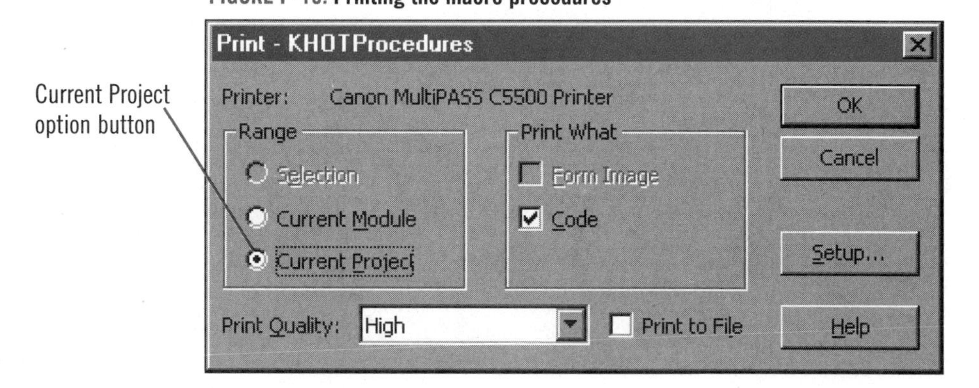

Excel 2000

Practice

► Concepts Review

Label each element of the Visual Basic Editor screen shown in Figure P-16.

FIGURE P-16

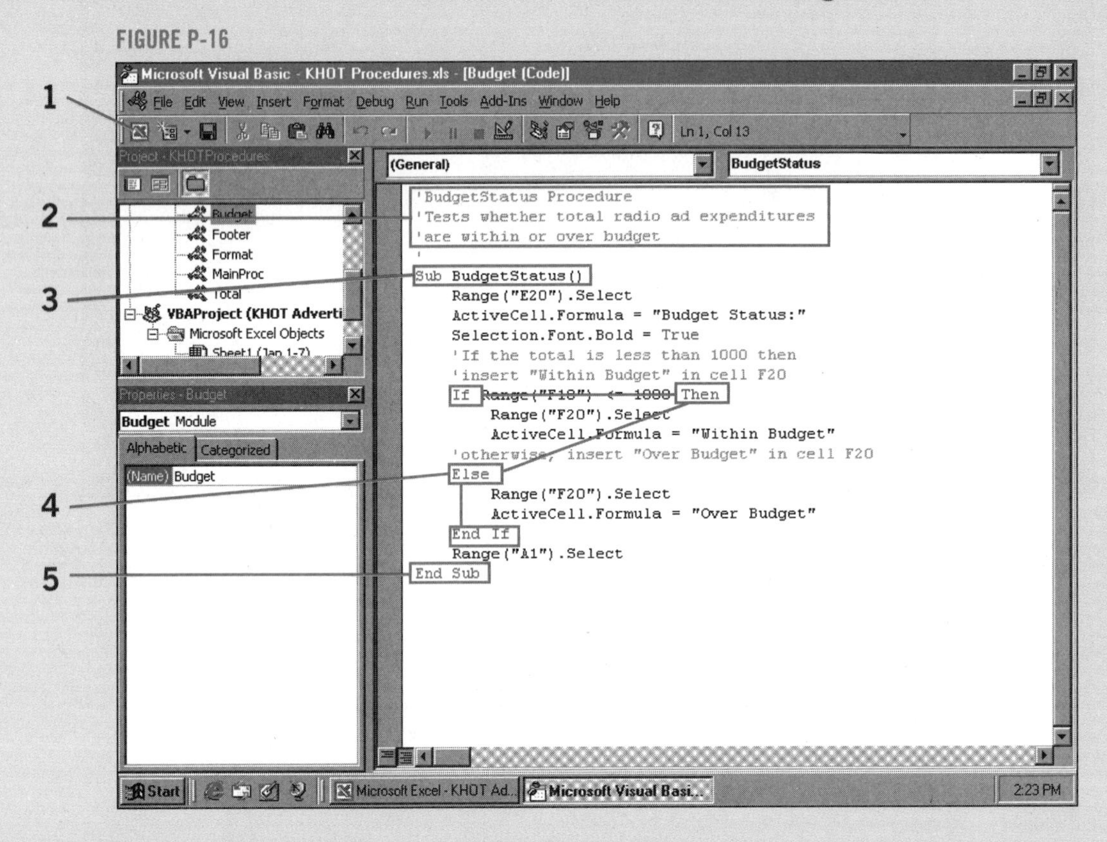

Match each term with the statement that describes it.

6. **Sub procedure**
7. **Procedure**
8. **Keywords**
9. **Function**
10. **Comments**

a. Another term for a macro in Visual Basic for Applications (VBA)
b. A procedure that returns a value
c. Words that are recognized as part of the programming language
d. A series of statements that perform an action but don't return a value
e. Descriptive text used to explain parts of a procedure

Select the best answer from the list of choices.

11. You enter the statements of a macro in
- **a.** The Macro dialog box.
- **b.** Any blank worksheet.
- **c.** The Properties window of the Visual Basic Editor.
- **d.** The Code window of the Visual Basic Editor.

12. What must you keep in mind when typing VBA code?
- **a.** Typographical errors can cause your procedures to fail.
- **b.** You can edit your code just as you would text in a word processor.
- **c.** The different parts of the code will appear in different colors.
- **d.** All of the above.

13. If your macro doesn't run correctly, you should
- **a.** Create an If . . . Then . . . Else statement.
- **b.** Select the macro in the Macro dialog box, click Step Into, and then debug the macro.
- **c.** Debug the macro in the worksheet window.
- **d.** Close the workbook and start over with a new macro.

▶ Skills Review

1. View and analyze VBA code.
- **a.** Open the workbook titled EX P-3, then save it as "Mission Medical Inc".
- **b.** Review the unformatted worksheet named Sheet1.
- **c.** Open the Visual Basic Editor.
- **d.** Select the ListFormat module.
- **e.** Insert comments in the List Format code describing what action you think each line of code will perform. (*Hint:* One of the statements will sort the list alphabetically by customer name.)
- **f.** Run the FormatList macro.
- **g.** Compare the results with the code and your comments.
- **h.** Save the workbook.

2. Write VBA code.
- **a.** Open Visual Basic Editor and insert a new module named "Total".
- **b.** Enter the Code exactly as shown in Figure P-17.
- **c.** Run the SalesTotal macro.
- **d.** Save the workbook.

FIGURE P-17

```
'SalesTotal Procedure
'Totals monthly sales
Sub SalesTotal()
  Range("F17").Select
  ActiveCell.Formula = "=SUM($F$2:$F$16)"
  Selection.Font.Bold = True
  With Selection.Borders(xlTop)
   .LineStyle = xlSingle
  End With
  Range("A1").Select
End Sub
```

3. Add a conditional statement.

a. Open Visual Basic Editor and insert a new module named "Goal".

b. Enter the procedure exactly as shown in Figure P-18.

c. Run the SalesGoal macro. If the procedure returns the message "Missed goal", the procedure worked as planned.

d. Save the workbook.

FIGURE P-18

```
'SalesGoal Procedure
'Tests whether sales goal was met
'
Sub SalesGoal()
  'If the total is >= 225000, then insert "Met Goal"
  'in cell G17
  If Range("F17") >= 225000 Then
   Range("G17").Select
   ActiveCell.Formula = "Met goal"
  'otherwise, insert "Missed goal" in cell G17
  Else
   Range("G17").Select
   ActiveCell.Formula = "Missed goal"
  End If
End Sub
```

4. Prompt the user for data.

a. Open Visual Basic Editor and insert a new module named "Header".

b. Enter the procedure exactly as shown in Figure P-19.

c. Run the HeaderFooter macro. When you encounter a runtime error, click End.

d. Save the workbook.

FIGURE P-19

```
'HeaderFooter Procedure
'Procedure to customize the header and footer
'
Sub HeaderFooter()
  'Inserts the filename in the header
  Worksheets("Sheet1").PageSetup.CenterHeader = "&F"
  'Declares the variable LeftFooterText as a string
  Dim LeftFooterText As String
  'Prompts user for left footer text
  LeftFooter = InputBox("Enter your full name:")
  'Inserts response into left footer
  Workbooks("Sheet1").PageSetup.LeftFooter = LeftFooterText
  Workbooks("Sheet1").PageSetup.CenterFooter = ""
  Workbooks("Sheet1").PageSetup.RightFooter = "&D"
End Sub
```

5. **Debug a macro.**
   a. Run the HeaderFooter macro. When you encounter a runtime error, click Debug.
   b. The statement selector is positioned on the incorrect procedure statement: *Workbooks("Sheet1").PageSetup.LeftFooter = LeftFooterText.* (*Hint:* Note that Workbooks, instead of Worksheets, was entered in the statement.)
   c. Change *Workbooks* in the incorrect line of code to *Worksheets.* Do the same in the two following lines of code.
   d. Rerun the HeaderFooter procedure.
   e. Check the header and footer. Notice that the procedure does not display your name in the left section of the footer.
   f. Use the Step Into feature to find the error in the code and then correct it. Make sure you leave Debugger mode by clicking the Reset button.
   g. Rerun the HeaderFooter procedure.
   h. Verify that your name now appears in the left section of the footer.
   i. Save the workbook.
6. **Create and run a main procedure.**
   a. Return to the Visual Basic Editor, insert a new module, and name it "MainProc".
   b. Enter comments that give the procedure's name (MainProcedure), and explain its purpose.
   c. Enter the following procedure header: *Sub MainProcedure ().*
   d. Enter four Call statements that will run the FormatList, SalesTotal, SalesGoal, and HeaderFooter procedures in sequence.
   e. Save the procedure and return to Excel.
   f. Open the EX P-3 workbook, then save it as Medical Mission Inc Version 2.
   g. Run the MainProcedure procedure. (*Hint:* In the Macro dialog box, the macro procedures you created will now have *'Medical Mission Inc.xls'!* as part of their names. That's because the macros are stored in the Medical Mission Inc workbook, and not in the Medical Mission Inc Version 2 workbook.)
   h. Save the Medical Mission Inc Version 2 workbook, print the worksheet, then close the workbook.
   i. Print the current project's code.
   j. Return to Excel and close any open workbooks.

Independent Challenges

1. Your officemate William is on vacation for two weeks, and you have taken over his projects. The office manager, Monique, asks you to document the Excel procedure that William wrote (called DoYourThing) for the company's auditors. You have located the workbook containing the procedure; now you will document it.

To complete this independent challenge:

a. Open the workbook titled EX P-4, then save it as "Mystery Procedure".
b. Run the DoYourThing procedure, noting anything you think should be mentioned in your documentation.
c. Review the procedure in the Visual Basic Editor.
d. Document the procedure by annotating the printed code, indicating the actions the procedure performs and the objects (ranges) that are affected.
e. Print the procedures code.
f. Save and close the workbook.

2. You work in the sales office of a large automobile dealership called Auto Heaven. Each month you are required to produce a report stating whether sales quotas were met for the following five vehicle categories: compacts, sedans, sports/utility, vans, and trucks. This quarter the sales quotas for each month are as follows: compacts 50, sedans 35, sports/utility 20, vans 19, and trucks 40. The results this month (Jan 1-7) were 53, 32, 12, 25, and 35, respectively. You decide to create a procedure to automate your monthly task of determining the sales quota status for the vehicle categories. You would like the new clerk to take this task over when you go on vacation next month. Because the clerk has no previous experience with Excel, you decide to add input boxes that prompt the user to enter the actual sales results for the month.

To complete this independent challenge:

a. Create a workbook to be used as a monthly template, then save it as "Sales Quota Status".
b. Create a procedure using multiple If... Then... Else statements to determine the sales quota status for each vehicle category automatically.
c. Add input boxes to prompt the user for the actual sales data for each vehicle category. (*Hint:* You can use a combination of statements using InputBox and ActiveCell.)
d. Record a new macro called Shortcut that assigns [Ctrl]+[Q] to run the Monthly Sales macro. Insert a line on the worksheet that tells the user to press [Ctrl]+[Q] to enter sales data.
e. Test the procedure. Correct any problems.
f. Save your work, insert your name in a "Created by" line below the procedure name, then print the code.
g. Close the workbook.

3. You are an internal auditor for a large food manufacturer called Earthly Treats. You are responsible for ensuring that staff members document their Excel worksheets properly. To help the staff document their worksheets more efficiently, you decide to create two procedures. The first procedure will automate the process of displaying worksheet formulas. The second will prompt the user for his or her department name and insert that information in the footer, then print the worksheet and delete it. The company name and the date should appear in the footer as well. After you create the two procedures, you will create a main procedure to run them in sequence.

To complete this independent challenge:

a. Create a workbook, then save it as "Documentation Procedures".
b. Create a procedure that opens a new worksheet, enters "Earthly Treats Report" in cell A1, turns on formula display in the new sheet, and uses AutoFit to fit the new sheet's columns.
c. Create a procedure that creates the footer as described above. The procedure should also print the new formula sheet, then delete the new sheet as the last step. (*Hint:* You can use the Macro Recorder to create the procedure.)
d. Create a main procedure that calls the new worksheet procedure and the footer/print procedure in sequence.
e. Save, test, then debug each procedure.
f. Insert your name in a "Created by" line under the procedure name, then print the code for the current project.
g. Save your work, then close the workbook.

4. Alice Wegman, MedialLoft's marketing manager, would like to know how important the radio spots on KHOT are to MediaLoft's marketing strategy. Jim Fernandez has asked you to get a copy of the MediaLoft Advertising Campaign chart and create a formatting procedure to highlight the KHOT radio spots.

To complete this independent challenge:

a. Connect to the Internet, and go to the MediaLoft intranet site at http://www.course.com/Illustrated/MediaLoft. Click the Marketing link, then click the MediaLoft Advertising Campaigns link.
b. Select the table and drag it into a blank Excel workbook and save the workbook as "MediaLoft Ad Campaign".
c. Insert a module and create a procedure that will insert rows above and below the KHOT radio spots information row, then change the text for the radio spot row to bold and the KHOT effectiveness rating to a 14-point font.
d. Run the procedure, add your name to the workbook footer, and print the results.
e. Save the workbook and close Excel.

► Visual Workshop

Open the workbook titled EX P-5 and save it as "Big Time Audio". Create a macro procedure that will format the worksheet as shown in Figure P-20.

FIGURE P-20

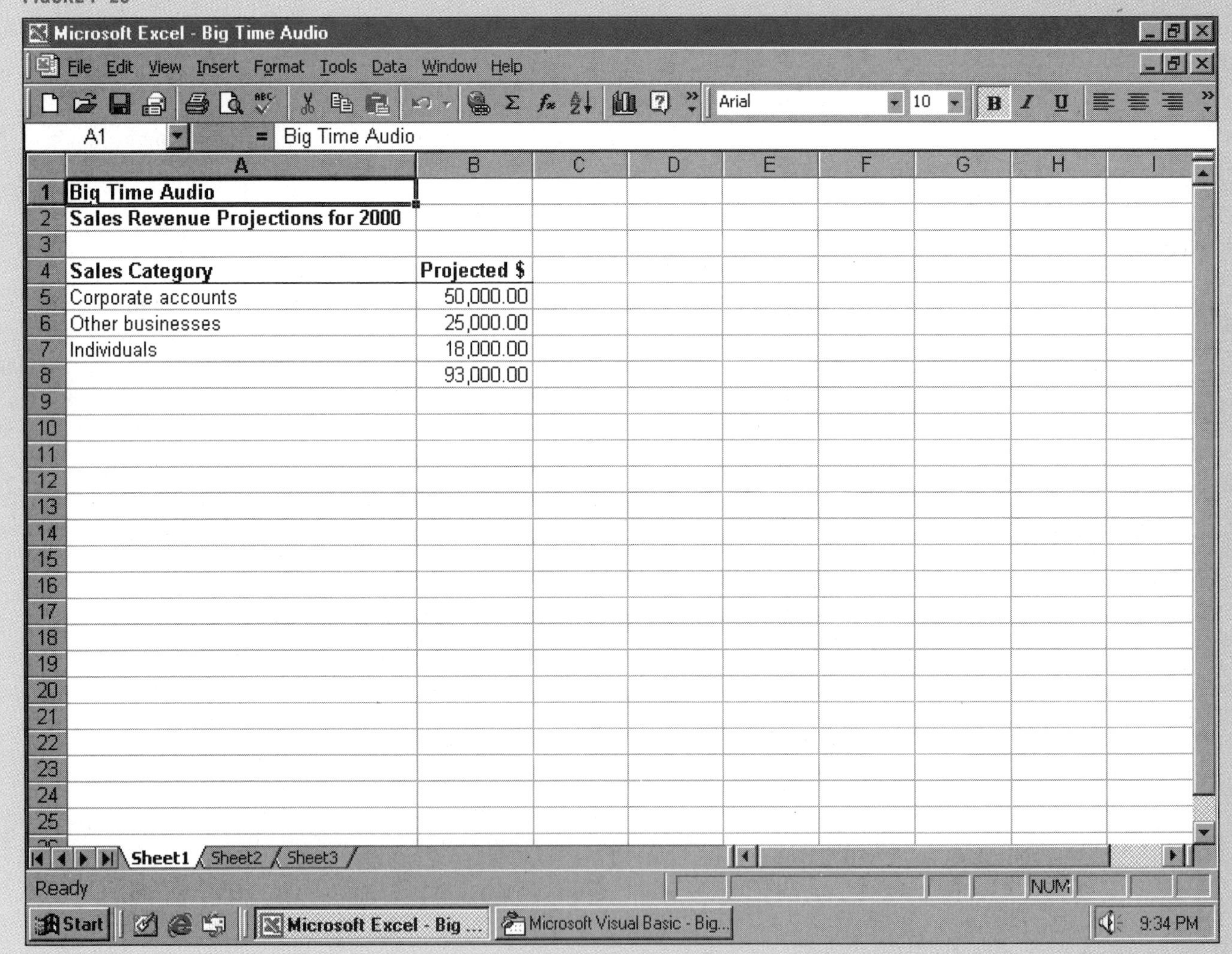

Excel 2000 MOUS Certification Objectives

Below is a list of the Microsoft Office User Specialist program objectives for Core and Expert Excel 2000 skills showing where each MOUS objective is covered in the Lessons and the Practice. This table lists the Core and Expert MOUS certification skills covered in the units in this book. For more information on which Illustrated titles meet MOUS certification, please see the inside cover of this book.

MOUS standardized coding number	Activity	Lesson page where skill is covered	Location in lesson where skill is covered	Practice
XL2000E.1	**Importing and exporting data**			
XL2000E.1.1	Import data from text files (insert, drag and drop)	Excel M-4 Excel M-5	Steps 1–5 Clues to Use	Skills Review 1, Independent Challenge 1
XL2000E.1.2	Import from other applications	Excel M-6	Steps 1–2	Skills Review 2, Independent Challenge 2
XL2000E.1.3	Import a table from an HTML file (insert, drag and drop — including HTML round tripping)	Excel M-9	Clues to Use	Independent Challenge 4
XL2000E.1.4	Export to other applications	Excel M-7 Excel M-16	Clues to Use Steps 1–9	
XL2000E.2	**Using templates**			
XL2000E.2.1	Apply templates	Excel O-17	Clues to Use	Skills Review 8, Independent Challenge 4
XL2000E.2.2	Edit templates	Excel O-17	Clues to Use	Skills Review 8, Independent Challenge 4
XL2000E.2.3	Create templates	Excel O-16	Steps 1–6	Skills Review 8, Independent Challenge 4
XL2000E.3	**Using multiple workbooks**			
XL2000E.3.1	Using a workspace	Excel F-11	Clues to Use	
XL2000E.3.2	Link workbooks	Excel F-14 Excel F-7	Steps 1–2 Clues to Use	Skills Review 7, Independent Challenge 4 Skills Review 3
XL2000E.4	**Formatting numbers**			
XL2000E.4.1	Apply number formats (Accounting, Currency, Number)	Excel C-2 (Currency) Excel M-4 (Currency) Excel M-4 (Number) Excel M-4 (Accounting)	Step 3 QuickTip Step 7 QuickTip	Skills Review 1, Independent Challenge 2 Independent Challenge 2 Skills Review 2
XL2000E.4.2	Create custom number formats	Excel E-9	Clues to Use	Independent Challenge 1
XL2000E.4.3	Use conditional formatting	Excel C-14	Steps 1–7	Skills Review 7, Independent Challenges 2, 4

MOUS standardized coding number	Activity	Lesson page where skill is covered	Location in lesson where skill is covered	Practice
XL2000E.5	**Printing workbooks**			
XL2000E.5.1	Print and preview multiple worksheets	Excel O-15	Clues to Use	Skills Review 7
XL2000E.5.2	Use the Report Manager	Excel F-10 Excel K-7	QuickTip Clues to Use	
XL2000E.6	**Working with named ranges**			
XL2000E.6.1	Add and delete a named range	Excel B-5 (Adding) Excel B-17 (Adding) Excel K-6 (Deleting)	Clues to Use Clues to Use QuickTip	Skills Review 1, Independent Challenge 1 Independent Challenge 1
XL2000E.6.2	Use a named range in a formula	Excel B-17 Excel I-14	Clues to Use Steps 2–3	Skills Review 6
XL2000E.6.3	Use Lookup Functions (HLOOKUP or VLOOKUP)	Excel I-13 (HLOOKUP) Excel I-12 (VLOOKUP)	Clues to Use Steps 1–8	Skills Review 5, Independent Challenge 3
XL2000E.7	**Working with toolbars**			
XL2000E.7.1	Hide and display toolbars	Excel G-16 Excel O-5	QuickTip Clues to Use	Skills Review 2
XL2000E.7.2	Customize a toolbar	Excel G-16	Steps 1–8	Skills Review 7, Independent Challenges 1, 2
XL2000E.7.3	Assign a macro to a command button	Excel G-16	Steps 1–8	Skills Review 7, Independent Challenges 1, 2
XL2000E.8	**Using macros**			
XL2000E.8.1	Record macros	Excel G-4	Steps 1–8	Skills Review 1
XL2000E.8.2	Run macros	Excel G-6	Steps 1–8	Skills Review 2
XL2000E.8.3	Edit macros	Excel G-8	Steps 1–6	Skills Review 3
XL2000E.9	**Auditing a worksheet**			
XL2000E.9.1	Work with the Auditing toolbar	Excel O-4	Step 2	Skills Review 2, Independent Challenge 1
XL2000E.9.2	Trace errors (find and fix errors)	Excel O-4	Step 3	Skills Review 2, Independent Challenge 1
XL2000E.9.3	Trace precedents (find cells referred to in a specific formula)	Excel O-4	Step 5	Skills Review 2, Independent Challenge 1
XL2000E.9.4	Trace dependents (find formulas that refer to a specific cell)	Excel O-4	QuickTip	Skills Review 2
XL2000E.10	**Displaying and Formatting Data**			
XL2000E.10.1	Apply conditional formats	Excel C-14	Steps 2–7	Skills Review 7, Independent Challenges 2, 4

MOUS standardized coding number	Activity	Lesson page where skill is covered	Location in lesson where skill is covered	Practice
XL2000E.10.2	Perform single and multi-level sorts	Excel H-12	Steps 1–6	Skills Reviews 4, 5, Independent Challenges 1–3
		Excel H-14	Steps 1–6	Skills Review 5, Independent Challenges 1–3
XL2000E.10.3	Use grouping and outlines	Excel I-10	Steps 1–7	Skills Review 4
XL2000E.10.4	Use data forms	Excel H-6	Steps 1–8	Skills Review 2, Independent Challenge 2
XL2000E.10.5	Use subtotaling	Excel I-10	Steps 1–7	Skills Review 4, Independent Challenge 3
XL2000E.10.6	Apply data filters	Excel I-2, I-4, I-6	Steps 1–7, 1–7, 1–5	Skills Reviews 1–3, Independent Challenges 1, 3
XL2000E.10.7	Extract data	Excel I-8	Steps 1–5	
XL2000E.10.8	Query databases	Excel M-6	QuickTip	
XL2000E.10.9	Use data validation	Excel I-16	Steps 1–7	Skills Review 7, Independent Challenges 1, 3
XL2000E.11	**Using analysis tools**			
XL2000E.11.1	Use PivotTable autoformat	Excel L-12	Steps 1–8	Skills Review 6, Independent Challenges 1, 2, 4
XL2000E.11.2	Use Goal Seek	Excel K-12	Steps 1–6	Skills Review 6, Independent Challenge 3
XL2000E.11.3	Create PivotChart reports	Excel L-14	Steps 1–6	Skills Review 7, Independent Challenges 2, 4
XL2000E.11.4	Work with scenarios	Excel K-4, K-6	Steps 1–8, 1–7	Skills Reviews 2, 3, Independent Challenges 1, 2
XL2000E.11.5	Use Solver	Excel K-14, K-16	Steps 1–8, 1–6	Skills Review 7, Independent Challenges 3, 4
XL2000E.11.6	Use data analysis and PivotTables	Excel L-1–L-12	All Steps	All Skills Reviews and Independent Challenges
XL2000E.11.7	Create interactive PivotTables for the Web	Excel N-12	Steps 1–7	Skills Review 5, Independent Challenge 3
XL2000E.11.8	Add fields to a PivotTable using the Web browser	Excel N-13	Clues to Use	
XL2000E.12	**Collaborating with workgroups**			
XL2000E.12.1	Create, edit, and remove a comment	Excel O-14 (Create)	Steps 1–6	Skills Review 7, Independent Challenge 1
		Excel O-14 (Edit)	QuickTip	Skills Review 7
		Excel O-16 (Remove)	Step 2	Skills Review 7
XL2000E.12.2	Apply and remove worksheet and workbook protection	Excel F-8	Steps 1–8, QuickTip	Skills Review 4

MOUS standardized coding number	Activity	Lesson page where skill is covered	Location in lesson where skill is covered	Practice
XL2000E.12.3	Change workbook properties	Excel F-9	Clues to Use	Independent Challenge 3
XL2000E.12.4	Apply and remove file passwords	Excel F-8	Table F-1, QuickTip	
		Excel N-8	Steps 1–6, Clues to Use	Skills Review 3, Independent Challenge 1
		Excel N-9	Clues to Use	
XL2000E.12.5	Track changes (highlight, accept, and reject)	Excel N-6 (Highlight)	Steps 1–2, 7	Skills Review 2, Independent Challenge 1
		Excel N-6 (Accept and Reject)	QuickTip	Skills Review 2
XL2000E.12.6	Create a shared workbook	Excel N-4	Steps 1–5	
XL2000E.12.7	Merge workbooks	Excel N-7	Clues to Use	

Project Files List

To complete many of the lessons and practice exercises in this book, students need to use a Project File that is supplied by Course Technology and stored on a Project Disk. Below is a list of the files that are supplied, and the unit or practice exercise to which the files correspond. For information on how to obtain Project Files, please see the inside cover of this book. The following list only includes Project Files that are supplied; it does not include the files students create from scratch or the files students create by revising the supplied files.

Unit	File supplied on Project Disk	Location file is used in unit
Windows 98 Unit A	No files supplied	
Windows 98 Unit B	WIN B-1.bmp	Lessons
	WIN B-2.bmp	Skills Review
Excel Unit A	EX A-1.xls	Lessons
	EX A-2.xls	Skills Review
Excel Unit B	EX B-1.xls	Lessons
	EX B-2.xls	Skills Review
	EX B-3.xls	Independent Challenge 3
Excel Unit C	EX C-1.xls	Lessons
	EX C-2.xls	Skills Review
	EX C-3.xls	Independent Challenge 1
	EX C-4.xls	Independent Challenge 2
	EX C-5.xls	Visual Workshop
Excel Unit D	EX D-1.xls	Lessons
	EX D-2.xls	Independent Challenge 1
	EX D-3.xls	Independent Challenge 2
	EX D-4.xls	Independent Challenge 3
	EX D-5.xls	Visual Workshop
Excel Unit E	EX E-1.xls	Lessons
	EX E-2.xls	
	EX E-3.xls	
	EX E-4.xls	
	EX E-5.xls	Skills Review
	EX E-6.xls	Independent Challenge 1
	EX E-7.xls	Independent Challenge 2
	EX E-8.xls	Independent Challenge 4

Unit	File supplied on Project Disk	Location file is used in unit
Excel Unit F	EX F-1.xls Pay Rate Classifications	Lessons
	EX F-2.xls Expense Details	Skills Review
	EX F-3.xls	Independent Challenge 1
Excel Unit G	No files supplied	
Excel Unit H	EX H-1.xls	Lessons
	EX H-2.xls	Independent Challenge 2
	EX H-3.xls	Independent Challenge 3
	EX H-4.xls	Independent Challenge 4
Excel Unit I	EX I-1.xls	Lessons
	EX I-2.xls	Skills Review
	EX I-3.xls	Independent Challenges 1–2
	EX I-4.xls	Independent Challenge 3
	EX I-5.xls	Independent Challenge 4
Excel Unit J	EX J-1.xls	Lessons
	EX J-2.xls	Skills Review
	EX J-3.xls	Independent Challenges 1–2
Excel Unit K	EX K-1.xls	Lessons
	EX K-2.xls	Skills Review
	EX K-3.xls	Independent Challenges 1–2
	EX K-4.xls	Independent Challenge 3
Excel Unit L	EX L-1.xls	Lessons
	EX L-2.xls	Skills Review
	EX L-3.xls	Independent Challenge 1
	EX L-4.xls	Independent Challenge 2
	EX L-5.xls	Independent Challenge 3
	EX L-6.xls	Independent Challenge 4
	EX L-7.xls	Visual Workshop
Excel Unit M	EX M-1.txt EX M-2.dbf EX M-3.jpg EX M-4.doc	Lessons

Unit	File supplied on Project Disk	Location file is used in unit
	EX M-5.xls	
	EX M-6.ppt	
	EX M-7.xls	
	EX M-8.xls	
	EX M-9.txt	Skills Review
	EX M-10.dbf	
	EX M-11.bmp	
	EX M-12.xls	
	EX M-13.ppt	
	EX M-14.xls	
	EX M-15.xls	
	EX M-16.prn	Independent Challenge 1
	EX M-17.wk1	Independent Challenge 2
	EX M-18.jpg	Visual Workshop
Excel Unit N	EX N-1.xls	Lessons
	EX N-2.xls	
	EX N-3.xls	Skills Review
	EX N-4.xls	Independent Challenge 1
	EX N-5.xls	Independent Challenge 2
	EX N-6.xls	Independent Challenge 3
Excel Unit O	EX O-1.xls	Lessons
	EX O-2.xls	Skills Review
	EX O-3.xls	Independent Challenge 1
	EX O-4.xls	Independent Challenge 2
	EX O-5.xls	Visual Workshop
Excel Unit P	EX P-1.xls	Lessons
	EX P-2.xls	
	EX P-3.xls	Skills Review

Windows 98

Glossary

Accessories Built-in progams that come with Windows 98.

Active Desktop The screen that appears when you first start Windows 98, providing access to your computer's programs and files and to the Internet. *See also* Desktop.

Active program The program that you are using, differentiated from other open programs by a highlighted program button on the taskbar and a differently colored title bar.

Active window The window that you are currently using, differentiated from other open windows by a differently colored title bar.

Address Bar The area below the toolbar in My Computer and Windows Explorer that you use to open and display a drive, folder, or Web page.

Back up To save files to another location in case you have computer trouble and lose files.

Browser A program, such as Microsoft Internet Explorer, designed to access the Internet.

Bullet mark A solid circle that indicates that an option is enabled.

Capacity The amount of information a disk can hold, usually measured in megabytes (Mb).

Cascading menu A list of commands from a menu item with an arrow next to it; pointing at the arrow displays a submenu from which you can choose additional commands.

Channel Bar The bar on the right side of the Active Desktop that shows buttons to access the Internet and view Web pages known as active channels (like those on television).

Check box A square box in a dialog box that you click to turn an option on or off.

Check mark A mark that indicates that a feature is enabled.

Classic style A Windows 98 setting in which you single-click to select items and double-click to open them.

Click To press and release the left mouse button once.

Clipboard Temporary storage space on your computer's hard disk containing information that has been cut or copied.

Close To quit a program or remove a window from the desktop. The Close button is usually located in the upper-right corner of a window.

Command A directive that provides access to a program's features.

Command button In a dialog box, a button that carries out an action. A command button usually has a label that describes its action, such as Cancel or Help. If the label is followed by an ellipses (...), clicking the button displays another dialog box.

Context-sensitive help Help that is specifically related to what you are doing.

Control Panel Used to change computer settings such as desktop colors or mouse settings.

Copy To place information onto the Clipboard in order to paste it in another location, but also leaving it in the original location.

Cut To remove information from a file and place it on the Clipboard, usually to be pasted into another location.

Default Settings preset by the operating system or program.

Delete To place a file or folder in the Recycle Bin, where you can either remove it from the disk permanently or restore it to its original location.

Desktop The screen that appears when you first start Windows 98, providing access to your computer's programs and files and to the Internet. *See also* Active Desktop.

Dialog box A window that opens when more information is needed to carry out a command.

Document A file that you create using a program such as WordPad.

Double-click To press and release the left mouse button twice quickly.

Drag To move an item to a new location using the mouse.

Drive A device that reads and saves files on a disk and is also used to store files; floppy drives read and save files on floppy disks, whereas hard drives read and save files on your computer's built-in hard disk.

Edit To change the content or format of an existing file.

Explorer Bar The pane on the left side of the screen in Windows Explorer that lists all drives and folders on the computer.

File An electronic collection of information that has a unique name, distinguishing it from other files.

File hierarchy A logical structure for folders and files that mimics how you would organize files and folders in a filing cabinet.

File management The process of organizing and keeping track of files and folders.

Floppy disk A disk that you insert into a disk drive of your computer (usually drive A or B) to store files.

Folder A collection of files and/or other folders that helps you organize your disks.

Font The design of a set of characters (for example, Times New Roman).

Format To enhance the appearance of a document by, for example, changing the font or font size, adding borders and shading to a document.

Graphical user interface (GUI) An environment made up of meaningful symbols, words, and windows in which you can control the basic operation of a computer and the programs that run on it.

Hard disk A disk that is built into the computer (usually drive C) on which you store files and programs.

Highlighting When an icon is shaded differently indicating it is selected. *See also* Select.

Icon Graphical representation of computer elements such as files and programs.

Inactive Refers to a window or program that is open but not currently in use.

Input device An item, such as a mouse or keyboard, that you use to interact with your computer.

Insertion point A blinking vertical line that indicates where text will appear when you type.

Internet A worldwide collection of over 40 million computers linked together to share information.

Internet style A Windows 98 setting in which you point to select items and single-click to open them. *See also* Web style.

Keyboard shortcut A keyboard alternative for executing a menu command (for example, [Ctrl][X] for Cut).

List box A box in a dialog box containing a list of items; to choose an item, click the list arrow, then click the desired item.

Maximize To enlarge a window so it fills the entire screen. The Maximize button is usually located in the upper-right corner of a window.

Menu A list of related commands in a program (for example, the File menu).

Menu bar A bar near the top of the program window that provides access to most of a program's features through categories of related commands.

Minimize To reduce the size of a window. The Minimize button is usually located in the upper-right corner of a window.

Mouse A hand-held input device that you roll on your desk to position the mouse pointer on the Windows desktop. *See also* Mouse pointer.

Mouse buttons The two buttons on the mouse (right and left) that you use to make selections and issue commands.

Mouse pointer The arrow-shaped cursor on the screen that follows the movement of the mouse. The shape of the mouse pointer changes depending on the program and the task being executed. *See also* Mouse.

Multi-tasking Working with more than one window or program at a time.

My Computer A program that you use to manage the drives, folders, and files on your computer.

Open To start a program or open a window; also used to describe a program that is running but not active.

Operating system A computer program that controls the basic operation of your computer and the programs you run on it. Windows 98 is an example of an operating system.

Option button A small circle in a dialog box that you click to select an option.

Paint A drawing program that comes with Windows 98.

Pane A section of a divided window.

Point To position the mouse pointer over an item on your computer screen; also a unit of measurement (1/72nd inch) used to specify the size of text.

Pointer trail A shadow of the mouse pointer that appears when you move the mouse; helps you locate the pointer on your screen.

Pop-up menu A menu that appears when you right-click an item on the desktop.

Program Task-oriented software that you use for a particular kind of work, such as word processing or database management. Microsoft Access, Microsoft Excel, and Microsoft Word are all programs.

Program button A button on the taskbar that represents an open program or window.

Properties Characteristics of a specific computer element (such as the mouse, keyboard, or desktop display) that you can customize.

Quick Launch toolbar A toolbar located next to the Start button on the taskbar that contains buttons to start Internet-related programs and show the desktop.

Random access memory (RAM) The memory that programs use to perform necessary tasks while the computer is on. When you turn the computer off, all information in RAM is lost.

Recycle Bin An icon that appears on the desktop that represents a temporary storage area on your computer's hard disk for deleted files, which remain in the Recycle Bin until you empty it.

Restore To reduce the window to its previous size before it was maximized. The Restore button is usually located in the upper-right corner of a window.

Right-click To press and release the right mouse button once.

ScreenTip A description of a toolbar button that appears when you position the mouse pointer over the button.

Scroll bar A bar that appears at the bottom and/or right edge of a window whose contents are not entirely visible; you click the arrows or drag the box in the direction you want to move. *See also* Scroll box.

Scroll box A rectangle located in the vertical and horizontal scroll bars that indicates your relative position in a window. *See also* Scroll bar.

Select To click and highlight an item in order to perform some action on it. *See also* Highlighting.

Shortcut A link that you can place in any location that gives you instant access to a particular file, folder, or program on your hard disk or on a network.

Shut down The action you perform when you have finished working with Windows 98; after you shut down it is safe to turn off your computer.

Slider An item in a dialog box that you drag to set the degree to which an option is in effect.

Spin box A box with two arrows and a text box; allows you to scroll in numerical increments or type a number.

Start button A button on the taskbar that you use to start programs, find and open files, access Windows Help and more.

Tab A place in a dialog box where related commands and options are organized.

Taskbar A strip at the bottom of the screen that contains the Start button, Quick Launch toolbar, and shows which programs are running.

Text box A rectangle in a dialog box in which you type text.

Title bar The area along the top of the window that indicates the filename and program used to create it.

Toolbar A strip with buttons that allow you to activate a command quickly.

Web page A document that contains highlighted words, phrases, and graphics that link to other documents on the Internet.

Web site A computer on the Internet that contains Web pages.

Web style A Windows 98 setting in which you point to select items and single-click to open them. *See also* Internet style.

Window A rectangular frame on a screen that can contain icons, the contents of a file, or other usable data.

Windows Explorer A program that you use to manage files, folders, and shortcuts; allows you to work with more than one computer, folder, or file at once.

Windows Help A "book" stored on your computer, complete with an index and a table of contents, that contains information about Windows 98.

WordPad A word processing program that comes with Windows 98.

World Wide Web Part of the Internet that consists of Web sites located on different computers around the world.

Zip disk A portable disk that can contain 100 Mb, far more than a regular floppy disk.

Zip drive A drive that can handle Zip disks.

Excel 2000

Glossary

3-D references A reference that uses values on other sheets or workbooks, effectively creating another dimension to a workbook.

Absolute reference A cell reference that contains a dollar sign before the column letter and/or row number to indicate the absolute, or fixed, contents of specific cells. For example, the formula $A$1+$B$1 calculates only the sum of these specific cells no matter where the formula is copied in the workbook.

Active cell The current location of the cell pointer.

Address The location of a specific cell or range expressed by the coordinates of column and row; for example, A1.

Alignment The horizontal placement of cell contents; for example, left, center, or right.

Analyze To manipulate data, such as a list, with Excel or another tool.

Anchors Cells listed in a range address. For example, in the formula =SUM(A1:A15), A1 and A15 are anchors.

Area chart A line chart in which each area is given a solid color or pattern to emphasize the relationship between the pieces of charted information.

Arguments Information a function needs to create the answer. In an expression, multiple arguments are separated by commas. All of the arguments are enclosed in parentheses; for example, =SUM(A1:B1).

Arithmetic operator A symbol used in a formula, such as + or -, / or *, to perform mathematical operations.

ASCII file A text file that contains data but no formatting; instead of being divided into columns, ASCII file data are separated, or delimited, by tabs or commas.

Attribute The styling features such as bold, italics, and underlining that can be applied to cell contents.

AutoComplete A feature that automatically completes labels entered in adjoining cells in a column.

AutoFill A feature that creates a series of text or numbers when a range is selected using the fill handle.

AutoFit A feature that automatically adjusts the width of a column to accommodate its widest entry when the boundary to the right of the column selector is double-clicked.

AutoFormat Preset schemes that can be applied to format a range instantly. Excel comes with 16 AutoFormats that include colors, fonts, and numeric formatting.

AutoSum A feature that automatically creates totals using the AutoSum button.

Background color The color applied to the background of a cell.

Backsolving A problem-solving method in which you specify a solution and then find the input value that produces the answer you want; sometimes described as a what-if analysis in reverse.

Bar chart A chart that shows information as a series of (horizontal) bars.

Border The edge of a selected area of a worksheet. Lines and color can be applied to borders.

Bug In programming, an error that causes a procedure to run incorrectly.

Cancel button The X in the formula bar; it removes information from the formula bar and restores the previous cell entry.

Cell The intersection of a column and row in a worksheet.

Cell address The unique location identified by intersecting column and row coordinates.

Cell comments Notes you've written about a workbook that appear when you place the pointer over a cell.

Cell pointer A highlighted rectangle around a cell that indicates the active cell.

Cell reference The address or name that identifies a cell's position in a worksheet; it consists of a letter that identifies the cell's column and a number that identifies its row; for example, cell B3. Cell references in worksheets can be used in formulas and are relative or absolute.

Change history A worksheet containing a list of changes made to a shared workbook.

Changing cells In what-if analysis, cells that contain the values that change in order to produce multiple sets of results.

Chart A graphic representation of information from a worksheet. Types include 2-D and 3-D column, bar, pie, area, and line charts.

Chart sheet A separate sheet that contains a chart linked to worksheet data.

Chart title The name assigned to a chart.

Chart Wizard A series of dialog boxes that helps create or modify a chart.

Check box A square box in a dialog box that can be clicked to turn an option on or off.

Clear A command on the Edit menu used to erase a cell's contents, formatting, or both.

Clipboard A temporary storage area for cut or copied items that are available for pasting. See *Office Clipboard.*

Clipboard toolbar A toolbar that shows the contents of the Office Clipboard; contains buttons for copying and pasting items to and from the Office Clipboard.

Close A command that closes the file so you can no longer work with it, but keeps Excel open so that you can continue to work on other workbooks.

Code window In the Visual Basic Editor, the window that displays the selected module's procedures, written in the Visual Basic programming language.

Column chart The default chart type in Excel that displays information as a series of (vertical) columns.

Column selector button The gray box containing the letter above the column.

Comments In a Visual Basic procedure, notes that explain the purpose of the macro or procedure; they are preceded by a single apostrophe and appear in green on a color monitor.

Conditional format The format of a cell based on its value or the outcome of a formula.

Conditional formula A formula that makes calculations based on stated conditions, such as calculating a rebate based on a purchase amount.

Consolidate To add together values on multiple worksheets and display the result on another worksheet.

Control menu box A box in the upper-left corner of a window used to resize or close a window.

Copy A command that copies the content of selected cells and places it on the Clipboard.

Criteria range A cell range containing one row of labels (usually a copy of column labels) and at least one additional row underneath it that contains the criteria you want to match.

Custom chart type A specially formatted Excel chart.

Cut A command that removes the cell contents from the selected area of a worksheet and places them on the Clipboard.

Data entry area The unlocked portion of a worksheet where users are able to enter and change data.

Data form In an Excel list (or database), a dialog box that displays one record at a time.

Data label Descriptive text that appears above a data marker in a chart.

Data map An Excel chart that shows information plotted on a map with symbols representing data points.

Data marker A graphical representation of a data point, such as a bar or column.

Data point Individual piece of data plotted in a chart.

Data series The selected range in a worksheet that Excel converts into a graphic and displays as a chart.

Data table A range of cells that shows the resulting values when one or more input values are varied in a formula; when one input value is changed, the table is called a one-input data table, and when two input values are changed, it is called a two-input data table.

Database An organized collection of related information. In Excel, a database is called a list.

Debug In programming, to correct an error in code.

Declare In the Visual Basic programming language, to define a text string as a variable.

Delete A command that removes cell contents from a worksheet.

Dependent cell A cell, usually containing a formula, whose value changes depending on the values in the input cells. For example, a payment formula or function that depends on an input cell containing changing interest rates is a dependent cell.

Destination program In a data exchange, the program that will receive the data.

Dialog box A window that opens when more information is needed to carry out a command.

Divide-by-zero error An Excel worksheet error that occurs when a formula attempts to divide a value by zero.

Document To make notes about basic worksheet assumptions, complex formulas, or questionable data.

Dummy column/row Blank column or row included at the end of a range that enables a formula to adjust when columns or rows are added or deleted.

Dynamic page breaks In a larger workbook, horizontal or vertical dashed lines that represent the place where pages print separately. They also adjust automatically when you insert or delete rows or columns, or change column widths or row heights.

Edit A change made to the contents of a cell or worksheet.

Electronic spreadsheet A computer program that performs calculations on data and organizes information into worksheets. A worksheet is divided into columns and rows, which form individual cells.

Embedding Inserting a copy of data into a destination document; you can double-click the embedded object to modify it using the tools of the source program.

Enter button The check mark in the formula bar used to confirm an entry.

Exploding pie slice A slice of a pie chart that has been pulled away from the whole pie to add emphasis.

External reference indicator The exclamation point (!) used in a formula to indicate that a referenced cell is outside the active sheet.

Extract To place a copy of a filtered list in a range you specify in the Advanced Filter dialog box.

Field In a list (an Excel database), a column that describes a characteristic about records, such as first name or city.

Field name A column label that describes a field.

Fill color Cell background color.

Fill Down A command that duplicates the contents of the selected cells in the range selected below the cell pointer.

Fill handle A small square in the lower-right corner of the active cell used to copy cell contents.

Fill Right A command that duplicates the contents of the selected cells in the range selected to the right of the cell pointer.

Filter To hide data in an Excel list that does not meet specified criteria.

Find A command used to locate information the user specifies.

Floating toolbar A toolbar within its own window that is not anchored along an edge of the worksheet.

Font The typeface or design of a set of characters (letters, numbers, symbols, and punctuation marks).

Footer Information that prints at the bottom of each printed page; on screen, a footer is visible only in Print Preview. To add a footer, use the Header and Footer command on the View menu.

Format The appearance of text and numbers, including color, font, attributes, borders, and shading. See also *Number format.*

Format Painter A feature used to copy the formatting applied to one set of text or in one cell to another.

Formula A set of instructions used to perform numeric calculations (adding, multiplying, averaging, etc.).

Formula bar The area below the menu bar and above the Excel workspace where you enter and edit data in a worksheet cell. The formula bar becomes active when you start typing or editing cell data. It includes the Enter button and the Cancel button.

Freeze To hold in place selected columns or rows when scrolling in a worksheet that is divided in panes. See also *panes.*

Function A special, predefined formula that provides a shortcut for a commonly used calculation; for example, AVERAGE. In the Visual Basic programming language, a predefined procedure that returns a value.

Goal cell In backsolving, a cell containing a formula in which you can substitute values to find a specific value, or goal.

Gridlines Horizontal and/or vertical lines within a chart that make the chart easier to read.

Header Information that prints at the top of each printed page; on screen, a header is visible only in Print Preview. To add a header, use the Header and Footer command on the View menu.

Hide To make rows, columns, formulas, or sheets invisible to workbook users.

HTML Hypertext Markup Language, the format of pages that a Web browser such as Internet Explorer or Netscape Navigator can read.

Hyperlink An object (a filename, a word, a phrase, or a graphic) in a worksheet that, when you click it, will display another worksheet, called the target.

If...Then...Else statement In the Visual Basic programming language, a conditional statement that directs Excel to perform specified actions under certain conditions; its syntax is "If *condition* Then *statements* Else [*elsestatements*].

Input Information that produces desired results in a worksheet.

Input cells Spreadsheet cells that contain data instead of formulas and that act as input to a what-if analysis; input values often change to produce different results. Examples include interest rates, prices, or other data.

Insertion point Blinking I-beam that appears in the formula bar during entry and editing.

Interactive Describes a worksheet saved as an HTML document and posted to an intranet or Web site that allows users to manipulate data using their browsers.

Internet A large computer network made up of smaller networks and computers.

Intranet An internal network site used by a particular group of people who work together.

Keywords In a macro procedure, words that are recognized as part of the Visual Basic programming language.

Label Descriptive text or other information that identifies the rows and columns of a worksheet. Labels are not included in calculations.

Label prefix A character that identifies an entry as a label and controls the way it appears in the cell.

Landscape orientation A print setting that positions the worksheet on the page so the page is wider than it is tall.

Legend A key explaining how information is represented by colors or patterns in a chart.

Line chart A graph of data that is mapped by a series of lines. Line charts show changes in data or categories of data over time and can be used to document trends.

Linking The dynamic referencing of data in other workbooks, so that when data in the other workbooks is changed, the references in the current workbook are automatically updated.

List The Excel term for a database, an organized collection of related information.

Lock To secure a row, column, or sheet so that data there cannot be changed.

Logical test The first part of an IF function; if the logical test is true, then the second part of the function is applied, and if it is false, then the third part of the function is applied. In the function IF(Balance>1,000,Rate*0.05,0), the 5% rate is applied to balances over $1,000.

Macro A set of instructions, or code, that performs tasks in the order you specify.

Main procedure A procedure containing several macros that run sequentially.

Mixed reference Formula containing both a relative and an absolute reference.

Mode indicator A box located at the lower-left corner of the status bar that informs you of the program's status. For example, when Excel is performing a task, the word "Wait" appears.

Model A worksheet used to produce a what-if analysis that acts as the basis for multiple outcomes.

Module In Visual Basic, a module is stored in a workbook and contains macro procedures.

More Buttons button A button you click on a toolbar to view toolbar buttons that are not currently visible.

Mouse pointer A symbol that indicates the current location of the mouse on the desktop. The mouse pointer changes its shape at times; for example, when you insert data, select a range, position a chart, change the size of a window, or select a topic in Help.

Moving border The dashed line that appears around a cell or range that is copied to the Clipboard.

Name box The left-most area in the formula bar that shows the cell reference or name of the active cell. For example, A1 refers to cell A1 of the active worksheet. You can also get a list of names in a workbook using the Name list arrow.

Named range A range of cells given a meaningful name; it retains its name when moved and can be referenced in a formula.

Number format A format applied to values to express numeric concepts, such as currency, date, and percentage.

Object A chart or graphic image that can be moved and resized and contains handles when selected. In object linking and embedding (OLE), the data to be exchanged between another document or program.

Object Linking and Embedding (OLE) A Microsoft Windows technology that allows you to transfer data from one document and program to another using embedding or linking.

Office Assistant An animated character that appears to offer tips, answer questions, and provide access to the program's Help system.

Office Clipboard A temporary storage area shared by all Office programs that can be used to cut, copy, and paste multiple items within and between Office programs. The Office Clipboard can hold up to 12 items collected from any Office program. See also *Clipboard toolbar.*

One-input data table A range of cells that shows resulting values when one input value in a formula is changed.

Open A command that retrieves a workbook from a disk and displays it on the screen.

Order of precedence The order in which Excel calculates parts of a formula: (1) exponents, (2) multiplication and division, and (3) addition and subtraction.

Output The end result of a worksheet.

Page field In a PivotTable or a PivotChart report, a field area that lets you view data as if it is stacked in pages, effectively adding a third dimension to the data analysis.

Panes Sections into which you can divide a worksheet when you want to work on separate parts of the worksheet at the same time; one pane freezes, or remains in place, while you scroll in another pane until you see the desired information.

Paste A command that moves information on the Clipboard to a new location. Excel pastes the formula, rather than the result, unless the Paste Special command is used.

Paste Function A series of dialog boxes that lists and describes all Excel functions and assists the user in function creation.

Pie chart A circular chart that represents data as slices of pie. A pie chart is useful for showing the relationship of parts to a whole; pie slices can be extracted for emphasis. See also *Exploding pie slice.*

PivotChart report An Excel feature that lets you summarize worksheet data in the form of a chart in which you can rearrange, or "pivot," parts of the chart structure to explore new data relationships.

PivotTable report An Excel feature that allows you to summarize worksheet data in the form of a table in which you can rearrange, or "pivot," parts of the table structure to explore new data relationships; also called a PivotTable.

PivotTable list An interactive PivotTable on a Web or intranet site that lets users explore data relationships using their browsers.

Plot area The area of a chart that contains the chart itself, its axes, and the legend.

Point A unit of measure used for fonts and row height. One inch equals 72 points.

Pointing method Specifying formula cell references by selecting the desired cell with your mouse instead of typing its cell reference; this eliminates typing errors.

Portrait orientation A print setting that positions the worksheet on the page so the page is taller than it is wide.

Precedence Algebraic rules that Excel uses to determine the order of calculations in a formula with more than one operator.

Procedure A sequence of Visual Basic statements contained in a macro that accomplishes a specific task.

Procedure footer In Visual Basic, the last line of a Sub procedure.

Procedure header The first line in a Visual Basic procedure.

Print Preview A command you can use to view the worksheet as it will look when printed.

Print title In a list that spans more than one page, the field names that print at the top of every printed page.

Program Task-oriented software (such as Excel or Word) that enables you to perform a certain type of task, such as data calculation or word processing.

Programs menu The Windows 95/98 Start menu that lists all available programs on your computer.

Project In the Visual Basic Editor, the equivalent of a workbook; a project contains Visual Basic modules.

Project Explorer In the Visual Basic Editor, a window that lists all open projects (or workbooks) and the worksheets and modules they contain.

Properties In the Visual Basic Editor, the characteristics associated with a module.

Properties window In the Visual Basic Editor, the window that displays a list of characteristics, or properties, associated with a module.

Range A selected group of adjacent cells.

Range object In Visual Basic, an object that represents a cell or a range of cells.

Range format A format applied to a selected range in a worksheet.

Record In a list (an Excel database), data about an object or a person.

Refresh To update a PivotTable so it reflects changes to the underlying data.

Relative cell reference A type of cell reference used to indicate a relative position in the worksheet. It allows you to copy and move formulas from one area to another of the same dimensions. Excel automatically changes the column and row numbers to reflect the new position.

Replace A command used to find one set of criteria and replace it with new information.

Reset usage data An option that returns personalized toolbars and menus to their default settings.

Route To send an e-mail attachment sequentially to each user in a list, who then forwards it to the next user on the list.

Routing slip A list of e-mail users who are to receive an e-mail attachment.

Row height The vertical dimension of a cell.

Row selector button The gray box containing the number to the left of the row.

Save A command used to permanently store your workbook and any changes you make to a file on a disk. The first time you save a workbook you must give it a filename.

Save As A command used to create a duplicate of the current workbook with a new filename. Used the first time you save a workbook.

Scenario A set of values you use to forecast results; the Excel Scenario Manager lets you store different scenarios.

Scenario summary An Excel table that compiles data from various scenarios so that you can view the scenario results next to each other for easy comparison.

Search criterion The specification for data that you want to find in an Excel list, such as "Denver" or "is greater than 1000."

Selection handles Small boxes appearing along the corners and sides of charts and graphic images that are used for moving and resizing.

Series of labels Pre-programmed series, such as days of the week and months of the year. They are formed by typing the first word of the series, then dragging the fill handle to the desired cell.

Shared workbook An Excel workbook that several users can open and modify.

Sheet Another term used for a *worksheet.*

Sheet tab A description at the bottom of each worksheet that identifies it in a workbook. In an open workbook, move to a worksheet by clicking its sheet tab. Also known as *Worksheet tab.*

Sheet tab scrolling buttons Buttons that enable you to move among sheets within a workbook.

Sort keys Criteria on which a sort, or a reordering of data, is based.

Source list The list on which a PivotTable is based.

Source program In a data exchange, the program used to create the data you are embedding or linking.

Spell check A command that attempts to match all text in a worksheet with the words in the dictionary.

standard chart type A commonly used column, bar, pie, or area chart in the Excel program; each type has several variations. For example, a column chart variation is the Columns with Depth.

Start To open a software program so you can use it.

Statement In Visual Basic, a line of code.

Status bar The bar at the bottom of the Excel window that provides information about various keys, commands, and processes.

Sub procedure A series of Visual Basic statements that perform an action but do not return a value.

Summary function In a PivotTable, a function that determines the type of calculation applied to the PivotTable data, such as SUM or COUNT.

Syntax In the Visual Basic programming language, the formatting rules that must be followed so that the macro will run correctly.

Table In an Access database, a list of data.

Target The location that a hyperlink displays after you click it.

Target cell In what-if analysis (specifically, in Excel Solver), the cell containing the formula.

Template A workbook containing text, formulas, macros, and formatting you use repeatedly; when you create a new document, you can open a document based on the template workbook. The new document will automatically contain the formatting, text, formulas, and macros in the template.

Text annotations Labels added to a chart to draw attention to a particular area.

Text color The color applied to the text within a cell.

Tick marks Notations of a scale of measure on a chart axis.

Title bar The bar at the top of the window that indicates the program name and the name of the current worksheet.

Toggle button A button that turns a feature on and off.

Toolbar A bar that contains buttons that give you quick access to the most frequently used commands.

Tracers In Excel worksheet auditing, arrows that point from cells that might have caused an error to the active cell containing an error.

Track To identify and keep a record of who makes which changes to a workbook.

Two-input data table A range of cells that shows resulting values when two input values in a formula are changed.

Truncate To shorten the display of a cell based on the width of a cell.

Uniform Resource Locator (URL) A unique address for a location on the World Wide Web; www.course.com is an example.

Values Numbers, formulas, or functions used in calculations.

Variable In the Visual Basic programming language, a slot in memory in which you can temporarily store an item of information; variables are often declared in Dim statements such as Dim variablename As datatype.

View A set of display or print settings that you can name and save for access at another time. You can save multiple views of a worksheet.

Visual Basic for Applications (VBA) A programming language used to create macros in Excel.

Web query An Excel feature that lets you obtain data from a Web, Internet, or intranet site and places it in an Excel workbook for analysis.

What-if analysis A decision-making feature in which data is changed and automatically recalculated.

Wildcard A special symbol you use in defining search criteria in the data form or Replace dialog box. The most common types of wildcards are the question mark (?), which stands for any single character, and the asterisk (*), which represents any group of characters.

Window A rectangular area of a screen where you view and work on a worksheet.

Workbook A collection of related worksheets contained within a single file.

Worksheet An electronic spreadsheet containing 256 columns by 65,536 rows.

Worksheet tab See *Sheet tab.*

Worksheet window The worksheet area in which data is entered.

World Wide Web A structure of documents, called pages, connected electronically over a large computer network called the Internet.

X-axis The horizontal line in a chart.

X-axis label A label describing the x-axis of a chart.

Y-axis The vertical line in a chart.

Y-axis label A label describing the y-axis of a chart.

Zoom A feature that enables you to focus on a larger or smaller part of the worksheet in Print Preview.

Index

Index

▶C

▶D

Index

▶E

▶F

Index

▶G

▶H

▶I

▶K

▶L

Index

▶M

▶N

▶O

▶P

Index

▶Q

▶R

Index

▶T

Index

►X

►Y

►Z